The IMA Volumes
in Mathematics
and Its Applications

Volume 21

Series Editors
Avner Friedman   Willard Miller, Jr.

Institute for Mathematics and
its Applications
IMA

The **Institute for Mathematics and its Applications** was established by a grant from the National Science Foundation to the University of Minnesota in 1982. The IMA seeks to encourage the development and study of fresh mathematical concepts and questions of concern to the other sciences by bringing together mathematicians and scientists from diverse fields in an atmosphere that will stimulate discussion and collaboration.

The IMA Volumes are intended to involve the broader scientific community in this process.

Avner Friedman, Director
Willard Miller, Jr., Associate Director

* * * * * * * * * *

IMA PROGRAMS

* * * * * * * * * *

SPRINGER LECTURE NOTES FROM THE IMA:

The Mathematics and Physics of Disordered Media

Editors: Barry Hughes and Barry Ninham
(Lecture Notes in Math., Volume 1035, 1983)

Orienting Polymers

Editor: J.L. Ericksen
(Lecture Notes in Math., Volume 1063, 1984)

New Perspectives in Thermodynamics

Editor: James Serrin
(Springer-Verlag, 1986)

Models of Economic Dynamics

Editor: Hugo Sonnenschein
(Lecture Notes in Econ., Volume 264, 1986)

Dijen Ray-Chaudhuri

Coding Theory and Design Theory

Part II
Design Theory

With 32 Illustrations

Springer-Verlag
New York Berlin Heidelberg
London Paris Tokyo Hong Kong

Dijen Ray-Chaudhuri
Department of Mathematics
Ohio State University
Columbus, Ohio 43210
USA

Series Editors

Avner Friedman
Willard Miller, Jr.
Institute for Mathematics and Its Applications
University of Minnesota
Minneapolis, MN 55455 USA

Mathematical Subject Classification Codes: 62Kxx, 05Bxx, 94C30.

Library of Congress Cataloging-in-Publication Data

Coding theory and design theory / Dijen Ray-Chaudhuri, editor.
    p. cm. — (The IMA volumes in mathematics and its
applications ; v. 20–21)
    "Based on the proceedings of a workshop which was an integral part
of the 1987–88 IMA program on applied combinatorics"—Foreword.
    Includes bibliographical references.
    Contents: v. 1. Coding theory — v. 2. Design theory.
    ISBN 0-387-97228-5 (v. 1 : alk. paper). — ISBN 0-387-97231-5 (v.
2 : alk. paper)
    1. Coding theory. 2. Experimental design. I. Ray-Chaudhuri,
Dijen, 1933– II. Series.
QA268.C68   1990
003'.54—dc20   89-26336

Printed on acid-free paper.

Camera-ready copy prepared by the IMA.
Printed and bound by Edwards Brothers, Inc., Ann Arbor, Michigan.
Printed in the United States of America.

9 8 7 6 5 4 3 2 1

ISBN 0-387-97231-5 Springer-Verlag New York Berlin Heidelberg
ISBN 3-540-97231-5 Springer-Verlag Berlin Heidelberg New York

The IMA Volumes
in Mathematics and its Applications

Current Volumes:

Nonlinear Evolution Equations that Change Type

Computer Aided Proofs in Analysis

Multidimensional Hyperbolic Problems and Computations (2 Volumes)

Microlocal Analysis and Nonlinear Waves

Summer Program 1989: *Robustness, Diagnostics, Computing and Graphics in Statistics*

Robustness, Diagnostics in Statistics (2 Volumes)

Computing and Graphics in Statistics

1989-1990: *Dynamical Systems and Their Applications*

Introduction to Dynamical Systems

FOREWORD

This IMA Volume in Mathematics and its Applications

Coding Theory and Design Theory Part II: Design Theory

is based on the proceedings of a workshop which was an integral part of the 1987-88 IMA program on APPLIED COMBINATORICS. We are grateful to the Scientific Committee: Victor Klee (Chairman), Daniel Kleitman, Dijen Ray-Chaudhuri and Dennis Stanton for planning and implementing an exciting and stimulating year-long program. We especially thank the Workshop Organizer, Dijen Ray-Chaudhuri, for organizing a workshop which brought together many of the major figures in a variety of research fields in which coding theory and design theory are used.

Avner Friedman

Willard Miller, Jr.

PREFACE

Coding Theory and Design Theory are areas of Combinatorics which found rich applications of algebraic structures. Combinatorial designs are generalizations of finite geometries. Probably, the history of Design Theory begins with the 1847 paper of Reverand T.P. Kirkman "On a problem of Combinatorics", Cambridge and Dublin Math. Journal. The great Statistician R.A. Fisher reinvented the concept of combinatorial 2-design in the twentieth century. Extensive application of algebraic structures for construction of 2-designs (balanced incomplete block designs) can be found in R.C. Bose's 1939 Annals of Eugenics paper, "On the construction of balanced incomplete block designs". Coding Theory and Design Theory are closely interconnected. Hamming codes can be found (in disguise) in R.C. Bose's 1947 Sankhyā paper "Mathematical theory of the symmetrical factorial designs". The same paper also introduced the packing problem in projective spaces - the central problem in the construction of optimum linear codes. Coding theory has developed into a rich and beautiful example of abstract sophisticated mathematics being applied successfully to solve real-life problems of communication. Applications of deep theorems of Algebraic Geometry for construction of linear codes by V.D. Goppa and others created much excitement. Much work remains to be done to make the algebraic geometric codes practical and implementable. Theory of t-designs for $t > 2$ is in a state of rapid development. The 1987-88 Applied Combinatorics Program of IMA decided to devote the period from May 1, 1988 to June 25, 1988 to concentration on Design Theory and Coding Theory. It was particularly appropriate as many of the specialists that were invited worked in both of these areas.

The purpose of this section of the Applied Combinatorics Year was to bring together Coding Theorists, Design Theorists and Statisticians in the area of experimental designs, to exchange informations and ideas on the latest developments, to encourage interactions and to create an inspiring and stimulating research environment. This purpose was well served. Before the beginning of the workshops from May 1 to June 10, 1988 the pace was relaxed with plenty of time for research exchanges. During this period lectures of J.H. van Lint on Algebraic Geometric Codes was a particularly popular event. In this period there were also lectures by E. Assmus, R.A. Bailey, C-S. Cheng, M. Deza, A.S. Hedayat, S.L. Ma, V. Pless, D.K. Ray-Chaudhuri, N. Singhi, R.M. Wilson and L. Teirlinck. The periods of workshops, Coding Theory, June 13–17, 1988 and Design Theory, June 20–25, 1988 were much more intense with forty (40) lectures altogether. Symposium on Statistical theory of Experimental Designs attracted many statisticians with lively lectures by eight prominent statisticians. Most of the participants submitted their papers for publication in this volume on Coding Theory and Design Theory. Unfortunately a few fine lectures are not submitted for inclusion in these Proceedings.

Thanks are due to IMA director Professor A. Friedman, Associate director W. Miller, Jr. and IMA staff for their extremely helpful attitude and generous assistance. I take this opportunity to offer special thanks to Mrs. P. Brick, Mr. S. Skogerboe, and Mrs. K. Smith for their preparation of the manuscripts.

CONTENTS — PART II

CONTENTS — PART I

RECENT RESULTS ON DIFFERENCE SETS*

K. T. ARASU†

DEDICATED TO THE MEMORY OF MY LOVING DAUGHTER LAVANYA

Abstract. We survey recent results on difference sets discovered after the two books by Beth, Jungnickel and Lenz [16] and Lander [49] were published. We also update Lander's table on abelian difference sets.

AMS(MOS) subject classifications. 05B10

1. Introduction. The classical papers on difference sets are Singer [75], Hall [34] and Bruck [20]. A lot of research activity took place in this area since these papers were written. Excellent surveys of Baumert [15] and Hall [35] provide all the relevant information. Recent books of Beth, Jungnickel and Lenz [16] and Lander [49] contain an extensive bibliography and treat the topic of difference sets using modern algebraic approaches. The aim of this paper is to gather all the results discovered after these two books got published.

In section 2, we give the basic results on difference sets by introducing the notion of multipliers, an ingenious discovery of Hall [34]. We take the approach of McFarland [58] and define multipliers for elements of the group ring ZG. This gives us an advantage of taling about "contracted" multipliers (in the terminology of Lander [49]), in general. For those readers who are not familiar with the theory, we provide existence and nonexistence examples of difference sets using multipliers, as applications of the first multiplier theorem.

We begin section 3 by referring the reader to an elegant proof of the first multiplier theorem given by Pott [68, 69]. We then mention the multiplier conjecture and attempts made by McFarland [58] to resolve this. We close section 3 by stating the "contracted" multiplier theorem of Lander [49], independently proved by Arasu and Ray–Chaudhuri [12]. While Lander's version applies only to abelian groups, the version proved by Arasu and Ray–Chaudhuri [12] has applications in some nonabelian groups, as well.

In section 4, we discuss planar ($\lambda = 1$) difference sets and provide the current status of the prime power conjecture which states that an abelian projective plane of order n exists if and only if n is a prime power. We also state a weaker form of a conjecture of Hall: For each fixed $\lambda > 1$, there exists only a finite number of (v, k, λ) abelian difference sets.

*Research supported in part by National Security Agency Grant #MDA 904–87–H–2018. The final version of this manuscript was written while the author was visiting the Institute for Mathematics and its Applications (IMA) at the University of Minnesota. The author gratefully acknowledges the hospitality and the financial support provided by the IMA.

†Math. Institut, Arndtstr 2, 6300 Giessen, Federal Republic of Germany

In section 5, we state a theorem of Wilbrink [81], its various generalizations thereof, due to Arasu [2, 3] and Pott [70]. Several interesting applications of this theorem which provide connections between certain well-known conjectures are also indicated.

In section 6, we state more nonexistence theorems, one of which is due to Ghinelli–Smit [32] and a generalization of it due to Arasu [4]. Lander [50] points out that results of [4] follow as a special case of a theorem of Mann [57]. Jungnickel and Pott [40] strengthened a result of Mann [57] and applied it to certain nonabelian groups. We provide examples of this.

Section 7 is completely devoted to difference sets in 2–groups. The only completely satisfactory result in the theory of difference sets is: Difference sets in abelian 2-groups exist if and only if the underlying group satisfies Turyn's exponent bound.

Davis's Ph.D. thesis [22] initiated an interest in settling the above problem. Dillon [27] gave a different construction of a result of Davis [22, 23] and Kraemer [48] finally finished off the problem. In section 8, we briefly discuss Menon difference sets (also known as H-sets or Hadamard difference sets).

Results of section 9 provide the current status of Lander's table on abelian difference sets. Section 10 is about extraneous multipliers (a concept introduced by Mann [56]). Various new results due to Wu [82], Ko [47] and Pott [71] are mentioned. An application to relative difference sets and a potential application to planar difference sets are given. A theorem of Ho [37] is quoted in this context.

Section 11 deals with difference sets which admit -1 as a multiplier. In section 12, we mention a theorem of Kantor [44] in which he proves that a finite projective plane admitting a flag–transitive collineation group is desarguesian, modulo a degenerate situation, which gives rise to a planar difference set with certain peculiar properties. We conclude by listing a few open problems in section 13.

2. Basic results. Let G be a group of order v, written multiplicatively. A subset D of G of size k is said to be a (v, k, λ) difference set if the list of "differences" xy^{-1} $(x, y \in D)$ contains each nonidentity element of G exactly λ times. An easy counting argument shows that

$$k(k-1) = \lambda(v-1).$$

We define $n = k - \lambda$; n is called the order of D. We say that D is cyclic (resp. abelian) if G is cyclic (resp. abelian).

THEOREM 2.1. *Let D be a (v, k, λ) difference set in a group G.*

(i) *(Schutzenberger [74]). If v is even, then n is a perfect square.*

(ii) *(Bruck–Ryser–Chowla [21]). If v is odd, then the equation*

$$x^2 = ny^2 + (-1)^{\frac{v-1}{2}} \lambda z^2$$

has a solution in integers x, y, z, not all zero.

REMARK. The above celebrated theorem 2.1 actually holds in a more general setting: i.e. the existence of a (v, k, λ) symmetric design implies the above conclusions. The equivalence of the existence of a (v, k, λ) symmetric design with a sharply transitive automorphism group to that of a (v, k, λ) difference set is due to Bruck [20].

It is easy to show that if D is a (v, k, λ) difference set in group G, then D', the complement of D in G, is a $(v, v - k, v - 2k + \lambda)$ difference set in G. Therefore, without loss of generality, we may assume that $k < v/2$. (Note: It can be easily shown that if $v > 2$, then $k = \dfrac{v}{2}$ is impossible.)

Let R be a commutative ring with unity 1 and G be a group. We let RG denote the group ring of G over R. We identify each subset S of G with the group ring element $S = \sum_{x \in S} x$. For $A = \sum_g a_g g \in RG$ and any integer t (resp. any automorphism a) we define $A^{(t)} = \sum_g a_g g^t$ (resp. $A^{(\alpha)} = \sum_g a_g g^\alpha$).

We usually work with the case $R = Z$, the ring of integers, or $R = GF(p)$, the finite field with p elements, p a prime.

The difference set condition for $D \subseteq G$ can be translated into

$$\text{D.} \quad D^{(-1)} = n + \lambda G \text{ in } ZG, \text{ where } n = n.1 \in ZG.$$

Given $A = \sum_g a_g g \in ZG$, an integer t with $(t, |G|) = 1$ is said to be numerical multiplier of A if $A^{(t)} = Ag_0$ for some $g_0 \in G$. More generally an automorphism α of G is said to be a multiplier of A if $A^{(\alpha)} = Ag_0$ for some $g_0 \in G$. We will suppress the prefix numerical when we talk about numerical multipliers and refer to them simply as multipliers. This should not cause any confusion. It is easy to see that the set M of all multipliers of $A \in ZG$ forms a group under composition. The set N of all numerical multipliers of A forms a subgroup of M.

REMARK. Let $D \subseteq G$. An integer t with $(t, |G|) = 1$ is a multiplier of D if $D^{(t)} = Dg$ for some $g \in G$.

Note. (1) Dg is called a translate of D. (2) An automorphism α of G is a multiplier of D if and only if it is an automorphism of the associated design.

THEOREM 2.2. (First multiplier theorem [36]) Let D be an abelian (v, k, λ) difference set. Let p be a prime, $p|n$, $p \nmid v$. If $p > \lambda$, then p is a multiplier of D.

There are various generalizations of theorem 2.2 due to Bruck [20] and McFarland [58]. An account of all this can be found in [16] and [49]. The concept of multipliers was first introduced by Hall [34] for (v, k, λ) difference sets with $\lambda = 1$. This ingenious discovery is quite useful in constructing or proving the nonexistence of a putative (v, k, λ) difference set D in a specified group of order v. To illustrate this, we first need a result on multipliers fixing a translate of D. There are several theorems of this type (see [16] and [49]). We mention:

3

THEOREM 2.3. (McFarland and Rice [59]) *Let D be a (v, k, λ) difference set in an abelian group G. The group of numerical multipliers fixes at least one translate of D.*

Examples. (1) We construct a (11, 5, 2) difference set in the additive group Z_{11}.

Let D be a hypothetical (11, 5, 2) difference set in Z_{11}. By theorem 2.2, 3 is a multiplier of D. By theorem 2.3, we may assume that D is fixed by the multiplier 3 (otherwise, replace D by such a translate). Then D must be a union of some of the orbits of Z_{11} under $< x \longrightarrow 3x >$, which are $\{0\}, \{1, 3, 9, 5, 4\}$ and $\{2, 6, 7, 10, 8\}$. We see that both $\{1, 3, 4, 5, 9\}$ and $\{2, 6, 7, 8, 10\}$ work.

(2) We prove the nonexistence of a (31, 10, 3) difference set in Z_{31}.

Let D be a putative (31, 10, 3) difference set in Z_{31}. 7 is a multiplier of D. Assume, as in example 1, that D is closed under multiplication by 7. But $x \longrightarrow 7x$ has, on Z_{31}, three orbits of sizes 1, 15 and 15. Therefore D cannot exist.

3. Multiplier theorems and the multiplier conjecture. Hall's proof of multiplier theorems [34] uses polynomial notations and rather involved calculations in the group ring ZG. Mann's treatment [54] uses character theory of abelian groups. We refer the reader to Lander [49] and Pott [68, 69] for an elegant and completely elementary proof of the first multiplier theorem (Theorem 2.2).

Multiplier Conjecture. The hypothesis "$p > \lambda$" in theorem 2.2 is unnecessary.

While all the known proofs (including Pott's) use the condition "$p > \lambda$" very crucially, all the known examples seem to suggest that the condition "$p > \lambda$" is superfluous. Early proofs of multiplier theorems reduce to obtaining only trivial solutions to $F^{(-1)} F = m^2, F \in ZG$. In an attempt to resolve the multiplier conjecture, McFarland [58] defined an integral valued function $M(m)$, $m \in N$, the set of positive integers, to obtain conditions for trivial solutions to the equation $F^{(-1)} F = m^2, F \in ZG$. This function is defined in

THEOREM 3.1. (McFarland [58]) *For every positive integer m and for every prime divisor p of m, there exists an integer $M(m)$ such that if G is a finite abelian group whose order v is relatively prime to $M(m)$, then the only solutions to*

$$F^{(-1)} F = m^2, F \in ZG, \text{ are } F = \pm mg, \ g \in G. \text{ We can define } M(m) \text{ inductively}$$
as follows:

$$M(1) = 1; M(2) = 2.7; M(3) = 2.3.11.13; M(4) = 2.3.7.31. \text{ For } m \geq 5, \ M(m)$$
is the product of the distinct prime factors of m, $M\left(\dfrac{m^2}{p^{2f}}\right)$, $p-1, p^2-1, \cdots, p^u-1$,

where $p^f | m, p^{f+1} \nmid m$ and $u = \dfrac{m^2 - m}{2}$.

Before we state the next multiplier theorem, we introduce one more concept: Let D be a (v, k, λ) difference set in a group G. Let H be a normal subgroup of G. The canonical homomorphism from $G \longrightarrow G/H$ extends to a homomorphism from $ZG \longrightarrow Z[G/H]$. An integer t with $(t, |G/H|) = 1$ is said to be a G/H-multiplier of D if t is a multiplier of $\overline{D}$ in $Z(G/H)$. (Here $\overline{D}$ denotes the image of D in $Z(G/H)$).

THEOREM 3.2. (Lander [49]) *Let D be a (v, k, λ) difference set in an abelian group G. Let n_1 be a divisor of n and let $n_1 = p_1^{\alpha_1} \cdots p_s^{\alpha_s}$ be its canonical prime factorization.*

Suppose that H is a subgroup of order h and index w. Suppose that $t \in Z$, $(t, w) = 1$.

If (i) for $i = 1, \cdots s$, there exists an integer $j = j(i)$ such that either $p_i^j \equiv t$ or -1 (mod exponent of G/H) and (ii) $n_1 > h\lambda$ or $\left(w, M\left(\dfrac{n}{n_1} \right) \right) = 1$, then t is a G/H-multiplier of D.

REMARKS. (i) If $H = (1)$ in theorem 3.2, t is just a multiplier of D, in the usual sense.

(ii) t is also referred to as a contracted multiplier of D.

(iii) Arasu and Ray-Chaudhuri [12] proved a variation of theorem 3.2, which only requires G/H to be abelian (G not necessarily abelian). Their version applied to some nonabelian groups and can be used to exclude certain nonabelian difference sets.

4. Planar difference sets. When $\lambda = 1$, the parameters of a (v, k, λ) difference set take the form $(n^2 + n + 1, n + 1, 1)$ and its existence is equivalent to that of a projective plane of order n which admits a sharply transitive automorphism group. Cyclic $(n^2 + n + 1, n + 1, 1)$ difference sets have been constructed for each prime power n (Singer [75]). If $n \equiv 1$ (mod 3) and if there exists an abelian planar difference set of order n, then there exists a nonabelian planar difference set of order n, as well. (Bruck [20])

If D is an abelian planar difference set of order n, then D^{-1} is an oval in the corresponding projective plane (see, Jungnickel and Vedder [41], for instance). This assertion is due to Bruck and is a vital ingredient in the proof of Theorem 4.1. Note that D^{-1} induces a second projective plane isomorphic to the one determined by D. Motivated by this fact, Pickert [66] introduces the notion of a "double plane" and gives a characterization of those projective planes belonging to an abelian difference set by using the configurational axioms involving lines and ovals. Pott [73] has shown that every cyclic planar difference set of order $n \equiv 1$ (mod 3) leads to a nonabelian difference set D such that D^{-1} is not an oval. Pott [73] also shows that the inverses of at least three translates of D are ovals in D.

We now state the prime power conjecture (PPC).

Prime Power Conjecture. If there exists a planar difference set of order n, then n is a prime power.

While the PPC is far from being resolved, several recently obtained results provide strong evidence for its validity. The first major progress toward this is given by

THEOREM 4.1. (Jungnickel and Vedder [41]) *If there exists an abelian planar difference set of even order n, then $n = 2, 4$ or $n \equiv 0$ (mod 8).*

The proof given by Jungnickel and Vedder is an example of a fascinating interplay between geometry and arithmetic. Using algebraic tools (see section 5 for details), Wilbrink [81] proved:

THEOREM 4.2. (Wilbrink [81]) *If there exists an abelian planar difference set of order n, then*

$$
\begin{array}{lll}
& (i) & \text{if } 2\|n, \text{ then } n = 2 \\
\text{and} & (ii) & \text{if } 3\|n, \text{ then } n = 3.
\end{array}
$$

REMARKS. (1) Part (i) of theorem 4.2 is already contained in theorem 4.1.

(2) Pless [67] gives a coding theoretic proof of (i) of theorem 4.2 in the cyclic case, which essentially runs along the same lines as that of [81]. Her proof, using the "G-code" terminology of Lander [49] carries over to the abelian case, as well.

We now mention another result in this direction, which has not appeared elsewhere in print.

PROPOSITION 4.3. *If there exists an abelian planer difference set D of order $n \equiv 16 \pmod{32}$ with $n \equiv 1 \pmod 3$, then $n = 16$.*

Proof. We note that $v = n^2 + n + 1 \equiv 0 \pmod 3$ and 2 is a multiplier of D by theorem 2.2. By theorem 6.4, n must be a square (because 2 has even order mod u^*, $u^* =$ exponent of the underlying group). Therefore there exists a planar difference set of order $\sqrt{n}$ (see [16], for instance). Since $\sqrt{n} \equiv 4 \pmod 8$, theorem 4.1 implies that $\sqrt{n} = 4$ or $n = 16$.

REMARKS. (i) The above proof works if we replace the condition $n \equiv 1 \pmod 3$ by any one of the conditions of theorem of VI.5.12 of [16], which would force n to be a perfect square.

(ii) Proposition 4.3 should be true without any additional assumptions like $n \equiv 1 \pmod 3$, if the PPC were true.

While there exists an infinite family of planar ($\lambda = 1$) difference sets (when $n =$ prime power), there is no known infinite family of difference sets for $\lambda > 1$. In this regard, we mention a conjecture of Hall (in a weak form).

Hall's Conjecture 4.4. For each fixed $\lambda \geq 2$, there exists only a finite number of (v, k, λ) difference sets.

The following nonexistence result is due to Hall [34].

THEOREM 4.5. *(Hall [34], Lander [49], Lander [49], Jungnickel and Pott [40]) Let D be an abelian planar difference set of order n Then n cannot be a multiple of 6, 10, 14, 15, 21, 22, 26, 33, 34, 35, 38, 39, 46, 55, 57, 58, 62 or 65.*

Theorem 4.5 for the cyclic case is due to Hall [34]. Lander [49] generalized it to the abelian case, with the three exceptions $n = 22, 46$ and 58. Jungnickel and Pott [40] finished off these three exceptions.

6

Until recently the only nonexistence results for an abelian planar difference set of square ordere are theorems 4.1, 4.2 and 4.5. Arasu [9] proved the following results which provide further restrictions on admissible orders for abelian projective planes.

THEOREM 4.6. (Arasu [9]) *Let* D *be a cyclic planar difference set of order* n *in a group* G. *Suppose that* $n = m^{2s}$ *where* $(s, 3) = 1$. *Let be a multiplier of* D. *Suppose that there exists a prime divisor* q *of* $m^2 - m + 1$ *such that* t *has odd order modulo* q. *Then* t *has odd order modulo* v, *where* $v = m^4 + m^2 + 1$, *and hence* t *has odd order modulo* p *for each prime divisor* p *of* v.

THEOREM 4.7. (Arasu [9]) *Let* D *be an abelian planar difference set of order* n. *Suppose that* $n = m^{2^r}$ *where* r *is a positive integer. Let* t *be a multiplier of* D *and* $v = m^4 + m^2 + 1$. *If there exists a prime* q *dividing* $m^2 - m + 1$ *such that* t *has odd order mod* q, *then* t *has odd order mod* v.

We provide a sample corollary of theorems 4.6 and 4.7.

COROLLARY 4.8. *Suppose that* $m \equiv 10$ *or* $12 \pmod{14}$. *Then (i) there does not exist a cyclic projective plane or order* m^{2r} *for each* r *with* $(r, 3) = 1$, *and (ii) there does not exist an abelian projective plane of order* m^{2^r} *for each positive integer* r.

Proof. Take $t = 2$ and $q = 7$ in theorems 4.6 and 4.7 and use the fact 3 cannot divide m.

We close this section by quoting a theorem of Ho [38], which provides certain restrictions on the multiplier group of a cyclic planar difference set.

THEOREM 4.9. (Ho [38]) *Let* G *be a cyclic group of order* $n^2 + n + 1$ *containing a planar difference set of order* n. *Let* M *be the multiplier group of* D. *Then the following hold:*

(i) The Sylow 2-subgroup T *of* M *is cyclic. If* $|T| = 2^a$ *for some integer* $a \geq 0$, *then* $n = m^{2^a}$ *for some integer* $m \geq 2$.

(ii) For $k = 3, 5$ *or* 2^a *for some integer* $a \geq 0$, *we have* $|M| = 3k$ *if and only if* $n = p^k$ *for some prime* p.

(iii) We have $|M| = \dfrac{|Aut\ (G)|}{2}$ *if and only if* $n = 2$ *or* 4. *Furthermore,* $n = 2$ *occurs if and only if* $|M| = odd$ *in this case.*

(iv) We have $|M| = \frac{|Aut\ (G)|}{4}$ *if and only if* $n = 3$.

5. Wilbrink's Theorem. Wilbrink [81] proved an important identity that has to be satisfied in $GF(p)G$ by an abelian planar difference set D of order n, when $p|n$ but $p^2 \nmid n$. This was generalized by Arasu [2, 3] to arbitrary λ. We state the general version in the following theorem.

THEOREM 5.1. (Wilbrink [81], Arasu [2, 3]) *Let* D *be an abelian* (v, k, λ) *differ- ence set in* G. *Let* p *be a prime with* $p \nmid v, p|n$ *and* $p^2 \nmid n$. *Assume that* $D^{(p)} = D$

(i.e. p is a multiplier fixing D). Then the following identity holds in $GF(p)G$:

$$D^{p-1} + (D^{(-1)p-1} = \begin{cases} 1 + \lambda^{p-2}G & \text{if } p \nmid \lambda \\ 1 - v^{p-2}G & \text{if } p \mid \lambda. \end{cases}$$

While the original proofs of theorem 5.1 are not particularly difficult, they are not completely elementary either: One uses a result due to Bridges, Hall and Hayden [19] about the dimension of the $GF(p)$-code of the associated symmetric design and the semisimplicity of the group algebra $GF(p)G$ by arguing about the unique idempotent generators of certain ideals in $GF(p)G$. Pott [68] has given an alternate proof of theorem 5.1 using discrete Fourier transform of G, but Pott's proof also requires the dimension argument of [19]. Pott also obtained a converse of theorem 5.1. Recently, Jungnickel [42] has given a completely elementary proof of theorem 5.1 which only uses a few computations in ZG mod p^2 and mod p.

An interesting application of theorem 5.1 was obtained by Arasu [2, 3].

THEOREM 5.2. (Arasu [2, 3]) *Let D be a (v, k, λ) difference set in an abelian group G. Suppose that $k - \lambda \equiv 2 \pmod 4$ and that 2 is a multiplier of D. Then $k = 2\lambda$ or $2\lambda + 1$ according as λ is even or odd. (Thus the corresponding design is Hadamard, up to complementation).*

In view of the above theorem, we obtain

COROLLARY 5.3. (Arasu [3]) *The multiplier conjecture implies Hall's conjecture 4.4, when $k - \lambda \equiv 2 \pmod 4$.*

To obtain another corollary, we mention a conjecture of Ryser.

Ryser's conjecture. [49] If there exists a cyclic (v, k, λ) difference set, then $(v, n) = 1$.

Lander's conjecture. [49] If D is an abelian difference set in a group G and p is a prime divisor of (v, n), then the Sylow p-subgroup of G is non-cyclic.

Clearly Lander's conjecture implies Ryser's.

COROLLARY 5.4. (Arasu [3]) *The multiplier conjecture implies the conjectures of Ryser and Lander, for the case $n \equiv 2 \pmod 4$.*

REMARK. Arasu [6, 7] verified Lander's conjecture for the case $\lambda = 3, k \leq 500$.

Pott [70] developed a new method to obtain Wilbrink-type identities in $GF(p)G$ satisfied by (v, k, λ) difference sets, when a higher power of p divides n. He gives explicit formulae if p^2 or p^3 is the exact p-power dividing n. His method of proof uses knowledge about field extensions of the p-adic numbers, their characters and discrete Fourier transforms. We now quote these theorems of Pott.

THEOREM 5.5. (Pott [70] *Let D be an abelian (v, k, λ) difference set of order n with $p^2 | n$ but $p^3 \nmid n$ and $D^{(p)} = D$. Then the following identity holds in $GF(p)G$:*

8

$$1 = D^{p-1} + (D^{(-1)})^{p-1} + \left[\frac{1}{p}(D^{p^2-p+1} - D)\right]^{p-1} + \gamma\frac{1}{v}G, \text{ where the calculations}$$

within the brackets [ ] are carried out in ZG and

$$\gamma = \left\{ \begin{array}{ll} -1 & \text{if } p \nmid k \\ 1 & \text{if } p \mid k. \end{array} \right.$$

THEOREM 5.6. (Pott [70]) Let D be as in the theorem 5.5 but assume $p^3 | n$ and $p^4 \nmid n$. Then the following identity holds in $GF(p)G$:

$$1 = D^{p-1} + (D^{(-1)})^{p-1} + \left(\frac{1}{p}(D^{p^2-p+1} - D)\right)^{p-1}$$
$$+ \left[\frac{1}{p}(D^{(-1)})^{p^2-p+1} - D^{(-1)})\right]^{p-2} + \gamma\frac{1}{v}G$$

where expressions in [ ] and γ have the same meaning as in theorem 5.5.

REMARKS. (i) Pott's approach does not need information about the dimension of the code of the associated symmetric design.

(ii) Pott's method would also provide formulae when $p^i | n$ and $p^{i+1} \nmid n$ for each $i (i \geq 4)$. But the identities would involve even more unpleasant looking expressions.

(iii) Unfortunately theorems 5.5 and 5.6 have not yet found applications. We believe that certain variations of Pott's approach to G/H-multipliers would give nonexistence applications. But the calculations are bound to be quite involved.

6. More nonexistence results. The following nonexistence theorem was proved by Ghinelli–Smit [32].

THEOREM 6.1. (Ghinelli–Smit [32]) Let D be an abelian planar difference set of order n. Assume that n is a nonsquare. Let p be a prime divisor of n. Then for each divisor h of $n^2 + n + 1$,

$$h(n^2 + n + 1)\,(-1)^{\left(\frac{n^2+n+1}{h} - 1\right)\frac{1}{2}}$$

is a square in the ring of p-adic integers.

An extension of theorem 6.1 to arbitrary (v, k, λ) abelian difference sets is given in:

THEOREM 6.2. (Arasu [4]) Let D be a (v, k, λ) difference set in an abelian group G. Let p be a prime divisor of n, where $n = k - \lambda$. Assume (i) $(v, k) = 1$, (ii) n is a nonsquare and (iii) p is a multiplier of D. Then, for each divisor h of v, $h(-1)^{\frac{h-1}{2}}$ is a square in the ring Z_p of p-adic integers.

The proof techniques use representation theory, Galois theory and elementary linear algebra.

The above theorem provides nonexistence applications in view of the following well–known result in number theory (see [17]), for instance).

9

THEOREM 6.3. (i) when $p \neq 2$, a unit σ of Z_p is a square if and only if σ is a square modulo p.

(ii) A unit σ of Z_2 is a square if and only if σ is a square modulo 8.

Lander [49] proves theorem 6.4 using a theorem of Mann [57] and quadratic reciprocity and shows in [50] that this is stronger than Theorem 6.2.

THEOREM 6.4. (Lander [49]) Let D be a (v, k, λ) difference set in an abelian group G with exponent v^*. Every multiplier m of D has odd order (mod v^*), provided neither of the following holds:

(i) n is a square, or

(ii) for some prime $q \equiv 1 \pmod 4$,

$n = qn_1^2, v = q^a v_1$, with $a \geq 1$ and m has odd order (mod v_1).

Pott [68], using discrete Fourier transforms, proved the following version of theorem 6.2, which also applies to nonabelian difference sets that admit G/H-multiplier, where G/H is abelian

THEOREM 6.5. (Pott [68]) Let D be a (v, k, λ) difference set of nonsquare order n in a group G. Let H be a normal subgroup of G of order h. Assume that G/H is abelian and $(v, n) = 1$. If the prime p is a G/H-multiplier of D, then $(-1)^{(\frac{v}{h}-1)\frac{1}{2}}$ is a square modulo p.

REMARKS. (i) If one drops the conditions that p is a multiplier and that $(v, n) = 1$, but assumes $p|n'$, the square free part of n, one also obtains the conclusions of theorem 6.5. But this variation gives no information beyond theorem 4.4 of Lander [49].

(ii) For $p = 2$, theorem 6.5 is weaker than theorem 6.2, when one considers abelian groups G and "usual" multipliers.

Our next result is due to Jungnickel and Pott [40]. It strengthens a well known result of Mann [57].

THEOREM 6.6. (Jungnickel and Pott [40]) Let D be a (v, k, λ) difference set in a group G, where $v > k$. Let $u \neq 1$ be a divisor of v, let U be a normal subgroup of index u of G. Let $H = G/U$. Assume that H is abelian and of exponent u^*. Finally, let p be a prime not dividing u^* and assume $tp^f \equiv -1 \pmod{u^*}$ for some G/U-multiplier t of D and a suitable nonnegative integer f. Then the following hold:

(i) p does not divide the square free part of n, say $p^{2j}\|n$ for some nonnegative integer j.

(ii) $p^j \leq v/u$, and

(iii) if $u > k$, then $p^{2j}|v\lambda$ (or equivalently $p^j|k$).

10

Mann [57] proved only the abelian version of theorem 6.6 (i) and a special case of (ii) with the stronger assumption that t is a multiplier of D. Jungnickel and Pott [40] obtained interesting applications of theorem 6.6. We mention two examples.

Example 1. There is no planar difference set of order 18: Here $n = 18$, $v = 343 = 7^3$; Let G be any group of order 7^3. It is easy to see that G has a normal subgroup of order 7. Select $p = 3$ and observe $3^{21} \equiv -1 \pmod{49}$; then (iii) implies $3|k = 19$, a contradiction. (This result has already been obtained by Arasu and Ray–Chaudhuri [12] using different methods.)

Example 2. Let D be a $(704, 38, 2)$ difference set in an abelian group G. Let U be a subgroup of index 64 and assume that $H = G/U$ has exponent $u^* = 2$ or 4. Choose $p = 3$; then $p^2 \| n, p \nmid k$ and $p \equiv -1 \pmod{u^*}$. Hence from (iii), we obtain a contradiction as $u > k$. This rules out the open cases no. 180–183 in table 6.1 of Lander [49]. These cases have been ruled out by Arasu [5], using different methods which involve detailed case analysis.

Recently Arasu, Davis, Jungnickel and Pott [10] obtained further results under the same hypothesis of theorem 6.6.

THEOREM 6.7. (Arasu, Davis, Jungnickel and Pott [10].) *With the same assumptions as in theorem 6.6, one has the following additional results:*

(i) *If $p^{2j} \| n$, then $|D \cap Ug| \equiv y \pmod{p^j}$, where y is a nonnegative integer independent of the choice of $g \in G$.*

(ii) *One has $yu \equiv k \pmod{p^j}$; if we choose y_0 as the smallest nonnegative integer solution of this congruence, we also have $y_0 u \leq k$.*

APPLICATIONS. (i) Let G be any group of order 204 with a normal subgroup of order k, i.e. of index $u = 17$. Then G cannot contain a $(204, 29, 4)$ difference set. Here we take $p = 5$ and note $5^8 \equiv -1 \pmod{17}$. We have $5^2 \| n$ i.e. $j = 1$. So theorem 6.7 gives $17y_0 \leq 29$, where y_0 is the smallest nonnegative integer solution of $17y \equiv 29 \pmod{5}$. But then $y_0 = 2$ and we obtain a contradiction. This example excludes some nonabelian groups also.

(ii) The argument in part (3) of Lander [49, pp212–213] for the nonexistence of $(352, 27, 2)$ difference sets in $Z_{11} \times U$, where U is one of $Z_8 \times Z_2^2, Z_4^2 \times Z_2, Z_8 \times Z_4$ or $Z_{16} \times Z_2$, contains several mistakes. The first two of these cases are ruled out by theorem 6.7 (see [10] for details). The other two cases need different arguments.

Arasu [8] has given a proof which includes all the abelian $(352, 27, 2)$ cases in a unified manner.

7. Difference sets in 2–groups. We begin by stating a well–known result of Mann.

THEOREM 7.1. (Mann [55]) *Every nontrivial difference set in a 2-group has parameters $(2^{2s+2}, 2^{2s+1} \pm 2^s, 2^{2s} \pm 2^s)$ for some nonnegative integer s.*

REMARK. Theorem 7.1 actually holds for any (v, k, λ) symmetric design, with v a power of 2.

The following theorem of Turyn [76] provides necessary conditions for the existence of difference sets in abelian 2-groups.

THEOREM 7.2. (Turyn [76]) *If there exists an abelian difference set in G with $v = 2^{2s+2}$, then the exponent of G is at most 2^{s+2}.*

Dillon [29] provided sufficient conditions under which 2–groups possess difference sets.

THEOREM 7.3. (Dillon [29]) *Let G be a group of order 2^{2s+2}. Assume that the center of G has rank at least $s + 1$. Then G contains a difference set.*

REMARK. Dillon [29] has conjectured that it suffices to have $E = Z_2^{s+1}$ to be a normal subgroup of G (a condition which is weaker than assuming the center of G to have rank at least $s + 1$). This conjecture has been verified for the first few values of s.

There is a wide gap that separates Turyn's bound of theorem 7.2 from Dillon's minimum rank requirement of theorem 7.3. The rank 2 case that satisfies the Turyn bound occurs when $G = Z_{2^{s+1}} \times Z_{2^{s+1}}$ or $G = Z_{2^s} \times Z_{2^{s+2}}$. When $s = 2$, the groups are $Z_8 \times Z_8$ and $Z_4 \times Z_{16}$. The question whether $Z_8 \times Z_8$ and $Z_4 \times Z_{16}$ contain difference sets remained open for a long time. Turyn [78, 79] using a systematic computer search discovered all the difference sets in $Z_8 \times Z_8$. Arasu and Reis [13] (and independently Turyn) discovered some difference sets in $Z_4 \times Z_{16}$, using a computer. But recently Davis [22] in his Ph.D. dissertation constructed difference sets in $Z_{2^{s+1}} \times Z_{2^{s+1}}$ and $Z_{2^s} \times Z_{2^{s+2}}$ for each positive integer s. His construction is rather involved; Dillon [27] has given a simpler construction for these difference sets and we state it in

THEOREM 7.4. (Dillon [27]) *Let $G = Z_{2^{s+1}} \times Z_{2^{s+1}}$. Let $\tau : Z_{2^{s+1}} \longrightarrow \{0, 1\}$ be defined by $\tau(x) = \left\lfloor \dfrac{x}{2^s} \right\rfloor$ and and $\pi : Z_{2^{s+1}} \longrightarrow Z_{2^{s+1}}$ be the permutation which maps the residue $2^r t(t \text{ odd})$ to the residue $2^r \bar{t}$, where $t\bar{t} \equiv 1 \pmod{2^{s+1}}$. Then $D = \{x, y) | \tau(\pi(x)y) = 1\}$ is a difference set in G.*

REMARKS. (1) D can also be interpreted as a difference set in $Z_{2^s} \times Z_{2^{s+2}}$. (see [27]).

(2) As a consequence of Theorem 7.4 and remark 1 (also of Davis' theorem [22]), we see that Turyn's bound is sharp for all $s \geq 1$, taking $G = Z_{2^{s+2}}$.

(3) Theorem 7.4 is a special case of the following result of Dillon – we quote it based on his lecture notes at IMA in June'88.

THEOREM 7.5. (Dillon) *Let $G = H \times H$, where $H = Z_{2^{s+2}}$. Let $f^* : H \longrightarrow \{\pm 1\}$ satisfy $f^*(x + 2^s) = -f^*(x)$ for all $x \in H$. Let $\pi : H \longrightarrow H$ be defined by $\pi(2^r t) = 2^r \bar{t}$, where notations are as in theorem 7.4. Then $D = \{(x, y) \in G | f^*(\pi(x)y) = -1\}$ is a difference set in G which is fixed by every numerical automorphism.*

REMARKS. 1) $f^*(x) = \left\lfloor \dfrac{x}{2} s \right\rfloor$ gives Theorem 7.4.

12

2) These difference sets have -1 as a multiplier (and hence admit every odd prime as an extraneous multiplier, see section 10).

3) There are exponentially many pairwise inequivalent difference sets in G. A similar result is given in

THEOREM 7.6. (Kantor [45]) *There are at least* $\displaystyle\binom{2^n + 1}{2^n - 1} / (2^n + 1) 2^n (2^n - 1)^2 n$ *pairwise inequivalent difference sets in elementary abelian 2–group of order* 2^{2n}.

Dillon's composition theorems and transfer theorems [28, 29] yield difference sets in other 2-groups, including some nonabelian ones. A remarkable result along these lines is given in

THEOREM 7.7. (Kramer [48]) *Abelian 2-groups admit difference sets if and only if they satisfy Turyn's exponent bound.*

In our opinion, theorem 7.7 is the only completely satisfactory result in the theory of difference sets when the question of existence is involved. We wish to remark that Yamamoto and Yamada [84] provide different constructions of certain difference sets in abelian 2-groups. We conclude this section by referring the reader to the works of Davis [24] and Pott [72] who constructed difference sets in nonabelian 2-groups. (*Note*: Pott [72] actually deals with other groups, too).

8. Menon difference sets. The parameters of theorem 7.1 (when $v = $ a power of 2) fall under a more general calss of parameters given in the following theorem.

THEOREM 8.1. (Menon [65]) *If there exists a* (v, k, λ) *difference set with* $v = 4n$, *then the parameters have the following form:*

(*)
$$(4m^2,\ 2m^2 \pm m,\ m^2 \pm m).$$

REMARKS. 1) Theorem 8.1 holds for (v, k, λ) symmetric designs in general (of course, when $v = 4n$).

2) $m = 1$ yields trivial difference sets.

3) $m \longrightarrow -m$ yields parameters of the complementary difference set.

Difference sets with parameters (*) are called Menon difference sets. We warn the reader that these are also referred to as H-sets or Hadamard difference sets. Some authors use the term "Hadamard" when $k = 2\lambda + 1$ and $v = 2k + 1$. Our terminology is chosen to agree with [16].

Menon difference sets for $m = 2$ and $m = 3$ are well–known (see Bruck [20] and Menon [65] respectively). We now state Menon's composition theorem.

THEOREM 8.2. (Menon [65]) *If there exists difference sets with parameters* (*) *with* $m = m_1$ *and* $m = m_2$ *in groups* G_1 *and* G_2 *then there is such a difference set with* $m = 2m_1 m_2$ *in* $G_1 \times G_2$.

Theorem 8.2 together with the following theorem of Turyn [77] provides construction of Hadamard difference sets for all $m = \pm 2^r 3^s, r \geq 0, s \geq 0$.

THEOREM 8.3. (Turyn [77]) *Menon difference sets exist for $m = 3^s$ for $s \geq 1$.*

All known constructions so far have m of the form $m = \pm 2^r 3^s$. McFarland has mae the following conjecture:

McFarland's conjecture. If there exists a Menon difference of order m^2, then $m = \pm 2^r 3^s, r \geq 0, s \geq 0$.

We now quote a few results of McFarland on Menon difference sets, based on the lecture given by McFarland at the IMA workshop on codes and designs.

THEOREM 8.3. (McFarland [16]) *If there exists a difference set in an abelian group of order $4p^2, p$ a prime, then it is a Menon difference set and $p = 2$ or $p = 3$.*

The proof of this result uses various results of Mann, McFarland and Turyn, some tools from algebraic number theory, finite geometry and abelian group characters. Theorem 8.3 in particular proves the nonexistence of $(100, 45, 20)$ difference set in $Z_4 \times Z_5 \times Z_5$, an open case in table 6.1 of Lander [49].

THEOREM 8.4. (McFarland [62]) *Suppose that $m = 2^e p, e \geq 0, p$ a prime, $p \neq 2$ or 3. let G be an abelian group of order $4m^2$. Assume that (i) the Sylow p-subgroup of G is $Z_p \times Z_p$ and (ii) the Sylow 2-subgroup of G has*

$$
\begin{array}{ll}
exponent\ 2 & if\ p \equiv 1 \pmod 4 \\
exponent\ 2\ or\ 4 & if\ p \equiv 3 \pmod 4
\end{array}
$$

Then G cannot contain a Menon difference set, unless $p + 1$ divides 2^e.

REMARK. $p + 1 | 2^e$ if and only if p is a Mersenne prime and the order of the Sylow 2-subgroup of G is $> 4p^2$.

THEOREM 8.5. (McFarland [63]) *Suppose that the abelian group G contains a Menon difference set. Let H be a subgroup of G such that*

    i) *$|H|$ is even and*

    ii) *$(|H|, |G/H|) = 1$*

Suppose furthermore that $|G/H|$ is a self-conjugate modulo the exponent of H(i.e. for each prime $p, p | \ |G/H|$, there exists an integer t depending on p such that $p^t \equiv -1 \pmod{exponent\ of\ H}$).

Then H contains a Menon difference set.

REMARK. Theorem 8.5 can be used to provide nonexistence results for Menon difference sets, as seen in the following:

COROLLARY 8.6. (McFarland [63]) *Let $p_1, p_2, \cdots, p_s$ be primes, $\neq 2$ or 5. Assume that $5 \nmid p_i - 1$ for each $i = 1, \cdots, s$. Let $G = Z_2^r \times Z_5 \times Z_5 \times K$, where K is an abelian group such that $(p | \ |K|, p$ a prime implies that $p = p_i$ for some $i = 1, \cdots, s)$ and Z_2^r denotes the elementary abelian 2-group of rank r. Then G does not contain a Menon difference set.*

A variation of theorem 8.5 is given theorem 11.1.

14

9. Lander's table. Lander [49] gives all parameter triples (v, k, λ) satisfying the basic equation $k(k-1) = \lambda(v-1)$, and which do not contradict the Bruck–Ryser–Chowla and Schutzenberger theorems in the range $k \leq 50, k < \frac{v}{2}$. For a fixed such triple, Lander considers all possible abelian groups of order v and obtains 268 possible cases. Of these, 65 correspond to known difference sets, 178 are known not to exist (four such cases are incorrectly proven; for correct proofs, see [8] and [10]) and 25 are undecided. We update Lander's table in this section.

Entry #34. There is no $(27, 13, 6)$ difference set in $Z_3 \times Z_9$.

Bozikov [18] proved this using a long, detailed case analysis. Kibler [46] obtained this result using a computer search. Arasu [5], DeCaen [25] and Wei [80] independently proved this theoretically using multiplier theorems and intersection numbers. (For more on intersection numbers, see [10] or [12]).

REMARK. This case has been given as an exercise in the lecture notes at Ohio State University, prepared by R.M. Wilson (see [82]).

Entries 48 and 49. $(81, 16, 3)$ difference sets do not exist in $Z_9 \times Z_9$ and $Z_3 \times Z_3 \times Z_9$.

This result was independently proved by Kibler [46] (using computers), Bozikov [18] and Arasu [1]. Methods of Arasu and Bozikov are quite different.

Entry #115. $(64, 28, 12)$ difference sets exist in $Z_8 \times Z_8$.

Turyn [78] discovered all of these difference sets using a systematic computer search. Davis [22, 23] and Dillon [27] provide different theoretical constructions. (cf: section 7)

Entry #113. $(64, 28, 12)$ difference sets exist in $Z_4 \times Z_{16}$.

Arasu and Reis [13] and Turyn [78] independently obtained examples of these using a computer. Davis [22, 23] and Dillon [27] provided theoretical constructions (cf. section 7).

Entry #147. $(375, 34, 3)$ difference sets do not exist in $Z_3 \times Z_5 \times Z_{25}$.

Arasu [5], DeCaen [25] and Wei [80] independently proved this using multipliers and intersection numbers.

Entries 180–183. $(704, 38, 2)$ difference sets do not exist in $Z_4^3 \times Z_{12}, Z_2^2 \times Z_4^2 \times Z_{11}, Z_2^4 \times Z_4 \times Z_{11}$ and $Z_2^6 \times Z_{11}$.

A computer search of Dickey and Hughes (see Hughes [39]) includes this result. The first theoretical proof of this result is due to Arasu [5], but methods used are rather involved. Wei [80] independently obtained this result. A short, elegant proof is due to Jungnickel and Pott [40] (see example 2 in section 6).

Entry #226. $(100, 45, 20)$ difference sets do not exist in $Z_4 \times Z_5 \times Z_5$.

A long proof of this result is due to McFarland [61] (see remarks after theorem 8.3 for details).

Thus, 14 more entries in Lander's table now need to be filled. We conclude this section by stating a result of Arasu and Stewart [14].

15

THEOREM 9.1. (Arasu and Stewart [14]) *If the multiplier conjecture is true, then 7 more entries in Lander's table (viz. #235–237, 245, 266–268) can be filled with answer "no".*

10. Extraneous multipliers. Let D be an abelian (v, k, λ) difference set in a group G. A prime $p, p \nmid n$, is said to be an *extraneous multiplier* of D if $D^{(p)} = Dg$ for some $g \in G$.

REMARK. A prime p is an extraneous multiplier of D if p actually is a multiplier of D and furthermore $p \nmid n$.

Even though Hall [34] had some results on extraneous multipliers, the term "extraneous" was first introduced by Mann [56]. Both Hall [34] and Mann [56] dealt with extraneous multipliers for cyclic planar difference sets. Wu [83] proved an extension of Mann's theorem [56].

THEOREM 10.1. (Wu [83]) *Let D be a cyclic (v, k, λ) difference set of order n. If a prime p is an extraneous multiplier of D, then $p \geq 5$. If, furthermore, $\lambda = 1$, then $p \geq 7$.*

REMARKS. 1) The $\lambda = 1$ case of theorem 10.1 concluding $p \geq 3$ was first proved by Hall [34] and Mann [56] was able to prove that $p \geq 5$.

2) Even though Wu proved theorem 10.1 only for cyclic difference sets, Wu's method also can be adapted to the abelian case.

THEOREM 10.2. (Ko [47], Pott [71]) *Let D be an abelian (v, k, λ) difference set. Then*

(i) *2 cannot be an extraneous multiplier of D.*

(ii) *if 3 is an extraneous multiplier of D, then -1 is a multiplier of D.*

(iii) *When $\lambda = 1$, 5 cannot be an extraneous multiplier of D.*

Examples. 1) $(11, 5, 2)$ difference set of Example 1, section 2, has 3 as a multiplier, by theorem 2.2. Therefore 5 which is $\equiv 3^3 \pmod{11}$ is an extraneous multiplier of this difference set.

2) As in example 1, one can show that 11 is an extraneous multiplier of a cyclic $(21, 5, 1)$ difference set.

3) By theorem 11.3, (ii), if D is an abelian (v, k, λ) difference set with -1 as a multiplier, then every integer t, with $(t, v) = 1$, is a multiplier of D. Hence these difference sets admit infinitely many extraneous multipliers (for instance, any prime $p, p \nmid n, p \nmid v$ would do). In section 11, we provide some examples of these difference sets.

The following theorem of Ho [37] will have potential applications only when the prime p under consideration is an extraneous multiplier. This seems to suggest that extraneous multipliers deserve further study.

16

THEOREM 10.3. (Ho [37]) *Let p be a prime, which is a multiplier of an abelian planar difference set of order n. If $3|n^2 + n + 1$ or $(p+1, n^2 + n + 1) \neq 1$, then n is a square in $GF(p)$.*

REMARK. If $p|n$, then $n \equiv 0 \pmod{p}$ and hence n is trivially a square in $GF(p)$. Hence, unless the prime p under discussion is an extraneous multiplier, Ho's theorem will not have any content.

Another application of extraneous multipliers is given in:

THEOREM 10.4. (Arasu, Davis, Jungnickel & Pott [11]) *Let D be an abelian $(m, n, k, 1)$ relative difference set. Then 2 is a multiplier of D if and only if D is affine difference set of even order k.*

REMARK. For the definition of relative and affine difference sets, we refer the reader to Elliott and Butson [30] and an excellent expository article by Jungnickel [43].

11. Difference sets with -1 as a multiplier. -1 plays a special role in nonexistence theorems, because "reversibility" entails severe restrictions. A detailed account of this topic can be found in section 4.5 of Lander [49]. In this section, we only mention the recent results in this direction.

We begin by quoting two theorems of McFarland.

THEOREM 11.1. (McFarland [63]) *Suppose that the abelian group G contains a Menon difference set which is fixed by the multiplier -1. Let H be a subgroup of G satisfying (i) $|H|$ is even and (ii) $(|H|, |G/H|) = 1$. Then H contains a Menon difference set which is also fixed by the multiplier -1.*

REMARK. Proof of theorem 11.1 runs along the same lines of theorem 8.5.

THEOREM 11.2. (McFarland [63]) *Let D be a Menon difference set of order m^2 fixed by the multiplier -1. Then the square-free part of m divides 6.*

REMARK. Consider the range $1 < m \leq 100$. Menon difference sets fixed by the multiplier -1 exist for all $m = \pm 2^r 3^s, r, s > 0$. This accounts for 19 values of m in the given range. Theorem 11.2 rules out all the remaining values of m in this range, except for the six values

$$m = 25, 49, 50, 75, 98, 100.$$

We now quote a well-known theorem (for instance, see [16]).

THEOREM 11.3. *Let D be an abelian (v, k, λ) difference set of order $n = k - \lambda$ in G admitting -1 as a multiplier. Then the following hold:*

(i) *v and λ are even and n is a square.*
(ii) *every integer relatively prime to v is a multiplier.*
(iii) *there exists $g \in G$ such that Dg is fixed by every multiplier.*
(iv) *if $p^{2i}|n$, then $p^{i+1}|v$.*

17

THEOREM 11.4. (Ghinelli–Smit [32], Pott [71]) *Let D be an abelian (v, k, λ) difference set with multiplier -1. Let p be an odd prime dividing v. Then $p|n$.*

REMARK. Ghinelli–Smit [32] proved this using character theory; her proof is quite long. An elementary proof of this is given by Pott [71]. Theorem 11.4 is a special case of theorem 11.5 below

THEOREM 11.5. (Ma [51]) *Let G be an abelian group of order v and exponent v^*. Let p be a prime divisor of v such that $p^t\|v$ and $p^r\|v^*$. If G contains a nontrivial difference set with -1 as a multiplier, then $p^{2r}|4n$ and $p^{2(t-r+1)} \nmid 4n$.*

COROLLARY 11.6. *Under the hypothesis of theorem 11.5, we must have $2r \leq t$.*

REMARKS. (1) Theorem 11.5 follows from a more general result on polynomial addition sets (see [5]).

(2) Further results with -1 as a multiplier can be found in [51].

We now quote another result of Pott [70], which is new.

THEOREM 11.7. (Pott [71]) *Let D be an abelian (v, k, λ) difference set with multiplier -1. Then 3 is a divisor of v, k or λ.*

REMARKS. (i) Difference sets in a group G with -1 as a multiplier give rise to strongly regular graphs admitting G as a regular automorphism group. Their connections to association schemes and schur rings can be found in Ma [52].

(ii) Most of the known examples of difference sets admitting -1 as a multiplier are Menon difference sets. (In fact, Menon difference sets of order $m^2, m = \pm 2^r 3^s, r \geq 0, s \geq 0$, admitting -1 as a multiplier do exist.) The only known exception is due to McFarland [60], who constructed a $(4000, 775, 150)$ difference set in $Z_5^3 \times Z_2^5$, with -1 as a multiplier. McFarland and Ma [64] have shown that except for two possible parameter triples (v, k, λ), with $v \neq 4n$, abelian difference sets with -1 as a multiplier, $n \leq 10^8$, the only parameter triple that admits a difference set with multiplier -1 is $(4000, 775, 150)$. McFarland has made the following conjecture.

Conjecture. (McFarland) If D is an abelian (v, k, λ) difference set, admitting -1 as a multiplier, then either $v = 4n$ or $v = 4000, k = 775, \lambda = 150$.

We finally remark that Ma [53] has constructed an infinite family of nonabelian difference sets which are invariant under $x \longrightarrow x^{-1}$. Since $x \longrightarrow x^{-1}$ does not induce an automorphism of the associated design, -1 is usually referred to as, in this case, a weak multiplier.

12. A related problem. In this section, we deal with a problem in finite geometry which reduces to a question on difference sets. It is widely conjectured that a finite projective plane admitting a flag transitive collineation group must be desarguesian. (e.g. see Dembowski [26]) Modulo a degenerate case, Kantor [44] proved the above conjecture. We state it in

THEOREM 12.1. [Kantor [44]] *Let π be a projective plane of order n and let F be a collineation group transitive on flags (i.e. incident point-line pairs). Then either*

$$(i)\pi \text{ is desarguesian and } F \geq PSL(3,n)$$

or (ii) F *is a Frobenius group of odd order* $(n^2 + n + 1)(n + 1)$ *and* $n^2 + n + 1$ *is a prime.*

The following description pinning down the structure of F in case (ii) is well-known (for instance, see Fink [31]):

Suppose that a finite projective plane of order n has a collineation group F of odd order which acts regularly on the flags of π. Then either $n = 2$ or 8 or else π is non-desarguesian cyclic plane determined by a difference set D in the cyclic group $(GF(p), +)$, where $p = n^2 + n + 1$ is a prime with n even. In fact D can be taken to be the set of nth powers in the multiplicative group of $GF(p)$, in which case D consists of all its own multipliers and contains all divisors of n.

If the conjecture we mentioned in the beginning of this section were true, one should be able to prove the nonexistence of such a difference set. But so far, this has remained as an open problem.

13. Open problems. We conclude this survey by listing a few open problems.

1. Prove or disprove the multiplier conjecture.
2. Prove or disprove Hall's conjecture: For each fixed $\lambda > 1$, there exists only a finite number of (v, k, λ) difference sets.
3. Prove or disprove Ryser's conjecture: If there exists a cyclic (v, k, λ) difference set, then $(v, n) = 1$.
4. Prove or disprove Lander's conjecture: (which includes Ryser's conjecture): If D is a v, k, λ abelian difference set in a group G and p is a prime divisor of (v, n), then the Sylow p-subgroup of G is non-cyclic.
5. Prove or disprove the prime power conjecture on planar difference sets.
6. Prove or disprove:

   If there exists a

   $$\left(\frac{n^m - 1}{n - 1}, \frac{n^{m-1} - 1}{n - 1}, \frac{n^{m-2}}{n - 1} \right) \text{ difference set}$$

   with $m \geq 3$, then n is a prime power. (This includes 5 above).

7. Remove the hypothesis $n \equiv 1 \pmod 3$ from proposition 4.3.
8. Generalize proposition 4.3 to include

   $$n \equiv 2^{2^r} \pmod{2^{2^r+1}}.$$

9. Fill in the remaining entries of Lander's table.
10. Determine all groups of order 64 that have difference sets.

19

11. Extend Lander's table to include nonabelian groups, as well. (This includes 10 above.)

12. By ad hoc arguments, produce multipliers for the difference sets in question of theorem 9.1 and finish off some of the open cases in Lander's table.

13. Find nonexistence applications of theorems 5.5 and 5.6 (Pott's generalization of Wilbrink's identities).

14. Try to apply Wilbrink's identity for primes $p, p \geq 5$.

15. Find applications of Ho's theorem (theorem 10.3) to obtain nonexistence results of abelian planar difference sets, supporting the prime power conjecture.

16. Prove or disprove McFarland's conjecture: If Menon difference sets of order m^2 exist, them $m = \pm 2^r 3^s$. $r \geq 0, s \geq 0$.

17. Find all parameter triples (v, k, λ) for which there exist difference sets admitting -1 as a multiplier.

18. Prove or disprove Dillon's conjecture: "Z_2^{s+1} is a normal subgroup of G" is a sufficient hypothesis in theorem 7.3 (instead of having the stronger hypothesis: the center G has rank at least $s + 1$).

19. Prove or disprove McFarland's conjecture:

    If D is an abelian (v, k, λ) difference set admitting -1 as a multiplier, then either $v = 4n$ or $v = 4000, k = 775, \lambda = 150$.

20. Prove the nonexistence of the difference sets described at the end of Chapter 12.

Acknowledgements. The author thanks Dr. J. F. Dillon and Professors D. Jungnickel and R. McFarland for reading the first version of this manuscript and providing very helpful suggestions. The author is very grateful to Professor W. M. Kantor for his suggestions regarding the material in section 12.

REFERENCES

[1] ARASU, K.T. (81, 16, 3), *abelian difference sets do not exist*, J. Comb. Th. Ser A 43 (1986), 350–353.

[2] ARASU, K.T., *On Wilbrink's theorem*, J. Comb. Th. Ser A, 44 (1987), 156–158.

[3] ARASU, K.T., *Another variation of Wilbrink's theorem*, Ars Combinatoria 25 (1988), 107–109.

[4] ARASU, K.T., *On abelian difference sets*, Arch. Math. vol 48 (1987), 491–494.

[5] ARASU, K.T., *More missing entries in Lander's table could be filled*, Arch. Math. vol. 49 (1988).

[6] ARASU, K.T., *On Lander's conjecture for the case* $\lambda = 3$, J. Comb. Math. and Comb. computing, vol. 1 (1987), 5-11.

[7] ARASU, K.T., *Validity of Lander's conjecture for* $\lambda = 3$ *and* $k \leq 500$, J. Comb. Math and Comb. computing, vol. 2 (1987), 73–76.

[8] ARASU, K.T., *Singer groups of biplanes of order 25*, submitted.

[9] ARASU, K. T., *Abelian projective planes of square order*, to appear in Europ J. Comb.

[10] ARASU, K. T., DAVIS, J., JUNGNICKEL, D. AND POTT, A., *A note on intersection numbers of difference sets*, submitted.

[11] ARASU, K. T., DAVIS, J., JUNGNICKEL, D. AND POTT, A., *Some nonexistence results on divisible difference sets*, submitted.

[12] ARASU, K. T. AND RAY–CHAUDHURI, D. K., *Multiplier theorem for a difference list*, Ars Comb. 22 (1986), 119–137.

[13] ARASU K.T. AND REIS, J., *On abelian groups of order 64 that have difference sets*, Wright State University Technical Report #1987.10 (1987).

[14] ARASU, K.T. AND STEWART, D., *Certain implications of the multiplier conjecture*, J. Comb. Math. and Comb. Computing, vol. 3 (1988).

[15] BAUMERT, L. D., *Cyclic difference sets*, In Lecture Notes in Mathematics, 182, New York: Springer-Verlag (1971).

[16] BETH, T. JUNGNICKEL, D. AND LENZ, H., *Design Theory*, Mannheim 1985, Cambridge 1986.

[17] BOREVICH, Z. I. AND SHAFAREVICH, I.R., *Number Theory*, New York: Academic Press (1966).

[18] BOZIKOV, Z., *Abelian Singer groups of certain symmetric block designs*, Radovi Matematiki 1 (1985), 247–253.

[19] BRIDGES, W.G., HALL M. JR. AND HAYDEN, J. L., *Codes and designs*, J. Comb. Th. Ser A, 31 (1981) 155–174.

[20] BRUCK, R.H., *Difference sets in a finite group*, Trans. Amer. Math. Soc 78 (1955), 464–481.

[21] CHOWLA, S. AND RYSER, H.J., *Combinatorial problems*, Canad. J. Math, 2 (1950), 93–99.

[22] DAVIS, J., *Difference sets in abelian 2-groups*, Ph.D. dissertation, U. of Virginia (1987).

[23] DAVIS, J., *Difference sets in abelian 2-groups*, submitted.

[24] DAVIS, J., *Difference sets in nonabelian 2-groups*, submitted.

[25] DECAEN, D., *Non-existence of Several Small abelian difference sets*, Abstract #153, 18th Southeastern Conference in Comb., (1987).

[26] DEMBOWSKI, P., *Finite geometrics*, Springer, Berlin/Heidelberg/New York (1968).

[27] DILLON, J.F., *Difference sets in 2-groups*, to appear in Contemporary Math. Finite Geometries and Designs, AMS (1988).

[28] DILLON, J.F., *Variations on a scheme of McFarland for Noncyclic Difference sets*, J. Comb. Th (A), 40 (1985).

[29] DILLON, J.F., *Elementary Hadamard difference sets*, Ph.D. thesis, University of Maryland (1974).

[30] ELLIOTT, J.E.H. AND BUTSON, A.T., *Relative difference sets*, Illinois J. Math., 10, 517–531 (1966).

[31] FINK, *A note on sharply flag-transitive projective planes*, In Finite geometries (Pullman, Wash. 1981), Lecture Notes in Pure and Applied Math 82, Dekker, New York (1983), 161–164.

[32] GHINELLI-SMIT, D., *On abelian projective planes*, Arch. Math. 44, (1985) 282–288.

[33] GHINELLI-SMITH, D., *A new result on difference sets with −1 as a multiplier*, Geo. ded. 23, (1987), 309–317.

[34] HALL, M. JR, *Cyclic projective planes*, Duke Math. J. 14 (1947), 1079–1090.

[35] HALL, M. JR., *Difference sets* In combinatorics, eds. M. Hall, Jr. and J. H. van Lint, (1975) Dordrecht: D. Reidel, 321–346.

[36] HALL, M. JR., *Combinatorial Theory*, 2nd edition, John Wiley and sons (1986).

[37] HO, C., *Some remarks on difference sets*, (to appear).

[38] HO, C., *On multiplier groups of finite cyclic planes*, to appear in J. algebra.

[39] HUGHES, D.R., eds. D.A. Holton and Jennifer Seberry, Lecture notes in mathematics, 686, Berlin-Heidelberg-New York (1978) 55–58, *On biplanes and semibiplanes:* In combinatorial mathematics.

[40] JUNGNICKEL, D. AND POTT, A., *Two results on difference sets*, to appear in Proc. 7th Hungarian Coll. on Combinatorics, Eger (1987).

[41] JUNGNICKEL, D. AND VEDDER, K., *On the geometry of planar difference sets*, Europ. J. Comb. 5 (1984), 143–148.

21

[42] JUNGNICKEL, D., *An elementary proof of Wilbrink's theorem*, to appear in Arch. Math..

[43] JUNGNICKEL, D., *On affine difference sets*, submitted.

[44] KANTOR, W.M., *Primitive permutation groups of odd degree, and an application to finite projective planes*, J. Algebra, 106 (1987), 15–45.

[45] KANTOR, W.M., *Exponential numbers of two-weight codes, difference sets and symmetric designs*, Discr. Math, 46, (1983), 95–98.

[46] KIBLER, R.E., *A summary of non-cyclic difference sets, $k < 20$*, J. comb. Th. A, 25 (1978), 62–67.

[47] KO, H.P., *A note on extraneous multipliers for difference sets*, submitted.

[48] KRAEMER, R.G., *Proof of a conjecture on Hadamard 2-groups*, submitted.

[49] LANDER, E.S., *Symmetric Designs: An algebraic Approach*, London Math. Society Lecture Note Series, 74 (1983).

[50] LANDER, E.S., *Restrictions upon multipliers of an abelian difference set*, Arch. Math., vol. 50 (1988) 241–242.

[51] MA, S.L., *Polynomial addition sets and symmetric difference sets*, submitted.

[52] MA, S.L., *On association schemes, Schur Rings, Strongly regular graphs and Partial difference sets*, to appear in Ars Comb..

[53] MA, S.L., *A family of difference sets having -1 as an invariant*, to appear in Europ. J. Comb..

[54] MANN, H.B., *Addition theorems*, New York: Interscience (1967).

[55] MANN, H.B., *Difference sets in elementary abelian groups*, Ill. J. Math. 9 (1965), 212–219.

[56] MANN, H.B., *Some theorems on difference sets*, Canad. J. Math. (1952), 222–226.

[57] MANN, H.B., *Balanced Incomplete block designs and abelian difference sets*, Ill. J. Math. 8 (1964), 252–261.

[58] MCFARLAND, R.L., *On multipliers of abelian difference sets*, Ph.D. dissertation, Ohio State University (1970).

[59] MCFARLAND, R.L. AND RICE, B.F., *Translates and multipliers of abelian difference sets*, Proc. AMS, 68 (1978), 375–379.

[60] MCFARLAND, R.L., *A family of difference sets in non-cyclic groups*, J. Comb. Theory, A., 15 (1973), 1–10.

[61] MCFARLAND, R.L., *Difference sets in abelian groups of order $4p^2$*, submitted.

[62] MCFARLAND, R.L., *Necessary Conditions for Hadamard difference sets*, submitted.

[63] MCFARLAND, R.L., *Subdifference sets of Hadamard difference sets*, to appear in J. Comb. Th(A).

[64] MCFARLAND, R.L. AND MA, S.L., *Abelian Difference sets with multiplier minus one*, submitted.

[65] MENON, P.K., *On difference sets whose parameters satisfy a certain relation*, Proc. AMS (1986), 13, 739–745.

[66] PICKERT, G, *Differenzmengen und ovale*, to appear in Discr. Math..

[67] PLESS, V., *Cyclic projective planes and binary, extended cyclic self-dual codes*, J. Comb. Th. (A), vol. 43 (1986), 331–333.

[68] POTT, A., *Applications of the DFT to abelian difference sets*, Arch. Math., 51 (1988), 283–288.

[69] POTT, A., *On multiplier theorems*, to appear in Proc. IMA workshop (1988).

[70] POTT, A., *New necessary conditions on the existence of abelian difference sets*, submitted.

[71] POTT, A., *On abelian difference sets with multiplier -1*, to appear in Arch. Math..

[72] POTT, A., *A generalization of a construction of Lenz*, submitted.

[73] POTT, A., *A note on nonabelian planar difference sets*, Europ. J. Comb. 9 (1988), 169–170.

[74] SCHUTZENBERGER, M.P., *A nonexistence theorem for an infinite family of symmetrical block design*, Ann. Eugenics, 14 (1949), 286–287.

22

[75] SINGER, J., *A theorem in finite projective geometry and some applications to number theory*, Trans. AMS 43 (1938), 377–385.

[76] TURYN, R.J., *Character sums and difference sets*, Pac. J. Math 15 (1965), 319–346.

[77] TURYN R.J., *A special class of Williamson matrices and difference sets*, J. Comb. Th. (A), vol. 36 (1984), 111–115.

[78] TURYN, R.J., Personal communication.

[79] TURYN, R.J., *Computer searches for difference sets*, Lecture notes of an unspoken lecture at IMA, June'88.

[80] WEI, R, *Nonexistence of some abelian difference sets*, to appear in Proc. International conf. comb. designs and applications, Anhui, China, August (1988).

[81] WILBRINK, H.A., *A note on planar difference sets*, J. Comb. Th. A. 38 (1985), 94–95.

[82] WILSON, R.M., Unpublished lecture notes on difference sets, Ohio State University (1973).

[83] WU, X., *Extraneous multipliers of cyclic difference sets*, J. Comb. Th., Ser A, 42, (1986), 259–269.

[84] YAMAMOTO, K. AND YAMADA, M, *Hadamard difference sets over an extension ring of $Z/4Z$*, submitted.

AUTOMORPHISM GROUPS OF BLOCK STRUCTURES WITH AND WITHOUT TREATMENTS

R. A. BAILEY*

Abstract. A designed experiment has two permutation groups associated with it. The first, consisting of all automorphisms of the block structure (ignoring the treatments) determines the strata for the subsequent analysis. The second, comprising all permutations of the plots which respect both the block structure and the treatment allocation, can help to simplify calculation of efficiency factors and hence assessment of designs.

Key words. automorphism, block structure, centralizer algebra, designed experiment, efficiency factor, multiplicity-free, permutation character, randomization, strata

AMS(MOS) subject classifications. 05B99, 20B25, 20C15, 65K99

§1. BACKGROUND

To a statistician, a *design* has three components: a set Ω of plots, a set T of treatments, and a function $\phi \colon \Omega \to T$ allocating treatments to plots. The sets Ω and T are both finite, and usually carry some sort of structure. This structure is often a semi-lattice of equivalence relations (partitions), but may include other relations, such as adjacency between plots in an agricultural field. For our purposes it is sufficient to consider *structure* to be a family of binary relations on a given set. The non-trivial structure on Ω which was first considered, and is still the most commonly used, is a single partition into *blocks*. For historical reasons, then, Ω and its structure are called the *block structure*. See [4], [5], [7], [26], [34], [47], [51], [52]. Similarly, T and its structure are called the *treatment structure*.

The treatment on plot ω is $\omega\phi$. Although as a general rule I write functions on the right of their arguments if they are likely to be composed with other functions, and on the left otherwise, I can afford to be rather cavalier in this paper because no proofs and few detailed formulas are included.

The real vector space $\mathbf{R}^\Omega$ consists of all functions from Ω to $\mathbf{R}$. Its canonical basis comprises the characteristic functions of the singleton subsets of Ω. An inner product can be uniquely defined on $\mathbf{R}^\Omega$ in such a way that the canonical basis is orthonormal: all future references to orthogonality in $\mathbf{R}^\Omega$ are with respect to this inner product.

An $\Omega \times \Omega$ real matrix is simply a function from $\Omega \times \Omega$ to $\mathbf{R}$. Together with the canonical basis, any such matrix defines a linear transformation from $\mathbf{R}^\Omega$ to itself; if the matrix is symmetric then the associated linear transformation does not depend on whether functions are written on the right or on the left. Thus I shall regard a symmetric $\Omega \times \Omega$ matrix and its associated (self-adjoint) linear transformation of $\mathbf{R}^\Omega$ as interchangeable. Similar remarks apply to $\mathbf{R}^T$.

Treatments are applied to plots according to ϕ, an experiment is conducted, and a single real-number measurement—such as yield of grain in tonnes per hectare—is

*Statistics Department, Rothamsted Experimental Station, Harpenden, Herts, AL5 2JQ, U.K.
This work was partly supported by the Institute for Mathematics and its Applications.

made on each plot (in general more than one measurement may be made, but that does not essentially affect the theory presented below). Let $y(\omega)$ be the real number recorded on plot ω: the function y is called the *data*. We assume that there is a real random variable Y defined on $\Omega \times T$ such that y is a realization of Y_ϕ, which is defined by

$$Y_\phi(\omega) = Y(\omega, \omega\phi) \qquad \text{for } \omega \text{ in } \Omega.$$

The basic assumptions on Y are that

(A) the effects of plots and treatments on the mean response are additive; that is, there are functions $f: T \to \mathbf{R}$ and $h: \Omega \to \mathbf{R}$ such that, for all ω in Ω and all t in T,

$$E(Y(\omega, t)) = h(\omega) + f(t);$$

(B) the covariance between components of Y depends only on the Ω-coordinate; that is, there is a function $C: \Omega \times \Omega \to \mathbf{R}$ such that, for all ω_1, ω_2 in Ω and all t_1, t_2 in T,

$$\text{Cov}\left(Y(\omega_1, t_1), Y(\omega_2, t_2)\right) = C(\omega_1, \omega_2).$$

If we know h then we can estimate f from the known data. If we also know C then we can obtain the "best" linear estimator of f (in the sense of having minimum variance) and also an estimate of the variance of that estimator.

Standard textbooks on the statistical design of experiments, such as [24] and [25], assume that h is in a known low-dimensional subspace of $\mathbf{R}^\Omega$ (possibly $h = 0$) and that $C = I\sigma^2$, where I is the identity function on $\mathbf{R}^\Omega$ and σ^2 may or may not be known. In these circumstances the procedures for estimating f and the variance of that estimator are well known.

However, it is more realistic to assume that C is unknown, or at least is not as well-specified as $I\sigma^2$. Suppose that C is unknown but we do know that a given subspace W of $\mathbf{R}^\Omega$ is an eigenspace of C, with (possibly unknown) eigenvalue ξ. Let $P: \mathbf{R}^\Omega \to \mathbf{R}^\Omega$ be the orthogonal projector onto W. Then it can be shown that

$$\text{Cov}(PY) = (I_W \oplus 0_{W^\perp})\xi,$$

where I_W is the identity function on W and $0_{W^\perp}$ is the zero function on the orthogonal complement $W^\perp$ of W. Thus we can use the projected data Py to perform estimation within W. See [34], [35] and [3] for more details.

Because of their importance in analyzing data from designed experiments, eigenspaces like W have acquired a special name.

DEFINITION. A *stratum* is an eigenspace of the covariance matrix C.

If all strata are known, then estimation can be performed in each one. If the eigenvalues of C are known up to a scalar multiple, information from the separate strata can then be combined; more generally, the relative values of these eigenvalues have to be estimated from the data before the information can be combined (see

[19], [32], [36], [37], [50] and [54]). Thus knowledge of the strata is the key to the whole analysis.

In §2 we shall show how to use the automorphism group of the block structure (ignoring treatments) to find the strata. In §3 we shall restrict to the subgroup which also preserves treatments and show how knowledge of this subgroup also gives helpful information about the design.

§2. STRATA

In this section we concentrate on finding the strata. Treatments are not involved in the definition of strata, and so are ignored for almost the whole of the section.

2.1. Randomization. If the covariance matrix C is not completely known, how can we expect to know its eigenspaces? This is not as unreasonable as it first appears: after all, C being $I\sigma^2$ with unknown σ^2 is equivalent to $\mathbf{R}^\Omega$ being the single eigenspace of C. However, as we said before, it is usually unrealistic to assume that C is as simple as $I\sigma^2$.

In [18] Fisher introduced *randomization*, partly as means of allowing for our lack of precise knowledge about h and C.

DEFINITION. Let G be a group of permutations of Ω. Then *randomization by G* consists of choosing g in G with probability $1/|G|$ and then using the design ϕ^g, where
$$\omega(\phi^g) = (\omega g^{-1})\phi \qquad \text{for } \omega \text{ in } \Omega.$$

Fisher advocated choosing a suitable group G and randomizing by it. This remains one of the cornerstones of statistical design. We delay for a moment consideration of what is suitable, and consider the theoretical consequences of randomization.

Randomization incorporates some extra randomness into the model given by Conditions (A) and (B). If the group G is used for randomization then h and C should be replaced by h^G and C^G respectively, which are defined as follows.

$$h^G(\omega) = \frac{1}{|G|} \sum_{g \in G} h(\omega g)$$

$$C^G(\omega_1, \omega_2) = \frac{1}{|G|} \left(\sum_{g \in G} C(\omega_1 g, \omega_2 g) + h(\omega_1 g)h(\omega_2 g) \right) - h^G(\omega_1)h^G(\omega_2).$$

(Kempthorne and his school derived this in [27] and [56] for the case that $C = 0$. However, this extra assumption makes very little difference to the inference from the experiment: see [3].) To avoid unwieldy notation, I shall henceforth write h and C for h^G and C^G.

If G is transitive on Ω then h is a constant vector. If G is not transitive then h cannot be assumed constant, and this has undesirable consequences for estimation (see [9]). Let V_0 be the 1-dimensional subspace of $\mathbf{R}^\Omega$ consisting of the constant vectors. It is usual in a designed experiment to assume that V_0 is a stratum.

26

However, V_0 is a stratum if and only if G is transitive on Ω (see [3]). Further, the desirable condition on G given in §2.3 implies transitivity. For all these reasons, we henceforth assume that G is transitive on Ω. Thus the model satisfies the following extra two conditions:

(C) h is constant;

(D) $C(\omega_1, \omega_2) = C(\omega_1 g, \omega_2 g)$ for all ω_1, ω_2 in Ω.

Condition (D) means that C is in the *centralizer algebra* of G.

No matter what transitive group G we choose for randomization, Conditions (C) and (D) remain true. However, if there is some structure on Ω then this gives us some information about the original C: for example, if Ω has a single sensible partition into blocks (see [40]) then plots within a block are more likely to be highly correlated than plots from different blocks. Randomizing by a group which does not preserve the structure on Ω destroys this knowledge about C. It is therefore absurd to use such a group.

DEFINITIONS. An *automorphism* of a block structure is a permutation of the underlying set Ω such that, for every binary relation ρ in the structure, $\rho^g = \rho$, where

$$\rho^g = \big\{ (\omega_1 g, \omega_2 g) : (\omega_1, \omega_2) \in \rho \big\}.$$

The *automorphism group* of a block structure is the group consisting of all its automorphisms.

We must restrict G to be a subgroup of the automorphism group of the block structure. Since G is assumed transitive, so must the latter be.

DEFINITION. (See [1].) A block structure is *homogeneous* if its automorphism group is transitive on the underlying set.

Our abstract problem now reduces to the following: given a homogeneous block structure, a known transitive subgroup G of its automorphism group, and an unknown symmetric matrix C in the centralizer algebra of G—what can we say about the eigenspaces of C?

2.2. Examples. The first three examples show that we often know a great deal about the strata when G is the full automorphism group of the block structure. In these examples all of the strata are known exactly, and they are precisely the subspaces found by Fisher by intuition in his early work [18, §§48–49].

Example 1. If Ω is completely unstructured of size n then we may take G to be the whole symmetric group $\mathbf{S}_n$. Then

$$C = \alpha I + \beta(J - I)$$

for some scalars α and β, where J is the constant function defined by

$$J(\omega_1, \omega_2) = 1 \qquad \text{for } \omega_1, \ \omega_2 \text{ in } \Omega.$$

27

The strata are V_0 and $V_0^\perp$, of dimensions 1 and $n - 1$ respectively.

Example 2. Let Ω consist of b blocks of size k. The automorphism group of this block structure is the permutation wreath product $\mathbf{S}_k \operatorname{wr} \mathbf{S}_b$. Let V_{blocks} be the b-dimensional subspace of $\mathbf{R}^\Omega$ defined by

$$V_{\text{blocks}} = \big\{ v : v(\omega_1) = v(\omega_2) \text{ if } \omega_1 \text{ and } \omega_2 \text{ are in the same block} \big\}.$$

It can readily be checked that there are three strata:

$$V_0$$

$$V_{\text{blocks}} \cap V_0^\perp$$

$$V_{\text{blocks}}^\perp$$

of dimensions 1, $b - 1$ and $b(k - 1)$ respectively.

Example 3. Suppose that Ω is a rectangular array with r rows and c columns, and that G is the full automorphism group, which is the permutation direct product $\mathbf{S}_r \times \mathbf{S}_c$. Define spaces V_{rows} and V_{cols} analogously to V_{blocks}. Then the strata, with their dimensions, are

$$V_0 \qquad\qquad 1$$

$$V_{\text{rows}} \cap V_0^\perp \qquad\qquad r - 1$$

$$V_{\text{cols}} \cap V_0^\perp \qquad\qquad c - 1$$

$$(V_{\text{rows}} + V_{\text{cols}})^\perp \qquad (r - 1)(c - 1).$$

Examples 1–3 are all *poset block structures* (see [4], [11], [47], [48]). The underlying set is a Cartesian product over a poset; and the structure is a lattice of partitions defined by the ancestral subsets (or *filters* or *admissible subsets*) of the poset. Such a lattice defines an orthogonal direct-sum decomposition of $\mathbf{R}^\Omega$ (see [7], [47], [52]). The automorphism group of a poset block structure is a *generalized wreath product* of symmetric groups ([11]). The strata of any matrix in the centralizer algebra of a generalized wreath product of symmetric groups are shown in [4] and [11] to be precisely the direct summands determined by the partition lattice. Thus the strata of poset block structures match the subspaces given by statisticians' intuition.

A wider class of block structures, known as orthogonal block structures ([2], [7]), also consists of lattices of partitions which are orthogonal in the statistical sense ([52, §3.2]): the corresponding equivalence relations are uniform and commute ([47]). The partition lattice again defines an orthogonal direct-sum decomposition of $\mathbf{R}^\Omega$, but the summands may no longer be strata of any group of automorphisms.

28

Example 4, which has been discussed in more detail in [8] and [41], shows the least that can go wrong.

Example 4. Let Ω be the Latin square in Figure 1. That is, Ω has 81 plots and there are three non-trivial partitions on Ω—into rows, columns and letters. Letters *do not* denote treatments in this experiment, although they may well represent treatments from a previous experiment on these plots: recall that we are ignoring treatments in this section.

A	B	C	D	E	F	G	H	I
B	C	A	E	F	D	H	I	G
C	A	B	F	D	E	I	G	H
D	E	F	G	H	I	A	B	C
E	F	D	H	I	G	B	C	A
F	D	E	I	G	H	C	A	B
G	H	I	A	B	C	D	E	F
H	I	G	B	C	A	E	F	D
I	G	H	C	A	B	F	D	E

FIG. 1. *Latin square in Example 4*

Since the Latin square in Figure 1 is the Cayley table of the elementary Abelian group $\mathbf{V}_9$, Section 10 of [42] shows that the automorphism group of this block structure is the semi-direct product $(\mathbf{V}_9 \times \mathbf{V}_9).(\text{Aut }\mathbf{V}_9)$. The strata, with their dimensions, are

$$V_0 \qquad\qquad 1$$

$$V_{\text{rows}} \cap V_0^{\perp} \qquad\qquad 8$$

$$V_{\text{cols}} \cap V_0^{\perp} \qquad\qquad 8$$

$$V_{\text{letters}} \cap V_0^{\perp} \qquad\qquad 8$$

$$V_{\text{greek}} \cap V_0^{\perp} \qquad\qquad 8$$

$$(V_{\text{rows}} + V_{\text{cols}} + V_{\text{letters}} + V_{\text{greek}})^{\perp} \qquad 48$$

where V_{letters} is defined analogously to V_{rows} and V_{greek} will be defined in a moment. Intuition suggests three 8-dimensional strata and one 56-dimensional stratum. There is a surprising extra stratum: where does it come from?

Figure 2 shows a Graeco-Latin square whose Latin part is precisely Figure 1. The 9-dimensional subspace V_{greek} is defined by the partition into Greek letters. It is shown in [6] that every automorphism of Figure 1 also preserves the partition into Greek letters. Thus the automorphism group gives strata which are not obvious from the pure combinatorics of the block structure.

29

A	α	B	β	C	γ	D	δ	E	ϵ	F	ζ	G	θ	H	η	I	λ
B	γ	C	α	A	β	E	ζ	F	δ	D	ϵ	H	λ	I	θ	G	η
C	β	A	γ	B	α	F	ϵ	D	ζ	E	δ	I	η	G	λ	H	θ
D	θ	E	η	F	λ	G	α	H	β	I	γ	A	δ	B	ϵ	C	ζ
E	λ	F	θ	D	η	H	γ	I	α	G	β	B	ζ	C	δ	A	ϵ
F	η	D	λ	E	θ	I	β	G	γ	H	α	C	ϵ	A	ζ	B	δ
G	δ	H	ϵ	I	ζ	A	θ	B	η	C	λ	D	α	E	β	F	γ
H	ζ	I	δ	G	ϵ	B	λ	C	θ	A	η	E	γ	F	α	D	β
I	ϵ	G	ζ	H	δ	C	η	A	λ	B	θ	F	β	D	γ	E	α

FIG. 2. *Graeco-Latin square in Example 4*

2.3 The permutation character. In the preceding examples the strata can all be found (or at least verified!) by a mixture of common sense and *ad hoc* methods. A general solution requires deeper group theory.

The permutation action of G on Ω naturally induces the permutation linear representation of G on $\mathbf{R}^\Omega$, by

$$v \mapsto v^g \qquad \text{for } v \text{ in } \mathbf{R}^\Omega$$

where

$$v^g(\omega) = v(\omega g^{-1}) \qquad \text{for } \omega \text{ in } \Omega.$$

This representation preserves orthogonality, and its permutation character π is given by

$$\pi(g) = \left| \{ \omega \in \Omega : \omega g = \omega \} \right| \qquad \text{for } g \text{ in } G.$$

It is easy to see that every stratum must be invariant under this linear action of G; that is, every stratum is a G-invariant subspace of $\mathbf{R}^\Omega$. It is not quite true that every stratum must be a G-irreducible subspace of $\mathbf{R}^\Omega$, because particular values for the entries in C can cause two eigenspaces to coalesce. In Example 1, if $\beta = 0$ then C has a single eigenspace, which *contains* both of the supposed strata V_0 and $V_0^\perp$. However, the stratum-projection method of analysis described in §1 depends only on W being *contained* in an eigenspace, not necessarily being a whole eigenspace. Estimation is more efficient if larger subspaces are used, so long as each one is contained in an eigenspace, but it is essential that C be a scalar on each subspace used. Thus a statistician who knows the pattern of C (from Condition (D)) but not the values of the entries in C should use a subspace only if it is contained in an eigenspace of every matrix in the centralizer algebra of G. Maximal such subspaces are indeed G-irreducible ([10]).

Standard representation theory tells us how to find the G-irreducible subspaces of $\mathbf{R}^\Omega$ in terms of the permutation character. (The corresponding theory for $\mathbf{C}^\Omega$ is in [53, §29], and modification for $\mathbf{R}^\Omega$ in [12].) Let $\mathcal{I}$ be the set of real-irreducible characters of G. Then there are non-negative integers $(a_\chi)_{\chi \in \mathcal{I}}$ such that

$$\pi = \sum_{\chi \in \mathcal{I}} a_\chi \chi.$$

30

THEOREM 1.

(1) *If $a_\chi = 1$ then the subspace of $\mathbf{R}^\Omega$ admitting χ is a stratum.*

(2) *If $a_\chi > 1$ then the subspace of $\mathbf{R}^\Omega$ admitting χ is the direct sum of a_χ strata, which cannot be further identified without more knowledge of C.*

(3) *If $a_\chi = 0$ then no subspace of $\mathbf{R}^\Omega$ admits χ.*

This theorem is of more than theoretical interest. For structured sets it is often possible to calculate the values of the a_χ without calculating π itself, for example by using the orthogonality relations among the irreducible characters and finding the number of orbits of G in various induced permutation actions. The *homogeneous* space W_χ admitting χ can, if necessary, be found by using the formula in Theorem 8 of [44, §2.6], but it can often be deduced from knowledge of its dimension $(a_\chi \chi(1))$ and its G-invariance.

It must be stressed that Theorem 1 is in terms of *real*-irreducible characters of G. Group theorists are more used to dealing with the *complex*-irreducible characters, and it is these that are to be found in character tables. The connection between the two sorts of irreducible character was spelt out in our context by [10], [33], [49]: see also [44, Chapters 12–13]. Each real-irreducible character of G is either

(1) a complex-irreducible character of G of real type;

(2) the sum of a pair of complex-conjugate complex-irreducible characters of G; or

(3) twice a complex-irreducible character of G of quaternionic type.

More details are given in [12].

If $a_\chi \leq 1$ for all χ in $\mathcal{I}$ then all the strata for every matrix in the centralizer algebra of G are known exactly: they are precisely the G-irreducible spaces of $\mathbf{R}^\Omega$. In this case G is said to be *real-multiplicity-free*. Thus our problem is entirely solved for real-multiplicity-free groups. The next example (from [2]) shows that all is not lost when G is not real-multiplicity-free.

Example 5. Let Ω be the set of $(q+1)(q^2+q+1)$ flags of the Desarguesian projective plane Π of order q. Then Ω can be regarded as a $(q^2+q+1) \times (q^2+q+1)$ rectangular array with holes. The rows and columns of the array are the lines and points of Π respectively; a given row and column have non-empty intersection (a single plot) if and only if the corresponding line and point are incident in Π. Figure 3 shows this block structure with $q = 2$.

Let G be the automorphism group of Ω, which is $\mathrm{PGL}(3, q)$. Let π' be the permutation character of G in its induced action on points. Using the fact ([43, Chapter IX, Theorem 2]) that G is transitive on ordered 4-tuples of points in general position and [20, Satz 20.2] we find that

$$\langle \pi, 1_G \rangle = \langle \pi', 1_G \rangle = 1,$$

$$\langle \pi', \pi' \rangle = 2, \qquad \langle \pi, \pi \rangle = 6, \qquad \langle \pi, \pi' \rangle = 3,$$

31

		X		X	X	X
X			X		X	X
X	X			X		X
X	X	X			X	
	X	X	X			X
X		X	X	X		
	X		X	X	X	

FIG. 3. *Array with holes in Example 5*

where 1_G is the principal character of G and $\langle \ , \ \rangle$ is the usual inner product on characters. Hence there are irreducible characters ψ and η of G, with degrees $q^2 + q$ and q^3 respectively, such that $\pi' = 1_G + \psi$ and

$$\pi = 1_G + 2\psi + \eta.$$

Strictly, the foregoing argument shows that ψ and η are *complex*-irreducible characters of G, because not all real-irreducible characters of G have unit length with respect to $\langle \ , \ \rangle$. However, since each of ψ and η occurs with multiplicity 1 in a permutation character, they must each be real-irreducible.

Thus $\mathbf{R}^\Omega = W_{1_G} \oplus W_\psi \oplus W_\eta$, where W_{1_G} is a 1-dimensional stratum, W_η is a q^3-dimensional stratum, and W_ψ is the direct sum of two $(q^2 + q)$-dimensional strata which cannot be further specified without more knowledge of C. (This decomposition is obtained, by a longer method, in [13], [14] and [15].)

Obvious G-invariant subspaces of $\mathbf{R}^\Omega$ are V_0, V_{rows} and V_{cols}, of dimensions 1, $q^2 + q + 1$ and $q^2 + q + 1$ respectively. The latter two intersect in V_0 and are not geometrically orthogonal ([52, §3.2]) in the sense that orthogonal complementation with respect to V_0 does not render them orthogonal. This is a sure sign of unidentifiable strata. In general, if there are two G-invariant subspaces of $\mathbf{R}^\Omega$ which are not geometrically orthogonal then each must contain a G-irreducible subspace belonging to the same homogeneous subspace W_χ whose multiplicity a_χ is more than 1.

Matching of dimensions shows that the strata are as follows.

W_{1_G}	V_0	1	one stratum
W_ψ	$(V_{\text{rows}} + V_{\text{cols}})^\perp \cap V_0^\perp$	$2(q^2 + q)$	direct sum of two unidentifiable strata
W_η	$(V_{\text{rows}} + V_{\text{cols}})^\perp$	q^3	one stratum

Dimensions (third column) allow us to match the known G-invariant spaces (second column), the homogeneous spaces (first column) and the strata (comments in the fourth column).

In spite of its two unidentifiable strata, this block structure is not unsuitable for experimentation. Any treatments would typically be applied so as to be orthogonal

32

to both rows and columns, as in Figure 4, for example, where numbers denote treatments. Then only the stratum W_η is used for analysis, and the non-identifiability of the unused strata is of no consequence. More generally, so long as the treatments are orthogonal to all unidentifiable strata, the design may be analyzed just like one in which all strata are identifiable.

1	2	X	3	X	X	X
X	3	2	X	1	X	X
X	X	1	2	X	3	X
X	X	X	1	3	X	2
3	X	X	X	2	1	X
X	1	X	X	X	2	3
2	X	3	X	X	X	1

FIG. 4. *Treatments applied to the array in Fig. 3 so as to be orthogonal to both rows and columns*

Example 6. Another rectangular array with holes is the $n \times n$ square with missing diagonal. The automorphism group is $\mathbf{S}_n$. As shown in [2] and [21], the strata for this, with dimensions, are

$$V_0 \qquad\qquad 1$$

$$(V_{\text{rows}} + V_{\text{cols}}) \cap V_0^\perp \qquad 2(n-1) \qquad \text{direct sum of two unidentifiable strata}$$

$$V_{\text{symm}} \qquad \frac{n(n-3)}{2}$$

$$V_{\text{antisymm}} \qquad \frac{(n-1)(n-2)}{2}$$

where

$$V_{\text{symm}} = \left\{ v \in (V_{\text{rows}} + V_{\text{cols}})^\perp : v(\omega) = v(\bar{\omega}) \text{ for all } \omega \text{ in } \Omega \right\}$$
$$V_{\text{antisymm}} = \left\{ v \in (V_{\text{rows}} + V_{\text{cols}})^\perp : v(\omega) = -v(\bar{\omega}) \text{ for all } \omega \text{ in } \Omega \right\}$$

and $^-$ represents reflection of the square array Ω in its missing diagonal. Thirty years earlier, Yates ([55]) had used 'common sense' to find the strata. He correctly gave the three identifiable strata, but he chose a particular G-invariant direct-sum decomposition of $(V_{\text{rows}} + V_{\text{cols}}) \cap V_0^\perp$ into a pair of orthogonal $(n-1)$-dimensional spaces. As James pointed out in [21], Yates's choice is arbitrary.

§3. TREATMENTS

In this section we assume that the strata and their projection matrices are known, and we consider the extra complications added to the geometry and algebra

33

of $\mathbf{R}^\Omega$ by the treatment set $\mathcal{T}$ and the design map ϕ. Because they now need to be composed with other functions, functions such as h and f from §1 will now be written on the right of their arguments, as will matrices when considered as linear transformations.

3.1 General balance and efficiency. The prime purpose of experiments is to estimate linear functions of f. Because $\mathbf{R}^\mathcal{T}$ has a canonical basis, we can regard any such linear function as $[x, f]$ for some x in $\mathbf{R}^\mathcal{T}$, where $[\ ,\ ]$ is the inner product on $\mathbf{R}^\mathcal{T}$ mentioned in §1. Usually estimates are found of $[x_1, f]$, $[x_2, f]$, $\ldots$ for some orthogonal basis $\{x_1, x_2, \ldots\}$ of $\mathbf{R}^\mathcal{T}$; from these, estimates of other linear functions of f are obtained by linear combination.

The design map ϕ has a dual-like map ϕ_* which embeds $\mathbf{R}^\mathcal{T}$ in $\mathbf{R}^\Omega$: it is defined by

$$(\omega)(x\phi_*) = (\omega\phi)x \qquad \text{for } x \text{ in } \mathbf{R}^\mathcal{T} \text{ and } \omega \text{ in } \Omega.$$

If all treatments are equally replicated then ϕ_* preserves orthogonality.

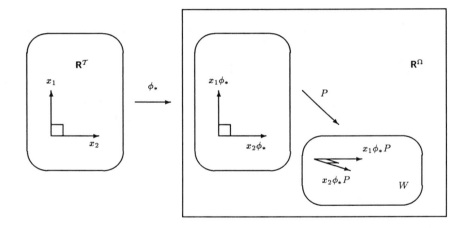

FIG. 5. *Linear transformations used in estimation*

Let W be a stratum, with projector P. For estimation in W, not only is the data projected onto W, but so are the linear functions x. Usually P does not preserve orthogonality among the elements of $\mathbf{R}^\mathcal{T}\phi_*$. However, James and Wilkinson ([22]) proved the following theorem (see Figure 5).

THEOREM 2. *There is an orthogonal basis* $\{x_1, x_2, \ldots\}$ *of* $\mathbf{R}^\mathcal{T}$ *such that* $x_i\phi_*P$ *is orthogonal to* $x_j\phi_*P$ *if* $x_i \neq x_j$.

Note that Theorem 2 does not imply that P is monomorphic on $\mathbf{R}^\mathcal{T}$. Certain of the x_iP may be zero: those that are not form an orthogonal basis for $\mathbf{R}^\mathcal{T}\phi_*P$.

The importance of Theorem 2 is that the estimators of $[x_i, f]$ and $[x_j, f]$ from stratum W are uncorrelated if and only if $x_i \phi_* P$ is orthogonal to $x_j \phi_* P$. Interpretation of results of experiments is much easier if uncorrelated estimators are used.

The linear transformation ϕ_* can be written with respect to the two canonical bases as a $\mathcal{T} \times \Omega$ matrix X, called the *design matrix*. It satisfies

$$X(t, \omega) = \begin{cases} 1 & \text{if } \omega\phi = t \\ 0 & \text{otherwise} \end{cases}$$

for t in $\mathcal{T}$ and ω in Ω. The symmetric $\mathcal{T} \times \mathcal{T}$ matrix XPX' is called the *information matrix* for stratum W. It is easy to see that a basis for $\mathbf{R}^{\mathcal{T}}$ satisfies the condition in Theorem 2 if and only if it consists of eigenvectors of the information matrix: hence Theorem 2 is a corollary of the diagonalizability of symmetric matrices.

When information from different strata is combined, it is obviously convenient if the *same* eigenvector basis can be used. This is intuitively attractive, and also has clear computational advantages. Furthermore, Houtman and Speed ([19]) showed that simple linear combination of information from different strata is best if *and only if* the same eigenvector basis can be used. Anticipating these developments, Nelder ([35]) made the following definition.

DEFINITION. A design is *generally balanced* if there is basis of $\mathbf{R}^{\mathcal{T}}$ which satisfies the condition in Theorem 2 for all strata; equivalently, if the information matrices for all of the strata have a common eigenvector basis.

General balance is a very important property, and the majority of designs in common use are generally balanced. But general balance alone does not make a design good. For each x_i, we need to know how much information on $[x_i, f]$ comes from each stratum.

For a given x, let θ be the angle between $x\phi_*$ and $x\phi_* P$. The *efficiency factor* for $[x, f]$ in stratum W is defined to be $\cos^2 \theta$. Thus the efficiency factor is 1 if $x\phi_* \in W$ and is 0 if $x\phi_* \in W^\perp$; and the sum, over the strata, of the efficiency factors for $[x, f]$ is equal to 1. The variance of the estimator of $[x, f]$ in W is inversely proportional to this efficiency factor, and directly proportional to the eigenvalue ξ of C on W. If there is any prior reason for thinking that ξ will be large, then good designers demand that all efficiency factors in that stratum should be as small as possible. However, it may not be possible for them all to be zero, and so the designer must use knowledge about the relative importance (to the purposes of the experiment) of the x_i. (See [22] for proofs of these statements, [38] for an explanation of the geometry, and [23] for a very clear exposition of the nature and meaning of efficiency factors.)

To assess whether a generally balanced design is good, then, the designer needs to know the common eigenvector basis and its associated two-way array of efficiency factors. So, even when the block structure, treatment structure and strata are established, questions still facing a statistician who is considering using a particular design map ϕ are:

(1) is the design generally balanced?

35

(2) if so, what is the common eigenvector basis $\{x_1, x_2, \ldots\}$?

(3) what are the efficiency factors for each x_i in each stratum?

3.2 Automorphisms preserving treatments. Although group theory does not provide a general answer to these questions, as it did to the problem of identifying strata, it is helpful in many specific instances. As treatments *and* strata are both involved in the concept of general balance, we must restrict the notion of automorphism accordingly.

DEFINITIONS. An *automorphism* of a design $(\Omega, \mathcal{T}, \phi)$ is an automorphism g of the block structure on Ω such that

$$\omega_1 \phi = \omega_2 \phi \quad \Longleftrightarrow \quad (\omega_1 g)\phi = (\omega_2 g)\phi \qquad \text{for } \omega_1, \omega_2 \text{ in } \Omega.$$

The *automorphism group* of the design is the group consisting of all its automorphisms.

Let H be the automorphism group of the design, and let $\bar{H}$ be the permutation group on $\mathcal{T}$ induced by H (so that $\bar{H}$ is the maximal quotient of H which acts faithfully on $\mathcal{T}$). Because all the strata are H-invariant, all the information matrices are centralized by $\bar{H}$. Let K be the group of all permutations of $\mathcal{T}$ which centralize all the information matrices.

In general, $\bar{H}$ is a proper subgroup of K. Indeed, there are designs for which $\bar{H}$ is trivial but K is the whole symmetric group on $\mathcal{T}$. Example 7 shows a less extreme difference.

Example 7. Let Ω consist of five blocks, each of which is divided into two subblocks of two plots each. Let $\mathcal{T} = \{0, 1, 2, 3, 4\}$ and let ϕ be the design map shown in Figure 6. Then $H = \bar{H}$, acting faithfully on $\mathcal{T}$ as the affine group $\mathrm{AGL}(1, 5)$. If either blocks or subblocks are ignored then the design is a balanced incomplete-block design, so the whole design is a nested balanced incomplete-block design (see [39]). In every information matrix of a balanced incomplete-block design all the diagonal elements are equal, as are all the off-diagonal elements. Hence $K = \mathbf{S}_5$.

FIG. 6. *Nested balanced incomplete-block design in Example 7*

For computational simplicity, many designs used in experiments are generated from a design on a subset of Ω by taking all translates under some permutation group $\tilde{K}$ on $\mathcal{T}$. In these circumstances $\tilde{K} \leq K$, and frequently $\tilde{K}$ is the whole of K.

Example 8. Suppose that Ω is a 4×12 rectangular array, and that pairs of columns are grouped into blocks. The structure on Ω consists of the four partitions whose classes are rows, columns, blocks and block-row intersections. Let $\tilde{K}$ be the Abelian group $\langle a \rangle \times \langle c \rangle$, where $a^2 = c^6 = 1$, and put $\mathcal{T} = \tilde{K}$. The design in Figure 7 consists of all translates under $\tilde{K}$ of any one of its blocks. It may be checked that $K = \tilde{K}$.

1	ac		c	ac^2		c^2	ac^3		c^3	ac^4		c^4	ac^5		c^5	a
a	c		ac	c^2		ac^2	c^3		ac^3	c^4		ac^4	c^5		ac^5	1
ac^4	c^5		ac^5	1		a	c		ac	c^2		ac^2	c^3		ac^3	c^4
c^4	ac^5		c^5	a		1	a		c	ac^2		c^2	ac^3		c^3	ac^4

FIG. 7. *Abelian-group design in Example 8*

Does knowledge of K enable us to deduce anything about the eigenspaces of information matrices centralized by K without examining the entries in those information matrices? This question is strikingly similar to the one posed at the end of §2.1, and is answered by using exactly the same theory.

THEOREM 3. *If K is real-multiplicity-free then the design is generally balanced. Each homogeneous space of K is then (contained in) an eigenspace of every information matrix. Efficiency factors may be found by applying each information matrix to any vector in each homogeneous space.*

Note that Theorem 3 is not an 'if and only if' theorem. Unlike the matrix C in §2, each information matrix has known entries, and it is quite possible for these matrices to have a common eigenvector basis even if K is not real-multiplicity-free. In this case, knowing the homogeneous spaces of K aids the search for such a basis.

Since Theorem 3 is permissive rather than prescriptive, it applies equally well to any subgroup of K, in particular to $\bar{H}$ or to $\tilde{K}$ in the construction exemplified by Example 8. A proper subgroup is less likely to be real-multiplicity-free: even if it is, its homogeneous spaces may be smaller than those of K. Nevertheless, the effort to find the whole group K may not be justified if a suitably large subgroup of it is already known.

3.3 Abelian-group designs. Designs like that in Example 8 are used so often for statistical experiments that we now specialize to them. We assume that the block structure is defined by a semi-lattice of orthogonal uniform partitions on Ω, in such a way that the information matrices are linear combinations of the concurrence matrices for the various partitions: all poset block structures come into this class.

The treatment set $\mathcal{T}$ is identified with an Abelian group. Each equivalence class of each partition defines a multiset on $\mathcal{T}$ (that is, a function from $\mathcal{T}$ to the natural numbers **N**), recording the number of plots in that class to which each treatment is allocated. Acting on itself by multiplication, $\mathcal{T}$ induces an action on these multisets. The design is defined to be an *Abelian-group design* if, for every partition, the (multi)set of multisets consists of (one or more copies of) complete orbits of $\mathcal{T}$. It may be verified that Example 8 is indeed an Abelian-group design. These designs are also called *cyclic* (see [30]) or *generalized cyclic* (see [17]), but both of these terms have other meanings. Relationships between these meanings, and implications among related definitions, are given in [12].

Let $\mathcal{J}$ be the set of complex-irreducible characters of $\mathcal{T}$. Because $\mathcal{T}$ is Abelian, every element of $\mathcal{J}$ is in $\mathbf{C}^{\mathcal{T}}$. Combining complex-irreducible characters with their complex conjugates gives an orthogonal basis of $\mathbf{R}^{\mathcal{T}}$ ([28], [29]).

THEOREM 4. ([12]) *Let* $(\Omega, \mathcal{T}, \phi)$ *be an Abelian-group design. Then*

(1) *the design is generally balanced;*

(2) *a common eigenvector basis which exhibits this general balance is*

$$\{\chi + \bar{\chi} : \chi \in \mathcal{J}\} \cup \{i(\chi - \bar{\chi}) : \chi \in \mathcal{J}, \chi \neq \bar{\chi}\};$$

(3) *if, for a given partition with b classes, the multisets form (one or more copies of) a single orbit of $\mathcal{T}$, then the eigenvalue of the corresponding concurrence matrix on $\chi + \bar{\chi}$ (and on $i(\chi - \bar{\chi})$ if $\chi \neq \bar{\chi}$) is*

$$\frac{b}{|\mathcal{T}|} \sum_{t \in \mathcal{T}} n_t \chi(t)$$

where

$$n_t = \left| \left\{ (\omega_1, \omega_2) \in \Delta \times \Delta : (\omega_1 \phi)(\omega_2 \phi)^{-1} = t \right\} \right|$$

and Δ is any equivalence class of the partition.

Since every $\chi(t)$ above is a $|\mathcal{T}|$-th root of unity, the efficiency factors of an Abelian-group design can also be expressed in terms of trigonometric functions of the angle $2\pi/|\mathcal{T}|$. For block structures consisting of a single partition, such formulas are given in [23, §4.3] for cyclic $\mathcal{T}$ and [23, §4.5] for general (finite) Abelian groups. The latter are rather cumbersome, being expressed in terms of the former for a (possibly arbitrary) set of generators of $\mathcal{T}$.

§4. DISCUSSION

We have shown in §2 that the representation theory of finite permutation groups is essential for a general solution to the problem of identifying the strata in randomized experiments. Identifying those strata whose sum contains the treatment space is sufficient for the analysis of the experiment. In §3 we showed that the same theory can be extremely helpful in deciding whether a design is generally balanced, and, if so, in finding its efficiency factors. However, the group theory is not essential here: it merely provides a short cut to tedious matrix calculations.

Although numerous unpublished reports by my collaborators and myself contain the theory in §2, the closest work in the published literature is Speed's approach to analysis of variance [45] and [46]. His covariance matrix C comes from a known association scheme, which may or may not be the set of adjacency matrices of a permutation group. He needs to identify all the strata. Treatments do not enter into his discussion, so he has no interest in examples like Examples 5 and 6.

A handful of authors has considered the automorphism group of the design, and related its homogeneous spaces to spaces traditionally used in the analysis of the experiment: see [13], [14], [15], [21], [31], [33]. However, none of these distinguishes the roles of the block structure on Ω and the partition induced on Ω by ϕ. I believe that this distinction is an essential part of a designed experiment, because the block structure on Ω is usually given while the statistician is free to choose ϕ to maximum advantage. By giving an easy method of calculating efficiency factors in many cases—particularly Abelian-group designs—, the theory of §3 helps this choice.

In [16], Dawid finds the homogeneous spaces of the automorphism groups of various structures on a set. He proposes using them to test hypotheses which are invariant under various of the groups. However, there are no treatments as such, and his structures are not obviously those of designed experiments. Moreover, all the groups in his example are real-multiplicity-free: it is not clear whether this is essential (as in identification of *all* strata under randomization), or merely convenient, as in our §3.

REFERENCES

[1] L. BABAI, *On the abstract group of automorphisms*, in *Combinatorics*, Ed. H. N. V. Temperley, London Mathematical Society Lecture Notes 52, Cambridge University Press, Cambridge, 1981, pp. 1–40.

[2] R. A. BAILEY, *Block strata and canonical strata in randomized experiments*, unpublished report, Edinburgh, 1978.

[3] ————, *A unified approach to design of experiments*, J. Roy. Statist. Soc. A, 144 (1981), pp. 214–223.

[4] ————, *Distributive block structures and their automorphisms*, in *Combinatorial Mathematics VIII*, Ed. K. L. McAvaney, Lecture Notes in Mathematics 884, Springer, Berlin, 1981, pp. 115–124.

[5] ————, *Block structures for designed experiments*, in *Applications of Combinatorics*, Ed. R. J. Wilson, Shiva, Nantwich, 1982, pp. 1–18.

[6] ————, *Latin squares with highly transitive automorphism groups*, J. Austral. Math. Soc., 33 (1982), pp. 18–22.

[7] ————, *Factorial design and Abelian groups*, Linear Algebra and its Applications, 70 (1985), pp. 349–368.

[8] ————, *Contribution to the discussion of "Symmetry models and hypotheses for structured data layouts" by A. P. Dawid*, J. Roy. Statist. Soc. B, 50 (1988), pp. 22–24.

[9] ————, *Strata for randomized experiments*, unpublished report, Rothamsted, 1988.

[10] R. A. BAILEY AND P. J. CAMERON, *The eigenspaces of averaged symmetric matrices*, unpublished report, Edinburgh, 1977.

[11] R. A. BAILEY, C. E. PRAEGER, C. A. ROWLEY AND T. P. SPEED, *Generalized wreath products of permutation groups*, Proc. London Math. Soc., 47 (1983), pp. 69–82.

[12] R. A. BAILEY AND C. A. ROWLEY, *General balance and treatment permutations*, Rothamsted and Open University, 1986.

[13] C. T. BURTON AND I. M. CHAKRAVARTI, *On the commutant algebras corresponding to the permutation representations of the full collineation groups of* PG(k, s) *and* EG(k, s), $s = p^r$, $k \geq 2$, J. Math. Anal. Appl., 89 (1982), pp. 489–514.

[14] I. M. CHAKRAVARTI AND C. T. BURTON, *Symmetries (groups of automorphisms) of Desarguesian finite projective and affine planes and their role in statistical model construction*, in Statistics and Probability: Essays in Honor of C. R. Rao, Ed. G. Kallianpur, P. R. Krishnaiah and J. K. Ghosh, North-Holland, Amsterdam, 1982, pp. 169–178.

[15] —————, *On the algebras of symmetries (groups of collineations) of designs from finite Desarguesian planes*, J. Math. Anal. Appl., 89 (1982), pp. 515–529.

[16] A. P. DAWID, *Symmetry models and hypotheses for structured data layouts*, J. Roy. Statist. Soc. B, 50 (1988), pp. 1–21.

[17] A. M. DEAN AND S. M. LEWIS, *A unified theory for generalized cyclic designs*, J. Statist. Plann. Inf., 4 (1980), pp. 13–23.

[18] R. A. FISHER, *Statistical Methods for Research Workers*, Oliver and Boyd, Edinburgh, 1925.

[19] A. M. HOUTMAN AND T. P. SPEED, *Balance in designed experiments with orthogonal block structure*, Ann. Statist., 11 (1983), pp. 1069–1085.

[20] B. HUPPERT, *Endliche Gruppen I*, Springer, Berlin, 1967.

[21] A. T. JAMES, *Analysis of variance determined by symmetry and combinatorial properties of zonal polynomials*, in Statistics and Probability: Essays in Honor of C. R. Rao, Ed. G. Kallianpur, P. R. Krishnaiah and J. K. Ghosh, North-Holland, Amsterdam, 1982, pp. 329–341.

[22] A. T. JAMES AND G. N. WILKINSON, *Factorization of the residual operator and canonical decomposition of nonorthogonal factors in the analysis of variance*, Biometrika, 58 (1971), pp. 279–294.

[23] J. A. JOHN, *Cyclic Designs*, Chapman and Hall, London, 1987.

[24] P. W. M. JOHN, *Statistical Design and Analysis of Experiments*, Macmillan, New York, 1971.

[25] O. KEMPTHORNE, *The Design and Analysis of Experiments*, Wiley, New York, 1957.

[26] —————, *Classificatory data structures and associated linear models*, in Statistics and Probability: Essays in Honor of C. R. Rao, Ed. G. Kallianpur, P. R. Krishnaiah and J. K. Ghosh, North-Holland, Amsterdam, 1982, pp. 397–410.

[27] O. KEMPTHORNE, G. ZYSKIND, S. ADDELMAN, T. N. THROCKMORTON AND R. F. WHITE, *Analysis of Variance Procedures*, ARL 149, Aeronautical Res. Lab., Wright-Patterson Air Force Base, Ohio, 1961.

[28] A. KOBILINSKY, *Orthogonal factorial designs for quantitative factors*, Statistics and Decisions, Supp. 2 (1985), pp. 275–285.

[29] —————, *Confounding in relation to duality of finite Abelian groups*, Linear Algebra and its Applications, 70 (1985), pp. 321–347.

[30] —————, *Complex linear models and cyclic designs*, unpublished report, I. N. R. A, Paris, 1987.

[31] W. LEDERMANN, *Representation theory and statistics*, unpublished report, Séminaire Dubreil-Pisot, Paris, Paper 15, 1967.

[32] F. B. MARTIN AND G. ZYSKIND, *On combinability of information from uncorrelated linear models by simple weighting*, Ann. Math. Statist., 37 (1966), pp. 1338–1347.

[33] A. D. MCLAREN, *On group representations and invariant stochastic processes*, Proc. Camb. Phil. Soc., 59 (1963), pp. 431–450.

[34] J. A. NELDER, *The analysis of randomized experiments with orthogonal block structure. I. Block structure and the null analysis of variance*, Proc. Roy. Soc. A, 283 (1965), pp. 147–162.

[35] —————, *The analysis of randomized experiments with orthogonal block structure. II. Treatment structure and the general analysis of variance*, Proc. Roy. Soc. A, 283 (1965), pp. 163–178.

[36] —————, *The combination of information in generally balanced designs*, J. Roy. Statist. Soc. B, 30 (1968), pp. 303–311.

[37] R. W. PAYNE AND R. D. TOBIAS, *General balance, combination of information and the analysis of covariance*, unpublished report, Rothamsted and North Carolina, 1988.

[38] R. W. PAYNE AND G. N. WILKINSON, *A general algorithm for analysis of variance*, Applied Statistics, 26 (1977), pp. 251–260.

[39] D. A. PREECE, *Nested balanced incomplete block designs*, Biometrika, 54 (1967), pp. 479–486.

[40] —————, *The design and analysis of experiments: what has gone wrong?*, Utilitas Mathematica, 21A (1982), pp. 201–244.

[41] D. A. PREECE, R. A. BAILEY AND H. D. PATTERSON, *A randomization problem in forming designs with superimposed treatments*, Austral. J. Statist., 20 (1978), pp. 111–125.

[42] E. SCHÖNHARDT, *Über lateinische Quadrate und Unionen*, J. Reine Angew. Math., 163 (1930), pp. 183–229.

[43] J. G. SEMPLE AND G. T. KNEEBONE, *Algebraic Projective Geometry*, Oxford University Press, Oxford, 1963.

[44] J.-P. SERRE, *Linear Representations of Finite Groups*, Springer, New York, 1977.

[45] T. P. SPEED, ANOVA *models with random effects: an approach via symmetry*, in *Essays in Time Series and Allied Processes: Papers in honour of E. J. Hannan*, Ed. J. Gani and M. B. Priestly, Applied Probability Trust, Sheffield, 1986, pp. 355–368.

[46] —————— , *What is an analysis of variance?*, Ann. Statist., 15 (1987), pp. 885–910.

[47] T. P. SPEED AND R. A. BAILEY, *On a class of association schemes derived from lattices of equivalence relations*, in *Algebraic Structures and Applications*, Ed. P. Schultz, C. E. Praeger and R. P. Sullivan, Marcel Dekker, New York, 1982, pp. 55–74.

[48] —————————— , *Factorial dispersion models*, Internat. Statist. Review, 55 (1987), pp. 261–277.

[49] T. P. SPEED AND D. E. TAYLOR, *Structure of the real adjacency algebra of a coherent configuration satisfying (PC)*, unpublished report, Canberra and Sydney.

[50] D. A. SPROTT, *A note on combined interblock and intrablock estimation in incomplete block designs*, Ann. Math. Statist., 27 (1956), pp. 633–641.

[51] T. N. THROCKMORTON, *Structures of classification data*, Ph. D. thesis, Iowa State University, 1961.

[52] T. TJUR, *Analysis of variance models in orthogonal designs*, Internat. Statist. Review, 52 (1984), pp. 33–65.

[53] H. WIELANDT, *Finite Permutation Groups*, Academic Press, New York, 1964.

[54] F. YATES, *The recovery of inter-block information in balanced incomplete block designs*, Ann. Eugen., 10 (1940), pp. 317–325.

[55] —————— , *Analysis of data from all possible reciprocal crosses between a set of parental lines*, Heredity, 1 (1947), pp. 287–301.

[56] G. ZYSKIND, O. KEMPTHORNE, R. F. WHITE, E. E. DAYHOFF AND T. E.DOERFLER, *Research on Analysis of Variance and Related Topics*, ARL 64-193, Aeronautical Res. Lab., Wright-Patterson Air Force Base, Ohio, 1964.

41

CHARACTERIZATION THEOREMS FOR FAILED PROJECTIVE AND AFFINE PLANES

AART BLOKHUIS, ANDRIES E. BROUWER
AND HENNY A. WILBRINK†

Abstract. We characterize the failed projective and affine planes introduced by Mendelsohn and Assaf [7]. It is shown that no non-trivial FPP exists, and that a non-trivial FAP is either of Baer type, or related to a certain type of Bhaskar-Rao Design, of which probably only one example exists.

1. INTRODUCTION

In [7] E. Mendelsohn and A. Assaf define a Failed Projective Plane of order n, a $FPP(n)$, as an incidence structure of points and lines satisfying the following axioms:

FP(1). *Each line is incident with $n + 1$ points.*

FP(2). *Through each pair of points there is at least one line.*

FP(3). *The number of points is $n^2 + n + 1$, the number of lines is $n^2 + n + 2$.*

A trivial example of a $FPP(n)$ is obtained from a projective plane of order n by adding a new line incident with an arbitrary set of $n + 1$ of the points. We show that this is the only example. More interesting is the concept of a Failed Affine Plane of order n, a $FAP(n)$, satisfying the axioms:

FA(1). *Each line is incident with n points.*

FA(2). *Through each pair of points there is at least one line.*

FA(3). *The number of points is n^2, the number of lines is $n^2 + n + 1$.*

Again a trivial example is obtained from an affine plane by adding a new line, but C. Baker [1] gives two non-trivial examples:

Example 1. Let the points of the plane be a set of $\sqrt{n}$ symbols plus the set of points of a projective plane of order n outside a Baer subplane. Lines will be of two types. The non-Baer lines are incident with the points on them, the Baer lines are in addition incident with the $\sqrt{n}$ symbols. One can check that this defines a $FAP(n)$. Such a $FAP(n)$ will be called of Baer type.

---

†Department of Mathematics and Computing Science, Eindhoven University of Technology, P.O. Box 513, 5600 MB Eindhoven, The Netherlands

Example 2. A $FAP(3)$ can be obtained from the incidence structure with point-line incidence matrix

$$A = \begin{pmatrix} F & I \\ I & J - F \end{pmatrix}$$

by deleting a line with 5 points. Here F stands for the point-line incidence matrix of the Fano plane $PG(2,2)$, while I and J are the 7 by 7 identity and all-one matrix.

We will show that a non-trivial FAP is either of Baer type or corresponds to a special type of Bhaskar-Rao Design, of which we conjecture the second example to be the only one.

2. NOTATION AND TERMINOLOGY

A point in a $FPP(n)$ (resp. a $FAP(n)$) is called an *i-point* if it is on $n+1+i$ lines. Note that $i \geq 0$; 0-points are called *ordinary*, i−points with $i \neq 0$ *special*. An ordinary point is joined to any other point by exactly one line. Let x_i denote the number of i−points. Counting flags one gets $\sum i x_i = n+1$ in a $FPP(n)$ and $\sum i x_i = n$ in a $FAP(n)$.

Hence the number of special points is at most $n+1$ (resp. n). A line is called *regular* if it contains only ordinary points and *almost-regular* if it contains exactly one special point. Two lines are called *parallel* if they do not intersect. (Parallellism is not an equivalence relation in this case.)

3. CHARACTERIZATION OF FAILED PROJECTIVE PLANES

THEOREM 1. *There is no non-trivial Failed Projective Plane.*

Proof. Let π be a $FPP(n)$. Suppose π does not contain a regular line. Then the $n+1$ lines through an ordinary point contain precisely one special point. Hence any line containing 2 special points contains $n+1$ (and hence all) of them. It follows that we have a $PG(2,n)$ with some line counted twice. Next assume there exists an ordinary line l. This line is intersected by $n(n+1)$ other lines, hence there is a unique line m parallel to it. Through an i−point there are exactly i parallels to l, hence m contains only (and all) special points. As a consequence all special points are 1-points.

CLAIM. *Each special point P lies on an almost-regular line.*

Proof. If not, then on each line through P there are at most $n-1$ ordinary points, while one of them, m contains no ordinary points. Hence P is joined to at most $(n+1)(n-1) = n^2 - 1$ ordinary points, contradiction. □

CLAIM. *Each pair of special points is joined by exactly two lines.*

Proof. Let P be a special point. Note that P is joined to the other special points twice on the average, since $\sum_{Q \neq P} \sigma(P,Q) = (n+2)n$ [where $\sigma(P,Q)$ denotes the number of lines through P and Q], and the contribution of the ordinary points in this sum is precisely n^2. Let a be an almost-regular line through P and let Q be another special point. Of the $n+2$ lines through Q, there are n that intersect a in an ordinary point. Hence at most 2 intersect a in P. □

As a consequence of the last claim, we may remove the line m containing all special points and still every pair of points will be joined by a line, so that we are left with a projective plane. This finishes the proof of Theorem 1. □

4. FAILED AFFINE PLANES WITH ALMOST-REGULAR LINES

Throughout this section α will be a Failed Affine Plane of order $n > 2$ containing at least one line a with exactly one special point.

LEMMA 2. *There are exactly $n - 1$ lines parallel to a.*

Proof. Through any ordinary point not on a there is exactly one parallel. Since there are at least $n^2 - n - (n-1)$ such points, there must be at least $n - 1$ parallels and so at most $n^2 + 1$ lines intersecting a. On the other hand, since a contains one special point, we have that at least $n^2 + 1$ lines intersect l. Hence there are exactly $n^2 + 1$ lines intersecting l and precisely $n - 1$ parallels. □

LEMMA 3. *If there is a regular line m parallel to the almost regular line a then there is a line containing all special points. Moreover, all other special points are joined twice to the special point on a.*

Proof. Through the special point, S say, of a there goes another line k parallel to m. If k contains an ordinary point P, then the line through P parallel to a, as well as k will be parallel to m, since two parallels of a never intersect in an ordinary point, and m has only ordinary points. This is a contradiction since through P there is only one parallel to m. Hence, k contains only (and hence all) special points, of which there are then precisely n, all being 1-points. Moreover, two parallels to a (being parallel to m also) do not intersect in a special point either (since through each special point there are two parallels to m, but one of them is the line containing all special points). Hence through each special point different from S there is exactly one parallel to l, and therefore precisely two lines joining it to S. □

LEMMA 4. *If there is no regular line parallel to a then all parallels are almost-regular and all special points are joined twice to the special point of a.*

Proof. Since the $n - 1$ parallels all have at most $n - 1$ ordinary points, and together $(n-1)^2$ they are almost regular. Now suppose there is a special point S' that is joined only once to S, the special point of a. Then S is on two parallels to a, n_1 and n_2 say. Now all other parallels to a are also parallel to n_1 (and n_2). But they cover the remaining ordinary points. Now through S there must be another parallel to n_1, but the only ordinary points left are those on n_2. Hence we get a line $(n_2 \backslash \{S'\}) \cup \{S\}$, a contradiction since $n > 2$. It follows that the other special points are joined at least (and therefore exactly) twice to S. □

LEMMA 5. *If there is a line l containing all special points then α is a trivial Failed Affine Plane .*

Proof. The only thing we have to show is that, after deletion of l, two special points are still joined by a line. Since each special point is on $n + 2$ lines, one of

44

which contains no ordinary points, it must be on an almost- regular line as well, otherwise it would be joined to at most $(n+1)(n-2) < n^2 - n$ ordinary points. Now Lemma 3 or Lemma 4 yields that the other special points are joined twice to it. ∎

We can summarize the contents of Lemmas 3,4 and 5 in

PROPOSITION 6. *If α is a non-trivial Failed Affine Plane of order n, containing an almost regular line, then*

(1) *each point is on the same number, c, of almost regular lines;*

(2) *the almost regular lines come in c parallel classes of n lines;*

(3) *there are n special points, all of them 1-points and any pair of them is on precisely 2 lines.*

Proof. If for some almost regular line l there is a regular parallel, then by Lemma 3 and 5 α is trivial. Hence we are in the case of Lemma 4 and (1), (2) and (3) follow. ∎

From now on we assume that α is non-trivial.

LEMMA 7. *A regular line l has exactly n parallels, two intersecting regular lines have precisely one common parallel, through each ordinary point there are at least two regular lines.*

Proof. Through each ordinary point not on l there is one parallel, through each special point exactly two. Hence

$$n.\#\text{parallels} = (n^2 - 2n).1 + n.2.$$

Let l,m be two intersecting regular lines. Through each of the $n-1$ points on $l\backslash m$ there is exactly one parallel to m, hence one parallel to m is also parallel to l. Finally, let P be an ordinary point; since non-regular lines join P to at most $n-2$ other ordinary points, P must be on at least 1 regular line. With equality if and only if P is on n almost regular lines. But then by Proposition 6 each point is on n almost regular lines, and it easily follows that α is trivial. ∎

LEMMA 8. *Let μ be the minimal number of special points on a non-regular, non-almost-regular line. Then $\mu(\mu+1) \le 2n$.*

Proof. Consider two intersecting regular lines l and m. We say that an (ordinary) point O is of type (P,Q) if the line through O parallel to m (or m if O is on m) intersects l in P, and the line through O parallel to l intersects m in Q. Obviously there is at most one ordinary point of given type (P,Q) for P on l and Q on m. Moreover, if for certain P there is a Q such that there is no point of type (P,Q), then there are at least μ such Q, for in that case, the parallel through P to m is not regular, and of course also not almost-regular, whence it contains at most $n - \mu$ ordinary points. It follows that, since not every pair (P,Q) occurs as a type, there ar at least μ^2 pairs not occurring, hence at most $n^2 - \mu^2$ ordinary points are of type (P, Q) for certain P and Q. The remaining ordinary points must all lie on the unique common parallel, which is obviously not regular (l and m are both parallel to it and intersect in an ordinary point) nor almost-regular. Hence at most $n - \mu$ ordinary points are added, giving

$$n^2 - \mu^2 + n - \mu \geq n^2 - n$$

i.e.

$$\mu^2 + \mu \leq 2n. \quad \square$$

We shall call a line with the minimal number μ of special points a μ−line.

LEMMA 9. A μ−line has at most $n + \mu(\mu - 3)/2$ parallels.

Proof. Let l be a μ−line. There are $(n - \mu)n$ lines $\neq l$ intersecting l in an ordinary point, while through each special point S there are $n + 1$ lines different form l. Some of them however may intersect l again. If we count the lines $m\ (\neq l)$ through S with multiplicity $1/|m \cap l|$, that is we compute

$$\sum_{S \in \mathbf{S}} \sum_{m \neq l, S \in m} \frac{1}{|m \cap l|}$$

where $\mathbf{S}$ denotes the set of all special points, we get the total number of lines intersecting l in a special point. Now since each pair of special points is on two lines,

$$\sum_{m \neq l, S \in m} (|l \cup m| - 1) = \mu - 1$$

(for fixed $S \in \mathbf{S}$), and from this it easily follows that

$$\sum_{m \neq l, S \in m} \frac{1}{|m \cap l|} \geq n + 1 - \frac{\mu - 1}{2}.$$

As a consequence the number of lines different from l intersecting l is at least $(n - \mu)n + \mu(n + 1 - (\mu - 1)/2)$, and hence l has at most $n + \mu(\mu - 3)/2$ parallels. $\square$

LEMMA 10. If $\mu = 2$ then $n = 3$ and α is uniquely determined.

Proof. Take a μ−line l. It has at least $n - 1$ parallels, since each ordinary point not on l is on at least one parallel. On the other hand

$$n + \frac{\mu(\mu - 3)}{2} = n - 1,$$

so l has exactly $n - 1$ parallels. Consider the other line, m through the two special points of l. Every special point outside m is on no other parallel (to l), every ordinary point outside m on exactly one. Hence through each ordinary point of m there are two parallels, which are regular, and do not intersect the other parallels. But this means that m has at most one ordinary point, and, since α is nontrivial,

46

exactly one. This shows that l has exactly 2 (intersecting) regular parallels, and counting the number of remaining points that must be covered ($= n^2 - n - (n-2) - (2n-1) = (n-3)(n-1)$) shows that the remaining parallels are almost-regular. This is impossible however, since an almost-regular line with regular parallel implies that α is trivial by Proposition 6. Hence there are no remaining parallels and $n = 3$. It is easy to see that the resulting configuration exists and is unique. It is example 2 from section 1. $\square$

LEMMA 11. *Any line intersects a $\mu-$line in at most two points.*

Proof. Let m intersect the $\mu-$line l in 3 or more points. Then through each ordinary point on m there are at least 3 parallels to l. Since the total number of parallels is at most $n + \mu(\mu - 3)/2$ by Lemma 9, the number of ordinary points on m is at most $n/3 + \mu(\mu - 3)/6$ [recall that each point is on c almost-regular lines]. Let S be a special point on m and count the number of ordinary points joined to S:

$$n^2 - n \leq \frac{n}{3} + \frac{\mu(\mu - 3)}{6} + c(n - 1) + (n + 1 - c)(n - \mu) =$$

$$= \frac{n}{3} + \frac{\mu(\mu - 3)}{6} + (n + 1)(n - \mu) + c(\mu - 1) \leq$$

$$\leq (n + 1)(n - \mu) + (\frac{n}{3} + \frac{\mu(\mu - 3)}{6})\mu \leq (n + 1)((n - \mu) + \frac{2(n - \mu)\mu}{3}.$$

Here we used $c \leq \frac{n}{3} + \frac{\mu(\mu-3)}{6}$ and $\mu(\mu + 1) \leq 2n$. Now the right hand side is a decreasing function of μ for $\mu > 2$. For $\mu = 3, 4, 5$ the previous estimate gives a contradiction, while for $\mu > 5$ the right hand side is always too small. $\square$

LEMMA 12. $\mu(\mu + 1) \geq 2n$.

Proof. Let S be a special point on a $\mu-$line l. Any line m through S that intersects l in one other point has at most $\frac{n}{2} + \frac{\mu(\mu-3)}{4}$ ordinary points, by Lemma 9, and the fact that through any ordinary point on m there are at least two parallels. By Lemma 11 there are precisely $\mu - 1$ such lines. Count the number of ordinary points joined to S:

$$n^2 - n \leq (\mu - 1)(\frac{n}{2} + \frac{\mu(\mu - 3)}{4}) + c(n - 1) + (n + 3\mu - c)(n - \mu),$$

using the estimate $c \leq \frac{n}{2} + \frac{\mu(\mu-3)}{4}$ this yields $\mu(\mu+1) \geq 2n$ if $\mu > 3$ and an identity for $\mu = 3$. $\square$

Together with Lemma 8 we get $\mu(\mu + 1) = 2n$, and all estimates are equalities, summarizing we get:

PROPOSITION 13. *If α is a non-trivial Failed Affine Plane of order n containing an almost-regular line, then*

(1) *each line contains 0,1 or μ special points and $\mu^2 + \mu = 2n$;*

(2) *each point is on $\frac{\mu(\mu-1)}{2}$ almost regular lines;*

(3) *each ordinary point is on one $\mu-$line and on μ regular lines;*

(4) *each special point is on $\mu + 2$ $\mu-$lines.*

47

Proof. Let T be the maximal number of special points on a line. Then $c \leq n - T$ and $c = \frac{n}{2} + \frac{\mu(\mu-3)}{4}$ It follows that $T \leq \mu$. Parts 2,3 and 4 can be verified by counting. □

A more symmetric description of the resulting structure can be given after the next lemma. For a regular line l let $\pi_l = \{l\} \cup \{$ the parallels to $l\}$.

LEMMA 14. *Let l be a regular line. Then*

(1) π_l contains $n - \mu$ regular lines and $\mu + 1$ μ-lines;

(2) any two μ-lines in π_l intersect in exactly one point;

(3) if m in π_l is regular then $\pi_l = \pi_m$;

(4) there are $\mu + 2$ regular parallel classes; each regular line is in exactly one, each μ-line in precisely two.

Proof. Through each ordinary point there is one parallel, through each special point there are two. Since a non-regular parallel to l is necessarily a μ-line this gives part (1). The counting arguments in Lemma 12, and the fact that we have equality everywhere shows that if n and m are two μ-lines intersecting in two points, then each parallel to m intersects n (since again by elementary counting two μ-lines always intersect in one or two points), so (2) is proved. Again by counting it follows that any pair of μ-lines that intersects in exactly one point is in precisely one regular parallel class π_l. (3) is obvious, (4) is again a counting argument. □

We now define a new structure α^* by adding $n + 2$ ideal points. One for each parallel class of almost-regular lines (accounting for $c = \frac{\mu(\mu-1)}{2}$ new points) and one for each regular parallel class π_l, accounting for $\mu + 2$ points. We also add a new line, incident with the ideal point if it belongs to the corresponding parallel class.

PROPOSITION 15.

(1) α^* has $n^2 + n + 2$ points and $n^2 + n + 2$ lines.

(2) There are $n + \mu + 2$ points on $n + 2$ lines each, the remaining points are on $n + 1$ lines.

(3) There are $n + \mu + 2$ lines with $n + 2$ points, the remaining lines have $n + 1$ points.

(4) The points on $n + 2$ lines and the lines on $n + 2$ points form a biplane of order μ, i.e. a $2 - ((\mu + 2)(\mu + 1)/2 + 1, \mu + 2, 2)$ design).

(5) A point on $n+1$ lines is joined to any other point by exactly one line and dually a line with $n + 1$ points intersects any other line in one point.

(6) Deletion of any line with $n + 2$ points, together with the incident points yields a Failed Affine Plane of order n.

Proof. (1) is obvious. To see (2) note that besides the n special points also the $\mu + 2$ regular parallel classes are on $n + 2$ lines. (3) The $n + \mu + 1$ μ-lines all have two ideal points by Lemma 14.4, the new line also has $n + 2$ points. The remaining lines are in one parallel class, hence have one ideal point. (4) If two μ-lines intersect in just one point in α then (see remark after the proof of Lemma 14.2) they are

48

in the same regular parallel class, hence in α^* they have two points of intersection. Conversely , the points on $n + 2$ lines in α^* are the old special points and the ideal points corresponding to regular parallel classes. It follows that any pair is on 2 lines: by Lemma 4 for two special points, for a special point S and a regular parallel class it follows from the fact that through S there are two parallels , and finally two intersecting regular lines have a unique common parallel by Lemma 7. and they also lie on the new line. (5) and (6) are obvious. □

In matrix terms the configuration α^* can be characterized by the fact that the point-line incidence matrix A satisfies

$$A.A^t = \begin{pmatrix} 2J + nI & J \\ J & J + nI \end{pmatrix} .$$

where the upper left hand corner is of size $n + \mu + 2$, while the lower right hand corner is of size $n^2 - \mu$.

One should expect that so much regularity conditions are enough to settle the possible existence of these objects, but this is as far as we got. Of course the Bruck Chowla Ryser condition for biplanes restrict the possibilities for μ (cf [3]). The state of affairs for small μ is as follows: For $\mu = 2, n = 3$ the configuration is unique and given in example 2. For $\mu = 3, n = 6$ existence of α^* would give a set of 35 subsets of size 7 of a 43-set, each pair intersecting exactly once, by taking all $(n + 1)-$ lines missing a particular $(n + 2)-$ point, together with the $\mu + 2$ $(n + 2)-$ lines through that point and deleting this point. By a result of van Lint, Janssen, Koolen and Hall [6] however there can be at most 32 such sets.

Another way to describe the structure is as a Bhaskar-Rao Design . A Bhaskar-Rao design (for the purpose of this paper) is a group divisible design with pointset $X * Q$ and groups $x * Q$ for $x \in X$ such that its collection of blocks can be partitioned into families of size $|Q|$ each, where the blocks in one family all meet the same set of groups. (It follows that projecting X yields a pairwise balanced design $(X, \mathcal{B})$.) Now let $(Q, .)$ be a quasigroup. A Bhaskar-Rao design of index λ over $(Q, .)$ is a pairwise balanced design $(X, \mathcal{B})$ together with a family $\Phi = \phi_B | B \in \mathcal{B}$ of maps $\phi_B : B \to Q$ such that for any two elements $x, y \in X$ and any two (not necessarily distinct) elements $\alpha, \beta \in Q$ there are precisely λ pairs $(\gamma, B) \in Q * \mathcal{B}$ such that $x, y \in B$ and $\gamma\phi_B(x) = \alpha, \gamma\phi_B(y) = \beta$. Clearly, any Bhaskar-Rao design over $(Q, .)$ yields a Bhaskar-Rao design. The structure we are interested in, is a Bhaskar-Rao design of index 1 with as underlying design a $2-(n+\mu+2, n, 2)$ design. Gibbons and Mathon [5], show for $(\mu, n) = (4, 10)$ and $Q = \mathbf{Z}_6$ or $Q = \text{Sym}(6)$ that a Bhaskar-Rao design over Q does not exist.

This concludes the determination of the structure of Failed Affine Planes with an almost regular line.

5. FAILED AFFINE PLANES WITHOUT ALMOST REGULAR LINES

In this section we show that if α has no almost regular lines, then it is of Baer type. To prove this, we show that α can be embedded, in a certain sense, in a projective plane.

DEFINITION. *An incidence structure of points and lines is called a partial projective plane of order n ($PPP(n)$) if*

(1) *two points are on exactly one line;*

(2) *each point is on $n + 1$ lines;*

(3) *there are $n^2 + n + 1$ lines.*

By a result of DOW [4] a $PPP(n)$ with more then $n^2 - 2\sqrt{n+3} + 6$ points can be embedded in a projective plane. A regular line has exactly n parallels, since it intersects precisely n^2 lines. Two intersecting regular lines have a unique common parallel, just as before and we recall the notion of a regular parallel class: $\pi_l = \{l\} \cup \{\text{the parallels to } l\}$. For regular lines m and l we have $\pi_l = \pi_m$ iff l is parallel to m. Let α be a Failed Affine Plane of order n.

PROPOSITION 16. *Define an incidence structure α^*: points are the ordinary points of $\alpha +$ the regular parallel classes, lines are the lines of α. A point P is incident with a line l if P is on l or l in P (corresponding to the case that P is a point or a parallel class). Then α^* is a partial projective plane of order n.*

Proof. We shall show that the three axioms are satisfied.

1. Two ordinary points lie on a unique line; through an ordinary point there is a unique line in a fixed regular parallel class; two intersecting regular lines have a unique common parallel.

2. This follows from the fact that a regular parallel class contains $n + 1$ lines, and ordinary points of α are by definition on $n + 1$ lines.

3. Obvious. □

Next we show that if α has no almost regular line, that α^* contains at least $n^2 - 1$ points and hence is embeddable.

LEMMA 17. *There are at least $n/2 + 1$ regular parallel classes.*

Proof. Since a line with special points covers at most $n - 2$ ordinary points, each ordinary point is on at least $n/2 + 1$ regular lines, which all determine a different parallel class. □

LEMMA 18. *If α contains no 1-point, then α^* is embeddable.*

Proof. Since $\sum i x_i = n$ the number of ordinary points is at least $n^2 - n/2$. It follows that α^* has at least $n^2 + 1$ points and is embeddable. □

LEMMA 19. *Let S be a 1-point of α, and T another special point. Then there is a line through S, not containing T, with exactly two special points.*

Proof. Counting the number of ordinary points covered by the $n + 2$ lines through S it follows that at least 6 of them contain just two special points. Let l and m be two of them and suppose both contain T. Through each ordinary point on m there are 2 parallels to l, together $2(n - 2)$ parallels. The number of lines intersecting l is at least $n(n - 2) + 2(n + 2) - \#\{$ lines through S and $T\}$,

50

with equality precisely when also T is a 1-point. Since the total number of lines is $n^2 + n + 1$, the number of lines through S and T is at least $n - 1$. If this number equals $n - 1$ then T is also a 1-point, and each of the 3 lines through S missing T contains at most 3 ordinary points, since the lines through T and each one of them are different and do not contain S. Also, counting all points joined to S (except T) with multiplicity, we find $n^2 - 1$. Hence, there is exactly one point different from T doubly joined to S. Since on each line through S but not T there are at least three special points, we find (allowing for the fact that one may be counted twice) $n \geq 7$. On the other hand, counting the number of ordinary points joined to S one gets $n^2 - n \leq n^2 - 3n + 11$, or $n \leq 5$. Contradiction.

Finally, if the number of lines through S and T is greater than $n - 1$, then similar but easier arguments lead to a contradiction. ☐

LEMMA 20. *A 1-point S and an i-point T are joined by at most $i + 3$ lines.*

Proof. By lemma 19 there is a line l through S with two special points not containing T. There are $n - 2$ lines through an ordinary point of l. Hence at most $i + 3$ through T and S. ☐

LEMMA 21. *A line l with 2 special points, a 1-point S and an i-point T, has at most $n + 1$ parallels. Through the two special points of l there is at least one more line.*

Proof. There are at least $(n - 2)n + (n + 2) + (n + 1 + i) - (i + 3) = n^2$ lines intersecting l. Note that if there are precisely $n + 1$ parallels, then there are at least 4 lines through the two special points of l. If there are only 3 lines through this pair, then there are at most n parallels. Less than 2 lines is impossible, since the line l has at least $n - 1$ parallels. ☐

We shall treat the three cases, i.e. at least 4 lines, 3 lines and 2 lines through the special points of l separately.

LEMMA 22. *It is not possible that there are three or more extra lines through the special pair on l.*

Proof. Through each ordinary point on such an extra line there are two parallels to l. Hence those lines contain at most $(n + 1)/2$ ordinary points , and since there are at least three of them, S is joined to at most

$$3(n + 1)/2 + (n - 1)(n - 2) = n^2 - 3n/2 + 7/2$$

ordinary points. From $n^2 - n \leq n^2 - 3n/2 + 7/2$ it follows that $n \leq 7$. Since there are at least 6 lines through S with just two special point, $n = 7$, all special points are 1-points, and each line contains 0,2 or 4 special points. But it is impossible to divide 7 special points on the 8 lines through an ordinary point in groups of even size. ☐

LEMMA 23. *It is not possible that there are two extra lines through the special pair on l.*

Proof. In this case l has at most n parallels, hence the extra lines through the special points of l contain at most $n/2$ ordinary points. Counting the number of ordinary points joined to S one gets $n^2 - n \leq 2.n/2 + n(n-2)$. Since we have equality, there are exactly $n^2 - n$ ordinary points and all special points are 1-points. Now through S there are n lines containing one additional special point, and 2 lines containing $n/2 - 1$ additional special points. Since each other special point is joined to S by at least one line with more then 2 special points we have a contradiction: $n - 1 > 2(n/2 - 1)$. So we are left with a configuration in which each 1-point is on a line l (at least 6 in fact) containing exactly one other special point T which is on exactly one extra line with S, L has $n - 1$ parallels and T is also a 1-point. $\square$

LEMMA 24. *It is not possible that there is just one extra line through the special pair $\{S, T\}$ on l.*

Proof. The other line through S and T contains at most $(n - 1)/2$ ordinary points, say τ. Since each special point U which is on a line l^* with S containing no further special points also determines a line through S (and U) with at most $(n - 1)/2$ ordinary points, while on the other hand there can be at most one such line through S (count the number of ordinary points joined to S) each point U like that is on that line already. The number of such points is therefore at most $n - 1 - \tau$. Hence S is joined to at most

$$(n - 1 - \tau)(n - 2) + (2 + \tau)(n - 3) + \tau = n^2 - n - 4$$

ordinary points. $\square$

We can combine Lemmas 18 to 24 in the following

THEOREM 25. *If α is a Failed Affine Plane of order n without almost-regular lines, then α has no 1-points, and α^* is embeddable in a projective plane of order n.* $\square$

We finish this section by showing that α is of Baer type

DEFINITION. *A subset B of a projective plane is called a blocking set if every line of the plane intersects both B and the complement of B.*

After completion of α^* to a projective plane π, there are 3 types of points. The ordinary points of α, the regular parallel classes of α and new points. The regular parallel classes + the new points form a blocking set fo π with less than $3n/2 + 1$ points. Also, since α contains no lines with $n - 1$ ordinary points, there are no lines with 2 points of the blocking set. Also if a line has precisely one point of the blocking set, this point corresponds to a regular parallel class. If a new point exists then each line through this new point would therefore contain at least 2 more points of the blocking set. Since $3n/2 + 1 < 2n + 3$ there are no new points.

THEOREM 26. *If α is a Failed Affine Plane of order n, without almost-regular lines, then α is of Baer type.*

Proof. Let P be an i-point ($i \geq 0$) of α. The $n+i+1$ lines through P, viewed as lines in the projective plane π cover the ordinary points exactly once, and the points of the blocking set (i.e. the regular parallel classes) exactly $i + 1$ times, because through an i−point there are $i + 1$ parallels to a regular line. Counting flags we get $n^2 + n + 1 + |B|.i = (n + 1)(n + i + 1)$, or $|B| = n + 1 + n/i$. In particular, i is constant. Looking at a line not containing the i−point P we see that this line contains one point of the blocking set (for such a point is covered $i + 1$ times by the lines through P, so on l there is at most one), on the other hand, a line containing P contains $a + 1$ points of B where $(a + 1)i + 1 = n + i + 1$ or $a = n/i$. Hence a line in α through a special point contains all of them (since $\sum j x_j = n$, there are just a special points since $ia = n$). Since all ordinary points must be joined to P we finally get

$$(n + i + 1)(n - a) = n^2 - a$$

together with $ia = n$ this yields $a = i = \sqrt{n}$; $|B| = n + \sqrt{n + 1}$.

Hence B is a Baer subplane by a theorem of Bruen [2] and α is of Baer type. □

REFERENCES

[1]   C. BAKER, *Failed Geometries*, Lecture given at 11th British Comb. Conf., London (1987).
[2]   A.A. BRUEN, *Blocking Sets in finite projective planes*, Siam J. Appl. Math., 21 (1971), pp. 380–392.
[3]   P.J. CAMERON, *Biplanes*, Math. Zeitung, 131 (1973), pp. 85–101.
[4]   S. DOW, *An improved bound for extending partial projective planes*, Discrete Math., 45 (1983), pp. 199– 207.
[5]   P.B. GIBBONS AND R.A. MATHON, *Group signings of symmetric balanced incomplete block designs*, Ars Combin., 23A (1987), pp. 123–134.
[6]   J.I. HALL, A.J.E.M. JANSEN, A.W.J. KOLEN AND J.H. VAN LINT, *Equidistant codes with distance 12*, Discrete Math, 17 (1977), pp. 71–83.
[7]   E. MENDELSOHN AND A. ASSAF, *Spectrum of Imbrical Designs*, Annals of Discrete Math., 34 (1987), pp. 363–370.

OPTIMAL PROPERTIES OF BALANCED INCOMPLETE BLOCK AND OTHER DESIGNS

CHING-SHUI CHENG*

Abstract. This paper reviews some optimal statistical properties of balanced incomplete block and other related designs. This includes applications to variety trials, weighing designs, and Hadamard transform optics in spectroscopy. Connections to some problems in graph theory, in particular the problem of maximizing the number of spanning trees in a graph, are also discussed.

Key words. Hadamard transform optics, optimal design, partially balanced incomplete block design, regular graph design, spanning tree, weighing design

AMS(MOS) subject classifications. 62K05, 62K10, 05B05

1. Introduction. The use of balanced incomplete block designs (BIBD), or 2-designs, in statistical experiments was first proposed by Yates [29]. Over the years, the study of BIBD's has occupied an important place in the theory of combinatorics. There has been a lot of literature on the combinatorial properties and construction of these and other related designs. In this paper, we shall review some results on optimal block designs, an aspect which is perhaps less known to combinatorialists. Some related combinatorial problems will also be discussed. The recent book by Constantine [12] also contains interesting discussions on combinatorial and statistical designs.

Section 2 discusses Kiefer's result on the optimality of BIBD's in variety trials [20, 22]. A graph-theoretic formulation of this result is given in Section 3. Section 4 considers optimal designs when a BIBD does not exist. Section 5 presents an application of BIBD's to optimal weighing designs and Hadamard transform optics [6, 13, 14].

The definition of a BIBD is reviewed in the following. A BIBD with v varieties and b blocks of size $k(k < v)$ is an arrangement of v varieties into b blocks of size k such that

(1) each variety appears at most once in each block,

(2) all the varieties appear in the same number of blocks,

and

(3) any pair of varieties appear together in the same number of blocks.

A design satisfying (1) is called a *binary* design, and one satisfying (2) is called an *equireplicated* design.

---
*Department of Statistics, University of California, Berkeley, California, 94720. This work was supported by National Science Foundation Grant No. DMS-8802640.

2. Kiefer's result on the optimality of BIBD's. Suppose v varieties (of grains, say) are to be compared on bk experimental units (plots) which are partitioned into b blocks of size k each, in such a way that the plots within the same block are more or less homogeneous. We shall assume $k < v$. The purpose of *blocking* is to increase the precision of the comparison. A design d is an assignment of the varieties to the plots such that each plot receives one variety. One observation is then taken on each plot. For any design d, we shall assume that the observation y_{ij} taken on the j-th plot in the i-th block is modeled by

$$(2.1) \qquad y_{ij} = \alpha_{d(i,j)} + \beta_i + \epsilon_{ij},$$

where $d(i,j) \in \{1, 2, \ldots, v\}$ is the label of the variety assigned to the j-th plot in the i-th block, $\alpha_1, \alpha_2, \ldots, \alpha_v$ are unknown constants representing the effects of the varieties, $\beta_1, \beta_2, \ldots, \beta_b$ are unknown constants representing the block effects, and the ϵ_{ij}'s are uncorrelated random errors with zero expectations and constant variance σ^2.

The purpose of the experiment is to compare the varieties. Consider a linear function $\mathbf{c}' \, \boldsymbol{\alpha} = \sum_{i=1}^{v} c_i \alpha_i$ of the variety effects. It can be shown that $\mathbf{c}' \, \boldsymbol{\alpha}$ is estimable, i.e., there exists a linear unbiased estimator, only if $\sum_{i=1}^{v} c_i = 0$. Such linear functions are called *contrasts*. For example, a simple contrast is $\alpha_i - \alpha_j$. A design is said to be *connected* if all the variety contrasts are estimable. We shall denote the collection of all connected designs with given values of v, b and k by $\mathcal{D}_{v,b,k}$.

Suppose one has equal interests in all the varieties. Let $\mathbf{c}_1, \mathbf{c}_2, \ldots, \mathbf{c}_{v-1}$ be $v-1$ orthonormal vectors such that $\mathbf{c}_i' \mathbf{1}_v = 0$, $\forall i$, where $\mathbf{1}_v$ is the $v \times 1$ vector of ones, and let $\mathbf{c}_1' \hat{\boldsymbol{\alpha}}, \mathbf{c}_2' \hat{\boldsymbol{\alpha}}, \ldots, \mathbf{c}_{v-1}' \hat{\boldsymbol{\alpha}}$ be the least squares estimators of $\mathbf{c}_1' \boldsymbol{\alpha}, \mathbf{c}_2' \boldsymbol{\alpha}, \ldots, \mathbf{c}_{v-1}' \boldsymbol{\alpha}$. Denote by $\mathbf{V}_d$ the covariance matrix of $\mathbf{c}_1' \hat{\boldsymbol{\alpha}}, \mathbf{c}_2' \hat{\boldsymbol{\alpha}}, \ldots, \mathbf{c}_{v-1}' \hat{\boldsymbol{\alpha}}$ under a design $d \in \mathcal{D}_{v,b,k}$. Then one would like to "minimize" $\mathbf{V}_d$ in a certain sense. A common approach is to choose an orthogonally invariant real-valued function Ψ (such as the trace or determinant) of $\mathbf{V}_d$ and minimize $\Psi(\mathbf{V}_d)$ over $d \in \mathcal{D}_{v,b,k}$. Such functions Ψ are called *optimality criteria*.

The covariance matrix $\mathbf{V}_d$ can be computed as follows. Let

$$\mathbf{C}_d = \mathbf{diag}(r_{d1}, r_{d2}, \ldots, r_{dv}) - k^{-1} \mathbf{N}_d \mathbf{N}_d',$$

where r_{di} is the number of times the i-th variety appears in the design, **diag** $(r_{d1}, r_{d2}, \ldots, r_{dv})$ is the diagonal matrix with diagonal entries $r_{d1}, r_{d2}, \ldots, r_{dv}$, and $\mathbf{N}_d$ is the $v \times b$ variety-block incidence matrix with the (i,j)-th entry equal to the number of times the i-th variety appears in the j-th block. We shall denote the (i,j)-th entry of $\mathbf{N}_d \mathbf{N}_d'$ by λ_{dij}, $i \neq j$. Note that if d is a binary design, then λ_{dij} is simply the number of blocks in which varieties i and j both appear. So for a BIBD, the λ_{dij}'s are constant. Now let $\mathbf{P} = [\mathbf{c}_1, \mathbf{c}_2, \ldots, \mathbf{c}_{v-1}]'$. Then it is known [20] that if d is connected, then

$$(2.2) \qquad \mathbf{V}_d = \sigma^2 (\mathbf{P} \mathbf{C}_d \mathbf{P}')^{-1}.$$

The matrix $\mathbf{C}_d$, which is symmetric, nonnegative definite, and has zero row sums, is called the *information matrix*, or *C-matrix* of design d. It is well known that d is connected if and only if rank $\mathbf{C}_d = v - 1$. Let $\mu_{d1} \geq \ldots \geq \mu_{d,v-1} > \mu_{dv} = 0$ be the eigenvalues of $\mathbf{C}_d$. Then the eigenvalues of $\sigma^{-2}\mathbf{V}_d$ are $\mu_{d1}^{-1}, \mu_{d2}^{-1}, \ldots, \mu_{d,v-1}^{-1}$. So orthogonally invariant functions of $\mathbf{V}_d$ can be defined as functions of $\mathbf{C}_d$ through its eigenvalues. To avoid inverting matrices, it is easier and more convenient to work with functions of $\mathbf{C}_d$. We shall call a design Φ-optimal if it minimizes a certain real-valued function $\Phi(\mathbf{C}_d)$ over $\mathcal{D}_{v,b,k}$. Some commonly used criteria are $\Phi_D(\mathbf{C}_d) \equiv \det \sigma^{-2}\mathbf{V}_d = \Pi_{i=1}^{v-1}\mu_{di}^{-1}$, $\Phi_A(\mathbf{C}_d) \equiv tr\sigma^{-2}\mathbf{V}_d = \sum_{i=1}^{v-1}\mu_{di}^{-1}$, and $\Phi_E(\mathbf{C}_d) \equiv \mu_{d,v-1}^{-1} =$ the maximum eigenvalue of $\sigma^{-2}\mathbf{V}_d$. These three functions Φ_D, Φ_A, Φ_E are called D-, A-, and E-criteria, respectively, and designs minimizing $\Phi_D(\mathbf{C}_d)$, $\Phi_A(\mathbf{C}_d)$, or $\Phi_E(\mathbf{C}_d)$ are said to be D-, A- or E-optimal, respectively.

Let $\mathcal{B}_{v,0}$ be the collection of all the $v \times v$ nonnegative definite symmetric matrices with zero row sums, and let $\mathcal{C}$ be a subset of $\mathcal{B}_{v,0}$. An important result by Kiefer [22] is the following

THEOREM 2.1. *If* $\mathcal{C}$ *contains a matrix* $\mathbf{C}^*$ *such that*

(i) $\mathbf{C}^*$ *is of the form* $a\mathbf{I}_v + b\mathbf{J}_v$, *where* $\mathbf{I}_v$ *is the identity matrix of order* v *and* $\mathbf{J}_v$ *is the* $v \times v$ *matrix of ones, and*

(ii) $\mathbf{C}^*$ *maximizes* $tr\,\mathbf{C}$ *over* $\mathbf{C} \in \mathcal{C}$,

then $\mathbf{C}^*$ *minimizes* $\Phi(\mathbf{C})$ *over* $\mathcal{C}$ *for all* $\Phi : \mathcal{B}_{v,0} \rightarrow [0, \infty]$ *such that*

(a) Φ *is convex,*

(b) $\Phi(\alpha\mathbf{C})$ *is nonincreasing in the scalar* $\alpha \geq 0$, *and*

(c) $\Phi(\mathbf{C})$ *is invariant under all simultaneous permutations of rows and columns of* $\mathbf{C}$.

Now take $\mathcal{C} = \{\mathbf{C}_d : d \in \mathcal{D}_{v,b,k}\}$ and let $\mathbf{C}^*$ be the C-matrix of a balanced incomplete block design in $\mathcal{D}_{v,b,k}$ if it exists. Then it is easy to verify that conditions (i) and (ii) in Theorem 2.1 are satisfied. Clearly (i) follows from (2) and (3) in the definition of a BIBD, while (ii) is satisfied by any binary design (condition (1) in the definition of a BIBD). Therefore we have

COROLLARY 2.2. *A BIBD minimizes* $\Phi(\mathbf{C}_d)$ *over* $d \in \mathcal{D}_{v,b,k}$ *for all* Φ *satisfying* (a), (b) *and* (c) *in Theorem 2.1.*

This is a remarkable result with a very simple proof. The same argument can be used to establish the optimality of Latin squares, orthogonal Latin squares and orthogonal arrays in more complex settings.

Note that (a), (b) and (c) are satisfied by the D-, A- and E-criteria. The optimality of a BIBD with respect to these three special criteria actually appeared in an earlier paper of Kiefer [20]. Some weaker results were also obtained independently by other authors at about the same time. Masuyama [25] and Mote [26] independently proved the E-optimality and Kshirsagar [24] proved the D- and A-optimality of a BIBD over *binary* designs.

56

This result on the optimality of a BIBD will be restated in graph-theoretic language in the next section.

3. Maximizing the number of spanning trees in a graph. Kiefer's result on the optimality of BIBD's reviewed in the preceding section and the general problem of finding D-optimal block designs have an interesting connection to the problem of maximizing the total number of spanning trees in a graph with fixed numbers of vertices and lines [18, 19]. Given a (simple or multiple) graph G with v vertices, let $\mathbf{C}(G)$ be the $v \times v$ matrix with the i-th diagonal entry equal to the degree of the i-th vertex and the (i,j)-th off-diagonal entry equal to -1 times the number of lines between the i-th vertex and the j-th vertex. Then it is known that the number of spanning trees in G is equal to $v^{-1} \prod_{i=1}^{v-1} \lambda_i(G)$, where $\lambda_1(G), \ldots, \lambda_{v-1}(G)$ are the $v-1$ largest eigenvalues of $\mathbf{C}(G)$; see [1]. Now each graph G with v vertices and l lines can be regarded as a block design with v varieties and l blocks of size *two*, each line considered as a block containing its two endpoints. Let this block design be denoted by $d(G)$. Then the matrix $\mathbf{C}(G)$ and the C-matrix $\mathbf{C}_{d(G)}$ of $d(G)$ are related by

$$\mathbf{C}(G) = 2\mathbf{C}_{d(G)}.$$

Therefore a graph G^* maximizes the total number of spanning trees among all the graphs with v vertices and l lines if and only if the corresponding block design $d(G^*)$ is D-optimal over $d \in \mathcal{D}_{v,l,2}$. Clearly a BIBD corresponds to a graph with equal number of lines between any two vertices. By Kiefer's result, such a graph has the maximum number of spanning trees among all the graphs with the same numbers of lines and vertices. This result was later re-proved by Kelmans [18].

4. Optimal designs when a BIBD does not exist. BIBD's can be constructed only for very restricted values of v, b and k, and do not exist in many practical situations. Likewise, one can put an equal number of lines between any two vertices in a graph if and only if $v(v-1)/2|l$. The search for an optimal design when a BIBD does not exist is a challenging problem. Intuitively, one would expect an optimal design to be combinatorially close to a BIBD. Indeed John and Mitchell [16] defined a *regular graph design* to be a design satisfying conditions (1), (2) in the definition of a BIBD and the following:

(4.1) $\quad |\lambda_{dij} - \lambda_{di'j'}| \leq 1$, for all $i \neq j$, $i' \neq j'$, i.e., $\lambda_{dij} = \lambda$ or $\lambda + 1$ for some λ.

Recall that λ_{dij} is the (i,j)-th entry of $\mathbf{N}_d\mathbf{N}_d'$. By slightly relaxing condition (3) in the definition of a BIBD, one obtains far greater availability of the designs. The reason such a design is called a regular graph design is that one can construct a regular simple graph with v vertices by putting a line between vertices i and j, $1 \leq i, j \leq v$, if and only if $\lambda_{dij} = \lambda$. Such a graph will be denoted by $G(d)$. Clearly $G(d)$ is a *strongly regular graph* if and only if d is a partially balanced incomplete block (PBIB) design with two associate classes. In case equal replication of the varieties is not possible (v does not divide bk), one can modify condition (2) in the definition of a BIBD to

(4.2) $\qquad\qquad |r_{di} - r_{di'}| \leq 1, \quad \text{for all } i \neq i',$

and replace (4.1) with

(4.3)   For any i, $|\lambda_{dij} - \lambda_{dij'}| \leq 1$, for all $j, j' \neq i$.

A binary design satisfying (4.2) and (4.3) is called a *nearly balanced incomplete block design* by Cheng and Wu [9].

    An interesting question is, are the best nearly balanced incomplete block designs, especially the best regular graph designs, always optimal? The latter was in fact the conjecture of John and Mitchell [16]. Unfortunately, it is not always true. In a computer search, Jones and Eccleston [17] found designs with unequal replications (i.e., the r_{di}'s are not all equal) which are better than the best regular graph designs under the A-criterion for $(v, b, k) = (10, 10, 2)$, $(11, 11, 2)$ and $(12, 12, 2)$. A counterexample for the E-criterion can be found in Constantine [11]. Another disturbing fact is that even a regular graph design which is also a two-associate-class PBIB design (i.e., the corresponding graph is strongly regular) can fail to be optimal over the regular graph designs. For example, when $v = 10$, $b = 30$ and $k = 2$, there exists a regular graph design which is a two-associate-class PBIB design of the triangular type. However, John and Mitchell's [16] computer search produced a better regular graph design which is not a PBIB design, under both the A- and D-criteria. These surprising results demonstrate that the determination of optimal block designs is a tricky and difficult problem.

    Some special regular graph designs have been shown to be optimal. For example, Cheng [4] proved that if $\mathcal{D}_{v,b,k}$ contains a group-divisible design with two groups and $\lambda_2 = \lambda_1 + 1$, then it minimizes $\sum_{i=1}^{v-1} f(\mu_{di})$ over $\mathcal{D}_{v,b,k}$ for any real-valued function f defined on $[0, \infty)$ such that $f' < 0, f'' > 0, f''' < 0$ and $\lim_{x \to 0+} f(x) = f(0) = \infty$. Such criteria are called type 1 criteria in [4]. One obtains the D- and A-optimalities by choosing $f(x) = -\log x$ and x^{-1}, respectively. The E-optimality is also included as a limiting case. An immediate corollary of the D-optimality result is that if G is a graph in which the vertices are divided into two groups of equal size such that there are λ lines between any two vertices in the same group and $\lambda + 1$ lines between any two vertices in different groups, then G has the maximum number of spanning trees among all the graphs with the same numbers of lines and vertices as G.

    Numerical evidences and intuition strongly suggest that the above result also holds in general for any group-divisible design with $\lambda_2 = \lambda_1 + 1$, not necessarily with two groups. However, a proof seems to be very difficult. Only some partial results are available. It can be shown that such designs are E-optimal over $\mathcal{D}_{v,b,k}$ (see [28]), and are also optimal *over the regular graph designs* in $\mathcal{D}_{v,b,k}$ with respect to all the type 1 criteria. A corollary of the latter result is that a regular complete multipartite graph G has the maximum number of spanning trees among all the *simple* graphs with the same numbers of vertices and lines as G; see [5]. Whether this result holds without restricting to simple graphs is an interesting and challenging problem. Likewise, it is unknown if a group-divisible design with $\lambda_2 = \lambda_1 + 1$ is optimal over the whole class $\mathcal{D}_{v,b,k}$, not just the regular graph designs.

    While attending the Design Theory Workshop at IMA where this paper was presented, Cheng and Bailey [7] proved that if $\mathcal{D}_{v,b,k}$ contains a two-associate-class

PBIB design with $\lambda_2 = \lambda_1 + 1$ or $\lambda_1 - 1$ such that $\mathbf{N}_d\mathbf{N}'_d$ is a *singular* matrix, then it is optimal over all the binary and equireplicated designs in $\mathcal{D}_{v,b,k}$ with respect to all the type 1 criteria. Furthermore, the duals of such designs are also optimal over the binary and equireplicated designs in $\mathcal{D}_{b,v,r}$ where $r = bk/v$. This result covers, for example, all the partial geometries introduced by Bose [2] and all the two-associate-class PBIB designs with $\lambda_2 = \lambda_1 \pm 1$ and $b < v$. The E-optimality of some of these designs over $\mathcal{D}_{v,b,k}$ has been established by Constantine [10].

Although the best nearly balanced incomplete block design may not be optimal, it can be shown that it is optimal if the number of blocks is sufficiently large. Cheng, Masaro and Wong [8] presented a graph theoretic version of such a result for the D-criterion. Let r_i be the degree of the i-th vertex in a graph and let λ_{ij} be the number of lines between vertices i and j. Then a graph is called *nearly balanced* if the following two conditions hold:

(i) $|r_i - r'_i| \le 1$, for all $i \ne i'$,
(ii) For any i, $|\lambda_{ij} - \lambda_{ij'}| \le 1$, for all j, $j' \ne i$.

It can easily be seen that for any v and l, there exists a nearly balanced graph with v vertices and l lines. Cheng, Masaro and Wong [8] showed that for any v, there exists a positive integer l^* such that as long as $l \ge l^*$, any nearly balanced graph with v vertices and l lines has more spanning trees than any non-nearly-balanced graph with the same numbers of lines and vertices. The proof does not give a useful bound for l^*, which deserves further investigation.

Another interesting connection to graph theory concerns the search for E-optimal designs. If d is a regular graph design, then the information matrix $\mathbf{C}_d$ is related to the adjacency matrix $\mathbf{A}_{G(d)}$ of $G(d)$ by

$$\mathbf{A}_{G(d)} = k\mathbf{C}_d - \{(k-1)r + \lambda + 1)\}I_v + (\lambda + 1)\mathbf{J}_v.$$

Therefore searching for an E-optimal design among the regular graph designs is equivalent to maximizing the smallest eigenvalue of $\mathbf{A}_{G(d)}$. It is easy to see that the smallest eigenvalue of $\mathbf{A}_{G(d)}$ cannot be greater than -1. This upper bound is achieved if d is a BIBD or a group-divisible design with $\lambda_2 = \lambda_1 + 1$. In fact, this is the idea behind the proof of the E-optimality of such designs. Many of the designs which have been proven E-optimal are regular graph designs with the smallest eigenvalues of $\mathbf{A}_{G(d)}$ greater than or equal to -2. This brings in the connection to the characterization of graphs whose adjacency matrices have the smallest eigenvalues ≥ -2; which was solved in [3]. Regular graph designs with the smallest eigenvalues of $\mathbf{A}_{G(d)}$ greater than or equal to -2 are also expected to perform very well under other criteria. We conjecture that a simple graph that has the maximum number of spanning trees with given numbers of lines and vertices can be found among those whose complementary graphs have the smallest eigenvalues greater than or equal to -2, if such graphs exist. In particular, we expect line graphs to play important roles in the determination of graphs with maximum number of spanning trees.

5. Applications to weighing design and Hadamard transform optics. In the monograph by Harwit ahd Sloane [14] and in an earlier paper [13], they posed the following conjecture: suppose $\mathbf{X}^* = \mathbf{N}_d$ is the $v \times v$ block-variety incidence matrix of a symmetric BIBD d of block size $k = (v+1)/2$; then it minimizes $tr(\mathbf{X}'\mathbf{X})^{-1}$ over all the $v \times v$ matrices $\mathbf{X}$ with entries $0 \leq x_{ij} \leq 1$. This arises from a problem in Hadamard transform optics as well as the statistical problem of weighing designs. For the latter, see Chapter 17 of [27]. The readers are referred to [14] for detailed discussions. The more restrictive problem of optimizing over matrices with $(0, 1)$-entries was treated by Jacroux and Notz [15].

This conjecture has recently been confirmed by Cheng [6]. In fact $\mathbf{X}^*$ not only minimizes $tr(\mathbf{X}'\mathbf{X})^{-1}$, but is also optimal with respect to many other criteria. Similar result holds for BIBD's with $b > v$ as well. Some optimal properties of the incidence matrices of BIBD's with $k > (v+1)/2$ can also be established.

To state the result, we need to define two sequences of numbers $f(k)$ and $g(k)$ for integers k such that $[(v+1)/2] \leq k \leq v-1$, where $[(v+1)/2]$ is the integral part of $(v+1)/2$:

$$f(k) = \begin{cases} \dfrac{ln\{(2k-1-v)/(2k-1)\}}{ln\{k(v-1)/(v-k)\}} + 1, & \text{if } [(v+1)/2]+1 \leq k \leq v-1 \\ -\infty, & \text{if } k = [(v+1)/2], \end{cases}$$

$$g(k) = \frac{ln\{(2k+1-v)/(2k+1)\}}{ln\{k(v-1)/(v-k)\}} + 1.$$

Note that $\{f(k)\}$ and $\{g(k)\}$ are interlacing, i.e., we have $f(k) < g(k) < f(k+1)$ for all k. Also, $f(k) < 1$ and $g(k) < 1$. Thus the intervals $\{[f(k), g(k)]\}_{k=[(v+1)/2]}^{v-1}$, $\{(g(k), f(k+1))\}_{k=[(v+1)/2]}^{v-2}$ and $(g(v-1), 1]$ form a partition of $[-\infty, 1]$.

In the rest of the paper, we shall denote the set of all the $b \times v$ matrices $\mathbf{X}$ with entries $0 \leq x_{ij} \leq 1$ by $\mathcal{M}_{b,v}$. We shall also assume $b \geq v$. Now for any p such that $-\infty \leq p \leq 1$ and any $\mathbf{X} \in \mathcal{M}_{b,v}$, define

(5.1) $$\phi_p(\mathbf{X}'\mathbf{X}) = \{v^{-1}tr(\mathbf{X}'\mathbf{X})^p\}^{1/p} \text{ if } -\infty < p \leq 1 \text{ and } p \neq 0,$$

(5.2) $$\phi_0(\mathbf{X}'\mathbf{X}) = \{det(\mathbf{X}'\mathbf{X})\}^{1/v},$$

and

(5.3) $$\phi_{-\infty}(\mathbf{X}'\mathbf{X}) = \text{ the minimum eigenvalue of } \mathbf{X}'\mathbf{X}.$$

In [6], Cheng considered the more general problem of

(5.4) $$maximizing \; \phi_p(\mathbf{X}'\mathbf{X}) \text{ over } \mathbf{X} \in \mathcal{M}_{b,v}.$$

For $-\infty < p < 0(p > 0)$, this is equivalent to minimizing (maximizing) $tr(\mathbf{X}'\mathbf{X})^p$, while choosing $p = 0$ amounts to maximizing $det(\mathbf{X}'\mathbf{X})$. In the application to Hadamard transform optics, $(\mathbf{X}'\mathbf{X})^{-1}$ is the covariance matrix of the least squares estimators of the intensities of the various frequency components in a spectrum. Therefore in this context $\mathbf{X}'\mathbf{X}$ plays the same role as the C-matrix in Section 2, and ϕ_0, ϕ_{-1} and $\phi_{-\infty}$ are the D-, A- and E-criteria, respectively.

The following was proved in [6]:

THEOREM 5.1. *let* $\mathbf{X}^*$ *be the block-variety incidence matrix of a BIBD with* v *varieties and* b *blocks of size* k. *If* $k \geq [(v+1)2]$, *then* $\mathbf{X}^*$ *maximizes* $\phi_p(\mathbf{X}'\mathbf{X})$ *over* $\mathbf{X} \in \mathcal{M}_{b,v}$ *for all* $p \in [f(k), g(k)]$.

If v is odd, then Theorem 5.1 implies that the block-variety incidence matrix $\mathbf{X}^*$ of a BIBD with v varieties and b blocks of size $(v+1)/2$ maximizes $\phi_p(\mathbf{X}'\mathbf{X})$ over $\mathbf{X} \in \mathcal{M}_{b,v}$ for all $p \in [-\infty, 1 - \ln(v/2+1)/\ln(v+1)]$. Since $1 - \ln(v/2+1)/\ln(v+1) > 0$, we conclude that $\mathbf{X}^*$ minimizes $tr(\mathbf{X}'\mathbf{X})^p$ for all $p < 0$, and also maximizes $det(\mathbf{X}'\mathbf{X})$ and $tr(\mathbf{X}'\mathbf{X})^p$ for all $0 < p \leq 1 - \ln(v/2 + 1)/\ln(v + 1)$ over all $\mathbf{X} \in \mathcal{M}_{b,v}$. In particular, $\mathbf{X}^*$ is A- and D-optimal. Since $\phi_{-\infty} = \lim_{p \to -\infty} \phi_p$, it is also E-optimal. Letting $p = -1$ and $b = v$, one proves Harwit and Sloane's conjecture. Furthermore, if $\mathbf{X}^*$ is the block-variety incidence matrix of a BIBD with v varieties and b blocks of size $k > (v+1)/2$, then $\mathbf{X}^*$ maximizes $tr(\mathbf{X}'\mathbf{X})^p$ over $\mathcal{M}_{b,v}$ for all $p \in [f(k), g(k)]$.

If v is even, then the block-variety incidence matrix $\mathbf{X}^*$ of a BIBD with v varieties and b blocks of size $v/2$ maximizes $\phi_p(\mathbf{X}'\mathbf{X})$ over $\mathbf{X} \in \mathcal{M}_{b,v}$ for all $p \in [-\infty, 1 - \ln(v + 1)/\ln(v - 1)]$. Since $1 - \ln(v + 1)/\ln(v - 1) < 0$, we conclude that $\mathbf{X}^*$ minimizes $tr(\mathbf{X}'\mathbf{X})^p$ for all $p < \ln(v + 1)/\ln(v - 1) - 1$. In particular, it is A- and E-optimal; but unlike the previous case, it is *not* D-optimal. In this case, 0 happens to lie in $(g(v/2), f(v/2 + 1))$; so the incidence matrix of a BIBD of the next larger block size $v/2 + 1$ is also not D-optimal. We shall present a D-optimal solution later.

The key idea in the proof of Theorem 5.1 is to use the approach of *approximate designs* and the celebrated Equivalence Theorem in the theory of optimal design due to Kiefer and Wolfowitz [23]; also see Kiefer [21]. Let $\mathcal{X}_v = \{\mathbf{x} = (x_1, x_2, \ldots, x_v)' : 0 \leq x_i \leq 1\}$ be the v-dimensional unit cube. For any $\mathbf{X} \in \mathcal{M}_{b,v}$, write

$$\mathbf{X} = [\mathbf{x}_1 \mathbf{x}_2 \cdots \mathbf{x}_b]'.$$

Then each $\mathbf{x}_i \in \mathcal{X}_v$. If $\xi_\mathbf{X}$ is the probability measure on $\mathcal{X}_v$ assigning probability $1/b$ to each $\mathbf{x}_i$, then we have

$$(5.5) \qquad b^{-1}\mathbf{X}'\mathbf{X} = b^{-1} \sum_{i=1}^{b} \mathbf{x}_i \mathbf{x}_i' = \int_{\mathcal{X}_v} \mathbf{x}\mathbf{x}' \xi_\mathbf{X}(d\mathbf{x}).$$

One can extend (5.5) to an arbitrary discrete probability measure ξ on $\mathcal{X}_v$ by defining

$$\mathbf{M}(\xi) = \int_{\mathcal{X}_v} \mathbf{x}\mathbf{x}' \xi(d\mathbf{x}).$$

Let Ξ be the set of all the discrete probability measures on $\mathcal{X}_v$. We shall consider the problem of

$$(5.6) \qquad \text{maximizing } \phi_p(\mathbf{M}(\xi)) \text{ over } \xi \in \Xi,$$

where ϕ_p, $-\infty \leq p \leq 1$; is defined as in (5.1), (5.2) and (5.3), with $\mathbf{X}'\mathbf{X}$ replaced by $\mathbf{M}(\xi)$. If the block-variety incidence matrix $\mathbf{X}^*$ of a BIBD with b blocks and v

61

varieties is such that $\xi_{\mathbf{x}^*}$ is a solution to (5.6), then $\mathbf{X}^*$ maximizes $\phi_p(\mathbf{X}'\mathbf{X})$ over $\mathbf{X} \in \mathcal{M}_{b,v}$. The advantage of solving (5.6) is that the set of all $\mathbf{M}(\xi)$'s is a convex set and ϕ_p is a concave function for $p \leq 1$; so one can use calculus.

Now we shall give an outline of the proof. Since ϕ_p is concave, a measure $\xi^* \in \Xi$ maximizes $\phi_p(\mathbf{M}(\xi))$ if and only if

(5.7) $$\partial\phi_p((1 - \alpha)\mathbf{M}(\xi^*) + \alpha\mathbf{M}(\xi))/\partial\alpha|_{\alpha=0+} \leq 0, \forall \xi \in \Xi.$$

A straightforward computation of the derivative shows that (5.7) is equivalent to

$$tr[\mathbf{M}(\xi^*)^{p-1}\{\mathbf{M}(\xi) - \mathbf{M}(\xi^*)\}] \leq 0, \quad \forall \xi \in \Xi.$$
$$\Leftrightarrow tr[\mathbf{M}(\xi^*)^{p-1}\mathbf{M}(\xi)] \leq tr\mathbf{M}(\xi^*)^p, \quad \forall \xi \in \Xi.$$

$$\Leftrightarrow \int_{\mathcal{X}_v} \mathbf{x}'\mathbf{M}(\xi^*)^{p-1}\mathbf{x}\xi(d\mathbf{x}) \leq tr\mathbf{M}(\xi^*)^p, \quad \forall \xi \in \Xi.$$
$$\Leftrightarrow \mathbf{x}'\mathbf{M}(\xi^*)^{p-1}\mathbf{x} \leq tr\mathbf{M}(\xi^*)^p, \quad \forall \mathbf{x} \in \mathcal{X}_v.$$
(5.8) $\quad\quad \Leftrightarrow \xi^*$ is supported on points which maximize $\mathbf{x}'\mathbf{M}(\xi^*)^{p-1}\mathbf{x}$

over $\mathbf{x} \in \mathcal{X}_v$.

The last equivalence follows from the identity

$$\int_{\mathcal{X}_v} \mathbf{x}'\mathbf{M}(\xi^*)^{p-1}\mathbf{x}\xi^*(d\mathbf{x}) = tr\mathbf{M}(\xi^*)^p.$$

Therefore to show the optimality of a given measure ξ^*, it is enough to verify (5.8). If $\mathbf{X}^*$ is the block-variety incidence matrix of a BIBD of block size k, then $\xi_{\mathbf{x}^*}$ is supported on points $\mathbf{x}$ with k components equal to 1 and $v - k$ components equal to zero, all of which have the same values of $\mathbf{x}'\mathbf{M}(\xi_{\mathbf{x}^*})^{p-1}\mathbf{x}$ since $\mathbf{M}(\xi_{\mathbf{x}^*})$ has constant diagonal entries and constant off-diagonal entries. To finish the proof, it is enough to show that such points maximize $\mathbf{x}'\mathbf{M}(\xi_{\mathbf{x}^*})^{p-1}\mathbf{x}$ over $\mathbf{x} \in \mathcal{X}_v$. It is easy to see that this is the case if and only if $p \in [f(k), g(k)]$.

The preceding argument solves (5.6), and therefore (5.4), for $p \in [f(k), g(k)]$. How about the solution for $p \in (g(k), f(k + 1))$? A similar argument shows that for any such p, a solution to (5.6) is a mixture $\epsilon\xi_{\mathbf{X}_k} + (1 - \epsilon)\xi_{\mathbf{X}_{k+1}}$, where $\mathbf{X}_k$ (respectively, $\mathbf{X}_{k+1}$) is the block-variety incidence matrix of a BIBD with v varieties and block size k (respectively, $k+1$). Cheng [6] gave an explicit expression of ϵ which is a strictly decreasing function of $p \in (g(k), f(k + 1))$. In fact, as p runs from $g(k)$ to $f(k + 1)$, ϵ exhausts all the numbers between 1 and 0. Generally speaking, the optimal weight ϵ is too complicated to provide simple solutions for (5.4). However, we shall record one rare case in which it does yield useful results. We pointed out earlier that for even v, no BIBD provides a D-optimal solution. In this case, the optimal weight in the solution to problem (5.6) for $p = 0$ as derived in [6] takes a very simple form. Let d_1 (respectively, d_2) be a BIBD with v varieties and b_1 (respectively, b_2) blocks of size $v/2$ (respectively, $v/2 + 1$). If $r_1 = r_2$, where r_i is the number of replications of each variety in d_i, then $\mathbf{X}^* = [\mathbf{N}_{d_1}\mathbf{N}_{d_2}]'$ maximizes $\det(\mathbf{X}'\mathbf{X})$ over $\mathbf{X} \in \mathcal{M}_{b_1+b_2,v}$, where $\mathbf{N}_{d_i}$ is the variety-block incidence matrix of d_i, $i = 1, 2$.

Although problem (5.6) has been completely solved, when a BIBD with the appropriate parameter values does not exist, the original problem (5.4) remains very difficult and no result is yet available.

REFERENCES

[1] N. BIGGS, *Algebraic Graph Theory*, Cambridge Univ. Press, London, 1974.

[2] R.C. BOSE, *Strongly regular graphs, partial geometries and partially balanced designs*, Pacific J. Math., 13 (1963), pp. 389–419.

[3] P.J. CAMERON, J.M. GOETHALS, J.J. SEIDEL AND E.E. SHULT, *Line graphs, root systems, and elliptic geometry*, J. Algebra, 43 (1976), pp. 305–327.

[4] C.S. CHENG, *Optimality of certain asymmetrical experimental designs*, Ann. Statist., 6 (1978), pp. 1239–1261.

[5] C.S. CHENG, *Maximizing the total number of spanning trees in a graph: two related problems in graph theory and optimum design theory*, J. Combinatorial Theory, Ser. B, 31 (1981), pp. 240–248.

[6] C.S. CHENG, *An application of the Kiefer-Wolfowitz equivalence theorem to a problem in Hadamard transform optics*, Ann. Statist., 15 (1987), pp. 1593–1603.

[7] C.S. CHENG AND R.A. BAILEY, *On the optimality of some two-associate-class partially balanced incomplete block designs*, submitted for publication.

[8] C.S. CHENG, J.C. MASARO AND C.S. WONG,, *Do nearly balanced multigraphs have more spanning trees?*, J. Graph Theory, 8 (1985), pp. 342–345.

[9] C.S. CHENG AND C.F. WU, *Nearly balanced incomplete block designs*, Biometrika, 68 (1981), pp. 493–500.

[10] G.M. CONSTANTINE, *On the E-optimality of PBIB designs with a small number of blocks*, Ann. Statist., 10 (1983), pp. 1027–1031.

[11] G.M. CONSTANTINE, *On the optimality of block designs*, Ann. Inst. Statist. Math., 38 (1986), pp. 161–174.

[12] G.M. CONSTANTINE, *Combinatorial Theory and Statistical Design*, Wiley, New York, 1987.

[13] M. HARWIT AND N.J.A. SLOANE, *Masks for Hadamard transform optics and weighing designs*, Appl. Optics, 15 (1976), pp. 107–114.

[14] M. HARWIT AND N.J.A. SLOANE, *Hadamard Transform Optics*, Academic Press, New York, 1979.

[15] M. JACROUX AND W.I. NOTZ, *On the optimality of Spring balance weighing designs*, Ann. Statist., 11 (1983), pp. 970–978.

[16] J.A. JOHN AND T.J. MITCHELL, *Optimal incomplete block designs*, J. Royal Statist. Soc. B., 39 (1977), pp. 39–43.

[17] B. JONES AND J.A. ECCLESTON, *Exchange and interchange procedures to search for optimal designs*, J. Royal Statist. Soc. B., 42 (1980), pp. 238–243.

[18] A.K. KELMANS, *On properties of the characteristic polynomial of a graph*, (Russian), Kibernetiku na službu Kommunizmu, 4 Gosénergoizdat, Moscow, 1967.

[19] A.K. KELMANS AND V.M. CHELNOKOV,, *A certain polynomial of a graph and graphs with an extremal number of trees*, J. Combinatorial Theory Ser. B., 16 (1974), pp. 197–214.

[20] J. KIEFER, *On the nonrandomized optimality and randomized nonoptimality of symmetrical designs*, Ann. Math. Statist., 29 (1958), pp. 675–699.

[21] J. KIEFER, *General equivalence theory for optimum designs (approximate theory)*, Ann. Statist., 2 (1974), pp. 849–879.

[22] J. KIEFER, *Construction and optimality of generalized Youden designs*, in *A Survey of Statistical Designs and Linear Models*, J. N. Srivastava, ed., North-Holland, Amsterdam, 1975, pp. 333–353.

[23] J. KIEFER AND J. WOLFOWITZ, *The equivalence of two extremum problems*, Canada. J. Math., 14 (1960), pp. 363–366.

[24] A.M. KSHIRSAGAR, *A note on incomplete block designs*, Ann. Math. Statist., 29 (1958), pp. 907–910.

[25]   M. MASUYAMA, *On the optimality of balanced incomplete block designs*, Rep. Statist. Appl. Res. Un. Japan Sci. Engrs., 5 (1957), pp. 4–8.

[26]   V. L. MOTE, *On a minimax property of a balanced incomplete block design*, Ann. Math. Statist. 29 (1958), pp. 910–914.

[27]   D. RAGHAVARAO, *Constructions and Combinatorial Problems in Design of Experiments*, Wiley, New York, 1971.

[28]   K. TAKEUCHI, *On the optimality of certain types of PBIB designs*, Rep. Statist. Appl. Res. Un. Japan Sci. Engrs., 8 (1961), pp. 140–145.

[29]   F. YATES, *Incomplete randomized blocks*, Annals of Eugenics, 7 (1936), pp. 121–140.

DIFFERENCE SETS IN NONABELIAN 2–GROUPS*

JAMES A. DAVIS†

Abstract. Difference sets have been found in all Abelian 2–groups meeting Turyn's exponent bound ([1], [2], [3], [6]). However, this still leaves many nonabelian 2–groups: this paper explores a technique for finding difference sets in nonabelian groups using the structure from the Abelian groups.

Section 1 The Abelian Case. For background on difference sets, see ([5], [7]). In this paper, we consider difference sets with parameters $(2^{2d+2}, 2^{2d+1} - 2^d, 2^{2d} - 2^d)$. In the Abelian case, we have the following results:

THEOREM 1. $\mathbf{Z}_{2^{d+2}} \times \mathbf{Z}_{2^d}$ and $\mathbf{Z}_{2^{d+1}} \times \mathbf{Z}_{2^{d+1}}$ both have nontrivial difference sets ([1], [2], [3])

THEOREM 2. An Abelian group of order 2^{2d+2} has a nontrivial difference set if and only if the exponent of the group is less than 2^{d+3} ([6]).

To show that we have a difference set in these groups, we can use a character theoretic result found in Turyn's paper ([8]).

THEOREM 3. $D \subset G$ is an Abelian difference set if and only if $|\chi(D)| = |\sum_{d \in D} \chi(d)| = \sqrt{n}$ for all nonprincipal characters χ, and $\sum_{d \in D} \chi_0(d) = K$.

Applying this to a specific example should give an idea how to generalize.

Example. $\mathbf{Z}_{16} \times \mathbf{Z}_4, a^{16} = b^4 = 1$, $H = \langle a^4, b^2 \rangle$. If we write $G = U g_i H$, we can write $D = U g_i D_i$ for

$$
\begin{array}{cccccc}
D_2 & D_3 & D_4 & D_5 & D_5' & D_6 \qquad D_6' \\
\langle a^4 \rangle & \langle a^8, b^2 \rangle & \langle a^4 b^2 \rangle & \left(\begin{array}{cc} \langle a^8 b^2 \rangle & a^{12} \langle a^8 b^2 \rangle \\ \cup & \cup \\ a^4 \langle a^8 b^2 \rangle & a^8 \langle a^8 b^2 \rangle \end{array} \right) & \left(\begin{array}{cc} \langle b^2 \rangle & a^{12} \langle b^2 \rangle \\ \cup & \cup \\ a^4 \langle b^2 \rangle & a^8 \langle b^2 \rangle \end{array} \right)
\end{array}
$$

$$g_2 = a \quad g_3 = ab \quad g_4 = a^3 \quad g_5 = 1 \quad g_5' = b \quad g_6 = a^2 \quad g_6' = a^6 b$$

I claim that $g_2 D_2 \cup g_3 D_3 \cup g_4 D_4 \cup g_5 D_5 \cup g_5' D_5' \cup g_6 D_6 \cup g_6' D_6'$ is a difference set in G. To see this, let $\chi \neq \chi_0$ be a character on G. We establish an equivalence relation on the characters of $G : \chi \equiv_H \chi'$ if $Ker(\chi|_H) = Ker(\chi'|_H)$. This partitions the characters into six equivalence classes; e_1 (characters principal on H), $e_2(Ker = \langle a^4 \rangle)$, $e_3(Ker = \langle a^8, b^2 \rangle)$, $e_4(Ker = \langle a^4 b^2 \rangle)$, $e_5(Ker = \langle a^8 b^2 \rangle)$, and $e_6(Ker = \langle b^2 \rangle)$. Note here the connections between the equivalence classes e_i and the subsets D_i; other than e_1, each e_i is associated to D_i (and D_i' in two cases) by the similar subgroups. This association is further shown in the next lemma.

---

*This paper was written while the author was visiting the Institute for Mathematics and its Applications (IMA) at the University of Minnesota. The author gratefully acknowledges the hospitality and financial support provided by the IMA.

†Department of Mathematics, University of Richmond, Richmond, VA 23173

LEMMA 4. *If $\chi \in e_i, i \neq 1$, then $\sum_{d_j \in D_j} \chi(d_j) = 0$ for every $i \neq j$.*

This effectively kills all of the D_j in the sum over all of D: we need only be concerned with what the characters from e_i do to the elements of D_i. If they give character sum of modulus 4 in every case, then D is a difference set. These split into two cases. The first case is exemplified by the class e_2: any character in e_2 kills $D_3, D_4, D_5, D_5', D_6, D_6'$. On D_2, that character is principal, so it has sum of modulus $|D_2| = 4$. Classes e_3 and e_4 can also be handled in this way.

Suppose $\chi \in e_5$. χ kills D_2, D_3, D_4, D_6, and D_6', but D_5 and D_5' survive. Looking at the way these are written, we can consider them as a matrix

$$
\begin{matrix}
1D_5 & bD_5' \\
\end{matrix}
$$
$$
\begin{pmatrix}
\langle a^8 b^2 \rangle & a^{12}\langle a^8 b^2 \rangle \\
a^4 \langle a^8 b^2 \rangle & a^8 \langle a^8 b^2 \rangle
\end{pmatrix}
$$

If we sum across the rows, one row will give a contribution of modulus four while the other will sum to 0. Thus, we again get the sum that we want. Class e_6 is also handled this way.

It is easy to check for $\chi \in e_1$ $\left(\left| \sum_{d \in D} \chi(d) \right| = 4 \left| \sum_{i \neq i'} \chi(g_i) \right| = 4 \left| - \chi(g_{i'}) \right| = 4 \right)$.
Thus, D is a difference set in $\mathbf{Z}_{16} \times \mathbf{Z}_4$. $\square$

The generalization of this example yields Theorem 1. The techniques are messy, so we will not explore the details here, but we do indicate the ideas. Partition the characters into equivalence classes $e_1, e_2, \ldots, e_m$, where each equivalence class is determined by the kernel of the character restricted to a subgroup H. If the group $G = Ug_iH$, we will write $D = Ug_iD_i$. The D_i are organized into K–matrices:

$$
\begin{pmatrix}
x_{11}K & \ldots & x_{1n}K \\
x_{21}K & & \vdots \\
\vdots & & \vdots \\
x_{n1}K & & X_{nn}K
\end{pmatrix}
$$

Each column is a D_i and the K is a kernel of one of the equivalence classes (hence, an association between the character classes and the K–matrices as in the example). If $\chi \neq \chi_0$ is a character not in the equivalence class of a K–matrix (or in e_1), then $\chi(D_i) = \sum_{d_i \in D_i} \chi(d_i) = 0$ for every D_i in that K–matrix. This is the generalization of the idea in Lemma 4. Any character χ in the equivalence class associated to a K–matrix will have sum 0 in every row except one, and that row will have sum of modulus 2^d. Since this is $\sqrt{n}$, $D = Ug_iD_i$ is a difference set in G. For more details on K–matrix structure, see ([1], [2]).

Section 2: The Nonabelian Case. We will consider the nonabelian 2–Group Case. First, we look at an example.

Example. $\overline{G} = \mathbf{Z}_{16} \rtimes \mathbf{Z}_4$, $\overline{a}^{16} = \overline{b}^4 = 1, \overline{b}\overline{a}\overline{b}^{-1} = \overline{a}^9, \overline{H} = \langle \overline{a}^4, \overline{b}^2 \rangle$. Notice the similarity of the Abelian case $G = \mathbf{Z}_{16} \times \mathbf{Z}_4$, including the fact that elements in $\overline{G}$ can be written uniquely as $\overline{g} = \overline{a}^i \overline{b}^j$, $i = 0, 1, 2, \ldots, 15; j = 0, 1, 2, 3$. Thus, we can take an element of $g = a^i b^j$ and map it to $\overline{g} = \overline{a}^i \overline{b}^j$ in a one–to–one map. Taking $D = U g_i D_i$ from the $\mathbf{Z}_{16} \times \mathbf{Z}_4$ example in Section 1 and applying this formal map, we get $\overline{D} = U \overline{g}_i \overline{D}_i$.

$$(*) \qquad \overline{D}\,\overline{D}^{(-1)} = \sum_i \overline{g}_i \overline{D}_i \sum_j \overline{D}_j^{(-1)} \overline{g}_j^{-1} = \sum_{i,j} \overline{g}_i \overline{D}_i \overline{D}_j^{(-1)} \overline{g}_j^{-1}$$
$$= \sum_{i,j} \overline{g}_i \overline{g}_j^{-1} \overline{D}_i \overline{D}_j^{(-1)}$$

The last equality holds since $\overline{H}$ is contained in the center of $\overline{G}$ (and so are all $\overline{D}_i \subset \overline{H}$).

LEMMA 6. *If G is an Abelian group with a difference set in K–matrix structure, and D_i and D_j are from different K–matrices, then $D_i D_j^{(-1)} = 2^{d-1} H$ ($|G| = 2^{2d+2}$)*

Proof. Let χ be a nonprincipal character on H. χ will be in an equivalence class e_n where $n \neq 1$.

Since D_i and D_j are from different K–matrices, at least one of these is in a K–matrix not associated to χ. Thus, either $\chi(D_i) = 0$ or $\chi(D_j) = 0$ (or both).

$\chi(D_i D_j^{(-1)}) = \chi(D_i)\overline{\chi(D_j)} = 0$ for every $\chi \neq \chi_0$. By the orthogonality relations for characters, this implies that $D_i D_j^{(-1)} = cH$. By counting, there are $(2^d)(2^d)$ elements on the left hand side of the equation and $c(2^{d+1})$ on the right hand side, so $c = 2^{d-1}$. □

Using Lemma 6 in $\mathbf{Z}_{16} \rtimes \mathbf{Z}_4$, $\overline{D}_i \overline{D}_j^{(-1)} = 2\overline{H}$ whenever $\overline{D}_i$ and $\overline{D}_j$ are from different K–matrices. When they are from the same K–matrix, $\overline{D}_i \overline{D}_j^{(-1)}$ will be the same as in the Abelian Case (since $\overline{H}$ is Abelian). Also, when they are from the same K–matrix, $\overline{g}_i \overline{g}_j^{(-1)}$ will be the same formal element as in the Abelian case. Therefore, when $\overline{D}_i$ and $\overline{D}_j$ are from the same K–matrix, we have the same formal sum. When they are from different K–matrices, we will have the same formal sum, even though the $\overline{g}_i \overline{g}_j^{-1}$ may be permuted. Thus, $\overline{D}$ is a difference set in the semidirect product. □

We now consider a generalization of this idea. We will use the K–matrix idea introduced at the end of Section 1.

THEOREM 7. *Suppose an Abelian group G has a nontrivial difference set $D = U g_i D_i$ using the K–matrix structure, relative to a subgroup H. Suppose $\overline{G}$ is a group with elements that are formally the same as the elements in G (i.e., if $g = a_1^{i_1} a_2^{i_2} \cdots a_n^{i_n}$ are all elements of G, then $\overline{g} = \overline{a}_1^{i_1} \overline{a}_2^{i_2} \ldots \overline{a}_n^{i_n}$ are all elements of $\overline{G}$, where the i_j have the same restrictions). If $\overline{H}$ is the set of elements mapped from H, $\overline{D} = U \overline{g}_i \overline{D}_i$ is a nontrivial diff. set in $\overline{G}$ if:*

(i) $\overline{H} \lhd \overline{G}$

67

(ii) $\overline{H}$ is Abelian

(iii) $\overline{g}_i\overline{g}_j^{-1}$ is the same formal element as $g_ig_j^{-1}$
    when $\overline{D}_i$ and $\overline{D}_j$ are from the same K–matrix.

(iv) $\overline{g}_i\overline{D}_i\overline{D}_j^{(-1)}\overline{g}_j^{-1} = \overline{g}_i\overline{g}_j^{-1}\overline{D}_i\overline{D}_j^{(1-)}$ for $\overline{D}_i$ and $\overline{D}_j$ from the same K–matrix.

Proof. $\overline{DD}^{(-1)} = \sum_{i,j} \overline{g}_i\overline{D}_i\overline{D}_j^{(-1)}\overline{g}_j^{-1}$. If $\overline{D}_i$ and $\overline{D}_j$ are from different K–matrices, Lemma 6 shows that $\overline{D}_i\overline{D}_j^{(-1)} = 2^{d-1}\overline{H}$. Since $\overline{H} \lhd \overline{G}$, $\overline{g}_i\overline{D}_i\overline{D}_j^{(-1)}\overline{g}_j^{(-1)} = \overline{g}_i\overline{g}_j^{-1}(2^{d-1}\overline{H})$. Even if the $\overline{g}_i\overline{g}_j^{-1}$ are permuted around, the sum will look the same (formally) as the Abelian case. Similarly, if $\overline{D}_i$ and $\overline{D}_j$ are from the same K–matrix, $\overline{g}_i\overline{D}_i\overline{D}_j^{(-1)}\overline{g}_j^{-1} = \overline{g}_i\overline{g}_j^{(-1)}\overline{D}_i\overline{D}_j^{(-1)}$, which is formally the same as Abelian by (ii) and (iii). Thus, since D is a difference set in G, $\overline{D}$ is a difference set in $\overline{G}$. $\square$

COROLLARY 8. *The following semidirect products have nontrivial difference sets:*

(1)(a) $\mathbf{Z}_{2^{d+2}} \rtimes \mathbf{Z}_{2^d}, a^{2^{d+2}} = b^{2^d} = 1, bab^{-1} = a^{2^d+1}$

   (b) $\mathbf{Z}_{2^{d+2}} \rtimes \mathbf{Z}_{2^d}, a^{2^{d+2}} = b^{2^d} = 1, bab^{-1} = a^{2^{d+1}+1}$

   (c) $\mathbf{Z}_{2^{d+2}} \rtimes \mathbf{Z}_{2^d}, a^{2^{d+2}} = b^{2^d} = 1, bab^{-1} = a^{3(2^d)+1}$

(2)(a) $\mathbf{Z}_{2^d} \rtimes \mathbf{Z}_{2^{d+2}}, a^{2^d} = b^{2^{d+2}} = 1, bab^{-1} = a^{2^{d-2}+1}$

   (b) $\mathbf{Z}_{2^d} \rtimes \mathbf{Z}_{2^{d+2}}, a^{2^d} = b^{2^{d+2}} = 1, bab^{-1} = a^{2^{d-1}+1}$

   (c) $\mathbf{Z}_{2^d} \rtimes \mathbf{Z}_{2^{d+2}}, a^{2^d} = b^{2^{d+2}} = 1, bab^{-1} = a^{3(2^{d-2})+1}$

(3) $\mathbf{Z}_{2^{d+1}} \rtimes \mathbf{Z}_{2^{d+1}}, a^{2^{d+1}} = b^{2^{d+1}} = 1, bab^{-1} = a^{2^d+1}$

Proof. We use the K–matrix structures for $\mathbf{Z}_{2^{d+2}} \times \mathbf{Z}_{2^d}$ and $\mathbf{Z}_{2^{d+1}} \times \mathbf{Z}_{2^{d+1}}$ found in ([1], [2]). Conditions (i), (ii), and (iv) from Theorem 7 are satisfied because H is contained in the center of those groups. To satisfy (iii), we need to examine more closely the coset representatives in the K–matrices. The coset representatives for D_i and D_j are $\overline{z}^m\overline{y}$ and $\overline{z}^n\overline{y}$ when D_i and D_j are from the same K–matrix. Moreover, $\overline{z}$ has a first component factor with exponent divisible by 4. In all the Cases (1) and (2), $\overline{a}^4$ is in the center of $\overline{G}$. Thus, $\overline{z}^m\overline{y}(\overline{z}^n\overline{y})^{-1} = \overline{z}^{m-n}$, which is the same formal element as the Abelian case. Case (3) has an analogous argument using $\overline{b}^2$ instead of $\overline{a}^4$. Thus, (iii) is satisfied, so Thm 7 applies. $\square$

In the groups of order 64, we can use Thm 7 to show that $\mathbf{Z}_8 \rtimes \mathbf{Z}_8, \overline{a}^8 = \overline{b}^8 = 1, \overline{b}\overline{a}\overline{b}^{-1} = \overline{a}^3$ and $\mathbf{Z}_8 \rtimes \mathbf{Z}_8, \overline{b}\overline{a}\overline{b}^{-1} = \overline{a}^{-1}$ also have difference sets. After considering nonexistence results by Dillon [4] and Ma (personal correspondence), the following semidirect products are unknown:

(1) $\mathbf{Z}_{32} \rtimes \mathbf{Z}_2, a^{32} = b^2 = 1 \quad bab^{-1} = a^{17}$ [Note that $\mathbf{Z}_{32} \times \mathbf{Z}_2$ does not have a difference set by Turyn's bound]

(2) $$\mathbf{Z}_{16} \rtimes \mathbf{Z}_4 \quad a^{16} = b^4 = 1 \quad bab^{-1} = a^3$$
$$\mathbf{Z}_{16} \rtimes \mathbf{Z}_4 \quad a^{16} = b^4 = 1 \quad bab^{-1} = a^7$$
$$\mathbf{Z}_{16} \rtimes \mathbf{Z}_4 \quad a^{16} = b^4 = 1 \quad bab^{-1} = a^{11}$$

REMARK. J. Dillon, in these proceedings, provides a construction that includes (1b), (2b), and (3) as well as many other situations.

REFERENCES

[1] DAVIS, J., *"Difference sets in Abelian 2–Groups"*, Ph.D. Dissertation, University of Virginia, 1987.

[2] DAVIS, J., *"Difference sets in Abelian 2–Groups"*, submitted.

[3] DILLON, J.F., *"Difference Sets in 2–Groups"*, to appear Proc. Amer. Math. Soc., 1988.

[4] DILLON, J.F., *"Variations on a Scheme of McFarland for Noncyclic Difference Sets"*, J. Comb. Th6 (A), 40, 1980.

[5] BETH, TH., JUNGNICKEL, D., AND LENZ, H., *Design Theory*, Mannheim 1985, Cambridge 1986.

[6] KRAEMER, R.G., *"Proof of a Conjecture on Hadamard 2–Groups,"* *paperinfo submitted.*

[7] LANDER, E.S., *Symmetric Designs: An Algebraic Approach*, London Math. Society Lecture Note Series, 74, 1983.

[8] TURYN, R.J., *"Character sums and Difference Sets,"*, Pac. J. Math, 15, 319–346 (1965).

ORTHOGONAL 1-FACTORIZATIONS OF THE COMPLETE MULTIGRAPH

JEFFREY H. DINITZ*

Abstract. A 1-factorization of the complete multigraph λK_n is called *decomposable* if some proper subset of the factors forms a 1-factorization of $\lambda' K_n$ for some $\lambda' < \lambda$; otherwise it is called *indecomposable*. In this paper the notion of orthogonal 1-factorizations of λK_n is defined. We describe direct starter constructions and recursive frame constructions for orthogonal 1-factorizations. We then determine the spectrum of orthogonal indecomposable 1-factorizations of $2K_n$.

1. Introduction and definitions. The complete multigraph λK_v has v vertices and λ edges joining each pair of vertices. A *1-factor* of λK_v is a set of edges which between them contain each vertex precisely once. A *1-factorization* is a set of 1-factors which partition the edges of λK_v.

Clearly v must be even for a 1-factor to exist; say $v = 2n$. It is well known that K_{2n} has a 1-factorization for every n. Taking λ copies of this factorization yields a 1-factorization of λK_{2n}. Thus every λK_{2n} has a 1-factorization.

Given a 1-factorization F of λK_{2n}, it may be that there exists an integer λ_1 ($\lambda_1 < \lambda$) such that $\lambda_1(2n - 1)$ of the 1-factors of F form a 1-factorization of $\lambda_1 K_{2n}$. In such a case F is called *decomposable*; otherwise it is termed *indecomposable*. We abbreviate indecomposable 1-factorization as IOF. A 1-factorization F of λK_{2n} is called *simple* if it has no repeated 1-factors. The following result of Colbourn, Colbourn and Rosa [3] and Archdeacon and Dinitz [1] deals with the existence of simple IOF of λK_n for small λ.

THEOREM 1.1. *A simple indecomposable 1-factorization of λK_{2n} exists as follows:*

$\lambda = 2$: *if and only if $2n \geq 6$;*
$\lambda = 3$ *or* 4: *if and only if $2n \geq 8$;*
$\lambda = 5$: *if $2n \geq 10$;*
$\lambda = 6, 8,$ *or* 9: *if $2n \geq 12$;*
$\lambda = 7$: *if $2n \geq 16$;*
$\lambda = 10$: *if $2n \geq 14$;*
$\lambda = 12$: *if $2n \geq 32$;*

In [1], Archdeacon and Dinitz also proved the following result for all λ.

THEOREM 1.2. *A simple indecomposable 1-factorization of λK_{2n} exists for all $n \geq 2(\lambda + p)$, where p is the smallest prime not dividing λ.*

Two 1-factorizations F_1 and F_2 of λK_n are said to be *orthogonal* if any 1-factor in F_1 and any 1-factor in F_2 have at most 1 edge in common. It is well known that

---

*Department of Mathematics, University of Vermont, Burlington, VT 05405

the existence of two orthogonal 1-factorizations of K_{2n} is equivalent to a Room square of side $2n - 1$, and that these exist if and only if $2n \geq 8$ [11, 15]. Clearly, if F_1 is orthogonal to F_2, then λ copies of F_1 and λ copies of F_2 will be orthogonal 1-factorizations of λK_n. However, these 1-factorizations will be decomposable and not simple. We will give constructions for orthogonal indecomposable simple 1-factorizations and will discuss the spectrum of these for $\lambda = 2$.

Given two orthogonal 1-factorizations of λK_{2n}, F and G, we can index the rows of a $\lambda(2n - 1)$ by $\lambda(2n - 1)$ square L by the 1-factors in F and the columns by the 1-factors in G. Since any edge $\{i, j\} \in \lambda K_{2n}$ occurs in exactly λ 1-factors in F and λ 1-factors of G, we get a λ by λ subarray of L determined by these 1-factors. Place the pair $\{i, j\}$ in the cells of any transversal of this subarray. If this is done for every edge in the graph, the resulting square L satisfies the following properties:

1) every cell of L is either empty or contains an unordered pair of symbols from $\{1, \ldots, 2n\}$,
2) each symbol of $\{1, \ldots, 2n\}$ occurs once in each row and column of L,
3) every unordered pair of symbols occurs in precisely λ cells of L,
4) if two pairs of symbols occur in two cells of the same row (column), then they do not occur in two cells of any column (row).

We define a λ-*square* $\lambda S(2n, \lambda)$ to be a $\lambda(2n - 1)$ by $\lambda(2n - 1)$ array satisfying the above four properties. In Figure 1 below we give a λ-square $\lambda S(12, 2)$.

It is clear that a Room square of side n is a $\lambda S(n, 1)$. λ-squares can also be thought of in terms of other generalizations of Room squares. A λ-square $\lambda S(n, \lambda)$ is a uniform generalized Room square grs $S_2(n, \lambda; n + 1)$ (see Rosa [12]) and is also a Room rectangle $RR(n, n; [2, 1, 1] - [n + 1, n + 1, n + 1], 2, [\lambda, 1, 1])$ [9,12]. It is also a Kirkman square $KS_2(n + 1, 1, \lambda)$ (see [10,14]). Actually, each of the above squares need only satisfy properties 1, 2 and 3 but not necessarily property 4 of the definition of λ-squares. The relationship between λ-squares and orthogonal 1-factorizations of λK_n is analogous to the relationship between Room squares and orthogonal 1-factorizations of K_n and is given in the following theorem.

THEOREM 1.3. *The existence of two orthogonal 1-factorizations of λK_{2n} is equivalent to the existence of a λ-square $\lambda S(2n - 1, \lambda)$.*

Proof. In the discussion preceding the definition of λ-square, it was shown that the existence of two orthogonal 1-factorizations of λK_{2n} implies the existence of a λ-square $\lambda S(2n - 1, \lambda)$. Given a λ-square $\lambda S(2n - 1, \lambda)$ it is also clear that the rows and columns give two orthogonal 1-factorizations of λK_{2n}. Note that condition 4 assures the orthogonality of the row and column 1-factorizations. $\square$

Obviously, λ-squares $\lambda S(n, \lambda)$ can be constructed for all odd $n \geq 7$ and all λ by merely putting λ copies of a Room square of side n down the diagonal of a $\lambda \times n$ by $\lambda \times n$ array and leaving the remainder of the array empty. Note that in this

71

FIGURE 1
A λ-square $\lambda S(12, 2)$

1	2	3	4	5	6	7	8	9	10	11	12	13	14	15	16	17	18	19	20	21	22
0,∞	9,10	6,7										5,8		1,3							2,4
	1,∞	10,0	7,8									3,5	6,9		2,4						
		2,∞		8,9			0,1					4,6	7,10			3,5					
			3,∞	1,2	9,10							5,7		8,0			4,6				
				4,∞	2,3	10,0							6,8	9,1		5,7					
			0,1		5,∞	3,4								7,9	10,2			6,8			
						6,∞	4,5	1,2							8,10	0,3			7,9		
							7,∞	5,6	2,3		8,10				9,0		1,4				
								6,7	3,4		9,0					10,1	8,∞	2,5			
4,5										9,∞	7,8		10,1					0,2			3,6
8,9	5,6									10,∞	4,7				0,2					1,3	
		3,7						8,2	10,4		0,∞							6,9			1,5
	2,6		4,8					9,3	0,5			1,∞							7,10		
			5,9					10,4	1,6		3,7	2,∞									8,0
2,7						6,10		0,5	9,1		4,8	3,∞									
1,6	3,8					7,0				10,2		5,9	4,∞								
	2,7	4,9				8,1				0,3		6,10	5,∞								
		3,8	5,10				9,2			1,4			7,0	6,∞							
10,3		4,9	6,0										2,5	8,1	7,∞						
	0,4		5,10	7,1			8,∞							3,6	9,2						
	1,5			6,0	8,2									4,7	10,3	9,∞					
				7,1	9,3					2,6					5,8	0,4	10,∞				

construction both the resulting row and column 1-factorizations are decomposable and not simple. Recently, Lamken [10] has constructed indecomposable Kirkman squares $KS_2(n+1, 1, \lambda)$ for all $n \geq 6$ and all $\lambda \geq 1$. In our context, these are squares satisfying properties 1, 2, and 3 above which can not be decomposed into Kirkman squares with smaller λ. In that construction, the row and column 1-factorizations are never simple but are possibly indecomposable.

We define a *simple indecomposable λ-square $SI\lambda S(n, \lambda)$* to be a $\lambda S(n, \lambda)$ in which the row and column 1-factorizations are both simple and indecomposable.

In this paper we will show the existence of $SI\lambda S(n, 2)$ for odd $n \geq 11$. In order to construct λ-squares for these orders we will require a direct construction to get the smaller orders and then a recursive construction for the larger orders. The direct construction is the λ analogue of starters (see [15, 5, 6]) and is discussed in Section 2 while the recursive construction is a frame type construction (see [7]) and is developed in Section 3. In Section 4 we give the spectrum of simple indecomposable λ-squares with $\lambda = 2$.

2. Starter construction. Let G be an additive abelian group of odd order n. A λ-starter in G (of order n) is a set $S = \{S_1, S_2, ...S_\lambda\}$ where each S_i is a set of unordered pairs $S_i = \{\{s_{ij}, t_{ij}\}, 1 \leq j \leq \frac{1}{2}(n-1)\}$ and which satisfies the following properties:

1) $\bigcup_j(\{s_{ij}\} \cup \{t_{ij}\}) = G - \{0\}$, for each $1 \leq i \leq \lambda$, and

2) Each $g \in G - \{0\}$ occurs as a difference $\pm(s_{ij} - t_{ij})$, $1 \leq i \leq \lambda$, $1 \leq j \leq \frac{1}{2}(n-1)$, exactly λ times.

We give an example from [3].

EXAMPLE 2.1. A 3-starter in the group Z_{11}.

$$S_1 = \{2,3\}, \ \{4,5\}, \ \{8,9\}, \ \{6,10\}, \ \{1,7\}$$
$$S_2 = \{1,7\}, \ \{2,9\}, \ \{4,6\}, \ \{3,5\}, \ \{8,10\}$$
$$S_3 = \{1,4\}, \ \{2,7\}, \ \{3,10\}, \ \{5,8\}, \ \{6,9\}$$

Note that on the vertices labelled by $Z_{11} \cup \{\infty\}$ that $S_i \cup \{0, \infty\}$ is a 1-factor for each i. Each translate of S_i, $S_i + g = \{s_{ij}+g, t_{ij}+g\} \cup \{g, \infty\}$ is also a 1-factor for every $g \in G$. In general we get the following relationship between λ-starters and 1-factorizations of λK_n.

THEOREM 2.2. *If there exists a λ-starter of order n then there exists a 1-factorization of λK_{n+1}.*

Proof. Let $S = \{S_1, S_2, ..., S_\lambda\}$ be a λ-starter of order n. As noted above, each S_i generates n 1-factors $S_i + g$ of λK_{n+1}. Each pair $\{a, b\} \subset G$, occurs exactly λ times in these 1-factors by property (2) of the definition. The pair $\{\infty, g\}$ also occurs exactly λ times as $\{\infty, g\} \in S_i + g$ for $1 \leq i \leq \lambda$. $\quad\square$

Notice that if the S_i's are distinct then the resulting 1-factorization will be simple. Under certain conditions the 1-factorization generated by the λ-starter will also be indecomposable. One of those conditions is given in the following theorem. We will say that a difference $d \in G$ is *entirely contained* in S_i if all λ occurrences of pairs with difference d are in S_i.

73

THEOREM 2.3. *Let* $S = \{S_1, S_2, ..., S_\lambda\}$ *be a* λ-*starter in the group* G, $|G| = n$. *If there exists a difference* $d \in G$ *which is entirely contained in* S_i *for some* i, *and if* $GCD(\lambda, n) = 1$, *then* S *generates an indecomposable 1-factorization of* λK_{n+1}.

Proof. Assume difference d is entirely contained in S_i. Also assume that the resulting 1-factorization F of λK_{n+1} contains a 1-factorization F' of $\lambda_1 K_{n+1}$ where $\lambda_1 \leq \lambda$. The total number of pairs occurring in F' with difference d is $\lambda_1 \times n$. If t translates of S_i are contained in F', then we get that the total number of pairs occurring in F' with difference d is $t \times \lambda$. Equating, we get $\lambda_1 \times n = t \times \lambda$. Since $GCD(\lambda, n) = 1$ and since $\lambda_1 \leq \lambda$, we conclude that $\lambda_1 = \lambda$ and thus F is indecomposable. $\square$

Notice that in Example 2.1 the difference 1 is entirely contained in S_1. Since $GCD(3,11) = 1$, we have by Theorem 2.3 that this starter generates a simple indecomposable 1-factorization of K_{12}. If a λ-starter S generates an indecomposable 1-factorization we will say S is an *indecomposable* starter. Next we will concentrate on the concept of orthogonal λ-starters.

Let $S = \{S_1, S_2, ..., S_\lambda\}$ and $T = \{T_1, T_2, ..., T_\lambda\}$ be λ-starters of order n (in the group G). We say that S and T are *orthogonal* if the following two conditions hold:
1) S_i and T_j have no pairs in common for all $1 \leq i, j \leq \lambda$,
2) If $\{a, b\}, \{e, f\} \in S_i$ with $b - a = d_1$ and $f - e = d_2$, and there exists a j such that $\{x, y\}, \{z, w\} \in T_j$ with $y - x = d_1$ and $w - z = d_2$, then we must have that $z - x \neq e - a$.

Notice again that the above definition is the same as the usual definition for orthogonal starters when $\lambda = 1$ (see [4,5,15]) for results on orthogonal starters).

EXAMPLE 2.4. Two orthogonal 2-starters in Z_{11}.

$$S_1 = \{6,7\},\ \{9,10\},\ \{1,3\},\ \{2,4\},\ \{5,8\}$$
$$S_2 = \{6,9\},\ \{3,7\},\ \{1,5\},\ \{10,4\},\ \{8,2\}$$
$$T_1 = \{4,5\},\ \{8,9\},\ \{10,3\},\ \{2,7\},\ \{1,6\}$$
$$T_2 = \{3,5\},\ \{8,10\},\ \{4,7\},\ \{9,1\},\ \{2,6\}$$

Just as orthogonal starters generate orthogonal 1-factorizations of K_n, orthogonal λ-starters generate orthogonal 1-factorizations of λK_n and thus also λ-squares $\lambda S(n-1, \lambda)$. We state the following theorem and leave the proof to the interested reader.

THEOREM 2.5. *If there exist* t *orthogonal* λ-*starters of order* n, *then there exist* t *pairwise orthogonal 1-factorizations of* λK_{n+1}.

The λ-square in Figure 1 was constructed by use of the two orthogonal 2-starters in Z_{11} given in Example 2.4. The rows of the square are the 1-factors obtained from translates of S_1 and S_2 and the columns are generated from the translates of T_1 and T_2. Combining Theorems 2.5 and 1.2 gives the following result concerning λ-squares.

PROPOSITION 2.6. *If there exists two orthogonal λ-starters of order n, then there exists a λ-square $\lambda S(n-1, \lambda)$. Furthermore, if the starters are both simple and indecomposable then there exists a $SI\lambda S(n-1, \lambda)$.*

Orthogonal indecomposable λ-starters can be constructed on the computer by means of a modified version of the hill-climbing algorithm for strong starters described in [6]. In the appendix we give two orthogonal 2-starters in Z_{2n-1} for $6 \le n \le 30$ (orthogonal 2-starters for $K_{2n}, 6 \le n \le 30$). Since $GCD(2, 2n-1) = 1$, by Theorem 2.3 we have that each of these starters is indecomposable. They are also clearly simple. Thus, by Proposition 2.6 we have

THEOREM 2.7. *There exists a $SI\lambda S(2n-1, 2)$ for all $6 \le n \le 30$.*

3. Subsquares and frame construction. Before beginning our discussion of frames, we first must make some remarks concerning subsquares. Let L be a λ-square $\lambda S(n, \lambda)$. A square $w\lambda$ by $w\lambda$ subarray M of L is said to be a *sub-λ-square* if it is itself a λ-square $\lambda S(w, \lambda)$ on a subset of $w + 1$ symbols. Of importance to our constructions will be the existence of sub-λ-squares of order 1 (i.e. $\lambda S(1, \lambda)$). In the case of Room squares it is obvious that there always exists a subsquare of side 1. It is not quite so obvious to see this when $\lambda \ne 1$, so we will give the short proof of this fact.

LEMMA 3.1. *Every $\lambda S(n, \lambda)$ contains a sub-$\lambda S(1, \lambda)$.*

Proof. Let L be a $\lambda S(n, \lambda)$ and let $\{a, b\}$ be any pair in L. Rearrange the rows and columns of L so that the first λ of the rows and of the columns are the ones which contain $\{a, b\}$. Call this λ by λ square M. We will be done if we can show that all the cells of M which do not contain the pair $\{a, b\}$ are empty. Assume the pair $\{c, d\} \ne \{a, b\}$ occurs in M. But since $\{a, b\}$ and $\{c, d\}$ both occur in a row *and* a column of L this violates condition 4 of the definition of λ-square and the result follows. ☐

The following result will be used to show that larger squares are indecomposable.

THEOREM 3.2. *If L is a $\lambda S(n, \lambda)$ which contains an indecomposable sub-$\lambda S(m, \lambda)$, then L is indecomposable.*

Proof. Let $M \subseteq L$ be an indecomposable sub-$\lambda S(m, \lambda)$. Since any decomposition of L induces a decomposition of M, the result follows. ☐

Our main recursive construction requires the use of a generalization of a Room square called a Room frame. Room frames have been extremely useful in problems related to Room squares [4, 7, 8] and are examples of the usefulness of "holes" in combinatorial designs. Let S be a set, and let $\{S_1, ..., S_n\}$ be a partition of S. An $\{S_1, ..., S_n\}$-*Room frame* is an $|S|$ by $|S|$ array, F, indexed by S which satisfies the following properties:

1) every cell of F either is empty or contains an unordered pair of symbols of S,

2) the subarrays $S_i \times S_i$ are empty, for $1 \leq i \leq n$ (these subarrays are referred to as holes),

3) each symbol of $S - S_i$ occurs once in row (column) s, for any $s \in S_i$, and

4) the pairs occurring in F are precisely those $\{s, t\}$, where

$$(s, t) \in (S \times S) - \bigcup_{1 \leq i \leq n} (S_i \times S_i).$$

The type of F is defined to be the multiset $\{|S_i| : 1 \leq i \leq n\}$. We usually use an "exponential" notation to describe types: a type $t_i^{u_i} \ldots t_k^{u_k}$ denotes u_i occurences of t_i, $1 \leq i \leq k$. A Room frame can be thought of as a Room square from which a spanning set of subsquares has been removed. A Room frame of type 1^v gives rise to a Room square of side v by filling in each diagonal cell (s, s) with the pair $\{\infty, s\}$, where ∞ is a new symbol. In Figure 2 we give a Room frame of type $2^5 4^1$.

We will make use of the following frames which were recently constructed by Dinitz and Stinson.

THEOREM 3.3. [8, THEOREM 2.3]. *There exist Room frames of types* 2^6, $2^5 4^1$, $2^4 4^2$, $2^3 4^3$, $2^2 4^4$, $2^1 4^5$, *and* 4^6.

In order to make use of these frames we need to define some design-theoretic terminology. Let X be a set of points. A group-divisible design (or GDD) is a triple (X, G, A), which satisfies the following properties:

1) G is a partition of X into subsets called *groups*,

2) A is a set of subsets of X (called *blocks*) such that a group and a block contain at most one point in common, and

3) every pair of points from distinct groups occurs in a unique block.

The *group-type*, of a GDD(X, G, A) is the multiset $\{|G| : G \in G\}$. As with Room frames, we shall use an exponential notation for group types, for convenience. We will say that a GDD is a k-GDD if $|A| = k$ for every $A \in A$.

A *transversal design* TD(k, m) can be defined to be a k-GDD of type m^k. It is well-known that a TD(k, m) is equivalent to $k - 2$ mutually orthogonal Latin squares of order m. For results on Latin squares and transversal designs we refer to [2]. The following is the main recursive construction for Room frames.

FIGURE 2

FIGURE 2
A Room Frame of Type $2^5 4^1$

1 - 2		10/12	3/13			8/11	7/14		4/6	5/9			
		7/11	9/13	6/14	4/12			8/10	3/5				
9/12		**3 - 4**		8/14		5/11		7/13	1/6				2/10
	9/14				10/11			6/12	1/13	5/7			2/8
8/12	1/14			**5 - 6**		10/13	9/11		2/3	4/7			
4/13	3/12	10/14						2/11		8/9			1/7
3/11		5/13		2/12	4/14	**7 - 8**				1/10			6/9
		2/13	1/11					3/14	5/12	4/9			6/10
5/14	4/11			1/12	6/13			**9 - 10**		2/7			3/8
		8/13		6/11		7/12	2/14			1/3			4/5
6/8	5/10			3/7	2/9			1/4					
	6/7	1/9	5/8		2/4	3/10							
	7/9	4/10	1/8		2/5	3/6		**11 - 14**					
7/10		2/6		3/9		1/5	4/8						

Construction 3.4. [13, Construction 2.2] Let (X, G, A) be a GDD, and let w: $X \to Z^+ \cup \{0\}$ (we say that w is a *weighting*). For every $A \in A$, suppose that there is a Room frame of type $\{w(x) : x \in A\}$. Then there is a Room frame of type $\{\sum_{x \in G} w(x) : G \in G\}$.

Once we have constructed the Room frames, we can fill in the holes. The next theorem is essentially [13, Corollary 4.9], however, we will take multiple copies of the frame in order to obtain a λ-square.

LEMMA 3.5. *Suppose there is a Room frame of type $t_i^{u_i} \dots t_k^{u_k}$. For $1 \le i \le k$, suppose there is a simple λ-square $\lambda S(t_i + 1, \lambda)$. Then there is a simple $\lambda S(\sum_{1 \le i \le k} t_i u_i + 1, \lambda)$. Furthermore, if any one of the λ-squares $\lambda S(t_i + 1, \lambda)$ is indecomposable, then so is the resulting λ-square.*

Proof. Let F be an $\{S_i, \ldots S_n\}$ frame of type $t_i^{u_i} \cdots t_k^{u_k}$ where $\bigcup_{1 \le i \le n} S_i = S$, $\sum_{1 \le i \le n} u_i = n$ and $|S| = s$. Let $T_1 = T_2 = \cdots = T_\lambda = S$ be λ identical copies of S and let L be a $\lambda s + \lambda$ by $\lambda s + \lambda$ array indexed by $(\bigcup_{1 \le i \le n} T_i) \cup \{\infty_1, \cdots, \infty_\lambda\}$. We begin filling in L by defining $L(x, y) = F(x, y)$ if $(x, y) \in \bigcup_{1 \le i \le \lambda} T_i^2$.

Next we must fill in the "holes" in the frames. By hypothesis there is a simple λ-square $\lambda S(|S_i| + 1, \lambda)$ for each i, $1 \le i \le n$. Thus by Lemma 3.1 there exists a simple $\lambda S(|S_i| + 1, \lambda)$ containing a subsquare of order 1 for each i, $1 \le i \le n$. Call these λ-squares $\Lambda_1, \ldots, \Lambda_n$ where Λ_i is indexed by $\{\infty_1, \ldots \infty_\lambda\} \cup S_i$ and each Λ_i has its sub-λ-square indexed by the ∞'s. Λ_i uses the symbol set $S_i \cup \{\infty\} \cup \{\omega\}$ where ω is a new symbol and has $\{\infty, \omega\} = \Lambda_i(\infty_j, \infty_j)$ for $1 \le j \le \lambda$. (Note that there are λ copies of the indices S_i, one in each T_i). Define $L(x, y) = \Lambda_i(x, y)$ if $(x, y) \in (\{\infty_1 \ldots, \infty_\lambda\} \cup S_i) \times (\{\infty_1, \ldots, \infty_\lambda\} \cup S_i)$.

It may be checked that L is the desired λ-square. Furthermore, since each Λ_i is a sub-λ-square, if any of these squares are indecomposable, then by Theorem 3.2, L is indecomposable. Note that this construction basically just puts λ copies of the frame down the diagonal of L and then fills in the holes with the small λ squares.

We apply Construction 3.4 and Lemma 3.5 to the frames given by Theorem 3.3 to obtain the following theorem, which is our main recursive construction.

THEOREM 3.6. *Suppose there exists a $TD(6, m)$, and suppose there exists a $SI\lambda S(2r + 1, \lambda)$ for all r such that $m \le r \le 2m$. Then there exists a $SI\lambda S(2s+1, \lambda)$ for all $6m \le s \le 12m$.*

Proof. Let (X, G, A) be a $TD(6, m)$. Give the points in the TD weights 2 and 4 in such a way that $\sum_{x \in X} w(x) = 2s$. Apply construction 3.4 with the Room frames supplied by Theorem 3.3. Note that the "holes" in this frame are of size $2r$ for $2m \le 2r \le 4m$. Now use Lemma 3.5 and the hypothesized $SI\lambda S$'s to complete the construction. $\square$

4. The Spectrum. In this section we will discuss the spectrum of $SI\lambda S(n, 2)$

LEMMA 4.1. *There exists a $SI\lambda S(2s + 1, 2)$ for $30 \le s \le 732$.*

Proof. We will use Theorem 3.6 to construct $SI\lambda S(2s + 1, 2)$. The ingredients are a $TD(6, m)$ and a $SI\lambda S(2r + 1, \lambda)$ for all r such that $2m + 1 \le 2r + 1 \le 4m + 1$.

Consider the following table

m	$2r + 1$	$2s + 1$	Comments
5	11–21	61–121	11-21 exist by Theorem 2.7
9	19–37	108–217	19-37 exist by Theorem 2.7
17	35–69	205–408	Theorem 2.7 and Line 1 in this table
31	63–125	372–745	Lines 1 and 2 in this table
61	123–245	732–1465	Lines 2 and 3 in this table

THEOREM 4.2. *There exists a $SI\lambda S(2s + 1, 2)$ for all $s \geq 5$.*

Proof. If $5 \leq s \leq 372$ the result follows from Theorem 2.7 and Lemma 4.1. We assume $s \geq 732$ and proceed by induction. Let $m = [s/10]$, where [ ] denotes the greatest integer function. Then, since $m \geq 73$, there exists a TD(6, m) [2]. By induction, there exist $SI\lambda S(2r + 1, 2)$ for all $m \leq r \leq 2m$. Thus, by Theorem 3.6 there exists a $SI\lambda S(2s + 1, 2)$. □

COROLLARY 4.3. *There exist two orthogonal indecomposable 1-factorizations of $2K_{2n}$ for all $n \geq 6$.*

Conclusion. In this paper we have constructed orthogonal indecomposable 1-factorizations of $2K_{2n}$ for all $n \geq 6$. We used starter techniques to construct the small orders of n and then used recursive frame techniques to complete the spectrum. We would have liked to solve this problem for all λ, however, finding pairs of orthogonal starters for $\lambda > 2$ proved to be difficult (on the computer). We would like to note that all the recursive constructions in Section 3 work for *all* λ. Thus, if methods can be found to find small orders for a given λ, then the recursive techniques of this paper can be used to construct the large orders.

REFERENCES

[1] D.S. ARCHDEACON AND J.H. DINITZ, *Constructing indecomposable 1-factorizations of the complete multigraph*, preprint.

[2] TH. BETH, D. JUNGNICKEL, H. LENZ, *Design Theory*, B.I. Wissenschaftsverlag, Mannheim, (1985).

[3] C.J. COLBOURN, M.J. COLBOURN, AND A. ROSA, *Indecomposable 1-factorizations of the complete multigraph*, J. Austral. Math. Soc. (Series A), 39 (1985), pp. 334–343.

[4] J.H. DINITZ, *The existence of Room 5-Cubes*, Journal of Combinatorial Theory (Series A), 45 (1987), pp. 125–138.

[5] J.H. DINITZ, *Room n-cubes of low order*, Jour. Austral. Math. Soc. (Series A), 36 (1984), pp. 237–252.

[6] J.H. DINITZ AND D.R. STINSON, *A fast algorithm for finding strong starters*, SIAM J. Alg. Disc. Meth., 2 (1981), pp. 50–56.

[7] J.H. DINITZ AND D.R. STINSON, *Further results on frames*, Ars Combinatoria, 11 (1981), pp. 275–288.

[8] J.H. DINITZ AND D.R. STINSON, *On the existence of room squares with subsquares*, Contemporary Math, to appear.

[9] E.S. KRAMER, D.L. KREHER, S.S. MAGLIVERAS, AND D.M. MESNER, *An assortment of room-type designs*, Ars Combinatoria, 11 (1981), pp. 9–29.

[10] E.R. LAMKEN, *Notes on indecomposable Kirkman squares*, preprint.

[11] R.C. MULLIN AND W.D. WALLIS, *The existence of Room squares*, Aequationes Math., 13 (1975), pp. 1–7.

[12] A. ROSA, *Room squares generalized*, Annals of Discrete Mathematics, 8 (1980), pp. 43–57.

[13] D.R. STINSON, *Some constructions for frames, Room squares and subsquares*, Ars Combinatoria, 12 (1981), pp. 229–267.

[14] S.A. VANSTONE AND A. ROSA, *Starter-adder techniques for Kirkman squares and Kirkman cubes of small sides*, Ars Combinatoria, 14 (1982), pp. 199–212.

[15] W.D. WALLIS, A.P. STREET, AND J.S. WALLIS, *Combinatorics: Room squares, sum-free sets and Hadamard matrices.* Lecture Notes in Mathematics, 292 (1972) Springer-Verlag, Berlin.

APPENDIX

orthogonal λ-starters of $2K_{12}$

S_1: 6,7 9,10 2,4 1,3 5,8
S_2: 6,9 3,7 1,5 10,4 8,2
T_1: 4,5 8,9 10,3 2,7 1,6
T_2: 3,5 8,10 4,7 9,1 2,6

orthogonal λ-starters of $2K_{14}$

S_1: 1,2 11,12 3,5 8,10 4,7 6,9
S_2: 5,9 10,1 3,8 2,7 6,12 11,4
T_1: 9,10 4,5 3,6 11,2 7,12 8,1
T_2: 4,6 5,7 11,1 8,12 10,2 3,9

orthogonal λ-starters of $2K_{16}$

S_1: 7,8 4,5 10,12 1,3 6,9 11,14 13,2
S_2: 6,11 9,14 1,7 12,3 10,2 13,5 4,8
T_1: 2,3 12,13 5,8 7,10 11,1 4,9 14,6
T_2: 9,11 12,14 3,7 1,5 2,8 4,10 6,13

orthogonal λ-starters of $2K_{18}$

S_1: 8,9 14,15 11,13 3,5 1,4 7,10 12,16 2,6
S_2: 8,13 7,12 14,3 4,10 15,5 16,6 1,9 11,2
T_1: 4,5 1,2 10,13 12,15 3,8 6,11 7,14 9,16
T_2: 8,10 9,11 3,7 14,1 16,5 13,2 4,12 15,6

orthogonal λ-starters of $2K_{20}$

S_1: 4,5 8,9 1,3 11,13 12,15 7,10 17,2 14,18 16,6
S_2: 2,7 9,14 6,12 11,17 3,10 13,1 16,5 15,4 18,8
T_1: 17,18 9,10 4,7 5,8 11,16 15,1 14,2 6,13 3,12
T_2: 3,5 7,9 12,16 11,15 14,1 2,8 10,18 17,6 4,13

orthogonal λ-starters of $2K_{22}$

S_1: 3,4 12,13 17,19 6,8 7,10 15,18 16,20 5,9 14,2 1,11
S_2: 8,13 19,3 16,1 6,12 2,9 11,18 7,15 17,4 5,14 10,20
T_1: 11,12 14,15 19,1 13,16 2,7 4,9 3,10 20,6 17,5 8,18
T_2: 18,20 14,16 1,5 4,8 9,15 7,13 11,19 2,10 3,12 17,6

orthogonal λ-starters of $2K_{24}$

S_1: 21,22 4,5 8,10 13,15 7,12 18,1 19,3 9,17 11,20 6,16 14,2
S_2: 6,9 22,2 7,11 14,18 8,13 15,21 17,1 19,4 3,12 10,20 5,16
T_1: 14,15 18,19 10,13 5,9 16,21 1,7 20,4 3,11 22,8 2,12 6,17

T_2: 6,8 9,11 17,20 10,14 21,3 7,13 18,2 16,1 19,5 12,22 4,15

orthogonal λ-starters of $2K_{26}$

S_1: 12,13 23,24 4,6 16,18 15,20 21,2 3,10 9,17 5,14 1,11 22,8 7,19

S_2: 7,10 19,22 17,21 24,3 1,6 9,15 11,18 12,20 5,14 23,8 2,13 4,16

T_1: 6,7 19,20 21,24 11,15 12,17 10,16 1,8 22,5 4,13 18,3 23,9 2,14

T_2: 12,14 2,4 15,18 3,7 17,22 10,16 13,20 1,9 24,8 21,6 19,5 11,23

orthogonal λ-starters of $2K_{28}$

S_1: 1,2 9,10 18,20 22,24 16,21 8,14 4,11 26,7 6,15 13,23 19,3 5,17 12,25

S_2: 9,12 15,18 2,6 16,20 21,26 5,11 24,4 14,22 10,19 25,8 23,7 1,13 17,3

T_1: 5,6 16,17 7,10 19,23 3,8 20,26 15,22 21,2 9,18 4,14 1,12 13,25 11,24

T_2: 13,15 12,14 4,7 26,3 23,1 19,25 17,24 8,16 2,11 10,20 22,6 9,21 5,18

orthogonal λ-starters of $2K_{30}$

S_1: 16,17 9,10 12,14 1,3 22,27 5,11 18,25 20,28 26,6 13,23 4,15 19,2 24,8 7,21

S_2: 10,13 23,26 3,7 20,24 6,11 15,21 9,16 17,25 28,8 4,14 19,1 22,5 18,2 27,12

T_1: 20,21 11,12 1,4 28,3 9,14 19,25 8,15 23,2 17,26 6,16 13,24 27,10 5,18 22,7

T_2: 8,10 7,9 17,20 21,25 14,19 28,5 4,11 23,2 15,24 3,13 16,27 18,1 22,6 12,26

orthogonal λ-starters of $2K_{32}$

S_1: 30,28 20,22 8,9 17,18 21,23 12,14 5,10 29,4 25,1 11,19 15,24 27,6 2,13 26,7 3,16

S_2: 22,25 3,6 7,11 5,9 21,26 2,8 13,20 15,23 18,27 19,29 1,12 16,28 4,17 10,24 30,14

T_1: 26,27 12,13 19,22 30,3 4,9 17,23 8,15 21,29 11,20 28,7 5,16 2,14 24,6 18,1 10,25

T_2: 24,26 11,13 18,21 10,14 7,12 23,29 1,8 9,17 28,6 20,30 25,5 15,27 22,4 2,16 19,3

orthogonal λ-starters of $2K_{34}$

S_1: 14,15 21,22 3,6 19,23 2,7 24,30 5,12 17,25 28,4 32,9 18,29 8,20 31,11 13,27 1,16 10,26

S_2: 9,11 29,31 24,27 3,7 30,2 15,21 12,19 14,22 8,17 16,26 28,6 25,4 10,23 32,13 5,20 18,1

T_1: 27,28 5,6 17,20 18,22 9,14 25,31 30,4 11,19 7,16 2,12 23,1 29,8 13,26 10,24 21,3 32,15

T_2: 13,15 28,30 16,19 6,10 7,12 8,14 20,27 21,29 22,31 1,11 24,2 26,5 23,3 4,18 17,32 9,25

orthogonal λ-starters of $2K_{36}$

S_1: 33,34 22,23 13,15 18,20 5,10 31,2 7,14 9,17 19,28 29,4 21,32 24,1 3,16 11,25 26,6 27,8 30,12

S_2: 2,5 23,26 28,32 12,16 20,25 18,24 3,10 21,29 33,7 4,14 11,22 31,8 6,19 34,13 15,30 1,17 27,9

T_1: 4,5 20,21 24,27 22,26 25,30 32,3 10,17 6,14 9,18 1,11 2,13 19,31 34,12 15,29 28,8 7,23 16,33

T_2: 10,12 11,13 24,27 17,21 29,34 14,20 23,30 28,1 32,6 33,8 26,2 4,16 9,22 5,19 3,18 15,31 25,7

orthogonal λ-starters of $2K_{38}$

S_1: 13,14 17,18 9,12 3,7 27,32 36,5 16,23 35,6 24,33 20,30 8,19 22,34 25,1 15,29 26,4 31,10
11,28 21,2

S_2: 33,35 11,13 27,30 5,9 19,24 22,28 18,25 8,16 23,32 7,17 1,12 29,4 34,10 26,3 6,21
36,15 14,31 2,20

T_1: 31,32 12,13 35,1 20,24 21,26 10,16 8,15 25,33 9,18 4,14 6,17 27,2 29,5 22,36 19,34 28,7
23,3 30,11

T_2: 1,3 26,28 7,10 14,18 29,34 35,4 25,32 12,20 15,24 21,31 2,13 11,23 9,22 5,19 30,8 27,6
16,33 36,17

orthogonal λ-starters of $2K_{40}$

S_1: 34,35 26,27 33,36 21,25 2,7 16,22 12,19 30,38 6,15 3,13 37,9 8,20 11,24 18,32 28,4
1,17 14,31 5,23 10,29

S_2: 6,8 26,28 24,27, 14,18 11,16 31,37 22,29 33,2 25,34 7,17 4,15 1,13 23,36 35,10 5,20
3,19 21,38 30,9 32,12

T_1: 18,19 7,8 9,12 27,31 20,25 32,38 6,13 26,34 1,10 5,15 22,33 17,29 28,2 23,37 35,11
14,30 4,21 24,3 36,16

T_2: 13,15 34,36 25,28 26,30 4,9 23,29 3,10 16,24 5,14 1,11 7,18 19,31 38,12 21,35 32,8
17,33 20,37 27,6 22,2

orthogonal λ-starters of $2K_{42}$

S_1: 10,11 29,30 9,12 27,31 39,3 40,5 18,25 26,34 23,32 7,17 4,15 35,6 20,33 14,28 21,36 8,24 37,13
1,19 38,16 2,22

S_2: 22,24 23,25 28,31 36,40 4,9 8,14 35,1 5,13 7,16 17,27 19,30 26,38 21,34 33,6 3,18 37,12 39,15
2,20 10,29 32,11

T_1: 34,35 8,9 3,6 38,1 17,22 25,31 26,33 2,10 15,24 11,21 29,40 4,16 7,20 23,37 12,27 14,30 19,36
28,5 13,32 39,18

T_2: 2,4 18,20 36,39 34,38 3,8 11,17 16,23 29,37 19,28 40,9 24,35 13,25 14,27 7,21 32,6 26,1 5,22 15,33
12,31 10,30

orthogonal λ-starters of $2K_{44}$

S_1: 21,22 7,8 3,6 27,31 13,18 34,40 4,11 29,37 26,35 15,25 5,16 41,10 39,9 24,38 17,32 20,36 28,2
12,30 14,33 42,19 23,1

S_2: 28,30 9,11 4,7 12,16 26,31 32,38 18,25 37,2 24,33 13,23 40,8 10,22 1,14 34,5 27,42 19,35 3,20
21,39 41,17 29,6 15,36

T_1: 5,6 17,18 33,36 24,28 30,35 23,29 13,20 42,7 37,3 21,31 8,19 40,9 34,4 1,15 11,26 39,12 10,27 14,32
22,41 25,2 38,16

T_2: 23,25 40,42 26,29 30,34 12,17 4,10 8,15 19,27 28,37 39,6 41,9 20,32 35,5 7,21 1,16 38,11 14,31
18,36 3,22 13,33 24,2

orthogonal λ-starters of $2K_{46}$

S_1: 40,41 30,31 19,22 43,2 12,17 38,44 7,14 28,36 9,18 25,35 21,32 3,15 16,29 42,11 24,39 4,20 33,5
37,10 8,27 6,26 13,34 1,23

S_2: 14,16 27,29 34,37 20,24 7,12 11,17 21,28 2,10 39,3 41,6 35,1 26,38 40,8 22,36 18,33 44,15 13,30
31,4 23,42 5,25 43,19 32,9

T_1: 43,44 24,25 12,15 33,37 26,31 16,22 35,42 32,40 10,19 7,17 30,41 8,20 36,4 14,28 39,9 2,18 6,23
3,21 27,1 38,13 29,5 34,11

T_2: 32,34 8,10 35,38 44,3 4,9 15,21 20,27 16,24 17,26 23,33 1,12 29,41 30,43 37,6 13,28 31,2 5,22
7,25 40,14 36,11 18,39 42,19

orthogonal λ-starters of $2K_{48}$

S_1: 32,33 23,24 40,43 14,18 37,42 39,45 31,38 21,29 10,19 7,17 44,8 3,15 12,25 35,2 5,20 6,22 41,11
16,34 27,46 28,1 9,30 4,26 13,36

S_2: 7,9 42,44 37,40 10,14 1,6 13,19 28,35 4,12 27,36 22,32 20,31 3,15 17,30 41,8 24,39 29,45 21,38
16,34 46,18 23,43 5,26 11,33 2,25

T_1: 10,11 26,27 39,42 31,35 2,7 45,4 22,29 16,24 19,28 15,25 1,12 38,3 30,43 46,13 6,21 36,5 17,34
14,32 37,9 20,40 23,44 33,8 18,41

T_2: 8,10 19,21 39,42 24,28 11,16 34,40 22,29 1,9 6,15 26,36 2,13 33,45 37,3 32,46 12,27 4,20 14,31
25,43 35,7 18,38 23,44 30,5 41,17

orthogonal λ-starters of $2K_{50}$

S_1: 29,30 16,17 28,31 44,48 8,13 34,40 36,43 18,26 38,47 9,19 35,46 42,5 2,15 10,24 12,27 39,6 3,20
7,25 22,41 33,4 11,32 1,23 14,37 21,45

S_2: 38,40 41,43 32,35 46,1 8,13 23,29 17,24 37,45 10,19 15,25 7,18 30,42 47,11 34,48 21,36 12,28 3,20
4,22 44,14 6,26 33,5 9,31 16,39 27,2

T_1: 23,24 45,46 15,18 48,3 30,35 32,38 47,5 43,2 22,31 40,1 28,39 8,20 12,25 13,27 11,26 17,33 4,21
41,10 36,6 14,34 37,9 7,29 42,16 44,19

T_2: 29,31 5,7 33,36 15,19 1,6 18,24 37,44 45,4 13,22 20,30 21,32 39,2 46,10 12,26 42,8 9,25 35,3 16,34
28,47 23,43 27,48 38,11 40,14 17,41

orthogonal λ-starters of $2K_{52}$

S_1: 48,49 28,29 30,33 42,46 8,13 31,37 3,10 12,20 36,45 22,32 5,16 6,18 25,38 39,2 11,26 7,23 35,1
9,27 21,40 50,19 34,4 43,14 24,47 44,17 41,15

S_2: 11,13 45,47 1,4 16,20 26,31 12,18 25,32 42,50 48,6 14,24 10,21 37,49 33,46 29,43 23,38 44,9 17,34
35,2 22,41 19,39 7,28 5,27 36,8 30,3 15,40

T_1: 16,17 38,39 50,2 9,13 10,15 36,42 14,21 27,35 49,7 34,44 32,43 28,40 11,24 12,26 4,19 41,6 29,46
5,23 18,37 25,45 33,3 30,1 8,31 47,20 48,22

T_2: 8,10 34,36 42,45 14,18 38,43 15,21 41,48 27,35 16,25 44,3 49,9 7,19 24,37 12,26 31,46 17,33 39,5
11,29 4,23 32,1 50,20 6,28 30,2 40,13 22,47

orthogonal λ-starters of $2K_{54}$

S_1: 39,40 47,48 5,8 28,32 21,26 37,43 50,4 15,23 10,19 45,2 11,22 6,18 25,38 51,12 27,42 20,36 14,31
34,52 41,7 24,44 49,17 13,35 46,16 9,33 29,1 30,3

S_2: 49,51 46,48 42,45 16,20 6,11 23,29 14,21 26,34 19,28 30,40 43,1 27,39 5,18 47,8 9,24 15,31 38,2
32,50 3,22 17,37 44,12 41,10 13,36 33,4 35,7 52,25

T_1: 20,21 29,30 35,38 4,8 49,1 9,15 33,40 31,39 18,27 7,17 23,34 43,2 19,32 50,11 37,52 6,22 46,10
47,12 26,45 28,48 3,24 36,5 44,14 42,13 16,41 25,51

T_2: 18,20 9,11 24,27 37,41 52,4 7,13 43,50 21,29 17,26 35,45 22,33 46,5 2,15 30,44 39,1 16,32 19,36
49,14 42,8 28,48 38,6 12,34 40,10 23,47 31,3 25,51

orthogonal λ-starters of $2K_{56}$

S_1: 13,14 3,4 23,26 2,6 5,10 37,43 46,53 21,29 7,16 38,48 9,20 35,47 32,45 19,33 27,42 34,50 8,25
52,15 22,41 31,51 28,49 17,39 1,24 30,54 11,36 18,44 40,12

S_2: 2,4 40,42 38,41 45,49 46,51 44,50 32,39 54,7 10,19 26,36 11,22 5,17 15,28 21,35 18,33 53,14 20,37
13,31 48,12 27,47 3,24 8,30 6,29 1,25 9,34 52,23 16,43

T_1: 20,21 39,40 10,13 48,52 37,42 23,29 31,38 11,19 18,27 41,51 53,9 3,15 46,4 16,30 7,22 33,49 26,43
54,17 50,14 36,1 24,45 25,47 44,12 8,32 35,5 2,28 34,6

T_2: 29,31 54,1 34,37 24,28 9,14 10,16 6,13 38,46 32,41 52,7 12,23 47,4 45,3 25,39 20,35 26,42 27,44
48,11 2,21 40,5 15,36 51,18 30,53 50,19 8,33 17,43 22,49

orthogonal λ-starters of $2K_{58}$

S_1: 15,16 46,47 39,42 14,18 17,22 3,9 12,19 56,7 54,6 38,48 44,55 20,32 24,37 35,49 11,26 45,4 10,27
25,43 34,53 21,41 29,50 8,30 36,2 28,52 33,1 5,31 13,40 23,51

S_2: 13,15 23,25 29,32 2,6 11,16 56,5 43,50 41,49 10,19 45,55 33,44 14,26 17,30 4,18 39,54 20,36 21,38
42,3 28,47 46,9 31,52 12,34 35,1 27,51 40,8 22,48 37,7 53,24

T_1: 51,52 43,44 17,20 12,16 49,54 41,47 8,15 24,32 19,28 25,35 26,37 33,45 1,14 53,10 3,18 11,27 22,39
46,7 23,42 36,56 9,30 48,13 40,6 38,5 34,2 29,55 4,31 50,21

T_2: 51,53 29,31 33,36 26,30 55,3 19,25 34,41 1,9 47,56 13,23 21,32 8,20 15,28 40,54 48,6 52,11 18,35
44,5 24,43 7,27 38,2 39,4 46,12 49,16 17,42 45,14 10,37 22,50

orthogonal λ-starters of $2K_{60}$

S_1: 15,16 43,44 32,35 36,40 7,12 54,1 21,28 26,34 39,48 52,3 22,33 51,4 25,38 50,5 57,13 2,18 20,37
24,42 10,29 11,31 46,8 56,19 45,9 41,6 30,55 47,14 49,17 58,27 53,23

S_2: 29,31 39,41 16,19 17,21 4,9 8,14 49,56 40,48 26,35 32,42 7,18 34,46 47,1 22,36 57,13 11,27 45,3
2,20 33,52 44,5 50,12 15,37 28,51 58,23 30,55 43,10 38,6 25,53 54,24

T_1: 8,9 19,20 3,6 26,30 35,40 11,17 15,22 4,12 48,57 13,23 25,36 32,44 39,52 41,55 58,14 50,7 28,45
31,49 27,46 33,53 56,18 42,5 24,47 37,2 29,54 34,1 16,43 10,38 51,21

T_2: 23,25 32,34 28,31 3,7 44,49 55,2 50,57 10,18 15,24 42,52 26,37 48,1 4,17 5,19 30,45 22,38 54,12
33,51 8,27 21,41 14,35 36,58 56,20 29,53 47,13 39,6 43,11 40,9 46,16

85

INFLUENTIAL OBSERVATIONS UNDER ROBUST DESIGNS

SUBIR GHOSH* AND HAMID NAMINI†

Key words. Arrays, Designs, Factorial Experiments, Influential Observations, Invariance, Linear Models, Robustness, Unavailable Observations

AMS(MOS) subject classifications. 1970 Primary and Secondary 62J05, 62K05, 62K15, 62K99

0. Summary. In this paper we present some new results in the comparison of influence of sets of observations under robust designs in terms of the fitting of the model to the data and also in terms of the prediction. We consider 2^m and $2^{m_1} \times 3^{m_2}$ factorial experiments using both orthogonal and nonorthogonal arrays. We also study the invariance problem of two matrices M and Q under certain mappings of one set of runs to another set of runs. The study results in enormous simplification in the comparison of influential observations.

1. Introduction. The influence of a set of observations under a design is measured in terms of both the fitting of the model to the data and the prediction using the fitted model. The influence is in fact the effect of deleting the set of observations on both the fitting and the prediction. In the problem of comparing the influence of sets of t (a positive integer) observations and identifying the most (or the least) influential set of t observations, it is very natural to assume that the underlying design is robust against the unavailability of any t observations [Ghosh (1979)]. We first present the definition under the standard linear model

$$(1) \qquad\qquad E(\underline{y}) = X\underline{\beta},$$

$$(2) \qquad\qquad V(\underline{y}) = \sigma^2 I,$$

$$(3) \qquad\qquad \text{Rank } X = p,$$

where $\underline{y}(N \times 1)$ is a vector of observations, $X(N \times p)$ is a known matrix, $\underline{\beta}(p \times 1)$ is a vector of fixed unknown parameters and σ^2 is a constant which may or may not be known. Let $\mathcal{D}$ be the underlying design corresponding to $\underline{y}$.

DEFINITION. [Ghosh (1979)] The design $\mathcal{D}$ under the model (1–3) is said to be robust against the unavailability of any t observations if the parameters in β are still unbiasedly estimable when any t observations in $\underline{y}$ are unavailable.

Notice that there are $\binom{N}{t}$ possible sets of t observations. The mathematical interpretation of the above definition is that the rank of the matrix X remains the same (i.e., p) when any set of t rows of X is deleted. A powerful characterization of the robustness property is presented in the following theorem.

---

*Department of Statistics, University of California, Riverside, California 92521, USA. The work of the first author is sponsored by the Air Force Office of Scientific Research under Grant AFOSR–88–0092

†Department of Statistics, University of California, Riverside, California 92521, USA.

THEOREM 1. [Ghosh (1979)] Let $Z((N-p) \times N)$ be a matrix with Rank $Z = (N-p)$ and $ZX = 0$. The design $\mathcal{D}$ under the model (1-3) is robust against the unavailability of any t observations if and only if the matrix Z has the property P_t (i.e., every set of t columns of Z is linearly independent).

This characterization of robustness is very useful in finding a value of t for a given design. The idea of "Robustness of designs against the unavailability of data" is fundamental in measuring the influence of observations. We measure the influence of a set of t observations by assuming the observations in the set unavailable and then assessing the model fitted with the remaining $(N-t)$ observations. We also assess the prediction of t unavailable observations in terms of $(N-t)$ available observations.

For simplicity of the presentation, we do not introduce any notation for the ith $\left(i = 1, \ldots, \binom{N}{t}\right)$ set of t observations. We denote the ith set of t observations in $\underline{y}$ by $\underline{y}_2$ and the remaining observations in $\underline{y}$ by $\underline{y}_1$. The corresponding submatrices of X are denoted by X_2 and X_1. The least squares estimator of β on the basis of $\underline{y}$ is $\underline{b} = (X'X)^{-1}X'\underline{y}$. When the observations in $\underline{y}_2$ are unavailable, the least squares estimator of β on the basis of available observations in $\underline{y}_1$ is $\underline{b}_1 = (X_1'X_1)^{-1}X_1'\underline{y}_1$. The variance-covariance matrix of $\underline{b}_1$ is $V(\underline{b}_1) = \sigma^2(X_1'X_1)^{-1}$. The following are some meaningful measures of influence of $\underline{y}_2$ on fitting the model (1-3) to the observations in $\underline{y}_1$:

(4)
$$\begin{aligned} I_1(\underline{y}_2) &= \text{Determinant of } V(\underline{b}_1) = |V(\underline{b}_1)|, \\ I_2(\underline{y}_2) &= \text{Trace of } V(\underline{b}_1) = Tr(V(\underline{b}_1)). \end{aligned}$$

Smaller values of $I_i(\underline{y}_2), i = 1, 2$, indicate less influence of $\underline{y}_2$ on the fitting of the model with the observations in $\underline{y}_1$. Larger values of $I_i(\underline{y}_2), i = 1, 2$, indicate more influence of $\underline{y}_2$. Notice that smaller values of measures in (4) attain an overall minimizations of variances for $\underline{b}_1$ (See Kiefer (1959)). These measures of influence were used in Ghosh (1982) for $t = 1$. When the observations in $\underline{y}_2$ are unavailable, the predicted values $\widehat{\underline{y}}_2$ of the unavailable observations from the available observations in $\underline{y}_1$ is

(5)
$$\widehat{\underline{y}}_2 = X_2\underline{b}_1$$

The variance of $\widehat{\underline{y}}_2$ is $V(\widehat{\underline{y}}_2) = X_2V(\widehat{\underline{b}}_1)X_2' = \sigma^2X_2(X_1'X_1)^{-1}X_2'$. A meaningful measure of influence of $\underline{y}_2$ on the prediction of t unavailable observations in terms of $(N-t)$ available observations is

(6)
$$I_3(\underline{y}_2) = \text{Trace } V(\widehat{\underline{y}}_2).$$

Again, smaller value of $I_3(\underline{y}_2)$ indicates less influence of $\underline{y}_2$ on the prediction. Larger value of $I_3(\underline{y}_2)$ indicate more influence of $\underline{y}_2$. Note that smaller values of measures in (5) attain an overall minimization of variances for $\widehat{\underline{y}}_2$.

87

When we compare the influence of sets of observations with respect to $(w.r.t)I_1, I_2$ and I_3, we find two matrices M and Q play an important role. We observe in Section 2 that the M matrix appears in comparison w.r.t. all three measures I_1, I_2 and I_3. The Q matrix appears in comparison w.r.t. I_2 only. We consider both orthogonal and non-orthogonal designs in our study. We investigate in detail for 2^m and $2^{m_1} \times 3^{m_2}$ factorial experiments. In this context we study the invariance problem of the matrices M and Q for sets of t observations or runs. The consideration of invariance leads to a major simplification in the comparison of influence of sets of observations. We also present examples to illustrate this fact. The invariance problems arise in many other factorial design problems different from the one considered in this paper. To cite a few references, we mention Srivastava, Raktoe and Pesotan (1976), Srivastava and Ghosh (1977), Pesotan and Raktoe (1988) and others.

In the case of robustness w.r.t. pairs of observations, we observe that for the special orthogonal designs with $X'X = NI$, the inner product of two rows of X plays an important role in comparing influences w.r.t. I_1, I_2 and I_3. In this sense and for this special case we make some additional contributions to the work of Moore (1988).

The importance of knowing influential sets of observations at the design stage is that (1) we can assess the influence of a set of unavailable observations in the planned analysis, (2) in the case of deficit of budget during a long term experiment using the robust design where it may be a good idea not to collect observations which are least influential and (3) in the case of planned industrial experiments where the runs must be made sequentially (see Moore (1988)) it is beneficial to collect influential observations at the earlier stages of experimentation.

2. General Results. In this section, we present some general results on comparison of influence of sets of observations. We have $X'X = X_1'X_1 + X_2'X_2$. For a design $\mathcal{D}$ robust against the unavailability of any t observations, the rank of X_1 is p. We denote $M = X_2(X'X)^{-1}X_2'$ and $Q = X_2(X'X)^{-2}X_2'$.

THEOREM 2. *The comparison of influence of two sets of t observations w.r.t. the measure I_1 in (4) is equivalent to the comparison w.r.t. $|I_t - M|^{-1}$.*

Proof. We first observe that $\sigma^{-2}I_1(\underline{y}_2) = |X_1'X_1|^{-1}$. We write

$$X_1'X_1 = X'X[I_p - (X'X)^{-1}X_2'X_2].$$

Thus $|X_1'X_1| = |X'X| \ |I_p - (X'X)^{-1}X_2'X_2|$. By the Result 1 in Appendix, it follows that $|X_1'X_1| = |X'X| \ |I_t - M|$. The rest is clear. This completes the proof.

THEOREM 3. *The comparison of influence of two sets of t observations w.r.t. the measure I_2 in (4) is equivalent to the comparison w.r.t. $Tr(I - M)^{-1}Q$.*

Proof. We observe that

$$(X_1'X_1)^{-1} = (X'X)^{-1} + (X'X)^{-1}X_2'(I - M)^{-1}X_2(X'X)^{-1}.$$

Thus $Tr(X_1'X_1)^{-1} = Tr(X'X)^{-1} + Tr(I - M)^{-1}Q$. The rest is obvious. This completes the proof.

88

THEOREM 4. *The comparison of influence of two sets of t observations w.r.t. the measure I_3 in (6) is equivalent to the comparison w.r.t. $Tr(I - M)^{-1}$.*

Proof. We notice that $\sigma^{-2} I_3(\underline{y}_2) = Tr\, X_2(X_1' X_1)^{-1} X_2'$. Now $X_2(X_1' X_1)^{-1} X_2' = M + M(I - M)^{-1} M$. By the Result 6 in Appendix, we have $X_2(X_1' X_1)^{-1} X_2' = (I - M)^{-1} M$. Suppose $\lambda_i, i = 1, \cdots, t$, are the characteristic roots of M. It follows from the Results 2,4 and 5 in Appendix that $0 \leq \lambda_i < 1$, $i = 1, \cdots, t$. We thus have $Tr(I - M)^{-1} M = \sum_{i=1}^{t}(1 - \lambda_i)^{-1} \lambda_i = -t + \sum_{i=1}^{t}(1 - \lambda_i)^{-1} = -t + Tr(I - M)^{-1}$. The rest is clear. This completes the proof.

THEOREM 5. *A set of t observations is least influential w.r.t. the measure I_1 in (4) if and only if (iff) the matrix M is a diagonal matrix.*

Proof. We notice that $\sigma^{-2} I_1(\underline{y}_2) = |X_1' X_1|^{-1} = |X'X|^{-1} |I - M|^{-1}$. For a least influential $\underline{y}_2, I_1(\underline{y}_2)$ is minimum and hence $|I - M|$ is maximum. It now follows from the Results 5 and 9 in Appendix that $|I - M|$ is maximum when $(I - M)$ [i.e., M] is a diagonal matrix. This completes the proof of the theorem.

THEOREM 6. *A set of t observations is least influential w.r.t. the measure I_3 in (6) iff the matrix M is a diagonal matrix.*

Proof. We observe in Theorem 4 that the minimization of $I_3(\underline{y}_2)$ is equivalent to the minimization of $Tr(I - M)^{-1}$. It now follows from the Result 10 in Appendix that $Tr(I - M)^{-1}$ is minimum when M is a diagonal matrix. This completes the proof.

3. Orthogonal Designs. In this section we consider the special case of orthogonal designs and interpret the meaning and usefulness of various results presented in section 2. For orthogonal designs, the matrix $X'X$ is a diagonal matrix. We first consider the situation where $X'X = NI$. We then have $M = \dfrac{1}{N}\, X_2 X_2'$ and $Q = \dfrac{1}{N^2}\, X_2 X_2'$.

REMARK 1. For I_2 and I_3 defined in (4) and (6), we have $N I_2 = I_3$.

The comparisons of influence are thus equivalent w.r.t. the measures I_2 and I_3. For orthogonal designs, it now follows from Theorems 2, 3 and 4 that the comparison of influence w.r.t. I_1 or I_2 (or equivalently I_3) is equivalent to the comparison w.r.t. $|I - M|^{-1}$ or $Tr(I - M)^{-1}$.

THEOREM 7. *For an orthogonal design satisfying $X'X = NI$ and $p \geq t$, the characteristic roots of the matrix $X_1' X_1$ are N with multiplicity $(p - t)$ and $N(1 - \lambda_i), i = 1, \cdots, t$, where λ_i's are the characteristic roots of M.*

Proof. We have $X'X = X_1' X_1 + X_2' X_2$ and thus $X_1' X_1 - \lambda I = NI - X_2' X_2 - \lambda I = (N - \lambda)I - X_2' X_2 = N\left[\dfrac{N - \lambda}{N} I - \dfrac{X_2' X_2}{N}\right]$. Now $|X_1' X_1 - \lambda I| = 0$ is equivalent to $\left|\dfrac{N - \lambda}{N} I_p - \dfrac{X_2' X_2}{N}\right| = 0$. It follows from the Result 1 in Appendix that

$$\left| \frac{N-\lambda}{N} I_p - \frac{X_2' X_2}{N} \right| = \left(\frac{N-\lambda}{N} \right)^p \left| I_p - \frac{1}{(N-\lambda)} X_2' X_2 \right|$$

$$= \left(\frac{N-\lambda}{N} \right)^p \left| I_t - \frac{1}{(N-\lambda)} X_2 X_2' \right| = \left(\frac{N-\lambda}{N} \right)^{p-t} \left| \left(\frac{N-\lambda}{N} \right) I_t - \frac{1}{N} X_2 X_2' \right|$$

$$= \left(\frac{N-\lambda}{N} \right)^{p-t} \left| I_t - M - \frac{\lambda}{N} I_t \right|.$$ The rest is clear. This completes the proof.

4. 2^m Factorial Designs. We now consider a 2^m factorial experiment under a completely randomized design. The runs (or treatments) are denoted by $\underline{t}_i' = (t_{i1}, \cdots, t_{iu}, \cdots, t_{im})$ where t_{iu} is the level of the factor u in the run i, $t_{iu} = 0, 1, u = 1, \cdots, m; i = 1, \cdots, N$. Let $T(N \times m)$ be a matrix whose ith row is $\underline{t}_i'$, $i = 1, \cdots, N$. The matrix T is called the array (or the design) for the experiment. Let y_i be the ith observation on the ith run in T, $i = 1, \cdots, N$. We denote $\underline{y} = (y_1, \cdots, y_i, \cdots, y_N)'$. We now consider the model (1–3). The vector $\underline{\beta}$ is the vector of factorial effects selected for the experiment. The matrix X depends on T and $\underline{\beta}$. The entries in the first column of X are all unity. The columns of X corresponding to the main effects are obtained from T replacing 0 by (-1). The column of X for a q-factor interaction is obtained by taking the Schur Product of the columns corresponding to q main effects [The Schur Product of two vectors $\underline{a} = (a_1, \cdots, a_N)'$ and $\underline{b} = (b_1, \cdots, b_N)'$ is the vector $(a_1 b_1, \cdots, a_N b_N)'$]. The set of observations in $\underline{y}_2$ corresponds to a set of t runs T_2 of the array T. The remaining $(N - t)$ runs in T corresponding to $\underline{y}_1$ is denoted by T_1. In this context, the influence of a set of t observations in $\underline{y}_2$ can also be expressed equivalently in terms of the influence of the corresponding set of t runs in T_2.

4.1 Orthogonal 2^m factorial designs. In this section we consider orthogonal arrays T which are complete or fractional factorials. We have for such orthogonal arrays T , $X'X = NI$. For $t = 1$, notice that $X_2 X_2' = p$ and $I - M = \left(1 - \frac{p}{N} \right)$.

REMARK 2. For all orthogonal 2^m factorial designs, the single observations (i.e., $t = 1$) are equally influential w.r.t. I_1, I_2 and I_3.

REMARK 3. For orthogonal 2^m factorial designs, the pairs of observations (i.e., $t = 2$) are not equally influential $w.r.t.$ I_1, I_2 and I_3.

For $t = 2$, we denote $X_2' = [\underline{x}_{21}, \underline{x}_{22}]$, where $\underline{x}_{21}(p \times 1)$ and $\underline{x}_{22}(p \times 1)$.

THEOREM 8. *For orthogonal 2^m factorial designs, the comparison of influence of every pair of observations (i.e., $t = 2$) w.r.t. I_1, I_2 and I_3 is equivalent to the comparison w.r.t. the absolute value of $\underline{x}_{21}' \underline{x}_{22}$.*

Proof. We observe that

$$I - M = I - \frac{1}{N} X_2 X_2' = \begin{bmatrix} 1 - \dfrac{p}{N} & \underline{x}_{21}' \underline{x}_{22} \\ \underline{x}_{21}' \underline{x}_{22} & 1 - \dfrac{p}{N} \end{bmatrix}$$

It is now easy to see that both $|I - M|^{-1}$ and $Tr[I - M]^{-1}$ are monotonically increasing functions of $(\underline{x}_{21}' \underline{x}_{22})^2$. This completes the proof of the theorem.

REMARK 4. The condition on the absolute value of $\underline{x}'_{21}\underline{x}_{22}$ w.r.t. I_1 is appeared in Theorem 1 in Moore (1988). In fact, the reference to the work of Ghosh (1979, 1982) on robustness of design is missing in Moore (1988).

REMARK 5. The $\underline{x}'_{21}\underline{x}_{22}$ is related to the number of level changes in the runs corresponding to $\underline{x}_{21}$ and $\underline{x}_{22}$ under the appropriate model. (See Theorem 2 in Moore (1988), Cheng (1985)).

Example 1. We now consider a complete 2^4 factorial experiement to illustrate the results presented in this section. We assume 3-factor and higher order interactions to be zero. Thus the vector $\underline{\beta}$ consists of the general mean, the main effects and the two-factor interactions. This plan is called a Resolution 5 (or Resolution V) plan. Thus $p = 11$, $N = 16$, $\underline{\beta}(11 \times 1)$ and $X(16 \times 11)$. The matrix Z is given below.

$$
\begin{bmatrix}
1 & 1 & -1 & -1 & -1 & -1 & -1 & 1 & -1 & 1 & 1 & 1 & 1 & 1 & -1 & -1 \\
1 & -1 & 1 & -1 & -1 & -1 & 1 & -1 & 1 & -1 & 1 & 1 & 1 & -1 & 1 & -1 \\
1 & -1 & -1 & 1 & -1 & 1 & -1 & -1 & 1 & 1 & -1 & 1 & -1 & 1 & 1 & -1 \\
1 & -1 & -1 & -1 & 1 & 1 & 1 & 1 & -1 & -1 & -1 & -1 & 1 & 1 & 1 & -1 \\
1 & -1 & -1 & -1 & -1 & 1 & 1 & 1 & 1 & 1 & 1 & -1 & -1 & -1 & -1 & 1
\end{bmatrix}
$$

Notice that the rows of the matrix Z correspond to 3-factor and 4-factor interactions. The matrix Z has the property P_3 but not P_4. The fact that it does not have P_4 can be seen by checking that the sum of 4 column vectors 1, 2, 3 and 6 is in fact a null vector. It now follows from Theorem 1 that the design is robust against the unavailability of any 3 observations. The absolute values of $\underline{x}'_{21}\,\underline{x}_{22}$ for two pairs of runs $\begin{pmatrix} 1 & 1 & 1 & 1 \\ 0 & 0 & 0 & 0 \end{pmatrix}$ and $\begin{pmatrix} 1 & 1 & 1 & 1 \\ 1 & 0 & 0 & 0 \end{pmatrix}$ are 3 and 1, respectively. Thus the observations for the runs $\begin{pmatrix} 1 & 1 & 1 & 1 \\ 0 & 0 & 0 & 0 \end{pmatrix}$ are more influential than the observations for the runs $\begin{pmatrix} 1 & 1 & 1 & 1 \\ 1 & 0 & 0 & 0 \end{pmatrix}$.

4.2 Nonorthogonal 2^m factorial designs. In this section we consider nonorthogonal 2^m factorial experiments under completely Randomized designs. For nonorthogonal array T, the matrix $X'X$ is not a diagonal matrix. We consider B-arrays of full strength (i.e. strength m) as nonorthogonal arrays. We first describe these arrays. Let S_i be the set of all $(1 \times m)$ vectors having weight i (i.e., i elements equal to 1 and the other $(m - i)$ elements equal to 0), $i = 0, 1, \cdots, m$. The sets S_i, $i = 0, 1, \cdots, m$, appear as rows in T with frequencies λ_i, where λ_i is a nonnegative integer. Clearly the number of vectors in S_i is $\binom{m}{i}$ and $N = \sum_{i=0}^{m} \lambda_i \binom{m}{i}$. We first calculate the matrix $I - M$ for such arrays. Note that the rows and columns of $(X'X)^{-1}$ correspond to the elements of $\underline{\beta}$. Let F and F' be any two (not necessarily distinct) elements of $\underline{\beta}$ and let $\varepsilon_1(F, F')$ be the corresponding element of $(X'X)^{-1}$. Notice that the rows and columns of X_2 correspond to the observations or the runs in T and the elements of $\underline{\beta}$, respectively. Let the element of X_2 corresponding to the run $\underline{t}$ in T and the element F in $\underline{\beta}$ be $\varepsilon_2(\underline{t}, F)$. Note that the elements $\varepsilon_2(\underline{t}, F))$

in X_2 and $\epsilon_2(F, \underline{t})$ in X_2' are identical and furthermore $\varepsilon_2(\underline{t}, F)$ equal $+1$ or -1. Notice that the rows and columns of the matrix $M = X_2(X'X)^{-1}X_2'$ corresponds to the runs in T. The element of M corresponding to the runs $\underline{t}$ and $\underline{t}'$ in T is

(7)
$$\sum_{F,F' \in \underline{\beta}} \varepsilon_2(\underline{t}, F)\varepsilon_1(F, F')\varepsilon_2(F', \underline{t}').$$

The diagonal element of M corresponding to the run $\underline{t}$ in T is

$$\sum_{F,F' \in \underline{\beta}} \varepsilon_2(\underline{t}, F)\varepsilon_1(F, F')\varepsilon_2(F', \underline{t})$$

(8)
$$= \sum_{F \in \underline{\beta}} \quad \cdots \quad + \sum_{\substack{F,F' \in \underline{\beta} \\ F \neq F'}}$$

$$= Tr(X'X)^{-1} + \sum_{\substack{F,F' \in \underline{\beta} \\ F \neq F'}} \varepsilon_2(\underline{t}, F)\varepsilon_1(F, F')\varepsilon_2(F', \underline{t}).$$

REMARK 6. For a B-array of full strength, the comparison of influence of single observations (i.e., $t = 1$) w.r.t. I_1, I_2 and I_3 is equivalent to the comparison w.r.t.

(9)
$$\sum_{\substack{F,F' \in \underline{\beta} \\ F \neq F'}} \varepsilon_2(\underline{t}, F)\varepsilon_1(F, F')\varepsilon_2(F', \underline{t}).$$

We now consider the Resolution $(2d + 1)$ plan for an integer $d(\geq 1)$. The vector $\underline{\beta}$ consists of d factors and lower order interactions. We assume $(d + 1)$-factor and higher order interactions are all zero.

REMARK 7. For Resolution $(2d + 1)$ plan, two observations on two runs with equal weights in a B-array of full strength are equally influential.

The cases $d = 1$ and $d = 2$ are practically important. For $d = 2$, the expression for (8) is given in Theorem 1 of Ghosh and Kipngeno (1985) and the Remark 7 is in fact Corollary 2 of Ghosh and Kipngeno (1985) in a different context.

Example 2. Consider $d = 1$ for a 2^4 factorial experiment. Suppose the B-array of full strength (i.e. strength 4) $T(10 \times 4)$ consists of S_0, S_1, S_3 and S_4. The matrix $Z(5 \times 10)$ is given below.

$$Z = \begin{bmatrix} 3 & -1 & -1 & -1 & -1 & 0 & 0 & 0 & 0 & 1 \\ 1 & -1 & 0 & 0 & 0 & -1 & 0 & 0 & 0 & 1 \\ 1 & 0 & -1 & 0 & 0 & 0 & -1 & 0 & 0 & 1 \\ 1 & 0 & 0 & -1 & 0 & 0 & 0 & -1 & 0 & 1 \\ 1 & 0 & 0 & 0 & -1 & 0 & 0 & 0 & -1 & 1 \end{bmatrix}$$

The matrix Z has the property P_3 but not the property P_4 or in other words, the design is robust against unavailability of any 3 observations. It now follows from the Remark 7 that the observations for any two runs in $S_i (i = 1$ or $3)$ are equally influential.

5. Invariance of M. In this section we consider the problem of identifying the sets of t runs in arrays of 2^m factorial experiments so that the corresponding M matrices are identical. This in turn implies that the sets of observations corresponding to the sets of t runs are equally influential.

THEOREM 9. *If one set of t runs in T can be mapped to another set of t runs in T by renaming factors and/or changing the levels of factors, then the corresponding $X_2 X_2'$ matrices are identical (or, in other words, $X_2 X_2'$ remains invariant under the mapping).*

Proof. By renaming the factors, the inner product of a row vector in X_2 with itself and the inner product of two row vectors in X_2 remain invariant. This implies that $X_2 X_2'$ remains invariant. The change of levels of factors means the postmultiplication of X_2 by a diagonal matrix D whose first diagonal element is 1 and the other diagonal elements are either 1 or -1. Notice that $D' = D$ and $D^2 = D$ and therefore $X_2 X_2' = X_2 D D' X_2'$. Thus $X_2 X_2'$ remains invariant. This completes the proof.

Recall that for 2^m orthogonal designs, $M = \dfrac{1}{N} X_2 X_2'$.

REMARK 8. *For 2^m orthogonal complete or fractional factorial designs, if one set of t runs in T can be mapped to another set of t runs in T by renaming factors and/or changing the levels of factors, then the sets of observations corresponding to those two sets are equally influential w.r.t. I_1, I_2 and I_3.*

Example 3. Consider in Example 1, two pairs of runs $\begin{pmatrix} 1 & 1 & 1 & 1 \\ 0 & 0 & 0 & 0 \end{pmatrix}$ and $\begin{pmatrix} 0 & 1 & 1 & 1 \\ 1 & 0 & 0 & 0 \end{pmatrix}$. Notice that the second pair is obtained from the first pair by changing levels of the first factor. Hence by Remark 8 two sets of observations corresponding to the pairs are equally influential. Consider now the pairs of runs $\begin{pmatrix} 1 & 1 & 1 & 1 \\ 1 & 0 & 0 & 0 \end{pmatrix}$ and $\begin{pmatrix} 1 & 1 & 1 & 1 \\ 0 & 1 & 0 & 0 \end{pmatrix}$. Note the the second pair is obtained from the first pair by renaming the first factor as the second factor. Hence the corresponding pairs of observations are equally influential. In fact it can be checked that out of $\binom{16}{2} = 120$ pairs of runs in T, we can take only 4 pairs $\begin{pmatrix} 1 & 1 & 1 & 1 \\ 0 & 0 & 0 & 0 \end{pmatrix}$, $\begin{pmatrix} 1 & 1 & 1 & 1 \\ 1 & 0 & 0 & 0 \end{pmatrix}$, $\begin{pmatrix} 1 & 1 & 1 & 1 \\ 1 & 1 & 0 & 0 \end{pmatrix}$ and $\begin{pmatrix} 1 & 1 & 1 & 1 \\ 1 & 1 & 1 & 0 \end{pmatrix}$ so that these pairs can not be mapped one to the other by changing levels and/or renaming factors. The other $(120 - 4) = 116$ pairs can be obtained from these 4 pairs by the mappings. This reduces enormously the labor for comparing influence w.r.t. I_1, I_2 and I_3 of so many pairs. For these 4 pairs, the comparison of influence can be done using the Theorem 8.

REMARK 9. *For 2^m fractional factorial designs which are B-arrays of full strength and of resolution $(2d + 1)$ for an integer $d(\geq 1)$, if one set of t runs in T can be mapped to another set of t runs in T by renaming factors, then the sets of ob-*

servations corresponding to those two sets are equally influential w.r.t. I_1, I_2 and I_3.

THEOREM 10. *If one set of t runs in T can be mapped to another set of t runs in T by changing the levels of factors then the matrix M remains invariant if $X'X = DX'XD$ where the matrix D is defined in the proof of Theorem 9.*

Proof. The change of levels of factors means the postmultiplication of X_2 by the matrix D where D is a diagonal orthonormal matrix. The M matrices for the two sets of t runs are $X_2(X'X)^{-1}X_2'$ and $X_2D(X'X)^{-1}DX_2'$. We have $X_2D(X'X)^{-1}DX_2' = X_2(DX'XD)^{-1}X_2'$. Hence the Theorem 10 is true.

Example 4. Consider the Example 2. We first take two runs $(0,0,0,0)$ and $(1,1,1,1)$. Notice that here $t = 1$ and the second run is obtained from the first run by changing the levels of all factors. It can be seen that $X'X = DX'XD$. Thus the observations for two runs $(0,0,0,0)$ and $(1,1,1,1)$ are equally influential. Similarly the observations for two runs $(1,0,0,0)$ and $(0,1,1,1)$ are equally influential. Thus combining our findings in the Example 2 and this example, we observe that the observations for runs in S_0 and S_4 are equally influential. Furthermore, the observations for runs in S_1 and S_3 are also equally influential.

6. Orthogonal $2^{m_1} \times 3^{m_2}$ factorial designs. In this section we consider orthogonal arrays T which are complete or fractional factorials for $2^{m_1} \times 3^{m_2}$ factorial experiments. All elements of the first column in X are unity. The columns of X corresponding to the main effects for factors with two levels are obtained from the corresponding columns of T replacing 0 by (-1). The columns of X corresponding to the main effects for factors with three levels are obtained from the corresponding columns of T replacing 0 by $(-1,1)$, 1 by $(0,-2)$ and 2 by $(1,1)$. Notice that the first entry in pairs represents the linear effect and the second entry represents the quadratic effect. The column of X for a q-factor interaction is obtained by taking the Schur Product of the columns corresponding to q main effects. The matrix $X'X$ is a diagonal matrix but $X'X \neq NI$. Let $\varepsilon_1(F, F')$ be the diagonal element of $(X'X)^{-1}$ for F and $\varepsilon_2(\underline{t}, F)$ be the element of X_2 for $\underline{t}$ and F. Let $\underline{\beta}(i_1, \cdots, i_s)$ be the set of factorial effects in which all s factors $i_1, \cdots, i_s$ are present.

REMARK 10. For $2^{m_1} \times 3^{m_2}$ orthogonal (complete or fractional) factorial designs which are Resolution $(2d + 1)$ plans, d is an integer (≥ 1), we have

$$(10) \qquad \sum_{F \in \underline{\beta}(i_1, \cdots, i_s)} \varepsilon_2(\underline{t}, F)\varepsilon_1(F, F)\varepsilon_2(\underline{t}', F),$$

is a constant for all $\underline{t} = \underline{t}'$. Furthermore, (10) remains invariant for two pairs $(\underline{t}, \underline{t}')$ if one pair can be mapped to the other pair by renaming factors and/or changing the levels of factors.

REMARK 11. For $2^{m_1} \times 3^{m_2}$ orthogonal (complete or fractional) factorial designs which are Resolution $(2d + 1)$ plans, d is an integer (≥ 1),

94

(i) M remains invariant if one set of t runs in T can be mapped to another set of t runs in T by renaming factors and/or changing the levels of factors.

(ii) the single observations (i.e. $t = 1$) are equally influential w.r.t. I_1 and I_3

(iii) if one set of t runs in T can be mapped to another set of t runs in T by renaming and/or changing the levels of factors then the observation vectors for the two sets are equally influential w.r.t. I_1 and I_3.

Example 5. We consider a complete $2^2 \times 3$ factorial experiment under the Resolution 3 (i.e., $d = 1$) plan. Thus $N = 12$, $p = 5$, $\underline{\beta}(5 \times 1)$ and $X(12 \times 5)$. The matrix $Z(7 \times 12)$ is given below.

$$
Z = \begin{bmatrix}
1 & 1 & 1 & -1 & -1 & -1 & -1 & -1 & -1 & 1 & 1 & 1 \\
1 & 0 & -1 & 1 & 0 & -1 & -1 & 0 & 1 & -1 & 0 & 1 \\
-1 & 2 & -1 & -1 & 2 & -1 & 1 & -2 & 1 & 1 & -2 & 1 \\
1 & 0 & -1 & -1 & 0 & 1 & 1 & 0 & -1 & -1 & 0 & 1 \\
\hline
-1 & 2 & -1 & 1 & -2 & 1 & -1 & 2 & -1 & 1 & -2 & 1 \\
-1 & 0 & 1 & 1 & 0 & -1 & 1 & 0 & -1 & -1 & 0 & 1 \\
1 & -2 & 1 & -1 & 2 & -1 & -1 & 2 & -1 & 1 & -2 & 1
\end{bmatrix}
$$

The matrix Z has the property P_3 but not P_4. Notice that the rows of Z correspond to 2-factor and 3-factor interactions. It follows from Theorem 1 that the design is robust against the unavailability of any 3 observations. We now consider the pairs of runs. There are $\binom{12}{2} = 66$ such pairs. We can take only 5 pairs $\begin{pmatrix} 0 & 0 & 0 \\ 0 & 0 & 1 \end{pmatrix}$, $\begin{pmatrix} 0 & 0 & 0 \\ 0 & 1 & 1 \end{pmatrix}$, $\begin{pmatrix} 0 & 0 & 0 \\ 0 & 1 & 1 \end{pmatrix}$, $\begin{pmatrix} 0 & 0 & 0 \\ 1 & 1 & 0 \end{pmatrix}$ and $\begin{pmatrix} 0 & 0 & 0 \\ 1 & 1 & 1 \end{pmatrix}$ so that these pairs can not be mapped one to the other by changing levels and/or renaming factors. the other $(66 - 5) = 61$ can be obtained from these 5 pairs by the mappings. In fact the pairs $\begin{pmatrix} 0 & 0 & 0 \\ 0 & 0 & 1 \end{pmatrix}$ and $\begin{pmatrix} 0 & 0 & 0 \\ 1 & 1 & 1 \end{pmatrix}$ have M matrices $\frac{1}{24} \begin{bmatrix} 10 & 4 \\ 4 & 10 \end{bmatrix}$ and $\frac{1}{24} \begin{bmatrix} 10 & -4 \\ -4 & 10 \end{bmatrix}$. The observations for those pairs are equally informative w.r.t. I_1 and I_3. The M matrix for the pair $\begin{pmatrix} 0 & 0 & 0 \\ 0 & 1 & 1 \end{pmatrix}$ is a diagonal matrix and hence by Theorems 5 and 6, the corresponding observations are the least influential. The observations for the pair $\begin{pmatrix} 0 & 0 & 0 \\ 0 & 1 & 0 \end{pmatrix}$ are the most influential.

6.1. Invariance of Q. For $2^{m_1} \times 3^{m_2}$ orthogonal factorial designs, the matrix Q plays an important role when we compare influence w.r.t. I_2.

REMARK 12. For $2^{m_1} \times 3^{m_2}$ orthogonal (complete or fractional) factorial design, the matrix Q remains invariant if one set of t runs in T can be mapped to another set of t runs in T by renaming factors and/or changing the levels 0 and 1 for factors with 2 levels and/or changing the levels 0 and 2 for factors with 3 levels.

Example 6. In Example 5, we can take only 10 pairs $\begin{pmatrix} 0 & 0 & 0 \\ 0 & 0 & 1 \end{pmatrix}$, $\begin{pmatrix} 0 & 0 & 0 \\ 0 & 0 & 2 \end{pmatrix}$,

$$\begin{pmatrix} 0 & 0 & 0 \\ 0 & 1 & 0 \end{pmatrix}, \begin{pmatrix} 0 & 0 & 1 \\ 0 & 1 & 1 \end{pmatrix}, \begin{pmatrix} 0 & 0 & 0 \\ 0 & 1 & 1 \end{pmatrix}, \begin{pmatrix} 0 & 0 & 0 \\ 0 & 1 & 2 \end{pmatrix}, \begin{pmatrix} 0 & 0 & 0 \\ 1 & 1 & 0 \end{pmatrix}, \begin{pmatrix} 0 & 0 & 1 \\ 1 & 1 & 1 \end{pmatrix}, \begin{pmatrix} 0 & 0 \\ 1 & 1 \end{pmatrix}$$

and $\begin{pmatrix} 0 & 0 & 0 \\ 1 & 1 & 2 \end{pmatrix}$ so that these pairs can not be mapped one to the other. The remaining $(66 - 10) = 56$ pairs can be obtained from them by the mapping described in Remark 12. It can be seen that the set of observations for the pairs $\begin{pmatrix} 0 & 0 & 0 \\ 0 & 1 & 0 \end{pmatrix}$ is the most influential w.r.t. I_2. The set of observations for the runs $\begin{pmatrix} 0 & 0 & 1 \\ 1 & 1 & 1 \end{pmatrix}$ is the least influential w.r.t. I_2. The set of observations for $\begin{pmatrix} 0 & 0 & 0 \\ 0 & 1 & 1 \end{pmatrix}$ is very close to least influence. The sets of observations for $\begin{pmatrix} 0 & 0 & 0 \\ 0 & 0 & 1 \end{pmatrix}$ and $\begin{pmatrix} 0 & 0 & 1 \\ 0 & 1 & 1 \end{pmatrix}$ are equally influential w.r.t. I_2.

Remark 13. We note that Remarks 10, 11 and 12 are valid for 3^m factorial experiments.

Acknowledgement. The first author would like to thank Professors Dijen Ray-Chaudhuri and Willard Miller, Jr. for inviting him at the workshop and for providing excellent research atmosphere at the IMA. We would like to thank Mrs. Patricia V. Brick for her kind help in typing the manuscript using the IMA style.

REFERENCES

ANDREWS, D.F. AND HERZBERG, A.M. (1979), *The robustness and optimality of response surface designs*, J. Statist. Plann. and Inference, 3, 249–257.

BOSE, R.C. (1947), *Mathematical Theory of the symmetrical factorial design*, Sankhyā, 8, 107–166.

CHATTERJEE, S. AND HADI, A.S. (1986), *Influential Observations, high leverage points and outliers in linear regression*, Statistical Science, 3, 379–416.

CHENG, C.S. (1985), *Run orders of factorial designs*, In proceedings of the Berkeley Conference in Honor of Jerzy Neyman and Jack Kiefer, Vol. II (Lecam et. al. editors), Wadsworth, 619–633.

COOK, R.D. AND WEISBERG, S. (1982), *Residuals and influence in regression*, Chapman and Hall. New York..

GHOSH, S. (1979), *On robustness of designs against incomplete data*, Sankhyā, Pts 3 and 4, 204–208.

GHOSH, S. (1982), *Information in an observation in robust designs*, Commun. Statist. – Theor. Meth., 11 (10), 1173–1184.

GHOSH, S. AND KIPNGENO, W.A.K. (1985), *On the robustness of the optimum balanced 2^m factorial designs of resolution V* (given by Srivastava and Chopra) in the presence of outliers. J. Statist. Plann. and Inference, 11, 119–129.

KIEFER, J. (1959), *Optimum experimental designs*, J. Roy. Statist. Soc., Ser. B, 21 273–319.

MOORE, L.M. (1988), *Singular factorial designs resulting from missing pairs of design points*, J. Statist. Plann. and Inference, 19, 325–340.

PESOTAN, H. AND RAKTOE, B.L. (1988), *On invariance and randomization in factorial designs with applications to D-optimal main effect designs of the symmetrical factorial*, J. Statist. Plann. and Inference, 19, 283–298.

RAO, C.R. (1973), *Linear Statistical Inference and Its Applications*, (2nd edition) J. Wiley, New York.

RAKTOE, B.L. HEDAYAT, A. AND FEDERER, W.T. (1981), *Factorial Designs*, J. Wiley, New York.

SRIVASTAVA, J.N., RAKTOE, B.L. AND PESOTAN, H. (1976), *On invariance and randomization in fractional replication*, Ann. of Statist., 4, 423–430.

SRIVASTAVA, J.N. AND CHOPRA, D.V. (1971), *Balanced optimal 2^m fractional factorial designs of resolution $V, m \leq 6$*, Technometrics, 13, 257–269.

SRIVASTAVA, J.N. AND GHOSH, S. (1977), *Balanced 2^m factorial designs of resolution V which allow search and estimation of one extra unknown effect, $4 \leq m \leq 8$. Commun. Stat.*, A6, 141–166.

APPENDIX

In this section we present some important mathematical results used in the main body of the paper

RESULT 1. For $A(m \times n)$ and $B(n \times m)$, we have

$$|I_m \pm AB| = |I_n \pm BA|.$$

RESULT 2. The matrix M defined in Section 2 is positive semi definite.

RESULT 3. If Rank $X_2 = t$ then the matrix M is positive definite.

RESULT 4. If λ is a characteristic root of M with the characteristic vector $\underline{x}$ then $(1 - \lambda)$ is a characteristic root of $(I - M)$ with the characteristic vector $\underline{x}$. Notice that $|X_1'X_1| = |X'X| \, |I - M|$. If Rank $X_1 = p$ then $|X_1'X_1| > 0$. We also have $|X'X| > 0$. Thus $|I - M| > 0$. Furthermore $I - X(X'X)^{-1}X'$ is positive semi definite. The matrix $I - M$ is a block diagonal matrix of $I - X(X'X)^{-1}X'$. Hence $I - M$ is positive definite.

RESULT 5. If Rank $X_1 = p$ then $(I - M)$ is a positive definite matrix.

RESULT 6. $M(I - M)^{-1}M = (I - M)^{-1}M - M = M(I - M)^{-1} - M$

RESULT 7. The matrices M and $(I - M)^{-1}$ are commutative.

RESULT 8. The matrices M and $(I - M)^{-1}$ are simultaneously diagonalizable by an orthonormal matrix P, i.e., $P'MP = D_1$ and $P'(I - M)^{-1}P = D_2$, where D_1 and D_2 are diagonal matrices with diagonal elements as the characteristic roots of M and $(I - M)^{-1}$, respectively

RESULT 9. If $A = (a_{ij})$ be a $(t \times t)$ positive definite matrix then

$$|A| \leq a_{11} \cdots a_{tt}.$$

The ' $=$ ' holds if and only if $a_{ij} = 0$.

RESULT 10. If A is p.d. and $A^{-1} = (a^{ij})$, then

(a) $a^{ii} \geq a_{ii}^{-1}$ with equality if and only if $a_{ij} = 0$ for $j = 1, \cdots, i-1, i+1, \cdots, m$;
(b) $a^{ii} = a_{ii}^{-1}$ for all i implies $a_{ij} = 0, i \neq j$.

AFFINE PLANES AND PERMUTATION POLYNOMIALS

DAVID GLUCK*

Abstract. We sketch the proof of a result (obtained independently by Y. Hiramine) on polynomials over $GF(p)$ which implies that every transitive affine plane of prime order is desarguesian.

AMS(MOS) subject classifications. 51E15

Let F be a finite field of odd cardinality. We call a polynomial $f(x)$ in $F[x]$ a difference permutation polynomial if $f(x + a) - f(x)$ is a permutation polynomial for every nonzero a in F. Quadratic polynomials are clearly difference permutation polynomials. If $F = GF(p^e)$ with e odd, then $f(x) = x^{p^k+1}$ is a difference permutation polynomial if $(k, e) = 1$.

THEOREM ([3], [4]). *Let f be a difference permutation polynomial over a prime field $GF(p)$. Suppose the degree of f is less then p. Then f is a quadratic polynomial.*

The idea of the proof is to show that the graph of f in $AG(2, p)$ is closely related to an oval in $PG(2, p)$. We then apply Segre's theorem to conclude that this oval is a conic. This implies that f is a quadratic polynomial. A more detailed sketch of the proof follows.

Let ζ be a primitive pth root of 1 and let U be the circulant matrix with (i, j) entry $\zeta^{f(j-i)}/\sqrt{p}$ for $0 \le i, j \le p - 1$. The definition of difference permutation polynomial implies that U is unitary. The all ones vector is an eigenvector for U, with eigenvalue $(\zeta^{f(0)} + \cdots + \zeta^{f(p-1)})/\sqrt{p}$. Since U is unitary, we have $|\zeta^{f(0)} + \cdots + \zeta^{f(p-1)}| = \sqrt{p}$. Let S be the Gauss sum $\zeta^{0^2} + \cdots + \zeta^{(p-1)^2}$. Then $\zeta^{f(0)} + \cdots + \zeta^{f(p-1)}$ and S are both algebraic integers in $Q(\zeta)$ of absolute value $\sqrt{p}$. Since only one prime ideal of $Q(\zeta)$ lies over (p), one can show that the quotient of these two algebraic integers is a unit, which must be a root of unity.

We then have

$$\zeta^{f(0)} + \cdots + \zeta^{f(p-1)} = \pm\zeta^s(\zeta^{0^2} + \cdots + \zeta^{(p-1)^2})$$

for some integer s. Since the pth roots of 1 satisfy only one rational linear dependence relation, we can sharpen the equation above. We conclude that there is a quadratic polynomial $m(x)$ over $GF(p)$ which assumes the same values, with the same multiplicities, as $f(x)$.

Hence $f(x)$ assumes no value in $GF(p)$ more than twice. Clearly $f(x) - (ax + b)$ is also a difference permutation polynomial for a, b in $GF(p)$. Thus $f(x) - (ax + b)$ never has more than two zeros in $GF(p)$. This implies that no three points of the graph of f in $AG(2, p)$ are collinear.

*Department of Mathematics, Wayne State University, Detroit, Michigan 48202. Research partially supported by NSA.

99

One then shows that the completion in $PG(2, p)$ of this graph is an oval. By Segre's theorem, the oval is a conic, which implies that $f(x)$ is a quadratic polynomial.

Having sketched the proof of our result, we now relate it to affine planes.

A difference permutation polynomial f over a field F gives rise to an affine plane $A(f)$. The set of points of $A(f)$ is the same as that of $AG(2, F)$. The vertical lines $L(c) = \{(c, y) | y \in F\}$ are also lines of $A(f)$. The remaining lines of $A(f)$ are of the form $L(a, b) = \{(x, f(x - a) + b) | x \in F\}$ for a, b in F.

When f is quadratic, $A(f)$ is desarguesian. When $f(x) = x^{p^k + 1}$ as above, $A(f)$ is a nondesarguesian commutative semifield plane.

Now let A be an affine plane of order p with a collineation group G transitive on the affine points of A. Then a p-Sylow subgroup of G has index prime to $|A|$, and thus is also transitive on A. Hence we assume G is a p-group.

Let $H \leq G$ be the pointwise stabilizer of the line at infinity. Since translation planes of prime order are desarguesian, we may assume that $|H| \leq p$. Since G/H is isomorphic to a p-subgroup of $\mathrm{Sym}(p + 1)$, we have $|G/H| \leq p$. Thus $|H| = p$ and $|G| = p^2$.

If G is cyclic, a result of A.J. Hoffman (1952) implies that $p = 2$. Thus G is elementary abelian. By [1, 5.1.13], $A \cong A(f)$ for a difference permutation polynomial f. By our result, f is quadratic. Thus A is desarguesian.

REFERENCES

[1]   P. DEMBOWSKI, *Finite Geometries*, Springer, Berlin (1968).

[2]   P. DEMBOWSKI AND T. OSTROM, *Planes of order n with collineation groups of order n^2*, Math. Z. 103 (1968), 239–258.

[3]   D. GLUCK, *A note on permutation polynomials and finite geometries*, (to appear in Discrete Math.).

[4]   Y. HIRAMINE, *Proof of a conjecture on affine planes*, (to appear in J.C.T. (A)).

THE THEORY OF TRADE-OFF FOR t-DESIGNS

A.S. HEDAYAT†‡

Abstract. A trade for a t-design consists of two disjoint collections of blocks, T_1, T_2 such that T_1 covers every t-subset of varieties as often as T_2 does. The theory of trade-off deals with building trades and using them for the purpose of constructing t-designs based on various numbers of distinct blocks. Special attention is given to 2-designs, that is BIB designs.

O. Introduction. In the application of t-designs we may be confronted with a situation where some blocks become too costly to be selected for experimentation. For example, combining certain tasks within one block may be unacceptable to the experimenter. Suppose the available t-designs in the literature contain such blocks and by renaming we cannot dispose of these undesirable blocks. How can we alleviate this problem? The theory of trade-off can tell us how to trade undesirable blocks with those which are acceptable to the experimenter. This theory can do other things also. For example, via this theory we can, in principle, construct all nonisomorphic t-designs with repeated blocks. In this paper we present this theory and demonstrate a few of its applications.

The paper consists of seven sections. Preliminary definitions and notations are presented in Section 1. A matrix formulation of BIB designs is given in Section 2. An important family of BIB designs called *fundamental* BIB designs is identified and its usefulness in the study of BIB designs is demonstrated. It is shown that all BIB designs can be generated by integer combinations of fundamental BIB designs. These results for BIB designs can easily be extended to arbitrary t-designs. But we leave this to our readers.

Trades and the method of trade-off are formally introduced in Section 3. To convey the basic ideas and key results concerning trades in a simple manner we use 2-designs. In a later section we generalize some of the essential ideas of trades and trade-off to t-designs. Trades which appear within a design are very interesting and important. They can be used to reduce the support of the design or manipulate the frequencies of blocks within the design. We also point out two general methods for searching for such trades. These can be exploited to construct other designs from the trivial ones. Finally, we demonstrate a connection between certain trades and algebraic topology and use this connection to show an interesting way of constructing trades or excluding the existence of certain trades.

Trades for general t-designs are introduced and studied in Section 4. Apart from a few concepts there is very little overlap between Section 3 and Section 4. Therefore, the reader should not skip Section 3 because Section 4 covers only the

†Department of Mathematics, Statistics and Computer Science, University of Illinois, Chicago, P.O. Box 4348, Chicago, Illinois 60680

‡The research is sponsored by Grants AFOSR 85-0320 and AFOSR 89-0221 at University of Illinois at Chicago and by the Institute for Mathematics and its Applications, University of Minnesota, Minneapolis, MN 55455

general theory. A polynomial representation of trades is given and used to generate the basis consisting of minimal trades. Also we point out where computer algorithms for generating trades and basis for trades can be found.

The set of all distinct blocks of a design is called the support of the design. The cardinality of this set is called the support size. A question of interest is: What are the possible support sizes? How small can a support be? These questions and many other ones are dealt with in Section 5. Again, we limit ourselves to BIB designs. Most of the stated results can easily be generalized to arbitrary t-designs. We shall show the relation between trades and support sizes. Some useful bounds on the minimum support size are provided. We take our readers on a tour covering the spectrum of support sizes in Section 6.

We know we could restate many excellent results on t-designs in the literature for our study here. But the limitation of space forced us to postpone this formidable and very important task to a future project on the same topic. However, if our reader has published results directly related to this topic and we missed it, we offer our apology and request to be informed so that we do not commit the same error in our future projects on this topic.

For our novice readers we recommend a short journey on the topic of t-designs via Hedayat and Kageyama [15], Kageyama and Hedayat [26] and the excellent paper of Wilson [39].

1. Preliminaries. Let $V = \{1, 2, \ldots, v\}$ and let $v\Sigma k$ be the set of all $\binom{v}{k}$ distinct subsets of size k based on V, $2 \leq k < v$. We shall refer to the elements of V by varieties and those in $v\Sigma k$ by blocks of size k and use B_i to designate the ith block in $v\Sigma k$. Suppose D is a *collection* (multiset) of blocks of $v\Sigma k$. Then we can tag D by the frequency vector $F = (f_1, f_2, \ldots, f_{\binom{v}{k}})$ if B_i occurs $f_i \geq 0$ times in D. In the language of design of experiments D is said to be a proper incomplete block design based on v and k. In particular, if D is formed such that

$$(i) \qquad \sum_{i: a \in B_i} f_i = r \text{ for all varieties } a,$$

and

$$(ii) \qquad \sum_{i: ab \subset B_i} f_i = \lambda \text{ for all pairs of varieties } ab$$

then D is said to be a balanced incomplete block (BIB) design with parameters v, b, r, k and λ where $b = f_1 + f_2 + \cdots + f_{\binom{v}{k}}$. We then refer to vector F as a BIB vector. Customarily, such a design is designated by BIB(v, b, r, k, λ). If only b^* components of F are nonzeros, then we denote our BIB design by BIB$(v, b, r, k, \lambda | b*)$ to indicate that the design is built on precisely b^* distinct blocks. The knowledge about b^* is extremely useful to design theorists in the field of statistics. Some results in this regard will be given later. We shall refer to the set consisting of these b^* distinct blocks as the *support* of the design since the design is based on these blocks only.

Here are some very useful, albeit very difficult, questions concerning the support. Q_1. Given a set of distinct blocks, how do we check whether or not we can build a BIB design based on them? Clearly these blocks should cover all $\binom{v}{2}$ pairs of varieties. But obviously this very weak necessary condition is rarely sufficient. What else do we need to check? For example, let $v = 8$, and $k = 3$. Can we build a BIB design using the following blocks as its support?

$$123 \quad 145 \quad 167 \quad 168 \quad 178$$
$$246 \quad 257 \quad 258 \quad 347 \quad 348$$
$$356$$

Though, all $\binom{8}{2} = 28$ pairs are covered here we cannot use these blocks as the support of a BIB design. More on this later.

Q_2. How small can the cardinality (b^*) of the support be? For example, for $v = 11$, $k = 3$, can we build a BIB design based on 24 or fewer blocks?

Q_3. What is the set of admissible support sizes? For example, if $v = 7$ and $k = 3$, then is $b^* = 16$ admissible? And for each admissible value of b^* how can we find a solution with the required number of blocks?

Q_4. Given that a set of blocks can serve as a support of a BIB design, how do we build a BIB design based on these blocks? How often should each block be copied?

Before we leave this section we introduce two more terms. If the nonzero components of F are all identical then we say the design is *uniform*. A BIB design with $f_1 = f_2 = \cdots = f_{\binom{v}{k}} = m(\geq 1)$ is called a *trivial* BIB design. A BIB design with $b < \binom{v}{k}$ is said to be a *reduced* BIB design. Trivial BIB designs can be used as starting points for building reduced BIB designs, as we shall see later.

2. Fundamental BIB Designs. For a given v and k let $\mathcal{F}$ be the set of all frequency vectors associated with BIB designs. Clearly, for any fixed λ there are only finitely many BIB vectors in $\mathcal{F}$. However, if λ is free to vary, there are infinitely many vectors in $\mathcal{F}$. For the purpose of cataloging and understanding BIB designs, should we list all BIB vectors in $\mathcal{F}$? Clearly the answer is no. We believe it will be enough to list those BIB vectors which can be used to generate the remaining ones. These special designs will be called *fundamental* BIB *designs*. A formal definition and some useful results will follow.

Let P_2 be the pair inclusion matrix associated with $v\Sigma k$. That is, P_2 is a matrix with $\binom{v}{2}$ rows and $\binom{v}{k}$ columns. The rows of P_2 are indexed by the elements of $v\Sigma 2$ and its columns are indexed by the elements of $v\Sigma k$. The (i, j) entry of P_2 is 1 if the ith element of $v\Sigma 2$ is contained in the jth element of $v\Sigma k$. Otherwise, this entry is 0. Throughout we assume that the elements in $v\Sigma 2$ and in $v\Sigma k$ are both lexicographically ordered. We mention that P_2 is a full row rank matrix.

Shortly, we will give a basic method for checking whether a given frequency vector is a BIB vector. Another theoretically useful method is given in Proposition 2.1. In the sequel we shall adopt the following notation concerning vectors. If $G = (g_1, \ldots, g_n)'$ and $H = (h_1, \ldots, h_n)'$ are two vectors, then we write $H \geq G$ if $h_i \geq g_i$ for all $i = 1, \ldots, n$. However, we write $H > G$ if $h_i \geq g_i$ for all i and $h_j > g_j$ for some j.

103

By inspection, it is easy to verify the following result.

PROPOSITION 2.1. *The frequency vector F is a BIB vector if and only if*

$$(2.1) \qquad\qquad P_2 F = \lambda \mathbf{1}$$

for some positive integer λ.

Thus the problem of constructing BIB designs based on v, k and λ is precisely the problem of finding all nonnegative integral solutions, F, to the equation $P_2 F = \lambda \mathbf{1}$. This observation can be rephrased in the language of mathematical programming. For each fixed value of λ, Proposition 2.1 says that each feasible integer solution of the system

$$(2.2) \qquad\qquad \begin{aligned} P_2 F &= \lambda \mathbf{1} \\ F &\geq 0 \end{aligned}$$

corresponds to the frequency vector of a BIB(v, b, r, k, λ) design. The set of all feasible rational solutions to this system corresponds to the set of BIB vectors based on v and k after an appropriate scaling. Now there is always at least one feasible rational solution to (2.2), namely the rescaled BIB vector associated with the trivial BIB design. This can be used to conclude that for a given v and k there is at least one reduced BIB design. This follows from the well-known fact that whenever there is a feasible solution to a system, then there is a basic feasible solution.

All feasible solutions are convex combinations of the basic feasible solutions, so the classification of all BIB designs based on v and k reduces to finding all basic feasible solutions to (2.2); that is, to finding all of the vertices of the polytope defined by (2.2).

Remark 2.1. When applying BIB designs with repeated blocks in practice, we are not, of course, interested in finding all solutions to (2.2). Rather, we seek a solution which excludes, or at least minimizes the occurrence of certain blocks. We may find such a design by introducing an objective function which assigns positive cost to the blocks which we wish to avoid and zero cost to the other blocks. The standard linear programming algorithms for minimizing this objective function will then produce the desired design. If we are limited to a certain number of blocks we then have the integer programming problem of minimizing the objective function over the feasible integer solutions to (2.2).

What kind of a geometrical creature is $\mathcal{F}$? Some of what we said before can be used to answer this question. We note that if $F_1, F_2, \ldots$ are in $\mathcal{F}$ and if $c_1, c_2, \ldots$ are nonnegative integers then $F = c_1 F_1 + c_2 F_2 + \ldots$ is also in $\mathcal{F}$. Therefore we have:

PROPOSITION 2.2. *The set of all BIB vectors for a given v and k forms a positive integer cone.*

$\mathcal{F}$ is also closed under another useful operation.

104

PROPOSITION 2.3. *If F_1 and F_2 are two BIB vectors in $\mathcal{F}$ with $F_2 > F_1$, then $F = F_2 - F_1$ is also a BIB vector.*

Components of F are not at total liberty to vary. Indeed, by the inequality of Mann [36], $f_j \leq \sum_i f_i/v$, $j = 1, 2, \ldots, \binom{v}{k}$.

As we have already mentioned, when λ is free to vary, there are infinitely many BIB vectors in $\mathcal{F}$. Clearly we are not going to bother about all these BIB vectors. We already know that some of these designs are linear combinations of others. Thus, it is natural to be concerned only with the smallest subset of BIB vectors in $\mathcal{F}$ which can be used to generate the remaining ones. These latter designs deserve to be identified and labeled. To be precise we make the following definition.

DEFINITION 2.1. A BIB design F in $\mathcal{F}$ is said to be a *fundamental* BIB design if there does not exist any BIB design F_1 such that $F > F_1$.

How many fundamental BIB designs are there in $\mathcal{F}$? This can be answered by relating the concept of a fundamental BIB design to that of an irreducible solution in nonnegative integers to a system of homogeneous linear equations. Consider the set of nonnegative integer solutions to the set of homogeneous linear equations

$$(2.3) \qquad AX = 0$$

where A is an $m \times n$ matrix of integers. A solution X_1 to (2.3) is called *irreducible* if for no other such solution, X_2, $X_1 > X_2$. It is well known that there are only finitely many irreducible solutions to (2.3) [see, for example, Grace and Young [8]]. We observe that, if F_1 and F_2 are two BIB vectors in $\mathcal{F}$ with $F_1 < F_2$ then $\lambda_1 < \lambda_2$. Therefore, each fundamental BIB design correspond to an irreducible solution to the system

$$(2.4) \qquad \begin{bmatrix} P & \vdots & -1 \end{bmatrix} \begin{bmatrix} F \\ \cdots \\ \lambda \end{bmatrix} = 0.$$

Thus, we conclude that:

THEOREM 2.1. *For given v and k there are only finitely many fundamental BIB designs.*

What is fundamental about fundamental BIB designs? This is answered in Theorem 2.2.

THEOREM 2.2. *Let $F_1^*, F_2^*, \ldots, F_n^*$ be the frequency vectors of all fundamental BIB designs based on v and k. Then, for any BIB design with frequency vector F there exist nonnegative integers $a_1, a_2, \ldots, a_n$ such that*

$$(2.5) \qquad F = a_1 F_1^* + a_2 F^* + \cdots + a_n F_n^*.$$

Proof. Suppose F is not a fundamental BIB design. Then we know that there is a BIB vector F_1 in $\mathcal{F}$ with $F_1 < F$. Thus, by Proposition 2.3, $F_2 = F - F_1$ is also a BIB vector in $\mathcal{F}$. Clearly, the number of blocks in F_1 and F_2 are less than the number of blocks in F. However, F is a nonnegative linear combinations of F_1 and F_2, namely

$$F = F_1 + F_2.$$

Now if both F_1 and F_2 are fundamental BIB designs then we are done. Otherwise, suppose F_1 is not a fundamental BIB design. We shall now work on F_1 and split it into two BIB vectors as we did for F. We continue this splitting process till all component BIB vectors become fundamental. □

Remark 2.2. If b for any BIB vector F in $\mathcal{F}$ is minimal then F is a fundamental design. If desired, this observation could be used to decide when the splitting process in the proof of Theorem 2.2 can be terminated.

We note that every fundamental BIB design is a vertex of the polytope defined by (2.2) for some value of λ. However, the converse does not hold. For example, if F_1 is a fundamental BIB design with parameters v, b, r, k, λ then $2F_1$ will still be a vertex for the polytope

$$P_2 F = (2\lambda)\mathbf{1}$$
$$F \geq 0.$$

3. Trades and the Method of Trade-off. Here is a little bit of history about the topic of trades and trade-off methodology. In one of my statistical consulting experiences in the early '60s I was asked an intriguing question by a practitioner. The problem was this. He wanted to run an experiment based on a BIB design with $v = 8$ and $k = 3$. However, he did not want to perform any experiment based on the block 578. The combination was unacceptable to him. He wanted me to devise a procedure by which he could replace the block 578 by one (or more if needed) other block and yet have a BIB design. Clearly, 578 could not be replaced by a single block. But could it be replaced by two or more blocks? Though, I was unable to answer the latter question then, it lead me and my students and several of my colleagues to introduce and study trades on designs. This will now be defined formally in two different ways.

Suppose that the BIB design D contains a set of (not necessarily distinct) blocks T_1. Suppose also that there exists another set of blocks, T_2, based on the same v and k such that $T_1 \cap T_2 = \phi$ and both sets contain the same pairs of varieties the same number of times. Clearly, if we remove T_1 from D and replace it by T_2, then the new design will still be a BIB design with the same parameters as in D, but with possibly a different support or support size.

Since trading T_1 for T_2 did not change the basic properties of our design as a BIB we call (T_1, T_2) a trade and the process of replacing T_1 by T_2 a trade-off. However, as we shall see shortly, it will be to our advantage to define a trade independent of a particular BIB at hand. We have two equivalent definitions of a trade. One is combinatorial in nature and the other is an algebraic definition. Each one has its own usefulness in the theory and applications of trades and trade-off.

106

DEFINITION 3.1. Let T_1 and T_2 be two disjoint collections of m blocks from $v \sum k$. We say (T_1, T_2) forms a trade if for every pair of varieties (member of $v\Sigma 2$) the number of blocks containing this pair is the same in both T_1 and T_2. Lack of appearance is allowed. We refer to such a trade as a $(v, k, 2)$ trade of *volume* m. A trade is called a *simple* trade if it has no repeated blocks.

We emphasize that we used the term collection in our definition of a trade to indicate that repeated blocks are allowed in a trade as illustrated in Example 3.2. The number 2 in a $(v, k, 2)$ trade is used to remind us that we are concerned about covering pairs of varieties. In Section 4 we generalize this concept for covering t-tuples. The covering property of pairs in a $(v, k, 2)$ trade forces T_1 and T_2 to have the same number of blocks. This number, which we refer to as the volume of the trade is an important characteristic of the trade. The numbers $v, k, 2$ and m are referred to as the parameters of the trade.

EXAMPLE 3.1. Let $v = 6$, $k = 3$, then

T_1	T_2
146	124
125	156
234	235
356	346

is a $(6, 3, 2)$ trade of volume 4. Note that in this trade not every pair is covered.

EXAMPLE 3.2. Let $v = 7$, $k = 3$, then

T_1		T_2	
123	123	124	124
247	247	237	237
145	146	135	136
357	367	457	467

is a $(7, 3, 2)$ trade of volume 8 with repeated blocks. Note that if we discard the duplicated blocks, the resulting structure is no longer a trade.

An immediate question is this: when and how can we construct trades? Before answering this question we shall give a linear algebraic version of a trade.

DEFINITION 3.1'. An integer vector T of dimension $\binom{v}{k}$ is called a $(v, k, 2)$ trade if $P_2 T = 0$. The sum of all positive entries (m) in a trade is called its *volume*. The numbers $v, k, 2$ and m are called the parameters of the trade (see Section 4 for a generalization). We shall refer to $T = 0$ as the void trade.

The equivalence of the above two definitions of a trade based on a given v and k can be demonstrated as follows. Let (T_1, T_2) be a $(v, k, 2)$ trade of volume m in the sense of Definition 3.1. Recall that T_1 and T_2 are in $v\Sigma k$ which is ordered. Now form a vector T of dimension $\binom{v}{k}$. Make a one-to-one correspondence between

107

the coordinates of T and the blocks in $v\Sigma k$. Let the entries of T corresponding to distinct blocks in T_1 be their frequencies in T_1. Similarly, for T_2 except that we shall negate these frequencies. Let all other entries of T be zero. Clearly then, T is a $(v, k, 2)$ trade of volume m as defined in Definition 3.1'. Conversely if T is a $(v, k, 2)$ trade of volume m in the sense of Definition 3.1', then form T_1 by taking as many copies of the blocks of $v\Sigma k$ as the positive entries of T dictate. T_2 is similarly formed by the negative components of T (ignore the negative signs). Then (T_1, T_2) is a trade of volume m in the sense of Definition 3.1.

Remark 3.1. Which representation of a trade should we use? We use the (T_1, T_2) approach when we actually want to present a trade. We use the vector notation when we want to study their algebraic properties.

Since P_2 has rank $\binom{v}{2}$, there are precisely $\binom{v}{k} - \binom{v}{2}$ independent $(v, k, 2)$ trades which form a basis of the kernel of P_2. Note that if F_1 and F_2 are two BIB vectors based on v, k and λ then $F_1 - F_2$ is a $(v, k, 2)$ trade. In Section 4 we give a method for producing a basis for the set of trades.

It is useful to note that if (T_1, T_2) is a $(v, k, 2)$ trade of volume m, then it is also a $(v', k, 2)$ trade of volume m for $v' > v$. In vector notation it is enough by inserting into T zero corresponding to the blocks of $v'\Sigma k$ which are not in $v\Sigma k$. Also, if (T_1, T_2) is a $(v, k, 2)$ trade of volume m and (T_1', T_2') is a $(v, k, 2)$ trade of volume n, then for any two nonnegative integers a and b, (T_1^*, T_2^*) is a $(v, k, 2)$ trade, where T_i^* is formed by taking a copies of T_i and b copies of T_i', $i = 1, 2$. This is much neater in vector notation. If T is a $(v, k, 2)$ trade of volume m and T' a $(v, k, 2)$ trade of volume n, then $aT + bT'$ is a $(v, k, 2)$ trade with a volume at most $am + bn$. However, note that in vector notation a and b are allowed to be negative integers.

The problem of constructing trades is a very difficult one. Some useful results are available in the literature. Selected results will be mentioned throughout the papers.

THEOREM 3.1. *For every integer i, there exists a $(v, 3, 2)$ trade of volume i if and only if, $i \neq 1, 2, 3, 5$.*

For volumes $1, 2, 3$ the result is self evident. For the nonexistence of volume 5 and the existence of the remaining volumes we refer the reader to Hedayat and Li [20] or Hedayat and Li [21]. In Section 3.4 we shall point out the correspondence between $(v, 3, 2)$ trades and compact surfaces without boundaries and show that we can generate trades by Eulerian triangulation of such surfaces.

Here is another useful result.

THEOREM 3.2. *Every $(v, 3, 2)$ trade is an integer combination of $(v, 3, 2)$ trades of volume 4.*

For example, to obtain the $(7, 3, 2)$ trade of volume 8 in Example 3.2 we can combine one copy of each of the following $(6,3,2)$ trades of volume 4.

T_1	T_2		T_1'	T_2'
123	124	,	123	124
145	135		247	237
247	237		146	136
357	457		367	467

The main usefulness of trades for the construction of BIB designs with various supports and support sizes is due to the following *mixing* lemma which is easy to establish.

LEMMA 3.1. *Let F be a frequency vector of a BIB design based on v and k and T a $(v, k, 2)$ trade. Then for all positive integers m and n, $mF + nT$ is a BIB design if and only if $mF + nT > 0$. The condition that $f_i > 0$ whenever $t_i < 0$ is necessary and sufficient for the existence of such m and n.*

Also, it is clear that any BIB design sharing the same parameters with F can be written in the form $F + T$ for some trade T. Therefore, in order to search for all BIB designs with the same parameters as F, it suffices to investigate the trades.

3.1. Trade on a Design. Trades for which the added blocks are already present in the support of a BIB design play an important role in the theory of BIB designs. We will say that $T = (t_1, t_2, \ldots, t_{\binom{v}{k}})'$ is a *trade on the design D* if $t_i = 0$ for all blocks not in the support of D and the frequencies of the blocks to be deleted do not exceed the corresponding frequencies in D.

Trades on the design D may be characterized as follows: remove from the P_2-matrix all columns corresponding to blocks absent from D^*, the support of D, and call the resulting matrix P_2^*. Then each vector T^* of integers satisfying $P_2^* T^* = 0$ corresponds to a trade T on the design D. To construct T from T^*, let $t_i = 0$ if the ith block is absent from D^*, and $t_i = t_j^*$ if the ith block in $v \Sigma k$ corresponds to the jth column of P_2^*. So sets of trades in general, correspond to the integer valued vectors in the null space of a matrix.

An alternative version of the following theorem proved in Foody and Hedayat [4] provides an application of trades on a design for the purpose of reducing the support size.

THEOREM 3.3. *Let F be a frequency vector of a BIB design D with support D^*. If T is a trade on D, then there exist positive integers m and n such that $mF + nT$ is a frequency vector of a BIB design whose support is properly contained in D^*.*

Proof. By Lemma 3.1, it is enough to identify a pair of positive integers m and n such that $mF + nT > 0$ and $mF + nT$ has at least one extra coordinate with zero entry than F. Since T is a trade on D, $mF + nT > 0$ can not have a block which is not in D^*. Our choice of m and n is any pair of positive integers which satisfy $mf_j + nt_j = 0$ where

$$t_j/f_j = \min\{t_i/f_i, f_i \neq 0\}.$$

For this pair of integers $mF + nT > 0$ and the jth block of $v\Sigma k$ is being deleted from the support of the new design. This follows from

$$mf_i + nt_i \geq f_i f_j^{-1}(mf_j + nt_j) = 0, i = 1, 2, \ldots, \binom{v}{k}$$

and that some of the t_i's are positive. □

3.2. Discovering Trades on a Design. How do we check whether or not there is a trade on a given design? Based on what we have learned so far we can recommend two methods.

Method 1. Suppose we are given a BIB design D with support D^*. We go to the pair inclusion matrix P_2 and identify all columns which are generated by blocks in D^*. If these columns are dependent, then there is a trade on D.

Method 2. Suppose we are given a BIB design D_1 with support D_1^*. If we can identify a BIB design D_2 with support D_2^* such that $D_2^* \subset D_1^*$, then there is a trade on D_1.

The description for Method 1 follows from Theorem 3.3. A direct proof of it can be found in Foody and Hedayat [4]. Here we give a constructive proof for Method 2. Let F_1 and F_2 be the frequency vectors of D_1 and D_2 respectively. Then $P_2 F_1 = \lambda_1 \mathbf{1}$ and $P_2 F_2 = \lambda_2 \mathbf{1}$, and there exist positive integers m and n such that $m\lambda_1 - n\lambda_2 = 0$. Thus $P_2(mF_1 - nF_2) = 0$, and $mF_1 - nF_2 \neq 0$, since for some i, $f_{1i} > 0$ but $f_{2i} = 0$. Consequently, $mF_1 - nF_2$ is a trade. And since $D_2^* \subset D_1^*$, it is a trade on D_1. Several techniques for producing BIB designs whose support is contained within a given BIB designs are given in Foody and Hedayat [4].

3.3. Trade-Off on Trivial Designs. We recall that the pair inclusion matrix P_2 is not a full column rank matrix when $k > 2$. The $\binom{v}{k}$ columns of P_2 represent the support of the trivial design based on v and k. Thus, by Method 1 there is a trade on the trivial design, that is, $P_2 T = 0$ has a nonzero rational solution. We can apply this trade to a multiple of the trivial design to produce a new design, D_1, as in Theorem 3.3, with a smaller support. Now we remove from P_2 the columns corresponding to the blocks absent from D_1^*, the support of D_1, to produce P_2^*. We then find a solution to $P_2^* T = 0$ and continue as above. This process will ultimately produce a design whose support cannot be reduced. Several catalogs of designs produced in this way, by a computer program, are available in Statistical Laboratory at the University of Illinois at Chicago.

For those who are interested in nonisomorphic BIB designs we would like to point out that designs with different support sizes based on the same v and k are nonisomorphic. Therefore, by the above procedure we can easily produce lots of (theoretically all) nonisomorphic BIB designs.

Before passing to the next section let us apply trades listed in Examples 3.1 and 3.2 to the trivial BIB design with $v = 8$ and $k = 3$. Note that for $v = 8$ and $k = 3$

110

there is no reduced BIB design. If we replace the 4 blocks in T_1 by the 4 blocks in T_2 in Example 3.1 we obtain a BIB(8, 56, 21, 3, 6|52). To do a trade-off based on the trade in Example 3.2 we need to take two copies of our design first since some blocks in the trade are duplicated. Then, upon removing T_1 and replacing it by T_2 we obtain a BIB(8, 112, 41, 3, 12|54). This latter design has the minimum number of blocks if we insist on support size 54 (see Theorem 3.1). By the way, this provides a solution to the consulting problem mentioned in the beginning of Section 3. Clearly, the trade in Example 3.1 can be applied to any trivial BIB design based on $v \geq 6$ and $k = 3$ to reduce its support size from $\binom{v}{3}$ to $\binom{v}{3} - 4$. By renaming the varieties in this trade we can reapply it again and again to reduce the support size much further. In many cases we may obtain reduced BIB designs in the process. Constantine and Hedayat [3] have used this approach to produce BIB designs with a block appearing the maximum number of times. Such BIB designs could be useful in controlled sampling as explained in Hedayat [11].

3.4. The Topology of $(v, 3, 2)$ Trades. Given a $(v, 3, 2)$ trade (T_1, T_2), we construct a compact surface without boundary as follows. First we create two collections of 2-simplexes (triangles) with their vertices labeled by elements of V. The 2-simplexis related to T_1 will be called the *negative triangles* and those related to T_2 will be called the *positive triangles*. For every block xyz in T_1, there corresponds a negative triangle with vertices labelled by x, y, and z. If there are $m > 1$ copies of xyz in T_1, then there are m copies of such a triangle. Similarly, for every block in T_2, there corresponds a positive triangle. So, every pair xy appears on the same number of triangles in both collections. Thus, there exists a one-to-one matching between the edges of positive triangles and the edges of negative triangles so that every matched pair shares the same two labels. When we identify every matched pair of edges in the natural way, we obtain a compact surface without boundary. Here we emphasize the possible *nonuniqueness of the matching*. Different matchings may lead to different geometric configurations. See Example 3.5 below.

Example 3.3. The $(6, 3, 2)$ trade in Example 3.1 is represented by the diamond-shaped topological sphere given in Fig. 1. Here, in the picture the shaded regions are positive triangles.

In general, a $(v, 3, 2)$ trade gives rise to a compact surface that is partitioned into positive triangles and negative triangles with the following two properties.

(1) Any two positive triangles can not intersect each other except possibly at their vertices. Neither can any two negative triangles.

(2) The intersection of a positive triangle with a negative triangle is vacuum, or one vertex, or two vertices, or an edge.

We shall refer to such a partition of surfaces, with or without boundary, as an *Eulerian triangulation*, although it is not quite a triangulation in the usual sense of algebraic topology. The edges of the triangles form an Eulerian graph on the surface, that is, a graph such that the degree (valency) of every vertex is an even integer. Also no vertex can have degree equal to two, because then there would be two triangles sharing two common edges.

111

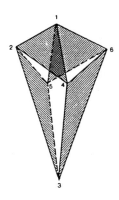

Figure 1

Example 3.4. The $(8, 3, 2)$ trade of volume 6

T_1	T_2
134, 156	138, 145
178, 238	167, 234
245, 267	256, 278

is obtained by triangulating a sphere as shown in Fig. 2.

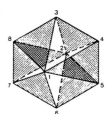

Figure 2

Example 3.5. The $(6, 3, 2)$ trade of volume 6

T_1	T_2
134, 146	124, 145
125, 236	136, 235
245, 356	256, 346

can be obtained by either Eulerian triangulation of a torus or the Klein bottle as shown in Fig. 3.

Using the correspondence between $(v, 3, 2)$ trades and the Eulerian triangulation of compact surfaces Hedayat and Li [21] gave a topological proof for the nonexistence of $(v, 3, 2)$ trades of volume 5 (see also Theorem 3.1) and the fact that every $(v, 3, 2)$

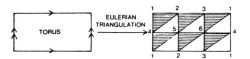 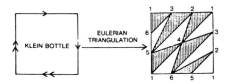

Figure 3

trade is a linear combination of trades of volume 4. In an algebraic setting and using a different language, Graver and Jurkat [10] proved that every $(v, k, 2)$ trade is a linear combination of trades of volume 4, $k \geq 3$.

In Section 4 we shall introduce and study trades which can be applied to t-designs, $t \geq 2$.

4. Trades for t-Designs.

In Section 3 we introduced and studied the notion of trades for BIB designs, that is 2-designs. We demonstrated the usefulness of this concept and associated methodologies for producing BIB designs with various support sizes. The block definition and its corresponding vector version of a trade for 2-designs can be naturally generalized to arbitrary t-designs. This shall be done in this section. Some well known and others not so well known results concerning such trades will be presented below.

DEFINITION 4.1. A (v, k, t) trade of volume m consists of two disjoint collections T_1 and T_2, each of m blocks, such that for every element of $v\Sigma t$ the number of blocks containing this element is the same in both T_1 and T_2. When $m = 0$, the trade is said to be void.

Throughout, we use the notation t - (v, k, λ) when we are referring to a block design based on $v\Sigma k$ in which every member of $v\Sigma t$ is contained in precisely λ blocks of the design, $t \geq 2$. Thus a 2 - (v, k, λ) design is simply a $\mathrm{BIB}(v, b, r, k, \lambda)$, where $b = rv/k$ and $r = \lambda(v - 1)/(k - 1)$. If the underlying parameters of the design is clear from the context or not important we will simply use the expression t-design.

We note that the definitions of t-designs and (v, k, t) trades allow repeated blocks. Moreover, a t-design is also a t'-design and a (v, k, t) trade is also a (v, k, t') trade for all t' with $0 < t' < t$. In addition, a (v, k, t) trade can serve as a (v', k, t) trade with $v' > v$. In a (v, k, t) trade, both collections of blocks must cover the same set of varieties. This set of varieties shall be called the *foundation* of the trade.

A vector version of a (v, k, t) trade can be given as follows. Let P_t be a matrix with $\binom{v}{t}$ rows and $\binom{v}{k}$ columns. As before, the elements of $v\Sigma t$ and $v\Sigma k$ are lexicographically ordered. Index the rows and the columns of P_t by the elements of $v\Sigma t$ and $v\Sigma k$ respectively. Insert 1 in the (i, j) entry of P_t if the ith element of $v\Sigma t$ is contained in the jth element of $v\Sigma k$; otherwise insert 0 in this entry. This matrix has rank $\binom{v}{t}$ [see for example, Foody and Hedayat [4]]. Now we may define

113

a (v, k, t) trade in the following way. A (v, k, t) trade is a nonzero integer vector T such that $P_t T = 0$. A parallel argument as in Section 3, for $(v, k, 2)$ trades, can be used to show that this definition and the one given in Definition 4.1 are identical, that is if (T_1, T_2) is a (v, k, t) trade, then from it we can construct a nonzero integer vector T such that $P_t T = 0$. Conversely, from any nonzero integer vector T with $P_t T = 0$ we can build two sets of blocks T_1 (from the negative entries of T) and T_2 (from the positive entries of T) so that (T_1, T_2) is a (v, k, t) trade.

In exhibiting (v, k, t) trades, it will be much more informative if we use its block definition. Indeed, in most situations it will be almost impossible to print their vector counterparts. However, for understanding the algebraic structure of (v, k, t) trades we will gain considerably if we work with their vector counterparts.

Example 4.1. Let $v = 8$, $k = 3$, then (T_1, T_2) with

T_1		T_2	
1357	2358	1358	2357
1368	2367	1367	2368
1458	2457	1457	2458
1467	2468	1468	2467

is a $(8, 4, 3)$ trade of volume 8 and foundation 8. Recall that this trade is also a $(v, 4, 3)$ trade with $v \geq 8$.

As in the case of 2-designs we can similarly represent t-designs by nonnegative integer vectors of dimension $v \Sigma k$. Conversely, a nonnegative integer vector F represents a t-design if $P_t F = \lambda \mathbf{1}$ for some positive integer λ. In terms of the vector representation, the relationship among t-designs and (v, k, t) trades can be summarized as:

1. If F_1 and F_2 are two t-designs based on the same v, k and λ then $F_1 - F_2$ is a (v, k, t) trade.

2. If F is a t-design based on v and k, and T is a (v, k, t) trade, then $F + T$ is a t-design if and only if $F + T$ has nonnegative components.

3. Any t - (v, k, λ) design differs from a given t - (v, k, λ') design by a trade.

4. If T_1 and T_2 are two (v, k, t) trades, then $T_1 + T_2$ and $T_1 - T_2$ are again (v, k, t) trades. Indeed, it is easily seen that the set of all (v, k, t) trades is a Z-module with dimension $\binom{v}{k} - \binom{v}{t}$.

Thus, the more we know about trades the better we will understand the structure of t-designs. In her Ph.D. dissertation Hwang [23], later formally published in Hwang [24], investigated the fundamental structure of (v, k, t) trades. Among other results she established the following results which we compile in one major theorem.

THEOREM 4.1. *For the family of (v, k, t) trades,*

   (i) *The minimum foundation size of a nonvoid trade is $k + t + 1$.*

   (ii) *For $v \geq k + t + 1$, the minimum volume of a nonvoid trade is 2^t.*

   (iii) *The nonvoid trades with the minimum foundation size $k+t+1$ and minimum volume 2^t, exist and have a unique structure.*

114

(iv) *There is no trade of volume* $2^t + 1$.

Result (iv) in Theorem 4.1 has been generalized by Khosrovshahi [27]. We also remark that a topological proof of the special case of (iv) with $k = 3$, $t = 2$ has appeared in Hedayat and Li [21]. A year after Hwang wrote her Ph.D. dissertation, Frankl and Pach [6] gave an independent and alternative proof of result (ii) in Theorem 4.1.

Result (iii) in Theorem 4.1 leads to the following definition.

DEFINITION 4.2. A (v, k, t) trade is called a minimal trade if its foundation size is $k + t + 1$ and its volume is 2^t.

Thus the $(8, 4, 3)$ trade listed in Example 4.1 is a minimal trade.

Theorem 3.2 for $(v, k, 2)$ trades can be generalized as follows.

THEOREM 4.2. *For* $v \geq k + t + 1$, *every* (v, k, t) *trade is an integer combination of minimal* (v, k, t) *trades.*

The family of (v, k, t) trades form a Z-module if we use their vector representations. A generating system for this Z-module based on a special construction called (t, k)-pods was obtained by Graver and Jurkat [10]. Within this algebraic setting Graver and Jurkat gave a proof of Theorem 4.2 (watch for different terminology and different notation). The generating system of Graver and Jurkat was reproduced later by Graham, Li and Li [9] in terms of homogeneous polynomials in a much more explicit and usable form. The following subsection will be devoted to this interesting result of Graham, Li and Li. The generators produced by these authors are minimal trades and thus can be used to generate all other trades.

As for BIB designs we can similarly define the concept of fundamental t-designs, trades on a t-design, etc. It is not surprising that all the results we mentioned for BIB designs can be restated for general t-designs. In particular, the counterpart of Theorem 3.3 for t-designs can be used to produce all possible t-designs with all possible support sizes. To save space we omit all these rephrasings.

Before leaving this topic we record a couple of new developments. Khosrovshahi [27] introduced an invariant of t-designs for testing design isomorphism called the *tradability index*. Among other interesting results the sensitivity of this invariant is discussed by this author. In another direction Singhi and Shrikhande [38] studied distinct t-designs. If F_1 and F_2 are two t - (v, k, λ) designs, then we say F_1 and F_2 are *distinct* if $F_1 \neq F_2$. Note that two distinct t - (v, k, λ) designs could be isomorphic in the usual sense. We may ask the following purely curious algebraic question. How many distinct t - (v, k, λ) designs are there? Singhi and Shrikhande [38] showed that as a function of λ, the number of distinct t - (v, k, λ) designs is a quasi-polynomial in λ, that is there are an integer m and polynomials $P_1, P_2, \ldots, P_m$ such that this number equals $P_i(\lambda)$ if $i \equiv \lambda \pmod{m}$. They also obtained some reciprocity relations for the numbers of distinct t - (v, k, λ) designs, which are analogous to Dehn Sommerville equations for a convex polytope.

4.1. A Basis for (v, k, t) Trades. As we mentioned before the set of all (v, k, t) trades form a Z-module of dimension $\binom{v}{k} - \binom{v}{t}$. By Theorem 4.2, all (v, k, t)

115

trades are integer combinations of minimal (v, k, t) trades. Consequently, it would be highly desirable to exhibit a basis for the Z-module consisting of minimal trades only. We shall present below one such basis. This interesting basis is a by product of the results of Graver and Jurkat [10] and Graham, Li, and Li [9] as we explained briefly before.

To avoid triviality, we shall assume that $v \geq k + t + 1$ and $k \geq t + 1$. To present a basis we will first introduce a polynomial that generates a minimal (v, k, t) trade. Then we give $\binom{v}{k} - \binom{v}{t}$ permutations which induce a basis after being applied to the given minimal trade. Here is the system. Consider the polynomial

$$(4.1) \quad \phi(x_1, x_2, \ldots, x_v) = (x_1 - x_2)(x_3 - x_4) \ldots (x_{2t+1} - x_{2t+2})x_{2t+3} \cdots x_{k+t+1}.$$

If we multiply the factors out and identify each x_i with i, the ith element in V, we shall obtain a (v, k, t) trade by taking the positive terms and negative terms separately. This trade will be denoted by $T_{\phi, v, k, t}$. For example, let $v = 8$, $k = 4$ and $t = 2$, then since $k + t + 1 = 4 + 2 + 1 = 7$, we obtain

$$\phi(x_1, x_2, \ldots, x_8) = (x_1 - x_2)(x_3 - x_4)(x_5 - x_6)x_7$$
$$= x_1 x_3 x_5 x_7 + x_2 x_4 x_5 x_7 + x_2 x_3 x_6 x_7 + x_1 x_4 x_6 x_7$$
$$- x_2 x_3 x_5 x_7 - x_1 x_4 x_5 x_7 - x_1 x_3 x_6 x_7 - x_2 x_4 x_6 x_7.$$

Thus by identifying x_i with i we shall obtain the following minimal $(8, 4, 2)$ trade.

T_1	T_2
1357	2357
2457	1457
2367	1367
1467	2467

To obtain the remaining independent minimal trades in the basis, we shall relabel the varieties in the trade generated by $T_{\phi, v, k, t}$ according to specific permutations on our v varieties. To do this let $T_{\phi, v, k, t}^{\sigma}$ be two sets of blocks generated by $T_{\phi, v, k, t}$ and relabeled according to permutation σ. Then, Graham, Li and Li [9] showed that if σ satisfies the following six conditions then $T_{\phi, v, k, t}^{\sigma}$ shall be another (v, k, t) trade which is independent of the trade $T_{\phi, v, k, t}$.

(1) $\sigma(1) < \sigma(3) < \cdots < \sigma(2t + 1)$;

(2) $\sigma(2) < \sigma(4) < \cdots < \sigma(2t + 2)$;

(3) $\sigma(2i - 1) < \sigma(2i), 1 \leq i \leq t + 1$;

(4) $\sigma(2t + 1) < \sigma(2t + 3) < \sigma(2t + 4) < \cdots < \sigma(k + t + 1)$;

(5) $\sigma(2t + 1) < \sigma(k + t + 2) < \sigma(k + t + 3) < \cdots < \sigma(v)$;

(6) if $2t + 3 \leq i \leq k + t + 1 < j \leq v$ and $\sigma(i) < \sigma(2t + 2)$ then $\sigma(i) < \sigma(j)$.

Among $v!$ permutations there are precisely $\binom{v}{k} - \binom{v}{t}$ permutations which satisfy these six conditions. By applying these permutations to $T_{\phi,v,k,t}$ we shall obtain the required basis for our (v,k,t) trades.

Clearly, it is not easy to exhibit these $\binom{v}{k} - \binom{v}{t}$ permutations. Hedayat and Hwang [12] presented a computer algorithm for identifying these special permutations. In Table 4.1 we present a basis for $(8,4,3)$ trades produced by their algorithm.

Khosrovshahi and Mahmoodian [30] followed a completely different approach and produced a simple linear algebraic algorithm for generating a basis for (v,k,t) trades. However, their generated basis may not consist of minimal trades. The computer algorithm of Khosrovshahi and Mahmoodian seems to be highly efficient. In collaboration with their graduate students and colleagues these authors have produced highly interesting computer softwares for trade-off methodology. In this list the paper by Khosrovshahi and Ajoodani-Namini [28] is highly interesting. It provides an ingenious and powerful algorithm for producing a family of bases consisting of minimal (v,k,t) trades. Their approach is free from any group theoretic arguments. Their algorithm gives an easy way of generating a matrix whose columns are independent minimal trades with the added property that these columns are in echelon form. This latter property reveals immediately the independence of these $\binom{v}{k} - \binom{v}{t}$ trades.

Our experience shows that minimal trades are very useful objects in the search of trades on t-designs and in the manipulation of the support of a given design. Indeed, it is very easy and highly rewarding to perform trade-off by hand or via a computer using minimal trades.

Table 4.1. A Basis Consisting of Minimal Trades for $(8,4,3)$ Trades

$$T_1 = + (1357) + (2457) + (2367) + (2358) + (1467) + (1458) + (1368) + (2468)$$
$$- (2357) - (1457) - (1367) - (1358) - (2467) - (2458) - (2368) - (1468)$$

$$T_2 = + (1257) + (3457) + (2367) + (2358) + (1467) + (1458) + (1268) + (3468)$$
$$- (2357) - (1457) - (1267) - (1258) - (3467) - (3458) - (2368) - (1468)$$

$$T_3 = + (1237) + (3457) + (2467) + (2348) + (1567) + (1358) + (1268) + (4568)$$
$$- (2347) - (1357) - (1267) - (1238) - (4567) - (3458) - (2468) - (1568)$$

$$T_4 = + (1347) + (2457) + (2367) + (2348) + (1567) + (1458) + (1368) + (2568)$$
$$- (2347) - (1457) - (1367) - (1348) - (2567) - (2458) - (2368) - (1568)$$

$$T_5 = + (1247) + (3457) + (2367) + (2348) + (1567) + (1458) + (1268) + (3568)$$
$$- (2347) - (1457) - (1267) - (1248) - (3567) - (3458) - (2368) - (1568)$$

$$T_6 = + (1234) + (3456) + (2457) + (2358) + (1467) + (1368) + (1278) + (5678)$$
$$- (2345) - (1346) - (1247) - (1238) - (4567) - (3568) - (2578) - (1678)$$

$$T_7 = + (1235) + (3456) + (2457) + (2348) + (1567) + (1368) + (1278) + (4678)$$
$$- (2345) - (1356) - (1257) - (1238) - (4567) - (3468) - (2478) - (1678)$$

$$T_8 = + (1245) + (3456) + (2357) + (2348) + (1567) + (1468) + (1278) + (3678)$$
$$- (2345) - (1456) - (1257) - (1248) - (3567) - (3468) - (2378) - (1678)$$

$$T_9 = + (1345) + (2456) + (2357) + (2348) + (1567) + (1468) + (1378) + (2678)$$
$$- (2345) - (1456) - (1357) - (1348) - (2567) - (2468) - (2378) - (1678)$$

$$T_{10} = + (1236) + (3456) + (2467) + (2348) + (1567) + (1358) + (1278) + (4578)$$
$$- (2346) - (1356) - (1267) - (1238) - (4567) - (3458) - (2478) - (1578)$$

$$T_{11} = + (1246) + (3456) + (2367) + (2348) + (1567) + (1458) + (1278) + (3578)$$
$$- (2346) - (1456) - (1267) - (1248) - (3567) - (3458) - (2378) - (1578)$$

$$T_{12} = + (1346) + (2456) + (2367) + (2348) + (1567) + (1458) + (1378) + (2578)$$
$$- (2346) - (1456) - (1367) - (1348) - (2567) - (2458) - (2378) - (1578)$$

$$T_{13} = + (1256) + (3456) + (2367) + (2358) + (1467) + (1458) + (1278) + (3478)$$
$$- (2356) - (1456) - (1267) - (1258) - (3467) - (3458) - (2378) - (1478)$$

$$T_{14} = + (1356) + (2456) + (2367) + (2358) + (1467) + (1458) + (1378) + (2478)$$
$$- (2356) - (1456) - (1367) - (1358) - (2467) - (2458) - (2378) - (1478)$$

5. The Support of BIB Designs. We present here a series of selected results concerning the supports of BIB designs. First, we examine the characteristic of BIB designs whose supports are minimal. Second we provide some lower bounds for the size of a support, and consider some conditions under which a given set of blocks may form the support of a BIB design. The case where the block size is equal to 3 and 4 will be discussed in greater detail. Most of the results presented for BIB designs can be generalized or applied directly to t-designs, $t \geq 3$. However, for the sake of simplicity we limit our discussion to BIB designs, that is 2-designs.

In the sequel we shall use the following shorthand notations. We use $\text{BIB}(v, k)$ to designate any BIB design based on v and k. In this case we have no particular interest in λ or equivalently in b. However, if the value of λ is needed to be specified, then we use $\text{BIB}(v, k, \lambda)$. Here we shall deal with the following types of design problems which have many implications in the statistical applications of such designs.

1. Given a BIB(v, k) with support D^*, how far can we reduce the support and still have a BIB(v, k)? As we shall see this heavily depends on the path we are taking to reduce D^*.

2. What is the minimum support size within the family of BIB(v, k) designs? We shall give a few exact answers and some useful bounds for this problem.

3. What are the possible support sizes for the family of BIB(v, k) designs? We know very little about this problem in general. Complete solutions are available for selected values of v and k. We shall take a tour on these discoveries.

4. Problem 3 is very difficult and it is fair to say that this problem will be with us for years to come. An easier version of problem 3 is to fix λ and seek the set of all possible support sizes for the family of BIB(v, k, λ) designs. We shall provide a few results in this domain of research.

5. Another interesting problem is this. Suppose a given support size b^* is possible for the family of BIB(v, k) designs. Find a design with this b^* whose λ is minimum, that is to say utilize the minimum number of blocks in building this design. Several results in this area will be given below. This problem is wide open.

5.1. Minimal Supports. For the family of BIB(v, k) designs we can partially order by set inclusion all of the supports within the family. We refer to the minimal elements under this ordering as *minimal* supports. The methodology we suggested in Section 3.3 provides a technique for generating designs with minimal supports.

The following theorem shows that all BIB designs with the same minimal support are, in a sense, the same.

THEOREM 5.1. *Let D be a BIB(v, k) design. Then D has minimal support if and only if any other BIB(v, k) design with the same support is a rational multiple of D.*

Proof. Suppose D^* is the support of D and D_1 is a BIB(v, k) design with support D^*, but D_1 is not a multiple of D. Further, we assume that D^* is a minimal support. Let F and G be the associated BIB vectors of these designs. Now $P_2 F = \lambda \mathbf{1}$ and $P_2 G = \lambda_1 \mathbf{1}$ for positive integers λ and λ_1. There exists positive integers q and s such that $q\lambda - s\lambda_1 = 0$. Let $T = qF - sG$. Since by assumption D_1 is not a multiple of D, it follows that T is a nonvoid trade. Thus T is a trade on D, and by Theorem 3.3, D^* cannot be minimal. The converse can be established via a contradiction. □

COROLLARY 5.1. *Let $\mathcal{D}$ be the set of all BIB(v, k) designs supported on the same minimal support. Then there exists a unique design D in $\mathcal{D}$ such that all other designs in $\mathcal{D}$ are integer multiples of D. Further, D is a fundamental BIB design.*

An interesting problem, for which we do not know the answer, is how to find the value of v and k for which all fundamental BIB(v, k) designs have minimal supports.

Based on Theorem 3.3 we can give an upper bound on the number of blocks in a minimal support. In fact, this bound depends only on v. In verifying this result we recall that rank of P_2 is $\binom{v}{2}$.

PROPOSITION 5.1. *For any BIB design with minimal support $b^* \leq \binom{v}{2}$.*

A result analogous to Proposition 5.1 has been proved by Wynn [40] using another technique in the context of probability sampling.

5.2. Lower Bounds on the Support Size of a BIB Design. Suppose we are given the parameters v, b, r, k and λ of a BIB design. With no additional knowledge about the design we can rely on Fisher's inequality and conclude that $b \geq v$ in the given design. Further information about the design can help us to improve on the Fisher inequality. For example, if we are told that one of the blocks in the design is being replicated f times, then by the inequality of Mann [36] we have $b \geq fv$. Note the practical meaning of this latter inequality. If for some reason we like to run multiple copies of a block, this might increase the size of our experiment very substantially. However, for sampling application this is not a problem at all, since all these frequencies will be converted to probabilities. For the application of t-designs with repeated blocks to controlled sampling the reader is referred to Hedayat [11].

In passing we should mention that if for some j, $f_j = \sum_i f_i/v$, then every block in the support intersects the jth block in the same number of elements. From Mann's inequality we obtain the following correlatives of Fisher's inequality.

PROPOSITION 5.2. *For the family of $BIB(v, k)$ designs every design is supported on at least v distinct blocks. If a design is supported on precisely v distinct blocks, then that design is a uniform design.*

Our experience shows that if a $BIB(v, k)$ cannot be built based on v distinct blocks, then it is impossible or very difficult to build such a design based on $(1 + \epsilon)v$ distinct bocks if ϵ is indeed too small. van Lint and Ryser [34] established this for $\epsilon = 1/v$. Let us record their result.

PROPOSITION 5.3. *Within the family of $BIB(v, k)$ designs there is no design which is supported on precisely $v + 1$ distinct blocks.*

What should be the counterpart of Proposition 5.3 for the family of t-designs, $t \geq 3$?

By observing that the support of a BIB design must cover all $\binom{v}{2}$ pairs of varieties we can put a lower bound on the cardinality of the support.

PROPOSITION 5.4. *The minimum support size for the family of $BIB(v, k)$ design is at least as large as $\lceil \frac{v}{k} \lceil \frac{v-1}{k-1} \rceil \rceil$, where $\lceil x \rceil$ is the smallest integer greater than or equal to x.*

It is interesting to note that any $BIB(v, k)$ design which is supported on precisely $\lceil \frac{v}{k} \lceil \frac{v-1}{k-1} \rceil \rceil$ distinct blocks is a uniform BIB design.

We have two lower bounds on the support size for the family of $BIB(v, k)$ designs, namely v (Proposition 5.2) and $\lceil \frac{v}{k} \lceil \frac{v-1}{k-1} \rceil \rceil$ (Proposition 5.4). Both bounds can be achieved for selected values of v and k. For example, for $v = 7$, $k = 3$, these bounds are equal and achievable. In general, if $v \geq k^2 - k + 1$, then $v \leq \lceil \frac{v}{k} \lceil \frac{v-1}{k-1} \rceil \rceil$. If, on the

120

other hand, v is small compared to $k^2 - k + 1$, then the bound given in Proposition 5.2 is sharper. It may be, however, that for a given v and k neither of these bounds is achieved. One such example is $v = 8$, $k = 3$. Indeed, for this case the smallest possible support size is 22.

Appealing to Mann's inequality and a few other arguments we can conclude that:

PROPOSITION 5.5. *If* $v < k^2 - k + 1$, *then the support of every design in the family of* $BIB(v, k)$ *designs consists of at least* $\frac{v}{k}\{\frac{2(v-1)}{k-1}\}$ *blocks. If a design is supported on precisely* $\frac{v}{k}\{\frac{2(v-1)}{k-1}\}$ *blocks then it is a uniform design.*

For example, consider the family of $BIB(6, 3)$ designs. Then by Proposition 5.5, every design in this family is supported on at least 10 distinct blocks, and based on 10 distinct blocks there is a uniform BIB design.

Thus far we have not put any restriction on λ. Having λ free allows us to capture all possible support sizes. For example, with $\lambda = 6$ we cannot have a BIB design based on $v = 8$, $k = 3$ which is supported on precisely 55 distinct blocks. However, this can be done if we allow $\lambda = 12$. Not specifying λ forced us to give relatively crude bounds on the minimum support size. If λ is specified and if some other auxiliary information about the design is available we can provide much better bounds than we have provided so far. This is considered next.

We now study some aspects of the supports for the family of $BIB(v, k, \lambda)$ designs. To do this we need a couple of new notations. Let E denote the support and E_ℓ be the set of blocks in the support that are repeated ℓ times in the design, $\ell = 1, 2, \ldots, \lambda$. For some designs and for some values of ℓ, it may happen that $E_\ell = \phi$. The set E_λ is an important set and reveals a great deal of information about the design. With respect to the size of the support we partition the family of $BIB(v, k, \lambda)$ designs. Let $D(i)$ denote the subfamily of $BIB(v, k, \lambda)$ designs all supported on $b^* = i$ distinct blocks, $i = v, v + 1, \ldots, \lambda\binom{v}{2}/\binom{k}{2} = b$.

$D(v)$	$D(v+1)$	$\ldots$	$\ldots$	$D(i)$	$\ldots$	$D(b)$

Family of $BIB(v, k, \lambda)$ designs

Denote by m_i the maximum cardinality of E_λ within $D(i)$. If $D(i)$ is empty then $m_i = 0$.

The following result is proved in Hedayat, Landgev and Tonchev [18].

THEOREM 5.2. *For the family of* $BIB(v, k, \lambda)$ *designs, the minimum support size is bounded below by*

(5.1)
$$2\frac{v(v-1)}{k(k-1)} - m$$

where $m = \max_i m_i$.

The inequality (5.1) involves the value of m, which is unknown. Note that whenever $v < k^2 - k + 1$, then we can utilize the inequality of Mann, and conclude that $m = 0$. This then coincides with the result in Proposition 5.5. Thus for example every BIB$(9,4)$ has at least 12 distinct blocks.

Hedayat, Landgev and Tonchev [18] obtained the following upper bounds on m for the family of BIB(v, k, λ) designs when $v \geq k^2 - k + 1$.

THEOREM 5.3. *For the family of BIB(v, k, λ) designs with $k \geq 3$, the following inequalities hold.*

$$(5.2) \qquad m \leq \frac{v}{k}(\lfloor \frac{v-1}{k-1} \rfloor - 1) \qquad if\ v - 1 \not\equiv 0 \ (\mathrm{mod}\ k - 1)$$

$$(5.3) \qquad m \leq \lfloor \frac{v(v-1)}{k(k-1)} - \frac{1}{\epsilon} \rfloor - 3 \ if\ v - 1 \equiv 0 \ (\mathrm{mod}\ k - 1)$$

where ϵ is the greatest common divisor of k and λ.

For example, we can apply Theorems 5.2 and 5.3 and conclude that: (1) For the family of BIB$(12, 3, \lambda)$ designs, $m \leq 16$. Indeed, there is a design which is supported on $2v(v-1)/k(k-1) - m = 44 - 16 = 28$ distinct blocks. One such design is listed in Hedayat, Landgev and Tonchev [18]. (2) For the family of BIB$(11, 3, \lambda)$ designs the bound (5.3) yields $m \leq 15$ and the bound (5.1) gives 21. While this is a very good lower bound on the minimum support size for this family, Hedayat, Landgev and Tonchev [18] showed that 25 is the minimum support size and presented one such design.

The techniques presented in this section and the previous ones can be used to study the spectrum of support sizes for the family of BIB(v, k) or at least the family of BIB(v, k, λ) designs. We reemphasize that it is easier to show the existence of a design with certain support size in BIB(v, k), where λ is free. However, it is by far much easier to prove the nonexistence of a design with certain support size within BIB(v, k, λ) designs where λ is fixed. The next section is concerned with this topic.

6. The Spectrum of Support Sizes for Selected Families of BIB Designs. In studying the possible support sizes of BIB designs, there are two avenues of research. Fix $v, k,$ and λ and seek all possible support sizes. We denote this set by $SS_2(v, k, \lambda)$. The subscript 2 stands for 2-designs. A better approach will be to fix v and k and let λ be free and seek all possible support sizes. We denote this latter set by $SS_2(v, k)$. After characterizing $SS_2(v, k)$, we should for each support size in $SS_2(v, k)$ search for a design with the smallest possible number of blocks, that is with the smallest λ. We note that $SS_2(v, k, \lambda) \subseteq SS_2(v, k)$. There are two major reasons for $SS_2(v, k, \lambda) \subseteq SS_2(v, k)$. First, it is possible that λ is too small to accommodate a given support size. For example, with $v = 7$, $k = 3$ and $\lambda = 2$ we cannot accomodate any support size beyond 14. Second, for some support size we require a much larger λ than the one specified in advance in $SS_2(v, k, \lambda)$. For example, when $v = 7$, $k = 3$, then $\lambda = 4$ is large enough to accomodate a design with support size 24. However, no design with these parameters can be constructed. The smallest λ which does the job is 5.

Within the family of BIB(v, k, λ) designs, the search for designs with allowable support sizes becomes very complicated when the parameters b, r, λ of the family are relatively prime, $r = \lambda(v-1)/(k-1)$ and $b = rv/k$. Shortly, we shall study two such families. Many interesting results concerning BIB designs with b, r, λ being relatively prime can be found in van Lint [33].

The results we shall present below are almost all based on the theory of trade-off. Before summarizing the available results we refer the reader to Hedayat and Pesotan [22] concerning the support matrices.

BIB$(6, 3)$ Family. Hedayat and Khosrovshahi [16] characterized the set $SS_2(6, 3)$ and for each support size found the smallest possible design. In this case $SS_2(6, 3) = \{10, 14, 16, 17, 18, 19, 20\}$.

BIB$(7, 3)$ Family. The characterization of $SS_2(7, 3)$ and the identification of the smallest design for each support size is due to Hedayat and Li [20]. For this family $SS_2(7, 3) = \{7, 11, 13, 14, 15, 17, 18, \ldots, 35\}$. The nonexistence of a design with support size 16 is complicated. A separate proof of this case is found in Foody and Hedayat [5].

BIB$(8, 3)$ Family. For any λ in this family, b, r, λ are relatively prime. And indeed this is the family with the smallest v which has this property. As we mentioned earlier the study of $SS_2(8, 3)$ becomes complicated. A complete characterization of $SS_2(8, 3)$ with the smallest design for each allowable support size is due to Foody and Hedayat [4], Hedayat and Hwang [13] and Hedayat, Landgev and Tonchev [18]. We would also like to mention that for this family of BIB designs the smallest possible design has $56 = \binom{8}{3}$ blocks. For this reason the literature prior to 1977 has left the wrong impression that the only design for this case is the trivial design. For this family $SS_2(8, 3) = \{22, 23, \ldots, 56\}$. Note that there is no hole in the range of support sizes. This is the only case known to us with this property. The fact that there is no design with support size below 22 is very complicated as has been demonstrated in Hedayat, Landgev and Tonchev [18].

BIB$(9, 3)$ Family. Such designs with support sizes belonging to $\{12, 18, 20, 21, \ldots, 84\}$ are constructed in Khosrovshahi and Mahmoodian [31]. According to them, Arian-nejad [1] has shown the nonexistence of designs with supports in $\{13, 14, 15, 16, 17, 19\}$. These two results yield $SS_2(9, 3) = \{12, 18, 20, 21, \ldots, 84\}$.

BIB$(10, 3, 2)$ Family. Hedayat and Hwang [13] studied this family of BIB designs since b, r, λ are relatively prime and $b = 30$ constitutes the smallest number of blocks with this property. Thus, in some sense this family of BIB designs is the counterpart of the family of BIB$(8, 3)$ designs as we discussed earlier. Hedayat and Hwang [13] proved that the support size 22 is impossible and $SS_2(10, 3, 2) = \{21, 23, 24, \ldots, 30\}$. Whether or not a BIB design with the support size 22 can be constructed with a larger λ is under investigation.

BIB$(11, 3, 3)$ Family. Hedayat, Landgev and Tonchev [18] showed that the minimum support size in $SS_2(11, 3)$ is 25 and they exhibited a design with support size 25 with $\lambda = 3$. Hedayat and Landgev [17] proved that $SS_2(11, 3)$ does not include 26 and 27 and $SS_2(11, 3, 3) = \{25, 28, 29, \ldots, 55\}$.

BIB(12, 3) Family. A full systematic study of this family in regard to possible support sizes is not being carried out. One of the results of Hedayat, Landgev and Tonchev [18] indicates that the minimum support size in $SS(12,3)$ is 28. They also exhibited one such design.

BIB(v, 3, 2) Family. For this family of BIB designs, $b = v(v-1)/3$. Let $n_v = v(v-4)/6$. If $v \equiv 0$ or $4 \pmod 6$, $v > 12$, then Rosa and Hoffman [37] proved that:

$$SS_2(v, 3, 2) = \{b - n_v, b - n_v + 2, b - n_v + 3, \ldots, b\} \text{ if } v \equiv 0 \pmod 4,$$

and

$$SS_2(v, 3, 2) = \{b - n_v + 1, b - n_v + 2, \ldots, b\} \text{ if } v \equiv 2 \pmod 4.$$

Concerning triple systems, that is BIB designs with $k = 3$, Alex Rosa and his co-researchers have obtained other interesting results in several areas directly and indirectly related to support sizes, though they do not use such terminology. Another paper of Rosa directly related to our study is by Ganter, Gülzow, Mathon and Rosa [7] from which the set $SS_2(10, 3, 2)$ can be extracted.

BIB(v, 3, 3) Family. During the workshop on design theory in IMA, University of Minnesota, Dr. E.S. Mahmoodian brought to our attention the IMA Preprint Series #378, dated January 1988. In this report Colbourn and Mahmoodian [2] study the support sizes for threefold triple systems. They have some interesting results concerning $v \equiv 1, 3, 5 \pmod 6$. Let $m_v = \lfloor v(v-1)/6 \rfloor$. Then for $v \equiv 1, 3 \pmod 6$,

$$SS_2(v, 3, 3) = \{m_v, m_v + 4, m_v + 6, m_v + 7, \ldots, 3m_v\} \text{ provided } v \neq 3, 7, 9.$$

and if $v \equiv 5 \pmod 6$

$$SS_2(v, 3, 3) = \{m_v + 7, m_v + 10, m_v + 11, \ldots, 3m_v + 1\}.$$

BIB(8, 4) Family. Hedayat and Hwang [14] proved that $\{14, 18, 20, 21, \ldots, 70\} \subseteq SS_2(8, 4)$. For each support size a design with the minimum number of blocks was presented. Later Hedayat, Landgev and Stufken [19] proved that $SS_2(8, 4)$ does not contain 15 and 16. However, support sizes 17 and 19 are in $SS_2(8, 4)$. For the latter two support sizes designs with the minimum number of blocks were constructed. In short, $SS_2(8, 4) = \{14, 17, 18, \ldots, 70\}$.

BIB(9, 4) Family. In Khosrovshahi and Mahmoodian [31] it is shown that $\{18, 22, 23, \ldots, 126\} \subseteq SS_2(9, 4)$. Apparently, Khosrovshahi and his coresearchers have been able to settle the undecided case namely $19, 20, 21$ and 23. At the time of this writing no further information is available to us except that Khosrovshahi and his coresearchers have been able to push the theory of trade off to a level which can answer many related problems in this area.

7. Closing Remarks. Almost all results we presented for 2-designs can be used directly or extended without much difficulties to t-designs, $t \geq 3$. Our emphasis was on 2-designs because it is easier to state and present many interesting results. Throughout the paper we stated many unsolved problems. We hope some of our readers become interested in tackling these problems. As we demonstrated, on many occasions the theory of trade-off is a simple yet powerful tool for constructing t-designs with various support sizes. Though many interesting results have been obtained via this theory, it is fair to say that it is in its infancy. It needs to be nourished by design lovers.

REFERENCES

[1] ARIANNEJAD, M., *On existence and nonexistence of some BIB designs with various support sizes*, Master of Science dissertation, University of Tehran, Iran. (1988).

[2] COLBOURN, C.J. AND MAHMOODIAN, E.S., *The spectrum of support sizes for threefold triple systems*, IMA Preprint Series, 378 (1988).

[3] CONSTANTINE, G.M. AND HEDAYAT, A., *Complete designs with blocks of maximal multiplicity*, J. Statist. Plann. and Inference, 7 (1983), pp. 289–294; Corrigendum, 7 (1983), p. 417.

[4] FOODY, W. AND HEDAYAT, A., *On theory and applications of BIB designs with repeated blocks*, Ann. Statist., 5 (1977), pp. 932–935; Corrigendum, 7 (1979), p. 925.

[5] FOODY, W. AND HEDAYAT A., *A graphical proof of the nonexistence of BIB($7, b, r, 3, \lambda|16$) designs*, J. Statist. Plann. and Inference, 20 (1988), pp. 77–90.

[6] FRANKL, P. AND PACH, J., *On the number of sets in a null t-design*, Europe. J. Combinatorics, 4 (1983), pp. 21–31.

[7] GANTER, B. GÜLZOW, A., MATHON, R. AND ROSA, A., *A complete census of $(10, 3, 2)$ designs and of Mendelsohn triple systems of order ten. IV. $(10, 3, 2)$ designs with repeated blocks*, Math. Schriften Kassel 5/78 (1978).

[8] GRACE, J.H. AND YOUNG, A., *The Algebra of Invariants*, Cambridge Univ. Press, (Reprinted by Strehart, New York, 1941), 1903.

[9] GRAHAM, R.I., LI, S.Y.R. AND LI, W.C.W., *On the structure of t-designs*, SIAM J. of Algebraic and Discrete Methods, 1 (1980), pp. 8–14.

[10] GRAVER, J.E. AND JURKAT, W.B., *The module structure of integral designs*, J. Combin. Theory, Ser. A, 15 (1973), pp. 75–90.

[11] HEDAYAT, A., *Sampling designs with reduced support sizes*, in *Optimizing Methods in Statistics*, (J. Rustagi, Ed.), 1979, pp. 273–288, Academic Press.

[12] HEDAYAT, A. AND HWANG, H.L., *An algorithm for generating a basis of the trades on t-designs*, Commun. Statist. - Simula., 12 (1983), pp. 109–125.

[13] HEDAYAT, A. AND HWANG, H.L., *BIB($8, 56, 21, 3, 6$) and BIB($10, 30, 9, 3, 2$) designs with repeated blocks*, J. Combin. Theory, Ser. A, 36 (1984), pp. 73–91.

[14] HEDAYAT, A. AND HWANG, H.L., *Construction of BIB designs with various support sizes with special emphasis for $v = 8$ and $k = 4$*, J. Combin. Theory, Ser. A, 36 (1984), pp. 163–173.

[15] HEDAYAT, A. AND KAGEYAMA, S., *The family of t-designs - Part I*, J. Statist. Plann. and Inference, 4 (1980), pp. 173–212.

[16] HEDAYAT, A. AND KHOSROVSHAHI, G.B., *An algebraic study of BIB designs: A complete solution for $v = 6$ and $k = 3$*, J. Combin. Theory, Ser. A, 30 (1981), pp. 43–52.

[17] HEDAYAT, A. AND LANDGEV, I.N., *Support sizes for BIB designs with $v = 11$ and $k = 3$*, Tech. Report, Institute of Mathematics, Sofia, Bulgaria (1987).

[18] HEDAYAT, A., LANDGEV, I.N., AND TONCHEV, V.D., *Results on the support of BIB designs*, J. Statist. Plann. and Inference, 22 (1989), pp. 295–306.

[19] HEDAYAT, A. LANDGEV, I.N. AND STUFKEN, J., *The possible support sizes for BIB designs with $v = 8$ and $k = 4$*, J. Combin. Theory, Ser. A, 51 (1989), pp. 258–267.

[20] HEDAYAT, A. AND LI, S.Y.R., *The trade-off method in the construction of BIB designs with variable support sizes*, Ann. Statist., 7 (1979), pp. 1277–1287.

[21] HEDAYAT, A. AND LI, S.Y.R., *Combinatorial topology and the trade-off method in BIB designs*, Ann. Discrete Math., 6 (1980), pp. 189–200.

125

[22] HEDAYAT, A., PESOTAN, H., *A study of BIB designs through support matrices*, J. Statist. Plann. and Inference, 11 (1985), pp. 363–372.

[23] HWANG, H.L., *Trades and the construction of BIB designs with repeated blocks*, Ph.D. dissertation, University of Illinois, Chicago (1982).

[24] HWANG, H.L., *On the structure of (v, k, t) trades*, J. Statist. Plann. and Inference, 13 (1986), pp. 179–191.

[25] HO, Y.S. AND MENDELSOHN, N.S., *Inequalities for t-designs with repeated blocks*, Aequationes Mathematicae, 10 (1974), pp. 212–222.

[26] KAGEYAMA, S. AND HEDAYAT, A., *The family of t-designs-part II*, J. Statist. Plann. and Inference, 7 (1983), pp. 257–287.

[27] KHOSROVSHAHI, G.B., *On trades and designs: Some recent results*, Computational Statistics and Data Analysis (1989) (to appear).

[28] KHOSROVSHAHI, G.B. AND AJOODANI-NAMINI, S., *A new basis for trades*, Tech. Report No. IC/88/206 at International Center for Theoretical Physics, Trieste, Italy [Also available through Dept. of Mathematics and Computer Science of Tehran, Iran].

[29] KHOSROVSHAHI, G.B. AND MAHMOODIAN, E.S., *A table of BIB$(10, 30t, 9t, 3, 2t)$ and BIB$(11, 55t, 15t, 3, 3t)$ designs*, Tech Report No. 2-1365, Sharif Univ. of Technology, Tehran, Iran (1987).

[30] KHOSROVSHAHI, G.B. AND MAHMOODIAN, E.S., *A linear algebraic algorithm for reducing the support size of t-designs and to generate a basis for trades*, Commun. Statist. - Simula., 16 (1987), pp. 1015–1038.

[31] KHOSROVSHAHI, G.B. AND MAHMOODIAN, E.S., *BIB$(9, 18t, 8t, 4, 3t)$ designs with repeated blocks*, J. Statist. Plann. and Inference, 18 (1988), pp. 125–131.

[32] KHOSROVSHAHI, G.B. AND MAHMOODIAN, E.S., *On BIB designs with various support sizes for $v = 9$ and $k = 3$*, Commun. Statist. Simula., 17 (1988), pp. 765–770.

[33] VAN LINT, J.H., *Block designs with repeated blocks and $(b, r, \lambda) = 1$*, J. Combin. Theory, Ser. A., 15 (1973), pp. 288–309.

[34] VAN LINT, J.H. AND RYSER, H.J., *Block designs with repeated blocks*, Discrete Math., 3 (1972), pp. 381–396.

[35] MAHMOODIAN, E.S., *On the support size of the 3-designs with repeated blocks*, Tech. Report, Depart. of Math. Sciences, Sharif Univ. of Technology, Tehran, Iran (1988).

[36] MANN, H.B., *A note on balanced incomplete block designs*, Ann. Math. Statist., 40 (1969), pp. 679–680.

[37] ROSA, A. AND HOFFMAN, D., *The number of repeated blocks in twofold triple systems*, J. Combin. Theory, Ser A, 41 (1986), pp. 61–88.

[38] SINGHI, N.M. AND SKRIKHANDE, S.S., *A reciprocity relation for t-designs*, Europe. J. Combinatorics, 8 (1987), pp. 59–68.

[39] WILSON, R.M., *On the theory of t-designs*, in: *Enumeration and Design* (Vanstone, S. and Jackson, D., Editors), Academic Press (1984), pp. 19–49.

[40] WYNN, H.P., *Convex sets of finite population plans*, Ann. Statist., 5 (1977), pp. 414–418.

TOTALLY IRREGULAR COLLINEATION GROUPS AND FINITE DESARGUESIAN PLANES

CHAT YIN HO†

Abstract. We verify the conjecture that a finite projective plan admits collineation group isomorphic to PSL(2,q) for a prime power q such that the stabilizer of each point in the group is not trivial, if and only if it is Desarguesian.

Key words. collineation group, projective plane, involution, orbit.

1. Introduction. In [4] we prove that the order of a finite projective plane admitting a group G as a collineation group is bounded by a function of $|G|$ and the number of the regular G-orbits of points. We call G *totally irregular* if each G-orbit of points is irregular (i.e., the stabilizer of a point in G is not trivial). Finite Desarguesian planes are closely related to totally irregular collineation groups. In fact these planes have been classified by various such collineation groups, e.g., a doubly transitive collineation group (Ostrom-Wagner [5]); a collineation group such that either each point is a center or each line is an axis of a perspectivity in this group (Cofman-Piper [5]). Using Hall's multiplier theorem [1], we see that planes with difference sets admit totally irregular collineation groups.

Each finite Desarguesian plane admits a totally irregular collineation group isomorphic to PSL(2,q) for some prime power q (see 2.2 in section 2). The following theorem provides some evidence that the converse of this might be true.

THEOREM. *A finite projective plane of order n admits PSL(2,q) for $q \leq 5$ as a totally irregular collineation group if and only if it is Desarguesian. Furthermore the following holds.*

(1) *$q = 2$ occurs if and only if $n = 2$ or 3.*

(2) *$q = 3$ occurs if and only if $n = 2, 3,$ or 4.*

(3) *$q = 4$ or 5 occurs if and only if $n = 4, 5, 9$ or 11.*

Observe that q and n might be different. We organize the paper in the following way. In section 2, some general lemmas are proved. Lemma 2.1 improves the bound of the order of a plane admitting a totally irregular collineation group. Examples for PSL(2,2), PSL(2,3) on planes of order 2,3 or 4 are given in 2.3. Section 3 treats PSL(2,2) and PSL(2,3) in general, and more information about these groups and planes are given in Propositions 3.3 and 3.4. A proof of the Theorem is presented in section 4.

---

†Department of Mathematics, University of Florida, Gainesville, Florida, 32611. This work is partially support by IMA and a grant from DSR, U. of Florida.

2. Preliminaries. Let Π be a finite projective plane of order n with point set P and line set L. Let G be a collineation group of Π. For any subset S of G, denote the set of fixed points (resp. lines) of S by $P(S)$ (resp. $L(S)$) and define $\Omega(S) := \cup_{\theta \in S} P(\theta)$. An element $\theta \in G, 1 \neq \theta$ is *planar* if the substructure $Fix(\theta) := (P(\theta), L(\theta))$ is a subplane.

2.1. LEMMA. *Let $c := c(G)$ be the number of cyclic subgroups of prime order in G. Suppose G is totally irregular. Then $\sqrt{n} \leq \frac{1}{2}(1 + \sqrt{4c-3})$. If in addition G does not contain any planar element, then $n \leq c$.*

Proof. Whenever $1 \neq \theta \in G$, we have $|P(\theta)| \leq n + \sqrt{n} + 1$. Let R be a set of elements of G which contains exactly one element from each cyclic subgroup of G of prime order. Since G is totally irregular, $P = \Omega(R)$. Hence $n^2 + n + 1 \leq |\Omega(R)| \leq c(n + \sqrt{n} + 1)$. Thus $n - \sqrt{n} + 1 \leq c$ which implies $\sqrt{n} \leq \frac{1}{2}(1 + \sqrt{4c-3})$.

Assume G does not contain any planar element. Then $|P(\theta)| \leq n + 2$ for $1 \neq \theta \in G$. This implies $n^2 + n + 1 \leq c(n+2)$. Hence $n - \frac{c-1}{2} \leq \sqrt{(\frac{c-1}{2} + 2)^2 - 3} < \frac{c+3}{2}$ completing the proof.

2.2. Remark. A Desarguesian plane of order n admits a collineation group G, isomorphic to PSL(2,n), leaving an oval invariant. So G acts on the set of exterior (resp. interior) points of this oval of cardinality $\frac{n(n+1)}{2}$ (resp. $\frac{n(n-1)}{2}$). This implies that G is totally irregular.

2.3. Examples. We call an element g of G a *flag* collineation if $Fix(g)$ is an incident point-line pair; a *perspectivity* if g fixes a line pointwise; *triangular* if $P(g)$ consists of three non-collinear points. For $B \in P$ and $b \in L$, let $[[B]] = \{l \in L | B \text{ is incident with } l\}$ and $(b) = \{X \in P | b \text{ is incident with } X\}$. If g is a perspectivity, then $P(g) = \{A\} \cup (a)$ and $L(g) = \{a\} \cup [[A]]$ for some $A \in P$ and $a \in L$. We call A the center, a the axis of g. A perspectivity is called an *elation* or a *homology* according as the center belongs to the axis or not. For brevity, 'the group generated by the matrices a,...,b' means 'the collineation group corresponding to the matrix group generated by the matrices a,...,b'.

2.3.1. Planes of order 2,3 and PSL(2,2).

Suppose $n = 2$. The group generated by $\begin{pmatrix} 1 & 1 & 0 \\ 0 & 1 & 0 \\ 0 & 0 & 1 \end{pmatrix}$ and $\begin{pmatrix} 1 & 0 & 0 \\ 1 & 1 & 0 \\ 0 & 0 & 1 \end{pmatrix}$ is totally irregular and is isomorphic to PSL(2,2). Its orbits of points have sizes 3,3,1.

Suppose $n = 3$. The group F generated by $\begin{pmatrix} 1 & 1 & 0 \\ 0 & 1 & 1 \\ 0 & 0 & 1 \end{pmatrix}$, $\begin{pmatrix} -1 & 0 & 0 \\ 0 & 1 & 0 \\ 0 & 0 & -1 \end{pmatrix}$; and the group T generated by $\begin{pmatrix} 1 & 1 & 0 \\ 0 & 1 & 0 \\ 0 & 0 & 1 \end{pmatrix}$, $\begin{pmatrix} -1 & 0 & 0 \\ 0 & 1 & 0 \\ 0 & 0 & -1 \end{pmatrix}$ are totally irregular and both are isomorphic to PSL(2,2). An element of order 3 of F (resp. T) is a flag collineation (resp. an elation). Point orbits of F have sizes 1,3,3,3. Point orbits of T have sizes 1,1,2,3,3,3.

2.3.2. Planes of order 2,3,4, and PSL(2,3).

Suppose $n = 2$. The group generated by $\begin{pmatrix} 1 & 1 & 0 \\ 0 & 1 & 0 \\ 0 & 0 & 1 \end{pmatrix}$, $\begin{pmatrix} 1 & 0 & 0 \\ 0 & 0 & 1 \\ 0 & 1 & 1 \end{pmatrix}$ is totally irregular and is isomorphic to PSL(2,3). Its point orbits have sizes 3,4. Suppose $n = 3$. The group generated by $\begin{pmatrix} -1 & 0 & 0 \\ 0 & -1 & 0 \\ 0 & 0 & 1 \end{pmatrix}$, $\begin{pmatrix} 0 & 1 & 0 \\ 0 & 0 & 1 \\ 1 & 0 & 0 \end{pmatrix}$ is isomorphic to PSL(2,3). It is totally irregular and its point orbits have sizes 3,3,3,4. An element of order 3 of this group is a flag collineation. Suppose $n = 4$. The group H generated by $\begin{pmatrix} 1 & 1 & 0 \\ 0 & 1 & 0 \\ 0 & 0 & 1 \end{pmatrix}$, $\begin{pmatrix} 1 & 0 & 0 \\ 0 & a & 0 \\ 0 & 0 & 1 \end{pmatrix}$, where $1 \neq a$ and $a^3 = 1$, is totally irregular and is isomorphic to PSL(2,3). Involutions in H are elations having a common center and a common axis. An element of H is a homology. The point orbits of H have sizes 1,1,3,4,4,4,4.

The group K generated by $\begin{pmatrix} 0 & 1 & 0 \\ 1 & 1 & 0 \\ 0 & 0 & 1 \end{pmatrix}$, $\begin{pmatrix} 1 & 0 & 1 \\ 0 & 1 & 0 \\ 0 & 0 & 1 \end{pmatrix}$ is totally irregular and is isomorphic to PSL(2,3). Involutions in K are elations having a common center but different axes. An element of order 3 in K is a triangular collineation. The point orbits of K have sizes 1,3,3,3,3,4,4.

3. PSL(2,2) and PSL(2,3). Notations and definitions of section 2 continued to be used in this section. We characterize PSL(2,2) and PSL(2,3) being totally irregular collineation groups in the following two propositions.

3.1. PROPOSITION. *The group $G \cong PSL(2,2)$ is a totally irregular collineation group if and only if $n = 2$ or 3. Furthermore, when $n = 3$ both possibilities for an element of order 3 of G being an elation or a flag collineation do occur.*

Proof. By the examples shown in 2.3.1, it remains to prove that $n \leq 3$, when G is totally irregular. Applying Lemma 2.1 with $c = 4$ yields $n \leq 5$. Suppose $n = 5$. Then G does not contain any planar element, which implies $n \leq 4$ by Lemma 2.1. This contradiction proves that $n \leq 4$.

Suppose $n = 4$. Then the plane is Desarguesian. Let β be an element of order 3 in G. Then β is either a triangular collineation or a homology. Since $< \beta >$ is normal in G, G acts on $P(\beta)$. This implies that in both cases G fixes a non-incident point-line pair B, b with $B \in P(\beta), b \in L(\beta)$ and $P(\beta) \subseteq \Delta := \{B\} \cup (b)$. Let $I(G) := \{$involutions of $G\}$. Suppose $I(G)$ consists of elations. Since $b = b^G$, b passes through all centers of $I(G)$. As $B \notin (b)$, B cannot be a common center for $I(G)$. Hence all 3 axes of $I(G)$ pass through $B = B^G$. Each of these axes has at most 4 points not in Δ. Since $\Omega(G) = \Delta \cup \Omega(I(G))$, so $|\Omega(G)| \leq |\Delta| + 3 \times 4 = 18 < 21 = |P|$. This proves that G is not totally irregular when $I(G)$ consists of elations. Therefore $I(G)$ consists of planar involutions (i.e. Baer involutions). For $\alpha \in I(G)$, $b = b^\alpha$ implies that b carries 3 points of $Fix(\alpha)$. Since $B = B^\alpha$, there are at most 3 points of $Fix(\alpha)$ not in Δ. Hence $|\Omega(G)| \leq |\Delta| + |\Omega(I(G))| \leq 6 + 3 \times 3 = 15 < 21 = |P|$. So G cannot be totally irregular. This contradiction proves that $n \neq 4$. Therefore $n \leq 3$, completing the proof.

3.2. PROPOSITION. *The group $G \cong PSL(2,3)$ is a totally irregular collineation group if and only if $n = 2, 3$, or 4. Furthermore, the following holds.*

(1) *When $n = 3$ an element of order 3 of G is a flag collineation.*

(2) *Suppose $n = 4$. If an element of order 3 of G is a homology, then involutions of G are elations having a common center and a common axis. If an element*

129

*of order 3 of G is a triangular collineation, then involutions of G are elations
having a common center but different axes. Both these possibilities do occur.*

Proof. By examples shown in 2.3.2, it remains to prove that $n \leq 4$ and the
restrictions on an element of order 2, or 3. Applying Lemma 2.1 with $c = 7$ yields
$n \leq 9$.

Assume $n = 9$. From $P = \Omega(G)$ and $91 = 7 \times 13$, we obtain that non-trivial
elements of G are planar. Each such subplane has order 3. The point sets of these
subplanes corresponding to the 7 subgroups of prime order are mutually disjoint.
However involutions of G commute with each orther, which implies that the point
sets of these three subplanes have common points. This contradiction proves $n \neq 9$.

Assume $n = 8$. Since 8 is not a square, involutions in G are elations. A planar
element of G fixes 7 points. Hence for $1 \neq g \in G, |P(g)| \leq n + 2$. This implies, as
in the proof of Lemma 2.1, that $n \leq 7$. This contradiction proves $n \neq 8$.

Assume $n = 7$. For $P = \Omega(G)$, the 7 subgroups of G of prime order must consist
of homologies whose axes are concurrent and distinct. The 7 remaining points must
be the centers of elements of these 7 subgroups as each of these points is fixed by
some non-trivial element in G. In particular centers and axes are never incident.
However this contradicts the fact that involutions in G commute. Therefore $n \neq 7$.

Assume $n = 5$. An element of order 3 fixes exactly one point. Involutions are
commuting homologies. Hence $|\Omega(G)| \leq 3(5 + 2) + 4 = 25 < 31$. So G cannot be
totally irregular. This proves $n \neq 5$.

Since $n \neq 6$, we have $n \leq 4$. Assume $n = 4$. [3,Theorem A] implies that
involutions are elations. So these three involutions either have a common center or
a common axis. Let $t \in G$ be an element of order 3. Then t is either a homology
or a triangular collineation. Suppose t is a homology. Assume involutions in G
have a common center A but different axes. Since t permutes the three involutory
axes, A is not the center of t. Hence the axis x of t passes through A. Thus
$x \in [[A]] \smallsetminus \{$ 3 involutory axes $\}$. Since the latter set has cardinality 2 and there
are 4 Sylow 3-subgroups of G, at least 2 Sylow 3-subgroups have elements with
a common axis. As these 2 Sylow 3-subgroups generate G, elements in G have a
common center. This contradiction proves that if involutions in G have a common
center, then they have a common axis. A dual argument shows that if involutions
have a common axis, then they have a common center. Therefore involutions always
have a common center and a common axis when t is a homology as, desired.

Suppose t is a triangular collineation. Assume involutions have a common axis
a. Then $a^t = a$. So t fixes 2 points on a. Hence there is exactly one point of $P(t)$
not on a. This implies $|\Omega(G)| \leq |(a)| + 4 = 9$. So G is not totally irregular. This
contradiction proves that involutions have different axes. Therefore they have a
common center as required.

Finally suppose $n = 3$. Assume an element t of order 3 of G is an elation.
If involutions have a common axis a. Then $a^t = a$ implies that the center C of
t is on a. Since G is generated by t and its involutions, $C^G = C$. Hence C is
a common center of elements of order 3 in G. This implies that C is a common

center of all non-trivial elements in G. But involutions are homologies and $C \in (a)$. This contradiction proves that involutions have different axes. If involutions have a common center, then using Maschke's theorem in the action of the matrix group $GL(3,3)$ on the natural 3-dimensional space we see that involutions will have a common axis. This contradiction proves that involutions have different centers. Since involutions commute, these 3 centers are not collinear. Hence t has an orbit of 3 non-collinear points. So t cannot be an elation. Therefore t is a flag collineation, completing the proof.

4. Proof of Theorem. Notations and definitions of section 2 continue to be used in this section. In addition, we assume $G \cong PSL(2,q)$ with $q \leq 5$ and G is totally irregular. We prove the Theorem in this section. Propositions 3.1, 3.2 take care of the cases $q = 2, 3$. [4, Theorem B] implies that $n = 4, 5, 9$, or 11 when $q = 4$ or 5. Suppose $G \cong PSL(2,4)=PSL(2,5)$. Lemma 2.2 takes care of the cases $n = 4, 5$. For $n = 9$, observe that $G \leq M \cong PSL(2,9)$, where M acts on an oval of 10 points. Hence G acts on the set of exterior points and the set of interior points of this oval. This implies that G cannot have any regular orbit of points. So G is totally irregular as desired. For $n = 11$, observe that $G \leq M \cong PSL(2,11)$, where M acts on an oval of 12 points. From [2], we see that G does not have any regular orbit of points. Therefore G is totally irregular, completing the proof of the Theorem.

REFERENCES

[1]   M. HALL JR., *Cyclic projective planes*, Duke Math. J., 14 (1947), pp. 1079–1090.

[2]   C.Y. HO, *Characterization of projective planes of small prime order*, J. Combinatorial Theory Ser. A, 41 (1986), pp. 189–220.

[3]   C.Y. HO, *Involutory collineations of finite planes*, Math. Z, 193 (1986), pp. 235–240.

[4]   C.Y. HO, *On the order of a projective plane and planes with a totally irregular collineation group*, Proc. Symposia in pure mathematics, A.M.S., 47 (1987), pp. 423–429.

[5]   D. HUGHES AND F. PIPER, *Projective planes*, Springer, New York, 1973.

REMARKS ON 2-(15,5,4) DESIGNS

S.A. HOBART AND
W.G. BRIDGES*

Abstract. There appear to be 88 2-(15,5,4) designs in the literature. We construct 15 new designs using three techniques: applications of coherent configurations, orbit matrix constructions, and Kreher's Design Toolchest computer software.

1. Introduction. Previous to the work of Mathon and Rosa [14], there appear to have been four generally available 2-(15,5,4) designs in the literature: two constructions by Hanani [5,6], one with a repeated block, a standard item in Hall [4], and a highly symmetric solution given in [2,13,16]. Mathon and Rosa recently enumerated all nonisomorphic 1-rotational 2-(15,5,4) designs. There are apparently 85. This, after isomorphism testing, brings the total known 2-(15,5,4) designs having no repeated blocks to 88.

We construct 16 designs with these parameters, 15 of them new, illustrating three construction techniques. The techniques, although not really new, have recently been refined, and have been productive. Two involve the presumption of automorphism groups which are reasonable. One of these uses the orbit matrix construction, as in [1,17] for example, to get a "homomorphic" image of the design which is then "lifted" to a design. The other employs the ideas of Kramer and Mesner [9,10] in a computer software package developed by Don Kreher [this proceedings].

The third technique utilizes an analysis of certain coherent configurations to "predict" a block intersection pattern which can yield a design and reveal a considerable amount of its structure. The 2-(15,5,4) design found in this way is the design of [2,13,16]; we show that it has automorphism group A_7, and give a construction using the Steiner system $S(5,8,24)$. We also use this design to construct three other 2-(15,5,4) designs.

The first two techniques are illustrated further in this proceedings by the papers of Tonchev, van Lint and Landgev, and Kreher. The coherent configuration approach is an outgrowth of the first author's Ph.D. thesis under the direction of D.G. Higman [8].

The results of this paper together with the literature give 103 nonisomorphic 2-(15,5,4) designs. (Nonisomorphim follows by inspection of block intersection patterns.) Our full list of designs has not yet been sorted with respect to isomorphism.

2. Lemmas on Design Automorphisms. Various cases of the following lemmas appear, at least implicitly, in the literature. We state and prove a general form for completeness.

---

*Department of Mathematics University of Wyoming Laramie, Wyoming 82071

LEMMA 2.1. *Let $D = (P, B)$ be a 2-design with point set P and block set B. Let σ be an automorphism of D viewed as a permutation on P, and let ρ be the corresponding block permutation. If σ has cycle type $m_1^{\alpha_1} m_2^{\alpha_2} \cdots m_t^{\alpha_t}$ then $\rho = \tau\gamma$ where τ has cycle type $(k_1 m_1)^{\alpha_1} (k_2 m_2)^{\alpha_2} \cdots (k_t m_t)^{\alpha_t}$ for integers $k_i \geq 1$, and τ and γ are disjoint.*

Proof. We first recall that the cycle type of a permutation is deducible from its spectrum as a permutation matrix, the number of ones giving the number of cycles, and a complete set of kth roots of unity indicating the presence of a k-cycle, *etc.* If P and Q are the v by v and b by b permutation matrices corresponding to σ and ρ, the claim will follow from the fact that P's spectrum is contained in Q's. If N is the incidence matrix, we have $PN = NQ$, from which it follows that the row space of N is Q-invariant, and P is the matrix of Q on the row space relative to the rows of N. Hence Q is similar to a block triangular matrix with P as a diagonal block. □

LEMMA 2.2. *Let D be a 2-design, and σ an automorphism of D of prime order $p > \max(k - 2, \lambda)$. Then the v' fixed points and the fixed blocks of D form a 2-(v', k, λ) design.*

Proof. Since $p > \max(k-2, \lambda)$, a block containing 2 fixed points consists entirely of fixed points. □

It follows from this second lemma that an automorphism of a 2-(15,5,4) design of prime order p must have $p \leq 7$; and if $p = 7$, it has only one fixed point.

If $p = 5$ and there are 10 fixed points, the subdesign of the lemma is a 2-(10,5,4) design. The 10 fixed points are each in 5 of the 24 nonfixed blocks and no two are in the same block, which is impossible. It follows easily that if $p = 5$, there are no fixed points.

3. The Orbit Matrix Constructions. In general if σ is an automorphism of a design D with point orbits $P_1, \cdots, P_t$ and block orbits $B_1, \cdots, B_s$, then the nonnegative integral t by s matrix $R = (r_{ij})$, where r_{ij} is the number of blocks of B_j containing any point from P_i, is referred to as the *orbit matrix* of σ. In an obvious way, the point orbits determine a t-dimensional subspace of $\mathbb{R}^v$ and the block orbits an s-dimensional subspace of $\mathbb{R}^b$. Viewing the design as a linear transformation from $\mathbb{R}^v$ to $\mathbb{R}^b$ (via its incidence matrix N), R is the matrix of the restriction of this transformation to these subspaces. From the design equation, $NN^t = (r - \lambda)I + \lambda J$, one then obtains a matrix equation involving R, called the *orbit matrix equation*. The orbit matrix technique amounts to solving the orbit matrix equation, and then constructing an N in block circulant form corresponding to the orbit decomposition. This is essentially the technique used in, for example, [1,17].

The orbit matrix equation for a 2-(15,5,4) design with an automorphism of order 3 which has no fixed points (and hence no fixed blocks) is $RR^t = 10I + 12J$, where R is 5 by 14. There are many solutions to this matrix equation. We list two, with corresponding designs.

$$
R = \begin{array}{rrrrrrrrrrrrrr}
3 & 1 & 0 & 2 & 1 & 0 & 0 & 1 & 1 & 1 & 1 & 1 & 1 & 1 \\
0 & 3 & 1 & 0 & 2 & 1 & 0 & 1 & 1 & 1 & 1 & 1 & 1 & 1 \\
1 & 0 & 3 & 1 & 0 & 2 & 0 & 1 & 1 & 1 & 1 & 1 & 1 & 1 \\
0 & 0 & 0 & 1 & 1 & 1 & 2 & 0 & 1 & 1 & 1 & 2 & 2 & 2 \\
1 & 1 & 1 & 1 & 1 & 1 & 3 & 2 & 1 & 1 & 1 & 0 & 0 & 0
\end{array}
$$

$$
N = \begin{array}{rrrrrrrrrrrrrr}
J & I & 0 & I+C & I & 0 & 0 & I & I & I & I & I & I & I \\
0 & J & I & 0 & I+C & I & 0 & I & I & C & C & C^2 & C^2 & C^2 \\
I & 0 & J & I & 0 & I+C & 0 & I & I & C^2 & C^2 & C & C & C \\
0 & 0 & 0 & I & I & C^2 & I+C & 0 & C & C & C^2 & I+C & I+C^2 & C+C^2 \\
I & I & I & C & C^2 & C^2 & J & I+C^2 & C & C^2 & C & 0 & 0 & 0
\end{array}
$$

where C is the 3 by 3 permutation circulant corresponding to (1 2 3).

$$
R = \begin{array}{rrrrrrrrrrrrrr}
0 & 0 & 0 & 0 & 2 & 2 & 2 & 2 & 1 & 1 & 1 & 1 & 1 & 1 \\
2 & 1 & 1 & 1 & 3 & 0 & 0 & 0 & 1 & 1 & 1 & 1 & 1 & 1 \\
1 & 2 & 1 & 1 & 0 & 3 & 0 & 0 & 1 & 1 & 1 & 1 & 1 & 1 \\
1 & 1 & 2 & 1 & 0 & 0 & 3 & 0 & 1 & 1 & 1 & 1 & 1 & 1 \\
1 & 1 & 1 & 2 & 0 & 0 & 0 & 3 & 1 & 1 & 1 & 1 & 1 & 1
\end{array}
$$

$N_1 =$

$$
\begin{array}{rrrrrrrrrrrrrr}
0 & 0 & 0 & 0 & C+C^2 & C+C^2 & C+C^2 & C+C^2 & I & I & I & I & I & I \\
C+C^2 & I & I & I & J & 0 & 0 & 0 & I & I & C & C & C^2 & C^2 \\
I & C+C^2 & I & I & 0 & J & 0 & 0 & I & C & I & C^2 & C & C^2 \\
I & I & C+C^2 & I & 0 & 0 & J & 0 & I & C^2 & C & C^2 & I & C \\
I & I & I & C+C^2 & 0 & 0 & 0 & J & I & C^2 & C^2 & C & C & I
\end{array}
$$

is a solution.

$$
N_2 = \begin{array}{rrrrrrrrrrrrrr}
0 & 0 & 0 & 0 & I+C & I+C & I+C & I+C & I & I & I & I & I & I \\
I+C & I & I & I & J & 0 & 0 & 0 & I & I & C & C & C^2 & C^2 \\
I & I+C & I & I & 0 & J & 0 & 0 & C & C^2 & I & C^2 & I & C \\
I & I & C+C^2 & C & 0 & 0 & J & 0 & I & I & C^2 & C^2 & C & C \\
I & I & C & C+C^2 & 0 & 0 & 0 & J & C & C^2 & C & I & C^2 & I
\end{array}
$$

is a second, nonisomorphic solution.

N_1 was constructed by hand, using methods similar to [17], while N and N_2 were found by computer.

4. The Toolchest Constructions. The Design Theory Toolchest software was developed to find t-designs and used to find a new simple 6-design [11,12]. It can be used successfully with $t = 2$ on appropriate machines.

Using the Apollo at the Institute for Mathematics and its Applications, and the Sun and Alliant at the Institute for Scientific Computation, University of Wyoming, we found at least 13 nonisomorphic 2-(15,5,4) designs, which are listed in the appendix. Four of these are 1-rotational and hence appear in [14].

134

5. Designs from Coherent Configurations. In this section we describe the construction of a 2-(15,5,4) design whose blocks form an association scheme. This design has previously appeared in [2,13,16]. We show this design has automorphism group A_7. Our motivation for studying this design came from a question about the existence of a particular coherent configuration, and we explain this connection. Finally, three related designs are described.

The construction of the design is as follows. Consider the Steiner system $S = S(5,8,24)$. Let B be a block of S, and choose two points x and y such that $x \in B$ and $y \notin B$. We define a new incidence structure D by taking the points to be the set of points of S outside of $B \cup \{y\}$, and the blocks to be those blocks of S which contain x and y and intersect B in two points. The incidence relation is that inherited from S. See [15] for similar geometric constructions using S.

THEOREM. *D is a 2-(15,5,4) design with automorphism group A_7.*

Proof. Clearly D has 15 points and 5 points per block. Suppose p and q are points of D. Then there are 5 blocks of S containing the points p, q, x, and y; we need only show that 4 of these intersect B in two points. Every block of S intersects B in an even number of points, thus each of these blocks must intersect B in 1 or 3 points other than x. Let m_i be the number of them intersecting B in i additional points. Then:

$$m_1 + m_3 = 5 , \quad \text{and}$$

$$m_1 + 3m_3 = 7 .$$

Therefore $m_1 = 4$ as claimed, and D is a 2-(15,5,4) design.

The subgroup of M_{24} which stabilizes B and fixes the points x and y is isomorphic to A_7 [3]; thus $A_7 \subseteq \text{Aut}(D)$.

Suppose σ is an automorphism of D. Define τ on the points of S as follows.

$$\tau(p) = \sigma(p) \text{ for all } p \text{ a point of } D.$$
$$\tau(x) = x$$
$$\tau(y) = y$$

$\tau(p)$ for $p \in B - \{x\}$ is defined using the following: If C is a block of D, there is a unique point p_C of B such that $C' = \{x, y, p_C\} \cup C$ is a block of S. If $p_C = p_D$ then C intersects D in one point. It follows that $\sigma(C)$ and $\sigma(D)$ must intersect in one point, and the corresponding blocks of S, $\sigma(C)'$ and $\sigma(D)'$, must intersect in four points, the fourth being a point other than x of B, *i.e.*, $p_{\sigma(C)} = p_{\sigma(D)}$. Let $\tau(p_C) = p_{\sigma(C)}$.

It is clear that τ acts on the blocks of S corresponding to blocks of D. To show that τ is an automorphism of S, we must show it takes all blocks of S to blocks of S.

First, suppose X is a block of S such that $|X \cap B| = 4$, and $x, y \in X$. We will show that $\tau(X)$ is a block of S.

135

Note that we showed earlier that of the five blocks containing x and y and two given points outside of B, four of them intersect B in one additional point and one intersects B in 3 additional points. These blocks partition the points of $B - \{x\}$.

Let $X = \{y, x, b_1, b_2, b_3, a_1, a_2, a_3\}$, where $X \cap B = \{x, b_1, b_2, b_3\}$. Thus X is the block containing x, y, a_1, and a_2 which intersects B in 4 points. Suppose the other 4 blocks containing these 4 points are B_4, B_5, B_6, and B_7, and the points of B they contain are b_4, b_5, b_6, and b_7 respectively.

Now the blocks $\tau(B_i)$ contain the four points x, y, $\tau(a_1)$ and $\tau(a_2)$ and they intersect B in 2 points; hence the block X' of S containing these four points which intersects B in four points must contain $\{x, y, \tau(a_1), \tau(a_2), \tau(b_1), \tau(b_2), \tau(b_3)\}$. A similar argument starting with the points x, y, $\tau(a_1)$, and $\tau(a_3)$ shows there must be a block of S containing $\{x, y, \tau(a_1), \tau(a_3), \tau(b_1), \tau(b_2), \tau(b_3)\}$, which intersects X' in at least 6 points so it must be X', and therefore $X' = \tau(X)$.

It is well-known that if X and Y are blocks of S which intersect in 4 points, then the symmetric difference of X and Y is a block of S, and if X and Y are disjoint blocks of S, then the set of points incident with neither X nor Y is a block of S. Using these two facts, it is now easy to show that the image under τ of every block is a block of S. Therefore, Aut $(D) = A_7$. $\quad\square$

We next define coherent configurations, and show the relationship of the design D to a particular one. If X is a finite set, we use diag (X^2) to denote the binary relation $\{(x, x) : x \in X\}$.

DEFINITION. Let X be a finite set, and $\{f_i\}_{i \in I}$ a set of binary relations on X. $(X, \{f_i\})$ is called a *coherent configuration* (c.c.) if the following conditions hold.

1. $\{f_i\}$ is a partition of X^2.
2. For all $i \in I$, $f_i^t = f_j$, for some $j \in I$.
3. $f_i \cap$ diag $(X^2) \neq 0$ implies $f_i \subseteq$ diag (X^2).
4. If $(x, y) \in f_k$, then $|\{z : (x, z) \in f_i$ and $(z, y) \in f_j\}|$ is a constant p_{ij}^k depending only on i, j, and k.

The coherent configuration is said to be *homogeneous* if diag $(X^2) = f_i$ for some i.

The set X can be partitioned into a disjoint union of sets $\{X_\alpha\}_{\alpha \in A}$, such that for every α, diag (X_α^2) is one of the relations f_i, and then for all $i \in I$, $f_i \subseteq X_\alpha \times X_b$ for some α, $\beta \in A$. If we let $r_{\alpha\beta} = |\{f_i : f_i \subseteq X_\alpha \times X_\beta\}|$, we say the c.c. has *type* $(r_{\alpha\beta})$.

Note that an association scheme with n associate classes is a homogeneous c.c. of type $(n+1)$. The sets X_α together with the relations $\{f_i \subseteq X_\alpha \times X_\beta\}$ are association schemes.

A standard reference for coherent configurations is [7], to which the reader is referred for more details.

In [8], Hobart studied coherent configurations of type $\left(\begin{smallmatrix} 2 & 2 \\ 2 & 4 \end{smallmatrix}\right)$. These correspond in a natural way to certain 2-designs having either two or three block intersection sizes. In particular,

THEOREM [8]. *Suppose* (P, B, F) *is a 2-design with three symmetric irreflexive binary relations* f_1, f_2, *and* f_3 *defined on the blocks, such that*

1. *For any two distinct blocks* B *and* C, $(B, C) \in f_i$ *for exactly one* i.
2. *If* $(B, C) \in f_i$, *then the number of points incident with both* B *and* C *is* a_i, *and* $a_2 \neq a_3$.
3. *If* p *is an point and* B *is a block, the number of blocks incident with* p *having relation* f_1 *to* B *depends only on whether* p *is incident with* B *or not.*
4. *If* B *and* C *are blocks, then the number of blocks* D *with* $(B, C) \in f_1$ *and* $(C, D) \in f_1$ *depends only on the relation between* B *and* C.

Then $(X, \{f_i\})$ *is a coherent configuration of type* $\left(\begin{smallmatrix} 2 & 2 \\ 2 & 4 \end{smallmatrix}\right)$, *where* $X = P \cup B$, *and the relations are* f_1, f_2, f_3, *identity on blocks, identity and nonidentity on points, and incidence and nonincidence of points and blocks.*

In particular, *the blocks of such a design form an association scheme with 3 associate classes.* ☐

$S(5, 8, 24)$ is an example of such a design; the relations on the blocks are defined by the three block intersection sizes.

The 2-(15,5,4) design D constructed in this section has intersection sizes 0, 1, and 2. We will show that it defines a c.c. of type $\left(\begin{smallmatrix} 2 & 2 \\ 2 & 4 \end{smallmatrix}\right)$, with parameters which are those of the smallest unknown case in Hobart's list [8, chapter 5].

THEOREM. *Any 2-(15,5,4) design with maximal block intersection size 2 defines a c.c. of type* $\left(\begin{smallmatrix} 2 & 2 \\ 2 & 4 \end{smallmatrix}\right)$.

Proof. Fix a block B of the design, and let n_i be the number of blocks intersecting B in i points. Then standard arguments show that for any block, $n_2 = 30$, $n_1 = 5$, and $n_0 = 6$.

Let B be a block, and let C_i, $1 \leq i \leq 6$, be the six blocks disjoint from B. Consider $C_i \cap C_j$. If $C_i \cap C_j = \phi$, then any C_k must intersect C_i or C_j in 3 points, a contradiction. If $C_i \cap C_j = \{p\}$, then there is one point, q, not in B, C_i, or C_j. Any other C_k cannot contain p, and must contain q and intersect both C_i and C_j in two points. It is impossible to find four blocks satisfying these conditions which intersect pairwise in no more than two points. Therefore, $|C_i \cap C_j| = 2$ for all $i \neq j$.

We now show that this design defines a c.c. Let f_1, f_2, and f_3 correspond to block intersection sizes 0, 1, and 2 respectively. Suppose B is a block. For $p \notin B$, let r_p be the number of blocks containing p which do not intersect B. Then by the usual counting arguments, $\sum_{p \notin B} (r_p - 3)^2 = 0$, hence $r_p = 3$ for all $p \notin B$ and (3) is satisfied.

137

Let B and C be blocks of the design. If $|B \cap C| = 0$ or 1, then clearly there are no blocks disjoint from both B and C. If $|B \cap C| = 2$, then there can be at most one block contained in the set of 7 points in neither B nor C. However for any block B there are 6 blocks disjoint from it and each of these is disjoint from 5 blocks which intersect B in 2 points. Thus for each of the 30 blocks intersecting B in 2 points there must be exactly one block disjoint from both of them, and (4) is satisfied. $\square$

In the proof of this theorem, we have established enough parameters to determine all the parameters of the c.c. using equations from [8]. In particular, the following two statements hold.

1. Given a block B and a point p, there are 2 or 1 blocks containing p intersecting B in 1 point, as p is an element of B or not.

2. Given two blocks which intersect in one point, there are 4 blocks intersecting both in one point.

Since a given block B intersects 5 blocks in one point, it follows that $\{C : |B \cap C| = 1\}$ is the dual of a 2-(6,2,1) design and such sets of blocks partition the blocks of the design. In addition, if $\{B_i : 1 \le i \le 6\}$ is such a set, the remaining blocks may be partitioned into six sets of the form $R_i = \{C : C \cap B_i = \phi\}$. This fact was used with a computer search to find the design D.

Starting from the dual of a 2-(6,2,1) design with blocks B_i, all possible sets R_i of 6 blocks disjoint from B_i, intersecting pairwise in 2 points, and intersecting B_j in 2 points for $i \ne j$, were found. The results are listed in Table 1; for each B_i there were two sets R_i. The R_i are arranged in the table so that blocks in the union of the R_i in column I intersect in at most 2 points; and similarly for column II. It is easily checked that this is not true for any other arrangement of the R_i's. Now either of these unions together with $\{B_i\}$ is a 2-(15,5,4) design, as will be shown below, and these two designs are isomorphic via any transposition of the original 6 blocks. Therefore there is a unique 2-(15,5,4) design with maximal block intersection size 2.

THEOREM. *Suppose $(P, \{B_i\})$ is the dual of the 2-(6,2,1) design, and there exist sets R_i of six 5-subsets of P such that if $D \in R_i$, then D is disjoint from B_i, $|D \cap B_j| = 2$ for $j \ne i$, and $|D \cap E| = 2$ for any $E \in R_i$, $D \ne E$. Then $(P, B = \{B_i\} \cup R_1 \cup \cdots \cup R_6)$ is a 2-(15,5,4) design.*

Proof. We need only check that any pair of points is in 4 blocks.

Let $C_i = P - B_i$. By the same reasoning as the previous theorem, any point of C_i is in 3 blocks of R_i. Any pair of points of C_i are in at most two blocks of R_i, hence 15 pairs of points occur in two blocks of R_i. There are then 30 pairs of points which occur in one block, and each of the 45 pairs of points of C_i are in either one or two blocks of R_i.

Suppose $\{p, q\} \subseteq C_1 \cap C_2$ for some C_1, $C_2 \in R_i$, and there is a block B_j with $\{p, q\} \subseteq B_j$. Then there must be a block D of R_i containing p, which contains at most one point each of C_1, C_2, and B_j. But this would require 11 points not in B_i.

138

Hence if a pair $\{p, q\}$ is in a block B_j, it is contained in one block of R_i. Note that $|R_i \cap B_j| = 4$ for all $j \neq i$, so the pairs of points of C_i contained in two blocks of R_i are precisely those not contained in any B_j.

If $\{p, q\} \subseteq B_i$, there are three blocks of $\{B_i\}$ containing neither of them, so $\{p, q\}$ is contained in 4 blocks of B. If $\{p, q\}$ is contained in no B_i, there are two blocks of $\{B_i\}$ containing neither, and again the points are in 4 blocks. $\square$

It follows from this theorem that any choice of an R_i for each B_i yields a 2-(15,5,4) design. However there are only four nonisomorphic ones among these, corresponding to 0, 1, 2 or 3 sets chosen from I. The isomorphisms are induced from permutations of the original 6 blocks, and the fact that these four are not isomorphic follows from looking at the block intersections.

Table 1

B_i	I					II				
	6	7	11	14	15	6	7	12	13	15
	6	8	12	13	14	6	8	10	14	15
$B_1 = 1\ 2\ 3\ 4\ 5$	6	9	10	13	15	6	9	11	13	14
	7	8	10	12	15	7	8	11	12	14
	8	9	10	11	14	8	9	10	12	13
	2	3	12	13	15	2	3	11	14	15
	2	4	10	14	15	2	4	12	13	14
$B_2 = 1\ 6\ 7\ 8\ 9$	2	5	11	13	14	2	5	10	13	15
	3	4	11	12	14	3	4	10	12	15
	3	5	10	11	15	3	5	11	12	13
	4	5	10	12	13	4	5	10	11	14
	1	3	8	14	15	1	3	9	13	15
	1	4	9	13	14	1	4	7	14	15
$B_3 = 2\ 6\ 10\ 11\ 12$	1	5	7	13	15	1	5	8	13	14
	3	4	7	9	15	3	4	8	9	14
	3	5	8	9	13	3	5	7	8	15
	4	5	7	8	14	4	5	7	9	13
	1	2	9	11	15	1	2	8	12	15
	1	4	6	12	15	1	4	9	11	12
$B_4 = 3\ 7\ 10\ 13\ 14$	1	5	8	11	12	1	5	6	11	15
	2	4	8	9	12	2	4	6	9	15
	2	5	6	8	15	2	5	8	9	11
	4	5	6	9	11	4	5	6	8	12
	1	2	7	12	14	1	2	9	10	14
	1	3	9	10	12	1	3	6	12	14
$B_5 = 4\ 8\ 11\ 13\ 15$	1	5	6	10	14	1	5	7	10	12
	2	3	6	9	14	2	3	7	9	12
	2	5	7	9	10	2	5	6	7	14
	3	5	6	7	12	3	5	6	9	10
	1	2	8	10	13	1	2	7	11	13
	1	3	6	11	13	1	3	8	10	11
$B_6 = 5\ 9\ 12\ 14\ 15$	1	4	7	10	11	1	4	6	10	13
	2	3	7	8	11	2	3	6	8	13
	2	4	6	7	13	2	4	7	8	10
	3	4	6	8	10	3	4	6	7	11

$|G|$	group generators	base blocks				
14	(1 2 3 4 5 6 7)(8 9 10 11 12 13 14)	1	4	5	6	9
	(1 8)(2 9)(3 10)(4 11)(5 12)(6 13)(7 14)	1	3	4	8	9
		0	1	4	8	10
		1	4	5	6	9
		0	1	4	8	10
		1	2	3	8	11
		1	3	4	5	9
		0	1	4	8	10
		1	2	3	10	13
		0	1	4	10	11
		1	2	4	6	8
		1	2	3	11	14
7	(1 2 3 4 5 6 7)(8 9 10 11 12 13 14)	1	3	4	5	10
		0	1	4	9	10
		0	1	4	9	11
		1	2	3	9	12
		4	6	8	10	14
		4	8	9	11	14
		1	4	6	8	9
		1	3	4	5	10
		0	1	2	8	10
		4	5	8	9	13
		0	1	4	9	14
		4	8	10	11	14
		0	1	2	5	9
		1	2	4	9	10
		1	2	3	8	12
		1	8	10	11	13
		0	4	8	9	14
		1	4	6	10	14
9	(1 2 3)(4 5 6)(7 8 9)(10 11 12)	1	4	7	10	11
	(1 4 7)(2 5 8)(3 6 9)(13 14 0)	1	2	4	6	12
		0	1	5	11	12
		0	1	2	3	14
		1	4	5	8	14
		0	5	7	10	14
		0	1	6	10	11
		1	4	7	10	11
		1	3	4	5	12
		0	1	2	3	14
		1	4	5	8	14
		0	5	7	10	14

$|G|$	group generators	base blocks				
		0	1	5	7	8
		1	3	4	5	12
		0	1	6	10	12
		1	4	7	11	12
		0	1	9	10	13
		0	1	2	3	14
		0	1	4	7	10
		0	2	5	8	11
12	(1 2 3)(4 5 6)(7 8 9)(10 11 12)(13 14 0)	0	2	3	4	12
	(1 4 7 10)(2 5 8 11)(3 6 9 12)	1	2	5	6	12
		0	3	7	8	14
		0	2	3	8	9
		0	1	2	6	10
		1	2	4	7	11
		0	2	3	4	13
		0	1	3	7	9
		0	2	3	6	10
		1	2	4	9	10
		0	1	2	4	14

Acknowledgements. The authors wish to thank Don Kreher for his kindness in providing the Design Theory Toolchest software associated with this research and his assistance in its use. We thank the Institute for Mathematics and its Applications, and the University of Wyoming's Institute for Scientific Computation for providing computer facilities and time.

We also thank Mark J. Oliver of the University of Wyoming's Institute for Scientific Computation for his helpful contributions.

REFERENCES

[1]   W.G. BRIDGES, MARSHALL HALL, JR., AND JACK L. HAYDEN, *Codes and Designs*, J. Combin. Theory, (A) 31, (1981) 155–174.

[2]   P.J. CAMERON AND J.H. VAN LINT, *Graphs, Codes and Designs*, in *London Math. Soc. Lecture Note 43*, Cambridge University Press, 1980.

[3]   J. CONWAY, *Three lectures on exceptional groups*, in *Finite Simple Groups*, (M.B. Powell and G. Higman editors), Academic Press, 1971.

[4]   MARSHALL HALL, JR., *Combinatorial Theory*, Blaisdell, Waltham, Massachusetts, 1967.

[5]   H. HANANI, *The existence and construction of balanced incomplete block designs*, Ann. Math. Stat. 32 (1961) 361–386.

[6]   H. HANANI, *Balanced incomplete block designs and related designs*, Discrete Math., 11 (1975) 255–369.

[7]   D.G. HIGMAN, *Coherent Algebras*, Lin. Alg. Appl., 93 (1987) 209–239.

[8]   S.A. HOBART, *Coherent configurations of type $\left(\begin{smallmatrix} 2 & 2 \\ & 4 \end{smallmatrix} \right)$ and designs*, Ph.D. thesis, University of Michigan, 1987.

[9]   E.S. KRAMER, *Some t-designs for $t \geq 4$ and $t = 17, 18$*, in *Proceedings of the Sixth Southeastern Conference on Combinatorics, Graph Theory and Computing*, Congressus Numerantium XIV (1975) 443–460.

[10] E.S. KRAMER AND D. MESNER, *t-designs on hypergraphs*, Discrete Math., 15, (1976), 263–296.

[11] D.L. KREHER AND S.P. RADZISZOWSKI, *The existence of simple 6-(14,7,4) designs*, J. Combin. Theory (A), 43 (1986) 237–244.

[12] D.L. KREHER AND S.P. RADZISZOWSKI, *Constructing 6-(14,7,4) designs*, (preprint).

[13] R. MATHON, *On linked arrays of pairs*, Ann. Discrete Math., 15 (1982) 273-292.

[14] R. MATHON AND A. ROSA, *On the (15,5,l) family of BIBDs*, (preprint).

[15] A. NEUMAIER, *Some sporadic geometries related to PG(3,2)*, Arch. Math., 42 (1984) 89–96.

[16] S.S. SANE AND S.S. SHRIKHANDE, *On generalized quasi-residual designs*, J. Stat. Plan. Infer., 17 (1987) 269–276.

[17] VLADIMIR D. TONCHEV, JACOBUS H. VAN LINT, AND I.N. LANDGEV, *A New Design*, in *Coding Theory, IMA Volumes in Mathematics and its Applications*, (D. Ray-Chauhduri, ed.), 20, Springer-Verlag, New York.

143

t-DESIGNS IN DELSARTE SPACES

S. G. HOGGAR*

Abstract. We survey results on t-designs on the sphere and in projective spaces over the real and complex numbers, quaternions, and Cayley numbers, with applications to combinatorics.

Key words. t-design, quaternions, Addition formula, scheme, graph.

AMS(MOS) subject classifications. 05B30 (05B25, 33A75).

Introduction. We explain a natural progression

Classical combinatorial t-designs

$\rightarrow$ Spherical t-designs

$\rightarrow$ t-designs in projective spaces over R, C, H, O

$\rightarrow$ t-designs in Delsarte spaces.

Here R, C are the real and complex numbers, H, O the quaternions and Cayley numbers (also known as octonions). We illustrate the use of Harmonic functions, Jacobi orthogonal polynomials, Addition formulae, Isometry groups and invariant integrals. We stress combinatorial applications, especially to association schemes and strongly regular graphs.

This mini-survey is organized as follows. In §1 we show how the combinatorial t-design leads naturally to a definition of spherical t-design in terms of harmonic functions. In §2 we illustrate how an Addition formula yields bounds for sets of lines in terms of the elements of $A = \{\cos^2 \emptyset\}$, where $\emptyset$ is the angle between a pair of lines. §3 charts progress up to the classification of tight t-designs in the sphere and projective spaces.

Combinatorial applications are given in §4, with useful explicit formulae, some new, along with discussion of examples such as reflection groups, and cross-connections.

In §5 we introduce Neumaier's 't-designs in Delsarte spaces', and their application to spheres and projective spaces.

Finally, we present 10 unsolved problems.

1. From classical to spherical. Spherical t-designs were introduced by Delsarte, Goethals and Seidel in a seminal paper [25]. Between them, they and others brought out connections and applications to the above list and to Extremal sets on the Euclidean sphere, Sphere packings, Geometrical configurations, Root systems, Finite (often simple) groups, Permutation groups, Approximation theory [12, 17,

*Department of Mathematics, Glasgow University, Glasgow G12 8QW, Scotland. This paper written on leave at: Department of Mathematics, Ohio State University, Columbus, Ohio 43210, USA.

26, 27]. We first recall that a *combinatorial* $t - (v, k, \lambda)$ *design* consists of a v-set **V** and a collection **B** of k-subsets called *blocks*, satisfying

(1.1) Every t-subset is contained in exactly λ blocks

Now, **B** can be represented as a set X of points on the discrete sphere

$$\Omega = \{(x_1, \ldots, x_v)| \text{ each } x_1 \text{ is 0 or 1 and } \sum x_i^2 = k\},$$

in R^v, by the correspondences:

$$
\begin{array}{lll}
\text{BLOCK} & \rightarrow & \text{POINT} \\
B = \{i_1, \ldots, i_k\} & & b = (b_1, \ldots, b_v), \; b_i = 1 \Leftrightarrow i \in B, \\
t\text{-SUBSET} & \rightarrow & \text{MONOMIAL} \\
J = \{j_1, \ldots, j_t\} & & f(x) = f_J(x) = x_{j_1} x_{j_2} \ldots x_{j_t}.
\end{array}
$$

Then $f(b) = 1 \Leftrightarrow$ coordinates $b_{j_1}, \ldots b_{j_t}$ all equal 1

$$\Leftrightarrow \{i_1, \ldots, i_k\} \supseteq \{j_1, \ldots, j_t\}.$$

EXAMPLE. $t = 2$, $v = 7$. The correspondence gives

$$
\begin{array}{lll}
\{1, 4\} & \rightarrow & x_1 x_4 = f(x) \\
\cap & & \\
\{1, 2, 4\} & \rightarrow & (1, 1, 0, 1, 0, 0, 0) = b
\end{array}
$$

The inclusion yields $f(b) = 1$.

Continuing the previous argument, we see that $\{j_1, \ldots, j_t\}$ is contained in λ blocks if and only if $f(b) = 1$ for λ points of X, and then condition (1.1): "each t-subset is in exactly λ blocks" becomes

$$\sum f(x) = \lambda \; (x \in X), \text{ for every monomial } f(x) \text{ of degree } t.$$

We can say more. Since the permutation group $\mathrm{Sym}(V)$ on the coordinates is transitive on such monomials, the condition for a t-design may be written

$$\sum_{x \in X} f(Tx) = \sum_{x \in X} f(x), \qquad \text{for all } T \text{ in } \mathrm{Sym}(\mathbf{V}), \; f \text{ in } \mathrm{Hom}(t),$$

where $\mathrm{Hom}(t)$ denotes the R-linear span of the monomials considered.

Finally, we observe that the above condition asserts that

(1.2) "the t'th moments of X are invariant under the action of $\mathrm{Sym}(V)$ on the coordinates"

In fact, invariance follows for $t - 1, \ldots, 2, 1$. Here a t-th moment of X is a sum $\sum f(x) \; (x \in X)$, where f is homogeneous of degree k in the coordinates, but no x_i appears to a power greater than unity. This last restriction is dropped below in the parallel definition we now introduce for t-designs on the continuous sphere, replacing v by d for dimension.

DEFINITION. Let X be a finite subset of the unit sphere Ω_d in R^d. Then X is a *spherical t-design*, or *t-design* on Ω, if

(1.3)   "the k'th moments of X are constant under orthogonal

           transformations $T \in O(d)$ for $k = 1, 2, \ldots, t$"

The harmonic connection. Powerful implications of the above definition follow from its relation to harmonic polynomials. Let $\hom(k)$ denote the linear space of functions on Ω which are given by homogeneous polynomials of degree k in the coordinates, and let $\operatorname{harm}(k)$ be the subspace of functions $g(x)$ which are harmonic, that is $\sum \partial^2 g / \partial x_i^2 = 0$. Then every $f(x)$ in $\hom(k)$ can be uniquely expressed as

$$f(x) = \sum (x, x)^i g_{k-2i}(x) \qquad (0 \le i \le k/2),$$

where (x, x) is the usual innerproduct and $g_r(x)$ is in $\operatorname{harm}(r)$. This gives condition (1.4) of the Theorem below.

THEOREM 1.1. [25]. *let X be a finite subset of the unit sphere Ω in R^d. Then X is a spherical t-design in Ω if and only if*

$$(1.4) \qquad \sum_{x \in X} g(x) = 0, \quad \text{for all } g \in \operatorname{harm}(k), \qquad k = 1, 2, \ldots, t.$$

EXAMPLES.

1-designs The condition (1.4) becomes $\sum x_i = 0$, $1 \le i \le d$, so X is a 'balanced' set of points on Ω, with the origin as centre of mass.

2-designs Here X is balanced, and in addition satisfies for $i \ne j$,

$$\sum_{x \in X} x_i x_j = 0, \qquad \sum_{x \in X} x_i^2 - x_j^2 = 0.$$

It can be shown that the additional conditions are equivalent to X being a *Eutactic star* of Schläfli [43]. That is, up to a constant multiple, the orthogonal projection of an orthonormal basis in some R^n, $n = |X|$, onto a d-dimensional subspace $(d < n)$. (This implies neither unit length nor the balanced property). Mimura [41] has given a systematic explicit construction for all cases of d, n in which a spherical 2-design can exist. The following previously known examples illustrate the significance of the concept. The precise overlap with [41] remains to be determined.

$d = 2$.	The vertices of a regular polygon centred at the origin.
$d = 3$.	The vertices of any regular polyhedron: tetrahedron, cube, octahedron, dodecahedron, icosahedron.
$d = 4, 6, 7, 8$.	The minimal vectors of respective lattices D_4, E_6, E_7, E_8. cf. [12].
$d = 24$.	A set of 2300 vectors in the Leech lattice with automorphism group Co. 2. [25].

Case $t \ge 3$. For plenty of examples on Ω see [25]. However the classification here is fairly wide open so far.

146

2. The Addition Formula. This is the key result for using the harmonic connection of t-designs. We require the innerproduct of functions f, g, in harm(k), namely

$$(2.1) \qquad (f,g) = \int f(x)g(x)d\omega(x) \qquad (x \in \Omega),$$

where $d\omega(x)$ is the unique $O(d)$-invariant measure on Ω [28]. Then for any orthogonal basis $f_1, \ldots, f_q$ of harm(k), with $(f_i, f_i) = |\Omega|$, and any pair x, y in Ω, and positive integer k, we have

$$(2.2) \qquad \sum f_i(x)f_i(y) = Q_k((x,y)) \qquad (1 \le i \le q),$$

where $Q_k(x)$ is a certain Gegenbauer polynomial [25]. The remarkable thing is that the left hand side seems to depend on the choice of basis $\{f_i\}$ and on x, y individually, yet it is expressible as a polynomial in a single variable, the innerproduct (x,y). Further information on such polynomials is found in [1, 49].

A simple example: the case d $= 2 = k$.

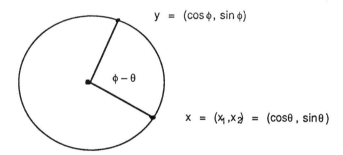

An orthogonal basis of harm(2) in case $d = 2$ is: $x_1^2 - x_2^2 = \cos 2\theta$, $2x_1 x_2 = \sin 2\theta$, and the addition formula is the well-known trigonometric formula in the first line of the argument below, with $Q_1(z) = 2z - 1$.

$$\cos 2\theta \cos 2\phi + \sin 2\theta \sin 2\phi = \cos(2\theta - 2\phi),$$
$$(2.3) \qquad\qquad = 2(x,y)^2 - 1, \text{ since } \cos(\theta - \phi) = (x,y),$$
$$= Q_1((x,y)^2)$$

The projective spaces. In the example above, (2.3) still holds with x replaced by its antipodal $-x$, since the innerproduct (x,y) appears only to an even power. Similarly for y. Thus we may view x, y as representative unit vectors for lines through the origin. In this way (2.3) and its higher-dimensional analogues are adapted towards getting results on projective spaces RP^{d-1}, with right hand side a

Gegenbauer polynomial of even powers only. An Addition formula using odd powers only, handles the real sphere Ω. To extend beyond the real case to projective spaces FP^{d-1}, $F = R, C, H, O$, we need

	(1)	a suitable space of functions on each FP^n,
(2.4)	(2)	a corresponding addition formula, and
	(3)	the polynomial Q_k known explicitly.

Such a formula was highlighted in the complex case by Koornwinder [37] for the space harm(p, q) of functions on the unit sphere in C^d, expressible as a polynomial g, homogeneous of degree p in the complex coordinates z_i and degree q in their conjugates w_i, and satisfying $\sum \partial^2 g/\partial z_i \partial w_i = 0$ (which implies the real and complex parts of g are harmonic in the usual sense).

EXAMPLE. harm$(1, 1)$ contains $z_1 w_1 - z_2 w_2$ and $z_1 w_2$.

This was used by J. J. Seidel and others [24] to establish bounds for systems of lines in R^n and C^n by a unified method. A unified extension to the Cayley numbers (see end of §5), and to t-designs for $F \neq R$, came with Neumaier's more general framework of t-designs in his concept of Delsarte Space [42]. For separate results in the quaternion case, see [29].

Application to bounds. Here is how an addition formula can give a bound for the size of line systems. Let X be a set of v unit vectors representing equiangular lines in F^d, say

$$(2.5) \qquad |(x, y)|^2 = \alpha, \text{ for all distinct } x, y \text{ in } X.$$

For $F = R, C, H$ the innerproduct (x, y) is given by $x^* y$, where x^* is the conjugate transpose of x as column vector. We write $\cos \emptyset = |(x, y)|$. Given that $\cos^2 \emptyset$ is well-defined even for $F = O$ (see (5,4)), and that $f_1, \ldots f_q$ is an orthogonal basis for an appropriate space of harmonic functions, the argument runs as follows.

$$
\begin{aligned}
0 &\leq \sum_i \left(\sum_{x \in X} f_i(x) \right) \left(\sum_{y \in X} f_i(y) \right), &&\text{a sum of squares,} \\
&= \sum_{x,y \in X} \sum_i f_i(x) f_i(y), &&\text{on reversing the order of summation,} \\
&= \sum_{x,y \in X} Q_k(\cos^2 \emptyset), &&\textbf{by the Addition Formula} \\
&= (v - 1) v Q_k(\alpha) + v Q_k(1), &&\text{since } \cos^2 0 = 1.
\end{aligned}
$$

It follows that $v[-Q_k(\alpha)] \leq Q_k(1) - Q_k(\alpha)$, so provided that the left hand side is positive we have $v \leq [Q_k(1) - Q_k(\alpha)]/ - Q_k(\alpha)$. It thus suffices simply to know $Q_1(x)$, and that up to a constant multiple. We earlier found for the real case $Q_1(x) = 2x - 1$. For general d we may use $dx - 1$. Indeed, with parameter m, where $2m = (F : R)$, the exact expression is $Q_1(x) = (md + 1)(dx - 1)$, so that we obtain (unusually) a bound independent of the choice of F. This is found in the top line of Table 1 following, with other bounds produced by further development of the technique above (see §5). We recall that the angle set for a subset of FP^{d-1} is $A = \{\cos^2 \emptyset\}$ where $\emptyset$ is the angle between a pair of lines. The special and absolute bounds agree at $A = \{1/5\}$, $d = 3$, realised by the six diagonals of an icosahedron. cf [39].

TABLE 1.Bounds for subsets of FP^{d-1}. $A = \{\cos^2 \emptyset\}$
$$N = md, \quad 2m = (F : R). \quad (x)_i = x(x+1)\ldots(x+i-1).$$

A	Special bound	Absolute bound
$\{a\}$	$\frac{d(1-a)}{1-da}$	$d(N - m + 1)$
$\{0,a\}$	$\frac{d(N+1)(1-a)}{m+1-(N+1)a}$	$\frac{d(N-m+1)(N+1)}{m+1}$
$\{a,b\}$	$\frac{(N)_2(1-a)(1-b)}{(m)_2-m(N+1)(a+b)+(N)_2 ab}$ *	$\frac{(N-m+1)_2(N)_2}{2(m)_2}$
$\{0,a,b\}$	$\frac{(N)_3(1-a)(1-b)}{(m)_3-(m)_2(N+2)(a+b)+m(N+1)_2 ab}$ **	$\frac{(N-m+1)_2(N)_3}{2(m)_3}$

* $a + b \leq 2(m+1)/(N+2)$,

** $a+b \leq 3(m+2)/(N+4)$ and $3(m+1)_2 - 2(m+1)(N+3)(a+b) + (N+2)_2 ab \geq 0$.

These restrictions, in addition to the denominators of the various bounds being positive ($a_0 > 0$), are the requirement $a_1, \ldots, a_{s-1} \geq 0$ of (3.2), of which Table 1 gives special cases. We note that $a_s > 0$ always. Results are obtained by expanding the annihilator polynomial in terms of Jacobi polynomials, with coefficients a_i. [24,42]. The conditions are satisfied by most known examples.

EXAMPLE 2.5. C^6, $A = \{0, 1/4\}$, $v = 126$. Number 7 of [31]. Diameters of the complex polytope with diagram [46],

whose vertices are also the minimal vectors of Coxeter's extreme form $K_{12}[22]$ (also used in sphere packing [17,28]). Projectively the centres of the homologies of the Mitchell-Hamill configuration; also realized by the normal vectors to hyperplanes of the complex reflection group from which the above polytope is formed by Wythoff's construction ([46], see also [19]). This even meets the absolute bound.

EXAMPLE 2.6. H^4, $A = \{1/9, 1/3\}$, $v = 64$. Number 22 in [31], fully described in [30, pp. 219-230]. Examples meeting the special bound with A consisting of

149

exactly two nonzero are very rare (cf [32, Example 33]) and this is one of them, from the quaternionic polytope with diagram

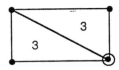

With H^4 as a right vector space, representative vertices are obtained from $(0, \omega^2, \omega, 1)$, $(\omega^2, 0, 1, \omega)$, $(\omega, 1, 0, \omega^2)$, $(1, \omega, \omega^2, 0)$ by *left* multiplication by $1, i, j, k$ and coordinate sign changes. Here $\omega = 1/2(-1 + i + j + k)$, a cube root of unity in H. As an additional benefit, the 64 complexified vectors span a subset of CP^7 meeting the *absolute* bound with $A = \{1/9\}$.

3. A Partial history.

3.1 Some definitions. For a finite nonempty subset X of Ω or FP^{d-1}, the *angle set* of X is $A = \{\cos \emptyset\}$ for Ω, $\{\cos^2 \emptyset\}$ for FP^{d-1}, where $\emptyset$ is the angle between distinct vectors or lines, and then

$$A^\circ = A \backslash \{0\}; \quad s = |A|; \quad e = |A^\circ|; \quad \varepsilon = s - e.$$

$Q_e(x)$ is the suitably normalized Jacobi polynomial in an Addition formula. $R_e(x) = Q_0(x) + Q_1(x) + \cdots + Q_e(x)$, also a Jacobi polynomial. The *annihilator polynomial* of A is $\text{ann}(x) = |X| \prod [(x - \alpha)/(1 - \alpha)]$. $(\alpha \in A)$, with expansion $\sum a_i Q_i(x)$ in Jacobi or (as a special case) Gegenbauer polynomials.

1975 [24]	P. Delsarte, J. M. Goethals, J. J. Seidel. Bounds for line systems in R^d and C^d via Gegenbauer/Jacobi polynomials $Q_k(x)$.
(3.1)	THEOREM: $|X| \leq R_e(1)$. (Absolute bound)
	THEOREM: Equality above implies $A^\circ = \{\text{all roots of } R_e(x)\}$
(3.2)	THEOREM: $a_0, a_1, \ldots, a_s \geq 0$ implies $a_0, a_1, \ldots, a_s \leq 1$.
	Explicit Special bounds in case $s \leq 3$, from $a_0 \leq 1$.

1977 [25]	SPHERICAL t-DESIGNS X defined by above authors.
(3.3)	THEOREM: $t \leq 2s - \varepsilon$. DEFINITION: X is *tight* if $t = 2s - \varepsilon$.
(3.4)	THEOREM: X is tight if and only if X meets the absolute bound.
(3.5)	THEOREM: If $a_0, \ldots, a_s > 0$ and $a_0 = \cdots = a_i = 1$, then X is an $s + i$-design.
(3.6)	THEOREM: If $t \geq s - 1$ then X is regular. If $t \geq 2s - 2$ then X is an association scheme.

Combinatorial applications included:

* If X is a 2-distance set ($s = 2$) and meets the special bound, then X is a strongly regular graph. Later [11]: If $t = 3$ then the subconstituents are also strongly regular.

* If X meets the absolute bound then X is an s-class association scheme.
* Related results and many examples, related to eg the Higman-Sims, McLaughlin, and Clebsch graphs, binary Golay code, Leech and Gossett lattices, n-dimensional polytopes, and to various simple groups [25].

1978 [29]   S. G. Hoggar. Special and Absolute bounds in the quaternion case by decomposing the $U(2n)$-irreducible space Harm(p, q)
into irreducibles under the symplectic subgroup $S_p(n)$, hence obtaining Addition formula.

1980 t-DESIGNS IN DELSARTE SPACES. A Neumaier [42] found a way to define t-designs on Ω and all FP^n simultaneously as special cases of his *Delsarte Spaces*, invented for the purpose. Derived general Addition Formula (without using groups) but minus explicit expression for polynomials $Q_k(x)$. Adapted and extended techniques of [25] to generalize (3.1)-(3.6) and later work on the Bose-Mesner Algebra of an association scheme (eg for $t \geq 2s - 2$ the scheme is even Q-polynomial [42]).

1982-3   S. G. Hoggar. Explicit $Q_k(x)$ for all FP^n at once using parameter $m = (F : R)/2$. For any set A: absolute and special bounds; coefficients a_i [31]; subdegrees of X if $t \geq s - 1$; classification of X with $A = \{0, a\}$, $t \geq 2$ [32]; intersection numbers if $t \geq 2s - 2$ [33].

1984 t-DESIGNS EXIST FOR ALL t. Follows for Ω and all FP^{d-1} from a theorem of P. D. Seymour and T. Zaslavsky (motivated by this consequence) [45].

1984   CONJECTURE [34]. For tight t-designs in FP^{d-1}, t is bounded:

$$t \leq 5$$

Proved using eg: The elements of A° are the roots of $R_e(x)$ and are *rational*; techniques with orthogonal polynomials, Newton polynomials, and squarefree integers.

*	1980	Case $F = R$	E. Bannai and R. M. Damerell	[3,4]
*	1984	Case $F = O$	S. G. Hoggar	[34]
*	1988	Case $F = C, H$	E. Bannai and S. G. Hoggar	[5,6,7]

COROLLARY. IF X is a *tight t-design in a projective space* then, for every pair of projective points in X,

$$\cos^2 \theta = 1/integer.$$

4. Applications to combinatorics. We take a little time to define and exemplify the combinatorial objects of special relevance here.

151

DEFINITION. The graph Γ, with no loops or multiple edges, is *strongly regular with parameters* (v, k, λ, μ) if [44]

(1) Γ has v vertices and is regular of degree k,
(2) the number of vertices of Γ joined to both of a pair x, y is λ if x and y are adjacent, μ if they are not; and both cases do occur (thus Γ is non-void and non-complete).

(a) (b)

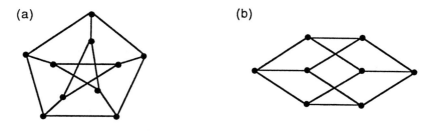

FIGURE 1. (a) The Petersen strongly regular graph, with $k = 3$, $\lambda = 0$, $\mu = 1$.
(b) An association scheme from a distance regular graph.

DEFINITION. An *s-class scheme* is a pair $(X, \{R_a\})$, where X is a finite nonempty set, a belongs to some index set Λ of size s, and the R_a partition the set of 2-subsets of X into s symmetric relations. Then x and y are called α-*associates* if (x, y) is in R_α. We often write just X for the scheme. The *subconstituents* of X are defined as

$$(4.1) \qquad X_a(x) = \{z \in X : (x, z) \in R_a\} \qquad (a \in \Lambda, \ x \in X)$$

Finally, X is called an *association scheme* if the *intersection number*

$$(4.2) \qquad p_{ab}(x, y) = \#\{z \in X : (x, z) \in R_a, \ (z, y) \in R_b\}$$

is a constant, Γ_{ab}^c, for all pairs x, y with $(x, y) \in R_c$. This implies that X is *regular*, that is, each *subdegree*

$$(4.3) \qquad d_a(x) = |X_a(x)|$$

is a constant, d_a, independent of x. Association schemes are intimately related to group theory [8], and error-correcting codes [48].

REMARK. A graph Γ with vertex set X is a scheme under $R_i = \{(x, y) :$ the shortest $x - y$ path has length $i\}$.

An association scheme which can be so obtained is called *metric* (the triangle inequality holds), and Γ is then called *distance regular*. Every strongly regular graph (see eg Fig. 1(a)) is a 2-class association scheme. Fig 1(b) is the graph for a metric 3-class association scheme, with points at a given distance from the lefthand point aligned vertically.

Delsarte [23] proved the important result for association schemes that

(4.4)   the combinatorial property of being metric is equivalent to the algebraic property of being P-polynomial.

P (or Q)-polynomial schemes. We need some preliminary definitions. The Bose-Mesner Algebra B of X is the real vector space generated by ℓ and the adjacency matrices $\{D_a\}$ ($a \in S$), where D_a, with rows and columns indexed by the elements of X, has (x, y) entry 1 if $(x, y) \in R_a$, otherwise 0. The reader may verify that relations (4.1) imply that $D_a D_b = \sum \Gamma_{ab}^c D_c$ ($c \in S$), and hence that B is a commutative algebra under matrix multiplication. It is then a standard consequence [8,48] that B has a unique basis of mutually orthogonal idempotents $E_0, \ldots, E_s$ (here we may assume that $E_0 = v^{-1}J$, where J is the all ones v by v matrix, $v = |X|$). Then the D_a are expressible as

$$(4.5) \qquad D_k = \sum_{j=0}^{s} P_k(j)E_j, \qquad \text{so that } D_k E_i = P_k(i)E_i,$$

for certain constants $P_k(i)$. Thus, for each $k = 1, 2, \ldots, s$, $P_k(i)$ is an eigenvalue of D_k with eigenspace spanned by the columns of E_i, and essentially, X is P-Polynomial if the $P_k(i)$ are polynomials:

DEFINITION. X is P-Polynomial if there are distinct real numbers $z_0 = 0$, $z_1, \ldots, z_s$ and polynomials $f_0, f_1, \ldots, f_s$ such that

$$(4.6) \qquad P_k(i) = f_k(z_i), \qquad 0 \le k, i \le s.$$

Delsarte's result implies that, for such a scheme, the relations of X can be ordered $R_1, \ldots, R_s$ so that the graph (X, R_1) is distance regular and relation R_i contains the pairs x, y joined by a path of minimum length i. Dually, X is called Q-Polynomial if a condition corresponding to (4.6) holds when we express the E_i in terms of the D_k. Here the combinatorial interpretation is less clear, but much is known about association schemes that are both Q and P-polynomial [9,50].

REMARK. We recall the notation of 3.1. The angle set of a potential t-design X is $A = \{\cos \emptyset\}$ for X in Ω and $A = \{\cos^2 \emptyset\}$ for X in FP^{d-1}, where $\emptyset$ is the angle between distinct vectors or lines x, y. Then X provides an s-class association scheme, where x, y are α-associates if and only if $\cos \emptyset$ (resp. $\cos^2 \emptyset$) equals α. In preparation for combinatorial implications we show how (the highest) t may be found.

The value of t. A more workable condition than (1.4) for X to be a t-design is, anticipating (5.11),

$$(4.7) \qquad \sum_{x,y \in X} Q_i((x, y)) = 0, \qquad 1 = 1, 2, \ldots, t$$

153

which, if X is known to be regular with subdegrees d_a, becomes

(4.8) $$\sum Q_i(a)d_a = 0, \quad (a \in A \cup \{1\}), \quad i = 1, 2, \ldots, t.$$

We give the first few polynomials $Q_i(x)$ for FP^{d-1} (notation of Table 1):

(4.9)
$$Q_0(x) = 1, \quad Q_1(x) = (md+1)(dx-1),$$
$$Q_2(x) = d(N+3)[(N+1)_2 x^2 - 2(m+1)(N+1)x + (m)_2]/2(m+1),$$

and for Ω:

$$Q_0(x) = 1, \quad Q_1(x) = dx, \quad Q_2(x) = (d/2+1)(dx^2 - 1).$$

Conditions (4.7), (4.8) are the 'bottom line'. In practice we can usually obtain the (highest possible) value of t from special or absolute bounds, as below.

THEOREM 4.1. *[25,42] In the notation of Section 3.1, let the Jacobi coefficients of the finite subset X of Ω of FP^{d-1} satisfy*

(4.10) $$a_0, a_1, \ldots, a_s > 0$$

Then X is an $(s+i)$-design if and only if $a_i = 1$ (cf. (3.5)).

Special case. If X meets the special bound ($a_0 = 1$) of Table 1, Section 2, and satisfies the conditions there with strict inequality (equivalent to (4.10)) then X is an s-design.

Proof. We use the Addition formula, plus positivity properties of a product of Jacobi polynomials.

JACOBI COEFFICIENTS a_i. For X in FP^{d-1} and general s, these are

(4.11) $$a_i = [\sum_{k=0}^{s-i}(-1)^k {}_i(s-k)(m)_{s-k}\sigma_k/(N)_{s-k+i}]/\prod(1-\alpha), \quad (\alpha \in A)$$

where σ_k denotes the elementary symmetric polynomial of degree k in the elements of A [31, page 245]. For the case of Ω see [36].

NOTATION 4.2.

$$(x)_i = x(x+1)\ldots(x+i-1), \quad {}_i(x) = x(x-1)\ldots(x-i+1)(i \in \mathbf{N}),$$
$$_0(x) = 1 = (x)_0.$$
$$2m = (F:R), \quad N = md, \quad c_i = (m)_i/(N)_i, \quad c_{ij} = (m)_i(m)_j/(N)_{i+j}.$$
$$d_{11}(x) = vc_{11}(x/m+1) - 2x,$$
$$d_{12}(x) = vc_{12}(2x/m+1) - x - x^2,$$
$$d_{22}(x) = vc_{22}(2x^2/(m)_2 + 4x/m + 1) - 2x^2.$$

154

THEOREM 4.3. Let X be a t-design of v points in Ω or FP^{d-1}, with angle set $A = \{a, b, \dots\}$, $s = |A|$. If $t \geq s - 1$ then X is regular [25,42] and [32,36] the subdegrees d_a are given by

$$[v(c_0\sigma_{s-1} + c_1\sigma_{s-3} + \dots) - F(1)]/F(a), \qquad \text{for } X \text{ in } \Omega,$$
$$[v(c_0\sigma_{s-1} - c_1\sigma_{s-2} + c_2\sigma_{s-3} - \dots\dots) - F(1)]/F(a), \quad \text{for } X \text{ in } FP^{d-1},$$

where σ_i is the i'th elementary symmetric polynomial in the elements of $A\backslash\{a\}$, the summation continuing while $i \geq 0$, and $F(x) = \prod(\lambda - x)$ $(\lambda \in A\backslash\{a\})$.

EXAMPLE 4.3A. [31] The double cover of the Hall-Janko group is generated by reflections in 315 hyperplanes in H^3 whose normal vectors define lines for which $A = \{0, 1/4, 1/2, (3 \pm \sqrt{5})/8\}$. Here $s = 5$, and by Theorem 4.1, $t = 5$. Now Theorem 4.3 gives the respective subdegrees d_a as: $10, 160, 80, 32$. Notice that, by (4.8) with $i = 1$, the algebraic conjugates have the same subdegree, which we calculate as 32.

REMARK 4.4. According to the results of Seymour-Zaslavski [45], t-designs exist in all our spaces for arbitrarily high t. Although so far no one has found a way to produce them explicitly, it is to be hoped that they will eventually be found, and that high t will not imply low t relative to s (a possible pessimistic conjecture), say $t < s - 1$. Meanwhile Table 2 gives some of the most useful d_a formula in more explicit form. The formula of Theorem 4.3 above for general s, and X in Ω, seems to be new (see [36]).

TABLE 2.   Subdegrees d_a for t-designs with $t \geq s - 1$

SPACE	A	d_a
Ω	$\{a, b\}$	$[1 + b(v - 1)]/(b - a)$
Ω	$\{a, b, c\}$	$[v(bc + 1/d) - (1 - b)(1 - c)]/(b - a)(c - a)$
FP^{d-1}	$\{0, a\}$	$(v - d)/ad$
FP^{d-1}	$\{a, b\}$	$(1 + b(v - 1) - v/d)/(b - a)$
FP^{d-1}	$\{0, a, b\}$	$\{1 - b - v[(m + 1)/(N + 1) - b]/d\}/a(b - a)$

EXAMPLE 4.4A. The Barnes-Wall Lattice [17] in R^{16}. The minimal vectors give 2160 lines with $A = \{0, 1/16, 1/4\}$. Proceeding as in Example 4.3A we obtain respective subdegrees 855, 1024, 280.

155

THEOREM 4.5. *Let X be a t-design of v points in Ω or FP^{d-1}. If $t \geq 2s - 2$ then X is a Q-polynomial association scheme [25,42], and we have the following:*

Case $s = 2$, $t \geqslant 2$, $A = \{a, b\}$. The graph $\Gamma = (X, R_a)$ is strongly regular[*], with

$$\lambda = [b^2(v - 2) + 2(ab + b - a) + av/d]/(b - a)^2, \qquad \text{for } X \text{ in } \Omega,$$

and for X in FP^{d-1} the term av/d becomes $v(m + a - 2b(N + 1))/d(N + 1)$. Now μ may be found from $\mu\ell = k(k - \lambda - 1)$, where ℓ is the complementary degree $v - k - 1$. Moreover [11,42], if $t \geq 3$ then each subconstituent of Γ is strongly regular.[*]

Case $s = 3$, $t = 5$, $A = \{0, a, b\}$. For X in FP^{d-1} the intersection numbers (4.2) of X as a 3-class association scheme are given in NOTATION 4.2 by [33]:

$$\Gamma^0_{aa} = vm^2[(N + 2)_2 b^2 - 2(m + 1)(N + 3)b + (m + 1)^2]/a^2(b - a)^2(N)_4,$$
$$\Gamma^0_{ab} = m(N - m + 1)(N + 3)(N + 4)^3/8(m + 1)(m + 2)^3,$$
$$\Gamma^a_{aa} = (b^2 d_{11} - 2bd_{12} + d_{22})/a^2(b - a)^2, \qquad d_{ij} = d_{ij}(a),$$

where Γ^0_{bb}, Γ^b_{bb} are obtained by interchanging a, b above, and the rest by using the well known relations, with intersection matrix $\Gamma^\gamma = [\Gamma^\gamma_{\alpha\beta}]$:

$$\text{row } \alpha \text{ of } \Gamma^\beta = d_\alpha(\text{row } \beta \text{ of } \Gamma^\alpha)/d_\beta,$$
$$\sum \Gamma^\gamma_{\alpha\beta} = d_\alpha - \delta_{\gamma\alpha} \qquad \text{(sum over all } \beta \text{ for fixed } \alpha, \gamma \text{ in } A\text{)},$$

where δ is the Kronecker symbol.

EXAMPLE 4.6. By Theorems 4.1, 4.5, our earlier Example 2.5 gives a strongly regular graph $\Gamma = (X, R_0)$ with parameters $(v, k, \lambda, \mu) = (126, 46, 12, 18)$. Since in fact $t = 3$, Γ has a strongly regular subconstituent $\Gamma_0 = (X_0, R_0)$ based on the 45 lines perpendicular to a fixed diameter of the polytope diagrammed. Hence Γ_0 has $d = 5$, and parameters $(45, 12, 3, 3)$. We note that Γ and Γ_0 can also be realized respectively by the vectors of the reflection group in the diagram, and that of the subgroup got by deleting the ringed vertex, cf. [31, Example 7].

REMARK 4.7. (1). Analogous formulae to the above hold for spherical t-designs and for general s with $t \geq 2s - 2$ [33,36].

(2) Case $s \geqslant 3$. So far all known examples in FP^{d-1} with $t \geq 2s - 2$ are **already tight**: $t = 2s - \varepsilon$ and hence (see §3) $t = 5$, $A = \{0, a, b\}$. It would be interesting to find examples that are not, or to prove that $t = 2s - \varepsilon - 1$ is impossible. Even the case $s = 4$, $t = 2s - 3$ of the *complex Leech lattice* [40] is unusual. On the other hand it means that the formulae of Theorem 4.5 cover more than is at first apparent. Referring to the Seymour-Zaslavsky result that "t-designs exist for all t", is it still true if we impose the condition $t = 2s - 2$? No one knows.

(3) Certainly $t \geq 2s - 2$ is not a necessary condition for an association scheme; Example 4.3A is an association scheme for group-theoretic reasons, yet $t = s$ only.

---

[*]If it is non-void and non-complete. cf Theorem 4.3.

(4)   On another tack, perhaps the definition of Delsarte spaces could be 'improved' to give a more delicate criterion for association schemes.

Tight t-designs

THEOREM 4.8. *In the notation of Section 3.1, X meets the absolute bound $R_e(1)$ if and only if X is a tight t-design, $t = 2s - \varepsilon$ [25,42]. Moreover, in case of equality we have (see §3)*

$$t \leq 5 \text{ for } FP^{d-1},$$

$$t \leq 11 \text{ for } \Omega,$$

and the nonzero elements of the angle set A are reciprocal integers, and are the roots of $R_e(x)$.

REMARK 4.9. Tight $(2n + 1)$-designs X in Ω must be antipodal $(x \in X \Rightarrow -x \in X)$ [25], hence equivalent to tight n-designs in RP^{d-1} [3]. For $d = 2$ the tight spherical t-designs are precisely the regular $(t+1)$-gons [25]. For $d \geq 3$ the only tight $2n$-designs in Ω are 4-designs [3]. One example is 4.10 below, with its surprising connections. By contrast, recent work shows that, in FP^{d-1}, tight 4-designs do not exist, and that tight $t = 5$ occurs uniquely [10 or 17, 35] in the two important examples 4.11, 4.12 below.

EXAMPLE 4.10. [19,20,21] A tight 4-design on Ω in R^6. The points are the vertices of the Gossett polytope 2_{21}, with $A = \{-1/2, 1/4\}$, in accordance with Theorem 4.8 and $R_2(x) = d((d + 2)x^2 + 2x - 1)/2$. It is interesting that the adjacencies of 2_{21}, given by $\cos \emptyset = 1/4$, correspond exactly to those among the 27 vertices of the Hessian complex polyhedron in C^3. A suitable vertex correspondence is obtained by taking the real form of the complex coordinates, which are the cyclic shifts of $(0, -\omega^m, \omega^n)$, where $m, n = 0, 1, 2$ and $\omega \neq 1$ is a cube root of unity. (Incidentally, the 9 diameters meet the absolute bound for equiangular lines in C^3).

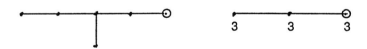

Coxeter diagrams for Gosset's polytope 2_{21}, and the Hessian polyhedron.

But furthermore, the adjacencies of both polytopes correspond to skewness among the celebrated 27 lines on a general cubic surface in C^4, via $(0, -\omega^m, \omega^n) \rightarrow 0mn$, where lines labelled abc, a', b', c' are incident if and only if exactly one of $a = a'$, $b = b'$, $c = c'$ holds.

157

By Theorem 4.5 this set of adjacencies yields a strongly regular graph, named the Schläfli graph [44], with strongly regular subconstituents. One of these has complement the Clebsch graph [44], which in turn contains the Petersen graph, and we are back to Figure 1 of §4.

EXAMPLE 4.11. For a tight 5-design in RP^{23}, Theorem 4.8 stipulates the values of $\cos^2\emptyset$ to be the roots of $xR_e(x) = x(x^2 - 5x/16 + 1/64)$, hence $A = \{0, 1/16, 1/4\}$. Also the size of X must be $R_e(1) = 98280$. This is realized by the minimal vectors of the Leech Lattice, which thus, by Theorem 4.5, gives a Q-polynomial 3-class association scheme. We recall that amongst many amazing properties, the Leech lattice yields Conways simple groups Co. 1, Co. 2, Co. 3 [16,17].

EXAMPLE 4.12. For a tight 5-design in the Cayley plane OP^2, Theorem 4.8 predicts $|X| = 819$, $A = \{0, 1/4, 1/2\}$. The details of a realization can be found in [15]. It is a set of points related to exceptional group $^3D_4(2)$, and forming a generalized hexagon with incidence based on $\cos^2\emptyset = 0$, where distances 2 and 3 correspond to respective values $1/4$ and $1/2$ of $\cos^2\emptyset$. By 4.5 it is also a 3-class Q-polynomial association scheme. The intersection numbers may be calculated from Theorem 4.5 as

$$\Gamma^0 = \begin{bmatrix} 1 & 0 & 16 \\ 0 & 256 & 256 \\ 16 & 256 & 16 \end{bmatrix}, \quad \Gamma^{1/4} = \begin{bmatrix} 0 & 9 & 9 \\ 9 & 304 & 198 \\ 9 & 198 & 81 \end{bmatrix}, \quad \Gamma^{1/2} = \begin{bmatrix} 1 & 16 & 1 \\ 16 & 352 & 144 \\ 1 & 144 & 142 \end{bmatrix}$$

We conclude this section with an expression that yields all the $Q_i(x)$ and $R_i(x)$ for FP^{d-1}.

$$Q_k^\varepsilon(x) = \frac{(N)_{2k+\varepsilon}}{(m)_{k+\varepsilon}k!} \sum_{i=0}^{k} (-1)^i \binom{k}{i} \frac{i(k+m+\varepsilon-1)}{i(2k+N+\varepsilon-2)} x^{k-i}$$

For the usual $Q_i(x)$ we set $\varepsilon = 0$ ($\varepsilon = 1$ is required for some proofs). For $R_e(x)$ as required by Theorem 4.8, we must (a) replace -2 by -1 in the bottom right hand of the expression, and (b) use $\varepsilon = 1$ if A contains 0. The polynomials for Ω are

$$Q_k(x) = \sum_{r=0}^{k/2} \frac{(-1)^r (N)_k}{r(N+k-2)r!} \frac{(2x)^{k-2r}}{(k-2r)!} \qquad (N = d/2)$$

5. Topology and Delsarte spaces.

We offer an approach to Neumaier's Delsarte space framework [42]. (cf [23]).

DEFINITION. Let E be a finite or infinite metric space with finite diameter d, finite measure ω and distance squared c_{xy}. Then E is called a *Delsarte space* if: for every pair of integers $i, j \geq 0$ there is a polynomial f_{ij} of degree $\geq i, j$ such that

(5.1)
$$\int_E c_{ax}^i c_{bx}^j d\omega(x) = f_{ij}(c_{ab}) \qquad \text{for all } a, b, \in E.$$

THEOREM 5.1. *The spaces Ω and FP^{d-1} are Delsarte spaces.*

REMARK 5.2. The spaces S of Theorem 5.1 in fact form a unity, they are precisely the compact connected symmetric spaces of rank 1 [28]. By an important theorem of H. C. Wang [52], they are also the compact connected spaces which are 2-point homogeneous, that is:

(5.2)
> the spaces S have an isometry group
>
> transitive on pairs x, y with c_{xy} fixed.

Combined with (5.3) to (5.6) below, this is a crucial property for proving Theorem 5.1.

(5.3) S has a unique measure (up to a constant multiple) which is invariant under any transitive group of isometries σ, that is

$$\int_S f(x^\sigma) d\omega(x) = \int f(x) d\omega(x) \qquad [28]$$

(5.4) Following Freudenthal, we define FP^{d-1} as the restriction to idempotents of trace 1, in the real vector space $H_d(F)$ of d by d hermitian matrices over F ($F = R, C, H, O$), with *real* innerproduct (A, B) as real part of the trace of AB. Now we can replace distances by innerproducts in (5.1) to get an equivalent condition.

NOTE: The connection with the usual definitions when $F = R, C, H$ is as follows: The matrices A, B correspond to unique lines, spanned say by unit (column) vectors a, b, via $A = aa^*$, $B = bb^*$, where a^* denotes the conjugate transpose of a. Then

$$|(a, b)| = |a^* b| = \cos \emptyset, \qquad \text{but } (A, B) = \cos^2 \emptyset.$$

The Cayley numbers O are described at the end of this section.

(5.5) The innerproduct in S may be viewed as a standard innerproduct of <u>real</u> vectors, where corresponding to a matrix A we write out the real components of each entry of A in turn.

(5.6) A power of the innerproduct of two real Euclidean vectors can be written as

$$(x, y)^r = (\otimes^r x, \otimes^r y)$$

where the tensor product $M \otimes N$ of matrices $M = (m_{ij})$ and $N = (n_{ij})$ is given by $(M \otimes N)_{ik,jl} = m_{ij} n_{kl}$, and $\otimes^r x$ is the r'th tensor power $x \otimes x \otimes \cdots \otimes x$.

Proof of Theorem 5.1. For a, b in S and integers $i, j \geq 0$ we define the function $f_{ij}(a, b) = \int (a, x)^i (b, x)^j d\omega(x)$. Then for any isometry σ of S,

$$\begin{aligned}
f_{ij}(a^\sigma, b^\sigma) &= \int^S (a^\sigma, x)^i (b^\sigma, x)^j d\omega(x) \\
&= \int^S (a^\sigma, x^\sigma)^i (b^\sigma, x^\sigma)^j d\omega(x), \quad \text{by (5.3)} \\
&= \int^S (a, x)^i (b, x)^j d\omega(x), \quad \text{since } \sigma \text{ is an isometry,} \\
&= f_{ij}(a, b), \quad \text{by definition,}
\end{aligned}$$

which, by 2-point homogeneity (5.2), depends only on the innerproduct (a, b). Now we make use of (5.5), and (5.6), viewing a, b, x as real column vectors, to write

$$f_{ij}(a, b) = \int (\otimes^i a, \otimes^i x)(\otimes^j b, \otimes^j x) d\omega(x)$$

$$= \int (\otimes^i a)^T (\otimes^i x)(\otimes^j x)^T (\otimes^j b) d\omega(x), \quad \text{in terms}$$

of matrices and their transposes.

$$= (\otimes^i a)^T [\int (\otimes^i x)(\otimes^j x)^T d\omega(x)](\otimes^j b)$$

$$= (\otimes^i a)^T M_{ij}(\otimes^j b),$$

where M_{ij} is a matrix with entries depending on i, j but not on a, b. From its form, and the definition of tensor product, the right hand side is a polynomial of degree $\leq i$ in the entries $a_1, a_2, \ldots$ of a and degree $\leq j$ in the entries $b_1, b_2, \ldots$ of b. But since it is expressible as a function of the innerproduct $(a, b) = a_1 b_1 + a_2 b_2 + \ldots$, it is a polynomial of degree $\leq i, j$ in (a, b). Thus we have proved Theorem 5.1.

Orthogonal polynomials. The measure ω on E induces a measure μ on $[0, \delta]$ by

$$(5.7) \qquad \int_0^\delta f(\alpha) d\mu(\alpha) = |E|^{-1} \iint_E f(c_{xy}) d\omega(x) d\omega(y),$$

hence an innerproduct $(f, g) = \int f(\alpha)g(\alpha)d\mu(\alpha)$ of functions $f, g : E \to R$, and from this a family of orthogonal polynomials $q_i(x)$ of degree $i = 0, 1, 2, \ldots$:

$$(5.8) \qquad\qquad (q_i, q_j) = \delta_{ij} \qquad \text{(the Kronecker delta)}.$$

DEFINITION. HARM(i) $(i = 0, 1, 2, \ldots)$ is the real vector space generated by the zonal harmonics $f_a : E \to R$, $x \to q_i(c_{ax})$, $\forall a \in E$.

LEMMA 5.3. For all a, b in E and $i, j = 0, 1, 2, \ldots$, we have

$$\int_E q_i(c_{ax})q_j(c_{bx})d\omega(x) = q_i(c_{ab})q_i(0)^{-1}\delta_{ij}.$$

Proof by double induction on pairs (i, j), for all $a, b \in E$ simultaneously, using (5.7) and (5.8). No group theory is used here.

THEOREM 5.4. (a) The spaces HARM(i) are orthogonal and HARM(i) has finite dimension $f_i = q_i(0)^2|E| > 0$.

(b) **The Addition Formula.** For an orthonormal basis $S_1, S_2, \ldots, S_f$ of HARM(i),

$$\sum_{r=1}^f S_r(x)S_r(y) = q_i(0)q_i(c_{xy}), \qquad \forall x, y \in E.$$

The definition of t-design. It is easy to see the equivalence of the following two conditions for a finite subset X of a Delsarte space E to be a t-design:

$$(5.9) \qquad \sum_{x \in X} g(x) = 0, \quad \text{for all } g \in \text{HARM}(i), \qquad i = 1, 2, \ldots, t$$

$$(5.10) \qquad \sum_{x \in X} q_i(c_{ax}) = 0, \quad \text{for all } a \in X, \qquad i = 1, 2, \ldots, t.$$

Indeed (5.10) is a special case of (5.9) but implies (5.9), since g is a sum $\sum f_a$ over a finite subset F of points a in E, thus $g(x) = \sum q_i(c_{ax})$. An application of the Addition formula proves a further equivalence,

$$(5.11) \qquad \sum_{x,y \in X} q_i(c_{xy}) = 0, \qquad i = 1, 2, \ldots, t,$$

and that, moreover, the given sum is in any case non-negative.

HARM(i) for spaces $S = \Omega$, FP^{d-1}. Let S be 2-point homogeneous under the action of an isometry group G. Then $\text{HARM}(i)$ is a real representation space for G via $(g.f_a)(x) = f_a(g^{-1}x)(a, x \in S, g \in G)$. Thus $g.f_a = f_{ga}$ and so, as G is transitive on S it is transitive on the set of all f_a. Therefore the representation is irreducible. By standard properties of orthogonal polynomials the f_a are harmonic, and we may make the first three identifications in Table 3 below using their description in Section 2.

TABLE 3. $\quad$ HARM(i) for the 2-point homogeneous spaces Ω, FP^{d-1}.

S	HARM(i)	group G
Ω	harm(i)	$O(d)$
RP^{d-1}	harm($2i$)	$O(d)$
CP^{d-1}	harm(i, i)	$U(d)$
HP^{d-1}	$Sp(d)$-irreducible subspace of above, with highest weight (i, i) [29]	$Sp(d)$
OP^2	identified by spherical zonal [28]	F_4

If we fix one point P in S as "pole" then f_p is invariant under the subgroup of G fixing P. In fact, as spherical zonal function in normal parlance [28], f_p determines which irreducible representation is generated, by its parameters as a Jacobi polynomial $P_i^{\alpha, \beta}(x)$. Indeed Ω gives the Gegenbauer case $\alpha = \beta = (d-3)/2$ [25],

161

whilst for FP^{d-1} we have $\alpha = m(d-1)-1$, $\beta = m-1$ (and argument $2x-1$) [31]. For working (equivalently) with inner products, we may set $\delta = 1$, $(a,b) = 1 - c_{ab}$, $Q_i(x) = |E|q_i(0)q_i(1-x)$, to give

$$(5.12) \qquad \text{dim. HARM}(i) = f_i = Q_i(1) \qquad (E = \Omega,\ FP^{d-1})$$

Embeddings. It follows from Lemma 5.3 that a general Delsarte space embeds isometrically into the unit sphere in R^{f_1}, identified as the real vector space HARM(i). For FP^{d-1} the dimension is $(md+1)(d-1)$, which is one less than that of $H_d(F)$, see (5.4).

The Cayley numbers, O. These form a non-associative 8-dimensional algebra over R, with basis $1 = e_0, e_1, \ldots, e_7$, and bilinear multiplication defined by $e_i^2 = -1$, $1 \le i \le 7$, and

$$(5.13) \qquad e_i e_j = -e_j e_i = e_k$$

whenever ijk is a cyclic permutation of one of $\{124, 235, 346, 457, 561, 672, 713\}$. Since the triples form a combinatorial $2 - (7,3,1)$ design, the multiplication is well-defined. For $a = \sum a_i e_i$ we define its *conjugate* $a^* = a_0 - a_1 e_1 - \ldots a_7 e_7$ and *norm* $|a|^2 = aa^* = a_0^2 + a_1^2 + \cdots + a_7^2$, whence

$$(5.14) \qquad |ab| = |a|.|b|, \qquad \text{therefore } O \text{ has no zero divisors,}$$

and there is a natural inclusion $O \supseteq H \supseteq C \supseteq R$, where C is generated by $1, e_1$ and H by $1, e_1, e_2, e_4$ (any such triple generates a copy of H).

PROBLEMS

We refer to t-designs in the unit sphere Ω, or projective spaces FP^{d-1}, for $F = R, C, H, O$. The following are sample problems, mostly with a variety of natural variations and extensions.

1. Prove that for t-designs in FP^{d-1} with $t \ge s$, we have

$$\cos^2 \emptyset = 1/integer$$

   for every distinct pair of projective points. A notable counterexample on Ω is the derived design [25] of Example 4.10, with $A = \{-3/5, 1/5\}$.

2. Find explicit t-designs for high t, say $t \ge 50$. They must exist [45], but are there limitations besides $t \le 2s - \varepsilon$?

3. Classify t-designs that are slightly less than tight, for $s \ge 3$. In particular, for $t = 2s - \varepsilon - 1$. None are presently known for FP^{d-1}. Can we prove they don't exist?

4. New t-designs from old. When do we get them (a) by some form of extension, contraction, or subconstituents in general Delsarte spaces or (b) by passing between R, C, H, O? Only a few <u>examples</u> known. cf 4.10 and Number 25 of [31], which yields the Barnes-Wall Lattice from quaternions.

162

5. Classify the tight 4-designs in Ω. cf. Remark 4.9.

6. Are there non-discrete Delsarte spaces besides the 2-homogeneous ones - or a better definition?

7. Prove results about *rigid t*-designs. cf Bannai [2].

8. When can a *t*-design have rational coordinates? How far need the rational field be extended? This should have bearing on Problem 2. cf Example 4.10 with irrational coordinates in R^6, but which can be written over the rationals in a 6-dimensional subspace of R^8 [21].

9. Characterize 3-designs in a way comparable to Seidel's eutactic star in case $t = 2$ [43].

10. Improve the special bounds, eg by optimizing over an extra angle. cf [31, Remark 5.7].

POSTSCRIPT. I should like to thank the Institute of Mathematics and its Applications, Minneapolis, for their hospitality during a week in June, 1988, which time was the inspiration for this manuscript.

REFERENCES

[1] R. Askey, *Orthogonal polynomials and special functions*, SIAM Regional conference in Applied Math., 21. Philadelphia, 1975.

[2] E. Bannai, *Rigid spherical t-designs and a theorem of Y. Hong*, J. Fac. Sci. Univ. Tokyo (Sect. 1A), 34 (1987), pp. 485-489.

[3] E. Bannai and R. M. Damerell, *Tight spherical designs, I*, J. Math. Soc. Japan, 31 (1979), pp. 199-207.

[4] ——————, *Tight spherical designs, II*, J. London Maths. Soc., 21 (1980), pp. 13-30.

[5] E. Bannai and S. G. Hoggar, *On tight t-designs in compact symmetric spaces of rank one*, Proc. Japan. Academy, 61A (1985), pp. 78-82.

[6] ——————, *Tight t-designs in projective spaces, and Newton polygons*, Proc. 10th British Combinatorial Conf., Glasgow 1985, Ars Combinatoria 20A (1985), pp. 43-49.

[7] ——————, *Tight t-designs and squarefree integers*, European J. Combinatorics, 9 (1988), pp. 1–23.

[8] E. Bannai and T. Ito, *Algebraic Combinatorics 1*, Benjamin/Cummings. Menlo Park, California, 1984.

[9] ——————, *Current research on Algebraic Combinatorics*, Graphs and Combinatorics, 2 (1986), pp. 287-308.

[10] E. Bannai and N. J. A. Sloane, *Uniqueness of certain spherical codes*, Can. J. Math., 33 (1981), pp. 437-449.

[11] P. J. Cameron, J. M. Goethals, and J. J. Seidel, *Strongly regular graphs having strongly regular subconstituents*, J. Algebra, 55 (1978), pp. 257-280.

[12] P. J. Cameron, J. M. Goethals, J. J. Seidel, and E. E. Shult, *Line graphs, root systems, and elliptic geometry*, J. Algebra, 43 (1976), pp. 305-327.

[13] A. M. Cohen, *Finite complex reflection groups*, Ann. Sci. École Norm. Sup. (4), 9 (1976), pp. 379-436.

[14] ——————, *Finite Quaternionic reflection groups*, J. Algebra, 64 (1980), pp. 293-324.

[15] A. M. Cohen and J. Tits, *On generalized hexagons and a near octagon whose lines have three points*, Europ. J. Combinatorics, 6 (1985), pp. 13-27.

[16] J. H. Conway, *A group of order 8, 315, 553, 613, 086, 720, 000*, Bull. London Math. Soc., 1 (1969), pp. 79-88.

[17] J. H. Conway and N. J. A. Sloane, *Sphere Packings, lattices and groups*, Springer-Verlag, New York, 1988.

[18] H. S. M. Coxeter, *Finite groups generated by unitary reflections*, Abh. Math. Sem. Univ. Hamburg, 31 (1967), pp. 125-135.

[19] ————————, *Regular complex polytopes*, Cambridge University Press, Cambridge, 1974.

[20] ————————, *The equianharmonic surface and the Hessian polyhedron*, Ann. Mat. Pura Appl. (IV), 98 (1974), pp. 77-92.

[21] ————————, *The polytope 2_{21}, whose twenty-seven vertices corresponds to the lines on the general cubic surface*, Amer. J. Math., 62 (1940), pp. 457-486.

[22] H. S. M. COXETER AND J. A. TODD, *An extreme duodenary form*, Canad. J. Math., 5 (1953), pp. 384-392.

[23] P. DELSARTE, *An algebraic approach to the association schemes of coding theory*, Philips Research Reports, Suppl., 10 (1973), pp. 1-97.

[24] P. DELSARTE, J. M. GOETHALS, AND J. J. SEIDEL, *Bounds for systems of lines, and Jacobi polynomials*, Philips Research Reports, 30 (1975), pp. 91-105. (Bouwkamp volume).

[25] ————————, *Spherical codes and designs*, Geom. Dedicata, 6 (1977), pp. 363-388.

[26] J. M. GOETHALS AND J. J. SEIDEL, *Spherical designs*, Proc. Symp. Pure Math., 34 (1979), pp. 255-272.

[27] ————————, *Cubature formulae, polytopes, and spherical designs, The geometric vein*, (Coxeter Festschrift, Toronto 1978), Spring-Verlag, New York, 1981.

[28] S. HELGASON, *Differential geometry, Lie groups, and symmetric spaces*, Academic Press, New York, 1978.

[29] S. G. HOGGAR, *Bounds for quaternionic line systems and reflection groups*, Math. Scand., 43 (1978), pp. 241-249.

[30] ————————, *Two quaternionic 4-polytopes, The geometric vein*, (Coxeter Festschrift, Toronto 1978), Springer-Verlag, New York, 1981.

[31] ————————, *t-designs in projective spaces*, Europ. J. Combinatorics, 3 (1982), pp. 233-254.

[32] ————————, *Parameters of t-designs in FP^{d-1}*, Europ. J. Combinatorics, 5 (1984), pp. 29-36.

[33] ————————, *Parameter of Association Schemes*, Proc. British Combinatorial Conf., 1983, Ars Combinatoria, 16B (1983), pp. 325-339.

[34] ————————, *Tight t-designs and octonions*, Coxeter Festschrift, Teil III, University of Giessen, 1984, pp. 1-16.

[35] ————————, *Tight 4 and 5-designs in projective spaces*, Graphs and Combinatorics (to appear).

[36] ————————. Preprint, in preparation.

[37] T. H. KOORNWINDER, *The Addition formula for Jacobi polynomials and spherical harmonics*, SIAM J. Appl. Math., 25 (1973), pp. 236-246.

[38] J. LEECH AND N. J. A. SLOANE, *Sphere packings and error-correcting codes*, Canad. J. Math., 23 (1971), pp. 718-745.

[39] P. W. H. LEMMENS AND J. J. SEIDEL, *Equiangular lines*, J. Algebra, 24 (1973), pp. 494-512.

[40] J. H. LINDSEY, *A correlation between $PSU_4(3)$, the Suzuki group and the Conway group*, Trans. Amer. Math. Soc., 157 (1971), pp. 189-204.

[41] Y. MIMURA, *A construction of spherical 2-designs*. submitted.

[42] A. NEUMAIER, *Combinatorial configurations in terms of distances*, Memorandum 81-09 (Dept. of Mathematics), Eindhoven University, 1981.

[43] J. J. SEIDEL, *Eutactic Stars*, Colloq. Math. Soc. Janos Bolyai, 18 (1976), pp. 983-999.

[44] ————————, *Strongly regular graphs, in Surveys in Combinatories*, ed. B. Bollobas, Camb. Univ. Press (1970), pp. 157-180.

[45] P. D. SEYMOUR AND T. ZASLAVSKY, *Averaging sets: a generalization of mean values and spherical designs*, Advances in Mathematics, 52 (1984), pp. 213-240.

[46] G. C. SHEPHARD, *Unitary groups generated by reflections*, Canad. J. Math., 5 (1953), pp. 364-383.

[47] G. C. SHEPHARD AND J. A. TODD, *Finite Unitary reflection groups*, Canad. J. Math., 6 (1954), pp. 274-304.

[48] N. J. A. SLOANE, *An introduction to association schemes and coding theory, in Theory and application of special functions*, ed., R. Askey, Academic Press, NY, 1975, pp. 225-260.

[49] G. SZEGÖ, *Orthogonal Polynomials*, 4th ed., Amer. Math. Soc., Providence, R.I., 1975.

[50] P. TERWILLIGER, *A characterization of P- and Q-polynomial association schemes*, J. Combin. Theory Ser. A, 45 (1987), pp. 8-26.

[51] L. TEIRLINK, *Nontrivial designs without repeated blocks exist for all t*, Discrete Mathematics, 65 (1987), pp. 301-311.

164

[52]   H. C. WANG, *Two-point homogeneous spaces*, Ann. of Math., 55 (1952), pp. 177-191.

LATIN SQUARES, THEIR GEOMETRIES AND THEIR GROUPS. A SURVEY*

DIETER JUNGNICKEL†

Abstract. We give a survey on the geometric and group theoretic aspects of Latin squares; thus we report on Bruck nets, transversal designs and their automorphism groups. In particular, we consider questions of existence, completion, geometrical configurations, translation nets and other types of nets and TD's with nice groups. We then indicate generalizations to arbitrary nets and TD's (with joining numbers not necessarily 0 or 1). In this connection we also discuss generalised Hadamard matrices.

Key words. Latin square, MOLS, net, transversal design, automorphism group, difference matrix, generalised Hadamard matrix, configuration, affine plane, affine space, orthogonal array, group partition

AMS(MOS) subject classifications. 05-02, 05 B 15, 05 B 20, 05 B 30, 20 B 25, 51 A 15 (primary), 05 B 05, 05 B 10, 05 B 25, 20 F 29, 51 A 20, 51 A 40, 51 A 45, 51 E 15, 51 E 20, 62 K 99 (secondary)

0. Introduction. Design Theory and Finite Geometries by now belong to the central areas of Discrete Mathematics, well worth studying both for their intrinsic interest and beauty as well as their importance in many applications; they are particularly useful in Statistics (see Raghavarao (1971)), Coding Theory (see MacWilliams & Sloane (1978)), Cryptography (see Simmons (1989a, 1989b), and Computer Science in general (see Colbourn & van Oorschot (1989)). The present survey will deal with one of the classical areas of Design Theory, i.e. with Latin squares (which were introduced by Euler in 1782, see Euler (1923)), their associated geometries (in particular (Bruck) nets and transversal designs) and their automorphism groups. We shall also consider generalizations to arbitrary nets and TD's (with λ not necessarily restricted to 1).

The standard reference on Latin squares is the 1974 book by Dénes & Keedwell [DK]. Our survey will, as indicated, have a somewhat different emphasis, as we are much more concerned with the geometric and group theoretic than the purely combinatorial aspect of Latin squares. In particular, we shall not discuss conjugacy, subsquares, squares with holes and similar aspects. Generally, we will not be very interested in single Latin squares (or quasigroups) but prefer to work with (large) sets of mutually orthogonal squares. On the other hand, we will not deal with the largest possible collections of MOLS either, since these correspond to affine and projective planes. The theory of finite planes is well-developed and much too large to be considered here. We refer the reader to Pickert (1955), Hughes and Piper (1973), Lüneburg (1980) and Kallaher (1981) for this topic. We shall also avoid discussing any applications of Latin squares and refer to [DK] for some results in

---

*This is a revised and updated version of a previous survey (in German), see Jungnickel (1984c). Since the writing of this earlier paper, quite a few new results have been obtained and several of the 20 open problems listed then have been (at least partially) solved.

†Mathematisches Institut, Justus-Liebig-Universität Giessen, Arndtstr. 2, D-6300 Giessen, F.R. Germany

this direction. In this connection, we also mention the forthcoming book by Hedayat & Stufken (1989).

The remainder of this survey consists of eight chapters (divided into sections) as follows: 1. Basics, 2. Existence, 3. Completion, 4. Configurations, 5. Translation Nets, 6. Automorphism Groups, 7. Generalizations, 8. Conclusion and Problems. We will in this survey rarely include proofs (and then sketches of proofs, mostly). Many of the results mentioned (and their proofs) can be found in [DK] or in the 1985 book on Design Theory by Beth, Jungnickel & Lenz [BJL], our main reference; thus, for such results, the reader need not consult the original papers.

1. Basics. In order to make this survey self-contained (and to introduce some notation) we will begin by recalling the fundamental definitions and some basic results on Latin squares, nets and transversal designs. Section 1 deals with the algebraic and combinatorial and Section 2 with the geometric aspects of our topic, respectively.

1.1 Latin Squares, Quasigroups and Orthogonal Arrays. Let S be a set of cardinality s, the elements of which will be called *symbols*. A *Latin square* (of *order* s) over S is an $(s \times s)$-matrix $Q = (q_{ij})_{i,j=1,\ldots,s}$ with entries from S satisfying the following condition:

(1.1)   Each line of Q contains each element of S (exactly once).

(Here a *line* of a matrix is either a row or a column.) Two Latin squares $Q = (q_{ij})$ and $Q' = (q'_{ij})$ over S are called *orthogonal* if one has

$$(1.2) \qquad \{(q_{ij}, q'_{ij}) : \ i,j = 1,\ldots,s\} = S \times S.$$

We also say that Q' is an *orthogonal mate* of Q, then. A set of Latin squares $\{Q_1, \ldots, Q_n\}$ is called a set of *mutually orthogonal Latin squares* (MOLS, for short) if Q_i and Q_j are orthogonal whenever $i,j \in \{1, \ldots, n\}$ and $i \neq j$.

1.1.1 Examples. We shall generally use $S = \{1, \ldots, s\}$.

2 MOLS of order 3:
$$\begin{pmatrix} 1 & 2 & 3 \\ 2 & 3 & 1 \\ 3 & 1 & 2 \end{pmatrix} \qquad \begin{pmatrix} 1 & 2 & 3 \\ 3 & 1 & 2 \\ 2 & 3 & 1 \end{pmatrix}$$

3 MOLS of order 4:
$$\begin{pmatrix} 1 & 2 & 3 & 4 \\ 2 & 1 & 4 & 3 \\ 3 & 4 & 1 & 2 \\ 4 & 3 & 2 & 1 \end{pmatrix} \qquad \begin{pmatrix} 1 & 3 & 4 & 2 \\ 2 & 4 & 3 & 1 \\ 3 & 1 & 2 & 4 \\ 4 & 2 & 1 & 3 \end{pmatrix} \qquad \begin{pmatrix} 1 & 4 & 2 & 3 \\ 2 & 3 & 1 & 4 \\ 3 & 2 & 4 & 1 \\ 4 & 1 & 3 & 2 \end{pmatrix}$$

A Latin square of order 4 without an orthogonal mate
$$\begin{pmatrix} 1 & 2 & 3 & 4 \\ 2 & 3 & 4 & 1 \\ 3 & 4 & 1 & 2 \\ 4 & 1 & 2 & 3 \end{pmatrix}$$

As the reader will surely have noticed, the first of each of these sets of MOLS is just a group table. This is not necessary, in general. We can, however, view every Latin square as the table of a "multiplication" on S; in view of (1.1), equations of the types $xa = b$ and $ay = b$, respectively, are then uniquely solvable. Such an algebraic structure is called a *quasigroup*. The study of (mutually orthogonal) Latin squares is thus equivalent to that of (mutually orthogonal) quasigroups. The reader is referred to [DK] and to Bruck (1958) for this point of view. This also leads to the possibility of approaching Latin squares with the methods of Universal Algebra; we mention T. Evans (1975, 1979) in this connection. We shall not pursue these topics here in any detail. We will, however, encounter one application of this algebraic interpretation of Latin squares in Chapter 2.

We now turn our attention to another combinatorial way of describing Latin squares. As before, let S be a symbol set of cardinality s. An *orthogonal array* $OA(s, r)$ over S is an $(r \times s^2)$-matrix $A = (a_{ij})_{i=1,\ldots,r, j=1,\ldots,s^2}$ with entries from S satisfying the following condition:

$$(1.3) \qquad \{(a_{ij}, a_{kj}) : j = 1, \ldots, s^2\} = S \times S$$

for any two distinct indices $i, k \in \{1, \ldots, r\}$.*)

Every orthogonal array can be *normalized*. As the first two rows contain each ordered pair of elements from S exactly once, we may assume (using a suitable permutation of the columns) that the first two rows of A are

$$\begin{array}{cccccc}
11\cdots 1 & 22\cdots 2 & 33\cdots 3 & \cdots & ss & \cdots & s \\
12\cdots s & 12\cdots s & 12\cdots s & \cdots & 12 & \cdots & s
\end{array}$$

(where we again take $S = \{1, \ldots, s\}$). It is easily seen that each further row of S then yields a Latin square over S: Take the "blocks" of s entries each as the rows of the square. To be precise, define Q_i for $i = 3, \ldots, r$ by

$$Q_i = \begin{pmatrix} a_{i,1} & \cdots & a_{i,s} \\ a_{i,s+1} & \cdots & a_{i,2s} \\ \vdots & & \\ a_{i,s^2-s+1} & \cdots & a_{i,s^2} \end{pmatrix}$$

then $\{Q_3, \ldots, Q_r\}$ is a set of $r - 2$ MOLS. This construction can be reversed; thus we have the following result.

1.1.2 LEMMA. *An $OA(s, r)$ is equivalent to a set of $r - 2$ MOLS of order s.*

Now let A be once more a normalized $OA(s, r)$. Clearly any permutation of the symbols $\{1, \ldots, s\}$ in a given row of A results in an $OA(s, r)$, again. Thus we may also assume that the first s entries in rows $3, \ldots, r$ are $12\ldots s$. Then each pair of rows distinct from the first row contains the pairs of symbols $(1, 1), \ldots, (s, s)$ in the first s columns. Hence the last $r - 1$ entries in column $s + 1$ have to be pairwise distinct (by (1.3)). In particular, we have $r - 1 \leq s$:

---

*)More precisely, the objects just defined are orthogonal arrays of *strength two*; there are also orthogonal array of strength t (with $t \geq 2$). We refer the reader to Hedayat & Stufken (1989) for a monograph on orthogonal arrays and their applications.

1.1.3 LEMMA. *There are at most $s - 1$ MOLS of order $s(s \geq 2)$.*

It is customary to denote by $N(s)$ the maximum cardinality of a set of MOLS of order $s(s \geq 2)$; usually one also puts $N(0) = N(1) = \infty$. So 1.1.3 may be rewritten as

(1.4) $N(s) \leq s - 1$ for $s \geq 2$.

In spite of much effort, our knowledge about the function $N(\cdot)$ is still rather limited. We shall discuss this question in Chapter 2. Before doing so, we now turn our attention to the geometric aspect of Latin squares.

1.2 Nets and Transversal Designs. It is rather remarkable that *infinite* nets were introduced first (under the German name "Gewebe"); they were used in certain topological investigations in Differential Geometry. We mention the books by Blaschke & Bol (1938) and Blaschke (1955) in this context. Finite sets (with three parallel classes seem to have been introduced by Reidemeister (1929).

We shall give the following definition of a *net* of *order* s and *degree* r (for short, an (s, r)-net): This is an incidence structure $\mathbf{D} = (V, \mathbf{L}, \in)$ consisting of *points* and *lines* and satisfying the following axioms

(N1) Any two points are on at most one common line.

(N2) $\mathbf{D}$ is *resolvable* (i.e. there is a partition of the line set $\mathbf{L}$ into *parallel classes* of lines, each of which in turn is a partition of the point set V; we write $\parallel$ to denote the associated equivalence relation on $\mathbf{L}$).

(N3) Any two non-parallel lines intersect (in a unique point by (N1)).

(N4) There are $r \geq 3$ parallel classes of s lines each.

1.2.1 Exercise. Show that it suffices to require that at least one parallel class contains exactly s lines (in (N4)).

1.2.2 Examples. An affine plane of order s is an $(s, s + 1)$-net, and conversely. Any $r \geq 3$ parallel classes of an affine plane of order s form an (s, r)-net. (We shall see very soon that a net, in general, cannot be obtained in this simple way, not even when an affine plane of order s exists.) In the language of Design Theory, an (s, r)-net is just an affine 1-design $S_r(1, s, s^2)$, cf. [BJL]. The term "net" seems to have been introduced by Baer (1939). It achieved popularity only after the work of Bruck (1951, 1963); indeed, nets as defined above are to this day frequently called *Bruck nets*. (We shall discuss a more general notion of "net" in Chapter 7.) We now show that nets and orthogonal arrays (and thus MOLS) are equivalent concepts.

1.2.3 PROPOSITION. *The existence of an $OA(s, r)$ is equivalent to that of an (s, r)-net.*

Proof. Let $\mathbf{D}$ be an (s, r)-net with parallel classes $\mathbf{L}_1, \ldots, \mathbf{L}_r$, and put $S = \{1, \ldots, s\}$. Label the lines in each $\mathbf{L}_i$ (arbitrarily) with the symbols from S, and label the points of $\mathbf{D}$ as $p_1, \ldots, p_{s^2}$. Now define $A = (a_{ij})_{i=1,\ldots,s^2}$ as follows: $a_{ij} = k$

if and only if p_j is on the line of $\mathbf{L}_i$ labelled k. As the points of $\mathbf{D}$ are in a one-to-one correspondence with the pairs (L, L') of lines from $\mathbf{L}_i$ and $\mathbf{L}_{i'}$ (where $i \neq i'$ and $i, i' \in \{1, \ldots, r\}$), one sees that A is the desired $OA(s, r)$. The converse is similar. □

In 1.1.1, we have exhibited a Latin square of order 4 without an orthogonal mate. By 1.1.2 and 1.2.3, this corresponds to a (4,3)-net which is not part of the affine plane of order 4. (We shall consider questions of "extending" and "completing" nets in Chapter 3.) In general, each single Latin square of order s (i.e., each quasigroup) yields an $(s, 3)$-net; in this way, quasigroups give rise to an interesting geometric interpretation. They may thus be studied by investigating corresponding *geometric invariants*, e.g. configurational axioms, the full automorphism group or the group of projectivities of the corresponding net. This approach goes back to Reidemeister (1929). We refer the reader to Barlotti & Strambach (1984) and to Strambach (1981) for a comprehensive study (and a list of references). We shall discuss a few elementary results in this area in Chapter 4.

Sometimes it is advantageous to work with the structures dual to nets, i.e. transversal designs. Thus a *transversal design* $TD[k, s]$ consists of k *point classes* (sometimes called "groups", or even "groops" in [BJL]) of s points each and has blocks of size k; no two points in the same class are joined, whereas any two points in distinct classes are on a unique block. (Thus a TD is a special type of group divisible design, i.e. a GDD where each block meets each point class.).

If a TD is in fact *resolvable* (i.e., the blocks satisfy (N2)), we may adjoin a new point to each of the s parallel classes of blocks and thus obtain a TD with one further point class (formed by the s new points). Thus a resolvable $TD[k, s]$ (for short, an $RTD[k, s]$) can be extended to a $TD[k + 1, s]$. Conversely, omitting one point class from a $TD[k + 1, s]$ gives an $RTD[k, s]$.

Let us collect the various descriptions of Latin squares we have obtained:

1.2.4 THEOREM. *The existence of each of the following structures implies that of all the remaining ones:*

(i) $r - 2$ *MOLS of order s;*

(ii) $r - 2$ *pairwise orthogonal quasigroups of order s;*

(iii) *An $OA(s, r)$;*

(iv) *an (s, r)-net;*

(v) *an affine $S_r(1, s, s^2)$:*

(vi) *a $TD[r, s]$;*

(vii) *an $RTD[r - 1, s]$*

We refer the reader to Hedayat & Shrikhande (1971) for connections of Latin squares to various other types of (combinatorial or experimental) designs.

2. Existence. In this chapter we shall report on known existence results; thus we will be interested in *lower* bounds on the function $N(\cdot)$ introduced in Section 1.1. (Except for the trivial upper bound $N(s) \leq s - 1$ of 1.1.3, there is only one other general nonexistence result; this will be discussed in Chapter 3, as it involves a completion result.) As usual in Design Theory, the known existence theorems are obtained by a combination of direct and recursive constructions. We shall begin with direct methods.

2.1 Direct Constructions. For small values of s, the only way of constructing Latin squares of order s is by direct methods. One of the most useful (and simple) tools is the concept of difference matrices. While this essentially goes back to Mann (1942) (who used the language of "complete mappings", cf. Section 6.1), the first explicit formulation in terms of matrices seem to be in Bose and Bush (1952). The present author has studied these in Jungnickel (1980). There are different notational conventions; we shall adopt that used in [BJL].

2.1.1 DEFINITION. Let G be an additively written group of order s, and let

$$D = (d_{ij})_{i=1,\ldots,r,j=1,\ldots,s}$$

be a matrix with entries from G. We call D an (s,r)-*difference matrix* (for short, a $DM(s,r)$) over G if the following condition holds:

(DM) $$\{d_{ih} - d_{jh} : h = 1, \ldots, s\} = G$$

for any two distinct indices $i, j \in \{1, \ldots, r\}$. Thus the differences arising from any two rows of D contain each group element exactly once.

2.1.2 *Examples.* (i) The multiplication table of the finite field $GF(q)$ is a (q,q)-difference matrix over the elementary abelian group $EA(q)$ of order q (i.e., the additive group of $GF(q)$). Condition (DM) is easily checked here, using the distributive law.

(ii) The following is a $DM(12,6)$ over $\mathbf{Z}_2 \oplus \mathbf{Z}_6$, where we write xy for the group element (x,y):

$$\begin{pmatrix} 00 & 00 & 00 & 00 & 00 & 00 & 00 & 00 & 00 & 00 & 00 & 00 \\ 00 & 01 & 02 & 03 & 04 & 05 & 10 & 11 & 12 & 13 & 14 & 15 \\ 00 & 03 & 10 & 01 & 13 & 15 & 02 & 12 & 05 & 04 & 11 & 14 \\ 00 & 12 & 01 & 15 & 05 & 13 & 03 & 14 & 02 & 11 & 10 & 04 \\ 00 & 04 & 15 & 14 & 02 & 11 & 12 & 10 & 13 & 01 & 03 & 05 \\ 00 & 10 & 12 & 02 & 11 & 01 & 13 & 15 & 04 & 14 & 05 & 03 \end{pmatrix}$$

(12,6)-difference matrices were obtained independently by Johnson, Dulmage and Mendelsohn (1961) and by Bose, Chakravarti and Knuth (1960).

(iii) Let A be the matrix below; then $D = (A \ -A \ 0)$ is a $DM(15,4)$ over $\mathbf{Z}_{15}$, due to Schellenberg, van Rees and Vanstone (1978):

$$A = \begin{pmatrix} 0 & 0 & 0 & 0 & 0 & 0 & 0 \\ 1 & 2 & 3 & 4 & 5 & 6 & 7 \\ 2 & 5 & 7 & 9 & 12 & 4 & 1 \\ 6 & 3 & 14 & 10 & 7 & 13 & 4 \\ 10 & 6 & 1 & 11 & 2 & 7 & 12 \end{pmatrix}$$

171

(iv) the following $DM(24,5)$ over $\mathbf{Z}_6 \oplus \mathbf{Z}_2 \oplus \mathbf{Z}_2 = G$ is due (in different notation) to Roth and Peters (1987); we write xyz for $(x,y,z) \in G$.

$$\begin{pmatrix} 000\ 000\ 000\ 000\ 000\ 000\ 000\ 000\ 000\ 000\ 000\ 000\ 000\ 000\ 000\ 000\ 000\ 000\ 000\ 000\ 000\ 000\ 000\ 000 \\ 000\ 001\ 010\ 011\ 100\ 101\ 110\ 111\ 200\ 201\ 210\ 211\ 300\ 301\ 310\ 311\ 400\ 401\ 410\ 411\ 500\ 510\ 510\ 511 \\ 000\ 010\ 011\ 001\ 200\ 210\ 211\ 201\ 400\ 510\ 511\ 401\ 501\ 111\ 110\ 500\ 311\ 101\ 100\ 310\ 410\ 300\ 301\ 411 \\ 000\ 011\ 001\ 010\ 300\ 401\ 411\ 310\ 510\ 111\ 101\ 500\ 201\ 410\ 400\ 211\ 210\ 501\ 511\ 200\ 301\ 110\ 100\ 311 \\ 000\ 101\ 401\ 300\ 210\ 310\ 010\ 510\ 211\ 200\ 500\ 511\ 411\ 311\ 011\ 111\ 501\ 001\ 301\ 201\ 110\ 100\ 400\ 410 \end{pmatrix}$$

We note the following simple but important result:

2.1.3 PROPOSITION. *Assume the existence of a $DM(s,r)$ over some group G. Then one has $N(s) \geq r - 1$.*

Proof. Write $G = \{g_1, \ldots, g_s\}$. Clearly $(D + g_1 \ \ D + g_2 \cdots D + g_s)$ is an $OA(s,r)$. Adding the row $(g_1g_2 \ldots g_s \ \cdots \ g_1g_2 \ldots g_s)$ yields an $OA(s, r+1)$. Apply Lemma 1.1.2. $\square$

2.1.4 COROLLARY. *One has the following*

(2.1) $N(s) = s - 1$ *for prime powers s;*

(2.2) $N(12) \geq 5, N(15) \geq 4, N(24) \geq 4.$

These results follow from the examples given in 2.1.2 together with (1.4). Note that (2.1) is equivalent to the well-known existence of an affine plane of order s for prime powers s. More about difference matrices is to be found in [BJL, Section VIII.3 and Section X.12] as well as in Jungnickel (1980). Further interesting examples of difference matrices were constructed by Mills (1977). Unfortunately, many small values of s require considerably more involved direct constructions. Two of the most important methods are due to Wilson (1974a) and to Wang (1978), respectively. These methods still use difference techniques in suitable groups; they may be conveniently described using so-called "quasi-difference matrices" and "partial quasi-difference matrices". We refer the reader to [BJL, Section VIII.8] for a detailed account of this topic, including many examples. We shall give a few examples, however, to convey the flavour of these constructions.

2.1.5 *Example.* Let G be a group of order $s-1$ and let $D = (d_{ij})_{i=1,\ldots,r, j=1,\ldots,s+1}$ be a matrix with entries from $G \cup \{\infty\}$. Assume that the following conditions hold:

(i) Each row of D contains exactly one entry ∞

(ii) Each column of D contains at most one entry ∞

(iii) $\{d_{ik} - d_{jk} : k = 1, \ldots, s+1; d_{ik}, d_{jk} \neq \infty\} = G$ for any two distinct indices $i, j \in \{1, \ldots, r\}$.

Then $A = (\infty \ D \ D + g_2 \cdots D + g_{s-1})$ is an $OA(s,r)$, where $\{g_2, \ldots, g_{s-1}\} = G \backslash \{0\}$. The following matrix D_1 over $\mathbf{Z}_{13}$ is due to Todorov (1985), whereas the matrix D_2 over $\mathbf{Z}_{19}$ is from Todorov (1989):

$$
D_1 = \begin{pmatrix}
\infty & 0 & 0 & 0 & 0 & 0 & 0 & 0 & 0 & 0 & 0 & 0 & 0 & 0 & 0 \\
0 & \infty & 0 & 1 & 3 & 2 & 4 & 5 & 6 & 7 & 8 & 9 & 10 & 11 & 12 \\
0 & 0 & \infty & 2 & 12 & 10 & 7 & 9 & 5 & 4 & 1 & 11 & 8 & 3 & 6 \\
0 & 1 & 2 & \infty & 9 & 5 & 3 & 12 & 7 & 11 & 0 & 4 & 6 & 8 & 10 \\
0 & 3 & 12 & 9 & \infty & 6 & 2 & 7 & 11 & 1 & 5 & 10 & 0 & 4 & 8
\end{pmatrix}
$$

$$
D_2 = \begin{pmatrix}
\infty & 0 & 0 & 7 & 1 & 11 & 1 & 7 & 11 & 2 & 14 & 3 & 4 & 9 & 6 & 5 & 16 & 17 & 10 & 13 & 15 \\
0 & \infty & 0 & 1 & 11 & 7 & 7 & 11 & 1 & 14 & 3 & 2 & 9 & 6 & 4 & 16 & 17 & 5 & 13 & 15 & 10 \\
0 & 0 & \infty & 11 & 7 & 1 & 11 & 1 & 7 & 3 & 2 & 14 & 6 & 4 & 9 & 17 & 5 & 16 & 15 & 10 & 13 \\
7 & 1 & 11 & \infty & 0 & 0 & 16 & 5 & 17 & 9 & 4 & 6 & 14 & 2 & 3 & 7 & 1 & 11 & 15 & 13 & 10 \\
1 & 11 & 7 & 0 & \infty & 0 & 17 & 16 & 5 & 6 & 9 & 4 & 3 & 14 & 2 & 11 & 7 & 1 & 10 & 15 & 13 \\
11 & 7 & 1 & 0 & 0 & \infty & 5 & 17 & 16 & 4 & 6 & 9 & 2 & 3 & 14 & 1 & 11 & 7 & 13 & 10 & 15
\end{pmatrix}
$$

These two matrices yield

$$(2.3) \qquad\qquad N(14) \geq 3,\, N(20) \geq 4.$$

The next example is a little more involved, since it contains different types of "infinite" entries:

2.1.6 Example. Let $G = \mathbf{Z}_7$ and consider the matrix

$$
D = \begin{pmatrix}
\infty_1 & 0 & 1 & 6 & \infty_2 & 0 & 2 & 5 & \infty_3 & 0 & 3 & 4 & 0 \\
0 & \infty_1 & 6 & 1 & 0 & \infty_2 & 5 & 2 & 0 & \infty_3 & 4 & 3 & 0 \\
1 & 6 & \infty_1 & 0 & 2 & 5 & \infty_2 & 0 & 3 & 4 & \infty_3 & 0 & 0 \\
6 & 1 & 0 & \infty_1 & 5 & 2 & 0 & \infty_2 & 4 & 3 & 0 & \infty_3 & 0
\end{pmatrix}
$$

Now form the matrix

$$A = (D \ D+1 \ D+2 \cdots D+6 \ B)$$

where B is an $OA(3,4)$ on the symbol set $\{\infty_1, \infty_2, \infty_3\}$. Then A is an $OA(10,4)$, and we have

$$(2.4) \qquad\qquad N(10) \geq 2.$$

The verification of this assertion is not too difficult, if one realizes that the differences from any two rows of D contain each $g \in G$ exactly once (disregarding differences involving an infinite entry ∞_i).

2.2 The MacNeish Theorem. The following is the most basic recursive construction. It is usually attributed to MacNeish (1922) though it may in fact have been known to Euler.

2.2.1 THEOREM. *One has*

(2.5) $$N(st) \geq \min\{N(s), N(t)\}.$$

Proof. If $Q_1, \ldots, Q_r$ and $Q'_1, \ldots, Q'_r$ are sets of mutually orthogonal quasigroups of order s and t, respectively, then $Q_1 \times Q'_1, \ldots Q_r \times Q'_r$ is a set of mutually orthogonal quasigroups of order st. □

2.2.2. COROLLARY. *Let $s = q_1 \cdots q_n$ be the canonical prime power factorization of s. Then one has*

(2.6) $$N(s) \geq \min\{q_i - 1 : i = 1, \ldots, n\}.$$

Proof. Use (2.2) and 2.2.1. □

MacNeish in fact published an erroneous proof for the *Euler conjecture* (stating $N(s) = 1$ for $s \equiv 2 \mod 4$) and, more generally, for the assertion that (2.6) holds with equality. Both assertions were disproved around 1960 by Bose, Shrikhande and Parker; cf. Parker (1959), Bose & Shrikhande (1960) and Bose, Shrikhande & Parker (1960). The main result of the last paper is the existence of a pair of orthogonal Latin squares of order s whenever $s \neq 2, 6$; cf. 2.4.3 below. The examples given in 2.1.4 and 2.1.5 already show that neither assertion can hold in general; both are true when one restricts attention to certain special classes of Latin squares, see Chapters 5 and 6. We mention that Theorem 2.2.1 has a difference matrix analogue due to Jungnickel (1980):

2.2.3 LEMMA. *The existence of both $DM(s,r)$ over G and $DM(t,r)$ over H implies that of $DM(st,r)$ over $G \oplus H$.*

Again, a direct product construction will suffice to prove this. In this context we mention another recursive construction for difference matrices; the proof uses Singer difference sets and may also be found in [BJL, IX.1.17].

2.2.4 THEOREM (Jungnickel 1980). *Let q be a prime power and assume that $N(q + 1) \geq r$. Then there exists a $DM(q^2 + q + 1, r + 1)$ over the cyclic group of order $q^2 + q + 1$; in particular, one has*

(2.7) $$N(q^2 + q + 1) \geq N(q + 1) \quad \text{for prime powers } q.$$

2.2.5 Examples. We obtain

(2.8) $$N(21) \geq 4, N(57) \geq 7, N(273) \geq 16.$$

A similar result for numbers of the form $N(q^2 - 1)$ yields the first interesting value only for $q^2 - 1 = 1023$, see Jungnickel (1980). A more involved result of this type (using quasi-difference matrices) is the following (see [BJL, VIII.8.23]): $N(q^2 + 2q + 2) \geq \min\{N(q + 2) - 1, N(q + 1)\}$ for prime powers q. This includes Example 2.1.6 and also gives $N(65) \geq 7$.

2.3 The Method of Bose and Shrikhande. The essential idea needed to disprove the Euler conjecture was the use of group divisible designs and pairwise balanced designs for constructing sets of MOLS, introduced by Bose and Shrikhande (1960). We recall the required definitions. Let V be a set of v points split into *point classes* with sizes from G; moreover, let **B** be a set of lines with sizes from K. If no two points in the same class are joined by a line in **B**, whereas any two points in distinct classes are joined by exactly one line, we call $(V, \mathbf{B})$ a *group divisible design* $GDD[K, G; v]$. A *pairwise balanced design* $B[K; v]$ is a GDD with $G = \{1\}$, i.e., any two points are joined. A *Steiner system* $S(2, k, v)$ is the special case $K = \{k\}$, i.e. a $B[\{k\}; v]$. Note that a $TD[k, s]$ is the same as a $GDD[\{k\}, \{s\}; ks]$. We mention some examples:

2.3.1 Examples. (i) An affine plane of order s is an $S(2, s, s^2)$.

(ii) A projective plane of order s is an $S(2, s+1, s^2+s+1)$.

(iii) Removing one point and all the lines incident with this point from an $S(2, k, v)$ yields a $GDD[\{k\}, \{k-1\}; v-1]$. Using this for affine planes yields the existence of $GDD[\{q\}, \{q-1\}; q^2-1]$ for every prime power q.

We need some more notation. A Latin square is called *idempotent* if it is the table of an idempotent quasigroup, i.e. a quasigroup satisfying the identity $xx = x$ for all x. The reader may verify the following result as an exercise:

2.3.2 LEMMA. *The existence of k idempotent MOLS of order s is equivalent to that of a $TD[k+2, s]$ with a parallel class (i.e. with s lines forming a partition of the point set).*

Note that there may exist a $TD[k, s]$ with a parallel class even if no $RTD[k, s]$ (i.e., no $TD[k+1, s]$, see 1.2.4) exists. We write $N^*(s)$ for the maximal number of idempotent MOLS of order s. Then always $N^*(s) \geq N(s) - 1$, by 1.2.4. We are now ready to state the fundamental construction of Bose and Shrikhande (1960).

2.3.3 THEOREM. *Let a $GDD[K, G; v]$ be given and assume $N^*(k) \geq n$ for all $k \in K$ and $N(g) \geq n$ for all $g \in G$. Then one also has $N(v) \geq n$. In case of a $B[K, v]$ one even has $N^*(v) \geq \min\{N^*(k) : k \in K\}$.*

Proof. We only consider the case of a $B[K; v]$ here. By hypothesis, we may define n mutually orthogonal idempotent quasigroup $Q_1^B, \ldots, Q_N^B$ on the point set of each line B of our $B[k, v]$. Now define operations $o_1, \ldots, o_n$ on all of the point set V as follows: $xo_ix = x$ for all x and $xo_iy = z$ if $xy = z$ in the quasigroup Q_i^B, where B is the unique line joining the distinct points x and y. It is not difficult to check that this gives n mutually orthogonal quasigroups on V. (The general case of a GDD is similar though more technical; we refer the reader to [BJL, Section X.1].) $\square$

2.3.4 Examples. (i) Let q be a prime power. Using the $GDD[\{q\}, \{q-1\}; q^2-1]$ of Example 2.3.1 in 2.3.3 shows that $N(q^2-1) \geq \min\{N^*(q), N(q-1)\}$ and thus (as $N^*(q) \geq N(q) - 1 = q - 2 \geq N(q-1)$)

(2.9) $$N(q^2-1) \geq N(q-1) \quad \text{for prime powers } q.$$

175

In particular, we have $N(80) \geq 7$.

(ii) Removing three non-collinear points and the lines joining them from an $S(2, k, v)$ gives a $GDD[\{k, k-1\}, \{1, k-2\}; v-3]$ and thus implies

$$N(v-3) \geq \min\{N^*(k), N^*(k-1), N(k-2)\}.$$

Using the projective planes of orders 4 and 8 shows

(2.10) $$N(18) \geq 2, N(7) \geq 6;$$

Using the affine planes of orders 5 and 9 gives

(2.11) $$N(22) \geq 2, N(78) \geq 6.$$

We remark that Theorem 2.3.3 shows that the set of all $s \in \mathbb{N}$ for which a set of k idempotent MOLS of order s exists is PBD-closed in the sense of Wilson's theory, see Wilson (1972a, 1972b, 1975) or [BJL, Ch. XI].

2.4 The Construction of Wilson. The next important breakthrough in recursive constructions of MOLS is due to Wilson (1974b). His result is more involved and we refer the reader to [BJL, X.3.1] for a proof.

2.4.1 THEOREM. *Let* **D** *be a* $TD[k+l, s]$ *with point classes* $P_1, \ldots, P_k, Q_1 \ldots, Q_l$. *Moreover, let* T *be a* t-subset *of* $Q_1 \cup \cdots \cup Q_l$, *and put* $u_L = |L \cap T|$ *for each line* L *of* **D**. *Assume the validity of the following conditions:*

  (i) *There exists a* $TD[k, t_i]$ *with* $t_i = |T \cap Q_i|$ *(for* $i = 1, \ldots, l$*).*
  (ii) *There exists a* $TD[k, m + u_L]$ *with* u_L *pairwise disjoint lines (for each line* L *of* **D***).*

Then there also exist $TD[k, ms + t]$.

We shall now give a few sample applications of Theorem 2.4.1. Using 2.4.1 with $l = 1$ and $T \subset Q_1$, we get the following result. (Note that always $u_L \in \{0, 1\}$, here.)

2.4.2 COROLLARY. *Let* $0 \leq t \leq s$. *Then one has*

$$N(ms + t) \geq \min\{N(m), N(m+1), N(s) - 1, N(t)\}$$

for all positive integers m.

As an application of 2.4.2, we can give a very short proof of the main result of Bose, Shrikhande and Parker (1960):

2.4.3 THEOREM. *One has* $N(n) \geq 2$ *for* $n \neq 2, 6$.

Proof. By Corollary 2.2.2, we need only consider values $n \equiv 2 \mod 4$. Let s be a positive integer congruent to $1,5,7,9,11,13$ or 17 modulo 18. Then $N(s) \geq 4$, by Corollary 2.2.2. Moreover, let $t \leq s$ be odd and thus $N(t) \geq 2$, again by Corollary 2.2.2. Then Corollary 2.4.2 yields $N(3s + t) \geq 2$, e.g. $N(18) \geq 2$ and $N(22) \geq 2$ (as $18 = 3.5 + 3$ and $22 = 3.7 + 1$). It is not too difficult to see that one obtains $N(n) \geq 2$ for $n \equiv 2 \pmod 4$, $n \geq 18$, in this way. This leaves only the cases $n = 10$ (see Example 2.1.6) and $n = 14$ (see Example 2.1.5). ∎

The reader may easily show that any TD contains at least two disjoint lines. Then one obtains from Theorem 2.4.1 (with $l = 2$) the following result:

2.4.4 COROLLARY. *Let $0 \le t \le s$ and $0 \le u \le s$. Then one has $N(ms+t+u) \ge \min\{N(m), N(m+1), N(m+2), N(s) - 2, N(u), N(t)\}$ for all positive integers m.*

2.4.5 Exercise. Show $N(51) \ge 4, N(62) \ge 4, N(58) \ge 5, N(96) \ge 7$ and $N(s) \ge 6$ for $s = 84, 85, 86, 87, 92, 93, 94, 95, 98$.

Wilson's method is strong enough to prove the following theorems, with the exception of a few direct constructions needed for some small cases.

2.4.6 THEOREM. *One has*

(i) $N(s) \ge 3$ for $s \ne 2, 6, 10$ *(Wang 1978, Todorov 1985)*;

(ii) $N(s) \ge 4$ for $s \ge 53$ *(Guérin 1966)*;

(iii) $N(s) \ge 5$ for $s \ge 63$ *(Hanani (1970))*;

(iv) $N(s) \ge 6$ for $s \ge 77$ *(Wilson 1974a, Wojtas 1978)*.

With the exception of $N(14) \ge 3$ (see (2.3)), all these results are proved in [BJL]. For the case of three MOLS, the reader might also want to consult Wallis (1984) or Street and Street (1987). The proofs are elementary but do require a lot of detailed considerations and thus are rather long.

2.5 Asymptotic Existence. Using Wilson's theorem 2.4.1, it is comparatively simple to prove the following famous result of Chowla, Erdös and Straus (1960), see [BJL, Section X.5]:

2.5.1 THEOREM. *One has $N(s) \to \infty$ for $s \to \infty$.*

Using more refined arguments, Chowla, Erdös and Straus in fact proved $N(s) \ge s^a$ with $a = \dfrac{1}{91}$ for all sufficiently large s. The value of a has been improved several times, since; the results of Wilson (1974b) brought a considerable progress, here. The best known value at present is due to Beth (1983) who gave $a = \dfrac{1}{14.8}$. All these results are quite non-trivial and use the sieve methods of number theory (in conjunction with Theorem 2.4.1). In view of Theorem 2.5.1, the following definition makes sense:

$$(2.12) \qquad n_k = \max\{s : N(s) < k\}.$$

Thus the results of Theorems 2.4.3 and 2.4.6 may be rewritten as

$$(2.13) \qquad n_2 = 6, n_3 \le 10, n_4 \le 52, n_5 \le 62, n_6 \le 76.$$

We shall now list all other results on n_k known at present. The proofs of these results require rather involved generalizations of Wilson's methods, e.g. the use of transveral designs with missing sub-TD's (equivalently, OA's with "holes"), and further direct constructions. It seems almost impossible to obtain these results without using a computer.

2.5.2 THEOREM. (Brouwer 1980b, Brouwer and van Rees 1982). *One has* $n_7 \leq$ 780, $n_8 \leq 4738$, $n_9 \leq 5842$, $n_{10} \leq 7222$, $n_{11} \leq 7478$, $n_{12} \leq 9286$, $n_{13} \leq 9476$, $n_{14} \leq n_{15} \leq 10632, n_{30} \leq 65278$.

2.6 MOLS of Small Orders. In Table A at the end of this paper, we give an updated version of Table H in [BJL] listing a lower bound on $N(s)$ for $s \leq 100, s$ not a prime power. If possible, we refer the reader to a bound mentioned in this survey and/or to a bound established in [BJL]. (References involving Roman numerals refer to [BJL].) A table of bounds for $N(s)$ with $s \leq 10,000$ was given by Brouwer (1979). Since then, there were a few improvements; we refer the reader to Brouwer (1980a, 1980b), Brouwer and van Rees (1982), Jungnickel (1981a) and Bennett (1987).

3. Completion. This chapter deals with the question of extending a net to a "larger" net and, if possible, of completing a net (i.e. embedding it into an affine plane of the same order).

3.1 Bruck's Completion Theorem. Let **D** be an (s, r)-net. We define a further parameter d, the *deficiency* of **D**, as follows:

$$(3.1) \qquad\qquad d = s + 1 - r.$$

The deficiency measures how far **D** falls short from being an affine plane of order s (which would have $s + 1$ instead of r parallel classes). We call **D** *step-t-extendable* if one can adjoin t new parallel classes of lines to **D** in such a way that one obtains an $(s, r + t)$-net **D**′. If **D**′ is an affine plane (i.e. if $t = d$), then **D** is called *embeddable* or *completable* and **D**′ is called a *completion* of **D**. Note that every line in **D**′**D** has to be a transversal for **D**, i.e. a set S of s points which intersects each line of **D** at most (and then precisely) once. A net **D** with deficiency $d \geq 1$ which is not step-1-extendable is called *maximal*; in particular, *transversal-free* nets are maximal. In this terminology, affine planes are *not* considered maximal nets; I prefer to call them *complete* nets. Of course, every affine plane is (trivially) transversal-free; we shall soon meet many non-trivial examples. Note that **D** is step-1-extendable if and only if it contains a set of s pairwise disjoint transversals.

Intuitively speaking, one might assume that both nets with a very small and with a large value of the deficiency should be extendable. In the first case, an affine plane with very few parallel classes missing should be reconstructable; in the second case, there are many points not yet joined to a given point and there should be a lot of choice in constructing new lines.

Only the first of these ideas works; it is the subject of the famous work of Bruck (1963a) on completing nets and will be discussed presently. Regarding the second idea, there are many maximal (even transversal-free) nets with 3 parallel classes only, as we shall see in Section 3.3.

3.1.1 THEOREM (Bruck's completion theorem). *Define the polynomial p by* $p(x) = \dfrac{1}{2}x^4 + x^3 + x^2 + \dfrac{3}{4}x$. *Then any (s, r)-net* **D** *of deficiency $d = s + 1 - r$ satisfying $p(d - 1) < s$ is completable.*

178

In particular, every (s, s)-net with $s \geq 5$ is embeddable into an affine plane of order s, a result due to Shrikhande (1961).* The proof of Theorem 3.1.1 uses methods from Graph Theory and is rather long; we refer the reader to Bruck (1963a) or to [BJL, Section X.7]. The "clique and claw"-method of Bruck (1963a) and Bose (1963) used to prove 3.1.1 has subsequently been used successfully for many other embedding theorems; we refer the reader to the survey by Shrikhande and Singhi (1981) and to Beutelspacher and Metsch (1986, 1987) for a recent application to linear spaces. Bruck (1963a) also proved the uniqueness of the completion in Theorem 3.1.1; in fact, he obtained the following stronger result.

3.1.2 THEOREM (Bruck's uniqueness theorem). *Let* $\mathbf{D}$ *be an* (s, r)-*net with deficiency* d *satisfying* $s > (d-1)^2$ *(or, equivalently,* $r > s - \sqrt{s}$*). Then any two transversals of* $\mathbf{D}$ *intersect in at most one point, and* $\mathbf{D}$ *has at most* sd *transversals. Equality holds if and only if* $\mathbf{D}$ *is completable; then the completion of* $\mathbf{D}$ *is obtained by adjoining all* sd *transversals of* $\mathbf{D}$*. In particular, the completion of* $\mathbf{D}$ *is unique (if it is at all possible).*

Theorem 3.1.2 is not too difficult to prove; we leave this as a more demanding exercise to the reader. Bruck (1963a) pointed out that the bound of 3.1.2 is best possible; we shall discuss the quality of the bound given by 3.1.1 in the next section. Nets satisfying $s = (d-1)^2$ have been studied by Ostrom (1964); he proved that such a net has at most $2sd$ transversals and admits at most two non-isomorphic completions. The case of equality coincides with the theory of derivations of projective planes, see Hughes and Piper (1973). This is a special case of Ostrom's theory of "net replacement", a very general construction method for projective planes; we refer the reader to Ostrom (1970) for this topic.

In view of the results discussed in this section, we shall call $\mathbf{D}$ a net of *critical deficiency* if $s = (d-1)^2$; a net of *small deficiency* if $s > (d-1)^2$; and a net of *very small deficiency* if $p(d-1) < s$.

3.2 Maximal Nets with Small Deficiency. The known examples of maximal nets of small deficiency are in fact all transversal-free. The first of these were constructed by Bruen (1971, 1972, 1975), using partial spreads in projective spaces $PG(3, q)$; we shall discuss this approach in Section 5.4. One has the following result:

3.2.1 THEOREM (Bruen). *For each prime* p *there exists a maximal net of order* p^2 *and deficiency* p*. For* $p \geq 5$*, there also exists a maximal net of order* p^2 *and deficiency* $p - 1$*.*

The proof of this result is comparatively involved, in particular in case $d = p - 1$. I shall sketch the methods employed and discuss a strengthening of 3.2.1 and some related results due to Jungnickel (1984) in Section 5.4. Some time ago Dow (1983) found a surprisingly simple construction which proves the following result:

3.2.2 THEOREM (Dow). *For each prime power* q*, there exists a maximal net of order* q^2 *and deficiency* q*.*

---

*As noted in §1.2, this is not true for $s = 4$. It holds trivially for $s = 3$.

Dow's proof uses the Desarguesian planes $AG(2, q^2)$ and their derivations, i.e. the Hall planes (see Hughes and Piper (1973)), together with results of Ostrom (1964): He adjoins to the $(q^2, q^2 - q)$-net common to both planes a further parallel class composed of some lines of each of these planes. Unfortunately, his method cannot be used for the case of deficiency $d = q - 1$; indeed, no comparable result is known for $d = q - 1$.

The examples given by Theorems 3.2.1 and 3.2.2 are all of small deficiency. However, d is in the order of magnitude of $\sqrt{s}$, whereas the bound in Bruck's completion theorem 3.1.1 is in the order of magnitude of $s^{1/4}$. Nevertheless, these examples show that Bruck's bound is reasonably good. In fact it is best possible for $s = 4, 9$ and 25, as the maximal (4,3)-, (9,7)- and (25,22)-nets provided by Theorem 3.2.1 show. For all other values of s, it is an open problem whether or not Bruck's bound is best possible. E.g., it is not known whether there is a maximal (8,6)-net. It would in any case be interesting to find further examples of nets of small deficiency; note that no such net is known if s is not a prime power.

3.3 Maximal Nets With Large Deficiency. In this section we mention some series of examples of maximal nets with large deficiency. The first two results will provide maximal nets with 3 parallel classes. Before stating these results, we note the following useful lemma:

3.3.1 LEMMA (Ostrom). *The existence of a maximal (s, r)-difference matrix (over some group G of order s) implies that of a transversal-free (and thus maximal) $(s, r + 1)$-net.*

Here, of course, a difference matrix D is called *maximal* if it cannot be enlarged by adding a further row subject to the condition in 2.1.1. Lemma 3.3.1 is a special case of a result due to Ostrom (1966), who used different terminology; see also [BJL,X.12.8]. Together with the following result it shows the existence of maximal $(s, 3)$-nets for even orders s:

3.2.2 THEOREM (Hall and Paige 1955). *Let G be a group of even order s, and assume that the Sylow 2-subgroup of G is cyclic. Then there is no $(s, 3)$-difference matrix over G.*

The special case $s \equiv 2 \mod 4$ of Theorem 3.3.2 is due to Mann (1942). Hall and Paige have stated their result in terms of "complete mappings" which are essentially the same as $(s, 3)$-difference matrices. A considerably simpler proof for Theorem 3.3.2 (or rather for a generalization of this result) was given by Drake (1979); see also [BJL, Section X.12]. The following second result on maximal $(s, 3)$-nets is due to Mann (1944); see also [BJL, X.8.5,8.6].

3.3.3 THEOREM (Mann). *Let $s \equiv 1 \mod 4$, say $s = 4n + 1$. Then there exists a Latin square of order s with a Latin subsquare of order $2n$. Each such square belongs to a maximal $(s, 3)$-net.*

3.3.4 COROLLARY. *Let $s \not\equiv 3 \mod 4$. Then there exists a maximal $(s, 3)$-net.*

It is not known whether a similar result holds for $s \equiv 3 \mod 4$. A maximal (7,3)-net is due to Sade (1951). The following result implies the existence of maximal nets satisfying the MacNeish bound 2.2.2 with equality (for all orders s which are not prime powers):

3.3.5 THEOREM (BRUCK 1951). *Assume the existence of an affine plane of order s and of a $(t, s+1)$-net. If s does not divide t, then there exists a transversal-free (and thus maximal) $(st, s+1)$-net.*

A simplified proof is due to Drake (1977), see also [BJL, X.8.9]. We finally mention that every $(s, 3)$-net contains at least a large "partial" transversal (in the obvious sense); the best known bound at present guarantees a partial transversal of size $s - c(\log s)^2$ for order s, see Shor (1982). No comparable result is known for nets with at least 4 parallel classes.

3.4 Existence. The only known general non-existence result for nets (or MOLS) arises from the famous Bruck-Ryser theorem in conjunction with Bruck's completion theorem.

3.4.1 THEOREM. *Let $s \equiv 1$ or $2 \mod 4$ and assume that s is not the sum of two squares. Moreover, let t be the largest positve integer satisfying $p(t) < s$, where p is the polynomial defined in Theorem 3.1.1. Then one has $N(s) \leq s - t - 3$.*

Proof. The theorem of Bruck and Ryser (1949) (see also [BJL, II.4.8,4.9] implies the non-existence of a (projective or affine) plane of order s. By Theorem 3.1.1, every (s, r)-net then has to have deficiency $d \geq t+2$ (otherwise it could be completed to an affine plane of order s). Thus $r \leq (s+1) - (t+2) = s - t - 1$ and therefore $N(s) \leq s - t - 3$. □

3.4.2 Examples. One has

(3.2)	$N(s) \leq s - 4$	for $s = 6, 14, 21, 22$;
(3.3)	$N(s) \leq s - 5$	for $s = 30, 33, 38, 42, 46, 54, 57, 62, \ldots$

The only other known upper bound on $N(s)$ occurs for $s = 6$:

$$(3.4) \qquad\qquad N(6) = 1;$$

this is due to Tarry (1900, 1901) who proved the non-existence of two MOLS of order 6 by a complete case analysis. Recently, much simpler proofs for this result were obtained by Betten (1983), see also [BJL, Section X.13], and by Stinson (1984). For more about Latin squares of order 6, see Betten (1984).

As the previous two sections indicate, it is also of interest to determine the numbers r for which a maximal (s, r)-net (equivalently, a maximal set of $r - 2$ MOLS of order s) exists (for given s). This has been considered for orders ≤ 8 by Drake (1977) and for $s = 9$ by Jungnickel and Grams (1986), see also [BJL, X.8.13]. The only two pairs with $s < 10$ for which the existence of a maximal set of k MOLS of order s is undecided are (8,4) and (9,4). We summarize the known results and simultaneously extend the discussion to $s = 12$ in the following table:

order s	exists	does not exist	undecided
2	1	-	-
3	2	1	-
4	1,3	2	-
5	1,4	2,3	-
6	1	2,3,4,5	-
7	1,2,6	3,4,5	-
8	1,2,3,7	5,6	4
9	1,2,3,5,8	6,7	4
10	1,2	7,8	3,4,5,6,9
11	2,3,4,10	8,9	1,5,6,7
12	1,2,3,5	9,10	4,6,7,8,11

Here the non-existence results come from Bruck's completion theorem 3.1.1 and for $s = 7, k = 3$ from Norton's (1939) classification of Latin squares of order 7 (see Drake (1977)). Existence comes from 3.2.1, 3.3.4, 3.3.5 and direct examples, often established from maximal difference matrices via 3.3.1; see Jungnickel and Grams (1986) for $s \leq 9$. For $s = 11$, there are maximal $(11, k)$-difference matrices with $k = 3, 4, 5$; see A.B. Evans and MacFarland (1984) and A.B. Evans (1987b) who state their results in the language of orthomorphism graphs. For $s = 12$, the value $k = 3$ is established from a maximal (12,4)-DM in the dihedral group of order 12 (see Chang, Hsiang and Tai (1965) who also use the language of "orthomorphisms"); the value $k = 5$ corresponds to the (12,6)-DM exhibited in 2.1.2 which is known to be maximal, see Johnson, Dulmage & Mendelsohn (1961) who cite unpublished work of Parker and van Duren or Baumert and Hall (1973). It would be desirable to remove some of the undecided cases and to extend the table above to somewhat larger values of s. Clearly this would require new methods for constructing maximal nets and/or difference matrices.

4. Configurations. In this chapter we will briefly consider some configuration theorems on nets. These conditions either guarantee the existence of certain automorphisms or the validity of algebraic conditions for the corresponding quasigroups. Since the role of configuration theorems in the study of affine and projective planes is well-known (see e.g. Hughes and Piper (1973), Pickert (1955) or Skornyakov (1953)), we shall mainly concentrate on nets with 3 parallel classes here.

4.1 Loops and Nets With 3 Parallel Classes. In this section, **D** will in general be an $(s, 3)$-net for some order s. Each $(s, 3)$-net is equivalent to a certain set of quasigroups of order s; conversely, any quasigroup of order s leads to an $(s, 3)$-net. One may assume that the quasigroup considered has a unit element, i.e. that it is a *loop*. Now let L be any (additively written) loop; we associate a net on $L \times L$ with L by choosing the following three parallel classes of lines:

(i) all lines of the form $\{x, y\} : x = c\}$ ($c \in L$);

(ii) all lines of the form $\{x, y\} : y = c\}$ ($c \in L$);

(iii) all lines of the form $\{x, y\} : y = x + c\}$ ($c \in L$)*.

We shall denote this net by $\mathbf{D}(L)$. This construction is essentially due to Reidemeister (1929). Of course, one immediate question is to determine when $\mathbf{D}(L)$ and $\mathbf{D}(L')$ are isomorphic. This has been done by Baer (1939):

4.1.1 THEOREM (Baer). *Let L and L' be two loops of order s. Then one has $D(L) \cong D(L')$ if and only if L and L' are isotopic, i.e. if there exist bijections $\rho, \sigma, \tau : L \rightarrow L'$ satisfying $(x + y)^\rho = x^\sigma + y^\tau$ for all $x, y \in L$.*

The most important geometric configuration in nets with 3 parallel classes has been introduced by Reidemeister (1929); it is used to ensure that the underlying loop is a group. We need two definitions before we can state Reidemeister's result. Let $\mathbf{P}_1, \mathbf{P}_2, \mathbf{P}_3$ be the 3 parallel classes of lines of $\mathbf{D}(L)$. The following axiom is called the *Reidemeister condition* (cf. Figure 1):

(RC) Assume that all of the lines pp', qq', rr', ss' belong to $\mathbf{P}_1$, that all of the lines $pr, p'r', qs, q's'$ belong to $\mathbf{P}_2$ and that all of the lines $ps, p's', qr$ belong to $\mathbf{P}_3$. Then $q'r'$ also belongs to $\mathbf{P}_3$.

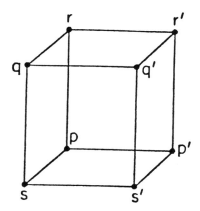

Figure 1

Even though (RC) is *not* symmetric in $\mathbf{P}_1, \mathbf{P}_2, \mathbf{P}_3$ (since $\mathbf{P}_3$ is special) it does in fact imply the validity of the corresponding two conditions where either $\mathbf{P}_1$ or $\mathbf{P}_2$ is the special parallel class; cf. Pickert (1955, pp. 52–53).

---

*Some authors choose instead the lines $\{(x, y) : x + y = c\}$.

183

Next let **D** be an (s,r)-net. An automorphism α of **D** is called *central translation** with respect to the parallel class **P** if α fixes every parallel class of **D** and also every line in **P**. The parallel class **P** is called the *direction* of α. We say that **D** is *transitive* in direction **P**, if there exists a central translation α with $p^\alpha = q$ whenever p and q are on a line in **P**.

The following result is essentially due to Reidemester (1929); see also Pickert (1955).

4.1.2 THEOREM. *Let L be a loop. Then the following conditions are equivalent:*

   (i) *L is associative, i.e. **L** is a group.*

  (ii) *$D(L)$ satisfies axiom (RC).*

 (iii) *$D(L)$ is transitive in each of the three directions.*

It is interesting to note that the automorphism group of L can be recovered from $D(L)$ if L is a group. It is in fact not too difficult to see that the stabilizer of the point $(0,0)$ in Aut $D(L)$ consists of the mappings $(x,y) \to (x\alpha, y\alpha)$ with $\alpha \in$ Aut L. Observing that the mappings $(x,y) \to (x+c, y+d)$ (with $c,d \in L$) are also in Aut $D(L)$ yields the following result:

4.1.3 THEOREM (Schönhardt 1930). *Let L be a group. Then the full automorphism group of $D(L)$ is a semidirect product of Aut L with $L \times L$.*

We next characterize abelian groups in a similar way. To this end, denote the three parallel classes of $D(L)$ by $\mathbf{P}_1, \mathbf{P}_2, \mathbf{P}_3$ (as before). The following axiom is called the *Thomsen condition* (cf. Figure 2):

(TC) Assume that all of the lines xx', yy', zz' belong to $\mathbf{P}_1$, that all of the lines $xy, y'z$ and $x'z'$ belong to $\mathbf{P}_2$ and that both xz and yz' belong to $\mathbf{P}_3$. Then $x'y'$ also belongs to $\mathbf{P}_3$.

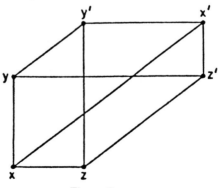

Figure 2

---

*Sometimes such automorphisms are just called "translations". Since this might lead to confusing them with the "translation nets" (see Chapter 5), I prefer the term "central translation".

4.1.4 THEOREM (Thomsen 1930). *Let L be a loop. Then L is an abelian group if and only if $\mathbf{D}(L)$ satisfies axiom (TC).*

4.1.5 COROLLARY. *If an $(s,3)$-net satisfies axiom (TC), then it also satisfies axiom (RC).*

Our final configuration theorem is called the *hexagon condition* (HC). It arises from axiom (RC) by specifying $r' = s$. Note that then p, q', s as well as p', q, s and r, s, s' are collinear triples of points; cf. Figure 3.

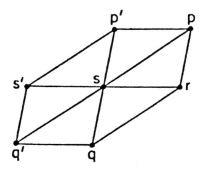

Figure 3

We now have the following theorem due to Bol (1937) and Pickert (1954):

4.1.6 THEOREM. *Let L be a loop. Then the following conditions are equivalent:*

(i) $\mathbf{D}(L)$ *satisfies axiom (HC).*

(ii) *Each loop isotopic to L is power-associative, i.e. each element x generates an associative sub-loop (and thus a subgroup) of L.*

(iii) *The identity $(x + x) + x = x + (x + x)$ holds in any loop L' isotopic to L.*

(iv) *For any loop L' isotopic to L and for any $x \in L'$, there exists an inverse $-x$ to x in L' (i.e. $x + (-x) = (-x) + x = 0$, where 0 is the unit element of L').*

For a detailed discussion of the axioms mentioned here (including proofs of the theorems stated above) and for further configuration theorems we refer the reader to Pickert (1955); see also Bruck (1963b).

4.2 Configurations in Nets with at Least 4 Parallel Classes. In this section, we shall consider the Desargues condition on (s, r)-nets with $r \geq 4$; this will turn out to be related to difference matrices. Let $\mathbf{D}$ be an (s, r)-net and let $\mathbf{P}$ be a parallel class of $\mathbf{D}$. The following axiom is called the *Desargues condition* for the direction $\mathbf{P}$ (cf. Figure 4):

(DC) Assume that all of the lines xx', yy' and zz' belong to $\mathbf{P}$ and that both $xy \| x'y'$ and $xz \| x'z'$. If y and z are on a line of $\mathbf{D}$, then y' and z' are also on a line of $\mathbf{D}$ and one has $yz \| y'z'$.

185

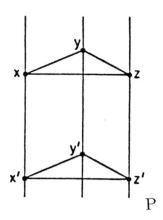

Figure 4

The following result is proved in Pickert (1974):

4.2.1 THEOREM. *Let* **D** *be an* (s,r)*-net, and let* **P** *be a parallel class of* **D**. *Then the following conditions are equivalent:*

(i) **D** *is transitive in direction* **P**.

(ii) **D** *satisfies axiom (DC) for the direction* **P** *and axiom (RC) with respect to* **P** *and any two further parallel classes.*

(iii) **D** *belongs to a set* $\{Q_1, \ldots, Q_{r-2}\}$ *of MOLS for which* Q_1 *is a group table and such that each of the Latin squares* $Q_2, \ldots, Q_{r-2}$ *arises from* Q_1 *by a suitable column permutation.*

The next result is implicitly contained in Jungnickel (1980); it was first explicitly stated in Jungnickel (1984c).

4.2.2 THEOREM. *The existence of an* (s,r)*-difference matrix* D *over* G *is equivalent to that of an* $(s, r + 1)$*-net* **D** *admitting* G *as a transitive group of central translations (for a suitable direction* **P***).*

For proof, one constructs **D** from D as in [BJL, X.12.8] and lets $g \in G$ operate according to $(i, x) \rightarrow (i, x + g)$ for all $x \in G$. The converse is similar. This construction also proves Lemma 3.3.1 (if D is maximal).

We finally mention a paper by Thiele (1979) who has characterized certain nets constructed from vector spaces which are important in the theory of net replacement, see Ostrom (1970).

5. Translation Nets. We have already seen a few connections between the geometric structure of nets and certain automorphisms. Both the present and the following chapter are devoted to the study of automorphism groups of nets. This type of question has only been investigated in recent years, and thus an elaborate general theory (as it exists for affine planes) cannot yet be expected. Still, there are already quite a few interesting results. For instance, "translation nets" are rather well understood by now; it is this class of nets that will be the topic of the present chapter.

5.1 Basics. Translation nets in general were first introduced explicitly by A. P. Sprague around 1979; his paper did not appear till some years later, see Sprague (1982). Implicitly, they were already considered by Drake and Jungnickel (1978) in the context of "Klingenberg structures". It should be noted that the study of single "translations" or, more generally, "dilatations" of nets does not seem to be very promising. The standard definition of a *dilatation* (as an automorphism preserving parallellism) and a *translation* (as a fixed-point-free dilation) leads to considerable difficulties. For instance, a dilatation can have more than one fixed point; a translation does not necessarily have a direction (which was the reason for introducing "central translations" in Chapter 4); and the translations do not in general form a group. Examples for these unpleasant situations are easy to construct. It is therefore reasonable to specify a "translation net" by requiring a regular group of translations to start with:

5.1.1. DEFINITION. Let **D** be a net and let G be a group of automorphisms of **D**. **D** is called a *translation net* with *translation group* G if G acts regularly (=sharply transitively) on the points of **D** and if G fixes each parallel class of **D**.

Note that 5.1.1. just generalizes the notion of translation planes (the case of complete translation nets); cf. Lüneburg (1980) for a comprehensive treatment of translation planes. It should be emphasized that a translation net is to be viewed as a pair $(\mathbf{D}, G)$. It is quite possible for a net to be a translation net with respect to distinct (even non-isomorphic) translation groups. Examples for this situation are given by Sprague (1982). We shall now show that the study of translation nets is equivalent to a combinatorial problem in group theory. We need a further definition:

5.1.2 DEFINITION. Let G be a (multiplicatively written) group of order s^2, and let $\mathbf{U} = \{U_1, \ldots, U_r\}$ be a set of $r \geq 3$ subgroups of order s of G. We call $\mathbf{U}$ a *partial congruence partition* with order s and degree r (for short, an (s,r)-PCP) of G, if the following condition holds:

$$(5.1) \qquad |U_i \cap U_j| = 1 \text{ (or, equivalently, } U_iU_j = G)$$

for any two distinct $i, j \in \{1, \ldots, r\}$. We also sometimes say that the subgroups U_i and U_j are *disjoint* if (5.1) holds. The U_i are called the *components* of **U**.

Note that the $(s, s+1)$-PCP's are just the "congruence partitions" introduced by André (1954) in his pioneering study of translation planes. PCP's in general were first introduced by Drake and Jungnickel (1978) who called them "uniform Klingenberg matrices". A well-known special class of PCP's are equivalent to "partial spreads" in projective spaces. These have been studied extensively since they were introduced by Mesner (1967); we will consider them in some detail in Section 5.3. The following result is simple but fundamental:

5.1.3 PROPOSITION (Sprague 1982). *Let* $\mathbf{U}$ *be an* (s,r)-*PCP in a group* G, *and define an incidence structure*

$$\mathbf{D}(\mathbf{U}) = (G, \{Ug : U \in \mathbf{U}, g \in G\}, \in).$$

Then $\mathbf{D}(\mathbf{U})$ *is a translation* (s,r)-*net with translation group* G. *Conversely, every translation net can be represented in this way.*

The *proof* that $\mathbf{D}(\mathbf{U})$ is a translation (s,r)-net is straightforward. We shall sketch the converse. Given a translation (s,r)-net $\mathbf{D}$ with translation group G, choose a "base point" p and identify the point q with the unique element $g \in G$ mapping p to q. Label the lines through p as $L_1, \ldots, L_r$ and let U_i be the (setwise) stabilizer of L_i in G (for $i = 1, \ldots, r$). It is not difficult to check that $\{U_1, \ldots, U_r\}$ is an (s,r)-PCP $\mathbf{U}$ in G and that $\mathbf{D} \cong \mathbf{D}(\mathbf{U})$.

Examples of non-complete translation nets can of course be obtained by omitting some parallel classes from an affine translation plane; all the corresponding PCP's are then defined in an elementary abelian group. We shall now mention a few non-trivial examples. As we shall see later, it is rather easy to obtain examples in abelian groups. Thus, let us start with a few non-abelian examples. (We refer the reader to Huppert (1967) for background from Group Theory.)

5.1.4 *Examples.* (i) Let H be any group of order s, and put $G = H \times H$. Then $U_1 = H \times \{1\}, U_2 = \{1\} \times H$ and $U_3 = \{(h,h) : h \in H\}$ form an $(s,3)$-PCP in G.

(ii) Let $G = \langle a, b, c, x, y, z \rangle$, where the square of each generator and the commutator of any two generators are 1 except for $[x,y] = a$ and $[x,z] = b$. Then the subgroups $\langle x, y \rangle, \langle cx, z \rangle, \langle ac, by, az \rangle$ and $\langle c, xyz \rangle$ form an (8,4)-PCP in G; they are, in turn, isomorphic to $D_4, D_4, \mathbf{Z}_2^3$ and $\mathbf{Z}_4 \times \mathbf{Z}_2$. (Here D_4 denotes the dihedral group of order 8.) This example is due to Sprague (1982) who has also shown that G is the only group of order 64 (apart from the elementary abelian group EA(64)) which contains an (8,4)-PCP. Moreover, G does not contain an (8,5)-PCP. These results were later rediscovered by Gluck (1989a).

(iii) Let G be a metacyclic group of order p^4 with exponent p^2 (p a prime), i.e. $G = \langle a, b \rangle$ with $a^{p^2} = 1$ and $a^b = a^{p+1}$. Then the subgroups $U_i = \langle ba^i \rangle (i = 1, \ldots, p)$ and $U_{p+1} = \langle a \rangle$ form a $(p^2, p+1)$-PCP in G; see Jungnickel (1981b).

Next we give a simple recursive construction which is the translation net analogue of the MacNeish theorem 2.2.1:

5.1.5 LEMMA. *Let* $\mathbf{U} = \{U_1, \ldots, U_r\}$ *and* $\mathbf{V} = \{V_1, \ldots, V_r\}$ *be* (s,r) - *and* (t,r)-*PCP's in* G *and* H, *respectively. Then* $\mathbf{U} \times \mathbf{V} = \{U_i \times V_i = 1, \ldots, r\}$ *is an* (st, r)-*PCP in* $G \times H$.

We now introduce some notation. Let G be any group of square order, say $|G| = s^2$, and write $T(G)$ for the maximal number of pairwise disjoint subgroups of order s of G. Also put $T(s) = \max\{T(G) : |G| = s^2\}$. Note that the existence of translation planes means $T(q) = q + 1$ for prime powers q and that therefore 5.1.5 immediately implies the following simple analogue of Corollary 2.2.2.

5.1.6 COROLLARY. *Let $s = q_1 \cdots q_n$ be the canonical prime power factorization of the positive integer s. Then*

$$(5.2) \qquad\qquad T(s) \geq \min\{q_i + 1 : i = 1, \ldots n\}.$$

We shall see in the next section that one always has equality in (5.2), a result already conjectured by Jungnickel (1981b) and finally proved by Jungnickel (1989a). We close this introductory section with a look at the relation between translations and central translations of a net. The following result is easily shown:

5.1.7 LEMMA. *Let $\mathbf{U} = \{U_1, \ldots, U_r\}$ be an (s, r)-PCP in G. Then $U_i^g = g^{-1}U_i g$ acts regularly on the line $U_i g$ of $\mathbf{D}(\mathbf{U})$. In particular: U_i consists of central translations (in which case $\mathbf{D}(\mathbf{U})$ is transitive in direction $\{U_i g : g \in G\}$) if and only if U_i is a normal subgroup of G. (Then $\{U_i g : g \in G\}$ is also called a normal direction of $\mathbf{D}(\mathbf{U})$.)*

The following results of Sprague (1982) show that the existence of normal directions severely restricts the structure of G:

5.1.8 THEOREM (Sprague). *Let $\mathbf{U} = \{U_1, \ldots, U_r\}$ be an (s, r)-PCP in G. Then the following assertions hold:*

(i) *If U_1 is a normal subgroup of G, then $U_2 \cong \cdots \cong U_r$.*

(ii) *If U_1 and U_2 are normal subgroups of G, then one has $G \cong U_1 \times U_2$ and $U_1 \cong U_2 \cong \cdots \cong U_r$.*

(iii) *If $\mathbf{U}$ has 3 normal components, then G is abelian*

The following result of Bailey & Jungnickel (1989) strengthens part (ii) of Theorem 5.1.8; it generalizes an argument of Jungnickel (1989b).

5.1.9 THEOREM. *Let H be a group of order s, and let $\alpha_1, \ldots, \alpha_r$ be automorphisms of H such that $\alpha_i \alpha_j^{-1}$ is fixed-point-free whenever $i \neq j$. Put $G = H \times H$, $U_i = \{(h, h^i) : h \in H\}$ for $i = 1, \ldots, r, U_{r+1} = H \times \{1\}$ and $U_{r+2} = \{1\} \times H$. Then $U_1, \ldots, U_{r+2}$ is an $(s, r + 2)$-PCP in G with normal components U_{r+1} and U_{r+2}. Conversely every $(s, r + 2)$-PCP with two normal components may be represented in this way.*

For obvious reasons, we call a translation net belonging to a PCP of the type described in 5.1.9 a *splitting* translation net. Theorem 5.1.9 shows that the splitting translation nets are equivalent to sets of MOLS constructible by the "automorphism method" of Mann (1942, 1943).

5.2 Non-Existence Results. Theorem 5.1.8 can be viewed as a non-existence result for translation nets which depends on the geometric structure of $\mathbf{D}$, more precisely on the existence of normal directions. In the present section, we shall first consider non-existence results which only depend on numerical conditions on s and r. The following simple auxiliary result is a slight generalization of a lemma of Sprague (1982); cf. Gluck (1989a).

5.2.1 LEMMA. *Let G be a finite group. Then one has the following:*

(i) *Assume $UV = G$ for subgroups U and V of G. Then $|U^g \cap V^h| = |U \cap V|$ for any two elements $g, h \in G$.*

(ii) *If $\{U_1, \ldots, U_r\}$ is an (s,r)-PCP in G, then so is $\{U_1^{g_1}, \ldots, U_r^{g_r}\}$ for any r elements $g_1 \ldots, g_r \in G$.*

The following application of 5.2.1 is of fundamental importance:

5.2.2 PROPOSITION. *Assume the existence of an (s,r)-PCP in G, and let P be a Sylow p-subgroup of G (for some prime p dividing s). Let $|P| = p^{2a}$. Then there also exists a (p^a, r)-PCP in P.*

Proof. Let $\{U_1, \ldots, U_r\}$ be an (s,r)-PCP in G. Then the Sylow p-subgroup P_i of U_i has order p^a. By the Sylow theorems, there exist $g_1, \ldots, g_r \in G$ such that $P_i^{g_i}$ is contained in P. By 5.2.1, $\{U_1^{g_1}, \ldots, U_r^{g_r}\}$ is also an (s,r)-PCP in G; then $\{P_i^{g_1} = U_i^{g_i} \cap P : i = 1, \ldots r\}$ is easily seen to be a (p^a, r)-PCP in P. $\square$

Sprague (1982) has proved 5.2.2 under the additional assumption that the Sylow p-subgroup P of G is normal. The present version of 5.2.2 appears in Jungnickel (1989a); it was inspired by an argument of Frohardt (1987). We obtain the following immediate consequence of 5.2.2. and 5.1.6:

5.2.3 THEOREM (Jungnickel 1989a). *Let G be a group of order s^2, and let $p_1^{a_1} \cdots p_n^{a_n}$ be the canonical prime power factorization of s. Let P_i be a Sylow p_i-subgroup of G for $i = 1, \ldots, n$. Then*

$$(5.3) \qquad T(G) \leq \min\{T(P_i) : i = 1, \ldots, n\} \leq \min\{p_i^{a_i} + 1 : i = 1, \ldots, n\}.$$

In particular,

$$(5.4) \qquad\qquad T(s) = \min\{p_i^{a_i} + 1 : i = 1, \ldots, n\}.$$

(5.4) shows that the MacNeish bound 2.2.2 is sharp for sets of MOLS belonging to translation nets. The abelian case of theorem 5.2.3 was already given by Drake and Jungnickel (1978) and the nilpotent case by Jungnickel (1981b). We have two comments regarding the bound (5.3) and (5.4). Equality (5.4) is demonstrated by using the fact $T(q) = q + 1$ for prime powers q which relies on PCP's in elementary abelian groups. It is however easy to construct examples of (nilpotent) groups G of order s^2 satisfying the same bound but not being a direct product of elementary abelian groups, cf. Jungnickel (1989a); thus Korollar 5.2.11 of Jungnickel (1984c) is not correct. It should also be noted that one may have $T(G) < \min\{T(P_i) : i = 1, \ldots, n\}$. The following unpublished result of Hayden (1987) will provide an example for this situation:

5.2.4 THEOREM (Hayden 1987). *Let H be a simple group of order s and let p be a prime dividing s. If all elements of order p of H are conjugate, then $T(H \times H) = 3$ (cf. Example 5.1.4).*

It should be noted that Theorem 5.2.4 also follows from a result of Mann (1942) in conjunction with Theorem 5.1.9 above. In particular 5.2.4 implies $T(A_n \times A_n) = 3$

for $n \geq 5$ (where A_n denotes the alternating group of order n). In case $n = 5$, we obtain the Sylow subgroups $P_1 \cong EA(2^4)$, $P_2 \cong EA(3^2)$ and $P_3 \cong EA(5^2)$; thus we have indeed $T(A_5 \times A_5) = 3 < 4 = \min\{T(P_i) : i = 1,2,3\}$. However, 5.1.5 and 5.2.3 show that this situation cannot arise for nilpotent groups (since they are the direct products of their Sylow subgroups):

5.2.5 THEOREM (Jungnickel 1981b). *Let G be a nilpotent group of order s^2, and let $s = p_1^{a_1} \cdots p_n^{a_n}$ be the canonical prime power factorization of s. If P_i is the Sylow p_i-subgroup of S, then $T(G) = \min\{T(P_i) : i = 1, \ldots, n\}$.*

Hence the determination of $T(G)$ for nilpotent groups G is reduced to the same problem for p-groups. Thus let G be a group of order p^{2a} (p prime). It is well-known that translation planes have elementary abelian translation groups (André 1954); thus we have $T(G) \leq p^a$ if G is not elementary abelian. The following result considerably improves this bound:

5.2.6 THEOREM (Jungnickel 1981b). *Let G be a group of order p^{2a}, p a prime. If G is not elementary abelian, one has*

$$(5.5) \qquad T(G) \leq p^{a-1} + \cdots + p + 1.$$

As Example 5.1.4 shows, (5.5) is best possible for $a = 2$. In general, not much is known about the quality of (5.5). The following result shows that (5.5) is rather weak for $p = 2$:

5.2.7 THEOREM (Frohardt 1987). *Let G be a group of order 2^{2a}. If G is not elementary abelian, then*

$$(5.6) \qquad T(G) \leq 2^{a-1};$$

for $a \geq 4$, one has strict inequality in (5.6).

Note that the case $a = 3$ can lead to equality, as the example of Sprague (1982) exhibited in 5.1.4 shows. Theorem 5.2.6 can be considerably improved for abelian groups:

5.2.8 THEOREM (Bailey & Jungnickel 1989). *Let G be an abelian group of order p^{2a}, p a prime, and let $U = \{U_1, \ldots, U_r\}$ be a (p^a, r)-PCP in G. Moreover, let the structure of the U_i (cf. 5.1.8) be as follows: There are exactly b_j invariants $p_j^{a_j}$ $(j = 1, \ldots, n)$. Then one has*

$$(5.7) \qquad T(G) = p^b + 1, \qquad \text{where } b = \min \{b_1, \ldots, b_n\}.$$

In particular

$$(5.8) \qquad T(G) \leq p^{\lfloor a/2 \rfloor} + 1,$$

191

provided that G is not elementary abelian.

More generally, Bailey & Jungnickel (1989) obtain improved bounds for splitting translation nets (also in the non-abelian case). The part "$\leq$" of (5.7) was already proved by Jungnickel (1981a), and the case $n = 1$ is due to Jungnickel (1989b) where PCP's in $\mathbf{Z}_q^{2a}$ with $q = p^b$ are studied using a matrix representation of PCP's for this special case which generalizes the approach of Bruck and Bose (1964, 1966) to the study of translation planes.

We finally state two results which show that the existence of relatively large PCP's forces an abstractly given group to be a p-group or even elementary abelian. Both theorems are consequences of results already stated, together with counting arguments.

5.2.9 THEOREM (Jungnickel 1989a). *Let G be a group of order s^2 admitting an (s,r)-PCP with $r \geq \lfloor \sqrt{s} \rfloor + 2$. Then G is a p-group; moreover, if G is abelian, then it is elementary abelian.*

5.2.10 THEOREM (Jungnickel 1981b, 1989a). *Let G be a group of order s^2 admitting an (s,r)-PCP, and let p be the smallest prime divisor of s. If*

$$r \geq \lfloor (2s - 2)/(p + 2) \rfloor + 3 \quad or \quad r \geq s/(p - 1),$$

then G is elementary abelian.

These bounds are best possible, see Jungnickel (1989a). This section has shown that there exists a rather well-developed existence theory for translation nets by now; nevertheless, further results on $T(G)$ (at least for p-groups) would be desirable.

5.3 Maximal Partial Spreads. In this section we consider PCP's related to projective geometry. Consider the $(2t+1)$-dimensional projective space $PG(2t+1, q)$ over $GF(q)$. A *partial t-spread* of $PG(2t + 1, q)$ is a collection $\mathbf{F}$ of pairwise disjoint t-dimensional subspaces (called the *components* of $\mathbf{F}$). In other words, $\mathbf{F}$ consists of disjoint $(t + 1)$-dimensional linear subspaces of the $(2t + 2)$-dimensional vector space $GF(q)^{2t+2}$; thus a partial t-spread is a special type of PCP in $EA(q^{2t+2})$. If q is a prime, then every PCP in $EA(q^{2t+2})$ is an fact a partial t-spread; this does not hold for proper prime powers q, since then a subgroup of order q^{t+1} is not necessarily a subspace of $GF(q)^{2t+2}$. But clearly each PCP is an elementary abelian group is a partial t-spread for an appropriate value of t.

A partial t-spread $\mathbf{F}$ in $PG(2t + 1, q)$ is called a t-*spread* if its components cover all points. It is called *maximal* if it is not a t-spread and if each t-dimensional subspace of $PG(2t + 1, q)$ meets at least one component of $\mathbf{F}$. The *deficiency* of $\mathbf{F}$ is the number $d = q^{t+1} + 1 - |\mathbf{F}|$, in analogy for nets. The terms "small deficiency", "very small deficiency" and "critical deficiency" are to be defined similarly.

We now start with results on the case $t = 1$; in this case, one usually omits the suffix "1-". Partial spreads in $PG(3, q)$ were introduced by Mesner (1967). A detailed study of (partial) spreads in $PG(3, q)$ is to be found in Hirschfeld (1985, Ch. 16). The following bounds are due to Glynn (1982), Mesner (1967) and Bruen (1975).

5.3.1 THEOREM. Let **F** be a maximal partial spread with r components in $PG(3, q)$. Then one has

$$(5.9) \qquad\qquad 2q \leq r \leq q^2 - \sqrt{q}.$$

If q is not a square, the upper bound can be improved to $p(d - 1) > q^2$, where $d = q^2 + 1 - r$ is the deficiency of **F** and where p is the polynomial introduced in Theorem 3.1.1.

A further improvement of the upper bound is discussed below, see Theorem 5.3.5. In the following, we list the known examples of maximal partial spreads of small deficiency (i.e., $d \leq q$); they are due to Bruen (1971), Bruen and Thas (1976) and Freeman (1980).

5.3.2 THEOREM. For $q \geq 3$, there exists a maximal partial spread with deficiency $d = q$ in $PG(3, q)$. For $q \geq 4$, there also exists a maximal partial spread with deficiency $d = q - 1$ in $PG(3, q)$.

The proof of 5.3.2 is relatively involved. Bruen's method is to discard $q + 1$ lines from a certain spread of $PG(3, q)$ and then to add one or two properly chosen other lines to obtain a maximal partial spread. The simplest case is that of deficiency q; this case can also be found in [BJL, Section X.9]. The most difficult case is $d = q - 1$ for $q = 2^a$ which was dealt with by Bruen and Thas (1976) and Freeman (1980); a simpler alternative proof for this case was given by Jungnickel (1984a). Beutelspacher (1980), Ebert (1978) and Heden (1989) constructed many examples of maximal partial spreads with $d > q$, a case which we will not discuss here. We now mention similar results for $t > 1$:

5.3.3 THEOREM (Beutelspacher 1980, Bruen 1980). Let **F** be a maximal partial t-spread with r components in $PG(2t + 1, q)$. Then one has

$$(5.10) \qquad\qquad q + \sqrt{q} \leq r \leq q^{t+1} - \sqrt{q};$$

for $q \geq 4$, the lower bound can be improved to $r \geq q + \sqrt{q} + 1$.

5.3.4 THEOREM (Beutelspacher 1980, Jungnickel 1984a). Let $t = 2a + 1$ with $a \geq 1$. For $q \geq 4$, there exists a maximal partial t-spread with deficiency $d = q^{a+1}$ in $PG(2t + 1, q)$. If q is not a prime, then there also exists a maximal partial t-spread with deficiency $d = q^{a+1} - 1$ in $PG(2t + 1, q)$.

Some interesting examples of maximal partial 2-spreads in $PG(5, q)$ were obtained by Bruen and Freeman (1982). Apart from these, no further examples of maximal partial t-spreads for t even seem to be known. For odd values of t, there are also interesting examples related to "orthogonal" spreads; see Dillon (1973). We finally mention that the upper bound in Theorem 5.3.1 has recently been somewhat improved by Heden (1986). A considerably simpler proof of this theorem which also resulted in a further improvement was given by Blokhuis, Brouwer & Wilbrink (1989) using a method of Blokhuis & Brouwer (1986). The present state of the art is as follows:

5.3.5 THEOREM. *Let* **F** *be a maximal partial spread of deficiency d in* $PG(3, q)$, *and assume that q is not a square. Then one has*

(5.11) $$d \geq \min\{1 + \sqrt{3q},\ \sqrt{pq}\ -p+2\},$$

where q is a power of the prime p.

5.4 Translation Nets of Small Deficiency. In this section we present the results of Jungnickel (1984a) on (maximal) translation nets of small deficiency. With two trivial exceptions, all such nets correspond to partial t-spreads:

5.4.1 THEOREM. *Let* **D** *be a translation net of small deficiency with translation group G. If the order s of* **D** *satisfies* $s \neq 2, 4$, *then G is elementary abelian.*

This is a consequence of 5.2.10 and 5.2.9. In what follows we shall always assume $s \geq 5$; in particular we may then use the fact that G has to be abelian by 5.4.1. The following result concerns the structure of completable translation nets of small deficiency; its proof uses Theorem 3.1.2.

5.4.2 THEOREM. *Let* **D** *be a completable net of small deficiency, say with completion* **E**. *Then one has Aut* **D** $\leq$ *Aut* **E**. *If* **D** *is a translation net with translation group G, then* **E** *is a translation plane with translation group G.*

Together with Theorem 3.1.1, we obtain the following consequence of 5.4.1 which was proved by Bruen (1975) under stronger assumptions.

5.4.3 THEOREM. *Any translation net of very small deficiency can be completed to a translation plane.*

Theorem 5.4.2 also implies that any maximal partial t-spread of small deficiency in $PG(2t + 1, p)$ (p a prime) yields a non-completable net. (Note that this will in general not be true for prime powers, since a maximal partial t-spread in $PG(2t + 1, q)$ is not necessarily maximal as a PCP.) To obtain a stronger result we need the following lemma of Ostrom (1966).

5.4.4 LEMMA (Ostrom). *Let* **U** *be a PCP with at least one normal component. Then* **D(U)** *is maximal if and only if it is transversal-free.*

Now assume that **U** is a maximal (s, r)-PCP of small deficiency and assume that **D(U)** is not transversal-free. Using 5.4.4, one can show that **D(U)** is step-x-extendable for some divisor $x \neq 1$ of s. If we have $s = p^2$ for a prime p, then this means that **D(U)** is completable which contradicts Theorem 5.4.2. Thus we have the following result:

5.4 THEOREM. *Let* **F** *be a maximal partial spread of small deficiency in* $PG(3, p)$, *p a prime. Then* **D**(F) *is transversal-free.*

Theorems 5.3.2 and 5.4.5 yield a proof of Theorem 3.2.1 on the existence of maximal nets of small deficiency. It is not possible to generalise Theorem 5.4.5

to arbitrary prime powers q. There are maximal partial $(2a + 1)$-spreads with deficiency $d = q^{a+1} - 1$ in $PG(4a + 3, q)$ which belong to completable translation nets (and hence are not maximal as PCP's) whenever q is a proper power of a prime. Examples for these can be constructed from suitable translation planes which are of dimension 2 over their kernel. However, in the case $d = q^{a+1}$ one can at least show that the corresponding nets are not completable.

5.4.6 THEOREM. *Let* $\mathbf{F}$ *be a maximal partial* $(2a + 1)$-*spread of deficiency* $d = q^{a+1}$ *in* $PG(4a + 3, q)$. *Then* $\mathbf{D}(\mathbf{F})$ *is not completable.*

The proof of this result uses Theorem 5.4.2 (which allows to extend the "dilatations" of $\mathbf{D}(\mathbf{F})$ to automorphisms of a hypothetical completion) together with the theorem of Zsigmondy (1892) - a number theoretic result which has surprisingly many applications in finite geometry. Johnson (1989) characterises the completable translation nets of small deficiency and constructs many example of maximal partial spreads of deficiency $q - 1$ in $PG(3, q)$ which belong to nets which are not completable.

5.5 Further Completion Results. In this section we state two further completion results. As was already mentioned in Section 3.1, Ostrom (1964) has proved that an arbitrary net of critical deficiency has at most two completions to an affine plane. In this connection, the following result of Bruen and Silverman (1974) is of interest:

5.5.1 THEOREM. *Let* $\mathbf{D}$ *be a net of order* p^2, *where* p *is a prime, and of deficiency* $d < 2p - 2$. *Then there are at most two non-isomorphic translation planes which are completions of* $\mathbf{D}$.

Now let $\mathbf{D}$ be a net of order p, p a prime. If $\mathbf{D}$ is a translation net, then $\mathbf{D}$ necessarily has translation group $EA(p^2)$ and thus clearly consists of some parallel classes of $AG(2, p)$. Further embeddings of $\mathbf{D}$ are only feasible if r is small:

5.5.2 THEOREM (Bruen 1975). *Let* $\mathbf{D}$ *be a translation net of order* p, p *a prime. If* $\mathbf{D}$ *has deficiency* $d < (p + 3)/2$, *then* $AG(2, p)$ *is the only completion of* $\mathbf{D}$ *and one has* $Aut\ \mathbf{D} \leq Aut\ AG(2, p)$.

Note that 5.5.2 would be a trivial consequence of the validity of the well-known conjecture that $AG(2, p)$ is the only plane of prime order p. We finally mention Bruen (1983), an interesting survey on translation nets, blocking sets and related questions.

5.6 Partial Spread Difference Sets. In this final section on translation nets, we shall discuss a connection to the theory of difference sets. We refer the reader to [BJL] and to Lander (1983) for detailed accounts of this area; see also Arasu (1989) for a survey of recent results. Nevertheless, we recall the required definition: Let G be a multiplicatively written group of order v, and let D be a k-subset of G. Then D is called a (v, k, λ)-*difference* set in G provided that the list of "differences" $de^{-1}(d, e \in D)$ contains each group element $g \neq 1$ exactly λ times. (The term "difference set" is due to the fact that the first examples, given by Singer (1938), were in additively written cyclic groups.) Difference sets are equivalent to symmetric designs with a regular automorphism group; their theory is one of the central parts of Finite Geometries and is also of interest for its many connections to Coding Theory. A special case of what is now called a partial congruence partition has in fact appeared earlier in a construction for difference sets:

5.6.1 THEOREM (Dillon 1973). *Let G be a group of order $4s^2$, and assume the existence of an $(2s, s)$-PCP in G. Then there also exists a $(4s^2, 2s^2 - s, s^2 - s)$-difference set in G.*

Proof. Let $U_1, \ldots, U_s$ be pairwise disjoint subgroups of order $2s$ of G, and put $D = (U_1 \cup \cdots \cup U_s) \backslash \{1\}$. It is not difficult to check that D is the desired difference set, distinguishing the case $g \in D$ and $g \notin D$. □

5.6.2 Example. The construction of Theorem 5.6.1 works in each of the following groups:

  (i) $G = \mathbb{Z}_4$ or $G = \mathbb{Z}_4 \times EA(4)$;
 (ii) $G = \mathbb{Z}_4 \times \mathbb{Z}_4, \mathbb{Z}_6 \times \mathbb{Z}_6$ or $S_3 \times S_3$;
(iii) G as in Example 5.1.4(ii);
 (iv) $G = EA(2^{2a})$, where a is any positive integer.

Note that (ii) is covered by Example 5.1.4(i) and that (i) is trivial. For (iv), one may use any 2^{a-1} lines of the affine plane $AG(2, 2^a)$ to define the required PCP; as this corresponds to the use of a partial $(a - 1)$-spread in $PG(2a - 1, 2)$, one calls the resulting difference sets *partial spread difference sets*. They were introduced by Dillon (1973, 1975) and have been studied extensively. Kantor (1984) proved that there are exponentially many inequivalent difference sets arising from lines of $AG(2, 2^a)$.

J.F. Dillon has posed the problem of classifying all groups G that admit a difference set as constructed in 5.6.1 (in other words, classifying all groups G of order $4s^2$ with a $(2s, s)$-PCP). This was in fact the motivation for the paper by Frohardt (1987), cf. Theorem 5.2.7. His answer is as follows:

5.6.3 THEOREM (Frohardt 1987). *Let G be a group of order $4s^2$ admitting a $(2s, s) - PCP$. Then G is one of the groups in Example 5.6.2.*

We note that Theorem 5.6.3 follows from Theorems 5.2.3 and 5.2.7 together with the results of Sprague (1982) and Gluck (1989a) discussed in Example 5.1.4. Difference sets with parameters $(4s^2, 2s^2 - s, s^2 - s)$ are called *Menon difference sets* in [BJL], since they were first studied by Menon (1962). Since there is also a close connection to Hadamard matrices, they are often also called "Hadamard" difference sets. Menon difference sets have found considerable interest; examples are known for all s of the form $s = 2^a 3^b$, a result due to Turyn (1984). Recent results give some reason to believe that there are no other examples, at least in the abelian case. We refer the reader to Dillon (1973, 1989), Turyn (1965, 1984), McFarland

(1989) and the papers cited there. An easy generalisation of the construction in 5.6.1 also provides a large family of "partial difference sets", see Ma (1984), and thus of strongly regular graphs with a regular group; the examples arising from abelian groups are then classified by the results of Bailey & Jungnickel (1989), cf. Theorem 5.2.8.

6. Automorphism Groups. After the detailed study of translation nets in the previous chapter, we shall now consider some other types of automorphism groups of nets and TD's which have been investigated.

6.1 Class Regular TD's. Let $\mathbf{D}$ be a transversal design $TD[k, s]$, and let G be a group of automorphisms of $\mathbf{D}$. Then $\mathbf{D}$ is called *class-regular* with respect to G if and only if G fixes the point classes of $\mathbf{D}$ and acts regularly on each point class. The following lemma is easy:

6.1.1 LEMMA. *Let $\mathbf{D}$ be a class-regular TD with respect to G. Then G acts semiregularly on the line set of $\mathbf{D}$ (i.e., only the identity fixes any line of $\mathbf{D}$.) The orbits of G on the set of lines are parallel classes, i.e. $\mathbf{D}$ is resolvable.*

Class-regular TD's afford yet another geometric interpretation of difference matrices, though it is essentially dual to Theorem 4.2.2:

6.1.2 THEOREM. *There exists a class-regular $TD[k, s]$ with respect to G if and only if there exists an (s, k)-difference matrix over G.*

Theorems 4.2.2 and 6.1.2 imply that difference matrices and class regular TD's generalize the well-known concept of (p, L)-transitivity of projective planes for $p \in L$ (cf. Hughes and Piper (1973)). An (s, s)-DM over G exists iff there exists a projective plane of order s which admits G as a (transitive) group of (p, L)-elations for some flag $(p, L)^*$; cf. Jungnickel (1979). Thus an (s, s)-DM is equivalent to a cartesian group of order s; in fact, a normalized difference matrix over G is just the multiplication table of a Cartesian group with additive group G. It is a long-standing problem to determine the possible orders of Cartesian groups; it is often conjectured that they only exist if s is a prime power and that the only Cartesian group of prime order p is $\mathbf{Z}_p$. Hayden (1989) characterizes the elementary abelian groups among the abelian Cartesian groups by a certain homogeneity condition which is equivalent to the existence of enough homologies of the corresponding plane: see A. B. Evans (1989d) for a much simpler proof. Hayden (1985) studies Cartesian groups using methods from Representation Theory. Difference matrices over $\mathbf{Z}_p$ or, more generally, $EA(p^a)$ are studied using the equivalent concept of "orthomorphism graphs" by A.B. Evans (1987a, 1987b, 1988, 1989a, 1989c) and by A.B. Evans and McFarland (1984). Mendelsohn and Wolk (1985) tried (without success) to find a non-Desarguesian plane of order $p = 13$ or $p = 17$ by finding a suitable $(p-1)$-clique in a portion of the orthomorphism graph of $\mathbf{Z}_p$ (equivalently, a

---

*An analogous generalization of (p, L)-transitivity for $p \notin L$ is given by suitable "generalized balanced weighing matrices" which however lead to GDD's which are not TD's; cf Jungnickel (1982b, Section 6).

197

suitable (p,p)-DM); this was generalized to $p \leq 47$ by A.B. Evans (1987b). Recently, using permutation polynomials, A.B. Evans (1989b) has shown that the approach of Mendelsohn and Wolk cannot work for any prime p. Of course, this still leaves the possibility of a suitable clique in another portion of the orthomorphism graph (which is known completely only for $p \leq 11$).

We now return to the question for which orders s an (s,s)-difference matrix over G can exist. Of course, Theorem 3.3.2 shows that for even s the Sylow 2-subgroup of G cannot be cyclic; in particular, $s \equiv 2 \mod 4$ is impossible. The only other known non-existence results are due to de Launey (1984a, 1984b):

6.1.3 THEOREM (de Launey). *Assume the existence of an (s,s)-DM over an abelian group G. Let $p \neq 2$ be a prime dividing s and suppose that $m \not\equiv 0 \pmod{p}$ is an integer dividing the square-free part of s. Then the order of m modulo p is odd (so m is a quadratic residue modulo p).*

Theorem 6.1.3 rules out all odd non-prime power values of $s \leq 100$, except for $s = 39, 55$ or 63. We mention another example which was rediscovered by Woodcock (1986) in the cyclic case:

6.1.4 COROLLARY. *There exists no (s,s)-difference matrix over an abelian group of order $s \equiv 15 \mod 18$.*

Proof. Write $s = 18a + 15 = 3(6a + 5)$ and choose $p = 3$. Clearly some prime $m \equiv 2 \mod 3$ has to divide the square-free part of $6a + 5$ (hence of s), and thus Theorem 6.1.3 gives a contradiction. □

As far as the author is aware, no further non-existence results for difference matrices are known. In particular, the only known non-existence result for (s,k)-difference matrices with $k < s$ is the Hall-Paige-Theorem 3.3.2. But even in the complete case we are still far from a satisfying existence theory.

6.2 Singer Groups. It is well-known that the plane $PG(2,q)$ admits a cyclic collineation group which acts regularly both on the points and on the lines of the plane; a similar result holds for the point-hyperplane design $PG_{d-1}(d,q)$. This famous result (which was the starting point of the theory of difference sets) is due to Singer (1938) (see[BJL, Ch. VI] for more on difference sets). It is therefore customary to call any automorphism group of an incidence structure **D** which acts regularly on both the points and the blocks of **D** a *Singer group*. Of course, in this situation the number of points equals the number of blocks. In this section, we shall consider (s,r)-nets with a Singer group; then necessarily $s = r$. Such a net is (for $s \neq r$) equivalent to an affine plane of order s from which one parallel class of lines has been discarded (c.f. the remark following Theorem 3.1.1). It is easy to see that an (s,s)-net is simultaneously an $RTD[s,s]$; such nets are called *symmetric nets*. The following construction of symmetric nets with a Singer group is basically due to Hughes (1956); see also Jungnickel (1982b).

6.2.1 THEOREM. *Let **A** be an affine plane of order q coordinatized by a semifield K (cf. Hughes and Piper (1973) who call semifields "division rings"). By discarding* a suitable parallel class of lines of **A**, one obtains a symmetric net **D** with a Singer group G. Moreover, G is abelian if and only if K is commutative; in this case, G is isomorphic to $EA(q^2)$ if q is odd and to $\mathbf{Z}_4 \oplus \cdots \oplus \mathbf{Z}_4$ if q is even.

Note in particular that a symmetric net with a Singer group can belong to a non-Desarguesian plane; this is in remarkable contrast to the well-known conjecture that the only projective planes with a Singer group are Desarguesian. It is well-known that a projective plane with a Singer group G may be represented by a "planar difference set" in G, see e.g. [BJL; Ch. VI]. Similarly, a symmetric net with a Singer group can be represented as follows, see e.g. Ganley (1976) or Jungnickel (1982b):

6.2.2. LEMMA. *Let G be a group of order s^2 with a normal subgroup N of order s, and let D be an s-subset of G satisfying the following condition:*

$$(6.1) \qquad \{d - d' : d, d' \in D; d \neq d'\} = G\backslash N.$$

Then

$$(6.2) \qquad dev D = (G, \{D + x : \ x \in G\}, \in)$$

is a symmetric net of order s with G as a Singer group. Conversely, every symmetric net with a Singer group can be represented in this way.

A set D as described in 6.2.2 is called an $(s, s, s, 1)$- *relative difference set* in G (with respect to the subgroup N). For relative difference sets in general, see Elliott and Butson (1966) and Jungnickel (1982b). The following theorem is due to Ganley (1976) building on previous work of Dembowski and Ostrom (1968). A considerably simpler proof was given by Jungnickel (1987).

6.2.3 THEOREM (Ganley). *Let D be an $(s, s, s, 1)$-relative difference set in an abelian group G (with respect to N), and assume that s is even. Then s is a power of 2, N is elementary abelian and G is a direct product of cyclic groups of order 4.*

In the odd order case, G cannot be cyclic (unless $s = 2$) by a result of Hoffman (1952) who in fact proved that no affine plane of order $s \neq 2$ admits a cyclic collineation group of order s^2. In general, the following restrictions can be derived; cf. Arasu, Davis, Jungnickel & Pott (1989).

6.2.4 THEOREM. *Let D be an $(s, s, s, 1)$-relative difference set in a group G relative to an abelian normal subgroup N, and assume that s is odd. If p is a prime divisor of the squarefree part of s, then p has odd order modulo q for every prime $q \neq p$ dividing s. In particular, p is a quadratic residue modulo q.*

Proof. It is easily seen that N acts regularly on each point class of the symmetric net dev D. By Theorem 6.1.2, this implies the existence of an (s, s)-difference matrix over N. Now the assertion follows from de Launey's result (Theorem 6.1.3). □

Using quadratic reciprocity, we note the following consequence of Theorem 6.2.4:

6.2.5 COROLLARY. *Let D be an abelian $(s,s,s,1)$-relative difference set, where s is odd. Then the squarefree part of s has at most one prime divisor $p \equiv 3 \pmod{4}$.*

No further restrictions on the possible orders of $(s, s, s, 1)$-relative difference sets seem to be known. In view of the known examples (cf. Theorem 6.2.1), the case of *splitting* $(s, s, s, 1)$-relative difference sets is of particular interest: Here one assumes that $G = N \oplus H$. These are equivalent to the "planar functions" of Dembowski & Ostrom (1968); see also Dembowski (1968). More precisely, if one has $D = \{(n_1, h_1), \ldots, (n_s, h_s)\} \subset N \oplus H$, then the mapping $f : H \to N$ defined by $f(h_i) = n_i$ is a planar function (and conversely).

Now let s be an odd prime p, and let D be a (necessarily abelian) $(p,p,p,1)$-relative difference set. As G cannot be cyclic by the result of Hoffman (1952), we have $G = EA(p^2)$; thus D is in fact splitting. J.F. Dillon posed the problem of classifying the possible planar functions of $\mathbf{Z}_p$, i.e. the possible $(p, p, p, 1)$-relative difference sets. Hiramine (1989) and Gluck (1989b) independently proved that only quadratic polynomials over $\mathbf{Z}_p$ can arise. In geometric language, this means the following:

6.2.6 THEOREM. *Let D be a $(p, p, p, 1)$-relative difference set, where p is an odd prime. Then the affine plane $\mathbf{A}$ belonging to the symmetric net dev D is the Desarguesian plane $AG(2, p)$.*

As Hiramine (1989) notes, this result in fact proves a conjecture of Kallaher (1981): Any affine plane of prime order with a transitive collineation group is Desarguesian. The reader may check as an exercise that $\{(x, f(x)) : x \in GF(q)\}$ is indeed a $(q, q, q, 1)$-relative difference set in $EA(q^2)$, q odd, provided that f is a quadratic polynomial.

6.3 Translation Transversal Designs. Let $\mathbf{D}$ be a resolvable transversal design $RTD[k, s]$. An analogy to Definition 5.1.1, we call $\mathbf{D}$ a *translation* transversal design if it admits an automorphism group G which acts regularly on the point set of $\mathbf{D}$ and which fixes every parallel class of $\mathbf{D}$. It should be noted that translation TD's are just a special case of the "translation structures" of André (1961); to see this, one only has to consider the point classes as lines. André's work has led to extensive considerations involving translation structures, kinematic spaces and the like; this is, however, outside the scope of the present survey. The first examples of translation TD's were exhibited by Jungnickel (1981a) using a construction involving Frobenius groups. Since then, they have been systematically studied by Schulz (1984, 1985a, 1985b) and Biliotti and Micelli (1985); these authors have obtained a very satisfactory theory. We shall now sketch some of their results, starting with a definition.

6.3.1 DEFINITION. Let G be a finite group. An (s, k)-*partition* of G is a set $\mathbf{U} = \{U_0, \ldots, U_s\}$ of $r + 1 \geq 2$ subgroups of G satisfying the following conditions:

(i) $|U_0| = s$ and $|U_j| = k$ for $j = 1, \ldots, s$:
(ii) $|U_i \cap U_j| = 1$ for $i \neq j$;

(iii) $U_0 \cup \cdots \cup U_s = G$.

One then has the following result:

6.3.2 PROPOSITION Schulz 1985a, Biliotti and Micelli 1985). *Let G be a finite group of order sk with an (s, k)-partition $\mathbf{U} = \{U_0, \ldots, U_s\}$. Then*

$$(G, \{U_i x : x \in G, i = 1, \ldots, s\}, \in)$$

is a translation $TD[k, s]$ with translation group G. Conversely, every translation TD can be represented in this way.

Thus G is a finite group with a (non-trivial) partition. All such groups have been classified (see Baer (1961a,b,c), Kegel (1961a) and Suzuki (1961)). Applying this classification leads to the following result:

6.3.3 THEOREM (Schulz 1985, Biliotti and Micelli 1985). *Let $\mathbf{D}$ be a translation TD with translation group G, represented as in 6.3.2. Then one has one of the following cases:*

(i) *G is a p-group with $H_p(G) \le U_0$. (Here $H_p(G)$ denotes the subgroup of G generated by all elements of order $\ne p$, where p is a fixed prime.).*

(ii) *G is a $HT(p)$-group, and $\mathbf{U}$ is the unique partition of G. (An $HT(p)$-group is a group G which is neither a p-group nor a Frobenius group and satisfies $[G : H_p(G)] = p$; cf. Hughes and Thompson (1959) and Kegel (1961b)).*

(iii) *G is a Frobenius group, and $\mathbf{U}$ is the Frobenius partition of G. (Cf. Huppert (1967) for Frobenius groups.)*

(iv) *G is a Frobenius group with Frobenius kernel K and Frobenius complement H, one has $U_0 < K$ and $U_i = K_i H$ for suitable $K_i < K$ with $K = U_0 U_i$ ($i = 1, \ldots, s$). In this case, $\mathbf{U}$ can be constructed from an "H-admissible triad for K". (Since a description of this construction would take up too much space we refer the reader to Biliotti and Micelli (1985)).*

Regarding existence, one has the following result:

6.3.4 THEOREM. *Let $\mathbf{D}$ be a translation $TD[k, s]$ of type (i), (ii), (iii) or (iv) (as in 6.3.3). Then the parameters k and s are as follows:*

(i) *This case arises if and only if s and k are powers of the same prime p, where $k \le s$. All these cases can be realized for G elementary abelian, but there are also some non-abelian examples, see Schulz (1985b).*

(ii) *This case arises if and only if $s = p^a t$ (where p does not divide $t \ge 2$) and if p divides $q_i - 1$ for $i = 1, \ldots, n$, where $t = q_1 \ldots q_n$ is the canonical prime power factorization of t; see Schulz (1984).*

(iii) *This case arises if and only if k divides $q_i - 1$ for $i = 1, \ldots, n$, where $s = q_1 \ldots q_n$ is the canonical prime power factorization of s; see Jungnickel (1981a).*

(iv) *Here necessarily $s = p^a$ for a prime p and $k = p^b h$ where $1 \leq b \leq a - 1$;
moreover, h divides $p^b - 1$ and $p^{a-b} \geq h > 1$. Examples with K elementary
abelian are known whenever h divides both $p^a - 1$ and $p^b - 1$, but there are
also some examples where K is non-abelian. See Schulz (1985a) and Biliotti
and Micelli (1985); an essential tool is a construction of Herzer (1980).*

6.4 Higher Transitivity. In this section we discuss a few results on nets with
large automorphism groups. There are several classes of transversal designs with
flag-regular automorphism groups (i.e. with a group G acting regularly on the set
of all incident point-line pairs). The following examples are given by Jungnickel
(1981a):

6.4.1 PROPOSITION. *Let $\mathbf{D}$ be a translation $TD[k, s]$ belonging to the Frobenius
partition of a Frobenius Group G (i.e. of type (iii) in 6.3.3). Then G is a subgroup
of a flag-regular automorphism group of $\mathbf{D}$.*

6.4.2 PROPOSITION. *Let $\mathbf{D}$ be a symmetric $TD[s, s]$ (s a prime power) with a
Singer group G obtained from a semifield as in 6.2.1. Then G is a subgroup of a
flag-regular automorphism group of $\mathbf{D}$.*

6.4.3 PROPOSITION. *Let s be a prime power and k a divisor of $s-1$. Then there
exists an $RTD[k, s]$ $\mathbf{D}$ admitting $G = \mathbf{Z}_k \oplus EA(s)$ as a point-regular automorphism
group respecting the parallelism of $\mathbf{D}$. Moreover, G is a subgroup of a flag-regular
automorphism group of $\mathbf{D}$.*

The RTD's of 6.4.3 can be obtained from the Desarguesian affine planes $AG(2, s)$.
In view of the diversity of the examples given above, a classification of flag-regular
(or even point-regular) TD's seems to be quite difficult. As far as the author is
aware, no further examples of such TD's are known, though.

We finally mention a theorem of Bailey (1982). Let D be any $(s, 3)$-net, and
let G be an automorphism group of G which fixes every parallel class. If $s \neq 2$,
then G clearly has at least 4 orbits on unordered pairs of points of D (three orbits
corresponding to the parallel classes and a further orbit on pairs of points which
are not joined). Bailey's result characterizes the case of exactly four orbits:

6.4.4 THEOREM. *Let D be an $(s, 3)$ net, and let G be an automorphism group
of D fixing every parallel class. If G has exactly 4 orbits on unordered pairs of
points of D, then D belongs to a group H (as in §4.1), where H is either $\mathbf{Z}_3$ or
$EA(2^a)$ with $a \neq 1$.*

We leave it to the reader to check that the groups H mentioned lead to nets
$\mathbf{D}(H)$ with a group G as described above.

7. Generalizations. The concepts discussed in the previous chapters admit
a natural generalization: The Bruck nets are the special case $\mu = 1$ of "(s, r, μ)-
nets" or, equivalently, affine designs $S_r(1, s\mu, s^2\mu)$. In this chapter we shall sketch
generalizations of previously discussed results to the case of arbitrary μ and also
mention a few other results.

202

7.1 Basics. We begin by giving the definition of an (s, r, μ)-*net*. This is an incidence structure $\mathbf{D} = (V, \mathbf{B}, \in)$ consisting of $s^2 \mu$ points and of blocks of size $s\mu$ satisfying the following axioms:

(7.1) $\mathbf{D}$ is resolvable (cf. (N2); we use the symbol $\parallel$ for paralellism of blocks, as in case $\mu = 1$);

(7.2) Any two non parallel blocks intersect in precisely μ points.

(7.3) There are $r \geq 3$ parallel classes (each containing s blocks, then).

In the language of Design Theory, an (s, r, μ)-net is nothing but an affine 1-design $S_r(1, s\mu, s^2\mu)$. The dual structure of an (s, r, μ)-net is again called a *transversal design*, more precisely a $TD_\mu[r, s]$. These structures were introduced by Hanani (1974), and the term "(s, r, μ)-net" appears first in Drake and Jungnickel (1978). They are, however, equivalent to *orthogonal arrays* $OA_\mu(s, r)$ (which can be defined in an obvious way, cf. Section 1.1), and in this language they have been studied since around 1945; the first references seem to be Plackett and Burman (1945) and Rao (1947). The following upper bound on r (which reduces to $r \leq s + 1$ for $\mu = 1$; cf. (1.4)) is due to Plackett and Burman (1945); the case of equality was characterised independently by Mavron (1972a) and by Drake and Jungnickel (1978). A proof may be found in [BJL, I.8.8].

7.1.1 THEOREM. *Let $\mathbf{D}$ be an (s, r, μ)-net. Then one has $r \leq (s^2\mu - 1)/(s - 1)$ with equality if and only if $\mathbf{D}$ is an (affine) 2-design. In this case, any two points of $\mathbf{D}$ are on precisely $\lambda = (s\mu - 1)/(s - 1)$ blocks. ($\mathbf{D}$ is also called a complete (s, μ)-net then.)*

Of course, we can only have equality in Theorem 7.1.1 if $s - 1$ is a divisor of $\mu - 1$. If this is not the case, one may somewhat improve the bound on r. We refer the reader to [BJL, Section X.6] for a proof of the following result.

1.1.2 THEOREM (Bose and Bush 1952). *Let $\mathbf{D}$ be an (s, r, μ)-net and assume $\mu - 1 = a(s - 1) + b$ for some b with $0 < b < s - 1$. Then one has $r \leq s\mu + \mu + a - \theta$, where*

$$\theta = -\left(s - b - \frac{1}{2}\right) + \sqrt{s(s - 1 - b) + (1/4)}.$$

In the next section we shall give some examples where the Bose-Bush bound on r is best possible. If an (s, r, μ)-net $\mathbf{D}$ contains a pair of points which are not joined by any block, one may further improve the bounds on r. The following result is due to Hine and Mavron (1980); cf. also [BJL, II.8.18].

7.1.3 THEOREM. *Let $\mathbf{D}$ be an (s, r, μ)-net containing a pair of points which are not joined by any block. Then one has $r \leq s\mu$. Moreover, for $r = s\mu$ the relation on V defined by*

(7.4) $$p \sim q \text{ if and only if } p = q \text{ or } p \text{ and } q \text{ are not joined}$$

is an equivalence relation. (*The classes of* $\sim$ *are then called the point classes of* **D**.)

We now call **D** a *symmetric* (s, μ)-*net* if **D** is an $(s, s\mu, \mu)$-net for which the dual structure is also an $(s, s\mu, \mu)$-net. In other words: The point classes of **D** have size s, and any two points in distinct classes are joined by exactly μ blocks. It can be shown that it is sufficient to require the first of these two conditions only; this is due to Hine and Mavron (1980) and to Jungnickel (1979), see also [BJL, II.8.21]. Equivalently, the following result holds:

7.1.4 THEOREM. *A* $TD_\mu[s\mu, s]$ *is in fact a symmetric* (s, μ)-*net if and only if it is resolvable.*

7.1.5 *Examples.* (i) Any affine 2-design with s blocks per parallel class and satisfying (7.2) is an $\left(s, \dfrac{s^2\mu - 1}{s - 1}, \mu \right)$-net, i.e. a complete (s, μ)-net. In particular: The design $AG_{d-1}(d, q)$ formed by the points and hyperplanes of the d-dimensional affine space over $GF(q)$ is a complete (q, q^{d-2})-net.

(ii) Omitting all hyperplanes parallel to a given fixed line L of $AG(d, q)$ from $AG_{d-1}(d, q)$ gives a symmetric (q, q^{d-2})-net, cf. [BJL, 1.7.18]. We shall see later (cf. 7.5.2 below) that a symmetric (s, μ)-net does not necessarily extend to a complete (s, μ)-net.

7.2 Existence. There are only two known general existence theorems for nets with arbitrary μ. The first of these results is due to Hanani (1974); a simplified proof may be found in [BJL, Section X.2].

7.2.1 THEOREM (Hanani). *Let* $\mu > 1$ *be an integer. Then there exists an* $(s, 7, \mu)$-*net for every positive integer* s.

The other general result is asymptotic; it is a special case of a result due to Ray-Chaudhuri and Singhi (1988).

7.2.2 THEOREM (Ray-Chaudhuri and Singhi). *Given* s *and* r, *there exists an* (s, r, μ)-*net whenever* μ *is sufficiently large.*

There are several known series of (s, r, μ)-nets with a large value of r. Let us first mention the known series of complete (s, μ)-nets:

7.2.3 *Examples.* Complete (s, μ)-nets exist in at least the following cases:

(i) $s = q$ a prime power and $\mu = s^{d-2}$ for some integer $d \geq 2$. Examples are given by the classical affine designs $AG_{d-1}(d, q)$, cf. 7.1.5. There are, however, many non-isomorphic examples with these parameters. For instance, there are at least $(k/2e)^k$ pairwise non-isomorphic complete (q, q^{d-2})-nets (with $k = q^{d-1}$) whenever $d \geq 3$ and $q \geq 8$; see Jungnickel (1984b).

(ii) $s = 2$ and 2μ is the order of a Hadamard matrix. (For an introduction to Hadamard matrices, see [BJL, Section 1.9], Street and Street (1987) or Hall (1986). For a recent survey, see e.g. Hedayat and Wallis (1978).) It is conjectured that Hadamard matrices exist for every order divisible by 4; a list of values n with $n \leq 500$ for which the existence of a Hadamard matrix of order $4n$ is still undecided may be found in [BJL, p. 622]. Of these, the values $n = 67, 103, 134$ and 268 are now known to exist, cf. Sawade (1985); thus the smallest open case at present is $n = 107$.

It has been conjectured by Shrikhande (1976) in his survey on affine designs that the examples given in 7.2.3 cover all possible parameters of complete (s, μ)-nets. Some non-existence results (for $\mu \neq 1$) were obtained by Shrikhande (1951, 1953). (The case $\mu = 1$ is covered by the Bruck-Ryser theorem (1949).) For more information regarding the structure of affine designs, see e.g. Mavron (1972b, 1977, 1984).

We next consider the known series of symmetric nets; to this end, we have to introduce a generalization of (s, r)-difference matrices (cf. 2.1.1) first. Thus let G be an (additively written) group of order s, and let $D = (d_{ij})$ be an $(r \times s\mu)$-matrix with entries from G. We call D an (s, r, μ)-*difference matrix* over G if the following condition holds:

(7.5) The list of differences $d_{ik} - d_{jk}(k = 1, \ldots, s\mu)$ contains each $g \in G$ precisely μ times (for any two distinct indices $i, j \in \{1, \ldots, r\}$).

Using 7.1.3 and 7.1.4, one obtains the following results; see [BJL, Section VII.3] for proofs.

7.2.4 THEOREM (Jungnickel 1979). *Let D be an (s, r, μ)-difference matrix. Then there exists a resolvable $TD_\mu[r, s]$. One has $r \leq s\mu$ with equality if and only if $-D^T$ is also an (s, r, μ)-difference matrix; in this case, there exists a symmetric (s, μ)-net.*

An $(s, s\mu, \mu)$-difference matrix is also called a *generalized Hadamard matrix* $GH(s, \mu)$. Note that the case $G = \mathbf{Z}_2$(written multiplicatively with elements $+1$ and -1 so that instead of differences we have quotients) just gives (ordinary) Hadamard matrices. We refer the reader to de Launey (1986) for a survey of GH-matrices; de Launey uses somewhat different notation, though. We shall now list most of the known series of GH-matrices; we first note two simple constructions:

7.2.5 LEMMA (Jungnickel 1979). *Let $D = (d_{ij})$ be an (s, r, μ)-difference matrix over G, and let H be a normal subgroup of order t of G. Then $D' = (d_{ij} + H)$ is an $(s/t, r, \mu t)$-difference matrix over G/H. If D is a generalized Hadamard matrix, then so is D'.*

7.2.6 LEMMA (Shrikhande 1964). *The existence of both (s, r, μ)- and (s, r', μ')-difference matrices over G implies that of an $(s, rr', s\mu\mu')$-difference matrix. In particular, the existence of $GH(s, \mu)$ and $GH(s, \mu')$ over G implies that of $GH(s, s\mu\mu')$.*

7.2.7 *Examples.* Let s be a power of the prime p and let G be the elementary abelian group of order s. Then $GH(s, \mu)$ over G exists in at least the following cases:

205

(i) $s = p^i, \mu = p^j$. For proof, apply 7.2.5 to a $GH(p^{i+j}, 1)$, cf. Example 2.1.2. (Drake 1979).

(ii) $\mu = 2$; cf. [BJL, VIII.3.14] (Jungnickel (1979); the case $s = p$ a prime is due to Masuyama (1957) and, independently, Butson (1962));

(iii) $\mu = 4$ (Dawson 1985);

(iv) The existence of $GH(s, \lambda)$ with $s\lambda - 1$ a prime power implies that of $GH(s, \mu)$ with $\mu = \lambda(s\lambda - 1)^n$ for all $n \geq 1$. (de Launey (1988), see also de Launey (1986); the special case of the existence of $GH(s, s-1)$ whenever $s-1$ is a prime power appears in Seberry (1980)).

Further constructions are given by de Launey (1989b, 1989d) and de Launey (1989c) who constructs the first examples of GH-matrices over groups G which are not elementary abelian; in all these cases G is a p-group, though, and one obtains only known parameters. Of course, one may apply 7.2.5 and 7.2.6 to the series given in 7.2.7. By Theorem 7.2.4, all these examples of GH-matrices immediately yield symmetric (s, μ)-nets. We note that the special case $\mu = 2$ yields examples of "divisible semibiplanes of elation type", structures which have found some interest lately; we refer the reader to Hughes (1978), Wild (1980, 1985) and Jungnickel (1982).

It is often possible to extend a symmetric net to an even larger net. To this purpose we require the following result of Jungnickel and Sane (1982) which is based upon ideas of Shrikhande (1964).

7.2.8 THEOREM. Let $\mathbf{D}$ be a symmetric (s, μ)-net. Then $\mathbf{D}$ can be extended to an $(s, s\mu + t, \mu)$-net $\mathbf{D}'$ (by adjoining t new parallel classes of blocks) with $t \geq 3$ if and only if s divides μ and there exists an $(s, t, \mu/s)$-net.

We sketch the proof: Choose a bijection α from the point set of an $(s, r, \mu/s)$-net $\mathbf{E}$ onto the set of point classes $\mathbf{D}$. For each block B of $\mathbf{E}$, adjoin to $\mathbf{D}$ the block $B^\alpha = \cup_{p \in B} p^\alpha$. It is not difficult to see that this yields the desired $(s, s\mu + t, \mu)$-net $\mathbf{D}'$; the converse is similar. We refer the reader to [BJL, X.11.4] for details. It is also easy to see that $\mathbf{D}'$ is maximal if and only if $\mathbf{E}$ is maximal. Moreover, if s does not divide μ, it is still possible to add one parallel class to $\mathbf{D}$. A recursive application of these results now yields the following:

7.2.9 THEOREM (Jungnickel and Sane 1982). Let s and t be positive integers with $s \geq 2$, and assume that s does not divide t. If there exists a symmetric (s, ts^n)-net for all $n \geq 0$, then there also exists a maximal $(s, t(s^{n+1}+s^n+\cdots+s)+1, ts^n)$-net (for all n).

7.2.10 Examples. Using 7.2.7, we can e.g. choose the following values of s and t:

(i) $s = p^i, t = p^j (p$ a prime and $i > j)$;

(ii) s an odd prime power, $t = 2$ or $t = 4$;

(iii) s and $t = s\lambda - 1$ prime powers provided that there exists $GH(s, \lambda)$.

206

Note that the examples with $t = 2$ in (ii) satisfy the Bose-Bush bound 7.1.2 with equality; this is due to Jungnickel (1979) simplifying a construction of Addelman and Kempthorne (1961). See also de Launey (1987) for related constructions.

The examples given in 7.2.7 show the existence of symmetric (s, μ)-nets for many values for which no complete net can exist (as $s - 1$ does not divide $\mu - 1$). As we have seen, one can still often extend such a symmetric net by a large number of parallel classes. On the other hand, there are complete (s, μ)-nets (for every prime power s) which do not contain any symmetric subnet, see Mavron (1984).

7.3 Completion. In this section, $\mathbf{D}$ always denotes an (s, r, μ)-net for which $s - 1$ divides $\mu - 1$ (so that a complete (s, μ)-net might exist). It then makes sense to study questions of completability, as we did in Chapter 3 in the special case $\mu = 1$. We now define the *deficiency* d of $\mathbf{D}$ as

$$d = \frac{s^2 \mu - 1}{s - 1} - r$$

and call $\mathbf{D}$ *completable* if it can be embedded into a complete (s, μ)-net by adjoining d new parallel classes of blocks. The completion problem for nets with $\mu > 1$ seems to be considerably more difficult than the corresponding problem for the case $\mu = 1$. Only the cases $d = 1$ and $d = 2$ are completely settled:

7.3.1 THEOREM (Shrikhande and Bhagwandas 1976, Shrikhande and Singhi 1979a). *A net of deficiency ≤ 2 is completable, unless $d = 2$ and $s = 4$.*

A comparatively simple (but still lengthy) proof of Theorem 7.3.1 is due to Jungnickel and Sane (1982); cf. [BJL, Section X.10]. The proof of the following theorem requires the use of strongly regular multigraphs.

7.3.2 THEOREM (Shrikhande and Singhi 1979b). *A (s, r, μ)-net of deficiency $d = 3$ is completable provided that $s \geq 104$.*

The only known result for $d \geq 4$ is for $s = 2$:

7.3.3 THEOREM (Verheiden 1978). *A $(2, r, \mu)$ net of deficiency $d \leq 6$ is completable.*

The following result of Jungnickel and Sane (1982) shows that the completion problem for $\mu > 1$ is indeed at least as difficult as the corresponding problem for $\mu = 1$:

7.3.4 THEOREM. *Let s be a prime power and assume the existence of a maximal Bruck net of order s and deficiency d. Then there also exists a maximal (s, r, s^n)-net of deficiency d for every positive integer n.*

This follows from Theorem 7.2.8. The results of Chapter 3 yield examples of maximal Bruck nets which can be used in 7.3.4:

(i) $s - p^2, d = p - 1$ for $p \geq 5$

(ii) $s = p^{2a}, d = p^a$

(iii) $s = 2^a, d = s - 2$

(iv) $s \equiv 1 \mod 4, d = s - 2$

(v) $s = 7, d = 4$;

(vi) $s = 8, d = 4$ or 5;

(vii) $s = 9, d = 3, 5$ or 6;

(viii) $s = 11, d = 6, 7$ or 8

In particualr, the case $s = 4$, $d = 2$ contained in (iii) shows that the exception in Theorem 7.3.1 is necessary.

7.4 Characterisations. In the case of Bruck nets, the study of configurations has led to some important characterisation theorems, cf. Chapter 4. It seems that configuration theorems have not been studied for the case $\mu > 1$. Thus we shall discuss characterisations using combinatorial properties or transitivity conditions. We recall the following definition: Let p and q be points of an incidence structure **D** which are joined by at least one block. Then the *line* pq is defined to the intersection of all blocks joining p and q. Note that this definition agrees with the old terminology used for Bruck nets; also, we obtain the usual notion of a line when considering the classical complete or symmetric (q, q^{d-2})-nets of Example 7.1.5. The reader may easily check that any two points are on a unique line provided that any two points are joined by either none or by a constant number λ of blocks ; in particular, this holds for complete and for symmetric (s, μ)-nets. We can now state the following famous characterization of the classical complete nets:

7.4.1 THEOREM (Dembowski 1964). *Let* **D** *be a complete* (s, μ)-net with $\mu > 1$ *and* $s \neq 2$. *Then the following assertions are equivalent:*

(i) *We have* $\mathbf{D} \cong AG_{d-1}(d, q)$ *for some prime power* $q \geq 3$ *and some* $d \geq 3$.

(ii) *Each line of* **D** *contains exactly* s *points.*

(iii) *Aut* **D** *acts transitively on triples of non-collinear points.*

(iv) *Each line meets each non-parallel block. (Here a line* L *is said to be parallel to a block* B *if* $L \subset C$ *for some block* $C \| B$.)

In fact one can somewhat weaken the hypothesis of Theorem 7.4.1; also there are other equivalent conditions (e.g. involving "planes"). A similar result holds for $s = 2$. A simple proof of 7.4.1 is due to Jungnickel and Lenz (1985), see also [BJL, Section XII.3]. As already mentioned in 7.2.3, there is in general a vast number of complete nets with the parameters of but not isomorphic to $AG_{d-1}(d, q)$. We next mention the following characterization of the classical symmetric nets (cf. 7.1.5):

7.4.2 THEOREM (Mavron 1981, Jungnickel 1981c). *Let* **D** *be a symmetric* (s, μ)-net with $\mu > 1$ *and* $s > 2$. *Then the following assertions are equivalent:*

(i) **D** *is constructed from some* $AG_{d-1}(d, q)$ *as in Example 7.1.5.*

(ii) *Each line of* **D** *has exactly s points.*

(iii) *Aut* **D** *acts transitively on non-collinear triples of points which are contained in a common block.*

The construction used in 7.1.5 can also be described within projective geometry: **D** arises from $PG_{d-1}(d,q)$ by omitting a hyperplane H_∞ with all its points and a point ∞ with all its hyperplanes, where $\infty \in H_\infty$. We remark that the analogous construction in the case $\infty \notin H_\infty$ yields the "biaffine geometries" characterised by Jungnickel and Vedder (1984). As in the case of complete nets, the number of non-isomorphic (q, q^{d-1})-nets $(d \geq 3)$ grows exponentially with $k = q^{d-1}$; see Jungnickel (1984b).

7.5. Translation Nets. The definition of a translation (s, r, μ)-net is analogous to that of a translation Bruck net given in 5.1.1. The notion of a PCP introduced in 5.1.2 has to be generalized as follows:

7.5.1 DEFINITION. Let G be a (multiplicatively written) group of order $s^2\mu$, and let $\mathbf{U} = \{U_1, \ldots, U_r\}$ be a set of r subgroups or order $s\mu$ of G. One calls $\mathbf{U}$ a *partial congruence partition* of *order* s, *degree* r and *index* μ (for short, an (s, r, μ)-PCP) of G if the following condition holds:

(7.6) $|U_i \cap U_j| = \mu$ (or, equivalently, $U_iU_j = G$) for any two distinct indices $i, j \in \{1, \ldots, r\}$.

Again, the U_i are called the *components* of $\mathbf{U}$

With this definition, Proposition 5.1.3 carries over to the case of arbitrary index μ. Note that the classical complete and symmetric nets of Example 7.1.5 are in fact translation nets. Some recursive constructions allow to construct further examples:

7.5.2 THEOREM (Jungnickel 1981b). *Let p be a prime, i a positive and j a non-negative integer. Moreover, let G be the elementary abelian group of order p^{2i+j}. Then there exist the following nets with translation group G:*

(i) *a symmetric (p^i, p^j)-translation net*

(ii) *a (p^i, r, p^j)-translation net with*

(7.7) $$r = p^{(a+1)i+b} + p^{ai+b} + \cdots + p^{i+b} + 1,$$

where $j = ai + b$ with $0 \leq b < i$.

Note that the construction of Lemma 5.1.5 carries over to arbitrary indices. If we define $T(s, \mu, G)$ to be the maximum value of r for which an (s, r, μ)-PCP in the group G of order $s^2\mu$ exists and if we put $T(s, \mu) = \max\{T(s, \mu, G) : G \text{ is a group of order } s^2\mu\}$ we thus obtain

(7.8) $$T(s, \mu) \geq \min\{T(p_i^a, p_i^{b_i}) : i = 1, \ldots, n\}$$

where $\{p_1, \ldots, p_n\}$ is the set of distinct primes dividing s and where $p^{a_i}\|s$ and $p^{b_i}\|\mu$. (We write $p^a\|x$ if p^a divides x but p^{a+1} does not divide x.) Note that 5.2.1 and 5.2.2. carry over to (s, r, μ)-PCP's to give the following results:

7.5.3 PROPOSITION (Jungnickel 1989a). *Assume the existence of an (s, r, μ)-PCP in G and let P be a Sylow p-subgroup of G for some prime p dividing s. Then there also exists and (p^a, r, p^b)-PCP in P where $p^a \| s$ and $p^b \| \mu$.*

As a consequence, we obtain the following generalization of Theorem 5.2.3:

7.5.4 THEOREM (Jungnickel 1989a). *Let $s = p_1^{a_1} \cdots p_n^{a_n}$ be the canonical prime power factorization of the positive integer s, and let $\mu = p_1^{b_i} \cdots p_n^{b_n}$. Then one has*

$$(7.9) \qquad T(s, \mu) = \min\{T(p^{a_i}, p^{b_i}) : i = 1, \ldots, n\}$$

This reduces the determination of $T(s, \mu)$ to the case of p-groups. Not surprisingly, $T(p^i, p^j, G)$ takes its maximal value for the elementary abelian group of order p^{2i+j}; this is shown by the following generalization of Theorem 5.2.6 together with Theorem 7.5.2.

7.5.5 THEOREM (Jungnickel 1981b). *Let $\mathbf{U}$ be a (p^i, r, p^j)-PCP in G. If G is not elementary abelian, then*

$$T(p^i, p^j, G) \leq p^{i+j-1} + \cdots + p + 1.$$

Thus the determination of $T(p^i, p^j, EA(p^{2i+j}))$ would complete the determination of $T(s, \mu)$ in general. Unfortunately, this problem is not yet completely solved. the present state of knowledge is as follows, cf. Jungnickel (1981b):

7.5.6 THEOREM. *One has the following:*

$$(7.10) \qquad T(q, q^d, EA(q^{d+2})) = q^{d+1} + \cdots + q^2 + q + 1 \text{ for prime powers } q;$$
$$(7.11) \qquad T(p^i, p^j, EA(p^{2i+j})) \leq p^{(a+1)i+b} + p^{ai+b} + \cdots + p^{i+b} + p^b - \theta \text{ where}$$
$$j = ai + b \text{ with } 0 < b < i \text{ and where}$$

$$2\theta = \sqrt{1 + 4p^i(p^i - p^b)} \; - (2p^i - 2p^b - 1);$$

$$(7.12) \qquad T(p^i, p^{ai+1}, EA(p^{(a+2)i+1})) = p^{(a+1)i+1} + p^{ai+1} + \cdots + p^{i+1} + 1 \text{ for } i \geq 2$$

Here (7.10) corresponds to complete translation nets and the upper bound (7.11) is just a consequence of the Bose-Bush bound of Theorem 7.1.2. A corresponding lower bound follows from 7.5.2. By a result of Drake and Freeman (1979), PCP's in elementary abelian groups are equivalent to certain partial t-spreads in a space $PG(n, p)$; then (7.12) follows from a result of Beutelspacher (1975). Using Proposition 7.5.3 and Theorem 7.5.5, one also obtains the following result:

7.5.7 THEOREM (Jungnickel 1989a). *Let G be a group of order $s^2\mu$ and assume the existence of an (s, r, μ)-PCP in G. If $r \geq s\mu$, then s and μ are powers of a prime p and G is elementary abelian.*

The following two interesting theorems follow easily from 7.5.7:

7.5.8 THEOREM (Jungnickel 1981b). *A complete (s, μ)-translation net (i.e. a translation affine 2-design) with translation group G exists if and only if the following conditions holds:*

(7.13)   *s is a prime power, μ is a power of s, and G is elementary abelian.*

7.5.9 THEOREM (Jungnickel 1982a). *A symmetric (s, μ)-translation net with translation group G exists if and only if the following condition holds:*

(7.14)   *s and μ are powers of the same prime p, and G is elementary abelian.*

The original proofs of 7.5.8 and 7.5.9 are much more involved since they use (in case of 7.5.8 via a result of Schulz (1967)) the classification of finite groups with a partition (cf. Section 6.3). An elementary but lengthy geometric proof of these two results was later given by Hine and Mavron (1983). As Theorem 7.5.7 shows, both results are special cases of a much more general result on PCP's which admits an elementary group theoretic proof.

7.6 Automorphism Groups. We conclude this chapter with a few remarks concerning other types of automorphism groups of (s, r, μ)-nets. As in Section 6.1, one may consider *class-regular transversal designs* $TD_\mu[r, s]$ which again are equivalent to (s, r, μ)-difference matrices, cf. Section 7.2. We refer the reader to Jungnickel (1979) for this result and for some construction methods not mentioned in Section 7.2. The following two non-existence results generalize the Hall-Paige-Theorem 3.3.2 and Theorem 6.1.3:

7.6.1 THEOREM (Drake 1979). *Let G be a group of even order s, and assume that the Sylow 2-subgroup of G is cyclic. Then there is no $(s, 3, \lambda)$-difference matrix over G whenever λ is odd.*

7.6.2 THEOREM (de Launey 1984a, 1984b). *Let G be an abelian group of odd order s, and let λ be odd. Furthermore let p be a prime dividing s and let $m \not\equiv 0$ (mod p) be an integer dividing the square-free part of $s\lambda$. If there exists $GH(s, \lambda)$ over G, then the order of m modulo p is odd.*

Recently, Brock (1988) proved a Bruck-Ryser type condition for GH-matrices:

7.6.3 THEOREM. *Assume the existence of $GH(s, \lambda)$ over a group G, where $h = s\lambda$ is odd. Then the equation*

$$z^2 = hx^2 + (-1)^{(t-1)/2} t y^2$$

has a non-trivial solution in integers x, y, z for every $t \neq 1$ which is the order of a homomorphic image of G.

For an interesting application of difference matrices to the existence problem for quasimultiples of affine and projective planes of arbitrary order n (i.e. designs

$S_\lambda(2, n, n^2)$ and $S_\lambda(2, n + 1, n^2 + n + 1)$, respectively) - even if no plane of order n exists - see Jungnickel (1989c).

We next mention symmetric (s, μ)-nets with a Singer group, cf. Section 6.2. The examples in 6.2.1 lead to symmetric (p^i, p^j)-nets with a Singer group for primes p (in suitable homomorphic images of the groups in 6.2.1). Except for these, one knows a few examples with $s = 2$ (and also a non-existence result) and with $s = 3$; cf. Jungnickel (1982b) and de Launey (1989d). Restrictions on s for odd s follow in analogy to Theorem 6.2.4, using Theorem 7.6.2. The cyclic case is again impossible by Elliott and Butson (1966).

One may consider translation TD's with $\lambda > 1$ and, more generally, translation divisible designs) and obtain results similar to those mentioned in Section 6.3: the Hughes-Thompson groups possible for $\lambda = 1$ (see 6.3.3) can then no longer occur as translation groups. We refer the reader to Schulz (1987a, 1987b, 1988) to Herzer and Schulz (1989) and Spera (1989).

As mentioned in Theorem 7.4.2 symmetric and complete nets with a highly transitive group are necessarily classical. There is one more family of examples with a large group due to Jungnickel (1981c):

7.6.4 THEOREM. *Let s and μ be powers of a prime p. Then there exists a symmetric (s, μ)-net with a group G which acts transitively on pairs of joined points.*

8. Conclusion. Let us conclude this survey with mentioning some other topics that have been studied and some open problems.

8.1 Further Topics. Many special types of Latin squares have been investigated, cf. [DK]. Among the most interesting are the *self-orthogonal* Latin squares (for short: SOLS), i.e. Latin squares L which are orthogonal to their transpose L^T. In particular we have the following stronger version of Theorem 2.4.3; see [BJL, IX.4.8] for a proof.

8.1.1 THEOREM (Brayton, Coppersmith and Hoffman 1976). *A SOLS of order s exists if and only if $s \notin \{2, 3, 6\}$.*

There is an intimate connection between SOLS and PBD's with block sizes $\neq 2, 3, 6$; cf. Drake and Larson (1983). For SOLS with sub-SOLS, see Drake and Lenz (1980). Other interesting classes of Latin squares related to groups can be constructed from "sequenceable" and "R-sequenceable" groups; see e.g. [DK], Friedlander, Gordon and Miller (1978), Keedwell (1981a, 1981b, 1983a, 1983b) and Anderson (1987a, 1987b).

There is a generalization of Bruck nets to higher dimensional objects introduced by Laskar (1974) for dimension 3 and by Laskar and Dunbar (1978) in arbitrary dimensions. We shall give the definition for $d = 3$:

8.1.2 DEFINITION. Let $V, \mathbf{L}$ and $\mathbf{P}$ be sets whose elements are called *points, lines* and *planes*, respectively, and let $(V, \mathbf{L}, I_1)$, $(\mathbf{L}, \mathbf{P}, I_2)$ and $(\mathbf{L}, \mathbf{P}, I_3)$ be incidence structures. Then $D = (V, \mathbf{L}, \mathbf{P}, I_1, I_2, I_3)$ is called a *3-net* with parameters

r, s and b (where r, s, b are integers ≥ 2) provided that the following axioms are satisfied.

(i) pI_1L and LI_2P imply pI_3P.

(ii) If two lines intersect, then they are contained in a common plane.

(iii) The points and lines of any plane form an $(s, r, 1)$-net.

(iv) The planes are partitioned into b classes such that each class in turn partitions V (so $(V, \mathbf{P}, I_3)$ is resolvable) and such that any two planes from distinct classes intersect in a line.

(v) Each line is contained in at least one plane.

8.1.3 Example. Let Π be a 3-dimensional projective space, P a plane of Π, $\Sigma = \Pi \backslash P$ and Q a subplane of P. Choosing as points, lines and planes of $\mathbf{D}$ respectively the points of Σ, the lines of Σ meeting P in a point of Q and the planes of Σ meeting P in a line of Q (with incidence relations induced from Π) yields a 3-net $\mathbf{D}$.

The following result is an analogue of the Main Theorem of Projective Geometry; a corresponding result for nets of arbitrary dimension d is due to Sprague (1981).

8.1.4 THEOREM (Sprague 1979). *Every finite 3-net with $r \geq 3$ is isomorphic to a 3-net constructed as in 8.1.3.*

Transversal designs are in some sense the closest analogue to 2-designs among the class of GDD's (cf. Section 2.3). It is, of course, quite possible to study similar analogues of t-designs, i.e. $t - TD$'s. As far as the author knows, this has not yet been done in a systematic way. Some early results (in the equivalent form of orthogonal arrays of strength t) have been obtained by Bose & Bush (1952), see also Hedayat & Stufken (1989). Hanani (1979) has explicitly considered $t - TD$'s as an ingredient in recursive constructions for t-designs. The case of $t - TD$'s with $\lambda = 1$ is also closely related to the MDS-codes studied in Coding Theory (cf. MacWilliams & Sloane (1978) for MDS-codes); we mention Bruen & Silverman (1983) as a more recent example of work in this direction (which could be translated into the language of $t - TD$'s).

A further generalization of nets are the so-called "transversal seminets" of Deza & Ihringer (1986). We finally mention a recent paper of Euler, Burkard and Grommer (1986) which studies a connection between Latin squares and Euclidean geometry by investigating certain associated polytopes.

8.2 Some Open Problems. We conclude this survey with a list of some open problems related to the questions discussed which we think are interesting. They range in difficulty from the manageable to the (at least at present) hopeless.

8.2.1   Find new upper bounds on the function $N(.)$. In particular, are there non-prime power values s with $N(s) = s - 1$?

8.2.2   Find new constructions for MOLS and thus new lower bounds on $N(.)$. In particular, find new bounds for the n_k of Section 2.5.

8.2.3 Improve the exponent a in the asymptotic existence theorem for MOLS discussed in Section 2.5.

8.2.4 Are there infinite sequences of non-prime powers s with $N(s) \geq \sqrt{s}$ or even $N(s) \geq cs$ for a constant c? In particular, is the conjecture $N(4p) \geq 2p - 1$ for primes p valid?

8.2.5 Find further examples of maximal nets of small deficiency, in particular for orders $s = p^{2a+1}$ (p a prime).

8.2.6 Is it true that there exists a maximal $(p^i, p, 1)$-difference matrix over $\mathbf{Z}_{p^i}$?

8.2.7 Try to prove an analogue of Corollary 3.3.4 in case $s \equiv 3 \mod 4$.

8.2.8 Fill in the missing cases in the table in Section 3.4.

8.2.9 Find a lower bound on the size of a partial transversal in an $(s, r, 1)$-net for $r \geq 4$.

8.2.10 Characterize all groups of order s^2 which admit an $(s, 3, 1)$-PCP.

8.2.11 Characterize the groups G with $T(G) = \min\{T(P_i) : i = 1, \ldots, n\}$ in Theorem 5.2.3.

8.2.12 Determine $T(H \times H)$ for all simple groups H; determine $T(P)$ for every Sylow subgroup P of such a group $H \times H$. Cf. 5.2.4.

8.2.13 Determine $T(P \times P)$ for all p-groups P. (Note that Theorem 5.2.8 covers the abelian case).

8.2.14 Find an analogue of Frohardt's theorem 5.2.7 for odd primes p.

8.2.15 All known examples of maximal partial spreads in $PG(3, q)$ have deficiency $d \geq q - 1$. Try to settle the conjecture that one has indeed $r \leq q^2 - q + 2$ instead of the bounds given in 5.3.1 and 5.3.5. Consider the analogous problem for partial t-spreads

8.2.16 Under which conditions is the net belonging to a maximal partial t-spread (or, more generally, to a maximal PCP) a maximal net?

8.2.17 Find further non-existence results for difference matrices with $\lambda = 1$. In particular, is there any $GH(s, 1)$ over a group G which is not elementary abelian? Is the plane belonging to a $GH(p, 1)$ (p a prime) always Desarguesian?

8.2.18 Classify the symmetric nets with a singer group (or at least their parameters).

8.2.19 Classify the flag-regular and the point-regular TD's.

8.2.20 Find further series of GH-matrices. In particular, does $GH(s, 8)$ exist for prime powers s?

8.2.21 Find further non-existence results for GH-matrices.

8.2.22 Can the Bose-Bush theorem 7.1.2 be strengthened? Alternatively, find new series of examples where 7.1.2 is best possible.

8.2.23   Are there any complete (s, μ)-nets with parameters not as in 7.2.3?

8.2.22   Can the Bose-Bush theorem 7.1.2 be strengthened? Alternatively, find new series of examples where 7.1.2 is best possible.

8.2.23   Are there any complete (s, μ)-nets with parameters not as in 7.2.3?

8.2.24   Settle the existence conjecture for Hadamard matrices.

8.2.25   Find an asymptotically correct bound on the number of complete or symmetric nets with classical parameters (as in 7.1.5).

8.2.26   Find completion results for (s, r, μ)-nets of deficiency $d \geq 4$.

8.2.27   Determine $T(p^i, p^j, EA(p^{2i+j}))$.

8.2.28   Classify the symmetric nets which admit a group G acting transitively on pairs of joined points (cf. 7.6.3). Is a symmetric net for which G also acts transitively on pairs of points which are *not* joined necessarily classical (as in 7.1.5)?

8.2.29   It has been conjectured by Jungnickel (1988c) that there always exists a $(2p, 2p, 2)$-difference matrix over $\mathbf{Z}_{2p}$. Settle this conjecture.

8.2.30   Can the bound in Bruck's theorem 3.1.1 be improved for translation nets?

The author hopes to have provided some evidence for his opinion that the geometries and groups belonging to Latin squares are interesting and deserve further study. The close connection and interplay of combinatorial, algebraic, geometric and number theoretic methods make this a fascinating area. In spite of much previous research (I have listed more than 250 references, and this is still not complete) there are still many open problems. If one of my readers is stimulated to solve one of the problems listed above, this survey will have served its purpose.

Acknowledgement. Most of the present survey was written while the author was a Visiting Professor at the University of Waterloo; the final revision was prepared during the author's visit to the Institute for Mathematics and its Applications at the University of Minnesota. He would like to thank both these institutions for their hospitality; he also gratefully acknowledges financial support by NSERC under grant IS–0367, by the Institute for Mathematics and its Applications and by the Deutsche Forschungsgemeinschaft.

Finally, the author is very much indebted to the following colleagues for their comments and suggestions: R.A. Bailey, A.E. Brouwer, M. Deza, J.F. Dillon, D.A. Drake, A.B. Evans, A.S. Hedayat, W.M. Kantor, G. Pickert, A. Pott, R.H. Schulz, M.S. Shrikhande, J.H. van Lint and C.F.J. Wu.

Table A

s	$N(s) \geq$	References	s	$N(s) \geq$	References
6	=1	(2.6), Section X.13	58	5	2.4.5, X(3.13.a)
10	2	(2.4),VIII.8.23	60	4	(2.5)
12	5	(2.2),VIII.3.13	62	4	2.45,X.(3.6.c)
14	3	(2.3)	63	6	(2.6)
15	4	(2.2),VIII.(3.20.b)	65	7	VIII.8.23
18	3	VIII.(8.24.a)	66	5	IX.4.4
20	4	(2.3)	68	5	IX.4.4
21	4	(2.8),IX.(1.19.c)	69	6	Zhu (1984)
22	3	VIII.(8.25.a)	70	6	(2.10),X.(1.3.b)
24	4	(2.2)	72	7	(2.6)
26	3	VIII.(8.25.b)	74	5	IX.4.4
28	3	(2.6)	75	5	IX.4.4
30	3	VIII.(8.25.c)	76	5	IX.4.4
33	4	VIII.(8.27.a)	77	6	(2.6)
34	3	VIII.(8.26.a)	78	6	(2.11),X.(1.3.b)
35	4	(2.6)	80	7	(2.9),X.(1.3.g)
36	4	VIII.(8.18.b)	82	8	VIII.(3.20.f)
38	3	VIII.(8.26.b)	84	6	2.4.5,X.(3.6.c)
39	4	Mills (1977)	85	6	2.4.5,X.(3.6.c)
40	4	(2.6)	86	6	2.4.5,X.(3.6.c)
42	3	VIII.(8.26.c)	87	6	2.4.5,X.(3.13.b)
44	3	(2.6)	88	7	(2.6)
45	4	(2.6)	90	6	X.(3.9.a)
46	4	VIII.(8.20.b)	91	7	X.(3.11.a)
48	4	Mills (1977)	92	6	2.4.5,X.(3.13.b)
50	6	VIII.(8.20.d)	93	6	2.4.5,X.(3.13.b)
51	4	2.4.5,X.(3.6.d)	94	6	2.4.5,X.(3.13.b)
52	3	(2.6)	95	6	2.4.5,X.(3.13.b)
54	4	X.(1.3.h)	96	7	2.4.5,X.(3.13.c)
55	5	Mills (1977)	98	6	2.4.5,X.(3.13.b)
56	7	Mills (1977)	99	8	(2.6)
57	7	(2.8),IX.(1.19.d)	100	8	VIII.(8.20.h)

REFERENCES

[BJL] BETH, T., JUNGNICKEL, D. AND LENZ, H., *Design Theory*, Bibliographisches Institut, Mannheim (1985) and Cambridge University Press, Cambridge (1986).

[DK] DÉNES, J. AND KEEDWELL, A.D., *Latin squares and their applications*, English Universities Press, London (1974).

Whenever possible we refer to these two books for proofs. For convenience, they will be referenced as [BJL] and [DK], respectively. All other references are by author's name and year, e.g. André (1954).

ADDELMAN, S. AND KEMPTHORNE, O., *Some main effect plans and orthogonal arrays of strength two*, Ann. Math. Stat. 32 (1961), 1167–1176.

ANDERSON, B.A., *Sequencings of dicylic groups*, Ars Comb. 23 (1987a), 131–142.

ANDERSON, B.A., *A fast method for sequencing low order non-abelian groups*, Ann. Disc. Math. 34 (1987b), 27–42.

ANDRÉ, J., *Über nicht-Desarguessche Ebenen mit transitiver Translationsgruppe*, Math. Z. 60 (1954), 156–186.

ANDRÉ, J., *Über Parallelstrukturen II, Translationsstrukturen*, Math. Z. 76 (1961), 155–165.

ARASU, K.T., *Recent results on difference sets*, This volume.

ARASU, K.T., DAVIS, J., JUNGNICKEL, D. AND POTT, A., *Some non-existence theorems for divisible difference sets*, (1989) (to appear).

BAER, R., *Nets and groups I*, Trans. Amer. Math. Soc. 46 (1939), 110–141.

BAER, R., *Partitionen endlicher Gruppen*, Math. Z. 75 (1961a), 333–372.

BAER, R., *Einfache Partitionen nicht-einfacher Gruppen*, Math. Z. 77 (1961b), 1–37.

BAER, R., *Einfache Partitionen endlicher Gruppen mit nicht-trivialer Fittingscher Untergruppe*, Archiv. Math. 12 (1961c), 81–89.

BAILEY, R.A., *Latin squares with highly transitive automorphism groups*, J. Austral. Math. Soc. (A) 33 (1982), 18–22.

BAILEY, R.A. AND JUNGNICKEL, D., *Translation nets and fixed-point-free group automorphisms*, J. Comb. Th. (A) (1989), (to appear).

BARLOTTI, A., AND STRAMBACH, K., *The geometry of binary systems*, Advances Math. 49 (1983), 1–105.

BAUMERT, L. AND HALL, M., *Nonexistence of certain planes of order 10 and 12*, J. Comb. Th. (A) 14 (1973), 273–280.

BENNETT, F.E., *Pairwise balanced designs with prime power block sizes exceeding 7*, Ann. Discr. Math. 34 (1987), 43–63.

BETH, T., *Eine Bemerkung zur Abschätzung der Anzahl der orthogonalen lateinischen Quadrate mittels Siebverfahren*, Abh. Math. Sem. Hamburg 53 (1983), 248–288.

BETTEN, D., *Zum Satz von Euler-Tarry*, Math. Nat. Unt. 36 (1983), 449–453.

BETTEN, D., *Die 12 Lateinischen Quadrate der Ordnung 6*, Mitt. Math. Sem. Giessen 163 (1984), 181–188.

BEUTELSPACHER, A, *Partial spreads in finite projective spaces and partial designs*, Math. Z. 145 (1975), 211–229. Correction: Math. Z. 147 (1976), 303.

BEUTELSPACHER, A, *Blocking sets and partial spreads in finite projective spaces*, Geom. Ded. 9 (1980), 425–449.

BEUTELSPACHER, A. AND METSCH, K, *Embedding finite linear spaces in projective planes*, Ann. Discr. Math. 30 (1986), 39–56.

BEUTELSPACHER, A. AND METSCH, K., *Embedding finite linear spaces in projective planes II*, Discr. Math. 66 (1987), 219–230.

BILIOTTI, M. AND MICELLI, G, *On translation transversal designs*, Rend. Sem. Mat. Univ. Padova 73 (1985), 217–229.

BLASCHKE, W., *Einführung in die Geometrie der Waben*, Birkhäuser, Basel-Stuttgart (1955).

BLASCHKE, W. AND BOL, G., *Geometrie der Gewebe*, Springer, Berlin (1938).

BLOKHUIS, A. AND BROUWER, A.E., *Blocking sets in Desarguesian projective planes*, Bull. London Math. Soc. 18 (1986), 132–134.

BLOKHUIS, A., BROUWER, A.E. AND WILBRINK, H.A., *Heden's bound on maximal partial spreads*, Discr. Math. 74 (1989), 335–339.

BOL, G., *Topologische Fragen der Differentialgeometrie*, 65. Gewebe and Gruppen. Math. Ann. 114 (1937), 414–431.

BOSE, R.C., *On the application of the properties of Galois fields to the construction of Hyper-Graeco-Latin-squares*, Sankhya 3 (1938), 323–338.

BOSE, R.C., *Strongly regular graphs, partial geometries and partially balanced designs*, Pacific J. Math. 13 (1963), 389–419.

BOSE, R.C. AND BUSH, K.A, *Orthogonal arrays of strength two and three*, Ann. Math. Stat. 23 (1952), 508–524.

BOSE, R.C., CHAKRAVARTI, I.M. AND KNUTH, D.E., *On methods of constructing sets of mutually orthogonal Latin squares using a computer I*, Technometrics 2 (1960), 507–516.

BOSE, R.C. AND SHRIKHANDE, S.S., *On the construction of sets of mutually orthogonal Latin squares and the falsity of a conjecture of Euler*, Trans. Amer. Math. Soc. 95 (1960), 191–209.

BOSE, R.C., SHRIKHANDE, S.S. AND PARKER, E.T., *Further results on the construction of mutually orthogonal Latin squares and the falsity of Euler's conjecture*, Canad. J. Math. 12 (1960), 189–203.

BRAYTON, R.K., COPPERSMITH, D. AND HOFFMAN, A.J., *Self-orthogonal Latin squares*, Atti del convegni Lincei 17 Tomo II (1976), 509–517.

BROCK, B.W., *Hermitian congruence and the existence and completion of generalized Hadamard matrices*, J. Comb. Th. (A) 49 (1988), 233–261.

BROUWER, A.E., *The number of mutually orthogonal Latin squares*, Math. Centrum Amsterdam Report ZW 123/79 (1979).

BROUWER, A.E., *A series of separable designs with application to pairwise orothogonal Latin squares*, Europ. J. Comb. 1 (1980a), 39–41.

BROUWER, A.E., *On the existence of 30 mutually orthogonal Latin squares*, Math. Centrum Amsterdam Report ZW 136/80 (1980b).

BROUWER, A.E. AND VAN REES, G.H., *More mutually orthogonal Latin squares*, Discr. Math. 39 (1982), 263–281.

BRUCK, R.H., *Finite nets I. Numerical invariants*, Canad. J. Math. 3 (1951), 94–107.

BRUCK, R.H., *A survey of binary systems*, Springer, Berlin-Göttingen-Heidelberg (1958).

BRUCK, R.H., *Finite nets II. Uniqueness and embedding*, Pacific J. Math. 13 (1963a), 421–457.

BRUCK, R.H., *What is a loop?* In: Studies in modern algebra, Math. Assoc. of America (1963b), 59–99.

BRUCK, R.H. AND BOSE, R.C., *The construction of translation planes from projective spaces*, J. Algebra 1 (1964) 85–102.

BRUCK, R.H. AND BOSE, R.C., *Linear representations of projective planes in projective spaces*, J. Algebra 4 (1966), 117–127.

BRUCK, R.H. AND RYSER, H.J., *The nonexistence of certain finite projective planes*, Canad. J. Math. 1 (1949), 88–93.

BRUEN, A.A., *Partial spreads and replaceable nets*, Canad. J. Math. 23 (1971), 381–391.

BRUEN, A.A., *Unimbeddable nets of small deficiency*, Pacific J. Math. 43 (1972), 51–54.

BRUEN, A.A., *Collineations and extensions of translation nets*, Math. Z. 145 (1975), 243–249.

BRUEN, A.A., *Blocking sets and skew subspaces of projective space*, Canad. J. Math. 32 (1980), 628–630.

BRUEN, A.A., *Blocking sets and translation nets*. In: Finite Geometries (Eds. N.L. Johnson, M.H. Kallaher, C.T. Long), Mercel Dekker, New York-Basel (1983), 77–92.

218

BRUEN, A.A. AND FREEMAN, J.W., *Intersections of t-reguli, rational curves, and orthogonal Latin squares*, Lin. Alg. Appl. 46 (1982), 103–116.

BRUEN, A.A. AND SILVERMAN, R., *Switching sets in* $PG(3, q)$, Proc. Amer. Math. Soc. 43 (1974), 176–180.

BRUEN, A.A. AND SILVERMAN, R., *On the non-existence of certain MDS-codes and projective planes*, Math. Z. 183 (1983), 171–175.

BRUEN, A.A. AND THAS, J.A., *Partial spreads, packings and Hermitian manifolds in* $PG(3, q)$, Math. Z. 151 (1976), 207–214.

BUTSON, A.T., *Generalized Hadamard matrices*, Proc. Amer. Math. Soc. 13 (1962) 894–898.

CHANG, L.Q., HSIANG, K. AND TAI, S., *Congruent mappings and congruence classes of orthomorphisms of groups*, Chinese Math. Acta 6 (1965), 141–152.

CHOWLA, S., ERDÖS, P. AND STRAUS, E.G., *On the maximal number of pairwise orthogonal Latin squares of given order*, Canad. J. Math. 12 (1960), 204–208.

COLBOURN, C.J. AND VAN OORSCHOT, P.C., *Applications of combinatorial designs in computer science*, (1989), (to appear).

DAWSON, J.E., *A construction for generalized Hadamard matrices* $GH(4q, EA(q))$, J. Stat. Planning Inf. 11 (1985), 103–110.

DE LAUNEY, W., *On the non-existence of generalized Hadamard matrices*, J. Stat. Planning Inf. 10 (1984a), 385–396.

DE LAUNEY, W., *On the non-existence of generalized weighing matrices*, Ars Comb. 17A, (1984b), 117–132.

DE LAUNEY, W., *A survey of generalized Hadamard matrices and difference matrices* $D(k, \lambda; G)$ *with large k*, Util. Math. 30 (1986), 5–29.

DE LAUNEY, W., *On difference matrices, transversal designs, resolvable transversal designs and large sets of mutually orthogonal F-squares*, J. Stat. Planning Inf. 16 (1987), 107–125.

DE LAUNEY, W., *(O,G)-designs with applications*, Ph.D. thesis, University of Sydney, Australia. (1988).

DE LAUNEY, W., *GBRD's: some new constructions for difference matrices, generalized Hadamard matrices and balanced weighing matrices*, Graphs Comb. (1989a), (to appear).

DE LAUNEY, W., *Some construction for square GBRD's and some new infinite families of generalized Hadamard matrices*, (1989b), (to appear).

DE LAUNEY, W., *Square GBRD's over non-abelian groups*, Ars Comb. 27 (1989c), 40–49.

DE LAUNEY, W., *Generalized Hadamard matrices which are developed modulo a group*, (1989d), (to appear).

DEMBOWSKI, P., *Eine Kennzeichnung der enlichen affinen Räume*, Archiv Math. 15 (1964). Correction: Archiv Math. 18 (1967), 111–112.

DEMBOWSKI, P., *Finite geometries*, Springer, Berlin-Heidelberg-New York (1968).

DEMBOWSKI, P. AND OSTROM, T.G., *Planes of order n with collineation groups of order* n^2, Math. Z. 103 (1968), 239–258.

DEZA, M. AND IHRINGER, T., *On permutation arrays, transversal seminets and related structures*, Ann. Discr. Math. 30 (1986), 185–202.

DILLON, J.F., *Elementary Hadamard difference sets*, Ph.D. thesis, Univ. of Maryland (1973).

DILLON, J.F., *Elementary Hadamard difference sets*, In: Proc. 6th Southeastern Conf. on Comb., Graph Th. and Comp. (1975), 237–249.

DILLON, J.F., *Difference sets in 2-groups*, Contemp. Math. (1989), (to appear).

DOW, S., *Transversal-free nets of small deficiency*, Archiv Math. 41 (1983), 472–474.

DRAKE, D.A., *Maximal sets of latin squares and partial transversals*, J. Stat. Planning Inf. 1 (1977), 143–149.

DRAKE, D.A., *Partial λ-geometries and generalized Hadamard matrices over groups*, Can. J. Math. 31 (1979), 617–627.

DRAKE, D.A. AND FREEMAN, J.W., *Partial t-spreads and group constructible* (s, r, μ)*-nets*, J. Geom. 13, (1979), 210–216.

DRAKE, D.A. AND JUNGNICKEL, D., *Klingenberg structures and partial designs II. Regularity and uniformity*, Pacific J. Math. 77 (1978), 389–415.

DRAKE, D.A. AND LARSON J.A., *Pairwise balanced designs whose line sizes do not divide six*, J. Comb. Th. (A) 34 (1983), 266–300.

DRAKE, D.A. AND LENZ, H., *Orthogonal Latin squares with orthogonal subsquares*, Archiv Math. 34 (1980), 565–576.

EBERT, G., *Maximal strongly partial spreads*, Canad. J. Math. 30 (1978), 483–489.

ELLIOTT, J.E.H. AND BUTSON, A.T., *Relative difference sets*, Illinois J. Math. 10 (1966), 517–531.

EULER, L., *Recherches sur une nouvelle espèce des quarrés magiques*, In: Leonardi Euleri opera omnia, Ser. I. Vol. 7, Teubner, Berlin-Leipzig (1923), 291–392.

EULER, R., BURKARD, R.E. AND GROMMES, R., *On Latin squares and the facial structure of related polytopes*, Discr. Math. 62 (1986), 155–181.

EVANS, A.B., *Generating orthomorphisms of $GF(q)^+$*, Discr. Math. 63 (1987a), 21–26.

EVANS, A.B., *Orthomorphisms of Z_p*, Discr. Math. 64 (1987b), 147–156.

EVANS, A.B., *Difference matrices, generalized Hadamard matrices and orthomorphism graphs of groups*, J. Comb. Math. Comb. Comp. 1 (1987c), 97–105.

EVANS, A.B., *Orthomorphisms of groups*, Proc. 3rd Conf. in Combinatorics New York 1985. Ars Comb. 25B (1988), 141–152.

EVANS, A.B., *Orthomorphisms in $GF(q)^+$*, Ars Comb. 27 (1989a), 121–132.

EVANS, A.B., *On planes of prime order with translations and honologies*, J. Geom. 34 (1988b), 36–41.

EVANS, A.B., *Orthomorphism graphs of groups*, J. Geom. (1989c), (to appear).

EVANS, A.B., *On elementary abelian Cartesian groups*, (1989d), (to appear).

EVANS, A.B. AND MCFARLAND, R.L., *Planes of prime order with translations*, Congr. Numer. 44 (1984), 41–46.

EVANS, T., *Algebraic structures associated with Latin squares and orthogonal arrays*, In: Proc. Conf. Alg. Asp. Comb. Toronto (1975), 31–52.

EVANS, T., *Universal algebra and Euler's officer problem*, Amer. Math. Monthly 86 (1979), 466–473.

FREEMAN J.W., *Reguli and pseudo-reguli in $PG(3, s^2)$*, Geom. Ded. 9 (1979), 267–280.

FRIEDLANDER, R.J., GORDON, B. AND MILLER, M.D., *On a group sequencing problem of Ringel*, Congressus Numerantium 21 (1978), 307–321.

FROHARDT, D., *Groups with a large number of large disjoint subgroups*, J. Algebra 107 (1987), 153–159.

GANLEY, M., *On a paper of Dembowski and Ostrom*, Archiv Math. 27 (1976), 93–98.

GLUCK, D., *Hadamard difference sets in groups of order 64*, J. Comb. Th. (A) 51 (1989a), 138–140.

GLUCK, D., *A note on permutation polynomials and finite geometries*, (1989b), (to appear).

GLYNN, D.G., *A lower bound for maximal partial spreads in $PG(3, q)$*, Ars Comb. 13 (1982), 39–40.

GUÉRIN, R., *Existence et propriétés des carrés Latin orthogonaux II*, Publ. Inst. Statist. Univ. Paris 15 (1982), 215–293.

HALL, M., *Combinatorial Theory* (2nd edition), Wiley, New York (1986).

HALL, M. AND PAIGE, L.J., *Complete mappings of finite groups*, Pacific J. Math. 5 (1955), 541–549.

HANANI, H., *On the number of orthogonal Latin squares*, J. Comb. Th. 8 (1970), 247–271.

HANANI, H., *On transversal designs*, In: Combinatorics. Math. Centre Tracts 55, Mathematisch Centrum, Amsterdam, (1974), 42–52.

HANANI, H., *A class of 3-designs*, J. Comb. Th. (A) 26 (1979), 1–19.

HAYDEN, J.L., *A representation theory for Cartesian groups*, Algebras, Groups and Geometries 2 (1985), 399–427.

HAYDEN, J.L., Personal communication (1987).

HAYDEN, J.L., *Elementary abelian cartesian groups*, (1989), (to appear).

HEDAYAT, A.S. AND SHRIKHANDE, S.S., *Experimental designs and combinatorial systems associated with Latin squares and sets of mutually orthogonal Latin squares*, Sankhya (A) 33 (1971), 423–432.

HEDAYAT, A.S. AND STUFKEN, J., *Orthogonal arrays and their applications*, (1989), (to appear).

HEDAYAT, A. AND WALLIS, W.D., *Hadamard matrices and their applications*, Ann. Stat. 6 (1978), 1184–1238.

HEDEN, O, *Maximal partial spreads and two-weight codes*, Discr. Math. 62 (1986), 277–293.

HEDEN, O., *Maximal partial spreads and the n-queen problem (1989), (to appear)*.

HERZER, A., *Endliche nicht-kommutative Gruppen mit Partition π und fixpunktfreiem π-Automorphismus*, Archiv Math. 34 (1980), 385–392.

HERZER, A. AND SCHULZ, R.-H., *Some new (s, k, λ)-translation transversal designs with non-abelian translation group*, J. Geom. (1989), (to appear).

HINE, T.C. AND MAVRON, V.C., *Embeddable transversal designs*, Discr. Math. 29 (1980), 191–200.

HINE, T.C. AND MAVRON, V.C., *Translations of symmetric and complete nets*, Math. Z. 182 (1983), 237–244.

HIRAMINE, Y., *A Conjecture on affine planes of prime order*, (1989), (to appear).

HIRSCHFELD, J.W.P., *Finite projective spaces of three dimensions*, Oxford University Press (1985).

HOFFMAN, A.J., *Cyclic affine planes*, Canad. J. Math. 4 (1952), 295–301.

HSU, D.F., *Generalized complete mappings*, Advances in Discrete Math. and Comp. Science, Vol. II. Hadronic Press, Nonantum, Mass. (1987).

HUGHES, D.R., *Partial difference sets*, Amer. J. Math. 78 (1956), 650–674.

HUGHES, D.R., *Biplanes and semibiplanes*, Lecture Notes in Math. 686 Springer (1978), 55–58.

HUGHES, D.R. AND PIPER, F.C., *Projective planes*, Springer, Berlin-Heidelberg-New York (1973).

HUGHES, D.R. AND THOMPSON, J.G., *The H_p-problem and the structure of H_p-groups*, Pacific J. Math. 9 (1959), 1097–1102.

HUPPERT, B., *Endliche Gruppen I*, Springer, Berlin-Heidelberg-New York (1967).

JOHNSON, D., DULMAGE, A.M. AND MENDELSOHN, N.S., *Orthomorphisms of groups and orthogonal Latin squares*, Canad. J. Math. 13 (1961), 356–372.

JOHNSON, N.L., *Maximal partial spreads and central groups*, (1989), (to appear).

JUNGNICKEL, D., *On difference matrices, resolvable transversal designs and generalized Hadamard matrices*, Math. Z., 167 (1979), 49–60.

JUNGNICKEL, D., *On difference matrices and regular Latin squares*, Abh. Math. Sem. Hamburg 50 (1980), 219–231.

JUNGNICKEL, D., *Einige neue Differenzenmatrizen*, Mitt. Math. Sem. Giessen 149 (1981a), 47–57.

JUNGNICKEL, D., *Existence results for translation nets*, In: Finite geometries and designs, London Math. Soc. Lecture Notes 49 (1981b), Cambridge University Press, 172–196.

JUNGNICKEL, D., *Transitive symmetric nets*, Archiv Math. 36 (1981c), 92–96.

JUNGNICKEL, D., *Transversal designs associated with Frobenius groups*, J. Geom 17 (1981d) 140–154.

JUNGNICKEL, D., *Symmetric translation nets*, J. Reine Angew. Math. 235 (1982a), 216–220.

JUNGNICKEL, D., *On automorphism groups of divisible designs*, Canad. J. Math. 34 (1982b), 257–297.

JUNGNICKEL, D., *Maximal partial spreads and translation nets of small deficiency*, J. Algebra 90 (1984a), 119–132.

JUNGNICKEL, D., *The number of designs with classical parameters grows exponentially*, Geom. Ded. 16 (1984b), 167–178.

JUNGNICKEL, D., *Lateinische Quadrate, ihre Geometrien und ihre Gruppen*, Jahresber. DMV 86 (1984c), 69–108.

JUNGNICKEL, D., *On a theorem of Ganley*, Graphs Comb. 3 (1987), 141–143.

JUNGNICKEL, D., *Existence results for translation nets II*, J. Algebra 122 (1989a), 288–298.

JUNGNICKEL, D., *Partial spreads over Z_q*, Linear Alg. Appl. 114/115 (1989b), 95–102.

JUNGNICKEL, D., *On the existence of small quasimultiples of affine and projective planes of arbitrary order*, Discr. Math. (1989c), (to appear).

JUNGNICKEL, D.AND GRAMS, G., *Maximal difference matrices of order ≤ 10*, Discr. Math. 54 (1986), 199–203.

JUNGNICKEL, D.AND LENZ, H., *Two remarks on affine designs with classical parameters*, J. Comb. Th. (A) 38 (1985), 105–109.

JUNGNICKEL, D.AND SANE, S.S., *On extensions of nets*, Pacific J. Math. 103 (1982), 437–455.

JUNGNICKEL, D.AND VEDDER, K., *Square divisible designs with $k = (n + 1)\mu$*, Archiv Math. 43 (1984), 275–284.

KALLAHER, M.J., *Affine planes with transitive collineation groups*, North Holland, Amsterdam-New York-Oxford (1981).

KANTOR, W.M., *Exponential numbers of two-weight codes, difference sets and symmetric designs*, Discr. Math. 46 (1984), 95–98.

KEEDWELL, A.D., *Sequenceable groups: A survey*, In: Finite Geometries and Designs. London Math. Soc. Lecture Notes 49 (1981a), 205–215.

KEEDWELL, A.D., *On the sequenceability of non-abelian groups of order pq*, Disc. Math. 37 (1981b), 203–216.

KEEDWELL, A.D., *On R-sequenceability and R_h-sequenceability of groups*, Annals Discr. Math. 18 (1983a), 535–548.

KEEDWELL, A.D., *On the existence of Super P-groups*, J. Comb. Th. (A) 35 (1983b), 89–97.

KEGEL, O.H., *Nicht-einfache Partitionen endlicher Gruppen*, Archiv Math. 12 (1961a), 170–175.

KEGEL, O.H., *Die Nilpotenz der H_p-Gruppen*, Math. Z. 75 (1961b), 373–376.

LANDER, E.S., *Symmetric designs. An algebraic approach*, Cambridge University Press (1983).

LASKAR, R, *Finite nets of dimension 3*, J. Algebra 32 (1974), 8–25.

LASKAR, R AND DUNBAR, J., *Finite nets of dimension d*, Discr. Math. 22 (1978), 1–24.

LÜNEBURG, H, *Translation planes*, Springer-Berlin-Heidelberg-New York (1980).

MA, S.L., *Partial difference sets*, Discr. Math. 52 (1984), 75–89.

MACNEISH, H.F., *Euler squares*, Ann. Math. 23 (1922), 221–227.

MACWILLIAMS, F.J. AND SLOANE, N.J.A., *The theory of error-correcting codes*, Amsterdam-New York-Oxford (1978).

MANN, H.B., *The construction of orthogonal Latin squares*, Ann. Math. Stat. 13 (1942), 418–423.

MANN, H.B., *On the construction of sets of mutually orthogonal Latin squares*, Ann. Math. Stat. 14 (1943), 401–414.

MANN, H.B., *On orthogonal Latin squares*, Bull. Amer. Math. Soc. 50 (1944), 249–257.

MASUYAMA, M., *On difference sets for constructing orthogonal arrays of index two and of strength two*, Rep. Stat. Appl. Res. JUSE 5 (1957), 27–34.

MAVRON, V.C., *Parallelisms in designs*, J. London Math. Soc. 4 (1972a), 682–684.

MAVRON, V.C., *On the structure of affine designs*, Math. Z. 125 (1972b), 298–316.

MAVRON, V.C., *Translations and parallel classes of lines in affine designs*, J. Comb. Th. (A) 22 (1977), 322–330.

MAVRON, V.C., *A characterization of some symmetric substructures of projective and affine geometries*, Archiv Math. 36 (1981), 281–288.

MAVRON, V.C., *On complete nets which have no symmetric subnets*, Mitt. Math. Sem. Giessen 165 (1984), 83–91.

MCFARLAND, R.L., *Difference sets in abelian groups of order $4p^2$*, Mitt. Math. Sem. Giessen (1989), (to appear).

MENDELSOHN, N.S. AND WOLK, B., *A search for a non-Desarguesian plane of prime order*, In: Proc. Conf. Finite Geometry, Winnipeg, Marcel Dekker, New York (1985), 199–208.

MENON, P.K., *On difference sets whose parameters satisfy a certain relation*, Proc. Amer. Math. Soc. 13 (1962), 739–745.

MESNER, D.M., *Sets of disjoint lines in $PG(3, q)$*, Canad. J. Math. 19 (1967), 273–280.

MILLS, W.H., *Some mutually orthogonal Latin squares*, In: Proc. 8th Southeastern Conf. on Comb., Graph Th. and Computing, Baton Rouge (1977), 473–487.

NORTON, H.W., *The 7×7 squares*, Ann. Eugenics 9 (1939), 269–307.

OSTROM, T.G., *Nets with critical deficiency*, Pacific J. Math. 14 (1964), 1381–1387.

OSTROM, T.G., *Replaceable nets, net collineations, and net extensions*, Canad. J. Math. 18 (1966), 666–672.

OSTROM, T.G., *Finite translation planes*, Lecture Notes in Math. 158, Springer, Berlin-Heidelberg-New York (1970).

PARKER, E.T., *Construction of some sets of mutually orthogonal Latin squares*, Proc. Amer. Math. Soc. 10 (1959), 946–949.

PICKERT, G., *Sechseckgewebe und potenz-assoziative Loops*, Proc. Int. Congr. Math. Amsterdam 2 (1954), 245–246.

PICKERT, G., *Einführung in die endliche Geometrie*, Klett, Stuttgart (1974).

PICKERT, G., *Projektive Ebenen*, Springer, Berlin-Göttingen-Heidelberg. 2nd edition (1955, 1975).

PLACKETT, R.L. AND BURMAN, J.P., *The design of optimum multi-factorial experiments*, Biometrika 33 (1945), 305–325.

RAGHAVARAO, D., *Constructions and combinatorial problems in design of experiments*, Wiley, New York (1971).

RAO, C.R., *Factorial experiments derivable from combinatorial arrangements of arrays*, J. Royal Stat. Soc. Suppl. 9 (1947), 128–139.

RAY-CHAUDHURI, D.K. AND SINGHI, N.M., *On existence and number of orthogonal arrays*, J. Comb. Th. (A) 47 (1988), 28–36.

REIDEMEISTER, K., *Topologische Fragen der Differentialgeometrie, V. Gewebe und Gruppen*, Math. Z. 29 (1929), 427–435.

ROTH, R. AND PETERS, M., *Four pairwise orthogonal Latin squares of order 24*, J. Comb. Th. (A) 44 (1987), 152–155.

SADE, A., *An omission in Norton's list of 7×7 squares*, Ann. Math. Stat. 22 (1951), 306–307.

SAWADE, K., *A Hadamard matrix of order 268*, Graphs Comb. 1 (1985), 185–187.

SCHELLENBERG, P.J., VAN REES, G.M.J. AND VANSTONE, S.A., *Four pairwise orthogonal Latin squares of order 15*, Ars Comb. 6 (1978), 141–150.

SCHÖNHARDT, E., *Über lateinische Quadrate und Unionen*, J. Reine Angew. Math. 163 (1930), 183–229.

SCHULZ, R.H., *Über Blockpläne mit transitiver Dilatationsgruppe*, Math. Z. 98 (1967), 60–82.

SCHULZ, R.H., *Transversal designs and Hughes-Thompson groups*, Mitt. Math. Sem. Giessen 165 (1984), 185–197.

SCHULZ, R.H., *Transversal designs and partitions associated with Frobenius groups*, J. Reine Angew. Math. 355 (1985a), 153–162.

SCHULZ, R.H., *On the classification of translation group divisible designs*, Europ. J. Comb. 6 (1985b), 369–374.

SCHULZ, R.H., *On translation transversal designs with $\lambda > 1$*, Archiv Math. 49 (1987a), 97–102.

SCHULZ, R.H., *Transversal designs with $\lambda > 1$ associated with Frobenius groups*, Results in Math. 12 (1987b), 401–410.

SCHULZ, R.H., *On the existence of generalized triads related to transversal designs*, Ars Comb. 25 B (1988), 203–209.

SEBERRY, J.S., *A construction for generalized Hadamard matrices*, J. Stat. Planning Inf. 4 (1980), 365–368.

SHOR, P.W., *A lower bound for the length of a partial transversal in a latin square*, J. Comb. Th. (A) 33 (1982), 1–8.

SHRIKHANDE, S.S., *On the non-existence of affine resolvable balanced incomplete block designs*, Sankhya 11 (1951), 185–186.

SHRIKHANDE, S.S., *The non-existence of certain affine resolvable balanced incomplete block designs*, Canad. J. Math. 5 (1953), 413–420.

SHRIKHANDE, S.S., *A note on mutually orthogonal Latin squares*, Sankhya (A) 23 (1961), 115–116.

SHRIKHANDE, S.S., *Generalized Hadamard matrices and orthogonal arrays of strength two*, Canad. J. Math. 16 (1964), 736–740.

SHRIKHANDE, S.S., *Affine resolvable balanced incomplete block designs. A survey*, Aequat. Math. 14 (1976), 251–269.

SHRIKHANDE, S.S. AND BHAGWANDAS, *On embeddings of orthogonal arrays of strength two*, In: Combinatorial mathematics and its applications. Univ. of North Carolina Press (1976), 256–273.

SHRIKHANDE, S.S. AND SINGHI, N.M., *A note on embeddings of orthogonal arrays of strength two*, J. Stat. Planning Inf. 3 (1979a), 267–271.

SHRIKHANDE, S.S. AND SINGHI, N.M., *Embedding of orthogonal arrays of strength two and deficiency greater than two*, J. Stat. Planning Inf. 3 (1979b), 367–379.

SHRIKHANDE, S.S. AND SINGHI, N.M., *Designs, adjacency multi-graphs and embeddings: A survey*, In: Combinatorics and graph theory. Lecture Notes in Math. 885 Springer-Berlin-Heidelberg-New York (1981), 113–132.

SIMMONS, G.J., *How to (really) share a secret*, Proc. of Crypto '88 Santa Barbara (1989a), (to appear).

SIMMONS, G.J., *Robust shared secret schemes*, 18th Conf. on Numerical Math. and Computing Winnipeg '88, Congr. Numer. (1989b), (to appear).

SINGER, J., *A theorem in finite projective geometry and some applications to number theory*, Trans. Amer. Math. Soc. 43 (1938), 377–385.

SKORNYAKOV, L.A., *Projective planes*, Amer. Math. Soc. Transl. 99 (1953).

SPERA, A.G., *On (s, k, λ)-partitions of a vector space*, (1989), (to appear).

SPRAGUE, A.P., *A characterization of 3-nets*, J. Comb. Th. (A) 27 (1979), 223–253.

SPRAGUE, A.P., *Incidence structures whose planes are nets*, Europ. J. Comb. 2 (1981), 193–204.

SPRAGUE, A.P., *Translation nets*, Mitt. Math. Sem. Giessen 157 (1982), 46–68.

STINSON, D.R., *A short proof of the non-existence of a pair of orthogonal Latin squares of order 6*, J. Comb. Th. (A) 36 (1984), 373–376.

STRAMBACH, K., *Geometry and Loops*, In: Geometries and groups. Lecture Notes in Mathematics 893, Springer, Berlin-Heidelberg-New York (1981), 111–147.

STREET, A.P. AND STREET, D.J., *Combinatorics of experimental design*, Oxford University Press (1987).

SUZUKI, M., *On a finite group with a partition*, Archiv Math. 12 (1961), 241–254.

TARRY, G., *Le problème des 36 officiers*, Compte Rendu Ass. Franc. pour l'avancement des Sciences 1 (1900), 122–123.

TARRY, G, *Le problème des 36 officiers*, Compte Rendu Ass. Franc. pour l'avancement des Sciences 2 (1901), 170–203.

THIELE, J., *Gewebe, deren Ternärkörper ans einem Vektorraum hervorgeht*, Mitt. Math. Sem. Giessen 140 (1979).

THOMSEN, G., *Topologische Fragen der Differentialgeometrie XII*, Schnittpunktsätze in ebenen Geometrien. Abh. Math. Sem. Hamburg 7 (1930), 99–106.

TODOROV, D.T., *Three mutually orthogonal Latin squares of order 14*, Ars Comb. 20 (1985), 45–48.

TODOROV, D.T., *Four mutually orthogonal Latin squares of order 20*, Ars Comb. 27 (1989), 63–65.

TURYN, R.J., *Character sums and difference sets*, Pacific J. Math. 15 (1965), 319–346.

TURYN, R.J., *A special class of Williamson matrices and difference sets*, J. Comb. Th. (A) 36 (1984), 111–115.

VERHEIDEN, E., *Integral and rational completion of combinatorial matrices*, J. Comb. Th. (A) 25 (1978), 267–276.

WALLIS, W.D., *Three orthogonal Latin squares*, Congr. Numer. 42 (1984), 69–86.

WANG, S.P., *On self-orthogonal Latin squares and partial transversals of Latin squares*, Ph.D. thesis, Ohio State University (1978).

WILD, P., *On semiplanes*, Ph.D. thesis, Univ. of London (1980).

WILD, P., *Biaffine planes and divisible designs*, J. Geom. 25 (1985), 121–130.

WILSON, R.M., *An existence theory for pairwise balanced designs I. Composition theorems and morphisms*, J. Comb. Th. (A) 13 (1972a), 220–245.

WILSON, R.M., *An existence theory for pairwise balanced designs II. The structure of PBD-closed sets and the existence conjectures*, J. Comb. Th. (A) 13 (1972b), 246–273.

WILSON, R.M., *A few more squares*, In: Proc. 5th Southeastern Conf. Comb., Graph Th. and Computing (1974a), 675–680.

WILSON, R.M., *Concerning the number of mutually orthogonal Latin squares*, Discr. Math. 9 (1974b), 181–198.

WILSON, R.M., *An existence theory for pairwise balanced designs III. Proof of the existence conjectures*, J. Comb. Th. (A) 18 (1975), 71–79.

WOJTAS, M., *A note on mutually orthogonal Latin squares*, Inst. matem. Politechniki Wroclawskiej, Kommunikat No. 236 (1978).

WOODCOCK, E.F., *On orthogonal Latin squares*, J. Comb. Th. (A) 43 (1986), 146–148.

ZHU, L., *Six pairwise orthogonal Latin squares of order 69*, J. Austral. Math. Soc. (A) 37 (1984), 1–3.

ZSIGMONDY, K., *Zur Theorie der Potenzreste*, Monatsh f. Math. u. Physik 3 (1892), 265–284.

A 4-(15,5,5) DESIGN

DONALD L. KREHER†

Abstract. A 4-(15,5,5) design is constructed using the algorithms in the design theory toolchest. This toolchest was presented at the Institute for Mathematics and its Applications Workshop on Coding Theory and Design Theory, June 13 - 25, 1988.

Key words. t-designs

For definitions and notation the reader is refered to [1] and [2]. The later publication appears in this very same volume.

Suppose that the 15 points of our desired $4 - (15, 5, 5)$ design is $X = \mathbf{Z}_{13} \cup \{+\infty, -\infty\}$ and assume that G the group of order 39 generated by $f : x \to x + 1$ and $g : x \to 3 \cdot x$ is an automorphism group. Then the $A_{4,5}$ matrix belonging to G has 43 rows and 85 columns. This results in a diophantine system of 43 equations in 85 unknowns $A_{4,5}U = 5J$ as described in [1,2]. This system was constructed and a solution was found by using the algorithms in the design theory toolchest [2]. The simple 4-(15,5,5) design coressponding to this solution is given in figure 1 as a list of orbit representatives. No other design with these parameters is known.

0 1 2 4 5	0 1 5 6 7	0 1 5 6 8	0 1 5 7 9	0 1 2 7 9
0 1 3 6 10	0 1 2 5 10	0 1 5 6 10	0 1 2 7 11	0 1 4 5 11
0 1 4 7 11	0 1 7 8 11	0 1 6 7 11	0 1 5 7 12	0 1 4 5 12
0 1 4 6 $+\infty$	0 1 4 5 $+\infty$	0 1 3 6 $+\infty$	0 1 2 7 $+\infty$	0 1 3 7 $+\infty$
0 1 3 9 $+\infty$	0 1 6 7 $+\infty$	0 1 5 9 $+\infty$	0 1 5 11 $+\infty$	0 1 8 10 $+\infty$
0 1 3 9 $-\infty$	0 1 7 12 $+\infty$	0 1 4 6 $-\infty$	0 1 3 6 $-\infty$	0 1 4 7 $-\infty$
0 1 5 12 $-\infty$	0 1 7 10 $-\infty$	0 1 7 9 $-\infty$	0 1 5 11 $-\infty$	0 1 8 10 $-\infty$
0 1 7 11 $-\infty$	0 1 7 12 $-\infty$	0 1 5 $+\infty$ $-\infty$	0 1 4 $+\infty$ $-\infty$	0 1 6 $+\infty$ $-\infty$
0 2 7 $+\infty$ $-\infty$	0 1 10 $+\infty$ $-\infty$	0 2 8 $+\infty$ $-\infty$		

Figure 1. Orbit representatives for a 4-(15,5,5) design

Acknowledgements. This research was supported under NSF grant number CCR-8711229 and completed during my stay at the Institute for Mathematics and Applications at University of Minnesota.

REFERENCES

[1] D. L. KREHER AND S. P. RADZISZOWSKI, *Constructing 6-(14,7,4) designs.*
[2] D. L. KREHER, *Design Theory Toolchest - User Manual and Report.*

†School of Computer Science, Rochester Institute of Technology, Rochester, New York 14623

DESIGN THEORY TOOLCHEST - USER MANUAL AND REPORT

DONALD L. KREHER†

Abstract. A package of algorithms that have been successful in constructing $t - (v, k, \lambda)$ designs is described and a user manual is also given. This package is available by contacting the author.

Key words. t-designs, automorphisms, algorithms

1. Introduction and theoretical overview. In this section we give a brief description of the theoretical background for the algorithms contained in this first version of the Design Theory Toolchest. A more complete description can be found in [2].

A *t-design* or *t-(v, k, λ) design* is a pair $(X, \mathcal{B})$ where X is a v-set of *points* and $\mathcal{B}$ is a family of k-subsets of X called *blocks* such that any t-points are contained in exactly λ blocks. A t-(v, k, λ) design is *simple* if no block in $\mathcal{B}$ is repeated and is said to have $G \leq Sym(X)$ as an *automorphism group* if whenever K is a block $K^\alpha = \{x^\alpha : x \in \mathcal{B}\}$ is also a block for all $\alpha \in G$.

Given a group $G \leq Sym(X)$ and integers $0 < t < v = |X|$, let $\Delta_1, \Delta_2, ... \Delta_{N_t}$ and $\Gamma_1, \Gamma_2, ... \Gamma_{N_k}$ be the the G-orbits of t and k-subsets of X. Define the N_t by N_k matrix $A_{tk} = A_{tk}(G|X)$ by $A_{tk}[\Delta_i, \Gamma_j] = |\{K \in \Gamma_j : K \supseteq T_0\}|$ where $T_0 \in \Delta_i$ is any fixed representative. Let $J_{N_t} = [1, 1, ..., 1]^T$. The following observation of Kramer and Mesner was given in 1976 [1].

A $t - (v, k, \lambda)$ designs exists with $G \leq Sym(X)$ as an automorphism group if and only if there is an integer solution U to the matrix equation

(1)
$$A_{tk}U = \lambda \cdot J_{N_t}$$

A $(0, 1)$-solution U to equation (1) represents a a simple design. A $(0,1)$-solution U that has some entry greater than 1 establishes the existence of a t-design with repeated blocks.

To solve equation (1) we use the following method. First the basis $\mathfrak{B}$ consisting of the columns of the matrix M below is constructed.

$$M = \begin{bmatrix} I & 0 \\ A_{tk} & -\lambda \cdot J \end{bmatrix}.$$

It now can be observed that if U is a solution to equation (1), then

$$M \cdot \begin{bmatrix} U \\ 1 \end{bmatrix} = \begin{bmatrix} U \\ 0 \end{bmatrix}.$$

Thus $U' = [U, 0] \in \mathcal{L} = Span_{\mathbf{Z}}(\mathfrak{B})$ and $\|U'\|^2 \leq N_k/2$. Hence our desired solution is a particular short vector "in" $\mathcal{L}$. Consequently we investigate transformations $\tau : \mathcal{L} \to \mathcal{L}$ that have the property the the "new" basis $\tau(\mathfrak{B})$ has shorter vectors then the "old" basis $\mathfrak{B}$. The belief is that it is likely that after applying several such transformations repeatedly to the basis that the desired solution will appear in it.

---

†School of Computer Science, Rochester Institute of Technology, Rochester, New York 14623

2. Users Guide and Example. In this section we describe how to use the package of computer programs which were developed to carry out the necessary operations presented in section 1.

The design Theory toolchest [version 1 , 1988] consists of the following 28 commands.

Auto	Fours	Info	L3	Makebasis
Move	Pairs	PartL3	Show	Sort
Sq	Swap	Triples	bnd_mat_grp	bnd_mat_list
create	cycletype	display	extract	gen
grplist	mat_grp	mat_list	norb_grp	norb_list
order	reps_grp	reps_list		

Figure 1. Commands available in the Design Theory Toolchest

Each of the commands in Figure 1 operate on and produce files with file names of the form *name.type*. We intend *name* to represent the problem name and *type* to be the type of data stored in that file. The meaning of *type* is given below.

gen - Generators of the group.

grp - Schrier-Sims compact representation of finite permutation groups.

list - List of all permutations in some group.

norb - Number of orbits of k-subsets, $k = 0, 1, 2, .., v$.

Rk - List of orbit representatives of k-subsets, k is an integer , $0 \le k \le v$.

mat - An A_{tk} matrix for some value of t and k.

basis - The basis $\mathfrak{B}$.

sol - Set of solutions U to equation (1) found so far.

desi - List of of orbit representatives of the blocks of the i-th design found.

cyc - List of cycle types obtained from some list of permutations.

A complete description of the commands in Figure 1 is given in section 3. Alternatively, the usage of a particular command can be obtained by simply entering the command without any arguments.

We now give a small example which we will call problem FANO. Suppose we suspect that $G = < (1\ 4\ 5)(2\ 0\ 6), (2\ 6)(4\ 5) >$ is an automorphism group of a 2-(7,3,1) design on $X = \{0, 1, 2, 3, 4, 5, 6\}$. The first thing that must be done is to enter the group. To enter the generators type

create FANO 7 2

since there are 7 points and 2 generators. This command will now promt you to input the group generators in cycle notation. Having done this they can be displayed with

display FANO.gen

Now the command

gen FANO

can be used to obtain the compact Schrier-Sims representation of the group. Finally, if we wish to have a list of all the elements in G the command

grplist FANO

is used. In general this is a good idea if the group is fairly small (say under 2000 for a small computer). At this point we have two representations for the group (i) FANO.grp the Schrier-Sims representation and (ii) FANO.list the list of all the group elements.

The second task is to construct the $A_{2,3}$ matrix. This requires executing the following three command.

norb_list FANO   or   norb_grp FANO

reps_list FANO 0 3   or   reps_grp FANO 0 3

mat_list FANO 2 3   or   mat_grp FANO 2 3

If the group is fairly small the commands ending in _list should be used otherwise one can use those ending with _grp. The parameters 0 3 are used to obtain all orbit representatives of i-subsets, $0 < i \leq 3$. The last command constructs the $A_{2,3}$ matrix and writes it to the file FANO.mat. Now we can seek a solution to equation (1) using the method described in Section 1. To obtain the basis $\mathfrak{B}$ the command

Makebasis FANO 2 7 3 1

is used. Then the transformations

L3 FANO

Pairs FANO

Triples FANO

and

Fours FANO

can be applied repeatedly in any order to the basis in hopes of obtaining a reduced basis in which the solution appears. L3 is the Lovász algorithm as described in [2,3] and the other transformations are what we call weight reduction and are described in [2]. To display the current basis the command

Show FANO

is available and to obtain statistics about the length of the basis vectors we have

Info FANO

229

This last command also checks for solutions U and appends them to the file FANO.sol. Warning if Info is executed many times during the course of applying the transformations the solution file FANO.sol may contain duplicate solutions and should be edited before proceeding. Finally to get the orbit representatives of say the first 2 solutions the command

extract FANO 2

will construct the files FANO.des1 and FANO.des2 containing these orbit representatives. The commands

Auto + 100 FANO

Auto - 100 FANO

and

Sq FANO

are also very useful. The first two do an automatic search with 100 iterations of L3, Pairs and Triples in the order we have found heristically most profitable. The command Sq preforms what is called size reduction in [2] and converts *a.basis* into a basis for the integer solution space to equation (1).

3. Manual. A complete description of the commands is given in this section. For clarity italics have been used to indicate the contents of a variable and not the name of the variable. In Figures 2 and 3 the interelationships between commands and files are given.

Auto + num name

Automatic search on *name*.basis with ascending sort and num iterations.

Auto - num name

Automatic search on *name*.basis with descending sort and num iterations.

Fours name

Replace *name*.basis with new basis obtained by looking at $+/-$ 1 combinations of four vectors at a time.

Info name

Display statistics about *name*.basis, e.g. length of vectors, total weight , e.t.c. This command also checks for solutions and writes them to the file *name*.sol.

L3 name

Replace *name*.basis with new basis obtained by Lovász algorithm.

Makebasis name t v k λ

Create *name*.basis from *name*.mat of the form

$$\begin{bmatrix} I & A^T \\ 0 & B^T \end{bmatrix}$$

230

where A^T is A_{tk} transpose and orbit lengths, B^T is $-[\lambda * J, b]$ where b is the number of blocks in a $t - (v, k, \lambda)$ design.

Makebasis name t v k λ f

Same as above except B^T is $-([\lambda * J, b] - H)$. where H is the $(n+1)$-dimensional vector in file f and n is the number of orbits of k-subsets.

Pairs name

Replace *name*.basis with new basis obtained by looking at $+/-$ 1 combinations of two vectors at a time.

PartL3 arg1 arg2 name

Replace *name*.basis with the reduced basis obtained from the Lovász algorithm applied only to the basis vectors between arg1 and arg2 (inclusive).

Show name

Display *name*.basis .

Sort + name

Replace *name*.basis with new basis obtained by an ascending sort of the basis vectors by their lengths.

Sort - name

Replace *name*.basis with new basis obtained by a descending sort of the basis vectors by their lengths.

Sq name

Replace *name*.basis with basis for for the lattice of integer solutions U to $A_{tk} cdot U - \lambda J = 0$.

Swap arg1 arg2 name

Replace *name*.basis with new basis obtained by interchanging basis vectors arg1 and arg2.

Triples name

Replace *name*.basis with new basis obtained by looking at $+/-$ 1 combinations of three vectors at a time

bnd_mat_list name t k bound

Create *name_bound*.mat and *name_bound*.Rk from *name*.list , *name*.Rt and *name*.Rk. Here *name_bound*.mat is the submatrix of the A_{tk} matrix obtained by deleting all columns which have an entry greater than *bound*. The file *name_bound*.Rk consist of the corresponding remaining orbit representatives of k-subsets. This command will instruct you to do minor editing of the output files.

bnd_mat_grp name t k bound

Create *name_bound*.mat and *name_bound*.Rk from *name*.grp, *name*.Rt and *name*.Rk. Here *name_bound*.*mat* is the submatrix of the A_{tk} matrix obtained by deleting all columns which have an entry less than *bound*. The file *name_bound*.Rk consist of the corresponding remaining orbit representatives of k-subsets. This command will instruct you to do minor editing of the output files.

create name v n

Create generator file *name*.gen of permutations, where $v =$ degree of the representation and $n =$ number of generators.

cycletype name

Create *name*.cyc from *name*.list. The j-th entry of the i-th line of this file is the number of cycles of length j contained in the i-th permutation on *name*.list.

display permutation_file

Displays permutations in cycle notation. This command is typically used with permutation_file being either *name*.gen or *name*.list.

extract name k Nsols

Create *name*.desi from *name*.sol, and *name*.Rk where k is the block size and $Nsols$ is the number of solutions. Then *name*.desi is a list of orbit representatives for the i-th solution found, $i = 1, 2, .., Nsols$.

gen name

Create *name*.grp from *name*.gen. This is the Schrier-Sims compact representation for a finite permutation group.

grplist name

Create *name*.list from *name*.grp. The resulting file *name*.list is a list of all group elements.

mat_grp name t k

Create *name*.mat from *name*.grp, *name*.Rt and *name*.Rk. The resulting file *name*.mat contains the transposed A_{tk} matrix.

mat_list name t k

Create *name*.mat from *name*.list, *name*.Rt and *name*.Rk. The resulting file *name*.mat contains the transposed A_{tk} matrix.

norb_grp name

Create *name*.norb from *name*.grp. The i-th entry of this file is the number of orbits of i-subsets, $0 \leq i \leq deg$.

norb_list name

Create *name*.norb from *name*.list . The i-th entry of this file is the number of orbits of i-subsets, $0 \leq i \leq deg$.

order name

Print the order of the group generated by gen and stored in *name*.grp.

reps_grp name start finish

Create *name*.R*i* from *name*.grp for each $i, start \le i \le finish$. These are orbit representatives. Usually *start* is 0 and *finish* is k, however, if the process is interrupted or if you wish to construct a design with larger block size k, then use $start = i + 1$ where *name*.R*i* is the last valid file of orbit representatives.

reps_list name start finish

Create *name*.R*i* from *name*.list for each $i, start \le i \le finish$. These are orbit representatives. Usually *start* is 0 and *finish* is k, however, if the process is interrupted or if you wish to construct a design with larger block size k, then use $start = i + 1$ where *name*.R*i* is the last valid file of orbit representatives.

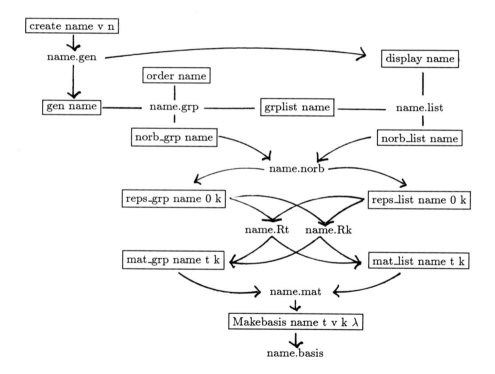

Figure 2. Toolchest file dependencies I

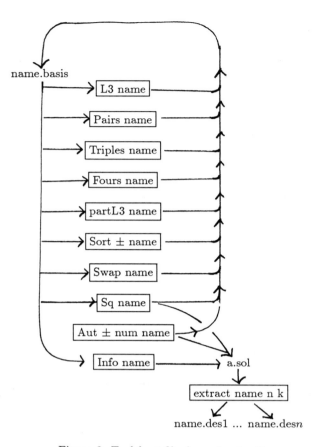

Figure 3. Toolchest file dependencies II

4. Hints. After constructing the basis the program "Sq" should almost always be run. This will not only reduce your file storage space, but will also often find a solution to equation (1). The program "Auto " is essentially the MSV algorithm in [2]. We run it only when "Sq" fails to find a solution.

The file *a.mat* constructed by either "mat_list a t k" or "mat_grp a t k" contains the entire A_{tk} matrix and this may not be what is wanted. There are two things which can be done. (1) Use "bnd_mat_list a t k λ" or "bnd_mat_grp a t k λ" as described above or (2) use the editor to delete unwanted orbits from *a.Rk* and the use "mat_list a t k" to construct the restricted matrix. Also, if some orbits of *t*-subsets should be covered more often than others, then this can be specified by the second form of "Makebasis " as described in the Manual.

5. Closing remarks. This is version 1 of the Design Theory Toolchest and contains a small number of algorithms or (if you like) *tools*. We hope to add many more tools and hope that other researchers will submit tools to be included in this package. The current package is implemented in C and can be obtained from the author at minimal charge by writing the author.

Acknowledgements. This research was supported under NSF grant number CCR-8711229 and completed during my stay at the Institute for Mathematics and Applications at University of Minnesota. I would also like to thank J. Dinitz, W. Bridges and especially S. Hobart for putting this package to the test and making helpful suggestions. I am also indebted to S. Radziszowski for his help in writing the initial version of the basis reduction algorithms.

REFERENCES

[1] E. S. KRAMER AND D. MESNER, *t-designs on Hypergraphs*, Discr. Math., 15 (1976), pp. 263-296.

[2] D. L. KREHER AND S. P. RADZISZOWSKI, *Constructing 6-(14,7,4) designs*.

[3] A. K. LENSTRA, H. W. LENSTRA AND L. LOVÁSZ, *Factoring Polynomials with Rational Coefficients*, Mathematische Annalen, 261 (1982), pp. 515-534.

CONSTRUCTIONS FOR RESOLVABLE AND NEAR RESOLVABLE $(v, k, k-1) - BIBDs$

E.R. LAMKEN*

Abstract. In this paper, we use resolvable transversal designs to construct resolvable, near resolvable and doubly resolvable $BIBDs$, as well as generalized and near generalized balanced tournament designs. We describe four basic constructions and show that they can be used to produce several new classes of these designs. Of particular interest are the first examples of $DR(v, k, \lambda) - BIBDs$ where the block size k is not a prime power and the first infinite classes of generalized and near generalized balanced tournament designs with block size k greater than 3. In addition, connections between the basic constructions for resolvable and near resolvable $BIBDs$ and constructions for generalized and near generalized balanced tournament designs are described.

1. Introduction. A group divisible design (GDD) is a collection B of subsets (blocks) of size k taken from a v-set V along with a partition of V into subsets (groups) $G_1, G_2, \ldots, G_m$ such that

(1) any two elements from distinct groups are contained in precisely λ_2 blocks of B, and

(2) any two distinct elements from the same group are contained in exactly λ_1 blocks of B $(\lambda_1 < \lambda_2)$.

We denote such a design by $GDD(v; k; G_1, G_2, \ldots, G_m; \lambda_1, \lambda_2)$. If $|G_i| = n$ for $i = 1, 2, \ldots, m$, we denote the design by $GDD(v; k; n; \lambda_1, \lambda_2)$. A transversal design, $TD(k, n)$, is a GDD which has k groups of size n, block size k, $\lambda_1 = 0$ and $\lambda_2 = 1$ or a $GDD(nk; k; n; 0, 1)$. It is well known that the existence of a $TD(k, n)$ is equivalent to the existence of a set of $k - 2$ mutually orthogonal Latin squares of side n.

A combinatorial design D with replication number r is said to be resolvable if the blocks of D can be partitioned into classes (called resolution classes) $R_1, R_2, \ldots, R_r$ such that each element of D is contained in precisely one block of each class. A resolvable $TD(k, n)$ is denoted by $RTD(k, n)$. The existence of a $RTD(k, n)$ is equivalent to the existence of a set of $k - 1$ mutually orthogonal Latin squares of side n.

Resolvable transversal designs can be used to construct resolvable, near resolvable and doubly resolvable balanced incomplete block designs, as well as generalized and near generalized balanced tournament designs. In this paper, we describe several of these constructions and show that they can be applied to produce new designs.

In order to describe our constructions, we will need several definitions and existence results for various types of resolvable designs. These are collected in the next section. We include in section 2 a survey of existence results for resolvable

---

*Institute for Mathematics and its Applications, University of Minnesota, Minneapolis, MN 55455. This research was supported by a Postdoctoral membership at the Institute for Mathematics and its Applications.

and near resolvable balanced incomplete block designs. The main constructions are contained in section 3, and in section 4 we describe some of the new designs that have been found using these constructions. Of particular interest to us are the first examples of $DR(v, k, \lambda) - BIBDs$ where k is not a prime power and the first infinite classes of generalized and near generalized balanced tournament designs with block size $k \geq 4$.

2. Preliminary definitions and results. A balanced incomplete block design $(BIBD)$ D is a collection B of subsets (blocks) taken from a v-set V with the following properties:

(1) Every pair of distinct elements from V is contained in precisely λ blocks of B.

(2) Every block contains exactly k elements.

We denote such a design as a $(v, k, \lambda) - BIBD$. It is well known that necessary conditions for the existence of a $(v, k, \lambda) - BIBD$ are

(1) $\qquad \lambda(v - 1) \equiv 0 \ (\mathrm{mod}(k - 1)) \quad \text{and} \quad \lambda v(v - 1) \equiv 0 \ (\mathrm{mod}\, k(k - 1)).$

A resolvable $(v, k, \lambda) - BIBD$ is denoted by $(v, k, \lambda) - RBIBD$. Necessary conditions for the existence of a $(v, k, \lambda) - RBIBD$ are that (1) be satisfied and that $v \equiv 0$ (mod k).

A $(v, k, \lambda) - BIBD$ D is said to be near resolvable (and denoted by $NR(v, k, \lambda) - BIBD$) if the blocks of D can be partitioned into classes $R_1, R_2, \ldots, R_v$ (resolution classes) such that for each element x of D there is precisely one class which does not contain x in any of its blocks and each class contains precisely $v - 1$ distinct elements of the design. Necessary conditions for the existence of $NR(v, k, \lambda) - BIBDs$ are $v \equiv 1$ (mod k) and $\lambda = k - 1$.

In general, the spectrum of resolvable and near resolvable $(v, k, \lambda) - BIBDs$ remains open. The existence of these designs has been established for several small values of k and λ. In this paper, we are primarily interested in the case $\lambda = k - 1$. For completeness, we include results for other values of λ. It is well known that there exists a $(v, 2, 1) - RBIBD$ for v a positive integer and $v \equiv 0$ (mod 2) and that there exists a $NR(v, 2, 1) - BIBD$ for v a positive integer and $v \equiv 1$ (mod 2). The existence of $RBIBDs$ and $NRBIBDs$ has also been established for block size $k = 3$; the necessary conditions are sufficient (with one exception).

THEOREM 2.1. (Ray–Chaudhuri and Wilson [17]). There exists a $(v, 3, 1) - RBIBD$ if and only if $v \equiv 3$ (mod 6).

THEOREM 2.2. (Hanani [8]). (i) There exists a $(v, 3, 2) - RBIBD$ if and only if $v \equiv 0$ (mod 3) and $v \neq 6$.
(ii) There exists a $NR(v, 3, 2) - BIBD$ if and only if $v \equiv 1$ (mod 3), $v \geq 4$.

For block size $k = 4$, the following results are known.

THEOREM 2.3. (Hanani, Ray–Chaudhuri and Wilson [9]). There exists a $(v, 4, 1) - RBIBD$ if and only if $v \equiv 4 \pmod{12}$.

THEOREM 2.4. (Baker [1]). There exists a $(v, 4, 3) - RBIBD$ if and only if $v \equiv 0 \pmod{4}$.

Less information is available for block size larger than 4. For block sizes 5, 6 and 8, resolvable $BIBDs$ have been investigated for $\lambda = 1$, 10 and 7 respectively.

THEOREM 2.5. (D. Chen and L. Zhu [4], D. Chen, B. Du and L. Zhu [6]). There exists a $(v, 5, 1) - RBIBD$ for every positive integer $v \equiv 5 \pmod{20}$ except for 147 possible exceptions for v, the largest of which is 23,085.

THEOREM 2.6. (R. Baker [1]). There exists a $(v, 6, 10) - RBIBD$ if and only if $v \equiv 0 \pmod{6}$.

THEOREM 2.7. (B. Rokowska [19]). If $v \equiv 0 \pmod{8}$ and v is not divisible by 3, 5 or 7, there exists a $(v, 8, 7) - RBIBD$.

Some other infinite classes of $RBIBDs$ are known to exist. We list one example below. Two other examples are included in our list of results for doubly resolvable $BIBDs$.

THEOREM 2.8. (B. Rokowska [18]). If p is a power of a prime number, there exists a $(2p^2, 2p, 2p - 1) - RBIBD$.

A combinatorial design D with replication number r is said to be doubly (near) resolvable if there exist two (near) resolutions R and R' of the blocks such that $|R_i \cap R'_j| \leq 1$ for all $R_i \in R, R'_j \in R'$. (It should be noted that the blocks of the design are considered as being labelled so that if a subset of the elements occurs as a block more than once the blocks are treated as distinct.) The (near) resolutions R and R' are called orthogonal resolutions of the design. In this paper, we restrict our attention to doubly resolvable $BIBDs$.

A doubly resolvable $(v, k, \lambda) - BIBD$ is denoted by $DR(v, k, \lambda) - BIBD$. Even less is known about the spectrum of doubly resolvable $(v, k, \lambda) - BIBDs$. Although several infinite classes of $DR(v, k, \lambda) - BIBDs$ are known to exist for $k \geq 2$ ([5,7,21]), the existence of $DR(v, k, \lambda) - BIBDs$ has been settled completely for only one set of parameters, $k = 2$ and $\lambda = 1$. ($DR(v, 2, 1) - BIBDs$ are also called Room squares.)

THEOREM 2.9. (Mullin and Wallis [16]). There exists a $DR(v, 2, 1) - BIBD$ for v a positive integer, $v \equiv 0 \pmod{2}$ and $v \neq 4$ or 6.

For block size $k = 3$ the problem is more difficult. The best result, thus far, for $\lambda = 1$ is asymptotic.

THEOREM 2.10. (Rosa and Vanstone [20]). There exists a constant v_1 such that for all $v_1 \leq v$ and $v \equiv 3 \pmod{6}$ there exists a $DR(v, 3, 1) - BIBD$.

The next parameter set to consider, $k = 3$ and $\lambda = 2$, is more tractable. Quite recently the spectrum of $DR(v, 3, 2) - BIBDs$ has been settled with a small number of possible exceptions, [12].

For $k \geq 3$, some infinite classes of $DR(v, k, \lambda) - BIBDs$ have been constructed. We include two of these results.

THEOREM 2.11. *(Fuji–Hara and Vanstone [7]). For p a prime power and n a positive integer greater than 2, there exists a $DR(p^n, p, 1) - BIBD$.*

THEOREM 2.12. *(Curran and Vanstone [5]). For k a prime power and $k \geq 3$ there exists a $DR(k^2 + k, \ k, k - 1) - BIBD$.*

We note that none of the $DR(v, k, \lambda) - BIBDs$ described above have block size k where k is *not* a prime power.

In the next section, we will also show how to modify our constructions for resolvable and near resolvable $BIBDs$ to produce various types of generalized balanced tournament designs. We include the necessary definitions in this section and refer to [10, 11, 13, 14] for further information and results about these designs.

A generalized balanced tournament design, $GBTD(n, k)$, defined on a kn-set V, is an arrangement of the blocks of a $(kn, k, k - 1) - BIBD$ defined on V into an $n \times (kn - 1)$ array such that

(1) every element of V is contained in precisely one cell of each column, and

(2) every element of V is contained in at most k cells of each row.

It is easy to see that a $GBTD(n, k)$ is a $(kn, k, k - 1) - RBIBD$ where the columns form the resolution classes of the $RBIBD$.

Let G be a $GBTD(n, k)$. An element which is contained in only $k - 1$ cells of row i of G is called a deficient element of row i. It is easily seen that each row of G contains exactly k deficient elements. These elements are called the deficient k-tuple of row i. An important observation is the following.

LEMMA 2.13. *The deficient k-tuples of G partition the set V into n k-tuples.*

Let $C = (C_1, C_2, \ldots, C_n)^T$ where C_i, $1 \leq i \leq n$, is the deficient k-tuple of row i of G. If C occurs as a column in G $k - 1$ times, then G is said to have Property C.

Suppose the blocks of row i of $G \cup C_i$, where C_i is the deficient k-tuple of row i, can be partitioned into k sets of n blocks each, $F_{i1}, F_{i2}, \ldots, F_{ik}$ so that every element of V occurs precisely once in F_{ij} for $j = 1, 2, \ldots k$. If every row of G has this property, then G is called a factored generalized balanced tournament design and is denoted by $FGBTD(n, k)$. We will call $F_{i1}, \ldots, F_{ik}$ the factors of row i. We note that if a $FGBTD(n, k)$ has Property C, then $C_i \in F_{ij}$ for all j.

A near generalized balanced tournament design, $NGBTD(n, k)$, defined on a $(kn + 1)$-set V, is an arrangement of the blocks of a $(kn + 1, k, k - 1) - BIBD$ defined on V into an $n \times (kn + 1)$ array so that

(1) every element of V occurs precisely k times in each row;

(2) every column of the array contains kn distinct elements of V; and

(3) the columns form a near resolution of the $(kn + 1, k, k - 1) - BIBD$.

Two examples of these definitions can be found in section 4; a $FGBTD(4,3)$ with Property C is displayed in Figure 1 and a $NGBTD(5,3)$ appears in Figure 2.

3. Main constructions. In this section, we describe four basic constructions for resolvable and near resolvable $BIBDs$ which use resolvable transversal designs. These constructions are applied in the next section to produce several new infinite classes of designs, including classes of $GBTDs$ and $NGBTDs$ as well as resolvable and near resolvable $BIBDs$.

The first construction is for resolvable $BIBDs$.

THEOREM 3.1. *If there exists a $NR(v, k, k-1) - BIBD$ and a $RTD(k,v)$, then there exists a $(kv, k, k-1) - RBIBD$.*

Proof. Let $V = \bigcup_{i=1}^{k} G_i$ where $G_i = \{x_{i1}, x_{i2}, \ldots, x_{iv}\}$. Suppose D_i is a $NR(v, k, k-1) - BIBD$ defined on G_i. The (near) resolution classes of D_i will be denoted by $R_{i1}, R_{i2}, \ldots, R_{iv}$ where the element x_{ij} does not occur in R_{ij} for $j = 1, 2, \ldots, v$.

Let Y_j be the k-tuple $\{x_{ij}|i = 1, 2, \ldots, k\}$. Suppose T is a $RTD(k,v)$ defined on V where the groups of T are $G_1, G_2, \ldots, G_k$ and such that T contains as a resolution class T_1 the k-tuples $Y_1, Y_2, \ldots, Y_v$. The remaining $v - 1$ resolution classes of T will be denoted by $T_2, T_3, \ldots, T_v$.

We construct a $(kv, k, k-1) - BIBD$ D from $k - 1$ copies of T together with $\bigcup_{i=1}^{k} D_i$. D is a resolvable $BIBD$; the resolution classes are constructed as follows.

(i) There are v resolution classes constructed from $\bigcup_{i=1}^{k} D_i$ and T_1. These are:

$$Y_j, R_{1j}, R_{2j}, \ldots, R_{kj} \quad \text{for} \quad j = 1, 2, \ldots, v.$$

(ii) There are $v - 1$ resolution classes, $T_2, T_3, \ldots, T_v$, from the first copy of T.

(iii) There are $(k - 2)v$ resolution classes from the remaining $k - 2$ copies of T.

□

This construction can be modified to use a $RBIBD$ in place of the $NRBIBD$.

THEOREM 3.2. *If there exists a $(v, k, k-1) - RBIBD$ and a $RTD(k,v)$, then there exists a $(kv, k, k-1) - RBIBD$.*

Proof. Let $V = \bigcup_{i=1}^{k} G_i$ where $G_i = \{x_{i1}, x_{i2}, \ldots, x_{iv}\}$. Suppose D_i is a $(v, k, k-1) - RBIBD$ defined on G_i. The resolution classes of D_i will be denoted by $R_{i1}, R_{i2}, \ldots, R_{i(v-1)}$. Suppose T is a $RTD(k,v)$ defined on V where the groups of T are $G_1, G_2, \ldots, G_k$. Let $T_1, T_2, \ldots, T_v$ denote the resolution classes of T.

We construct a $(kv, k, k-1) - RBIBD$ D from $k-1$ copies of T together with $\bigcup_{i=1}^{k} D_i$. In this case, D will have $v-1$ resolution classes which are constructed from the $(v, k, k-1) - RBIBDs$ (i.e. these resolution classes are $\bigcup_{j=1}^{k} R_{ji}$, $1 \le i \le v-1$) and $(k-1)v$ resolution classes from the $k-1$ copies of T. $\qquad\square$

The next construction is used to find $NRBIBDs$.

THEOREM 3.3. *If there exists a $NR(v, k, k-1) - BIBD$ and a $RTD(k,v)$, then there exists a $NR((k+1)v, k, k-1) - BIBD$.*

Proof. Let $V = \bigcup_{i=1}^{k+1} G_i$ where $G_i = \{x_{i1}, x_{i2}, \ldots, x_{iv}\}$. Suppose D_i is a $NR(v, k, k-1) - BIBD$ defined on G_i. The (near) resolution classes of D_i will be denoted by $R_{i1}, R_{i2}, \ldots, R_{iv}$ where the element x_{ij} does not occur in R_{ij} for $j = 1, 2, \ldots, v$.

Let T_i be a $RTD(k, v)$ defined on $V - G_i$ where the groups of T_i are $G_1, G_2, \ldots, G_{i-1}$, $G_{i+1}, \ldots, G_{k+1}$. Let $S_{i1}, S_{i2}, \ldots, S_{iv}$ denote the resolution classes of T_i.

We construct a $((k+1)v, k, k-1) - BIBD$ D from $\bigcup_{i=1}^{k+1} D_i$ and $\bigcup_{i=1}^{k+1} T_i$. D is a $NR((k+1)v, k, k-1) - BIBD$. The (near) resolution classes of D are

$$R_{ij} \cup S_{ij} \qquad \text{for} \qquad i = 1, 2, \ldots, k+1 \quad \text{and} \quad j = 1, 2, \ldots, v.$$

$$\square$$

The following construction is the analogue of Theorem 3.3 for $RBIBDs$.

THEOREM 3.4. *If there exists a $(v+1, k, k-1) - RBIBD$ and a $RTD(k,v)$, then there exists a $(v(k+1)+1, k, k-1) - RBIBD$.*

Proof. Let $V = \bigcup_{i=1}^{k+1} G_i \cup \{\infty\}$ where $G_i = \{x_{i1}, x_{i2}, \ldots, x_{iv}\}$. Suppose D_i is a $(v+1, k, k-1) - RBIBD$ defined on $G_i \cup \{\infty\}$. The resolution classes of D_i will be denoted by $R_{i1}, R_{i2}, \ldots R_{iv}$.

Let T_i be a $RTD(k, v)$ defined on $V - (G_i \cup \{\infty\})$ where the groups of T_i are $G_1, G_2, \ldots, G_{i-1}, G_{i+1}, \ldots, G_{k+1}$. Let $S_{i1}, S_{i2}, \ldots, S_{iv}$ denote the resolution classes of T_i.

We construct a $(v(k+1)+1, k, k-1) - RBIBD$ D defined on V from $\bigcup_{i=1}^{k+1} D_i$ and $\bigcup_{i=1}^{k+1} T_i$. The resolution classes of D are

$$R_{ij} \cup S_{ij} \quad \text{for} \quad i = 1, 2, \ldots, k+1 \quad \text{and} \quad j = 1, 2, \ldots, v.$$

$$\square$$

4. Applications. In this section, we apply the constructions described in section 3 to produce several new classes of designs. It is interesting and somewhat surprising that even simple examples of these constructions provide previously unknown designs. We begin with an application of Theorem 3.1.

THEOREM 4.1. *Let $k+1$ be a prime power. Then there exists a $(k(k+1), k, k-1) - RBIBD$.*

Proof. In order to apply Theorem 3.1, we require the existence of a $RTD(k, k+1)$ and a $NR(k+1, k, k-1) - BIBD$. If $k+1$ is a prime power, then there exists a set of k mutually orthogonal Latin squares of side $k+1$ and, therefore, a $RTD(k, k+1)$. It is easy to construct a $NR(k+1, k, k-1) - BIBD$ by taking the $k+1$ distinct k–subsets of a $(k+1)$ element set. Thus, we can apply Theorem 3.1 to construct a $(k(k+1), k, k-1) - RBIBD$. □

We note that if k is also a prime power, then these designs have the same parameters as the $RBIBDs$ described in Theorem 2.12. (The designs produced by Theorem 4.1 are not isomorphic to the ones constructed by Theorem 2.12.) However, if k is not a prime power, the $(k(k+1), k, k-1) - RBIBDs$ were not previously known to exist. The two smallest of these new designs are a $(42, 6, 5) - RBIBD$ and a $(110, 10, 9) - RBIBD$.

Applying Theorem 3.1 with $k+1$ a prime power actually produces designs with quite a bit more structure than we described in Theorem 4.1. In particular, we can use the same construction to show that there exist $DR(k(k+1), k, k-1) - BIBDs$.

THEOREM 4.2. *Let $k+1$ be a prime power, $k \geq 3$. Then there exists a $DR(k(k+1), k, k-1) - BIBD$.*

Proof. Let $k+1$ be a prime power. Let $V = \bigcup_{i=1}^{k} G_i$ where $G_i = \{x_{i1}, x_{i2}, \ldots, x_{i(k+1)}\}$. Let D_i be a $NR(k+1, k, k-1) - BIBD$ defined on G_i. The (near) resolution classes of D_i will be denoted by $R(x_{i1}), R(x_{i2}), \ldots, R(x_{i(k+1)})$ where the element x_{ij} does not occur in the block contained in $R(x_{ij})$ for $j = 1, 2, \ldots, k+1$ $(1 \leq i \leq k)$. Let X_j be the k–tuple $\{x_{ij} \mid i = 1, 2, \ldots, k\}$ $1 \leq j \leq k+1$.

Since $k+1$ is a prime power, there exists a set of k mutually orthogonal Latin squares of side $k+1$ and therefore, a doubly resolvable $TD(k, k+1)$, $\mathcal{T}$. Suppose $\mathcal{T}$ is defined on V where the groups of $\mathcal{T}$ are $G_1, G_2, \ldots, G_k$ and such that one of the resolutions, T, contains as a resolution class, T_1, the $k+1$ k–tuples $X_1, X_2, \ldots, X_{k+1}$. Let $T_2, T_3, \ldots, T_{k+1}$ denote the remaining resolution classes of T. We will distinguish a second resolution class of T, T_2. Suppose the blocks in T_2 are $Y_j = \{y_{ij} \mid i = 1, 2, \ldots, k\}$ where $y_{ij} \in G_i$, $1 \leq j \leq k+1$. $\mathcal{T}$ has a second resolution S which is orthogonal to T. The resolution classes of S will be denoted by $S_1, S_2, \ldots, S_{k+1}$. We recall that since $\mathcal{T}$ is a doubly resolvable $TD(k, k+1)$, $|S_i \cap T_j| = 1$ for all i, j.

We construct a $(k(k+1), k, k-1) - BIBD$ D from $k-1$ copies of $\mathcal{T}$ together with $\bigcup_{i=1}^{k} D_i$. D is a $DR(k(k+1), k, k-1) - BIBD$. In order to describe the pair

242

of orthogonal resolutions, we will distinguish between the copies of $\mathcal{T}$ by labelling them $\mathcal{T}^1, \mathcal{T}^2, \ldots, \mathcal{T}^{k-1}$.

The first resolution, $\mathcal{R}^1$, has the following resolution classes.

(i) $\mathcal{R}^1_i = \{X_i, R(x_{1i}), R(x_{2i}), \ldots, R(x_{ki})\}$ for $i = 1, 2, \ldots, k+1$
where X_i is a block in the resolution class T_1 of $\mathcal{T}^2$.

(ii) $\mathcal{R}^1_{k+1+i} = T_{1+i}$ for $i = 1, 2, \ldots, k$
where T_{1+i} is a resolution class of $\mathcal{T}^2$.

(iii) $\mathcal{R}^1_{2k+1+i} = S_i$ for $i = 1, 2, \ldots, k+1$
where S_i is a resolution class of $\mathcal{T}^1$.

(iv) The remaining $k^2 - 2k - 3$ resolution classes are the resolution classes $T_1, T_2, \ldots, T_{k+1}$ from $\mathcal{T}^3, \mathcal{T}^4, \ldots, \mathcal{T}^{k-1}$.

The second resolution, $\mathcal{R}^2$, has the following resolution classes.

(i) $\mathcal{R}^2_i = \{Y_i, R(y_{1i}), R(y_{2i}), \ldots, R(y_{ki})\}$ for $i = 1, 2, \ldots, k+1$
where Y_i is a block in the resolution class T_2 of $\mathcal{T}^1$.

(ii) $\mathcal{R}^2_{k+2} = T_1$ and $\mathcal{R}^2_{k+2+i} = T_{2+i}$ for $i = 1, 2, \ldots, k-1$
where $T_1, T_3, \ldots, T_{k+1}$ are resolution classes of $\mathcal{T}^1$.

(iii) $\mathcal{R}^2_{2k+1+i} = S_i$ for $i = 1, 2, \ldots, k+1$
where S_i is a resolution class of $\mathcal{T}^2$.

(iv) The remaining $k^2 - 2k - 3$ resolution classes are the resolution classes $S_1, S_2, \ldots, S_{k+1}$ from $\mathcal{T}^3, \mathcal{T}^4, \ldots, \mathcal{T}^{k-1}$.

We now verify that $\mathcal{R}^1$ and $\mathcal{R}^2$ are a pair of orthogonal resolutions for D. We first consider $|\mathcal{R}^1_i \cap \mathcal{R}^2_j|$ for $1 \leq i, j \leq k+1$. Since T_1 and T_2 are resolution classes of $\mathcal{T}$, $X_i \neq Y_j$ for all i, j. Suppose $|\mathcal{R}^1_i \cap \mathcal{R}^2_j| = m$ where $m \geq 2$. Then $|X_i \cap Y_j| = m$ and there exists (at least) a pair (a, b) where $a \in G_w$ and $b \in G_z$, $w \neq z$, which occurs twice in $\mathcal{T}$. Since $\mathcal{T}$ is a $TD(k, k+1)$, this cannot occur, and therefore $|\mathcal{R}^1_i \cap \mathcal{R}^2_j| \leq 1$ for $1 \leq i, j \leq k+1$. It is straightforward to check that $|\mathcal{R}^1_i \cap \mathcal{R}^2_j| \leq 1$ for $1 \leq i \leq k+2$ and $k + 2 \leq j \leq k(k+1) - 1$ and similarly that $|\mathcal{R}^2_i \cap \mathcal{R}^1_j| \leq 1$ for $1 \leq i \leq k+2$ and $k + 2 \leq j \leq k^2 + k - 1$. It is also easy to check that $|\mathcal{R}^1_i \cap \mathcal{R}^2_j| \leq 1$ for $i, j \geq k+2$. This verifies that $\mathcal{R}^1$ and $\mathcal{R}^2$ are a pair of orthogonal resolutions for D. $\square$

As in the case of Theorem 4.1, if k is also a prime power, these designs have the same parameters as the doubly resolvable designs described in Theorem 2.12. (However, the designs are not isomorphic.) If k is not a prime power, the designs constructed using Theorem 4.2 are the first known examples of $DR(v, k, \lambda) - BIBDs$ with k *not* a prime power power. The smallest example of this construction is a $DR(42, 6, 5) - BIBD$.

We can also use the same construction, Theorem 3.1, with $k + 1$ a prime power to produce $FGBTDs$.

THEOREM 4.3. Let $k + 1$ be a prime power. Then there exists a $FGBTD(k + 1, k)$ with Property C.

243

Proof. We use the notation and terminology described in the proof of Theorem 4.2. We construct a $FGBTD(k+1)$ with Property C, F, using the $(k(k+1), k, k-1)-BIBD$ D. Recall that D contains the blocks from $k-1$ copies of $\mathcal{T}$ and $\bigcup_{i=1}^{k} D_i$. For notational convenience, we will think of $\mathcal{T}$ as the $k+1$ square array formed by the superposition of k mutually orthogonal Latin squares where the columns of $\mathcal{T}$ form the resolution T and the rows of $\mathcal{T}$ the resolution S. (We label the columns $T_1, T_2, \ldots, T_{k+1}$ and the rows $S_1, S_2, \ldots, S_{k+1}$). In addition, the blocks X_i and Y_i will occur in row i of $\mathcal{T}$.

The columns of F will contain the following resolution classes of D.

(1) $\mathcal{R}_i = \{X_i, R(x_{1i}), R(x_{2i}), \ldots, R(x_{ki})\}$ for $i = 1, 2, \ldots, k+1$.

(2) $\mathcal{R}_{k+1+i} = T_{1+i}$ for $i = 1, 2, \ldots, k$.

(3) The remaining $k^2 - k - 2$ resolution classes are the $k-2$ copies of $T_1, T_2, \ldots, T_{k+1}$ from the $k-2$ copies of $\mathcal{T}$.

The column of deficient k–tuples for F will be $C = [Y_1 Y_2 \ldots Y_{k+1}]^T$ where Y_i occurs in row i of F.

We now describe how to place blocks in the rows of F. Row i of F will contain $k - 2$ copies of S_i and an additional copy of $S_i - X_i$. This places $k - 1$ copies of Y_i in row i of F. We must be also place one block from each of the resolution classes $\mathcal{R}_1, \mathcal{R}_2, \ldots, \mathcal{R}_{k+1}$ in row i. We will show that there is precisely one block B in $\mathcal{R}_j$ such that $B \cap Y_i = \emptyset$. B is then put in row i of F.

We consider $\mathcal{R}_j = \{X_j, R(x_{ij}), \ldots, R(x_{kj})\}$. ($R(x_{ij})$ is a block of size k.) We first show that there is at most one block B in $\mathcal{R}_j$ such that $B \cap Y_i = \emptyset$. Suppose there are two such blocks. There are two cases to consider.

Case (i) There exist m and n such that $R(x_{nj}) \cap Y_i = \emptyset$ and $R(x_{mj}) \cap Y_i = \emptyset$. Then the pair $\{x_{nj}, x_{mj}\}$ is contained in both Y_i and X_j. This cannot occur since $\mathcal{T}$ is a $TD(k, k+1)$.

Case (ii) There exists an m such that $R(x_{mj}) \cap Y_i = \emptyset$ and $X_j \cap Y_i = \emptyset$. Then $G_m \cap Y_i = \emptyset$. Again, this cannot occur if $\mathcal{T}$ is a $TD(k, k+1)$.

Next we show that there must be at least one B in $\mathcal{R}_j$ such that $B \cap Y_i = \emptyset$. We consider two cases.

Case (i) Suppose $X_j \cap Y_i \neq \emptyset$. Then there exists an n such that $x_{nj} \in Y_i$, and therefore $\mathcal{R}(x_{nj}) \cap Y_i = \emptyset$.

Case (ii) Suppose $R(x_{\ell j}) \cap Y_i \neq \emptyset$ for $1 \leq \ell \leq k$. This means that $x_{\ell j} \notin Y_i$ for $1 \leq \ell \leq k$ and $X_j \cap Y_i = \emptyset$.

This shows that there is precisely one block B in $\mathcal{R}_j$ such that $B \cap Y_i = \emptyset$.

We now verify that the rows of F have the required properties: (1) every element of V occurs at most k times in each row and (2) the rows can be partitioned into

244

factors. We first look more carefully at the $k+1$ square array A constructed from the columns of $\mathcal{R}_1, \mathcal{R}_2, \ldots, \mathcal{R}_{k+1}$. Row i of A does not contain any element of Y_i. There is precisely one block (or resolution class) in D_ℓ which does not contain any element of Y_i, $R(y_{\ell i})$. Thus, the blocks in row i of A are $R(y_{1i}), R(y_{2i}), \ldots, R(y_{ki})$ and X_i. Note that $R(y_{mi}) \cap R(y_{ni}) = \emptyset$ for $m \neq n$ and $1 \leq m, n \leq k$. Every element of $V - Y_i$ occurs precisely once in the blocks $R(y_{1i}), \ldots, R(y_{ki})$. Now consider row i of F. Row i of F contains the following blocks.

(1) $k-1$ copies of the block in S_i.

(2) $R(y_{1i}), R(y_{2i}), \ldots, R(y_{ki})$.

Thus, every element in $V - Y_i$ occurs k times in row i of F and every element in Y_i occurs $k-1$ times in row i. It is now easy to write down the factors for row i of F: $F_{ij} = S_i$ for $j = 1, 2, \ldots, k-1$ and $F_{ik} = Y_i \cup \{R(y_{1i}), \ldots, R(y_{ki})\}$.

This completes our verification that F is a $FGBTD(k+1, k)$ with Property C defined on V. □

To illustrate this construction, a $FGBTD(4,3)$ with Property C is displayed in Figure 1. The first 4 rows and columns of this design form the $TD(3,4)$, $\mathcal{T}$. The column of deficient triples $C = T_2 = [\{0,4,8\} \{1,5,9\} \{2,6,10\} \{3,7,11\}]^T$ and the other distinguished resolution class $T_1 = [\{3,5,10\} \{2,4,11\} \{1,7,8\} \{0,6,9\}]^T$.

0 4 8	1 6 11	2 7 9	3 5 10	0 4 8	1 6 11	2 7 9	3 5 10	1 2 3	9 10 11	5 6 7
1 5 9	0 7 10	3 6 8	2 4 11	1 5 9	0 7 10	3 6 8	4 6 7	8 10 11	2 3 0	2 4 11
2 6 10	3 4 9	0 5 11	1 7 8	2 6 10	3 4 9	0 5 11	8 9 11	4 5 7	1 7 8	3 0 1
3 7 11	2 5 8	1 4 10	0 6 9	3 7 11	2 5 8	1 4 10	0 1 2	0 6 9	4 5 6	8 9 10

Figure 1

A $FGBTD(4,3)$ with Property C

This existence result can now be used in recursive constructions for $FGBTDs$ to produce new infinite classes of $FGBTDs$ and, therefore, new classes of $RBIBDs$. We will use the following two recursive constructions for $FGBTDs$.

THEOREM 4.4. ([11]). If there exist k mutually orthogonal Latin squares of side nk and a $FGBTD(n, k)$, then there is $FGBTD(nk, k)$.

THEOREM 4.5. (Direct Product [11]). If there exists a $GBTD(n, k)$ with Property C, a $GBTD(m, k)$ with Property C and a set of k mutually orthogonal Latin squares of side m, then there is $GBTD(mn, k)$ with Property C.

The first class of previously unknown $RBIBDs$ which can be constructed using Theorems 4.3 and 4.4 is described in the next result.

LEMMA 4.6. Let i be a non-negative integer and let $k \in \{3, 4, 7\}$. Then there exists a $FGBTD((k+1)k^i, k)$.

Proof. Let $k \in \{3, 4, 7\}$. There exists $FGBTD((k + 1, k)$ by Theorem 4.3. We use Theorem 4.4 recursively; each time using a $FGBTD((k+1)k^i, k)$ and k mutually orthogonal Latin squares of side $(k + 1)k^{i+1}$ ([2,3]) to construct a $FGBTD((k + 1)k^{i+1}, k)$. □

All of these $FGBTDs$ for $k > 3$ are new designs. In addition, for $k = 7$ the $FGBTD(8 \cdot 7^i, 7)$ for $i \geq 0$ are also $(8 \cdot 7^{i+1}, 7, 6) - RBIBDs$ which were not previously known to exist.

The direct product construction can be used to provide new designs for all k where $k + 1$ is a prime power, $k \geq 2$.

LEMMA 4.7. *Let $k + 1$ be a prime power. There exists a $FGBTD((k + 1)^i, k)$ with Property C for i a positive integer.*

Proof. We use Theorem 4.5 recursively; each time we use a $FGBTD(k + 1, k)$ with Property C, a set of k mutually orthogonal Latin squares of side $k + 1$ and a $FGBTD((k+1)^i, k)$ with Property C to construct a $FGBTD((k+1)^{i+1}, k)$. □

Again, all of these $FGBTDs$ for $k > 3$ are new designs. For $k \geq 5$, the underlying $(k(k + 1)^i, k, k - 1) - RBIBDs$ are also new designs. We note that for $k = 8$ this construction produces designs which are in a class not covered by Theorem 2.7.

Finally, we note that Theorem 3.1 can also be thought of as a generalization of a frame construction for partitioned $GBTDs(PGBTDs)$ ([11]). This frame construction has been quite useful in finding $PGBTDs$ (and $DRBIBDs$). We refer to [10, 11] for the necessary definitions and details of these results.

We now consider applications of the second basic construction, Theorem 3.2. In the first application, we use the $((k + 1)^i k, k, k - 1) - RBIBDs$ from Lemma 4.7.

LEMMA 4.8. *Suppose k and $k + 1$ are prime powers, and let i and j be integers, $j \geq 1$ and $i \geq 0$. Then there exists a $((k + 1)^i k^j, k, k - 1) - RBIBD$.*

Proof. If $i = 0$ and k is a prime power, then it is easy to construct $(k^j, k, k - 1) - RBIBDs$ for $j \geq 1$ using Theorem 3.2. (This is equivalent to taking $k - 1$ copies of the $(k^j, k, 1) - RBIBDs$.) The cases $i \geq 1$ and $j = 1$ are covered by Lemma 4.7. To take care of the remaining cases for $i \geq 1$, we apply Theorem 3.2 recursively. Each time we use a $((k + 1)^i k^j, k, k - 1) - RBIBD$ to construct a $((k + 1)^i k^{j+1}, k, k - 1) - RBIBD$. The standard direct product construction for orthogonal Latin squares is used to construct a set of $k - 1$ mutually orthogonal Latin squares of side $(k + 1)^i k^j$, $i \geq 1$ and $j \geq 1$. □

The first two values of k for which Lemma 4.8 provides new designs are $k = 7$ and $k = 8$. The classes of designs are:

(1) there exist $(7^j 8^i, 7, 6) - RBIBDs$ and

(2) there exist $(8^j 9^i, 8, 7) - RBIBDs$ where $j \geq 1$ and $i \geq 0$.

Another example of constructing designs using Theorem 3.2 is to apply Theorem 3.2 recursively starting with a $(20, 5, 4) - RBIBD$.

246

LEMMA 4.9. *Let i be a positive integer, $i \geq 1$. There exists a $(4 \cdot 5^i, 5, 4) - RBIBD$.*

As in the case of Theorem 3.1, Theorem 3.2 is a generalization of a construction for generalized balanced tournament designs. In particular, if the $(v, k, k-1) - RBIBD$ is a $FGBTD(n, k)$ (where $v = nk$) and the $TD(k, v)$ is doubly resolvable, then Theorem 3.2 is equivalent to Theorem 4.4.

The third basic construction for resolvable $BIBDs$, Theorem 3.4, is more difficult to apply, and it does not appear to have a nice analogue for $GBTDs$. The next result comes from using the $RBIBDs$ described in Lemma 4.7 and 4.8 in Theorem 3.4

LEMMA 4.10. *(i)* *Let i be a positive integer, and let $k+1$ be a prime power. If there exist $k-1$ mutually orthogonal Latin squares of side $(k+1)^i k - 1$, then there is a $((k+1)((k+1)^i k - 1) + 1, k, k-1) - RBIBD$.*

(ii) *Let i be a non–negative integer and let j be a positive integer. Suppose $k+1$ and k are prime powers. If there exist $k-1$ mutually orthogonal Latin squares of side $(k+1)^i k^j - 1$, then there is a $((k+1)(k^j (k+1)^i - 1) + 1, k, k-1) - RBIBD$.*

For block size larger than 4, the three smallest $RBIBDs$ constructed by Lemma 4.10 have the following parameter sets: $(288, 6, 5)$, $(385, 7, 6)$ and $(640, 8, 7)$. For additional examples of $RBIBDs$ which can be constructed using Theorem 3.4, we use some of the known $(v, 5, 4) - RBIBDs$ and $(v, 6, 5) - RBIBDs$ where v is small. (All of these smaller designs are taken either from [15] or previous results listed in this paper.) Parameter sets for some of the resulting $RBIBDs$ are:

$$(115, 5, 4) , (145, 5, 4) , (175, 5, 4) \quad \text{and}$$
$$(78, 6, 5) , (120, 6, 5).$$

The remaining basic construction from section 3, Theorem 3.3, is for near resolvable $BIBDs$. As noted in section 2, there is considerably less information available about the spectrum of near resolvable $BIBDs$. Although algebraic constructions (starter–adder) for $NR(v, k, k-1) - BIBDs$ are known to exist ([22]), no general results on $NRBIBDs$ appear in the literature. Thus, it is likely that the majority of the designs described below were not previously known to exist.

The analogue of Theorem 4.1 for $NRBIBDs$ is the following.

THEOREM 4.11. *Let $k+1$ be a prime power. Then there exists a $NR((k+1)^i, k, k-1) - BIBD$ for i a positive integer.*

Proof. We apply Theorem 3.3 recursively. Each time we use a $NR((k+1)^i, k, k-1) - BIBD$ to construct a $NR((k+1)^{i+1}, k, k-1) - BIBD$. Since $k+1$ is a prime power, there exists a set of k mutually orthogonal Latin squares of side $k+1$ or a $RTD(k, k+1)$. A $NR(k+1, k, k-1) - BIBD$ is easily constructed by taking all the distinct k–subsets of a $(k+1)$–element set. So we have the designs needed to apply Theorem 3.3. □

As in the case of the first two constructions for $RBIBDs$, Theorems 3.1 and 3.2, Theorem 3.3 can be viewed as a generalization of a construction for generalized balanced tournament designs, this time for $NGBTDs$. The next result is equivalent to a special case of the direct product for $NGBTDs$ ([13]).

THEOREM 4.12. *Let $v = nk + 1$. If there exists a $NGBTD(n,k)$ and a doubly resolvable $TD(k,v)$, then there exists a $NGBTD(nk + n + 1, k)$.*

Proof. Let $V = \bigcup_{i=1}^{k+1} G_i$ where $G_i = \{x_{i1}, x_{i2}, \ldots, x_{iv}\}$ Suppose N_i is a $NGBTD$ (n,k) defined on G_i. N_i is an $n \times nk + 1$ array.

Since there exists a doubly resolvable $TD(k,v)$, there is a set of k mutually orthogonal Latin squares of side v. Let T_i denote the $v \times v$ array formed by the superposition of a set of k mutually orthogonal Latin squares of side v, $T_i = L_1 \circ L_2 \cdots \circ L_{i-1} \circ L_{i+1} \circ \cdots \circ L_{k+1}$ where L_i is defined on G_i.

Let N be the following $(v + n) \times (k + 1)v$ array.

$$
N = \begin{bmatrix} T_1 & T_2 & \ldots & T_{k+1} \\ N_1 & N_2 & & N_{k+1} \end{bmatrix}
$$

It is straightforward to verify that N is a $NGBTD(kn + n + 1, k)$ defined on V. $\square$

To illustrate this construction, the array $[B_1 \ B_2]$ is a $NGBTD(5,3)$ where B_1 and B_2 are displayed in Figure 2.

0 4 8	1 6 11	2 7 9	3 5 10	4 8 A	6 11 B	7 9 C	5 10 D
1 5 9	0 7 10	3 6 8	2 4 11	5 9 B	7 10 A	6 8 D	4 11 C
2 6 10	3 4 9	0 5 11	1 7 8	6 10 C	4 9 D	5 11 A	7 8 B
3 7 11	2 5 8	1 4 10	0 6 9	7 11 D	5 8 C	4 10 B	6 9 A
A B C	B C D	C D A	D A B	0 1 2	1 2 3	2 3 0	3 0 1

$$B_1$$

0 8 A	1 11 C	2 9 D	3 10 B	0 4 A	1 6 D	2 7 B	3 5 C
1 9 B	0 10 D	3 8 C	2 11 A	1 5 B	0 7 C	3 6 A	2 4 D
2 10 C	3 9 A	0 11 B	1 8 D	2 6 C	3 4 B	0 5 D	1 7 A
3 11 D	2 8 B	1 10 A	0 9 C	3 7 D	2 5 A	1 4 C	0 6 B
4 5 6	5 6 7	6 7 4	7 4 5	8 9 10	9 10 11	10 11 8	11 8 9

$$B_2$$

Figure 2

We can use Theorem 4.12 recursively to produce some infinite classes of $NGBTDs$.

THEOREM 4.13. *Let $k + 1$ be a prime power. Then there exists a* $NGBTD \left(\dfrac{(k + 1)^i - 1}{k}, k \right)$ *for i a positive integer.*

Proof. We first consider the case $i = 1$. Let V be a $(k + 1)$ element set, and let $b_1, b_2, \ldots, b_{k+1}$ denote the $k + 1$ distinct subsets of V of size k. Then the array $N = [b_1 b_2 \ldots b_{k+1}]$ is a $NGBTD(1, k)$ defined on V.

248

We now apply Theorem 4.12 recursively. Let $v = (k+1)^i$ when $k+1$ is a prime power. Then there exists a set of k mutually orthogonal Latin squares of side $(k+1)^i$ for $i \geq 1$. In each application of Theorems 4.12, a $NGBTD\left(\dfrac{(k+1)^i - 1}{k}, k\right)$ is used to construct a $NGBTD\left(\dfrac{(k+1)^{i+1} - 1}{k}, k\right)$. $\square$

The next class of new $NGBTDs$ is produced by applying a recent construction from [10] which uses $NGBTDs$ to construct $NRBIBDs$.

THEOREM 4.14. ([10]). If there is a $NGBTD(n, k)$, a $(kn+1, k+1, 1)-RBIBD$ and a $NR(n, k+1, k) - BIBD$, then there is a $NR(kn + n + 1, k+1, k) - BIBD$.

THEOREM 4.15. Let i be a positive integer, $i \geq 2$, and let $k+1$ be a prime power. Then there exists a $NR\left(\dfrac{(k+1)^i - 1}{k}, k+1, k\right) - BIBD$.

Proof. We will apply Theorem 4.14 recursively. Let $n = \dfrac{(k+1)^i - 1}{k}$ where i is a positive integer and $k+1$ is a prime power. The existence of $N\overset{\cdot}{G}BTD$ $\left(\dfrac{(k+1)^i - 1}{k}, k\right)$ is provided by Theorem 4.13. The existence of the $RBIBDs$, $((k+1)^i, k+1, 1) - RBIBDs$, follows immediately from the existence of a set of k mutually orthogonal Latin squares of side $k+1$. If $i = 2$, then $n = k+2$ and it is easy to construct a $NR(k+2, k+1, k) - BIBD$. The first application of Theorem 4.14 produces a $NR(k(k+2) + k + 2 + 1, k+1, k) - BIBD$ or a $NR\left(\dfrac{(k+1)^3 - 1}{k}, k+1, k\right) - BIBD$. Thus, in each application of Theorem 4.14, a $NR\left(\dfrac{(k+1)^i - 1}{k}, k+1, k\right) - BIBD$ is used to construct a $NR\left(\dfrac{(k+1)^{i+1} - 1}{k}, k+1, k\right) - BIBD$. $\square$

5. **Summary.** In this paper, we have used resolvable transversal designs to construct resolvable, near resolvable and doubly resolvable $(v, k, k-1) - BIBDs$, as well as generalized balanced and near generalized balanced tournament designs. The basic constructions described in section 3 were used to produce several new classes of designs; these include the first examples of $DR(v, k, k-1) - BIBDs$ where k is not a prime power and the first infinite classes of $FGBTDs$ and $NGBTDs$ with block size $k \geq 4$. We have also shown that the additional structure of $GBTDs$ and $NGBTDs$ can be quite useful in constructing resolvable and near resolvable $BIBDs$. $GBTDs$ and $NGBTDs$ are related to several types of combinatorial designs including resolvable, near resolvable and doubly resolvable $BIBDs$. We have indicated some of the connections to resolvable and near resolvable $BIBDs$, and we refer to [10–14] for further information and results on $GBTDs$ and $NGBTDs$.

REFERENCES

[1]   R.D. BAKER, *Resolvable BIBDs and SOLS*, Discrete Math 44 (1983) 13–29.

249

[2] A.E. BROUWER, *The number of mutually orthogonal Latin squares – a table up to order 10000*, Research report ZW 123/79, Mathematical Centrum, Amsterdam, June 1979.

[3] A.E. BROUWER AND G.H.J. VAN REES, *More mutually orthogonal Latin squares*, Discrete Math 39 (1982) 263–281.

[4] DEMENG CHU AND LIE ZHU, *Existence of resolvable balanced incomplete block designs with $k = 5$ and $\lambda = 1$*, Ars Combinatoria 24 (1987) 185–192.

[5] D.G. CURRAN AND S.A. VANSTONE, *Doubly resolvable designs from Bhaskar Rao designs*, Annals of Discrete Math, to appear..

[6] BEILING DU, JIANXING YIN AND LIE ZHU, *On the existence of $(v, 5, 1)$-resolvable BIBDs*, J. Suzhou University, to appear.

[7] R. FUJI–HARA AND S.A. VANSTONE, *On the spectrum of doubly resolvable designs*, Congressus Numerantium 28 (1980) 399–407.

[8] H. HANANI, *On resolvable balanced incomplete block designs*, J. Combinatorial Theory (A) 17 (1974) 275–289.

[9] H. HANANI, D.K. RAY–CHAUDHURI AND R.M. WILSON, *On resolvable designs*, Discrete Math 3 (1972) 343–357.

[10] E.R. LAMKEN, *Generalized balanced tournament designs*, preprint.

[11] E.R. LAMKEN, *Constructions for generalized balanced tournament designs*, in preparation.

[12] E.R. LAMKEN, *The existence of doubly resolvable $(v, 3, 2) - BIBDs$*, in preparation.

[13] E.R. LAMKEN, *On near generalized balanced tournament designs*, in preparation.

[14] E.R. LAMKEN, *Existence results for generalized balanced tournament designs with block size 3*, in preparation.

[15] R. MATHON AND A. ROSA, *Tables of Parameters of BIBDs with $r \leq 41$ including existence, enumeration and resolvability results*, Annals of Discrete Math 26 (1985) 275–308.

[16] R.C. MULLIN AND W.D. WALLIS, *The existence of Room squares*, Aequationes Math 1 (1975) 1–7.

[17] D.K. RAY–CHAUDHURI AND R.M. WILSON, *Solutions of Kirkman's school girl problem*, Proc. Symp. Pure Math 19 (1971) 187–203.

[18] B. ROKOWSKA, *The construction of resolvable block systems*, Colloq. Math. 49 (1985) 295–297.

[19] B. ROKOWSKA, *Resolvable systems of 8–tuples*, J. Statist. Planning Info. 9 (1984) 131–141.

[20] A. ROSA AND S.A. VANSTONE, *Starter-adder techniques for Kirkman squares and Kirkman cubes of small sides*, Ars Combinatoria 14 (1982) 199–212.

[21] S.A. VANSTONE, *Doubly resolvable designs*, Discrete Math 29 (1980) 77–86.

[22] S.A. VANSTONE, *On mutually orthogonal resolutions and near resolutions*, Annals of Discrete Math 15 (1982) 357–369.

A NEW DESIGN

JACK H. VAN LINT†, VLADIMIR D. TONCHEV‡
AND IVAN N. LANDGEV*

Abstract. We construct the first example of a quasi-residual design with $k < v/2$ for which the corresponding symmetric design cannot exist by the Bruck-Ryser-Chowla theorem. We also construct two new group-divisible designs.

Key words. block design, group-divisible design

AMS(MOS) subject classifications. 05B05

1. Introduction. The main result of this paper is the construction of a block design 2-(28,10,5). Among the designs for which the existence was unknown until now, only the elusive parameter set 2-(22,8,4) has a smaller value of v. The construction answers a question (that was open) concerning quasi-residual designs. This design is the first one that has been constructed with the properties : (i) $k < v/2$ and (ii) the design is quasi-residual and the corresponding symmetric design (in this case a 2-(43,15,5) design) does not exist by the Bruck-Ryser-Chowla theorem.

The idea of the construction is as follows. Assume that the design has a sufficiently nice automorphism group that fixes many blocks. This makes it possible to analyse the structure of the design and to find related designs by computer search. Once the existence of the design had been established we were able to give a completely computer-free description. In fact we believe that infinitely many designs with the same structure exist. A known 2-(10,4,2) design is of the same type as our design. Together they would be the cases $m = 1$ and $m = 3$ of a sequence (with $m = 3^s$). We remark that the method of Section 3 also works for $m = 5$, producing a third example of the group-divisible designs of Theorem 2.1. However, this does not lead to a quasi-symmetric design although a design with the corresponding parameters is known (see [2]).

2. Designs with an automorphism of order 3. It is not very difficult, although quite tedious, to show that the only primes which can be orders of an automorphism of a 2-(28,10,5) design are 2 and 3. The following lemma has played a crucial role in our construction of a design with an automorphism of order 3 (also cf. [3]).

---

†Department of Mathematics and Computing Science, Eindhoven University of Technology, Eindhoven, Netherlands

‡Bulgarian Academy of Sciences, Sofia and Eindhoven University of Technology, Eindhoven, Netherlands

*Bulgarian Academy of Sciences, Sofia

LEMMA 2.1. *An automorphism of order 3 of a* $2 - (v, k, \lambda)$ *design fixes at most* $b - 3r + 3\lambda$ *blocks.*

Proof. Consider a 3-cycle of points and count the blocks that contain all three points or none of them. □

We shall now consider the extremal case, first for the parameters 2-(28,10,5).

LEMMA 2.2. *Suppose that there exists a 2-(28,10,5) design with an automorphism* f *of order 3 fixing exactly one point and the maximum number of blocks, i.e.* $b - 3r + 3\lambda = 12$ *blocks. Then the cycles of* f *considered as "points" and the fixed blocks form a 2-(9,3,1) design, i.e. an affine plane of order 3, while the orbit matrix of the non-fixed points and blocks is a 9 by 10 matrix of the following form:*

$$(2.1) \qquad \begin{pmatrix} 1 & 2 & 1 & 1 & \ldots & 1 \\ 1 & 1 & 2 & 1 & \ldots & 1 \\ \vdots & \vdots & \vdots & \vdots & \ddots & \vdots \\ 1 & 1 & 1 & 1 & \ldots & 2 \end{pmatrix}.$$

In the above matrix each entry "1" has to be replaced by an appropriate power of the matrix

$$(2.2) \qquad C = \begin{pmatrix} 0 & 1 & 0 \\ 0 & 0 & 1 \\ 1 & 0 & 0 \end{pmatrix}.$$

and each entry "2" by $J - I$ to obtain the incidence matrix of non-fixed points and non-fixed blocks of the design. In fact, Lemma 2.2 is a particular case of a more general construction described in the next theorem.

THEOREM 2.1. *Suppose that there exists a* $2 - (9m + 1, 3m + 1, (3m + 1)/2)$ *design* (*m odd*), *with an automorphism* f *of order 3 fixing one point and the maximum number of blocks, i.e.* $3(3m - 1)/2$ *blocks. Then the cycles of* f *considered as "points" and the fixed blocks form a* $2 - (3m, m, (m - 1)/2)$ *design. The orbit matrix of the non-fixed points and blocks is a* $3m$ *by* $3m + 1$ *matrix of the form* (2.1), *and the incidence structure of the non-fixed points and blocks is a partially balanced group divisible design with group size 3,* $v = 9m$, $b = 3(3m + 1)$, *three blocks of size* $3m$ *and* $9m$ *blocks of size* $3m + 1$, $\lambda_1 = 1$, $\lambda_2 = m + 1$.

Proof. Consider the unique point, say P, fixed by f. Since $r = 3(3m + 1)/2$, P is contained in all $3(3m - 1)/2$ fixed blocks plus 3 non-fixed blocks. Since there are $3m$ block orbits of length 3 not containing P and $r - \lambda = k = 3m + 1$, for each 3-cycle of f there is a non-fixed block not containing P and containing at least two points from that cycle. Consequently, since $\lambda = (3m + 1)/2$, a 3-cycle can be contained in at most $\lambda - 1 = (3m - 1)/2$ fixed blocks. Therefore, the unique block orbit of length 3 containing the fixed point must meet each cycle of f in at least one point. Since there are $3m$ 3-cycles and $k = 3m + 1$, each non-fixed point occurs together with P in exactly one non-fixed block. Therefore, each 3-cycle is contained in exactly $\lambda - 1 = (3m - 1)/2$ fixed blocks, and each pair of points belonging to one and the same cycle occur together in exactly one non-fixed block not containing P, while each block from the remaining $3m - 1$ block orbits of length 3 must contain exactly one point from the same cycle. Hence, a row of the orbit matrix of the non-fixed points and blocks consists of one 2 and $3m$ 1's. Since $k = 3m + 1$, the same holds for the columns of the orbit matrix except the column corresponding to the orbit containing P which consists entirely of ones. Consequently, the orbit matrix is of the form (2.1). The scalar product of two rows of (2.1) is $3m + 3 = 3(m + 1)$. This implies that a pair of non-fixed points belonging to different cycles must occur together in exactly $m + 1$ blocks not containing P. Therefore, each two 3-cycles occur together in exactly $\lambda - m + 1 = (m - 1)/2$ fixed blocks. Hence the 3-cycles and the fixed blocks form a $2 - (3m, m, (m-1)/2)$ design, while the non-fixed points and blocks form a partially balanced design such that a pair of points belonging to one and the same cycle occur in one block, while pairs of points from different cycles occur in $m + 1$ blocks. This completes the proof. $\square$

COROLLARY. *A sufficient condition for the existence of a $2 - (9m + 1, 3m + 1, (3m + 1)/2)$ design is the existence of a $2 - (3m, m, (m - 1)/2)$ design and a symmetric group divisible design with group size 3, $v = 9m + 3$, $k = 3m + 2$, $\lambda_1 = 1$, $\lambda_2 = m + 1$.*

A class of $2 - (3m, m, (m - 1)/2)$ designs is provided by the affine geometry over $GF(3)$. Namely, if $m = 3^s$, then a $2 - (3^{s+1}, 3^s, (3^s - 1)/2)$ design is formed by the hyperplanes in $AG(s + 1, 3)$. The corresponding symmetric group divisible design has the following parameters :

$$v = 3^{s+2} + 3, \quad k = 3^{s+1} + 2, \quad \lambda_1 = 1, \quad \lambda_2 = 3^s + 1.$$

A symmetric group divisible (12,5,1,2) design corresponding to $s = 0$ is given in Bose, Clatworthy and Shrikhande [1]. Together with the trivial 2-(3,1,0) design this leads to a 2-(10,4,2) design.

3. A symmetric group divisible design (30,11,1,4). We shall construct the required group divisible design D represented as a 10 by 10 matrix A^* in which the entries on the diagonal are $C + C^2$ and all the others are $I, C,$ or C^2 (where C is as in (2.2)). Then $A^* A^{*\top}$ has diagonal entries $10I + J$ and all the other entries are $4J$. We now replace C by $\zeta = e^{2\pi i/3}$ (since $C^3 = I$, $\zeta^3 = 1$) noting that $J = I + C + C^2$ should be replaced by $0 = 1 + \zeta + \zeta^2$. The matrix A^* is then replaced by a 10 by 10 matrix A with -1 on the diagonal, cube roots of unity elsewhere and we must have $A\tilde{A} = 10I$. Note that a matrix of this kind of order 4 is $J - 2I$, providing an independent solution for the case $s = 0$ in Section 2.

We construct A by assuming even more regularity. Let C_5 denote the 5 by 5 circulant analogous to (2.2), so $C_5^5 = I_5$. We shall assume that there is a solution A with

(3.1) $\qquad A = I_5 \otimes P + (C_5 + C_5^4) \otimes Q + (C_5^2 + C_5^3) \otimes \overline{Q} = M(P, Q),$

where P is a symmetric real matrix (with -1 on the diagonal) and Q is a symmetric matrix with cube roots of unity as entries, both of size 2 by 2. As usual $\otimes$ denotes the Kronecker product. We have

$$(3.2) \qquad M(P,Q) \cdot \widetilde{M(P,Q)} = M(R,S),$$

where

$$R = PP^\top + 2Q\overline{Q} + 2\overline{Q}Q,$$
$$S = P\overline{Q} + QP + Q^2 + \overline{Q}Q + \overline{Q}^2.$$

Substitution of $P = \begin{pmatrix} -1 & 1 \\ 1 & -1 \end{pmatrix}$, $Q = \begin{pmatrix} \zeta & \zeta \\ \zeta & 1 \end{pmatrix}$ yields $R = 10I$, $S = O$ and hence $A = M(P,Q)$ solves our problem!

It has been checked by Kapralov (private communication) using a computer, that up to isomorphism the group divisible (30,11,1,4) design D is unique under the assumption of an automorphism of order 3 without fixed points. The full automorphism group of this design is a semi-direct product of a cyclic group of order 15 with the cyclic group of order 4, splitting the 30 points into two orbits of length 15.

We could have constructed our design in another way, again assuming high regularity, by using the orbits of length 15. One proceeds as follows. Let P be the permutation matrix of order 15 of the type of (2.1), i.e. $P_{i,j} = 1$ if and only if $j = i + 1$ (mod 15). We define

$$P_1 = P + P^2 + P^4 + P^8, \, P_2 = P^3 + P^6 + P^9 + P^{12}, \, P_3 = P^5 + P^{10}, \, P_4 = P^7 + P^{11} + P^{13} + P^{14}$$

It is well known that I and P_1, P_2, P_3, P_4 form a 5-dimensional algebra of matrices of order 15. We consider a 30 by 30 matrix $A = \begin{pmatrix} X & Y \\ Y & Z \end{pmatrix}$ where each entry is of the form $\epsilon_0 I + \epsilon_1 P_1 + \epsilon_2 P_2 + \epsilon_3 P_3 + \epsilon_4 P_4$, ($\epsilon_i = 0$ or 1). This reduces the number of possibilities to a reasonable number. A multiplication table for $P_i P_j$ is easily found. We now calculate $AA^\top$. If this is to be the incidence matrix of D, then we should have

$$AA^\top = \begin{pmatrix} A_1 & A_2 \\ A_3 & A_4 \end{pmatrix} \quad \text{with} \quad \begin{aligned} A_2 &= A_3 = 4J, \\ A_1 &= A_4 = 7I + 4J - 3P_3 \end{aligned}$$

(where the $-3P_3$ accounts for the inner products 1 of rows from the same 3-cycle). These equations are easily solved. We find the (essentially unique) solution : $X = P_1 + P_3$, $Y = I + P_1$, $Z = P_2 + P_3$. This method may be easier to generalize to other orders than the first one.

4. On group divisible designs with v = 9m, b = 3(3m + 1), $\lambda_1 = 1$, $\lambda_2 = m + 1$.

We consider the group divisible designs of Theorem 2.1, i.e. we assume that they have the form of (2.1) where each 1 represents an appropriate power of C and each 2 denotes $C + C^2$.

THEOREM 4.1. *If a group divisible design of type (2.1) with* $v = 9m$, $b = 3(3m + 1)$ *exists, then a symmetric group divisible design of size* $9m + 3$ *with "structure"* $I + J$ *exists.*

Proof. We use the method of Section 3 and replace C by ζ. So we now have a $3m$ by $3m + 1$ matrix G of type (2.1), where each 2 is replaced by -1 and each 1 by a power of ζ and furthermore $G\tilde{G} = (3m + 1)I$. Let $\mathbf{x}_i = (x_{i0}, x_{i1}, \ldots, x_{i,3m})$ denote the i-th row of G $(1 \le i \le 3m)$. Then $(\mathbf{x}_i, \overline{\mathbf{x}}_i) = 3m + 1$ and $(\mathbf{x}_i, \overline{\mathbf{x}}_j) = 0$ if $i \ne j$. Define

$$(4.1) \qquad \mathbf{x}_0 = \sum_{i=1}^{3m} \mathbf{x}_i - (3m + 1)(1, 0, 0, \ldots, 0).$$

(Note that $x_{00} = -1$.) By (4.1) we have

$$(4.2) \quad (\mathbf{x}_0, \overline{\mathbf{x}}_0) = 3m(3m + 1) + (3m + 1)^2 - 2(3m + 1)3m = 3m + 1,$$
$$(4.3) \quad (\mathbf{x}_0, \overline{\mathbf{x}}_i) = (\mathbf{x}_i, \overline{\mathbf{x}}_i) - (3m + 1) = 0 \qquad \text{for} \qquad i > 0.$$

It follows that if we form G' by adjoining $\mathbf{x}_0$ as top row to G, then $G'\tilde{G}' = (3m+1)I$. From (4.2) we know that $\sum_{j=1}^{3m} |x_{ij}|^2 = 3m$. Each entry is a sum of $3m + 1$ cube roots of unity (using $-1 = \zeta + \zeta^2$). But a sum of this number of cube roots of unity is either again a cube root of unity or it has absolute value greater than 1. It follows that all x_{ij} $(j = 1, 2, \ldots, 3m)$ are cube roots of unity and we are done. □

In the introduction we remarked that the method of Section 3 also works for $m = 5$. We shall now give the details.

THEOREM 4.2. *There exists a group divisible design (48,17,1,6).*

Proof. Consider the matrix of (3.1) but now substitute

$$P = -I + 2J, \quad Q = (1 - \zeta)I + \zeta J, \qquad \text{where } I \text{ and } J \text{ are 3 by 3.}$$

We find

$$PP^{\mathsf{T}} = 4I - J, \qquad\qquad Q^2 = -3\zeta I + (-1 + \zeta)J,$$
$$P\overline{Q} = (-2 + 2\zeta)I + J, \qquad Q\overline{Q} = \overline{Q}Q = 3I$$

and then by substitution (from (3.2)) : $R = 16I - J, S = -J$. Now define

$$(4.4) \qquad\qquad A = \begin{pmatrix} -1 & \mathbf{j}^{\mathsf{T}} \\ \mathbf{j} & M(P, Q) \end{pmatrix}.$$

Then $A\tilde{A} = 16I$. Just as in Section 3 this now yields the desired group divisible design (48,17,1,6). □

We have checked that the methods of Section 3 and Theorem 4.2 do not work for other "Paley type" matrices than (3.1) and also only for the two choices of P and Q that we have used.

REFERENCES

[1]   R.C.BOSE, W.H.CLATWORTHY AND S.S.SHRIKHANDE, *Tables of partially balanced designs with two associate classes*, North Carolina Agricultural Experiment Station Techn.Bull., 107 (1954).

[2]   Z.JANKO AND TRAN VAN TRUNG, *The existence of a symmetric block design for (70,24,8)*, Mitteilungen aus dem Mathem.Seminar Giessen, 165 (1984), pp. 17–18.

[3]   V.D.TONCHEV, *Combinatorial Structures and Codes*, Sofia University Press, Sofia, 1988.

NECESSARY CONDITIONS FOR HADAMARD DIFFERENCE SETS*

ROBERT L. M^cFARLAND†

Abstract. Difference sets with parameters of the form $(v, k, \lambda, n) = (4m^2, 2m^2 - m, m^2 - m, m^2)$ are called *Hadamard difference sets*. Constructions for these difference sets have been given for all values of m of the form $\pm 2^r 3^s$, where r and s are nonnegative integers. It is not known whether there exist Hadamard difference sets for any other values of m. In this paper we consider the case $m = \pm 2^e p$, where e is a nonnegative integer and p is an odd prime. We assume that the group G containing the difference set is the direct product of an elementary abelian p-group of order p^2 and an abelian 2-group with exponent 2 if $p \equiv 1 \pmod 4$ and exponent 2 or 4 if $p \equiv 3 \pmod 4$. We show that necessary conditions for the existence of a Hadamard difference set in G are that p be a Mersenne prime and if $p > 3$ then the order of the Sylow 2-subgroup of G must be larger than $4p^2$.

Key words. Hadamard difference set, difference set

AMS(MOS) subject classifications. 05B10

1. Introduction. A *difference set* is a combinatorial configuration that is defined as a subset D of a finite group G such that the differences of distinct elements of D replicate each nonidentity element of G the same number of times. In other words, the equation

$$d - d' = g$$

has the same number of solution pairs (d, d') in $D \times D$ for each nonidentity element g in G. The cardinalities of G and D are denoted by v and k, respectively, while the replication number is denoted by λ. Counting the total number of differences in two ways yields

$$(1.1) \qquad k(k - 1) = \lambda(v - 1).$$

The quantity $k - \lambda$ is called the *order* of the difference sets and is denoted by n:

$$(1.2) \qquad n = k - \lambda$$

For later use we note that (1.1) and (1.2) yield

$$(1.3) \qquad k^2 = n + \lambda v.$$

We call (v, k, λ, n) the *parameters* of the difference set.

The $(1, -1)$-incidence matrix M of a difference set D in a group G is the matrix

$$M = \sum_{g \notin D} [g] - \sum_{g \in D} [g],$$

*Research supported by the National Security Agency OCREAE Program Grant No. MDA 904-87-H-2014

†Department of Mathematics and Statistics, University of Minnesota at Duluth, Duluth, MN 55812

where $[g]$ is the $(0, 1)$-permutation matrix associated with the group element g in a right regular matrix representation of G. Since the transpose of $[g]$ is $[g]^T = [g]^{-1} = [-g]$, the difference set property implies that

$$MM^T = 4nI + (v - 4n)J,$$

where I is the identity matrix and J is the matrix of all 1's. Thus M is a Hadamard matrix of order $v > 1$ if and only if $v = 4n$. Menon [15] has shown that the parameters of a difference set must be of the form

(1.4) $$(v, k, \lambda, n) = (4m^2, 2m^2 - m, m^2 - m, m^2)$$

when $v = 4n$. Consequently, difference sets with the parameters (1.4) are called *Hadamard difference sets*. However, Turyn [18] calls these difference sets *H-sets*, while Beth, Jungnickel, and Lenz [1] suggest the name *Menon difference sets*.

Bruck [2] gives an example of a Hadamard difference set with $m = 2$, while Menon [15] gives some examples for $m = 2$ and 3. Menon [15] also shows that if there exist Hadamard difference sets in groups G_1 and G_2 with m values m_1 and m_2, respectively, then there exists a Hadamard difference set in the direct product group $G_1 \times G_2$ with m value $2m_1m_2$. Turyn [17] constructs Hadamard difference sets with $m = 3^s$ for all $s \geq 0$. Replacing m by $-m$ in (1.4) yields the parameters of the complementary Hadamard difference set. Thus Hadamard difference sets exist for $m = \pm 2^r 3^s$ for all $r, s \geq 0$. Whether there can exist Hadamard difference sets for any other values of m is an open problem. However, there are many other constructions for Hadamard difference sets: Davis [3], Dillon [4], [5], [6], [7], Kibler [8], McFarland [14], Rothaus [16], and Turyn [18].

We consider the existence of Hadamard difference sets for which $m = 2^e p$, where e is a nonnegative integer and $p > 3$ is a prime. We assume that the group containing the difference set is the direct product of an elementary abelian group of order p^2 and an abelian 2-group G_2 of exponent 2 if $p \equiv 1 \pmod 4$ and exponent 2 or 4 if $p \equiv 3 \pmod 4$. We prove that a necessary condition for existence is that $p + 1$ divides 2^e. In other words, if there exists a Hadamard difference set in such a group, then p must be a Mersenne prime and if $p > 3$ then the order of G_2 must be larger than $4p^2$. The case $e = 0$ of this result was first proved by Turyn [18, Theorem 12 and Corollary]. Subsequently, a simplified proof for this case was given by Mann and McFarland [11]. This latter proof was the motivation for this paper.

Other nonexistence theorems for Hadamard difference sets are McFarland [12], [13], and Turyn [18, Theorem 6 and its Corollaries].

2. The Group Ring and Abelian Characters. Group rings have become the standard setting for studying difference sets. Let ZG denote the group ring of the finite group G over the ring Z of rational integers. We assume that multiplication is the group operation in order that it can be identified with multiplication in ZG. A typical element A in ZG is of the form

(2.1) $$A = \sum_{g \in G} a_g g,$$

where the coefficients, a_g, belong to $\mathbf{Z}$. We identify each subset S of G with its characteristic function in $\mathbf{Z}G$, that is S denotes the element in $\mathbf{Z}G$ that has coefficient 1 on those group elements that belong to the subset S, and remaining coefficients 0. In particular, G itself denotes the element in $\mathbf{Z}G$ that has all coefficients equal to 1. Each n in $\mathbf{Z}$ is identified with the element $n1_G$ in $\mathbf{Z}G$, where 1_G is the identity element of G. Let D be a difference set in G with parameters (v, k, λ, n). Then, considering D as an element of $\mathbf{Z}G$,

$$
\begin{aligned}
DD^{(-1)} &= k1_G + \lambda(G - 1_G) \\
&= n + \lambda G,
\end{aligned}
$$

(2.2)

where $D^{(-1)}$ denotes the image of D under the inversion mapping $g \mapsto g^{-1}$, g in G.

Let H be a normal subgroup of G. Then the group homomorphism from G onto the factor group G/H induces a natural group ring homomorphism from $\mathbf{Z}G$ onto $\mathbf{Z}[G/H]$. We write A/H to denote the image of an arbitrary element A in $\mathbf{Z}G$ under this homomorphism. In particular, the image of the group ring element G under this homomorphism is

$$
G/H = |H|[G/H],
$$

where $|H|$ is the order of H and $[G/H]$ denotes the indicated quotient group. Hence (2.2) yields

$$
\begin{aligned}
(D/H)(D/H)^{(-1)} &= (D/H)(D^{(-1)}/H) \\
&= (DD^{(-1)})/H \\
&= (n + \lambda G)/H \\
&= n + \lambda |H|[G/H].
\end{aligned}
$$

Since a difference set has coefficients 0 and 1, the coefficients of D/H are no larger than $|H|$.

Now assume that G is a finite abelian group. A *character* χ of G is a homomorphism from G into the multiplicative group of complex roots of unity. Let e_G be the *exponent* of G, that is the order of the largest cyclic subgroup of G. Then the image of a group element g under χ, written $\chi(g)$, must be an e_G-th root of unity. It is well known that under pointwise multiplication the characters of G form a group that is isomorphic to G. This group is called the *character group* of G and it will be denoted by G^*. The identity of G^* is the *principal character*, denoted χ_0, that maps every element of G to 1. The *orthogonality relations* are

(2.3)
$$
\sum_{g \in G} \chi(g) = \begin{cases} |G|, & \text{if } \chi = \chi_0, \\ 0, & \text{if } \chi \neq \chi_0, \end{cases}
$$

and

(2.4)
$$
\sum_{\chi \in G^*} \chi(g) = \begin{cases} |G|, & \text{if } g = 1_G, \\ 0, & \text{if } g \neq 1_G. \end{cases}
$$

259

The characters of G can be extended linearly to the group ring $\mathbb{Z}G$:

$$\chi(\sum_{g \in G} a_g g) = \sum_{g \in G} a_g \chi(g)$$

Thus each character of G maps $\mathbb{Z}G$ into the order $\mathbb{Z}[\zeta]$, where ζ is a primitive e_G-th root of unity.

A straight forward application of the orthogonality relations (2.4) yields an expression for the coefficients a_g of a group ring element $A = \sum a_g g$ in terms of the values of the *character sums* $\chi(Ag^{-1})$, namely

(2.5)
$$a_g = \frac{1}{|G|} \sum_{\chi \in G^\bullet} \chi(Ag^{-1}), \quad g \in G.$$

This result is called the *inversion formula* for $\mathbb{Z}G$.

A character χ of G has a kernel, say K, that is a subgroup of G. Then χ has the same value on all the elements in each coset of K in G. Hence χ can be considered a character of the quotient group G/K, and therefore a character of the group ring $\mathbb{Z}[G/K]$. Thus for any A in $\mathbb{Z}G$,

$$\chi(A) = \chi(A/K)$$

and, more generally,

$$\chi(A) = \chi(A/K_1)$$

for any subgroup K_1 of K.

Now suppose that the group G is the direct product $H \times K$. Then an arbitrary element A in $\mathbb{Z}G$ can be written as

$$A = \sum_{h \in H} \sum_{k \in K} a_{hk} hk, \quad a_{hk} \in \mathbb{Z}.$$

For each character ψ of K define

$$\psi(A) = \sum_{h \in H} \psi(\sum_{k \in K} a_{hk} k) h.$$

If ψ has order d then ψ defines a group ring homomorphism from $\mathbb{Z}G$ onto $\mathbb{Z}[\zeta_d]H$, where ζ_d is a primitive d-th root of unity. We call ψ a *partial character* of G. Note that if ψ_0 is the principal character of K, then ψ_0 defines a homomorphism from $\mathbb{Z}H$ onto $\mathbb{Z}H$ and $\psi_0(A) = A/K$.

For a more detailed discussion of group rings and abelian group characters as they relate to difference sets, see Mann [9, Chapter 7].

3. Two Lemmas On Cyclotomic Fields. We begin by reviewing some basic facts about cyclotomic fields. For proofs and further information see, for example, Mann [10, Chapter 8] or Weiss [19, Chapter 7].

Let p be an odd prime and let ζ be a primitive p-th root of unity. The minimal-irreducible polynomial for ζ over $\mathbf{Q}$ is the cyclotomic polynomial

$$(3.1) \qquad\qquad 1 + x + \cdots + x^{p-1}.$$

Hence the cyclotomic field $\mathbf{Q}(\zeta)$ is of degree $p - 1$ over $\mathbf{Q}$. An integral basis for $\mathbf{Q}(\zeta)$ over $\mathbf{Q}$ is $\zeta, \zeta^2, \ldots, \zeta^{p-1}$. Thus the order $\mathbf{Z}[\zeta]$ is the ring of algebraic integers in $\mathbf{Q}(\zeta)$. Note that (3.1) implies that

$$(3.2) \qquad\qquad 1 + \zeta + \cdots + \zeta^{p-1} = 0.$$

LEMMA 3.1. *Let p be an odd prime and suppose that each of $\alpha_1, \ldots, \alpha_t$ is the sum of $\frac{1}{2}(p-1)$ or $\frac{1}{2}(p+1)$ distinct p-th roots of unity. If $\sum_{i=1}^{t} \alpha_i \overline{\alpha}_i$ is rational, then it is equal to $t(p+1)/4$.*

Proof. If α_i is the sum of $\frac{1}{2}(p+1)$ distinct p-th roots of unity, then (3.2) implies that $-\alpha_i$ is the sum of $\frac{1}{2}(p-1)$ distinct p-th roots of unity. Thus it is no restriction to assume that each α_i is the sum of

$$(3.3) \qquad\qquad s \;=\; \frac{1}{2}(p-1)$$

distinct p-th roots of unity. Hence each $\alpha_i \overline{\alpha}_i$ is the sum of s^2 p-th roots of unity of which s are equal to 1 (since the s roots of unity in α_i are distinct) and $s^2 - s$ are primitive p-th roots of unity. Thus

$$\sum_{i=1}^{t} \alpha_i \overline{\alpha}_i = st + \sigma,$$

where σ is the sum of $t(s^2 - s)$ primitive p-th roots of unity. A rational number b has the unique representation

$$b = -b(\zeta + \cdots + \zeta^{p-1})$$

as a linear combination over $\mathbf{Q}$ of primitive p-th roots of unity. Since σ must be rational in order that $\sum \alpha_i \overline{\alpha}_i$ be rational, we conclude that

$$\sigma = -t(s^2 - s)/(p - 1).$$

Then

$$\sum_{i=1}^{t} \alpha_i \overline{\alpha}_i = st + \sigma = st(p - s)/(p - 1).$$

Using (3.3) to eliminate s yields

$$\sum_{i=1}^{t} \alpha_i \overline{\alpha}_i = t(p+1)/4. \qquad\qquad \square$$

LEMMA 3.2. *Let p be an odd prime and let ζ be a primitive p-th root of unity. Define the weight, $\text{wt}(\alpha)$, of an algebraic integer*

$$(3.4) \qquad \alpha = \sum_{i=1}^{p-1} a_i \zeta^i, \quad a_i \in \mathbf{Z},$$

in the cyclotomic field $\mathbf{Q}(\zeta)$ to be the least nonnegative residue of $\sum_{i=1}^{p-1} a_i$ modulo p. Then for all algebraic integers α, β in $\mathbf{Q}(\zeta)$ and all c in $\mathbf{Z}$:

$$(3.5) \qquad \text{wt}(\alpha + \beta) \equiv \text{wt}(\alpha) + \text{wt}(\beta) \pmod{p}$$

$$(3.6) \qquad \text{wt}(c\alpha) \equiv c\,\text{wt}(\alpha) \pmod{p}$$

$$(3.7) \qquad \text{wt}(c) \equiv c \pmod{p}$$

$$(3.8) \qquad \text{wt}(\alpha\beta) \equiv \text{wt}(\alpha)\text{wt}(\beta) \pmod{p}$$

Proof. Since the representation (3.4) is unique, the weight function is well defined. Congruences (3.5) and (3.6) are obvious. Let $a_0, a_1, \ldots, a_{p-1}$ be arbitrary rational integers. Then (3.2) implies that

$$\sum_{i=0}^{p-1} a_i \zeta^i = \sum_{i=1}^{p-1} (a_i - a_0) \zeta^i.$$

Hence

$$\text{wt}\left(\sum_0^{p-1} a_i \zeta^i\right) = \text{wt}\left(\sum_1^{p-1}(a_i - a_0)\zeta^i\right)$$

$$\equiv \sum_1^{p-1}(a_i - a_0)$$

$$= -(p-1)a_0 + \sum_1^{p-1} a_i$$

$$\equiv \sum_0^{p-1} a_i \pmod{p}.$$

Thus (3.7) holds. Furthermore,

$$\text{wt}(\alpha\zeta^i) = \text{wt}(\alpha)$$

for all rational integers i. Therefore, if

$$\beta = \sum_{i=1}^{p-1} b_i \zeta^i,$$

then

$$\begin{aligned}
\mathsf{wt}(\alpha\beta) &= \mathsf{wt}(\alpha \sum b_i \zeta^i) \\
&= \mathsf{wt}(\sum \alpha b_i \zeta^i) \\
&\equiv \sum \mathsf{wt}(\alpha b_i \zeta^i) \\
&= \sum \mathsf{wt}(\alpha b_i) \\
&\equiv \sum \mathsf{wt}(\alpha) b_i \\
&= \mathsf{wt}(\alpha) \sum b_i \\
&\equiv \mathsf{wt}(\alpha)\mathsf{wt}(\beta) \pmod{p}. \qquad \square
\end{aligned}$$

4. Main Result. We prove the following necessary condition for the existence of certain Hadamard difference sets. Recall that the *exponent* of an abelian group is the order of the largest cyclic subgroup.

THEOREM 4.1. *Let $m = 2^e p$, where e is a nonnegative integer and p is an odd prime. Suppose that there exists a difference set D with the parameters*

$$(v, k, \lambda, n) = (4m^2, 2m^2 - m, m^2 - m, m^2)$$

in the direct product group $G = G_p \times G_2$, where G_p is an elementary abelian group of order p^2 and G_2 is an abelian group of order 2^{2e+2} with exponent 2 if $p \equiv 1 \pmod 4$ and exponent 2 or 4 if $p \equiv 3 \pmod 4$. Then $p = 3$ or $p + 1$ divides 2^e.

Note that the conclusion of the Theorem is equivalent to the assertion that p is a Mersenne prime and if $p \neq 3$, then the order of G_2 is greater than $4p^2$. The proof of the Theorem is broken up into a sequence of four lemmas.

LEMMA 4.2. *Let D/G_p be the image of the difference set D of Theorem 4.1 in the group ring $\mathbb{Z}G_2$. Then the coefficients of D/G_p are $\frac{1}{2}p(p \pm 1)$. Let A and B be the subsets of G_2 consisting of the group elements on which D/G_p has coefficients of $\frac{1}{2}p(p+1)$ and $\frac{1}{2}p(p-1)$, respectively. Then A and B are complementary Hadamard difference sets in G_2 with parameters*

(4.1) $$(v, k, \lambda, n) = (4m^2, 2m^2 - m, m^2 - m, m^2),$$

where $m = 2^e$ and -2^e, respectively.

Proof. Let ψ be any character of G_2 and let χ_0 be the principal character of G_p. Then (1.3), (2.2), and (2.3) imply that

(4.2) $$\psi\chi_0(D)\psi\chi_0(D^{(-1)}) = \psi\chi_0(n + \lambda G) \equiv 0 \pmod{2^{2e}p^2}.$$

The character sum $\psi(D/G_p) = \psi\chi_0(D)$ is a rational integer or a Gaussian integer depending on the order of ψ. Since a rational prime $p \equiv 3 \pmod 4$ cannot factor in

263

the Gaussian integers, (4.2) and the hypotheses of Theorem 4.1 imply that $\psi(D/G_p)$ is divisible by p. Then the inversion formula for $\mathbf{Z}G_2$ implies that the coefficients of D/G_p are divisible by p. Let

(4.3)
$$A = p^{-1} D/G_p - \tfrac{1}{2}(p-1)G_2.$$

Then A has integral coefficients and

$$AA^{(-1)} = n/p^2 + aG_2 = 2^{2e} + aG_2$$

for some integer a. Apply the principal character, ψ_0, of G_2 to $AA^{(-1)}$ and use the fact that

(4.4)
$$\psi_0(A) = k/p - \tfrac{1}{2}(p-1)2^{2e+2} = 2^{2e+1} - 2^e$$

to obtain $a = 2^{2e} - 2^e$. Hence

(4.5)
$$AA^{(-1)} = 2^{2e} + (2^{2e} - 2^e)G_2.$$

Consequently the coefficients of A have the same sum — $\psi_0(A)$ — as sum of squares — the coefficient of $AA^{(-1)}$ on the identity of G_2. Therefore A has coefficients 0 and 1. Then (4.4) and (4.5) imply that A is a difference set in G_2 with parameters (4.1), where $m = 2^e$. Furthermore, (4.3) implies that the coefficients 0 and 1 of A correspond to the coefficients $\tfrac{1}{2}p(p-1)$ and $\tfrac{1}{2}p(p+1)$, respectively, of D/G_p. □

LEMMA 4.3. *Let G_p be an elementary abelian group of order p^2 and let K_1, $\ldots$, K_{p+1} be the distinct subgroups of order p in G_p. If there exists a difference set D as described in Theorem 4.1, then $p+1$ divides 2^{2e+2} and D is of the form*

$$D = \sum_{i=1}^{p+1} \sum_{g \in S_i} gD_g,$$

where $\{S_1, \ldots, S_{p+1}\}$ is a partition of the 2-group G_2 with each S_i of cardinality $2^{2e+2}/(p+1)$ and each D_g in $\{D_g \mid g \in S_i\}$ is the sum of $\tfrac{1}{2}(p-1)$ or $\tfrac{1}{2}(p+1)$ distinct cosets of K_i in G_p, $i = 1, \ldots, p+1$.

For $i = 1, \ldots, p+1$ let pE_i be the image of D under the partial character χ_i, where χ_i is a character of G_p that has the subgroup K_i, defined above, as its kernel. Then

$$E_i = \sum_{g \in S_i} g\alpha_{ig},$$

where each α_{ig} is the sum of $\tfrac{1}{2}(p-1)$ or $\tfrac{1}{2}(p+1)$ distinct p-th roots of unity. Moreover,

$$E_i \overline{E_i}^{(-1)} = 2^{2e},$$

264

where the bar denotes complex conjugation of the coefficients α_{ig}.

Proof. Let h be an element of G_2, let ψ be a character of G_2, and let χ_i be one of the characters $\chi_1, \ldots, \chi_{p+1}$ specified in the statement of the Lemma. Then

$$\psi\chi_i(h^{-1}D)\overline{\psi\chi_i(h^{-1}D)} = \psi\chi_i(h^{-1}D)\psi\chi_i(hD^{(-1)})$$

$$(4.6) \qquad\qquad = \psi\chi_i(DD^{(-1)})$$

$$= \psi\chi_i(n + \lambda G)$$

$$= n$$

$$= 2^{2e}p^2.$$

Let ρ be a primitive p-th root of unity if G_2 has exponent 2 and a primitive $4p$-th root of unity if G_2 has exponent 4. By hypothesis $p \equiv 3 \pmod 4$ if G_2 has exponent 4, so the principal ideal generated by p factors in the cyclotomic field $\mathbb{Q}(\rho)$ as a power of a principal prime ideal — see Mann [10, Chapter 8] or Weiss [19, Chapter 7]. Hence (4.6) implies that $\psi\chi_i(h^{-1}D)$ is divisible by p, say

$$(4.7) \qquad\qquad \psi\chi_i(h^{-1}D) = p\alpha_\psi$$

for some algebraic integer α_ψ in $\mathbb{Q}(\rho)$ that satisfies

$$(4.8) \qquad\qquad \alpha_\psi\overline{\alpha}_\psi = 2^{2e}.$$

Write D in the form

$$(4.9) \qquad\qquad D = \sum_{g \in G_2} gD_g,$$

where each D_g is a subset of G_p, that is an element of the group ring $\mathbb{Z}G_p$ with coefficients 0 and 1. Then, from (4.7) and (4.9),

$$(4.10) \qquad p\alpha_\psi = \psi\chi_i(h^{-1}D) = \sum_{g \in G_2} \psi(h^{-1}g)\chi_i(D_g).$$

The orthogonality relations (2.4) for the characters ψ of G_2 then yield

$$p \sum_{\psi \in G_2^*} \alpha_\psi = \sum_{\psi \in G_2^*} \sum_{g \in G_2} \psi(h^{-1}g)\chi_i(D_g)$$

$$(4.11) \qquad\qquad = \sum_{g \in G_2} \chi_i(D_g) \sum_{\psi \in G_2^*} \psi(h^{-1}g)$$

$$= 2^{2e+2}\chi_i(D_h).$$

For each $i = 1, \ldots, p+1$ there is a g in G_2 for which $\chi_i(D_g) \neq 0$; for otherwise α_ψ would be zero in (4.10) and (4.8). Now fix i and let g be an element in G_2 for which

$$(4.12) \qquad\qquad \chi_i(D_g) \neq 0.$$

Let

$$(4.13) \qquad D_g/K_i = \sum_{j=0}^{p-1} a_j k_i^j, \quad a_j \in \mathbf{Z},$$

where k_i is a generator of the group G_p/K_i. Since D_g has coefficients 0, 1 and K_i is a subgroup of order p, the coefficients of D_g/K_i satisfy

$$(4.14) \qquad 0 \le a_j \le p, \quad j = 0, \dots, p-1.$$

Let $\chi_i(k_i) = \zeta$. Note that ζ is a primitive p-th root of unity since k_i does not belong to K_i — the kernel of χ_i in G_p. Then

$$(4.15) \qquad \chi_i(D_g) = \chi_i(D_g/K_i) = \sum_{j=0}^{p-1} a_j \zeta^j = \sum_{j=1}^{p-1} (a_j - a_0) \zeta^j.$$

Since $\zeta, \dots, \zeta^{p-1}$ is an integral basis for $\mathbf{Q}(\zeta)$ over $\mathbf{Q}$ and (4.11) implies that p divides $\chi_i(D_g)$, we conclude that

$$a_j - a_0 \equiv 0 \,(\mathrm{mod}\ p), \quad j = 1, \dots, p-1.$$

Hence

$$(4.16) \qquad a_0 \equiv a_1 \equiv \cdots \equiv a_{p-1}\,(\mathrm{mod}\ p).$$

If $a_0 = a_1 = \cdots = a_{p-1}$, then (4.15) would imply that $\chi_i(D_g) = 0$ — contrary to the assumption (4.12). Hence the only possible values for the a_j's that satisfy (4.14) and (4.16) are 0 and p. Then (4.13) implies that

$$(4.17) \qquad D_g = K_i \sum_{j=0}^{p-1} b_j(g) k_i^j,$$

where each $b_j(g)$ is 0 or 1. We assert that

$$(4.18) \qquad \sum_{j=0}^{p-1} b_j(g) = \tfrac{1}{2}(p \pm 1).$$

Let χ_0 be the principal character of G_p. The image of D in $\mathbf{Z}G_2$ is $D/G_p = \chi_0(D)$, which by (4.9) can be written as

$$D/G_p = \sum_{g \in G_2} g\chi_0(D_g).$$

Lemma 4.2 states that the coefficients of D/G_p are $\frac{1}{2}p(p \pm 1)$. Hence

$$(4.19) \qquad \chi_0(D_g) = \tfrac{1}{2}p(p \pm 1), \quad g \in G.$$

From (4.17), $\chi_0(D_g) = p \sum b_j(g)$. This proves (4.18).

To summarize, we have shown that for each $i = 1, \dots, p+1$ there is a g in G_2 such that $\chi_i(D_g) \neq 0$; and every D_g for which $\chi_i(D_g) \neq 0$ must be the sum of $\frac{1}{2}(p-1)$ or $\frac{1}{2}(p+1)$ distinct cosets of K_i in G_p.

For $i = 1, \dots, p+1$ let

$$S_i = \{g \in G_2 \mid \chi_i(D_g) \neq 0\}.$$

We assert that $\{S_1, \dots, S_{p+1}\}$ is a partition of G_2. The previous paragraph states that no S_i is empty. Suppose that S_i and S_j are not disjoint. Then there is a D_g for which $\chi_i(D_g) \neq 0$ and $\chi_j(D_g) \neq 0$. Hence D_g is the sum of $\frac{1}{2}(p \pm 1)$ cosets of K_i and the sum of $\frac{1}{2}(p \pm 1)$ cosets of K_j. This is impossible if $i \neq j$. Thus the S_i's are pairwise disjoint. Suppose that there is a g in G_2 that does not belong to any S_i. Then

$$\chi_1(D_g) = \cdots = \chi_{p+1}(D_g) = 0.$$

Applying automorphisms of $\mathbb{Q}(\zeta)$ yields $\chi_i^j(D_g) = 0$ for $i = 1, \dots, p+1$ and $j = 1, \dots, p-1$, that is $\chi(D_g) = 0$ for all nonprincipal characters χ of G_p. Hence by the inversion formula, $D_g = aG_p$ for some integer a. But this contradicts (4.19). Therefore $\{S_1, \dots, S_{p+1}\}$ is a partition of G_2, as asserted. Consequently, (4.9) and (4.17) yield

$$D = \sum_{g \in G_2} gD_g = \sum_{i=1}^{p+1} \sum_{g \in S_i} gD_g = \sum_{i=1}^{p+1} K_i \sum_{g \in S_i} g \sum_{j=0}^{p-1} b_j(g) k_i^j.$$

Since the kernels of the characters $\chi_1, \dots, \chi_{p+1}$ are $K_1, \dots, K_{p+1}$, respectively,

$$\chi_i(K_j) = \begin{cases} p, & \text{if } i = j, \\ 0, & \text{if } i \neq j. \end{cases}$$

Hence the image of D under the partial character χ_i is

$$\chi_i(D) = p \sum_{g \in S_i} g\alpha_{ig},$$

where by (4.18) each α_{ig} is the sum of $\frac{1}{2}(p-1)$ or $\frac{1}{2}(p+1)$ distinct p-th roots of unity. Let

$$E_i = \sum_{g \in S_i} g\alpha_{ig}, \quad i = 1, \dots, p+1.$$

Then

(4.20)
$$\begin{aligned} E_i \overline{E}_i^{(-1)} &= p^{-2} \chi_i(D) \chi_i(D^{(-1)}) \\ &= p^{-2} \chi_i(n + \lambda G) \\ &= p^{-2} n \\ &= 2^{2e}. \end{aligned}$$

Equating coefficients on the identity of G_2 in (4.20) yields

$$\sum_{g \in S_i} \alpha_{ig} \overline{\alpha}_{ig} = 2^{2e}.$$

Then Lemma 3.1 yields $2^{2e+2}/(p+1)$ as the cardinality of each S_i. □

267

LEMMA 4.4. *Let G_2 be a finite abelian group with exponent 2 or 4 and let p be an odd prime. Then G_2 cannot contain a subset S of cardinality $p+1$ such that the multi-set*

$$T = \{gh^{-1} \mid g \in S, \ h \in S, \ g \neq h\}$$

contains exactly $p+1$ distinct elements with each occurring exactly p times.

Proof. Suppose that the group G_2 contains a subset S of cardinality $p+1$ for which the multi-set T has the stated property. For any g in G_2, S can be replaced by

$$gS = \{gs \mid s \in S\}$$

without changing the multi-set T. Hence it is no restriction to assume that S contains the group identity element 1. We assert that neither S nor T can contain an element of order 2. For suppose g in S has order 2. Then $g = g \cdot 1^{-1}$ belongs to T. If $g_1 g_2^{-1} = g$, then $g_2 g_1^{-1} = (g_1 g_2^{-1})^{-1} = g^{-1} = g$. Thus g occurs an even number of times in T instead of the required p times. Therefore $S = \{1, g_1, \ldots, g_p\}$, where each g_i has order 4. No g_i^{-1} can belong to S since otherwise $g_i(g_i^{-1})^{-1} = g_i^2$ would be an element of order 2 in T. Thus T contains at least $2p$ distinct elements, namely $g_i \cdot 1^{-1}$ and $1 \cdot g_i^{-1}$ for $i = 1, \ldots, p$ — a contradiction. $\square$

LEMMA 4.5. *If there exists a difference set as described in Theorem 4.1 for a prime $p > 3$, then $p+1$ divides 2^e.*

Proof. Choose i in $\{1, \ldots, p+1\}$. Then, to avoid subscripts, let $S = S_i$ and let

$$(4.21) \qquad E = E_i = \sum_{g \in S} g \alpha_g$$

be as defined in Lemma 4.3. Furthermore, by Lemma 4.3 the weight (see Lemma 3.2) of each coefficient α_g of E is $\frac{1}{2}(p \pm 1)$. Let x and y be the number of coefficients of E that have weight $\frac{1}{2}(p-1)$ and $\frac{1}{2}(p+1)$, respectively. Then

$$(4.22) \qquad x + y = |S|,$$

where $|S|$ denotes the cardinality of S. Let $\mathcal{A}$ be the multi-set

$$(4.23) \qquad \mathcal{A} = \{\alpha_g \overline{\alpha}_h \mid g \in S, \ h \in S, \ g \neq h\}.$$

Note that $p \equiv 3 \pmod 4$ by Lemma 4.3. Thus if the coefficients α_g and α_h of E have the same weight, then $\mathsf{wt}(\alpha_g \overline{\alpha}_h) = \frac{1}{4}(p+1)$ since

$$\left(\frac{p-1}{2}\right)^2 \equiv \left(\frac{p+1}{2}\right)^2 \equiv \frac{1}{4}(p+1) \pmod p;$$

while if α_g and α_h have different weights, then $\mathsf{wt}(\alpha_g \overline{\alpha}_h) = \frac{1}{4}(3p-1)$ since

$$\left(\frac{p-1}{2}\right)\left(\frac{p+1}{2}\right) \equiv \frac{1}{4}(3p-1) \pmod p.$$

The coefficient of $E\overline{E}^{(-1)}$ on the identity element of G_2 is the sum of $|S|$ terms, $\alpha_g\overline{\alpha}_{g^{-1}}$, all of which have weight $\frac{1}{4}(p+1)$. Thus the multi-set $\mathcal{A}$ contains $x^2+y^2-|S|$ elements of weight $\frac{1}{4}(p+1)$ and $2xy$ elements of weight $\frac{1}{4}(3p-1)$.

We now determine the distribution of the weights of the elements of $\mathcal{A}$ by group element. Let k be a nonidentity group element in

$$SS^{-1} = \{gh^{-1} \mid g \in S,\ h \in S\}.$$

Then

$$(4.24) \qquad \sum_{\substack{g,h \in S \\ gh^{-1}=k}} \alpha_g\overline{\alpha}_h = 0,$$

since the summation is the coefficient of

$$E\overline{E}^{(-1)} = 2^{2e}$$

(see Lemma 4.3) on k. Let $w_0(k)$ and $w_1(k)$ be the number of ordered index pairs (g, h) in the summation (4.24) for which $\mathrm{wt}(\alpha_g\overline{\alpha}_h)$ is equal to $\frac{1}{4}(p+1)$ and $\frac{1}{4}(3p-1)$, respectively. Then Lemma 3.2 implies that

$$\tfrac{1}{4}(p+1)w_0(k) + \tfrac{1}{4}(3p-1)w_1(k) \equiv 0 \pmod{p}.$$

Hence

$$(4.25) \qquad w_0(k) \equiv w_1(k) \pmod{p}.$$

For each of the $|S|$ indices g in the summation (4.21) there is at most one index h in the summation

$$\overline{E}^{(-1)} = \sum_{h \in S} h^{-1}\overline{\alpha}_h$$

for which $gh^{-1} = k$. Thus there are at most $|S|$ terms in the summation (4.24). Therefore

$$(4.26) \qquad w_0(k) + w_1(k) \leq |S|.$$

Assume that $p + 1$ does not divide 2^e. We prove the Lemma by showing that this assumption implies that $p = 3$. By Lemma 4.3, $p+1 = 2^d$ for some integer d. Thus the assumption is equivalent to $e + 1 \leq d$. Then Lemma 4.3 yields

$$(4.27) \qquad |S| = 2^{2e+2}/(p+1) = 2^{2e+2-d} \leq 2^d = p+1.$$

Conditions (4.25) – (4.27) imply that there are three possible sets of values for $w_0(k)$ and $w_1(k)$ for each nonidentity k in SS^{-1}:

$$(4.28) \qquad w_0(k) = p,\ w_1(k) = 0$$
$$(4.29) \qquad w_0(k) = 0,\ w_1(k) = p$$
$$(4.30) \qquad w_0(k) = w_1(k)$$

Let a, b, c be the number of nonidentity k in $S^{-1}S$ for which (4.28), (4.29), (4.30) holds, respectively. Thus the multi-set $\mathcal{A}$ defined in (4.23) has

$$pa + \sum w_0(k)$$

elements of weight $\frac{1}{4}(p+1)$ and

$$pb + \sum w_1(k) = pb + \sum w_0(k)$$

elements of weight $\frac{1}{4}(3p-1)$, where all summations are over those nonidentity k in SS^{-1} for which (4.30) holds. Therefore, using the previously derived expressions for the weight distributions in $\mathcal{A}$,

(4.31)
$$x^2 + y^2 - |S| = pa + \sum w_0(k)$$

and

(4.32)
$$2xy = pb + \sum w_0(k).$$

Subtracting (4.32) from (4.31) yields

(4.33)
$$(x-y)^2 = |S| + p(a-b).$$

Since $|S| \leq p + 1$ by (4.27), we must have $|S| < p$ or $|S| = p$ or $|S| = p + 1$. Suppose that $|S| < p$. Then (4.25) and (4.26) imply $w_0(k) = w_1(k)$ for all k. Hence (4.28) and (4.29) cannot occur, that is $a = b = 0$. Then (4.33) implies that $|S|$ is a square. The first equality in (4.27) then implies that $p + 1$ is an even power of 2, say $p + 1 = 2^{2f}$. Hence $p = (2^f - 1)(2^f + 1)$, which is possible only if the prime p is equal to 3. If $|S| = p$, then (4.27) yields $p(p+1) = 2^{2e+2}$, which is impossible. Hence assume that

(4.34)
$$|S| = p + 1.$$

Then (4.33) implies that

$$x - y \equiv \pm 1 \pmod{p}.$$

Since x and y are nonnegative integers that satisfy $x + y = |S| = p + 1$ (see (4.22) and (4.34)), there are only the following four sets of values for x, y:

$$
\begin{aligned}
&\text{Case I:} \quad x = 0, \, y = p + 1 \\
&\text{Case II:} \quad x = 1, \, y = p \\
&\text{Case III:} \quad x = p, \, y = 1 \\
&\text{Case IV:} \quad x = p + 1, \, y = 0
\end{aligned}
$$

Assume that Case I or IV holds. Then (4.32) yields

$$0 = 2xy = pb + \sum w_0(k).$$

Hence $b = 0$ and $\sum w_0(k) = 0$, so $c = 0$. Then (4.31) yields

$$(p+1)^2 - (p+1) = pa,$$

so $a = p + 1$. Thus, from (4.28), there are exactly $p + 1$ nonidentity values of k in SS^{-1} for which $w_0(k) = p$ and $w_1(k) = 0$. Since $b = c = 0$, this accounts for all nonidentity values of k in SS^{-1}. Hence the multi-set

$$T = \{gh^{-1} \mid g \in S, \ h \in S, \ g \neq h\}$$

contains exactly $p + 1$ distinct elements and each of them occurs exactly $w_0(k) = p$ times. This is impossible by Lemma 4.4. Thus only Cases II and III are possible. Therefore each E_i in $\{E_1, \ldots, E_{p+1}\}$ (see Lemma 4.3) has either $x = 1$ coefficient of weight $\frac{1}{2}(p-1)$ and $y = p$ coefficients of weight $\frac{1}{2}(p+1)$, or else $x = p$ coefficients of weight $\frac{1}{2}(p-1)$ and $y = 1$ coefficient of weight $\frac{1}{2}(p+1)$. Therefore, for $i = 1, \ldots, p+1$, the set $\{D_g \mid g \in S_i\}$ contains either

(4.35)
$$\begin{cases} \text{one } D_g \text{ that is the sum of } \dfrac{1}{2}(p-1) \text{ cosets of } K_i \text{ and} \\ p \ D_g\text{'s that are the sum of } \dfrac{1}{2}(p+1) \text{ cosets of } K_i, \end{cases}$$

or

(4.36)
$$\begin{cases} p \ D_g\text{'s that are the sum of } \dfrac{1}{2}(p-1) \text{ cosets of } K_i \text{ and} \\ \text{one } D_g \text{ that is the sum of } \dfrac{1}{2}(p+1) \text{ cosets of } K_i. \end{cases}$$

Let z_1 and z_2 be the number of times (4.35) and (4.36) occur, respectively. Then D/G_p has $z_1 + pz_2$ coefficients that are equal to $\frac{1}{2}p(p-1)$ and $pz_1 + z_2$ coefficients that are equal to $\frac{1}{2}p(p+1)$. By Lemma 4.2, D/G_p has coefficients $\frac{1}{2}p(p-1)$ and $\frac{1}{2}p(p+1)$, with the former occurring $2 \cdot 2^{2e} + 2^e$ times and the latter occurring $2 \cdot 2^{2e} - 2^e$ times. Eqs. (4.27) and (4.34) yield

$$p + 1 = 2^{e+1}.$$

Hence

$$z_1 + pz_2 = 2 \cdot 2^{2e} + 2^e = \frac{1}{2}(p+1)(p+2),$$

$$pz_1 + z_2 = 2 \cdot 2^{2e} - 2^e = \frac{1}{2}(p+1)p.$$

These equations have the unique solution

$$z_1 = \frac{p+1}{2} \cdot \frac{p-2}{p-1} = 2^e \frac{p-2}{p-1},$$

$$z_2 = \frac{p+1}{2} \cdot \frac{p}{p-1} = 2^e \frac{p}{p-1}.$$

Thus z_1 and z_2 are integral if and only if $p - 1$ divides 2^e. Since $p + 1 = 2^{e+1}$, this is possible only if $p = 3$. $\quad\square$

REFERENCES

[1] T. BETH, D. JUNGNICKEL, AND H. LENZ, *Design Theory*, Cambridge Univ. Press, New York, 1986.

[2] R. H. BRUCK, *Difference sets in a finite group*, Trans. Amer. Math. Soc., 78 (1955), pp. 464–481.

[3] J. A. DAVIS, *Difference Sets in Abelian 2-Groups*, Ph. D. Thesis, Univ. of Virginia, (1987).

[4] J. F. DILLON, *Difference sets in 2-groups*, in *Proc. NSA Mathematical Sciences Meetings*, 6 & 7 January 1987 and 7 & 8 October 1987, R. L. Ward, (ed.), Ft. George Meade, Maryland, 1987, pp. 165–172.

[5] J. F. DILLON, *Variations on a scheme of McFarland for noncyclic difference sets*, J. Combin. Theory Ser. A, 40 (1985), pp. 9–21.

[6] J. F. DILLON, *Elementary Hadamard difference sets*, in *Proc. 6th S-E Conf. Combinatorics, Graph Theory and Computing*, (Utilitas Math.), Winnipeg, 1975, pp. 237–249.

[7] J. F. DILLON, *Elementary Hadamard Difference Sets*, Ph. D. Thesis, Univ. of Maryland, 1974.

[8] R. E. KIBLER, *A summary of noncyclic difference sets, $k < 20$*, J. Combin. Theory Ser. A, 25 (1978), pp. 62–67.

[9] H. B. MANN, *Addition Theorems*, Wiley, New York, 1965.

[10] H. B. MANN, *Introduction to Algebraic Number Theory*, The Ohio State Univ. Press, Columbus, Ohio, 1955.

[11] H. B. MANN AND R. L. McFARLAND, *On Hadamard difference sets*, in *A Survey of Combinatorial Theory*, J. N. Srivastava et al., (eds.), American Elsevier, New York, 1973, pp. 333–334.

[12] R. L. McFARLAND, *Difference sets in abelian groups of order $4p^2$*, Mitt. Math. Sem. Giessen (to appear).

[13] R. L. McFARLAND, *Sub-difference sets of Hadamard difference sets*, J. Combin. Theory Ser. A (to appear).

[14] R. L. McFARLAND, *A family of difference sets in non-cyclic groups*, J. Combin. Theory Ser. A, 15 (1973), pp. 1–10.

[15] P. KESAVA MENON, *On difference sets whose parameters satisfy a certain relation*, Proc. Amer. Math. Soc., 13 (1962), pp. 739–745.

[16] O. S. ROTHAUS, *On "bent" functions*, J. Combin. Theory Ser. A, 20 (1976), pp. 300–305.

[17] R. J. TURYN, *A special class of Williamson matrices and difference sets*, J. Combin. Theory Ser. A, 36 (1984), pp. 111–115.

[18] R. J. TURYN, *Character sums and difference sets*, Pacific J. Math., 15 (1965), pp. 319–346.

[19] E. WEISS, *Algebraic Number Theory*, McGraw-Hill, New York, 1963.

272

POLYNOMIAL ADDITION SETS AND
SYMMETRIC DIFFERENCE SETS

S. L. MA*

Abstract. Let $f(x)$ be an integral polynomial and G be a group of order v. A subset D of G with $|D| = k$ is called a $(v, k, f(x))$-polynomial addition set if $f\left(\sum_{g \in D} g\right) = \lambda \sum_{g \in G} g$ for some integer λ. In this paper, we give a survey on the cases where G is abelian and $f(x) = x^2 + bx + c$ or $x^m - d$. The results are applied to difference sets to yield some conditions on the existence of symmetric difference sets. Furthermore, a new result on symmetric Hadamard difference sets is proved.

Key words. polynomial digraphs, polynomial addition sets, difference sets.

AMS(MOS) subject classifications. 05B10, 05B30

1. Polynomial Addition Sets. Let $f(x)$ be an integral polynomial. A digraph Γ with v vertices is called a $f(x)$-**digraph** if $f(A) = \lambda J$ for some integer λ where A is the adjacency matrix of Γ and J is the $v \times v$ matrix with all entries equal to 1. (Usually, we may allow Γ to have self-loops so that A can be regarded as some $(0, 1)$-matrix.) This object is first studied by Hoffman [8] and Hoffman and McAndrew [9] for graphs and digraphs respectively with $\lambda \neq 0$.

In the studies of $f(x)$-digraphs, we always face the problem that, given a particular polynomial $f(x)$, we want to know whether there exists a $f(x)$-digraph. There are two special cases which have been studied extensively:

(I) $f(x) = x^2 + bx + c$ (i.e. $A^2 + bA + cI = \lambda J$): If $A^T = A$ and $\mathrm{tr}\, A = 0$, then Γ is a strongly regular graph and it is a well-known combinatorial object (see [10]). Recently, Duval [6] has tried to study the case with $A^T \neq A$.

(II) $f(x) = x^m - d$ (i.e. $A^m = dI + \lambda J$): The orientation of the problem is the studies of the matrix equation $A^2 = J$ by Knuth [12] and Ryser [23]. Later, Lam [13, 15] generalizes to the matrix equations $A^2 = dI + \lambda J$ and $A^m = dI + \lambda J$.

Remark. There is a generalization of $f(x)$-digraphs given by Bridges [1]. However, we are not going to deal with it.

Let G be a finite group and D be a subset of G. A **Cayley digraph generated by** D is a digraph whose vertex set is G and, for $g,\ h \in G$, g is joined to h if $g^{-1}h \in D$.

NOTATIONS. For any subset S of G, we define

(a) $\bar{S} = \sum_{g \in S} g \in \mathbf{Z}[G]$; and
(b) $S^{(t)} = \{g^t | g \in S\}$ for any integer t.

Note that a Cayley digraph generated by D is a $f(x)$-digraph if and only if $f(\bar{D}) = \lambda \bar{G}$ for some integer λ. If we are interested in Cayley $f(x)$-digraphs only, then we may formulate our problem using the language of the group algebra $\mathbf{Z}[G]$.

*Department of Mathematics, National University of Singapore, Kent Ridge, Singapore 0511.
The work was done when the author visited the IMA.

DEFINITION. Let G be a group of order v and D be a subset of G with $|D| = k$. Then D is called a $(v, k, f(x))$-**polynomial addition set** if $f(\bar{D}) = \lambda \bar{G}$ for some integer λ. (For detail discussion, please see [19].)

In this paper, we only consider the case where G is an abelian group so that we can make use of the characters of G. Let X be any character of G and $z = \sum_{g \in G} a_g g \in \mathbf{Z}[G]$. Define $X(z) = \sum_{g \in G} a_g Xg \in \mathbf{C}$.

PROPOSITION 1.1. *Let G be an abelian group of order v and D be a subset of G with $|D| = k$. Then D is a $(v, k, f(x))$-polynomial addition set if and only if $X(\bar{D})$ is a zero of $f(x)$ for each nontrivial character X of G.*

2. On Quadratic Polynomial. Now, let us consider the case $f(x) = x^2 + bx + c$. Suppose D is a $(v, k, x^2 + bx + c)$-polynomial addition set in an abelian group G. Without loss of generality, we may assume that the identity element 1_G of G is not contained in D. Then it can be shown that $D^{(-1)} = D$ or $G - D - \{1_G\}$. Thus $\{1_G, \bar{D}, \bar{G} - \bar{D} - 1_G\}$ spans a subalgebra of $\mathbf{Z}[G]$ which is known as a Schur ring of dimension 3 (see [20]). Using a result on Schur rings, we have the following theorem.

THEOREM 2.1. *(Wielandt [26]) Let G be an abelian group of order v. Let p be a prime such that G consists a nontrivial cyclic p-Sylow subgroup. Then the only possible $(v, k, x^2 + bx + c)$-polynomial addition sets in G are of the form H, $H \cup \{1_G\}$, $G - H$ or $G - H - \{1_G\}$ where (a) $H \cup \{1_G\}$ is a subgroup of G; or (b) $G \cong \mathbf{Z}_p$ and H corresponds to the set of nonzero quadratic residues.*

Remark. As a consequence of Theorem 2.1, we can completely characterize all $(v, k, x^2 + bx + c)$-polynomial addition set in cyclic groups.

Note that the polynomial $x^2 + bx + c$ in case (a) of Theorem 2.1 is reducible while it is irreducible in case (b). In the following, we shall discuss the irreducible and reducible cases separately.

Firstly, let $x^2 + bx + c$ be irreducible. Suppose there is a $(v, k, x^2 + bx + c)$-polynomial addition set D exists in an abelian group G. By the fact that the zeros of $x^2 + bx + c$ are conjugate, we find that the following conditions must be satisfied (see, for example, [18] and [19]):

(i) $v = p^t$ where p is an odd prime and t is an odd number;

(ii) $k = \begin{cases} (p^t - 1)/2 & \text{if } 1_G \notin D \\ (p^t + 1)/2 & \text{if } 1_G \in D; \end{cases}$

(iii) $x^2 + bx + c = \begin{cases} x^2 + x - \frac{p^t - 1}{4} & \text{if } p \equiv 1 \mod 4 \text{ and } 1_G \notin D \\ x^2 - x - \frac{p^t - 1}{4} & \text{if } p \equiv 1 \mod 4 \text{ and } 1_G \in D \\ x^2 + x + \frac{p^t + 1}{4} & \text{if } p \equiv 3 \mod 4 \text{ and } 1_G \notin D \\ x^2 - x + \frac{p^t + 1}{4} & \text{if } p \equiv 3 \mod 4 \text{ and } 1_G \in D; \end{cases}$

(iv) $D^{(t)} = D$ if t is a nonzero quadratic residue modulo p.

Up to now, all the known examples of this type are found in elementary p-groups. Thus, we have the following question.

Open problem. Is it true that elementary p-groups are the only abelian groups that consist $(v, k, x^2 + bx + c)$-polynomial addition sets where $x^2 + bx + c$ is irreducible?

Remark. Actually, for an irreducible polynomial $f(x)$ of degree at least 2, we also want to ask if there exists a $(v, k, f(x))$-polynomial addition set in an abelian group which is not an elementary p-group.

Now, let $x^2 + bx + c$ be reducible. Since all the zeros of $x^2 + bx + c$ are rational, it is known that if D is a $(v, k, x^2 + bx + c)$-polynomial addition set in an abelian group, then $D^{(t)} = D$ for all t relatively prime to v. Using this observation, Bridges and Mena prove the following.

THEOREM 2.2. *(Bridges and Mena [4]) Let G be an abelian group containing a nontrivial Sylow p-subgroup P where p is a prime. Suppose $P \cong \mathbf{Z}_{p^r} \times \mathbf{Z}_{p^s}$ with $r \neq s$. Then, for any $(v, k, x^2 + bx + c)$-polynomial addition set D in G where $x^2 + bx + c$ is reducible, either $D \cup \{1_G\}$ or $(G - D) \cup \{1_G\}$ must be a subgroup of G.*

Remark. If $|G| = w^2$ and $H_1, \ldots, H_m$ are subgroups of order w such that $H_i \cap H_j = \{1_G\}$ whenever $i \neq j$, then $D = H_1 \cup \ldots \cup H_m$ is a polynomial addition set of the required type. Hence, Theorem 2.2 does not hold if $r = s$.

The following is a more general result.

THEOREM 2.3. *(Ma [19]) Let G be an abelian group of order v and exponent v^*. Let p be a prime such that p^t strictly divides v and p^r strictly divides v^*. If there exists a $(v, k, x^2 + bx + c)$-polynomial addition set D in G such that $x^2 + bx + c$ is reducible and both $D \cup \{1_G\}$ and $(G - D) \cup \{1_G\}$ are not subgroup of G, then $p^{2r} | b^2 - 4c$ and $p^{2(t-r+1)} \nmid b^2 - 4c$.*

Remark. By Theorem 2.3, if $2r > t$, then, for any $(v, k, x^2 + bx + c)$-polynomial addition set D in G where $x^2 + bx + c$ is reducible, either $D \cup \{1_G\}$ or $(G - D) \cup \{1_G\}$ must be a subgroup of G. Since $(v, k, x^2 + bx + c)$-polynomial addition sets in abelian groups are related to Schur rings of dimension 3, one may want to ask if this result can be extended to Schur rings in general.

Open problem. Let G be an abelian group of order v and exponent v^*. Let p be a prime such that p^t strictly divides v and p^r strictly divides v^*. If $v \neq p$ and $2r > t$, does there exist a nontrivial primitive Schur ring over G? (For reference, see [20] and [26].)

3. On Cyclic Polynomial. For $f(x) = x^m - d$, the first published result is by Lam [14] who proves that no $(v, k, x^2 - d)$-polynomial addition set exists in cyclic groups with $1 < k < v - 1$. However, this result is only a consequence of Theorem 2.1.

Using a result on x^m-digraphs, we have the following interesting theorem.

THEOREM 3.1. *(Bridges and Mena [2]) If D is a $(v, k, x^m - d)$-polynomial addition set in an abelian group G, then D is a difference set in G.*

Remark. Difference sets will be discussed in Section 4. However, we want to point out that diference sets constructed by McFarland [21] and Spence [24] are $(v, k, x^m - d)$-polynomial addition sets for some even number m.

Summarizing the results in [19], we have some conditions on the existence of $(v, k, x^m - d)$-polynomial addition sets.

THEOREM 3.2. *(Ma [19]) Let G be an abelian group of order v and exponent v^*. If there is a $(v, k, x^m - d)$-polynomial addition set in G with $d \neq 0$, then $d = a^m$ where $|a|$ is the greatest common divisor of v and k. Furthermore, if p is a prime divisor of v such that p^t strictly divides v and p^r strictly divides v^*, then $p^{t-r+1} \nmid a$.*

Remark. Note that if G is cyclic, then, by Theorem 3.2, $d = 0$ or 1 and this implies $k = 0, 1, v - 1$ or v. That is, no $(v, k, x^m - d)$-polynomial addition set in cyclic groups with $1 < k < v - 1$ (also see [17]).

It is interesting to note that all the known nontrivial examples of $(v, k, x^m - d)$-polynomial addition sets have an even m, for example, see the remark of Theorem 3.1. Therefore, we may ask the following.

Open problem. Are there $(v, k, x^m - d)$-polynomial addition sets with $1 < k < v - 1$ such that m is odd?

4. Symmetric Difference Sets. Let G be a group of order v and D be a subset of G with $|D| = k$. D is called a (v, k, λ)-**difference set** if expressions $d_1 d_2^{-1}$, $d_1, d_2 \in D$ and $d_1 \neq d_2$, represent all non-identity elements in G exactly λ times (see [16]). Also, D is called **symmetric** if $D^{(-1)} = D$. Note that a symmetric (v, k, λ)-difference set is a $(v, k, x^2 - n)$-polynomial addition set where $n = k - \lambda$.

If G is abelian of order v and exponent v^*, and if there exists a symmetric (v, k, λ)-difference set D in G with $1 < k < v - 1$, then, using results in Sections 2 and 3, we have the following necessary conditions:

(i) $D^{(t)} = D$ for all t relatively prime to v;

(ii) $n = k - \lambda = a^2$ where $a = (v, k)$; and

(iii) if p is a prime divisor of v such that p^t strictly divides v and p^r strictly divides v^*, then $2r \leq t$, $p^r | 2a$ and $p^{t-r+1} \nmid 2a$.

Remark. The condition (iii) can be regarded as an improved version of theorems by Ghinelli-Smit [7] and Jungnickel [11].

Furthermore, if D is a Hadamard difference set, that is, $(v, k, \lambda, n) = (4N^2, 2N^2 \pm N, N^2 \pm N, N^2)$, then we can say more about the structure of G.

THEOREM 4.1. *Let q be a prime power and $G = K_1 \times K_2$ be an abelian group where K_1 is a cyclic group of order q and $q \nmid$ exponent of K_2. If $q \neq 4$, then no symmetric Hadamard difference set exists in G.*

Proof. Suppose there exists a symmetric Hadamard difference set D in G. Without loss of generality, let $(v, k, \lambda, n) = (4N^2, 2N^2 - N, N^2 - N, N^2)$. Let $q = p^r$ (where p is a prime), $K_1 = \langle g \rangle$ and $H = \langle g^p \rangle \times K_2$. By the condition (iii), $r \geq 2$

and hence $g^p \neq 1_G$. Put $D = A + B$ where A contains all elements in D with order divisible by q. Note that $B \subset H$ and $A \subset G - H$.

For $0 \leq i \leq q - 1$ and $(i, p) = 1$, choose integers t_i such that $(t_i, v) = 1$, $t_i \equiv i$ mod q and $t_{i+p^{r-1}} \equiv t_i$ mod $|K_2|$. Define

$$S_h = \{g^i h^{t_i} \,|\, 0 \leq i \leq q - 1 \text{ and } (i, p) = 1\}$$

for $h \in K_2$. We have the following observations:

(a) $D^{(t_i)} = D$ for all t_i implies that A is the disjoint union of some S_h's.

(b) The number of solutions $(x, y) \in S_h \times S_{h'}$ with $xy^{-1} \in H$ is equal to $p^{2r-2}(p - 1)$. Hence the number of solutions $(x, y) \in A \times A$ with $xy^{-1} \in H$ is equal to $|A|^2/(p - 1)$.

(c) If X is a character of G with $X g^{p^{r-1}} \neq 1$, then $X S_h = 0$ for all $h \in K_2$ and hence $X A = 0$.

By (b), $\frac{|A|^2}{p-1} + |B|^2 = n + \lambda|H| = n + \lambda\frac{v}{p}$. With $|A| + |B| = k$, we have

$$|B| = \frac{k \pm (p-1)\sqrt{n}}{p} = \frac{2N^2 + (p-2)N}{p} \text{ or } \frac{2N^2 - pN}{p}.$$

Let $X \in H^* =$ the group of characters of H. Extend X to a character of G by defining $X g$ to be a primitive p^{th} root of $X g^p$. By (c), we have $|XB|^2 = n$ if $X g^{p^{r-1}} \neq 1$. Let E be the set of all nontrivial characters of H with $X g^{p^{r-1}} = 1$. Then

$$|B| = \frac{1}{|H|} \sum_{X \in H^*} |XB|^2 = \frac{1}{|H|} \left\{ |B|^2 + n \left(\frac{p-1}{p} \right) |H| + \sum_{X \in E} |XB|^2 \right\}$$

and hence

$$0 \leq \sum_{X \in E} |XB|^2 = |B||H| - |B|^2 - n \left(\frac{p-1}{p} \right) |H|$$

$$= -\frac{N^2}{p^2}[4N^2(p-2) + (p-2)^2] \text{ or } -\frac{N^2}{p^2}[4N^2(p-2) + p^2].$$

The only possible solution is $p = 2$ and $XB = 0$ if $X \in E$.

Using $p = 2$, we have $\bar{A}\bar{A}^{(-1)} + \bar{B}\bar{B}^{(-1)} = n1_H + \lambda\bar{H}$. Using $XB = 0$ whenever $X \in E$, we have $(1 + g^{2^{r-1}})\bar{B} = \mu\bar{H}$ where $\mu = 2|B|/|H|$. Also, by (a), we can write $\bar{A} = g(1 + g^{2^{r-1}})\bar{C}$ for some $C \subset H$.

Consider the natural epimorphism $\rho : H \to L$ where $L = H/(\langle g^{2^{r-1}} \rangle \times K_2)$. Extend ρ to a homomorphism $\mathbf{Z}[H] \to \mathbf{Z}[L]$. Let $y = \rho\bar{C}$, $z = \rho\bar{B}$ and $g_0 = \rho g^2$. Note that $L = \langle g_0 \rangle$ is of order 2^{r-2} and

$$\begin{cases} 4yy^{(-1)} + zz^{(-1)} = n1_L + 2|K_2|\lambda L \\ 2z = 2|K_2|\mu L \end{cases}$$

where $y^{(-1)} = \rho \bar{C}^{(-1)}$ and $z^{(-1)} = \rho \bar{B}^{(-1)}$. Also, $A^{(-1)} = A$ implies $y^{(-1)} = g_0 y$.

Let X be any nontrivial character of L and $\zeta = X g_0$. Then $\frac{n}{4} = |Xy|^2 = \zeta (Xy)^2$ implies $\zeta = \left(\frac{N}{2Xy} \right)^2$. Since $\frac{N}{2Xy} \in \mathbb{Q}(\zeta)$, ζ is a square in $\mathbb{Q}(\zeta)$. The only possible case is $\zeta = 1$. Thus $X g_0 = 1$ for all characters X of L and hence $g_0 = 1_L$, that is, $r = 2$. It follows that $q = p^r = 4$. □

Up to now, all the known examples of abelian groups containing symmetric Hadamard difference sets are as follows:

(I) $\mathbb{Z}_4$ (trivial case).

(II) $\mathbb{Z}_{2^r}^2$ (constructed by Dillon [5]).

(III) $\mathbb{Z}_2^2 \times \mathbb{Z}_3^{2t}$ (constructed by Turyn [25]).

(IV) Direct product of groups in (I), (II) and (III) (using the method given by Menon [22]).

Together with the non-existence results, we list all the abelian groups with nontrivial symmetric Hadamard difference sets for $N = 2, 3, 4, 6, 8$ and 9.

v	k	λ	n	group
16	6	2	4	$\mathbb{Z}_2^4, \mathbb{Z}_2^2 \times \mathbb{Z}_4, \mathbb{Z}_4^2$
(16	10	6	4)	
36	15	6	9	$\mathbb{Z}_2^2 \times \mathbb{Z}_3^2$
(36	21	12	9)	
64	28	12	16	$\mathbb{Z}_2^6, \mathbb{Z}_2^4 \times \mathbb{Z}_4, \mathbb{Z}_2^2 \times \mathbb{Z}_4^2,$
(64	36	20	16)	$\mathbb{Z}_4^3, \mathbb{Z}_8^2$
144	66	30	36	$\mathbb{Z}_2^4 \times \mathbb{Z}_3^2, \mathbb{Z}_2^2 \times \mathbb{Z}_4 \times \mathbb{Z}_3^2$
(144	78	42	36)	unknown case: $\mathbb{Z}_4^2 \times \mathbb{Z}_3^2$
256	120	56	64	$\mathbb{Z}_2^8, \mathbb{Z}_2^6 \times \mathbb{Z}_4, \mathbb{Z}_2^4 \times \mathbb{Z}_4^2,$
(256	136	72	64)	$\mathbb{Z}_2^2 \times \mathbb{Z}_4^3, \mathbb{Z}_4^4, \mathbb{Z}_2^2 \times \mathbb{Z}_8^2,$
				$\mathbb{Z}_4 \times \mathbb{Z}_8^2, \mathbb{Z}_{16}^2$
324	153	72	81	$\mathbb{Z}_2^2 \times \mathbb{Z}_3^4$
(324	171	90	81)	unknown case: $\mathbb{Z}_2^2 \times \mathbb{Z}_9^2$

Remark. In here, we have a counter example for a conjecture by Bridges and Mena [3] which states that, for two groups G and H of order p^r, if the elementary divisors of G are a finer partition than the elementary divisors of H, then G spectrally dominates H. Let us put $G = \mathbb{Z}_2^3 \times \mathbb{Z}_8$ and $H = \mathbb{Z}_8^2$. Certainly, the elementary divisors of G are a finer partition than the elementary divisors of H. Since a symmetric Hadamard difference set exists in H, there is a Cayley graph generated by a subset of H with spectrum $28, 4, -4$. However, no Cayley graph of this spectrum can be generated by subsets of G by Theorem 4.1. Thus, G is not spectrally dominates H.

REFERENCES

[1] W. G. BRIDGES, *The polynomial of non-regular graph*, Pacific J. Math., 38 (1971), pp. 325-342.

[2] W. G. BRIDGES AND R. A. MENA, x^k-*digraph*, J. Combin. Theory Ser. B, . 30 (1981), pp. 136-143.

[3] W. G. BRIDGES AND R. A. MENA, *On rational spectra of graphs with abelian Singer groups*, Linear Algebra Appl., 46 (1982), pp. 51-60.

[4] W. G. BRIDGES AND R. A. MENA, *Rational G-matrices with rational eigenvalues*, J. Combin. Theory Ser. A, 32 (1982), pp. 264-280.

[5] J. F. DILLON, *Difference sets in 2-groups*, Proceeding of NSA Mathematical Sciences Meeting, 1987, pp. 165-172.

[6] A. M. DUVAL, *A directed graph version of strongly regular graphs*, J. Combin. Theory Ser. A, 47 (1988), pp. 71-100.

[7] D. GHINELLI-SMIT, *A new result on difference sets with* −1 *as a multiplier*, Geometriae Dedicata, 23 (1987), pp. 309-317.

[8] A. J. HOFFMAN, *On the polynomial of a graph*, Amer. Math. Monthly, 70 (1963), pp. 30-36.

[9] A. J. HOFFMAN AND M. H. MCANDREW, *On the polynomial of a directed graph*, Proc. Amer. Math. Soc., 16 (1965), pp. 303-309.

[10] X. L. HUBAUT, *Strongly regular graphs*, Discrete Math., 13 (1975), pp. 357-381.

[11] D. JUNGNICKEL, *Difference sets with multiplier* −1, Arch. Math., 38 (1982), pp. 511-513.

[12] D. E. KNUTH, *Notes on central groupoids*, J. Combin. Theory, 8 (1970), pp. 376-390.

[13] C. W. H. LAM, *Rational g-circulants satisfying the matrix equation* $A^2 = dI + \lambda J$, Ph.D. Thesis, Calif. Inst. Tech., 1974.

[14] C. W. H. LAM, *On rational circulants satisfying* $A^2 = dI + \lambda J$, Linear Algebra Appl., 12 (1975), pp. 139-150.

[15] C. W. H. LAM, *On some solutions of* $A^k = dI + \lambda J$, J. Combin. Theory Ser. A, 23 (1977), pp. 140-147.

[16] E. S. LANDER, *Symmetric designs: an algebraic approach*, Cambridge University Press, 1983.

[17] S. L. MA, *On rational circulants satisfying* $A^m = dI + \lambda J$, Linear Algebra Appl., 62 (1984), pp. 155-161.

[18] S. L. MA, *Partial difference sets*, Discrete Math., 52 (1984), pp. 75-89.

[19] S. L. MA, *Polynomial addition sets*, Ph.D. Thesis, University of Hong Kong, 1985.

[20] S. L. MA, *On association schemes, Schur rings, strongly regular graphs and partial difference sets*, to appear in Ars Combinatoria.

[21] R. L. MCFARLAND, *A family of difference sets in non-cyclic groups*, J. Combin. Theory Ser. A, 15 (1973), pp. 1-10.

[22] P. K. MENON, *On difference sets whose parameters satisfy a certain relation*, Proc. Amer. Math. Soc., 13 (1962), pp. 739-745.

[23] H. J. RYSER, *A generalization of the matrix equation* $A^2 = J$, Linear Algebra Appl., 3 (1970), pp. 451-460.

[24] E. SPENCE, *A family of difference sets*, J. Combin. Theory Ser. A, 22 (1977), pp. 103-106.

[25] R. J. TURYN, *A special class of Williamson matrices and difference sets*, J. Combin. Theory Ser. A, 36 (1984), pp. 111-115.

[26] H. WIELANDT, *Finite permutation groups*, Academic Press, New York, 1964.

RECONSTRUCTING PROJECTIVE PLANES
FROM SEMIBIPLANES

G. ERIC MOORHOUSE*

Abstract. ¿From a projective plane Π with a homology τ of order 2, one obtains an incidence system having as points and blocks the $\langle\tau\rangle$-orbits of length 2 on the points and lines of Π, and with incidence inherited from Π. The resulting structure, denoted by Π/τ, is an example of a homology semibiplane.

We have shown that a Desarguesian projective plane of odd prime order is uniquely reconstructible from its homology semibiplane (although such a reconstruction is not in general unique for other planes). This is one step towards classifying projective planes of prime order which admit a collineation of order 2.

More generally we reduce the problem of 'lifting' semibiplanes to projective planes, to an equivalent (but better codified) problem in linear algebra. Conceivably this technique may produce new projective planes from the semibiplanes of known planes.

Key words. semibiplane, projective plane, homology

AMS(MOS) subject classifications. 51E15, 05B30, 05B20

1. Homology Semibiplanes. A **semibiplane** is an incidence system $\Sigma = (\mathcal{P}, \mathcal{B})$ consisting of a set $\mathcal{P}$ of **points**, and a set $\mathcal{B}$ consisting of certain subsets of $\mathcal{P}$ called **blocks**, such that

(i) any two distinct points lie in either 0 or 2 common blocks;

(ii) any two distinct blocks meet in either 0 or 2 points;

(iii) Σ is connected; and

(iv) every block contains at least 3 points.

(See Hughes [5].) It is easy to show that given any semibiplane $\Sigma = (\mathcal{P}, \mathcal{B})$, there exist integers v, k such that $|\mathcal{P}| = |\mathcal{B}| = v$, each block contains exactly k points, and each point belongs to exactly k blocks.

EXAMPLE 1.1. Take vertices of the regular icosahedron as points, and the regular pentagons among its edge circuits as blocks. This forms a semibiplane with $v = 12$, $k = 5$.

Two blocks $L, L' \in \mathcal{B}$ are **parallel** if $L = L'$ or $L \cap L' = \emptyset$. Each block is parallel to exactly $t = v - \binom{k}{2}$ blocks. If parallelism is an equivalence relation on the blocks, then the dual relation on the points ($P \sim P' \iff P = P'$ or P, P' are unjoined) is also an equivalence relation. In this case the semibiplane Σ is said to be **divisible**, and each class (of points or of blocks) has size $t = v - \binom{k}{2}$. (Observe that Example 1.1 is divisible with $t = 2$. Antipodal vertices are unjoined points; pentagons lying in parallel planes are parallel blocks.)

* Department of Mathematics, University of Oregon, Eugene OR 97403. Supported by NSERC of Canada under a postdoctoral fellowship.

Suppose now that Π is a projective plane of order n, admitting an **involutory homology** τ (so that n is odd). That is, τ is a collineation of order 2, fixing pointwise some line of Π and an additional point of Π. (Our terminology concerning projective planes is standard and follows [6].) As in [5], we may construct a divisible semiplane with $v = \frac{1}{2}(n^2 - 1)$, $k = n$, $t = \frac{1}{2}(n-1)$ as follows: 'points' and 'blocks' are the $\langle \tau \rangle$-orbits of length 2 on the points and lines of Π, and incidence is inherited from Π. We denote the resulting semiplane by Π/τ. This motivates the definition: a **homology semibiplane** is a divisible semiplane with $t = \frac{1}{2}(k-1)$ (i.e. k is odd, $v = \frac{1}{2}(k^2 - 1)$). Its **order** is k. This suggests the following

PROBLEM 1.2. Given a homology semibiplane Σ, is $\Sigma \cong \Pi/\tau$ for some Π, τ? Moreover, how many *nonequivalent* pairs (Π, τ) yield Σ in this way?

(We say that the pairs (Π_1, τ_1), (Π_2, τ_2) are **equivalent** if there exists an isomorphism $\psi : \Pi_1 \to \Pi_2$ such that $\psi \circ \tau_1 = \tau_2 \circ \psi$; clearly in this case $\Pi_1/\tau_1 \cong \Pi_2/\tau_2$.) In [11] we prove

THEOREM 1.3. *If $\Pi/\tau \cong \Pi'/\tau'$ where Π' is Desarguesian of odd prime order, then $\Pi \cong \Pi'$.*

Under the broader hypothesis '... odd prime *power* order', we failed to obtain the same conclusion (the 'linear algebra' becomes much more involved in this case); see remarks in Section 2 concerning the case $n = 9$.

We indicate in Section 2 how these methods apply to the problem of classifying projective planes with involutory homologies. Section 3 describes the key idea in the proof of 1.3, namely the reduction of Problem 1.2 to a linear algebra problem. In Section 4 we remark on the situation for involutory collineations *other than* homologies. And Section 5 places our Problem 1.2 in the context of a more general 'lifting' problem.

2. Classifying planes with involutory homologies. We point out that Problem 1.2 is a subproblem of

PROBLEM 2.1. Given an odd integer n, how many (isomorphism classes of) projective planes of order n exist, admitting an involutory homology?

To solve 2.1 for a particular value of n, one proceeds in two steps:
  (i) First find all homology semibiplanes of order n (up to isomorphism). Then
  (ii) 'lift' each such semiplane, in as many (essentially different) ways as possible, to obtain projective planes (this is Problem 1.2).

For instance Matulić-Bedenić [10] shows the uniqueness of a projective plane of order 11 admitting an involutory homology, by first proving the uniqueness of the homology semibiplane Σ of order 11, then showing that Σ lifts uniquely. Note that Theorem 1.3 generalizes step (ii) of this argument. To attempt to prove that all projective planes of prime order admitting an involutory collineation are Desarguesian, amounts to generalizing step (i); however this is evidently too difficult for current methods.

281

Also interesting is the case $n = 9$ treated in [7], where Janko and van Trung show that

(i) there are precisely three homology semibiplanes of order 9, and

(ii) they lift as follows:

$$\Sigma_1 \longrightarrow \text{Desarguesian plane PG(2,9)}$$
$$\Sigma_2 \longrightarrow \text{Hughes plane of order 9}$$

$$\Sigma_3 \nearrow \text{Hall plane of order 9}$$
$$\searrow \text{dual Hall plane of order 9}$$

(In particular the only planes of order 9 admitting involutory homologies are the four known planes of order 9.) The example of Σ_1 above suggests that Theorem 1.3 might possibly extend to any Desarguesian plane Π', although not to an arbitrary plane Π' (in view of the case Σ_3 above).

3. 'Linearizing' the lifting problem. Let us see how Problem 1.2 reduces to a linear problem. The general case is formally treated in [11], and here we illustrate the key idea with particular reference to the case of $\Pi' = \text{PG}(2,5)$, the unique (Desarguesian) projective plane of order 5. The incidence matrix of Π', as shown in Figure 3.1, makes evident the action of an involutory homology τ' which fixes the seven points (resp., lines) corresponding to the first seven rows (resp., columns) of the matrix, and permuting the remaining points (resp., lines) in pairs corresponding to adjacent rows (resp., columns). From the bottom-right 24×24 submatrix thereof

FIGURE 3.1.
Incidence matrix
of $\Pi' = \text{PG}(2,5)$

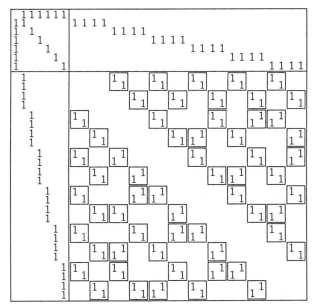

we obtain the incidence matrix of the resulting homology semibiplane $\Sigma' = \Pi'/\tau'$, shown as Figure 3.2. It turns out that Σ' is isomorphic to Example 1.1, this being in fact the unique homology semibiplane of order 5. (*Aside.* Using the construction of Σ' from Π' we see that $\text{Aut}\,\Sigma' \supseteq C_{\text{Aut}\,\Pi'}(\tau')/\langle\tau'\rangle \cong \text{GL}(2,5)/Z_2$ where $Z_2 \subset Z(\text{GL}(2,5))$ is of order 2; cf. [5]. It may in fact be shown that $\text{Aut}\,\Sigma' \cong$

GL(2, 5)/Z_2. Meanwhile from the earlier construction it is evident that Aut Σ' contains the isometry group of the icosahedron, namely $A_5 \times Z_2$, which is a subgroup of index 2 in GL(2, 5)/Z_2.)

FIGURE 3.2. Incidence matrix of the homology semibiplane Σ'

		1		1		1		1		1	
			1		1		1		1		1
1				1			1		1	1	
	1				1	1		1			1
1		1				1			1		1
	1		1				1	1		1	
1			1	1				1			1
	1	1			1				1	1	
1			1		1	1				1	
	1	1		1			1				1
1		1			1		1	1			
	1		1	1		1			1		

Consider now the reverse problem of trying to lift Σ' to a projective plane Π of order 5. To obtain (a 24×24 submatrix of) an incidence matrix for Π, each '1' in the incidence matrix of Σ' (see Fig. 3.2) must be replaced by either $\left(\begin{smallmatrix}1&0\\0&1\end{smallmatrix}\right)$ or $\left(\begin{smallmatrix}0&1\\1&0\end{smallmatrix}\right)$. Furthermore it is clear that the four 1's corresponding to any digon $(P, Q; L, M)$ of Σ' must be replaced by three $\left(\begin{smallmatrix}1&0\\0&1\end{smallmatrix}\right)$'s and one $\left(\begin{smallmatrix}0&1\\1&0\end{smallmatrix}\right)$, or by one $\left(\begin{smallmatrix}1&0\\0&1\end{smallmatrix}\right)$ and three $\left(\begin{smallmatrix}0&1\\1&0\end{smallmatrix}\right)$'s. (We call $(P, Q; L, M)$ a **digon** of Σ' if $P \neq Q$ are points of Σ', joined by the blocks $L \neq M$.)

Now let $\mathcal{F} \subset \mathcal{P} \times \mathcal{B}$ be the set of **flags** of Σ', i.e. the set of pairs (P, L) such that P is a point contained in the block L. Let $F = \mathrm{GF}(2)$, the field of order 2. The above remarks show firstly that any plane Π obtained from Σ' is determined by a corresponding function $\alpha : \mathcal{F} \to F$, namely $\alpha(P, L) = 0$ or 1 according as the (P, L)-entry of the incidence matrix of Σ' is replaced by $\left(\begin{smallmatrix}1&0\\0&1\end{smallmatrix}\right)$ or $\left(\begin{smallmatrix}0&1\\1&0\end{smallmatrix}\right)$; and secondly that

$$\alpha(P, L) + \alpha(P, M) + \alpha(Q, L) + \alpha(Q, M) = 1$$

for any digon $(P, Q; L, M)$ of Σ'.

Let V be the vector space of all functions $\mathcal{F} \to F$, with standard basis $\{\chi_{P,L} : (P, L) \in \mathcal{F}\}$, where

$$\chi_{P,L}(Q, M) = \begin{cases} 1, & \text{if } (Q, M) = (P, L); \\ 0, & \text{otherwise.} \end{cases}$$

Note that $\dim V = |\mathcal{F}| = 60$ (or in general $\frac{1}{2}k(k^2 - 1)$). Define an inner product on V by

$$(\beta, \gamma) = \sum_{(P,L) \in \mathcal{F}} \beta(P, L)\gamma(P, L), \qquad \text{for } \beta, \gamma \in V.$$

Then we require that $(\alpha, \delta) = 1$ for all $\delta \in \mathcal{D}$, where

$$\mathcal{D} = \{\chi_{P,L} + \chi_{P,M} + \chi_{Q,L} + \chi_{Q,M} : (P, Q; L, M) \text{ is a digon in } \Sigma'\}.$$

In particular

$$\alpha \in \langle \delta + \delta' : \delta, \delta' \in \mathcal{D} \rangle^{\perp}.$$

This is now a linear condition on α, which provides the basic key to limiting the possibilities for Π. Note however that distinct α's may yield isomorphic planes Π. In [11] we consider how to suppress these redundant solutions for α in the general case of Problem 1.2, as well as prove Theorem 1.3 in case Π' is Desarguesian of odd prime order.

4. Elation and Baer semibiplanes. An **elation semibiplane** is a divisible semibiplane with $t = k/2$ (i.e. k is even, $v = k^2/2$). Examples with $k = n$ may be constructed (cf. [5]) from projective planes of even order n with involutory elations; however other constructions are known. Indeed Jungnickel [9] (and implicitly Drake [2]) construct elation semibiplanes with $k = 2q$, q an odd prime power, using generalized Hadamard matrix constructions [8] (for q an odd prime the latter matrix constructions are due to Butson [1]). This family of elation semibiplanes was independently constructed by Wild [12]. By [3], none of the semibiplanes in this family 'lift' to projective planes with involutory elations. We wish to thank Dieter Jungnickel for bringing these examples to our attention. This presents a contrast with the situation for homology semibiplanes, where all constructions known to us arise from projective planes with involutory homologies.

As with homology semibiplanes, the problem of lifting elation semibiplanes (also 'Baer' semibiplanes; cf. [5]) reduces to a problem in linear algebra by the same method of Section 3.

5. Classifying planes with given groups. Our interest in lifting semibiplanes stems from a consideration of the more general

PROBLEM 5.1. Given an abstract finite group G and integer $n > 1$, classify (up to equivalence) all projective planes of order n which admit G as a collineation group.

Each solution to this problem may be expressed in the form of a matrix $\mathcal{A}$, a sort of *generalized incidence matrix* with entries in the group algebra $\mathbf{Q}G$ over the rational field $\mathbf{Q}$, as proposed by Hughes [3], [4], who showed that such matrices satisfy certain relations. If $P_1, P_2, \ldots, P_w$ and $L_1, L_2, \ldots, L_w$ are representatives of the distinct point and line orbits of G, then by definition the (i, j)-entry of $\mathcal{A}$ is

$$\sum \{g \in G : P_i^g \in L_j\}.$$

Another $w \times w$ matrix A (with integer entries) is defined as the homomorphic image of $\mathcal{A}$ under the homomorphism $\mathbf{Q}G \to \mathbf{Q}$, $\sum a_g g \mapsto \sum a_g$; i.e. the (i, j)-entry of A is $|\{g \in G : P_i^g \in L_j\}|$.

To illustrate we return to the example of Section 3 in which $G = \langle \tau' \rangle$, τ' an involutory homology of $\Pi' = \mathrm{PG}(2, 5)$. In this case the matrix $\mathcal{A}$ is given by Figure 5.2, in which $\gamma = 1 + \tau' \in \mathbf{Q}G$. To obtain A from $\mathcal{A}$ simply replace each τ' entry by 1, and each γ entry by 2. The relations of [3], [4] amount to

$$\mathcal{A}D^{-1}\mathcal{A}^{\mathrm{T}} = \mathcal{A}^{\mathrm{T}}D^{-1}\mathcal{A} = 5\mathcal{D} + \gamma \mathrm{J}, \qquad AD^{-1}A^{\mathrm{T}} = A^{\mathrm{T}}D^{-1}A = 5D + 2\mathrm{J},$$

where $\mathcal{D} = \begin{pmatrix} \gamma \mathrm{I}_7 & 0 \\ 0 & \mathrm{I}_{12} \end{pmatrix}$, $D = \begin{pmatrix} 2\mathrm{I}_7 & 0 \\ 0 & \mathrm{I}_{12} \end{pmatrix}$, I_r = identity matrix of order r, and J is the 19×19 matrix whose every entry is 1.

To solve 5.1 in general,

(i) first determine all possibilities for A, using the necessary relations for A (as in [3], [4]) and various arguments based on the structure of G. Then

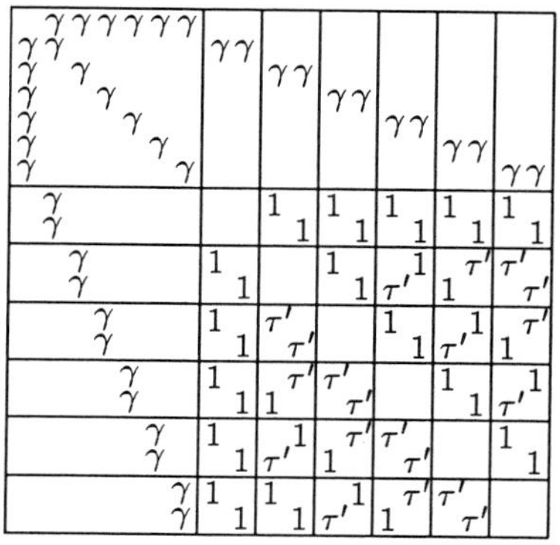

FIGURE 5.2. Generalized incidence matrix $\mathcal{A}$ for the action of an involutory homology τ' on $\Pi' = \mathrm{PG}(2,5)$

(ii) 'lift' each such A to as many $\mathcal{A}$'s as possible.

Step (ii) is very difficult in general, although for $|G| = 2$ we have seen that step (ii) reduces to a linear problem, which is much more tractable. Returning to our example, the lifting of A to $\mathcal{A}$ is accomplished by our function α. Namely, the bottom-right 12×12 submatrix of A is identical to Figure 3.2. An entry '1' thereof, say in the (P, L)-position where (P, L) is a flag of Σ', lifts to an entry '1' or 'τ'' of $\mathcal{A}$ according as $\alpha(P, L) = 0$ or 1 (cf. Figure 3.1).

REFERENCES

[1] A. T. BUTSON, *Generalized Hadamard matrices*, Proc. Amer. Math. Soc., **13** (1962), pp. 894–898.

[2] D. A. DRAKE, *Partial λ-geometries and generalized Hadamard matrices over groups*, Can. J. Math., **31** (1979), pp. 617–627.

[3] D. R. HUGHES, *Generalized incidence matrices over group algebras*, Ill. J. Math., **1** (1957), pp. 545–551.

[4] ————, *Collineations and generalized incidence matrices*, Trans. Amer. Math. Soc., **86** (1957), pp. 284–296.

[5] ————, *Biplanes and semibiplanes*, in *Combinatorics*, Lecture Notes in Mathematics No. 686, pp. 55–58, Springer-Verlag, Berlin, 1978.

[6] D. R. HUGHES AND F. C. PIPER, *Projective planes*, Springer-Verlag, New York, 1973.

[7] Z. JANKO AND T. VAN TRUNG, *The classification of projective planes of order 9 which possess an involution*, J. Comb. Theory Series A, **33** No. 1 (1982), pp. 65–75.

[8] D. JUNGNICKEL, *On difference matrices, resolvable transversal designs and generalized Hadamard matrices*, Math. Z., **167** (1979), pp. 49–60.

[9] ————, *On automorphism groups of divisible designs*, Can. J. Math, **34** (1982), pp. 257–297.

[10] I. MATULIĆ-BEDENIĆ, *The classification of projective planes of order 11 which possess an involution*, Radovi Matematički, **1** (1985), pp. 149–157.

[11] G. E. MOORHOUSE, *On the construction of finite projective planes from homology semibiplanes*, submitted.

[12] P. WILD, *Biaffine planes and divisible semiplanes*, J. Geom., **25** (1985), pp. 121–130.

ON MULTIPLIER THEOREMS

ALEXANDER POTT[†]

I. Introduction. A subset D of a multiplicative group G is called an (m, n, k, λ)-*relative difference set* (RDS) with respect to a normal subgroup N of G, if $|G| = mn$, $|N| = n$, $|D| = k$ and every element outside N has exactly λ representations as a difference $d_1 d_2^{-1}$ with elements $d_1, d_2 \in D$, whereas no element of $N \setminus \{1\}$ has such a representation. Relative difference sets are for instance the affine difference sets introduced by Bose [3]. In the case $n = 1$ this is the usual definition of an ordinary difference set, see for instance [2]. It is well-known that the existence of (m, n, k, λ)-RDS's is equivalent to the existence of (m, n, k, λ)-group divisible designs (GDD) with G acting as a regular automorphism group, such that $g \in G$ fixes *all* point classes whenever it fixes some point class [10]. We refer the reader to [2,10,12] for background from design theory and for a detailed discussion of the connections between symmetric and divisible designs and (relative) difference sets. Throughout this paper we will often make use of the following obvious equation

$$(1) \qquad k(k-1) = \lambda(v - n) = \lambda n(m - 1)$$

connecting the parameters of a GDD. Given a ring R, a subset $A \subseteq G$ will be identified with an element $\sum_{g \in A} g$ in a group ring RG which we also denote by A. For $t \in \mathbb{Z}$ we define $A^{(t)} := \sum_{g \in A} g^t$. Then we can translate the definition of RDS's into an equation in $\mathbb{Z}G$:

$$DD^{(-1)} = k + \lambda(G - N)$$

If $\varphi : G \to H$ is a group homomorphism we extend φ to a homomorphism from RG to RH. In particular, if φ is the canonical epimorphism $G \to G/N$ it is easy to check that D^φ is an element in $\mathbb{Z}G/N$ with coefficients 0 and 1. Thus D^φ corresponds to an $(m, 1, k, n\lambda)$-RDS in G/N, since

$$(2) \qquad (DD^{-1})^\varphi = (k - n\lambda) + n\lambda G/N \in \mathbb{Z}G/N.$$

A *multiplier* of an RDS D is a group automorphism φ, such that $D^\varphi = Dg$ for some $g \in G$. From now on we consider only abelian groups and are concerned with *numerical* multipliers, i.e. group automorphisms of the type $g \mapsto g^t$.

Multipliers for ordinary difference sets (i.e. $n = 1$) have been introduced by Hall [6], who has proved the so-called "first multiplier theorem". This has been generalized by Hall, Ryser [8], Bruck [4], Hall [7] and Menon [12] to what is now called the "second multiplier theorem". The corresponding result for RDS's is due to Elliott and Butson [5] and is proved in the special case of affine difference sets by Hoffman [9]. A more recent investigation of multipliers can be found in Ko and Ray-Chaudhuri [11] as well as in Arasu and Ray-Chaudhuri [1]. Lander [12] has given a more transparent proof of the second multiplier theorem, that has inspired this paper. His main idea was to use the following result on ideals in $\hat{\mathbb{Z}}_p G$, where $\hat{\mathbb{Z}}_p$ denotes the ring of p-adic integers.

†Mathematisches Institut der Universität Gießen, Arndtstraße 2, 6300 Gießen, West Germany

RESULT. Every ideal I in $\hat{Z}_pG$ is fixed by the map

$$\tau : \hat{Z}_pG \to \hat{Z}_pG$$
$$A \mapsto A^{(p)}, \quad \text{if } (p, v) = 1 \text{ and } G$$
$$\text{is an abelian group of order } v.$$

For a proof we refer the reader to Lander's book [12]. It is the aim of this paper to show that Lander's approach works for RDS's, too. We also include a slightly simplified version of Lander's proof of the second multiplier theorem, which is similar to the proof of the first multiplier theorem that the author has given in [14].

THEOREM 1. ("second multiplier theorem", Menon [13])

Let D be an $(m, 1, k, \lambda)$-difference set in an abelian group of order v with exponent v^*. Let $\ell = p_1^{a_1} \cdot \ldots \cdot p_s^{a_s}$ be a divisor of $k - \lambda$, where the p_i's are distinct primes. Then $t \in \mathbb{Z}$ is a multipier if the following hold:

(i) $(t, v) = 1$;

(ii) for every p_i there exists a $j_i \in \mathbb{Z}$ such that $t \equiv p_i^{j_i} \mod v^*$;

(iii) $\ell > \lambda$.

THEOREM 2. (Elliott, Butson [5])

Let D be an (m, n, k, λ) - RDS in an abelian group of order $v = mn$ and exponent $v*$ with respect to a normal subgroup N. Assume that the integer $t \in \mathbb{Z}$ is a multiplier of the difference set corresponding to D in G/N (see (2)). Let $\ell = p_1^{a_1} \cdot \ldots \cdot p_s^{a_s}$ be a divisor of k, where the p_i's are distinct primes. We assume $(\ell, v) = 1$. Then t is a multiplier if (i), (ii) and (iii) of Theorem 1 holds.

II. Proofs of the Theorems. The following Lemma is basically proved in [14].

LEMMA 1. Let M be the $\mathbb{Z}$-module generated by the rows of an incidence matrix of a symmetric (v, k, λ)-design. If $\mathbf{a} = (a_1, \ldots, a_v)$, $\mathbf{b} = (b_1 \ldots, b_v) \in M$ then $k < \mathbf{a}|\mathbf{b} > \equiv (\sum a_i)(\sum b_i) \mod k - \lambda$, where $\langle\ |\ \rangle$ denotes the usual scalar product.

Proof. We denote by $\mathbf{e}_1, \ldots \mathbf{e}_v$ the rows of the incidence matrix. Then $\mathbf{a} = \sum_{i=1}^{v} x_i\mathbf{e}_i$, $\mathbf{b} = \sum_{i=1}^{v} y_i\mathbf{e}_i$, thus $\langle\mathbf{a}|\mathbf{b}\rangle = \sum_{i,j=1}^{v} x_iy_j\langle\mathbf{e}_i|\mathbf{e}_j\rangle \equiv k(\sum x_i)(\sum y_i) \mod n$, since $\langle\mathbf{e}_i|\mathbf{e}_j\rangle \equiv k \mod n$. Observing $\sum_{i=1}^{v} a_i = k\sum_{i=1}^{v} x_i$ proves the Lemma. $\square$

The first part of the next Lemma is in Lander [12], the second part is the analogous statement about GDDs which we will require in the proof of Theorem 2.

LEMMA 2.

(i) Let $\mathcal{D}$ be a symmetric (v, k, λ)-design and R a set of k points. If R meets every block in at least λ blocks then R is itself a block.

(ii) Let $\mathcal{D}$ be a symmetric (m, n, k, λ)-GDD (i.e. the dual of $\mathcal{D}$ is also a GDD with the same parameters). We assume that R is a set of k points contained in the union of blocks $B_1, \ldots, B_n$ forming a block class. If every other block intersects R in at least λ points and if every two points of R are joined by a block then R is one of the blocks $B_1, \ldots, B_n$.

Proof (only (ii)). We denote the intersection number $|R \cap B_i| = t_i$, where $B_1, \ldots, B_v$ are the blocks of $\mathcal{D}$. We observe

$$(3) \qquad \sum_{i=1}^{n} t_i = k.$$

We count the number of flags (B_i, p) where $p \in R$ is a point on B_i in two ways and obtain

$$(4) \qquad \sum_{i=1}^{v} t_i = k^2,$$

since there are exactly k blocks through every point. Using (1), (3) and (4) we derive $\sum_{i=n+1}^{v} t_i = n(m-1)\lambda$, hence

$$(5) \qquad t_i = \lambda \qquad (i > n),$$

since $t_i > \lambda$ $\quad (i > n)$. A similar counting argument (for triples (B_i, p, q) with $p, q \in B_i \cap R$, $p \neq q$) yields

$$(6) \qquad \sum_{i=1}^{v} t_i(t_i - 1) = k(k-1)\lambda,$$

and, using (5),

$$(7) \qquad \sum_{i=n+1}^{v} t_i(t_i - 1) = \lambda(\lambda - 1)n(m-1) = k(k-1)(\lambda - 1).$$

Subtracting (7) from (6) and adding to (3) show $\sum_{i=1}^{n} t_i^2 = k^2$, which is possible only if $t_i = k$ for some $i \leq n$ (see (3)). $\square$

Proof of Theorem 1. The map $\varphi_t : G \to G$

$g \mapsto g^t$ is a group automorphism and fixes every ideal in $\hat{\mathbf{Z}}_{p_i} G$ according to the result of Lander, since $t \equiv p_i^{j_i} \mod v^*$. The ring $R_i := \mathbf{Z}_{p_i^{a_i}}$ of integers modulo $P_i^{a_i}$ is a homomorphic image of $\hat{\mathbf{Z}}_{p_i}$, hence $D^{(t)} \in\, < D >_{R_i G}$ for every $i = 1, \ldots, s$. We conclude from Lemma 1 that $\langle D^{(t)} | Dg \rangle \equiv \lambda \mod p_i^{a_i}$. Since $\ell > \lambda$ we obtain that $D^{(t)}$ meets every block in at least λ points and Lemma 2 (ii) is applicable. $\square$

Proof of Theorem 2. We denote by $\overline{D}$ the image of D under the canonical epimorphism $G \to G/N$, see (1). We may assume $\overline{D}^{(t)} = \overline{D}$ (this is well-known, see VI.2.3 in [2]). Then it is easy to see that $D^{(t)}$ is covered by the n blocks $Dg, g \in N$. To apply Lemma 2 (ii) it is enough to show that $D^{(t)}$ meets every block $Dg, g \notin N$, in t_g points with $t_g \equiv \lambda \mod p_i^{a_i}, i = 1, \ldots s$. Then we can finish the proof as above, since $\ell > \lambda$. We know that $D^{(t)} \in\, < D >_{\hat{\mathbf{Z}}_{p_i} G}$, thus we can write $D^{(t)} = \sum a_g Dg \in \hat{\mathbf{Z}}_{p_i} G$. Then $\langle D^{(t)} | Dg \rangle = a_g k + \lambda \sum_{hg^{-1} \notin N} a_h \in \hat{\mathbf{Z}}_{p_i}$, $g \notin N$, since $\langle Dh | Dg \rangle = \lambda$ if and only if $gh^{-1} \notin N$. Now we have to calculate

$s_g := \sum_{hg^{-1} \in N} a_h$. Note that the s_g's satisfy $\overline{D} = \sum_{\overline{g} \in G/N} s_g \overline{Dg}$ or, in other words: The vector $\mathbf{s} := (s_g)_{\overline{g} \in G/N}$ is a solution of $A\mathbf{s}^T = A \cdot (1, 0, \ldots 0)^T$, where $A \in \hat{\mathbf{Z}}_{p_i}^{(m,m)}$ is the incidence matrix of the design associated with $\overline{D}$ and the first column corresponds to $\overline{D}$. It is well-known that the rank of A is m, thus there is only one solution $(1, 0, \ldots 0)$ of the equation and $< D^{(t)} | Dg > = a_g k + \lambda$ with $g \notin N$. $\square$

As Lander points out, it is worth to note that we don't need his non-trivial result for a proof of special cases of the multiplier theorem, namely assuming $m = t = p$. Then we require only a trivial version of his result obtained by replacing $\hat{\mathbf{Z}}_p$ by $GF(p)$ giving very elementary proofs of the "first multiplier theorem" for both difference sets and relative difference sets.

Acknowledgement.

The author thanks Prof. D. Jungnickel for some helpful discussions. He also thanks the Institute for Mathematics and its Applications at the University of Minnesota for its hospitality and financial support during writing this paper.

REFERENCES

[1] ARASU, K.T., RAY-CHAUDHURI, D.K., *Divisible quotient lists and their multipliers*, Congr. Numer., 49 (1985), pp. 321–338.

[2] BETH. TH., JUNGNICKEL, D., LENZ, H., *Design Theory*, Bibliographisches Institut, Zürich 1985. Cambridge University Press, Cambridge, 1986.

[3] BOSE, R.C., *An affine analogue of Singer's theorem*, Journ. Ind. Math. Soc., 6 (1942), pp. 1-15.

[4] BRUCK, R.H., *Difference sets in a finite group*, Trans. Amer. Math. Soc., 78 (1955), pp. 464–481.

[5] ELLIOTT, J.E.H., BUTSON, A.T., *Relative difference sets*, Illinois J. Math., 10 (1966), pp. 517–531.

[6] HALL, M.JR., *Cyclic projective planes*, Duke Math. J., 14 (1947), pp. 1079—1090.

[7] HALL, M. JR., *A survey of difference sets*, Proc. Amer. Math. Soc., 7 (1956), pp. 957–986.

[8] HALL, M. JR., RYSER, H.J., *Cyclic incidence matrices*, Canad. J. Math., 3 (1951), pp. 495–502.

[9] HOFFMAN, A.J., *Cyclic affine planes*, Canad. J. Math., 4 (1952), pp. 295–301.

[10] JUNGNICKEL, D., *On automorphism groups of divisible designs*, Canad. J. Math., 34 (1982), pp. 257–297.

[11] KO, H.P., RAY-CHAUDHURI, D.K., *Multiplier theorems*, JCT (**A**), 30 (1981), pp. 134–157.

[12] LANDER, E.S., *Symmetric Designs: An Algebraic Approach*, Cambridge University Press, Cambridge, 1983.

[13] MENON, K., *Difference sets in abelian groups*, Proc. Amer. Math. Soc., 11 (1960), pp. 368–376.

[14] POTT, A., *Applications of the DFT to abelian difference sets*, Arch. Math., 51 (51), pp. 283–288.

ON λ-DESIGNS WITH $\lambda = 2P$*

ÁKOS SERESS†

Abstract. A λ-design is a family $B_1, B_2, ..., B_v$ of subsets of $X = \{1, 2, ..., v\}$ such that $|B_i \cap B_j| = \lambda$ for all $i \neq j$ and not all blocks are of the same size. Ryser's and Woodall's λ-design conjecture states that each λ-design can be obtained from a symmetric block design by complementing with respect to a fixed block. We prove some results on λ-designs in the case when λ is twice a prime number. In particular, we prove the λ-design conjecture for $\lambda = 10$, which was the smallest unsolved case.

1. Introduction and statement of results.

Definition 1.1. A λ-design D is a pair (X, L) such that (i) $X = \{1, 2, ..., v\}$, $|L| = v$, and the elements of L are subsets of X (The elements of X are called *treatments* and the elements of L are *blocks*.)

(ii) For all $B_i, B_j \in L, i \neq j, |B_i \cap B_j| = \lambda$

(iii) For all $B_j \in L, |B_j| = k_j > \lambda$ and not all k_j are equal.

λ-designs were first defined by Ryser[Ry] and Woodall[Wo70]. The only known examples are obtained from symmetric block designs by the following complementation procedure. Let (X, S) be a symmetric (v, k, λ') design and let $C_0 \in S$ be fixed. Then $L = \{B \subset X : B = X \setminus C_0$ or $B = (C \setminus C_0) \cup (C_0 \setminus C)$ for some $C \in S\}$ is the block system of a $(k - \lambda')$-design. λ-designs obtained by this procedure are called *type*-1 designs. The λ-*design conjecture* [Ry],[Wo70] states that all λ-designs are type-1. The conjecture was proven by deBruijn and Erdős [BE] for $\lambda = 1$, by Ryser [Ry] for $\lambda = 2$, and, in a series of papers by Bridges and Kramer [Br70], [Kr69], [BK], for $3 \leq \lambda \leq 9$. Singhi and Shrikhande [SS76] showed the validity of the conjecture for $\lambda =$prime.

Throughout the paper, D denotes a λ-design on v points. Ryser and Woodall independently proved the following theorem.

THEOREM 1.2. [Ry],[Wo70] *If D is a λ-design then there exist integers r_1, r_2 such that $r_1 + r_2 = v + 1$ and every treatment occurs either in r_1 blocks or in r_2 blocks.*

We say that a treatment i is in *class* n if its replication number is r_n and use the notation $i \in C_n$.

The present paper contains partial results of an attempt to prove the λ-design conjecture when λ is twice a prime. Our starting point is the following result of Singhi and Shrikhande.

---

*This research was supported in part by the Institute of Mathematics and its Applications with funds provided by the National Science Foundation.

†Mathematical Institute of the Hungarian Academy of Sciences, Budapest, Hungary, H-1053 and The Ohio State University, Columbus, OH 43210

THEOREM 1.3. [SS84] *Let D be any λ-design. Suppose that $r_1 > r_2$ and let* $\rho = \frac{r_1 - 1}{r_2 - 1} = \frac{x}{y}$, $(x, y) = 1$. *If $(\lambda, x - y) = 1$ then D is type-1.*

It is easy to see (cf. [SS76]) that $x - y < \lambda$ and $y < \lambda$. Hence in the case $\lambda = 2P$, P is an odd prime, Theorem 1.3 leaves open the following three possibilities:

Case 1: x, y are odd, $y > 1$;

Case 2: x is odd, $y = 1$; and

Case 3: $x - y = P$.

We are able to handle Case 1 and a part of Case 2. More precisely, we prove the following theorem:

THEOREM 1.4. *Let D be a λ-design with $\lambda = 2P$, P an odd prime and let* $\rho = \frac{x}{y}$, $(x, y) = 1$. *If either x, y are odd, $y > 1$ or $x \geq P$, $y = 1$ then D is type-1.*

The method of proof is a mixture of divisibility considerations (in the spirit of [SS76], [SS84]) and the analytic methods of [Se]. The main difficulty in proving the conjecture for $\lambda = 2P$ lies in Case 3 where all block sizes are divisible by P and the methods of Singhi and Shrikhande break down. However, using the analytic methods, we are able to handle the smallest unsolved value of P.

THEOREM 1.5. *The λ-design conjecture is true for $\lambda = 10$.*

The organization of the paper is as follows. In Section 2, we give the relations among the parameters of λ-designs and list the results of [Se] used in this paper. In Section 3, we prove some results valid for all values of λ. Section 4 contains the proof of Theorem 1.4 while the proof of Theorem 1.5 is given in Section 5.

2. Previous results. The parameters of λ-designs are most often expressed as functions of v, λ, ρ. For our purposes, it will be more convenient to use $d = e_1 - r_2$ and write the other parameters as functions of d, λ, ρ. Let e_1, e_2 be the number of class 1 and class 2 treatments, respectively. Wlog, we may assume that a treatment i is in class 1 if and only if $i \leq e_1$. We denote by k'_m, k^*_m the number of class 1 and class 2 treatments in B_m, respectively. Clearly, $k_m = k'_m + k^*_m$. The following equations were essentially obtained in [Ry] and [Wo70] (cf. [SS76],[Kr74]).

$$(2.1) \qquad k'_m = \lambda - \frac{k_m - 2\lambda}{\rho - 1},$$

$$(2.2) \qquad k^*_m = \lambda + \frac{(k_m - 2\lambda)\rho}{\rho - 1},$$

$$(2.3) \qquad e_1 = \lambda + \frac{\lambda + d}{\rho},$$

$$(2.4) \qquad e_2 = \lambda\rho - d\rho - \rho + \lambda,$$

291

$$(2.5) \qquad r_1 = \lambda\rho - d\rho - \rho + \lambda + d + 1,$$

$$(2.6) \qquad r_2 = \lambda - d + \frac{\lambda + d}{\rho},$$

$$(2.7) \qquad \frac{r_1^2 - r_1}{v - 1} = \frac{r_1\rho}{\rho + 1} = \lambda\rho - (d+1)\rho\frac{\rho - 1}{\rho + 1},$$

$$(2.8) \qquad \frac{r_1(r_2 - 1)}{v - 1} = \frac{r_1}{\rho + 1} = \lambda - (d+1)\frac{\rho - 1}{\rho + 1},$$

$$(2.9) \qquad \frac{r_2^2 - r_2}{v - 1} = \frac{r_2}{\rho + 1} = \frac{\lambda}{\rho} - \frac{d}{\rho}\frac{\rho - 1}{\rho + 1},$$

and

$$(2.10) \qquad \frac{r_2\rho}{\rho + 1} = \lambda - d\frac{\rho - 1}{\rho + 1}.$$

Let
(2.11)
$$R_{ij} = \sum_{\{m:i,j \in B_m\}} \frac{1}{k_m - \lambda}, \quad R_{i\bar{j}} = \sum_{\{m:i \in B_m, j \notin B_m\}} \frac{1}{k_m - \lambda}, \quad R_{\bar{i}\bar{j}} = \sum_{\{m:i,j \notin B_m\}} \frac{1}{k_m - \lambda}.$$

Then $R_{ij}, R_{i\bar{j}}$, and $R_{\bar{i}\bar{j}}$ depend only on the class of i and j. We use the notation $R_{ij} = R(1)$ if $i = j$ and i is in class 1; $R_{ij} = R(1,1)$ if $i \neq j$ and they are both in class 1; etc.

$$(2.12) \qquad R(1) = \rho + 1, \quad R(2) = \frac{1}{\rho} + 1,$$

$$(2.13) \qquad R(1,1) = \rho, \quad R(1,2) = 1, \quad R(2,2) = \frac{1}{\rho},$$

$$(2.14) \qquad R(1,\bar{1}) = 1, \quad R(1,\bar{2}) = \rho, \quad R(\bar{1},2) = \frac{1}{\rho}, \quad R(2,\bar{2}) = 1,$$

$$(2.15) \qquad R(\bar{1},\bar{1}) = \frac{1}{\rho} - \frac{1}{\lambda}, \quad R(\bar{1},\bar{2}) = 1 - \frac{1}{\lambda}, \quad R(\bar{2},\bar{2}) = \rho - \frac{1}{\lambda},$$

$$(2.16) \qquad R(\bar{1}) = 1 + \frac{1}{\rho} - \frac{1}{\lambda}, \quad R(\bar{2}) = 1 + \rho - \frac{1}{\lambda},$$

and

$$(2.17) \qquad \sum_{m=1}^{v} \frac{1}{k_m - \lambda} = \rho + 2 + \frac{1}{\rho} - \frac{1}{\lambda}.$$

We need the following result of Kramer.

THEOREM 2.1. [Kr74] (a) If $\rho \geq \lambda - 1$ then D is type-1.
(b) If $\rho = \frac{\lambda}{2}$ and $e_1 \geq \lambda + 2$ then D is type-1.

We shall also use the following results of [Se]. Let r_{ij} denote the number of blocks containing the treatments i and j. Moreover, let $x_1 = d\frac{\lambda\rho - \lambda}{\lambda\rho + \lambda - \rho}$ and $x_2 = (d + 1)\frac{\lambda\rho - \lambda}{\lambda\rho + \lambda - 1}$.

THEOREM 2.2. D is type-1 if and only if one of the following holds:
(i) $d \in \{0, -1\}$;
(ii) $\frac{r_1}{\rho + 1}$ or $\frac{r_2}{\rho + 1}$ is an integer; (let us note that (i) and (ii) were also announced in [Wo71])
(iii) $\frac{\lambda - x_1}{\rho}$ or x_2 is an integer;
(iv) there exists a treatment i such that r_{ij} depends only on the class of j.

THEOREM 2.3. (a) Let $i \in C_1$. Then more than half of the numbers $\{r_{ij} : j > e_1\}$ are equal to $\lceil \frac{r_1}{\rho + 1} \rceil$.
(b) Let $i \in C_2$. Then more than half of the numbers $\{r_{ij} : j > e_1\}$ are equal to $\lceil \frac{r_2}{\rho + 1} \rceil$.

LEMMA 2.4. $0 \leq \lceil \frac{r_2}{\rho + 1} \rceil - \frac{r_2}{\rho + 1} \leq \frac{\rho - 1}{\rho + 1}$.

We define

(2.18)
$$U_i = \sum_{\{m : i \in B_m\}} (k_m - \lambda - \frac{r_1}{\rho + 1}), \quad i \in C_1,$$

(2.19)
$$V_i = \sum_{\{m : i \notin B_m\}} (k_m - 2\lambda + x_1), \quad i \in C_1,$$

(2.20)
$$U_i = \sum_{\{m : i \in B_m\}} (k_m - \lambda - \frac{r_2 \rho}{\rho + 1}), \quad i \in C_2,$$

and

(2.21)
$$V_i = \sum_{\{m : i \notin B_m\}} (k_m - 2\lambda + x_2), \quad i \in C_2.$$

THEOREM 2.5. $U_i \geq 0$ and $V_i \geq 0$ for all i. D is type-1 if and only if $U_i = 0$ or $V_i = 0$ for some i.

Also, the following equalities hold.
For all $i \in C_1$,

(2.22)
$$U_i + V_i = \frac{(\rho - 1)^2 (e_1 - 1)e_2}{(\rho + 1)(\lambda\rho + \lambda - \rho)},$$

293

$$(2.23) \qquad \sum_{j \leq e_1, j \neq i} r_{ij} = \frac{r_1 \rho}{\rho + 1}(e_1 - 1) - \frac{U_i}{\rho - 1},$$

$$(2.24) \qquad \sum_{j > e_1} r_{ij} = \frac{r_1 e_2}{\rho + 1} + \frac{U_i \rho}{\rho - 1},$$

$$(2.25) \qquad U_i + V_i = \sum_{j \leq e_1, j \neq i} \left((r_{ij} - \frac{r_1 \rho}{\rho + 1})^2 + (r_{ij} - r_1 + \lambda - x_1)^2 \right) +$$

$$\sum_{j > e_1} \left((r_{ij} - \frac{r_1}{\rho + 1})^2 + (r_{ij} - r_2 + \frac{\lambda - x_1}{\rho})^2 \right),$$

and
$$(2.26)$$
$$\sum_{j \leq e_1, j \neq i} (r_{ij} - r_1 + \lambda - x_1)^2 + \sum_{j > e_1} (r_{ij} - r_2 + \frac{\lambda - x_1}{\rho})(r_{ij} - r_2 + \frac{\lambda - x_1}{\rho} + 1) = -\frac{V_i}{\rho - 1}.$$

For all $i \in \mathcal{C}_2$,

$$(2.27) \qquad U_i + V_i = \frac{(\rho - 1)^2 e_1 (e_2 - 1)}{(\rho + 1)(\lambda \rho + \lambda - 1)},$$

$$(2.28) \qquad \sum_{j \leq e_1} r_{ij} = \frac{r_2 \rho}{\rho + 1} e_1 - \frac{U_i}{\rho - 1},$$

$$(2.29) \qquad \sum_{j > e_1, j \neq i} r_{ij} = \frac{r_2(e_2 - 1)}{\rho + 1} + \frac{U_i \rho}{\rho - 1},$$

$$(2.30) \qquad U_i + V_i = \sum_{j \leq e_1} \left((r_{ij} - \frac{r_2 \rho}{\rho + 1})^2 + (r_{ij} - r_1 + \lambda \rho - \rho x_2)^2 \right) +$$

$$\sum_{j > e_1, j \neq i} \left((r_{ij} - \frac{r_2}{\rho + 1})^2 + (r_{ij} - r_2 + \lambda - x_2)^2 \right),$$

and
$$(2.31)$$
$$\sum_{j \leq e_1} (r_{ij} - r_1 + \lambda \rho - \rho x_2)^2 + \sum_{j > e_1, j \neq i} (r_{ij} - r_2 + \lambda - x_2)(r_{ij} - r_2 + \lambda - x_2 + 1) = -\frac{V_i}{\rho - 1}.$$

3. Some results valid for all values of λ. By Theorem 2.2(i), the λ-design conjecture is equivalent to the fact that $d = e_1 - r_2 \in \{0, -1\}$. The main purpose of this section is to give a non-trivial lower bound for d (cf. Theorem 3.5). We shall use this result in the next two sections and it may well be a part of the final resolution of the λ-design conjecture.

Let $t_1 = \lceil \frac{r_1}{\rho+1} \rceil - \frac{r_1}{\rho+1}$, $t_2 = \lceil \frac{r_2}{\rho+1} \rceil - \frac{r_2}{\rho+1}$, $s_1 = \lceil \frac{\lambda - x_1}{\rho} \rceil - \frac{\lambda - x_1}{\rho}$, and $s_2 = \lceil \lambda - x_2 \rceil - (\lambda - x_2)$.

LEMMA 3.1. $t_1 + t_2 = \frac{\rho-1}{\rho+1}$.

Proof: By (2.8) and (2.10), $r_2 - \frac{r_2}{\rho+1} - \frac{r_1}{\rho+1} = \frac{\rho-1}{\rho+1}$. Thus $t_1 + t_2 = \frac{\rho-1}{\rho+1}$ or $1 + \frac{\rho-1}{\rho+1}$; since, by Lemma 2.4, $t_2 \leq \frac{\rho-1}{\rho+1}$, $t_1 + t_2 = \frac{\rho-1}{\rho+1}$. $\square$

THEOREM 3.2. (a) Let $i \in C_1$. Then more than half of the numbers $\{r_{ij} : j > e_1\}$ are equal to $r_2 - \lceil \frac{\lambda-x_1}{\rho} \rceil$.
(b) Let $i \in C_2$. Then more than half of the numbers $\{r_{ij} : j > e_1\}$ are equal to $r_2 - \lceil \lambda - x_2 \rceil$.

Proof: (a) Let $i \in C_1$. We can suppose that $s_1 > 0$ and $V_i > 0$ otherwise, by Theorems 2.2(iii) and 2.5, the design is type-1 and all r_{ij} are equal to the stated value. From (2.26), we obtain

$$(3.1) \qquad \sum_{j>e_1} (r_{ij} - r_2 + \frac{\lambda-x_1}{\rho})(r_{ij} - r_2 + \frac{\lambda-x_1}{\rho} + 1) < 0.$$

If $r_{ij} = r_2 - \lceil \frac{\lambda-x_1}{\rho} \rceil$ for some $j > e_1$ then $(r_{ij} - r_2 + \frac{\lambda-x_1}{\rho})(r_{ij} - r_2 + \frac{\lambda-x_1}{\rho} + 1)$ contributes $-s_1(1-s_1)$ to the left-hand-side of (3.1); for all other $j > e_1$, $(r_{ij} - r_2 + \frac{\lambda-x_1}{\rho})(r_{ij} - r_2 + \frac{\lambda-x_1}{\rho} + 1)$ contributes at least $\min\{s_1(1+s_1),(1-s_1)(2-s_1)\} > s_1(1-s_1)$. Hence, for more than $e_2/2$ treatments j of class 2, $r_{ij} = r_2 - \lceil \frac{\lambda-x_1}{\rho} \rceil$.
(b) This part follows similarly from (2.31). $\square$

COROLLARY 3.3. (a) $s_1 + t_1 = \frac{\rho-1}{\rho+1} \frac{\lambda\rho+\lambda-\rho+d}{\lambda\rho+\lambda-\rho}$.
(b) $s_2 + t_2 = \frac{\rho-1}{\rho+1} \frac{\lambda\rho+\lambda+d}{\lambda\rho+\lambda-1}$.

Proof: (a) By Theorems 2.3(a) and 3.2(a), for each $i \in C_1$ there exists $j \in C_2$ such that $r_{ij} = \lceil \frac{r_1}{\rho+1} \rceil = r_2 - \lceil \frac{\lambda-x_1}{\rho} \rceil$. Therefore $s_1 + t_1 = r_2 - \frac{r_1}{\rho+1} - \frac{\lambda-x_1}{\rho} = \frac{\rho-1}{\rho+1} \frac{\lambda\rho+\lambda-\rho+d}{\lambda\rho+\lambda-\rho}$.
(b) Similar to the proof of (a). $\square$

LEMMA 3.4. $-\lambda\rho - \lambda < d < \lambda + \frac{\lambda}{\rho} - 1$.

Proof: From the inequalities $e_1 > 0$ and $e_2 > 0$. $\square$

THEOREM 3.5. $d \geq -\frac{1}{2}\lambda\rho - \frac{1}{2}\lambda + \frac{\lambda(\rho-1)}{4\lambda-2}$.

Proof: By Lemma 3.1 and Corollary 3.3, $\frac{\rho-1}{\rho+1} \leq \frac{\rho-1}{\rho+1} \frac{\lambda\rho+\lambda-\rho+d}{\lambda\rho+\lambda-\rho} + \frac{\rho-1}{\rho+1} \frac{\lambda\rho+\lambda+d}{\lambda\rho+\lambda-1}$. Solving this inequality for d, we obtain the stated bound. $\square$

PROPOSITION 3.6.

$$(3.2) \qquad \frac{\rho}{\rho-1} \sum_{i \leq e_1} U_i + \frac{1}{\rho-1} \sum_{i > e_1} U_i = e_1 e_2 \frac{\rho-1}{\rho+1}.$$

Proof: By equating the right-hand-sides of (2.24) and (2.28). $\square$

PROPOSITION 3.7. If $\rho = 3$ then the design is type-1.

Proof: By (2.8) and (2.10), $\rho = 3$ implies that either $\frac{r_1}{\rho+1}$ or $\frac{r_2}{\rho+1}$ is an integer. Hence, by Theorem 2.2(ii), the design is type-1. $\square$

LEMMA 3.8. *(a) If $d > 0$ then there exists B_m with $k'_m > \lambda$.*
(b) $\rho > \frac{\lambda}{2}$ and $e_1 \geq \lambda + 2$ is impossible.

Proof: (a) Let $i \in \mathcal{C}_2$. By (2.6) and (2.12), $d > 0$ implies that $\sum_{\{m:i \in B_m\}} \frac{1}{k_m - \lambda} > \frac{r_2}{\lambda}$. Therefore, there exists m such that $\frac{1}{k_m - \lambda} > \frac{1}{\lambda}$ or, equivalently, $k_m < 2\lambda$, $k'_m > \lambda$.
(b) If $\rho \geq \lambda - 1$ then Theorem 2.1(a) implies that the design is type-1 and, from Theorem 2.2(i), $e_1 = \lambda + 1$. Suppose that $\rho < \lambda - 1$. By (2.3), $e_1 \geq \lambda + 2$ implies $d > 0$. By (a), there exists B_m with $k'_m > \lambda$. $k'_m > \lambda + 1$ is impossible because (2.1),(2.2) would imply $k^*_m < 0$. Hence $k'_m = \lambda + 1$ and $\frac{1}{k_m - \lambda} = \frac{1}{\lambda - \rho + 1}$. Since $\rho < \lambda - 1$, there exist $i, j \in \mathcal{C}_2$ such that $i, j \in B_m$. Therefore $\frac{1}{\lambda - \rho + 1} \leq R(2, 2) = \frac{1}{\rho}$, implying $\rho \leq \frac{\lambda + 1}{2}$. Since $x - y < \lambda$, the only possibility is $\rho = \frac{\lambda + 1}{2}$. By Theorem 1.3, the design is type-1, contradicting $d > 0$. $\square$

4. The case $\lambda = 2P$. Throughout this section P always denotes an odd prime and $\lambda = 2P$.

LEMMA 4.1. *Suppose that $\rho = \frac{x}{y}$, x, y are odd, and $y > 1$. Then $P | (k_m - \lambda)$ if and only if $k_m = 2\lambda$.*

Proof: By (2.1), $\frac{k_m - 2\lambda}{\rho - 1}$ is an integer, i.e. $k_m - 2\lambda = (x - y)l_m$ for some integer l_m. $P \nmid (x - y)$, so $P | (k_m - \lambda)$ implies $P | l_m$. If $|l_m| \geq P$ then (2.1) or (2.2) gives negative value for k'_m or k^*_m; hence $l_m = 0$. $\square$

THEOREM 4.2. *If $\rho = \frac{x}{y}$, x, y are odd, $y > 1$, and $P \nmid x$ then $x = 2P - 1$, $y = P$, and the design is type-1.*

Proof: Suppose that x, y satisfy the conditions of the theorem. Let us fix $i \in \mathcal{C}_1$. By (2.16),

$$(4.1) \qquad \sum_{\{m:i \notin B_m\}} \frac{1}{k_m - \lambda} = 1 + \frac{y}{x} - \frac{1}{2P}.$$

Let a be the number of blocks B_m such that $P | (k_m - \lambda)$ and $i \notin B_m$. By Lemma 4.1, $k_m = 2\lambda$ for these blocks. Moreover, let $M = \{m : i \notin B_m \wedge P \nmid (k_m - \lambda)\}$. By (4.1),

$$(4.2) \qquad \frac{a + 1}{2P} = 1 + \frac{y}{x} - \sum_{\{m \in M\}} \frac{1}{k_m - \lambda}.$$

The denominator of the fraction on the right-hand-side of (4.2) is not divisible by P, so $P | (a + 1)$. Now let $j \in \mathcal{C}_1, j \neq i$, and let b be the number of blocks B_m such that $P | (k_m - \lambda)$ and $i, j \notin B_m$. Similarly to the previous argument, we obtain from (2.15) that $P | (b + 1)$. $b \geq 2P - 1$ is impossible because $\frac{y}{x} - \frac{1}{2P} < 1 - \frac{1}{2P}$. Hence $b = P - 1$ and $\frac{y}{x} - \frac{1}{2P} \geq \frac{P - 1}{2P}$, so $\rho < 2$. $a > b$ since we can choose j such that $j \in B_m$ for some m with $k_m = 2\lambda$. By (4.1), $a \geq 4P - 1$ would imply $\frac{4P - 1}{2P} \leq 1 + \frac{y}{x} - \frac{1}{2P}$, a contradiction, so the possible values for a are $a = 3P - 1$ and $a = 2P - 1$.

If $a = 3P - 1$ then $\sum_{\{m \in M\}} \frac{1}{k_m - \lambda} = \frac{1}{\rho} - \frac{1}{2} < \frac{1}{2}$. By (2.14), $R(\bar{1}, 2) = \frac{1}{\rho}$, hence $j \in B_m$ for all $j \in \mathcal{C}_2$ and $m \in M$. Similarly, $R(\bar{1}, 1) = 1$ implies that $j \notin B_m$ for

296

all $j \in \mathcal{C}_1$ and $m \in M$. Therefore, for all $m \in M$, $k'_m = 0$ and $k^*_m = e_2$. By (2.1), $k'_m = 0$ implies $k_m = \lambda\rho + \lambda$, so (2.4) gives $d = -1$. By Theorem 2.2(i), the design is type-1. From the integrality of e_2 we obtain that $y|2P$, so $y = P$. Moreover, $x|2P - 1$ since e_1 is an integer and $x > y$ implies $x = 2P - 1$.

Finally, we prove that $a = 2P - 1$ is impossible. In this case, each $j \in \mathcal{C}_1, j \neq i$ is contained in exactly P blocks with $k_m = 2\lambda$ and not containing i. Conversely, each such block contains exactly $2P$ treatments of class 1, hence $P(e_1 - 1) = (2P - 1)2P$, i.e. $e_1 = 4P - 1$. From (2.3), we obtain that $\rho = 1 + \frac{d+1}{2P-1}$ and, from (2.4), $e_2 = 4P - \frac{d(d+1)}{2P-1}$. $d \geq 0$ because $\rho > 1$; moreover, $d \neq 0$ since we assumed that $P \nmid x$. Therefore $d(d+1) > 0$ and even so $e_2 \leq 4P - 2$.

Let us denote the number of blocks with $k_m = 2\lambda$ by c. For each pair $h, j \in \mathcal{C}_1$, there are exactly $P - 1$ such blocks B_m with $h, j \notin B_m$. On the other hand, for fixed B_m there are $\binom{e_1 - 2P}{2}$ pairs $h, j \in \mathcal{C}_1$ with $h, j \notin B_m$. Thus $\binom{e_1}{2}(P - 1) = c\binom{e_1 - 2P}{2}$ and, using $e_1 = 4P - 1$, we obtain $c = 4P - 1$. Therefore there are $2P$ blocks with $k_m = 2\lambda$ and containing the fixed $i \in \mathcal{C}_1$. Each of these $2P$ blocks contains $2P$ treatments of class 2. Conversely, each treatment of class 2 is contained in $0, P$, or $2P$ of these blocks (since the denominator of $R(1,2)$ is not divisible by P). Since $e_2 \leq 4P - 2$, there are two treatments $h, j \in \mathcal{C}_2$ contained in all of these $2P$ blocks, contradicting $R(2,2) = \frac{1}{\rho} < 1$. $\square$

LEMMA 4.3. *Suppose that* $\rho = \frac{x}{y}$, x, y *are odd*, $y > 1$, *and* $P|x$. *Then* $P = x$.

Proof: $x \geq 5P$ is impossible since $x - y < \lambda$ and $y < \lambda$. If $x = 3P$ then $P < y < 2P$, and, by (2.1) and (2.2), the only possible values for k'_m are $2P$ and $2P - y$. Moreover, since e_1 is an integer, $3P|2P + d$. $d > 0$ contradicts Lemma 3.8(a). If $d \leq -2P$ then $e_1 \leq 2P$ and all blocks not containing a fixed $i \in \mathcal{C}_1$ are of the same size. Therefore r_{ij} depends only on the class of j, contradicting Theorem 2.2(iv). $\square$

THEOREM 4.4. *If* $\rho = \frac{P}{y}$, y *is odd, and* $y > 1$ *then* $y|2P - 1$ *and the design is type-1.*

Proof: We distinguish the following two cases: (i) $y \leq \frac{P-1}{2}$ and (ii) $y \geq \frac{P+1}{2}$.
(i) Let $i \in \mathcal{C}_1$ be fixed. For $j \in \mathcal{C}_1, j \neq i$, let us denote the number of blocks with $k_m = 2\lambda$ and $i, j \notin B_m$ by a_j. By (2.15), $\frac{2y-1-a_j}{2P}$ is a non-negative fraction with denominator not divisible by P, so it must be equal to 0. Hence $a_j = 2y - 1$ for all $j \in \mathcal{C}_1$, all blocks B_m with $i, j \notin B_m$ are of size 2λ, and r_{ij} is constant for all j in class 1. Similarly, for $j \in \mathcal{C}_2$, let b_j be the number of blocks with $k_m = 2\lambda$, $i \notin B_m$, and $j \in B_m$. From $R(\bar{1}, 2) = \frac{y}{P}$ we obtain that $P|(2y - b_j)$; thus all blocks containing a fixed treatment $j \in \mathcal{C}_2$ and not containing i are of size 2λ, and r_{ij} is constant for all j in class 2. Therefore, by Theorem 2.2(iv), the design is type-1. From the integrality of e_1 and e_2 we get $d = 0$ and $y|2P - 1$.
(ii) As above, we can conclude that $P|(2y - b_j)$ for all $j \in \mathcal{C}_2$. In particular, $b_j > 0$, hence there exists a block of size 2λ not containing a treatment of class 1. This implies $e_1 \geq \lambda + 1$ and $d > -2P$. On the other hand, Lemma 3.4 gives $d < 2P + 2y - 1 < 4P$. The integrality of e_1 implies $P|d$. Thus the possible values

for d are $3P, 2P, P, 0$ and $-P$. We examine the integrality condition given by e_2. If $d = 3P$ then $y|(-P-1)$. Since $y \geq \frac{P+1}{2}$, the only possibility is $y = \frac{P+1}{2}$ implying $e_2 = 0$, a contradiction. If $d = 2P$ then $y|(-1)$, a contradiction. If $d = P$ then $y|P-1$, a contradiction. If $d = 0$ then, by Theorem 2.2(i), the design is type-1. Finally, if $d = -P$ then $y|3P-1$. Since $y \geq \frac{P+1}{2}$, the only possibilities are $y = \frac{3P-1}{5}$ and $y = \frac{3P-1}{4}$. We prove that these cases are impossible.

If $d = -P$ and $y = \frac{3P-1}{5}$ then $r_1 = 6P + 1$ and

$$(4.3) \qquad \frac{r_1}{\rho + 1} = \frac{(6P+1)(3P-1)}{8P-1} = \frac{9}{4}P - \frac{1}{32}\left(3 + \frac{35}{8P-1}\right).$$

Thus $t_1 \geq \frac{11}{32}$. On the other hand, Corollary 3.3(a) gives $t_1 \leq \frac{(2P+1)(13P-6)}{(8P-1)(16P-7)}$, a contradiction. If $d = -P$ and $y = \frac{3P-1}{4}$ then $r_1 = 5P + 1$ and

$$(4.4) \qquad \frac{r_1}{\rho + 1} = \frac{(5P+1)(3P-1)}{7P-1} = \frac{15}{7}P + \frac{1}{7}\frac{P-7}{7P-1}.$$

Thus $t_1 \geq \frac{1}{7} - \frac{1}{7}\frac{P-7}{7P-1} = \frac{6(P+1)}{7(7P-1)}$. From Corollary 3.3(a) we obtain $t_1 \leq \frac{(P+1)(11P-5)}{(7P-1)(14P-6)}$ which leads to a contradiction. $\square$

THEOREM 4.5. *If $\rho = P$ then the design is type-1.*

Proof: By Theorem 2.1(b), it is enough to prove that $e_1 \leq 2P + 1$ is impossible. So let us suppose that $e_1 \leq 2P + 1$ and let us fix $i, j \in \mathcal{C}_1, i \neq j$. If $i, j \notin B_m$ for some block B_m and $P|(k_m - \lambda)$ then, similarly to the proof of Lemma 4.1, we can deduce that either $k'_m = P$ and $k_m - \lambda = P(P+1)$ or $k'_m = 0$ and $k_m - \lambda = 2P^2$. Let a be the number of blocks B_m with $k'_m = 0$ and $i, j \notin B_m$. Moreover, let b be the number of blocks B_m with $k'_m = P$ and $i, j \notin B_m$. By (2.15),

$$(4.5) \qquad \frac{1}{\rho} - \frac{1}{\lambda} - \frac{a}{2P^2} - \frac{b}{P(P+1)} = \frac{\frac{P(P+1)}{2} - a\frac{P+1}{2} - bP}{P^2(P+1)}$$

is a non-negative fraction with denominator not divisible by P; hence $P^2|(\frac{P(P+1)}{2} - a\frac{P+1}{2} - bP)$. The only possibility is that

$$(4.6) \qquad \frac{P(P+1)}{2} - a\frac{P+1}{2} - bP = 0;$$

in particular, the size of all blocks which do not contain i and j is divisible by P. (4.6) implies that $P|a$ so $a = 0$ or $a = P$.

If $a = 0$ then, for all $h \in \mathcal{C}_1$, the blocks not containing i and h must be of size $P(P+3)$. In particular, r_{ih} is constant for all $h \in \mathcal{C}_1, h \neq i$. Moreover, all blocks not containing i must satisfy $k'_m = P$ or $k'_m = e_1 - 1$. In the latter case,

$$(4.7) \qquad k_m - \lambda = P + 1 - d + \frac{d}{P}.$$

For $h \in \mathcal{C}_2$, let us denote by b_h the number of blocks satisfying $h \in B_m, i \notin B_m$, and $k'_m = P$. By (2.14), the denominator of $\frac{1}{P} - \frac{b_h}{P(P+1)} = \frac{P+1-b_h}{P(P+1)}$ is not divisible

298

by P; hence $b_h = 1$ or $b_h = P+1$. If $b_h = P+1$ for all $h \in \mathcal{C}_2$ then r_{ih} is constant for all $h \in \mathcal{C}_2$ and Theorem 2.2(iv) leads to a contradiction with $e_1 \leq \lambda + 1$. If there exists $h \in \mathcal{C}_2$ with $b_h = 1$ then, by (4.7),

$$(4.8) \qquad \frac{1}{P} - \frac{1}{P(P+1)} = c\frac{1}{P+1-d+\frac{d}{P}}$$

for some integer c. Solving this equation for c, we obtain $c = 1 + \frac{d}{P}\frac{1-P}{1+P} \cdot (\frac{P-1}{2}, \frac{P+1}{2}) = 1$ implies $\frac{P(P+1)}{2}|d$. $d < 0$ since $e_1 \leq \lambda + 1$ and $d \leq -P^2 - P$ contradicts Theorem 3.5. Hence the only possibility is $d = -\frac{P^2+P}{2}$ implying $\frac{r_2}{\rho+1} = \frac{P+3}{2}$. From Theorem 2.2(ii), we obtain a contradiction anyway.

If $a = P$ then, for all $h \in \mathcal{C}_1$, the only blocks not containing i and h are the same P blocks of size $2P^2 + 2P$. Hence there are $P+1-d+\frac{d}{P}$ blocks containing all class 1 treatments except i. The reciprocal sum of the $(k_m - \lambda)$'s for these blocks is 1. Repeating this argument with all class 1 treatments in the place of i, we obtain that each class 1 treatment is contained in exactly $(e_1 - 1)(P+1-d+\frac{d}{P})$ blocks satisfying $k'_m = e_1 - 1$ and the reciprocal sum of the $(k_m - \lambda)$'s for these blocks is $e_1 - 1$. By (2.12), $e_1 - 1 \leq P + 1$ which is equivalent to $d \leq -P^2$. Theorem 3.5 gives $d > -P^2 - P$. Since, from the integrality of e_1, $P|d$, the only possibility is $d = -P^2$. This implies $\frac{r_1}{\rho+1} = P^2 + 1$, contradicting Theorem 2.2(ii). $\square$

THEOREM 4.6. $\frac{\lambda}{2} < \rho < \lambda - 1$ is impossible.

Proof: $\frac{\lambda}{2} < \rho < \lambda - 1$ is impossible in type-1 designs. Hence, by Theorem 1.3, we have to prove that the assumption ρ is an odd integer, $P + 2 \leq \rho \leq 2P - 3$ leads to a contradiction. Also, by Lemma 3.8(b), we can suppose that $e_1 \leq 2P + 1$.

Three possible values of $k_m - \lambda$ are divisible by P: (i) $k_m - \lambda = 2P$ which is equivalent to $k'_m = 2P$; (ii) $k_m - \lambda = P(\rho+1) \iff k'_m = P$; and (iii) $k_m - \lambda = 2P\rho \iff k'_m = 0$. However, among blocks not containing two fixed treatments i, j of class 1, only cases (ii) and (iii) are possible.

Claim: There exists a block of size $2P\rho + 2P$.

Proof of the Claim: Suppose that there is no block of size $2P\rho + 2P$ and let a be the number of blocks not containing $i, j \in \mathcal{C}_1$ and of size $P(\rho+1) + 2P$. By (2.15),

$$(4.9) \qquad \frac{a}{P(\rho+1)} + \frac{1}{2P} = \frac{a + \frac{\rho+1}{2}}{P(\rho+1)}$$

is a fraction $\leq \frac{1}{\rho}$ and its denominator is not divisible by P. This implies $a = P - \frac{\rho+1}{2}$. Moreover, there exist some blocks not containing i and j such that the reciprocal sum of the $(k_m - \lambda)$'s for these blocks is $\frac{1}{\rho(\rho+1)}$. Since the smallest possible value of $\frac{1}{k_m - \lambda}$ is $\frac{1}{2P\rho}$ and $\frac{1}{\rho(\rho+1)} < 2\frac{1}{2P\rho}$, there must be a unique block satisfying $\frac{1}{k_m - \lambda} = \frac{1}{\rho(\rho+1)}$. Since, by (2.1), $(\rho-1)|(k_m - 2\lambda)$, we obtain $(\rho-1)|(\rho(\rho+1) - 2P)$ which is equivalent to $(\rho-1)|(2P-2)$. However, this fact contradicts $P+2 \leq \rho \leq 2P - 3$. $\square$

Let b be the number of blocks of size $2P\rho + 2P$. The Claim implies that $b > 0$. On the other hand, by (2.15), $\frac{1}{\rho} - \frac{1}{\lambda} \geq \frac{b}{2P\rho}$ implying $b \leq 2P - \rho$. Let us fix a block B_m of size $2P\rho + 2P$. Then B_m contains $2P\rho + 2P$ treatments of class 2. If all of these treatments were contained in at least one other block of size $2P\rho + 2P$ then at least $\frac{2P\rho+2P}{2P-\rho-1} > 2P$ of them would be contained in a block B_n contradicting $|B_m \cap B_n| = \lambda$. Therefore we can fix $h \in C_2$ such that B_m is the only block of size $2P\rho + 2P$ containing h. Let c be the number of blocks of size $P(\rho+1) + 2P$ and containing h. Moreover, for all $j \in C_2$, let c_j be the number of blocks B_n with $h, j \in B_n$ and $k_n = P(\rho+1) + 2P$. For $j \in C_1$, let c_j be the number of blocks B_n with $h \in B_n$, $j \notin B_n$, and $k_n = P(\rho+1) + 2P$. Now be distinguish three cases: 1) $e_1 < 2P$, 2) $e_1 = 2P$, and 3) $e_1 = 2P + 1$.

Case 1: $e_1 < 2P$. In this case, there are no blocks of size $4P$. If $j \in C_2$ and $j \notin B_m$ then $c_j = 0$. Indeed, $\frac{c_j}{P(\rho+1)}$ must be a fraction $\leq \frac{1}{\rho}$ and denominator not divisible by P implying $c_j = 0$ or $c_j = P$. As in the proof of the Claim, $c_j = P$ leads to contradiction. On the other hand, if $j \in B_m$ then

$$(4.10) \qquad \frac{c_j}{P(\rho+1)} + \frac{1}{2P\rho} = \frac{c_j\rho + \frac{\rho+1}{2}}{P\rho(\rho+1)}$$

is a fraction $\leq \frac{1}{\rho}$ and denominator not divisible by P. Therefore $c_j = c^*$ where c^* is the unique positive solution of the system

$$(4.11) \qquad P|(c^*\rho + \frac{\rho+1}{2}), \quad c^* < P.$$

There are $2P\rho + 2P - 1$ treatments with $c_j = c^*$. On the other hand, each of the c blocks of size $P(\rho+1) + 2P$ contains $P(\rho+2) - 1$ class 2 treatments beside h so

$$(4.12) \qquad c^*(2P\rho + 2P - 1) = c(P\rho + 2P - 1).$$

This implies $c - c^* = lP$ for some positive integer l so (4.12) is equivalent to $c^*\rho = l(P\rho + 2P - 1)$, contradicting $c^* < P$.

Case 2: $e_1 = 2P$. Since none of the class 1 treatments are in B_m, $c_j = c^*$ for all $j \in C_1$. On the other hand, each block of size $P(\rho+1) + 2P$ leaves out $e_1 - P$ treatments of class 1 so $e_1 c^* = c(e_1 - P)$, $c = 2c^*$. Now let c^{**} be the number of blocks of size $4P$ and containing h. Since $e_1 = 2P$, these blocks contain all treatments of class 1. This implies $c^{**} \leq 1$ since otherwise the intersection of two such blocks would contain $\geq 1 + 2P$ treatments. Because of $c = 2c^*$ and $R(1,2) = 1$, $\frac{c^*}{P(\rho+1)} + \frac{c^{**}}{2P}$ is a fraction with denominator not divisible by P implying

$$(4.13) \qquad P|(c^* + c^{**}\frac{\rho+1}{2}).$$

Thus $c^{**} = 0$ is impossible, i.e. $c^{**} = 1$. Adding (4.11) and (4.13), we obtain $P|(\rho+1)(c^*+1)$, $c^* = P-1$. So (4.13) gives $P|(P-1+\frac{\rho+1}{2})$ which is a contradiction.

Case 3: $e_1 = 2P + 1$. Then $d = -2P + \rho$ and $r_2 = 4P - \rho + 1$. Moreover, $\frac{e_2}{2} < 2P\rho + 2P$ so more than half of the class 2 treatments are contained in B_m. By Theorem 2.3(b), there exists $i \in B_m$ such that $r_{ih} = \lceil \frac{r_2}{\rho+1} \rceil = \lceil \frac{4P+2}{\rho+1} \rceil - 1$. Since $\rho \geq P + 2$, the possible values for r_{ih} are 2 and 3. $k_m^* \geq 2P$ for all blocks

300

otherwise the intersection with B_m could not be of size λ. This implies that $r_{ih} = 2$ is impossible since $\frac{1}{2P\rho} + \frac{1}{2P} = \frac{\rho+1}{2P\rho} < \frac{1}{\rho}$. If $r_{ih} = 3$ then there must be at least one block besides B_m containing i and h and of size divisible by P. If the size of this block is $4P$ then the third block B_n satisfies

$$(4.14) \qquad \frac{1}{k_n - \lambda} = \frac{1}{\rho} - \frac{1}{2P\rho} - \frac{1}{2P} = \frac{2P - \rho - 1}{2P\rho}.$$

Thus $P|(k_n - \lambda)$; however, both the assumptions $k_n - \lambda = 2P$ and $k_n - \lambda = P(\rho+1)$ lead to a contradiction easily. If the size of the second block is $P(\rho + 1) + 2P$ then we obtain

$$(4.15) \qquad \frac{1}{k_n - \lambda} = \frac{1}{\rho} - \frac{1}{2P\rho} - \frac{1}{P(\rho+1)} > \frac{1}{2P},$$

again a contradiction. ☐

PROPOSITION 4.7. (a) If $x - y = P$ then $y < P$.
(b) If $x - y = P$, $y < P$ then $d < 0$.

Proof: $x - y = P$ implies that each k_m is a multiple of P.
(a) Suppose that $y > P$. Then the only possible values for k_m' are $2P$ and $2P - y$, hence $\frac{1}{k_m - \lambda} = \frac{1}{2P}$ or $\frac{1}{3P}$. Let $i \in C_2$ and denote by a and b the number of blocks containing i and of size $4P$ and $5P$, respectively. By (2.12), $1 + \frac{y}{P+y} = \frac{3a+2b}{6P}$ implying that $(P + y)|6$. However, this is in contradiction with $y > P \geq 3$.
(b) Suppose that $d \geq 0$. From the integrality of e_1, we obtain $(P + y)|(2P + d)$; moreover, by Lemma 3.4, $d < 2P + \frac{2Py}{P+y} - 1 < 2P + 2y$. Thus the possible values for d are $d = P + 3y$ and $d = 2y$.

If $d = P + 3y$ then $r_2 = P$. The greatest possible value of $\frac{1}{k_m - \lambda}$ is $\frac{1}{P}$; hence, for any treatment i in class 2, $\sum_{i \in B_m} \frac{1}{k_m - \lambda} \leq P\frac{1}{P}$ contradicting (2.12). If $d = 2y$ then $r_2 = 2P$ and $e_1 = 2P + 2y$. Therefore, $k_m = k_n = 3P$, i.e. $k_m' = k_n' = 2P + y$ implies that the intersection of B_m and B_n consists of $2P$ treatments of class 1. In particular, any treatment i of class 2 is contained in at most one block of size $3P$. Thus $\sum_{i \in B_m} \frac{1}{k_m - \lambda} \leq \frac{1}{P} + (2P - 1)\frac{1}{2P}$ contradicting (2.12). ☐

5. The case $\lambda = 10$. By Theorem 1.4 and Propositions 3.7 and 4.7, the only possible values for ρ in a non-type-1 λ-design with $\lambda = 10$ are $\frac{9}{4}, \frac{8}{3}, \frac{7}{2}$, and 6. Moreover, in each case, d must be negative. In this section we shall eliminate these possibilities.

PROPOSITION 5.1. $\rho = \frac{9}{4}$ is impossible.

Proof: By Theorem 3.5, $d \geq -15$. From the integrality of e_1 and e_2, we obtain $9|(10 + d)$ and $4|(9 - d)$. However, this congruence system has no solution in the range $-15 \leq d \leq -1$. ☐

PROPOSITION 5.2. $\rho = \frac{8}{3}$ is impossible.

Proof: Theorem 3.5 gives $d \geq -17$. The integrality of e_1 and e_2 imply $8|(10+d)$ and $3|(9 - d)$. However, this congruence system has no solution in the range $-17 \leq d \leq -1$. ☐

301

PROPOSITION 5.3. $\rho = \frac{7}{2}$ is impossible.

Proof: In this case, Theorem 3.5 gives $d \geq -21$. The congruences are $7|(10 + d)$ and $2|(9 - d)$ with solutions $d = -3$ and $d = -17$ in the range $-21 \leq d \leq -1$. If $d = -3$ then $r_2 = 15$ and $t_2 = \frac{6}{9}$, contradicting Lemma 3.1. If $d = -17$ then $r_2 = 25$ and $t_2 = \frac{4}{9}$. However, Corollary 3.3(b) implies $t_2 \leq \frac{35}{99}$; we obtained a contradiction. $\square$

THEOREM 5.4. $\rho = 6$ is impossible.

Proof: Theorem 3.5 gives $d \geq -33$ and the integrality of e_1 implies $6|(10 + d)$. Thus the possible values for d are $-4, -10, -16, -22$, and -28. If $d = -4$ then $r_2 = 15$ and $t_2 = \frac{6}{7}$, contradicting Lemma 3.1. If $d = -22$ then $\frac{r_1}{\rho+1} = 25$ and if $d = -28$ then $\frac{r_2}{\rho+1} = 5$, contradicting Theorem 2.2(ii). The cases $d = -10$ and $d = -16$ require more careful considerations.

If $d = -10$ then $e_1 = 10$, $e_2 = 124$, $r_1 = 115$, and $r_2 = 20$. The possible values of $\frac{1}{k_m - \lambda}$ are $\frac{1}{10}, \frac{1}{15}, \frac{1}{20}, \cdots, \frac{1}{60}$; however, blocks not containing two fixed treatments of class 1 must satisfy $\frac{1}{k_m - \lambda} \leq \frac{1}{20}$. Therefore, $R(\bar{1}, \bar{1}) = \frac{1}{15}$ implies that there are at least two blocks not containing i and j for any $i, j \in \mathcal{C}_1$; hence $r_{ij} \geq 98$ for all $i, j \in \mathcal{C}_1$. By (2.23) and (2.24), for fixed $i \in \mathcal{C}_1$,

$$(5.1) \qquad \sum_{j \leq e_1, j \neq i} r_{ij} = 9 \cdot (98 + \frac{4}{7}) - \frac{U_i}{5} = 9 \cdot 98 + \frac{36}{7} - \frac{U_i}{5}$$

and

$$(5.2) \qquad \sum_{j > e_1} r_{ij} = 124 \cdot (16 + \frac{3}{7}) + \frac{6U_i}{5} = 124 \cdot 17 - 71 + \frac{1}{7} + \frac{6U_i}{5}.$$

Therefore $\frac{U_i}{5} \leq \frac{36}{7}$ and $\sum_{j > e_1} r_{ij} \leq 124 \cdot 17 - 40$. By (2.25),
$$(5.3)$$
$$U_i + V_i = \sum_{j \leq e_1, j \neq i} \left((r_{ij} - 98 - \frac{4}{7})^2 + (r_{ij} - 97 - \frac{3}{16})^2 \right) + \sum_{j > e_1} \left((r_{ij} - 16 - \frac{3}{7})^2 + (r_{ij} - 17 - \frac{1}{32})^2 \right) \geq$$

$$9 \cdot (\frac{4}{7})^2 + 9 \cdot (\frac{13}{16})^2 + 40 \cdot (\frac{3}{7})^2 + 40 \cdot (\frac{33}{32})^2 + 84 \cdot (\frac{4}{7})^2 + 84 \cdot (\frac{1}{32})^2 = 86 + \frac{31}{112}.$$

However, (2.22) implies that $U_i + V_i = 62 + \frac{31}{112}$, we obtain a contradiction.

If $d = -16$ then $e_1 = 9$, $e_2 = 160$, $r_1 = 145$, and $r_2 = 25$. By (2.28) and (2.29),

$$(5.4) \qquad \sum_{j \leq e_1} r_{ij} = 9 \cdot (21 + \frac{3}{7}) - \frac{U_i}{5} = 9 \cdot 21 + 4 - \frac{1}{7} - \frac{U_i}{5}$$

and

$$(5.5) \qquad \sum_{j > e_1, j \neq i} r_{ij} = 159 \cdot (3 + \frac{4}{7}) + \frac{6U_i}{5} = 159 \cdot 4 - 69 + 6 \cdot (\frac{1}{7} + \frac{U_i}{5})$$

302

hold for all $i \in \mathcal{C}_2$. In particular, $\frac{1}{7} + \frac{U_i}{5}$ is an integer. By Theorem 2.5 and Proposition 3.6, there exists $i \in \mathcal{C}_2$ satisfying $\frac{U_i}{5} \leq e_1 \frac{\rho-1}{\rho+1} = \frac{45}{7}$, or, because of the integrality condition, $\frac{1}{7} + \frac{U_i}{5} \leq 6$. For this particular i, (5.5) gives $\sum_{j > e_1, j \neq i} r_{ij} \leq 159 \cdot 4 - 33$. By (2.30),

$$(5.6) \qquad U_i + V_i > \sum_{j > e_1, j \neq i} \left((r_{ij} - 3 - \frac{4}{7})^2 + (r_{ij} - 4 - \frac{3}{23})^2 \right) \geq$$

$$33 \cdot (\frac{4}{7})^2 + 33 \cdot (\frac{26}{23})^2 + 126 \cdot (\frac{3}{7})^2 + 126 \cdot (\frac{3}{23})^2 > 78.$$

However, (2.27) implies that $U_i + V_i = 74 + \frac{11}{161}$, we obtain a contradiction. $\square$

REFERENCES

[Br70]   W. G. BRIDGES, *Some results on λ-designs*, J. of Comb. Th. 8 (1970), pp. 350–360.

[Br77]   W. G. BRIDGES, *A characterization of type-1 λ-designs*, J. of Comb. Th. (A), 22 (361–367).

[BK]   W. G. BRIDGES AND E. S. KRAMER, *The determination of all λ-designs with $\lambda = 3$*, J. of Comb. Th., 8 (1970), pp. 343–349.

[BE]   N. G. DEBRUIJN AND P. ERDÖS, *On a combinatorial problem*, Indagationes Math., 10 (1948), pp. 421–423.

[H]   M. HALL, *Combinatorial Theory*, Blaisdell, Waltham, Mass., 1967.

[Kr69]   E. S. KRAMER, *On λ-designs*, Ph. D. dissertation, Univ. of Michigan.

[Kr74]   E. S. KRAMER, *On λ-designs*, J. of Comb. Th. (A), 16 (1974), pp. 57–75.

[Ry]   AN EXTENSION OF A THEOREM OF DEBRUIJN AND ERDÖS ON COMBINATORIAL DESIGNS, J. Algebra, 10 (1968), pp. 246–261.

[Se]   Á. SERESS, *Some characterizations of type-1 λ-designs*, J. of Comb. Th. (A), submitted.

[SS76]   S. S. SHRIKHANDE AND N. M. SINGHI, *On the λ-design conjecture*, Utilitas Math., 9 (1976), pp. 301–318.

[SS84]   S. S. SHRIKHANDE AND N. M. SINGHI, *Some combinatorial problems*, Indian Statistical Institute (1984), pp. 340–359, in *Combinatorics and its Applications,*, pp..

[Wo70]   D. R. WOODALL, *Square λ-linked designs*, Proc. London Math. Soc., 20 (1970), pp. 669–687.

[Wo71]   D. R. WOODALL, *Square λ-linked designs: a survey*, in *Combinatorial Mathematics and its Applications*, Academic Press, 1971, pp. 349–355.

DESIGNS, INTERSECTION NUMBERS, AND CODES

M.S. SHRIKHANDE*

Abstract. Block intersection numbers provide a very useful tool in the study of combinatorial designs. In this paper we discuss some recent work on 2- and 3–designs having at most two intersection numbers. We include connections with M. Hall, Jr.'s conjecture: for fixed $\lambda \geq 2$, there are finitely many symmetric $2 - (v, k, \lambda)$ designs; results on quasi–symmetric $3 - (v, k, \lambda)$ designs with positive intersection numbers; results of Tonchev and Calderbank which use codes as their main tools and some results on quasi–symmetric 2–designs with intersection numbers 0 and 2 which satisfy configuration conditions.

Key words. design, intersection number, quasi–symmetric design, code

AMS(MOS) subject classifications. 05 B05 (primary), 05 B25 (secondary)

0. Introduction. The (block) intersection numbers $|B_i \cap B_j|$ provide a powerful tool in the study of combinatorial designs. For instance, symmetric $2-(v, k, \lambda)$ designs are characterized amongst $2 - (v, k, \lambda)$ designs by having exactly one intersection number. Quasi–symmetric $t - (v, k, \lambda)$ designs are those having exactly two intersection numbers. Cameron's famous result [9] on the possible extensions of symmetric $2 - (v, k, \lambda)$ designs can be viewed as a classification theorem of quasi-symmetric 3–designs with an intersection number zero.

Ray–Chaudhuri and Wilson [26] showed that a 2s–design has at least s intersection numbers and in the extremal case there are exactly s intersection numbers iff the design is tight. The famous $4 - (23, 7, 1)$ design has only two intersection numbers. The combined efforts of Ito, Enomoto, Noda [14, 18] and Bremner [4] have shown that up to complementation it is the unique quasi–symmetric 4–design. Cameron [11] has shown that no quasi–symmetric t–designs exist for $t \geq 5$. The classification problem for quasi–symmetric 3–designs with positive intersection numbers is open. Some progress has recently been made on this problem by Sane and Shrikhande [28].

The classification of quasi–symmetric 2–designs is another difficult open problem [21]. The block graph Γ of a quasi–symmetric 2–design is a strongly regular graph and provides one of the standard tools used in this area. One of the common themes is to put some additional structure on Γ and then try to pin down parametrically or otherwise the quasi–symmetric design (see for instance the fundamental paper of Goethals and Seidel [15]). The recent work in [20], [24] and [27] can be traced back to this idea, which was considerably exploited in Baartmans and Shrikhande [1].

The paper [1] is concerned with quasi–symmetric 2–designs having an intersection number zero and possessing no three mutually disjoint blocks. One of the

---

*Department of Mathematics, Central Michigan University, Mt. Pleasant, MI 48859.

The author gratefully acknowledges the hospitality of the Institute for Mathematics and its applications at the University of Minnesota. He is indebted to this institution and a Central Michigan University Research Professorship for financial support.

results of [1] is that for a fixed value ≥ 2 of the other intersection number there are finitely many such designs and the extremal designs are related to those occurring in Cameron's theorem [9]. Using a suitably modified quadratic polynomial occuring in [1], Sane and Shrikhande [27], showed for instance, that the well known open conjecture of M. Hall, Jr. that for a fixed $\lambda \geq 2$, there are finitely many symmetric $2 - (v, k, \lambda)$ designs is in fact equivalent to another conjecture of Singhi concerning certain quasi–symmetric 2–designs.

Recently I have learned from Cameron [12] of a result of his dealing with the other extreme than that considered in [1]–namely quasi–symmetric 2–designs with a spread. We refer to this in section 1 (Theorem 1.9).

The paper of Neumaier [25] contains a possible approach to classying quasi–symmetric 2–designs. In [25], Neumaier introduces the notion of a regular set in a strongly regular graph and then uses among other tools a result of Bridges and Shrikhande [5] on special partially balanced incomplete block designs to prove properties and parameter relations involving a quasi–symmetric 2–design and its block graph Γ. He then considers four classes of well known quasi–symmetric 2–designs. A classification result (Thm. Q. [25]) is then obtained by imposing some structural restrictions on Γ or the intersection numbers. Neumaier [25] calls a quasi–symmetric 2–design exceptional if neither the design nor its complement belongs to one of his four classes. A list of exceptional parameters with ≤ 40 points is given [25]. This table of Neumaier has resulted in much recent interest in quasi–symmetric 2–designs.

In attempting to settle some cases in Neumaier's table, Tonchev [33] showed connections with an important area from Coding Theory–namely self–dual codes. We discuss some of these results. Motivated I think, in part by the paper [33], Calderbank [7] has recently proved some powerful non–existence results involving the intersection numbers of a 2–design. These results (proved by using invariant theory) give new non–existence criteria depending on the parity of the intersection numbers. The results of Tonchev [33], and Calderbank [7] when specialized to quasi–symmetric designs rule out some designs in Neumaier's table. In another recent paper Calderbank [6] considers the case where the intersection numbers are all congruent modulo an odd prime. The results of Calderbank [6, 7] rule out, for example some feasible quasi–symmetric designs occurring in [31], [29] and [1].

The interplay between designs, intersection numbers and codes is thus the main theme of this paper. The breakdown of the present paper is the following: In section 1 we briefly discuss the results of [20], [24], and [27]. These all rest on the "polynomial method" which was the main tool of [1]. Cameron's result on spreads (Theorem 1.9) is then put at the other extreme of results [1]. In section 2 we give a partial result (Proposition 2.4) about a conjecture of Sane and Shrikhande [28] on quasi–symmetric 3–designs with smaller intersection number one. Section 3 briefly outlines some of Neumaier's ideas from [25]. Some important recent results of Tonchev and Calderbank referred to earlier are then discussed in sections 4 and 5. These are used to show in Corollaries 5.6 and 5.7 the non–existence of certain parameters of designs occurring in papers [1, 29, 31]. Finally in section 6 we outline some recent work of Mavron and Shrikhande [23] concerning the classification of quasi–symmetric 2–designs with intersection numbers 0 and 2 which satisfy certain configuration properties.

1. The Polynomial Method. We mention Beth et al [3] for general background on Designs.

Let D be a $t - (v, k, \lambda)$ design with blocks $B_1, B_2, \ldots, B_b$. The distinct cardinalities $|B_i \cap B_j|$, $i \neq j$ are called the (block) intersection numbers of the design. D is called quasi–symmetric (q.s.) if it has exactly two intersection numbers which are then commonly denoted by x, y with $x < y$.

If D is q.s. 2–design, then its block graph Γ is a graph with vertex set the blocks of D and where distinct blocks B_i, B_j are adjacent iff $|B_i \cap B_j| = y$. Then Γ is a strongly regular graph with usual parameters (n, a, c, d) (see e.g. Cameron and van Lint [8] or Shrikhande [29]). The following result of P.J. Cameron [9] gives the classification of q.s. 3–designs with $x = 0$:

THEOREM 1.1. *If D is a q.s. $3 - (v, k, \lambda)$ design with $x = 0$, then one of the following holds:*

   (i) $v = 4(\lambda + 1)$, $k = 2(\lambda + 1)$;

   (ii) $v = (\lambda + 1)(\lambda^2 + 5\lambda + 5)$, $k = (\lambda + 1)(\lambda + 2)$;

   (iii) $v = 112$, $k = 12$, $\lambda = 1$;

   (iv) $v = 496$, $k = 40$, $\lambda = 3$.

REMARKS 1.2. Designs occuring in (i) of above theorem are the so called Hadamard 3–designs which exist infinitely often. Lam et al [19], using a computer have ruled out (iii), which would be an extension of a projective plane of order 10. The design in (ii) for $\lambda = 1$ is the (unique) extension of the projective plane of order 4. Recently Bagchi [2] has proved the non–existence of (ii) for $\lambda = 2$, using the ternary code of the design; the situation for $\lambda \geq 3$ is open. Nothing is known about the case (iv)

Motivated partly by Theorem 1.1, Baartmans and Shrikhande [1] considered q.s. 2–designs with $x = 0$ and having no three mutually disjoint blocks. We also refer to such q.s. designs as triangle–free designs, as the complement of Γ has no triangles. The major tool of [1] is the next lemma:

LEMMA 1.3. *Let D be a q.s. $2 - (v, k, \lambda)$ design with intersection numbers 0 and $y \geq 2$. Suppose D has no three mutually disjoint blocks. Then k, λ, and y satisfy the diophantine equation (*)*

$$(*) \quad [k^2 - y(y+1)k + y^2]\lambda^2 + y[2k^2 - 2(y^2+1)k + y(y+1)]\lambda + y^2(k-y)(k-1) = 0.$$

Using among other things the discriminant of (*), the following results were proved in [1]:

THEOREM 1.4. *Under the hypothesis of Lemma 1.3, the following hold:*

306

(i) $2y \le k \le y(y+1)$;

(ii) $k = 2y$ iff D is a Hadamard 3–design;

(iii) $k = y(y+1)$ iff D has parameters of case (ii) in Theorem 1.1 or its residual;

(iv)   For a fixed value of y, there are finitely many such 2–designs D.

We call a design satisfying the hypothesis of Theorem 1.4 *exceptional* if $2y < k < y(y+1)$. Exceptional parameter sets seem to be quite rare. The paper [1] lists the following for $2 \le y \le 199$, found by a computer search.

Table I

(Table of exceptional triangle–free parameters with $2 \le y \le 199$).

No.	v	k	λ	y
1.	232	36	15	6
2.	5290	345	56	23
3.	1174581	13770	392	162

REMARK 1.5. We will show in section 5, that the first two parameter sets are impossible by a recent result of Calderbank [6]. This settles two of the three cases raised in Problem 5 of Shrikhande [30]. The paper [30] is a survey on such "polynomial methods".

In a recent paper [20], Limaye, Sane, and Shrikhande studied the structure of such triangle–free q.s. designs and developed some machinery towards resolving the following conjecture which is still open.

Conjecture 1.6. There are only finitely many exceptional triangle–free q.s. 2–designs with positive intersection number ≥ 2.

Symmetric $2 - (v, k, \lambda)$ designs can be regarded as improper q.s. designs having only one intersection number. Using a variant of the polynomial equation (*) in Lemma 1.3, Sane and Shrikhande [27] showed the following.

THEOREM 1.7. *The two open conjectures below are equivalent.*
M. Hall, Jr.'s conjecture: For a fixed $\lambda \ge 2$, there are finitely many symmetric $2 - (v, k, \lambda)$ designs.

Singhi's conjecture. For a fixed $\lambda \ge 2$, there are finitely many proper or improper q.s. $2 - (v, k, \lambda)$ designs having an intersection number zero.

Using MACSYMA to handle the tedious symbolic calculations, Meyerowitz, Sane and Shrikhande [24] proved the theorem below. This includes some results of [1], [20], and [27] as special cases.

THEOREM 1.8. *For fixed values of x, y, and $\bar{c}$ with $y \geq 2, \bar{c} \geq 0$ and $y > x \geq 0$, there are only finitely many q.s. 2–designs with intersection numbers x, y and having $\bar{c}$ triangles on any edge of $\overline{\Gamma}$, the complement of block graph Γ.*

The paper [1] deals with q.s. 2–designs with $x = 0$ and having no three mutually disjoint blocks. Recently P.J. Cameron [12] informed me of an unpublished result of his dealing with the other extreme. Recall that a spread is a family of pairwise disjoint blocks with the property that any point lies in one of them (such blocks are usually called a parallel class).

THEOREM 1.9. *Let D be a q.s. $2 - (v, k, \lambda)$ design with intersection numbers 0 and y, possessing a spread. Then one of the following holds:*

(i) *$\lambda = 1$ (and hence $y = 1$);*
(ii) *D is affine (i.e. $v = m^2 y$, $k = my, \lambda = (my - 1)/(m - 1)$) and any two blocks disjoint from a common block are disjoint from each other;*
(iii) *$v = y(2y + 1)\,(2y + 3)$, $k = y(2y + 1)$, $\lambda = y(2y - 1)$.*

REMARKS 1.10. Many examples are known for cases (i), (ii). Affine planes are the only designs satisfying both (i) and (ii). No design in (iii) is affine. The case $v = 15$, $k = 3, \lambda = 1$ (i.e. Kirkman's school girl problem) is in both (i) and (iii) and is the only case of a design with parameters (iii) which is known to exist. The first open case of (iii) has $y = 2$ and the design D has parameters $2 - (70, 10, 6)$. The binary code of D might be helpful for further analysis.

2. Quasi–symmetric 3–designs with x=1. Cameron's theorem 1.1 classifies q.s. 3–designs with smaller intersection number $x = 0$. One of the aims of a recent paper [28] of Sane and Shrikhande was to develop some machinery to investigate q.s. $3 - (v, k, \lambda)$ designs with $x \geq 1$. Their main tool (Theorem 3.2, [28]) asserts that in this case, the intersection numbers are roots of a quadratic $f(\alpha) = A\alpha^2 + B\alpha + C$, where A, B, C are explicit (known) functions of v, k, and λ. To be specific:

$$A = (v - 2)[\lambda(v - 1)(v - 2) - k(k - 1)(k - 2)],$$
$$B = -[(v - 2) + 2(k - 1)^2](v - 1)(v - 2)\lambda + [k(v - 2) + (k - 1)^2]k(k - 1)(k - 2)$$

and

$$C = (k - 1)^2 k^2 [\lambda(v - 2) - (k - 1)(k - 2)].$$

We remark that this fact already follows from Delsarte [13], section 5, however the derivation given in [28] is purely elementary. Using the quadratic $f(\alpha)$, Sane and Shrikhande proved the following:

THEOREM 2.1. *If D is a q.s.* $3 - (v, k, \lambda)$ *with intersection numbers* $x = 1$ *and* $y \geq 2$, *then*

(i) $yv^2 - y(k^2 - k + 3)v + k(k - 1)^2(k - 2) + 2y(k^2 - k + 1) = 0$

(ii) $\lambda = \dfrac{(k - 2)\,(k - y)}{(k - 2)^2 - (v - 2)\,(y - 2)}$

(iii) $y \geq 3$. *Moreover equality holds iff D is the Witt* $4 - (23, 7, 1)$ *design or residual a* $3 - (22, 7, 4)$ *design.*

(iv) $\lambda \geq 4$. *Furthermore equality holds iff D is the* $3 - (22, 7, 4)$ *design.*

(v) $v \leq 3 + \dfrac{(k - 2)\,(k - 3)}{(y - 2)}$. *Moreover equality holds iff D is the Witt 4–design.*

The paper [28] contains the following conjecture

Conjecture 2.2. Any q.s. $3 - (v, k, \lambda)$ design with $x = 1$ is either the $4 - (23, 7, 1)$ design or its residual a $3 - (22, 7, 4)$ design.

REMARK 2.3. I strongly suspect that conjecture 2.2 is true. In fact, a recent computer search verified this for block size $k \leq 200,000$.

I give below the following small observation concerning Conjecture 2.2.

PROPOSITION 2.4. *Let D be a q.s.* $3 - (v, k, \lambda)$ *design with* $x = 1$ *and* $v > \dfrac{1}{2}(k^2 - k + 3)$. *Then D is the* $4 - (23, 7, 1)$ *design.*

Proof. By Theorem 2.1, part (v) we have $y \leq 2 + \dfrac{2(k - 2)\,(k - 3)}{(k^2 - k + 3)}$. This yields $y \leq 3$, since we assume $k \geq 3$. Using part (iii), this implies D is either the $4 - (23, 7, 1)$ or $3 - (22, 7, 4)$ design. Since $v > \frac{1}{2}(k^2 - k + 3)$, this forces D to be the $4 - (23, 7, 1)$ design.

The paper [28] also contains the following stronger

Conjecture 2.5. Let D be a q.s. $3 - (v, k, \lambda)$ design. Then one of the following holds:

(i) $x = 0$ and D is a design occurring in Theorem 1.1.

(ii) $x = 1$ and D is the $4 - (23, 7, 1)$ design or its residual.

(iii) D is the complement of some design occurring in (i) or (ii) above.

REMARK 2.6. The recent note of Shrikhande and Singhi [32] contains an elementary proof of the previously mentioned result of Delsarte [13, Thm. 5.23]: Let D be a $(2s+1) - (v, k, \lambda)$ design with exactly $s+1$ intersection numbers. Then these intersection numbers are roots of a polynomial of degree $s + 1$ whose coefficients depend only on the design parameters v, k and λ. The case $s = 1$ gives the main tool of Sane and Shrikhande [28].

3. Neumaier's results on regular sets and q.s. designs. The paper [25] of Neumaier presents a possible approach towards the classification problem of general q.s. 2–designs. In this paper the notion of a regular set in a strongly regular graph is important. For convenience we follow Neumaier's notation. Let Γ be any strongly regular graph with parameters (v, k, λ, μ). Let $r \geq 0$ and $s \leq -1$ denote the "proper" eigenvalues of Γ. Suppose f is the multiplicity of r. A non–empty subset B of Γ is called a regular set of valency d and nexus e if the number of vertices of B adjacent with any vertex x of Γ is one of two constants $d(< k)$ or $e > 0$ depending on whether $x \in B$ or not. Neumaier calls a regular set positive (negative) if $d \geq e(d < e)$.

REMARK 3.1. The notion of a regular set in a strongly regular graph generalizes the concept of special partially balanced incomplete block design (s.p.b.i.b.d.) of Bridges and Shrikhande [5]. Neumaier shows (using [5]) that a p.b.i.b.d. is an s.p.b.i.b.d. iff every block is regular set. The paper [5] has also been useful in a recent paper of Haemers and Higman [16] on strongly regular decompositions of strongly regular graphs.

Following the notation of [25], let D be a q.s. $2 - (v^*, k^*, \lambda^*)$ design with point set P and block set β. Let $p, q(p < q)$ be the intersection numbers of D, and Γ the block graph of D. The next lemma of [25] is well known and follows by usual counting arguments.

LEMMA 3.2. Let $D = (P, \beta)$ be a $2 - (v^*, k^* \lambda^*)$ q.s. design. Then for each $x \in P$, the set of blocks through x is a positive regular set of Γ of valency d and nexus e, where

$$d = ((k^* - 1)\,(\lambda^* - 1) - (r^* - 1)\,(p - 1))/(q - p),$$
$$\text{and } \ e = (k^* \lambda^* - r^* p)/(q - p).$$

Using Lemma 3.2 and [5] among other things, Neumaier shows

PROPOSITION 3.3. All the parameters of a q.s. 2–design can be expressed in terms of the parameters of Γ as follows:

$$v^* = f + 1, \ k^* = \frac{(f + 1)e}{(k - r)}, \ p = k^* + st, \ q = k^* + (s + 1)t,$$
$$b^* = v, r^* = \frac{ve}{k - r}, \ \lambda^* = r^* - (r - s)t, \ d = e + r$$

where $t = \dfrac{k^*(k - r - e)}{k(-s - 1)}$ is a positive integer.

Next, Neumaier considers the following well known classes of q.s. 2–designs:

Class 1: Multiples of symmetric $2 - (v^*, k^* \lambda^*)$ designs (here $p = \lambda^*, q = k^*, \Gamma$ is a disjoint union of cliques).

Class 2: Strongly resolvable designs – i.e. $2 - (v^*, k^*, \lambda^*)$ designs with b^* blocks partitioned into $b^* - v^* + 1$ classes such that every point occurs the same number of times in each class (here the design is q.s. by a result of Hughes and Piper [17] and Γ is complete multipartite).

Class 3: Steiner systems $2 - (v^*, k^*, 1)$ which are not projective planes (here $p = 0, q = 1$).

Class 4: Residuals of biplanes ($= 2 - (v^*, k^*, 2)$ symm. designs) (here $p = 1, q = 2$).

Using Proposition 3.3 as one of his tools, Neumaier obtains the following type of classification result:

THEOREM 3.4.

   (i)   *A q.s. 2–design with Γ disconnected is of class 1.*

   (ii)   *A q.s. 2–design with Γ complete multipartite is of class 2.*

   (iii)   *A q.s. 2–design with $p = 0, q = 1$ is of class 3.*

   (iv)   *A q.s. 2–design with $p = 1, q = 2$ is of class 4 or a $2 - (5, 3, 3)$ design.*

In [25], Neumaier calls a q.s. 2–design exceptional if neither D nor its complement belongs to any of the above four classes. The paper [25] contains a table of all feasible exceptional parameters on $v^* \leq 40$ points, $k^* \leq \dfrac{v}{2}$. The table contains 23 parameter sets whose existence cannot be ruled out using various non–existence criteria of strongly regular graphs. Of these 23 cases, 8 parameter sets are known to exist and the remaining cases were left open. This table of Neumaier has resulted in much recent activity on q.s. 2–designs, which we shall discuss next.

4. Q.S. designs and self dual codes – Tonchev's results. We intend in this section to discuss some elegant recent work of Tonchev [33,34] on q.s. designs. In [33], Tonchev showed how tools from coding theory, in particular self dual codes can be effectively used in studying q.s. 2–designs. Using the classification of certain self–dual codes, he rules out some cases in Neumaier's table referred to earlier and proves uniqueness of certain cases.

As usual a binary code C of length n and dimension k is a k–dimensional subspace of the n dimensional vector space V_n over $GF(2)$. We also refer to C as a (n, k)–code. The (binary) code of a design D is the code generated by the rows of its $b \times v$ incidence matrix. A code C is self–orthogonal if $C \subseteq C^\perp$ and self–dual if $C = C^\perp$, when $C^\perp$ is the usual dual code of C.

In the following lemma from [33], the link between q.s. designs and codes is established.

LEMMA 4.1. *Let A be a $b \times v$ incidence matrix of a q.s. $2 - (v, k, \lambda)$ design with intersection numbers x, y satisfying $k \equiv x \equiv y \pmod 2$.*

   (i) *If k is even, then the binary code of length v with generator matrix A is self–orthogonal.*

(ii) If k is odd, then the matrix $\begin{pmatrix} 1 \\ 1 \\ \cdot & A \\ \cdot \\ \cdot \\ 1 \end{pmatrix}$ generates a binary self–orthogonal

code of length $v + 1$.

Notice that if further $k \equiv 0 \pmod 4$ (resp. $k \equiv 3 \pmod 4$) then the code in (i) (resp. (ii)) is doubly even–i.e. all weights in the code are divisible by 4.

The next two lemmas from [33] are about general $2 - (v, k, \lambda)$ designs.

LEMMA 4.2. *If A is the $b \times v$ incidence matrix of a $2 - (v, k, \lambda)$ design, then the dual of the binary code with generator matrix A has minimum weight $d \geq \dfrac{(r + \lambda)}{\lambda}$, where r is the number of blocks on a point.*

LEMMA 4.3. *If A is the $b \times v$ incidence matrix of a $2 - (v, k, \lambda)$ design, then the dual of the binary code with generator matrix* $\begin{pmatrix} 1 \\ 1 \\ \cdot & A \\ \cdot \\ \cdot \\ 1 \end{pmatrix}$ *has minimum weight*

$$ d \geq \min\left\{ \frac{(b + r)}{r}, \frac{(r + \lambda)}{\lambda} \right\}. $$

Using the above lemmas, the following is obtained in [33]:

COROLLARY 3.4. *If E is a self–dual code containing the code from Lemma 4.1, then the minimum weight of E is $\geq \dfrac{(r + \lambda)}{\lambda}$ in case (i), and is*

$$ \geq \min\left\{ \frac{(b + r)}{r}, \frac{(r + \lambda)}{\lambda} \right\} \quad \text{in case (ii).} $$

The following result is crucial for the proofs of the main results of Tonchev [33]. See also section 5.

Result 4.5. MacWilliams and Sloane, [[22], chapter 19, sec. 6]. Every self–orthogonal code of even length is contained in a self–dual code, and every doubly–even code of length divisible by 8 is contained in a doubly–even self–dual code of the same length.

The paper [33] also needs the results of Conway and Pless; Pless and Sloane [see ref. [2], [11] in [33]] on the enumeration of certain self–dual codes. Using all these tools Tonchev [33] obtains

THEOREM 4.6.

(i) The following q.s. 2–designs with intersection numbers x, y are unique: $2 - (21, 6, 4)$, $x = 0$, $y = 2$; $2 - (21, 7, 12)$, $x = 1, y = 3$; and $2 - (22, 7, 16)$, $x = 1$, $y = 3$.

(ii) Q.S. $2 - (29, 7, 12)$ and $2 - (28, 7, 16)$ (both with $x = 1, y = 3$) do not exist.

Working with the same methods on q.s. $2 - (31, 7, 1)$ designs with $x = 1, y = 3$ and using the classification of doubly–even $(32, 16, 8)$ codes Tonchev obtains in [34] the next

THEOREM 4.7. *There are exactly five non–isomorphic q.s. 2-(31,7,7) designs, and they all have rank 16 over GF (2).*

One of the above five designs is formed by the points and planes of $PG(4, 2)$. Tonchev thus provides in [34] a counterexample to the 'only if' part of the well known Hamada's conjecture: "If $N(D)$ is an incidence matrix of a design D having the same parameters as those of the design G defined by the flats of any given dimension in $PG(t, q)$ or $AG(t, q)$, then $\text{rank}_q N(D) \geq \text{rank}_q N(G)$, with equality if and only if D is isomorphic with G."

5. Calderbank's non–existence results. Recently Calderbank [6, 7] has proved some powerful non–existence results on 2–designs. The paper [7] concerns 2–designs whose intersection numbers $s_1, s_2, \ldots, s_n$ satisfy $s_1 \equiv s_2 \equiv \cdots \equiv s_n$ (mod 2). The proofs of the main theorems of the paper [7] depend on some deep results of Gleason and Mallows and Sloane [see [7]] on weight enumerators of certain self–dual codes. The other paper [6] addresses the case where $s_1 \equiv s_2 \equiv \cdots \equiv s_n$ (mod p), where p is an odd prime.

In this section we wish to discuss these two important results dealing with intersection numbers. Calderbank's results when applied to q.s. 2–designs ruled out some further cases in Neumaier's table. As a further application we immediately get (in Corollary 5.6) the non–existence of some feasible q.s. 2–designs which were mentioned in [29] and [31]. As another direct application we show (in Corollary 5.7) the non–existence of two 'exceptional' parameter sets which were referred to in section 1.

Let D be any $2 - (v, k, \lambda)$ design with intersection numbers $s_1, s_2, \ldots, s_n$ and $b \times v$ incidence matrix N. Let $\Gamma_i (i = 1, 2, \ldots, n - 1)$ be the block graphs where blocks E, F of D are adjacent iff $|E \cap F| = s_i$. If A_i is the adjacency matrix of Γ_i, then clearly

(1) $$N'N = (r - \lambda)I + \lambda J$$

and

(2) $$NN' = kI + s_1 A_1 + s_2 A_2 + \cdots + s_{n-1} A_{n-1} + s_n (J - \sum_{i=1}^{n-1} A_i - I)$$

As Calderbank notes, the next lemma from [7] weakens one of Tonchev's conditions (see Lemma 4.1, previous section).

LEMMA 5.1. *Let p be prime and D a $2 - (v, k, \lambda)$ design whose intersection numbers $s_1, s_2, \ldots, s_n$ satisfy $s_1 \equiv s_2 \equiv \cdots \equiv s_n \equiv s \pmod{p}$. Then*

(1) $k \equiv s \pmod{p}$

(2) $r \equiv \lambda \pmod{p}$.

The proof of Lemma 5.1 uses equations (1), (2) concerning $N'N$ and NN' and arguments involving their ranks over $GF(p)$. Calderbank then uses a counting argument and Lemma 5.1 to obtain

LEMMA 5.2. *Let D be a $2 - (v, k, \lambda)$ design, C the code spanned by the blocks of D and $z \epsilon C^{\perp}$. Then*

(1)   *If $wt(z) \equiv 2 \pmod 4$, then $r \equiv \lambda \pmod 4$;*

(2)   *If $wt(z) \equiv 1 \pmod 4$, then $r \equiv 0 \pmod 8$;*

(3)   *If $wt(z) \equiv -1 \pmod 4$, then $2\lambda + r \equiv 0 \pmod 8$.*

Using the above lemmas 5.1, 5.2, Result 4.5, the results of Gleason on weight enumerators and Mallows, Sloane (Theorem 3 in [7]), Calderbank proves the next two fundamental results.

THEOREM 5.3. *Let D be a $2-(v, k, \lambda)$ design with intersection numbers $s_1, s_2, \ldots s_n$. If $s_1 \equiv s_2 \equiv \cdots \equiv s_n \equiv 0 \pmod 2$, then*

either   *(1) $r \equiv \lambda \pmod 4$*

or   *(2) $k \equiv 0 \pmod 4$ and $v \equiv \pm 1 \pmod 8$*

THEOREM 5.4. *Let D be a $2-(v, k, \lambda)$ design with intersection numbers $s_1, s_2, \ldots, s_n$. If $s_1 \equiv s_2 \equiv \cdots \equiv s_n \equiv 1 \pmod 2$, then*

either   *(1) $r \equiv \lambda \pmod 4$*

or   *(2) $k \equiv v \pmod 4$ and $v \equiv \pm 1 \pmod 8$*

Using the above two theorems on q.s $2-(v, k, \lambda)$ designs, Calderbank [7] immediately rules out q.s. $2 - (21, 8, 14), 2 - (21, 9, 12)$ and $2 - (35, 7, 3)$ designs from Neumaier's table. With considerable further effort he also rules out q.s. $2 - (24, 8, 7)$, $2 - (33, 9, 6), 2 - (22, 8, 12)$, and $2 - (19, 9, 16)$ designs.

We mention another beautiful recent result of Calderbank [6] dealing with intersection numbers.

THEOREM 5.5. *Let p be an odd prime and D be a $2 - (v, k, \lambda)$ design with intersection numbers $s_1, s_2, \ldots, s_n$ satisfying $s_1 \equiv s_2 \equiv \cdots \equiv s_n \equiv s \pmod{p}$. Then either*

(1) $r \equiv \lambda \pmod{p^2}$,

(2) $v \equiv 0 \pmod 2$ $v \equiv k \equiv s \equiv 0 \pmod p$, $(-1)^{v/2}$ is a square in $GF(p)$,

(3) $v \equiv 1 \pmod 2$, $v \equiv k \equiv s \not\equiv 0 \pmod p$, $(-1)^{(v-1)/2}$. s is a square in $GF(p)$,

(4) $r \equiv \lambda \equiv 0 \pmod p$ and either

    (a) $v \equiv 0 \pmod 2$, $v \equiv k \equiv s \not\equiv 0 \pmod p$,

    (b) $v \equiv 0 \pmod 2$, $k \equiv s \not\equiv 0 \pmod p$, v/s is a non–square in $GF(p)$,

    (c) $v \equiv 1 \pmod{2p}$, $r \equiv 0 \pmod{p^2}$, $k \equiv s \not\equiv 0 \pmod p$,

    (d) $v \equiv p \pmod{2p}$, $k \equiv s \equiv 0 \pmod p$,

    (e) $v \equiv 1 \pmod 2$, $k \equiv s \equiv 0 \pmod p$, v is a non–square in $GF(p)$,

    (f) $v \equiv 1 \pmod 2$, $k \equiv s \equiv 0 \pmod p$, v and $(-1)^{(v-1)/2}$ are squares in $GF(p)$.

As an application of Calderbank's results we also rule out some q.s. designs mentioned in Shrikhande [29, 31].

COROLLARY 5.6. The following q.s. $2-(v, b, r, k, \lambda)$ designs D with intersection numbers s_1, s_2 do not exist

    (i) $D(21, 105, 65, 13, 39)$ with $s_1 = 7, s_2 = 9$;

    (ii) $D(41, 205, 85, 17, 34)$ with $s_1 = 5, s_2 = 8$;

    (iii) $D(43, 301, 175, 25, 100)$ with $s_1 = 13, s_2 = 16$.

Proof. For (i), apply Theorem 5.4. For (ii) and (iii) use Theorem 5.5 with $p = 3$.

We also get the non–existence of the first two exceptional parameters in [1] (see Table I in section 1).

COROLLARY 5.7. The following quasi–symmetric $2 - (v, b, r, k, \lambda)$ designs with intersection numbers s_1, s_2 do not exist:

    (1) $2 - (232, 638, 99, 36, 15)$, $s_1 = 0, s_2 = 6$.

    (2) $2 - (5290, 13202, 861, 345, 56)$, $s_1 = 0, s_2 = 23$.

Proof. Apply Theorem 5.5 with $p = 3$ and 23.

6. Designs with intersection numbers 0 and 2. As mentioned earlier, while Cameron [9] classified q.s. 3–designs having an intersection number zero, the corresponding question for q.s. 2–designs seems to be a very difficult problem. Even the very special case of intersection numbers 0 and 2 presents difficulties for a complete classification. In forthcoming paper [23] Mavron and Shrikhande imposed one of three "extra properties" on such designs and obtained a complete classification. We outline some of these results. We regard symmetric $2 - (v, k, 2)$ designs (= biplanes) as improper q.s. 2–designs with intersection numbers 0 and 2.

The following lemma is crucial:

LEMMA 6.1. Let D be a (proper or improper) q.s. $2 - (v, k, \lambda)$ design with intersection numbers $0, y (\geq 2)$. Then the following properties hold.

(i) $(r-1)(y-1) = (k-1)(\lambda-1)$;

(ii)   *If D is proper, then y divides k;*

(iii) k divides $y(\lambda-y)(\lambda-1)$.

Proof. (i): this is well known [8, Prop. 3.5] and follows easily by considering the derived design through any point. For (ii), which is also a standard result, use the eigenvalues of the block graph Γ (see, for example, [29], Cor. 2.6). For the remaining part, use (i), the basic parameters relations and congruences modulo k.

The next lemma is an easy consequence of a result of Hughes ([8], Thm. 1.11) and the result of Lam et al [19], mentioned in section 1.

LEMMA 6.2. *Let D be a q.s. $2 - (v,k,\lambda)$ design with $v - 1 > k > 3$, and with intersection numbers 0 and 2. Then $k = \lambda + 1$ iff D is the extension of a projective plane of order 2 or 4.*

We assume from now on that D is a proper or improper q.s. $2 - (v,k,\lambda)$ with $v - 1 > k > 3$ and having intersection numbers 0 and 2. The first "extra property" we impose is the following:

Property I. D is said to have Property I if given any 4 distinct points p,q,r, and s, then whenever s lies on a bock with each of two pairs from $\{p,q,r\}$, then s is also on a block with the third pair.

THEOREM 6.3. *D has Property I iff D is the extension of the projective plane of order 2 or 4.*

The above follows easily upon noting that Property I implies D is a 3–design. Then use the result of Lam et al [19] and Lemma 6.2

Property I is a global property. We next localize this property.

Property II. D has Property II for some non–flag (s, B) if whenever p, q, r are three distinct points on B, and s lies on blocks through any two of the pairs from $\{p, q, r\}$ then s lies on a block through the third pair.

Our second result is

THEOREM 6.4. *Suppose D has Property II for some non–flag. Then one of the following holds:*

(i)   *D is the extension of the projective plane of order 2 or 4*

(ii)   *D is a biplane (of characteristic 3, if D has a characteristic).*

(iii)   *D is a $2 - (100, 12, 5)$ design.*

Outline of Proof. Let D have Property II for some non–flag (s, B). Define a relation $\sim$ on the points of B as follows: If $i, j \epsilon B$, then $i \sim j$ if either $i = j$, or i, j, s are contained in a block of D. Then one can show that $\sim$ is an equivalence relation and the size of any equivalence class is $\lambda + 1$. Consequently $\lambda + 1$ divides k. Now use Lemmas 6.1, 6.2 in analyzing the possibilities.

REMARKS 6.5. Refer to [10] for Cameron's definition of the characteristic of a biplane. No example of the third possibility in the above theorem is known (to us).

The last configurational property is the following:

Property III. The design D has Property III for a non–flag (s, B) if whenever p,q,r are 3 distinct points on B and s is on none of the blocks through two of the pairs of points from $\{p,q,r\}$, then s is on none of the blocks through of the third pair.

The final result whose proof depends on similar ideas is

THEOREM 6.5. If D has property III, then one of the following holds:

(i) D is the extension of the projective plane of order 2 or 4;

(ii) D is the complement of the projective plane of order 2;

(iii) D is the unique q.s. $2 - (21, 6, 4)$ derived from the Witt $3 - (22, 6, 1)$.

REFERENCES

[1] A. BAARTMANS AND M.S. SHRIKHANDE, Designs with no three mutually disjoint blocks, Discrete Math. 40, (1982), pp. 129–139.

[2] B. BAGCHI, No extendable biplane of order 9, Preprint (1986).

[3] T.BETH, D. JUNGNICKEL AND H. LENZ, Design Theory, B.I. Wissenschaftverlag, Mannheim, 1985 and Cambridge University Press, Cambridge, 1986.

[4] A. BREMNER, A diophantine equation arising from tight 4–designs, Osaka J. Math. 16, (1979), pp. 353–356.

[5] W.G. BRIDGES AND M.S. SHRIKHANDE, Special partially balanced incomplete block designs and associated graphs, Discrete Math. 9, (1974), pp. 1–18.

[6] A.R. CALDERBANK, Geometric invariants for quasi–symmetric designs, J. Comb. Theory (A) 47, (1988), pp. 101–110.

[7] A.R. CALDERBANK, The application of invariant theory to the existence of quasi–symmetric designs, J. Comb. Theory (A) 44, (1987), pp. 94–109.

[8] P.J. CAMERON AND J.H. VAN LINT, "Graph Theory, Coding Theory and Block Designs", Lon. Math. Soc. Lecture Notes Series 43, Cambridge Univ. Press, London/New York, 1980.

[9] P.J. CAMERON, Extending symmetric designs, J. Comb. Theory (A) 14, (1973), pp. 215-220.

[10] P.J. CAMERON, Biplanes, Math. Z., 131, (1973) pp. 85–101.

[11] P.J. CAMERON, Near regularity conditions for designs, Geometriae Dedicata 1, (1973), pp. 213–223.

[12] P.J. CAMERON, Quasi–symmetric designs possessing a spread, Preprint (1987).

[13] P. DELSARTE, "An Algebraic Approach to the Association Schemes of Coding Theory", Philips Research Reports Supplements No. 10, (1973).

[14] H. ENOMOTO, N. ITO AND R. NODA, Tight 4–designs, Osaka J. Math. 16, (1979), pp. 39–43.

[15] J.M. GOETHALS AND J.J. SEIDEL, Strongly regular graphs derived from combinatorial designs, Canad. J. Math. 22, (1970), pp. 597–614.

[16] W.H. HAEMERS AND D.G. HIGMAN, Strongly regular graphs with strongly regular decomposition, Preprint (1987).

[17] D.R. HUGHES AND F.C. PIPER, On resolutions and Bose's theorem, Geometriae Dedicata 5, (1976), pp. 129–133.

[18] N. ITO, On tight 4–designs, Osaka J. Math. 12, (1975), pp. 493–522 (corrections and supplements, Osaka J. Math. 15, (1978), pp. 693–697).

[19] C.W.H. LAM, L. THIEL, S. SWIERCZ AND J. McKAY, *The non–existence of ovals in the projective plane of order 10*, Discrete Math. 45, (1983), pp. 319–322.

[20] N.B. LIMAYE, S.S. SANE, M.S. SHRIKHANDE, *Discrete Math. 64, (1987), pp. 199–207.*

[21] S. KAGEYAMA AND A. HEDAYAT, *The family of t–designs–Part I*, J. Statis. Plann. and Inference 4, (1980), pp. 173–212 (Part II, vol. 7, (1983) pp. 257–287.

[22] F.J. MACWILLIAMS AND N.J.A. SLOANE, *The Theory of Error Correcting Codes*, North–Holland, Amsterdam, 1977.

[23] V.C. MAVRON AND M.S. SHRIKHANDE, *Designs with intersection numbers 0 and 2*, Archiv der Math, (to appear).

[24] A. MEYEROWITZ, S.S. SANE AND M.S. SHRIKHANDE, *New results on quasi–symmetric designs–an application of MACSYMA*, J. Comb. Theory (A) 43, (1986), pp. 277–290.

[25] A. NEUMAIER, *Regular sets and quasi–symmetric 2–designs*, in: Combinatorial theory (D. Jungnickel and K. Vedder, eds.) Lecture notes in Math. 969, (1982), pp. 258–275.

[26] D.K. RAY–CHAUDHURI AND R.M. WILSON, *On t–designs*, Osaka J. Math. 16, (1975), pp. 737–744.

[27] S.S. SANE AND M.S. SHRIKHANDE, *Finiteness questions in quasi–symmetric designs*, J. Comb. Theory (A) 42, (1986), pp. 252–258.

[28] S.S. SANE AND M.S. SHRIKHANDE, *Quasi–symmetric 2,3, 4–designs*, Combinatorica 7 (3), (1987), pp. 291–301.

[29] M.S. SHRIKHANDE, *A survey of some problems in combinatorial designs–a matrix approach*, Linear Algebra and Appl., 79, (1986), pp. 215–247.

[30] M.S. SHRIKHANDE, *Quasi–symmetric designs and quadratic polynomials*, Proceedings of the 7th Hungarian Colloquium on Combinatorics (1987), pp. 471–480.

[31] M.S. SHRIKHANDE, *Strongly regular graphs and quasi–symmetric designs II*, unpublished, (1973).

[32] M.S. SHRIKHANDE AND N.M. SINGHI, *An elementary derivation of the annihilator polynomial of extremal $(2s + 1)$ – designs*, Discrete Math. (to appear).

[33] V.D. TONCHEV, *Quasi–symmetric designs and self–dual codes*, Europ, J. Combin. 7, (1986), pp. 67–73.

[34] V.D. TONCHEV, *Quasi–symmetric $2-(31,7,7)$ designs and a revision of Hamada's conjecture*, J. Comb. Theory (A), 42, (1986), pp. 104–110.

318

INVARIANT MOMENTS AND CUMULANTS

T.P. SPEED†

Abstract. We study the joint moments and cumulants of finite arrays of random vectors whose distribution is invariant under the action of a finite group permuting the index set of the array. The relations connecting the invariant moments with the corresponding cumulants are first considered, and then the question of finding symmetric unbiased estimates of the cumulants (k–statistics) is answered for a class of examples. Simple formulae for the k–statistics and expansions for the products of k–statistics are then discussed. The paper closes with some remarks on extensions and open problems in this area.

Key words. moment, cumulant, permutation group, partition lattice, k–statistic.

1. Introduction. Suppose that a finite group G acts transitively on a finite set I, and that $X = (X_i : i \in I)$ is an array of random vectors indexed by I whose distribution is invariant under all permutations $g \in G$. Then the joint moments and cumulants of X will be invariant functions defined on the product space $I^r = I \times \cdots \times I$ (r times), and they are the objects of interest to us in this paper. Throughout we will assume that $|I| \geq r$.

The motivation for this work comes from a series of papers by the present author and others, see references [7] to [14], in which certain special problems concerning invariant moments and cumulants, and related entities were studied when G was a symmetric group or a generalized wreath product of symmetric groups. The motivation for that work was certain very specific problems in statistics involving variances and covariances of mean squares in the analysis of variance [14], asymptotic expansions for the randomization distribution of an F–ratio [3], and the analysis of a class of matrices of important in the analysis of variance [11], [12]. Our aim in this paper is to put this earlier material in a more general setting, and pose a range of problems which are of interest whenever the situation mentioned in the first paragraph arises. At the same time we present one new theorem, see §5, which completes some results in these earlier papers in an entirely satisfactory way.

This paper is organized as follows. We begin by defining a group action and the notion of orbit, and then go on to illustrate the ideas in some examples of statistical interest. Moments and cumulants are defined for random variables, random vectors, arrays of random variables and finally, arrays of random vectors, in each case the cumulants being given via their generating functions, which are defined to be the logarithms of the corresponding moment generating functions. Explicit formulae for the cumulants are presented. We then turn to the situation outlined at the beginning of this section: arrays of random vectors whose distribution is invariant under a group permuting the index set of the array. We ask after an invariant moment–cumulant relationship which is appropriate to this situation. The classical problem of finding symmetric unbiased estimates of cumulants i.e. of generalised

---

†Department of Statistics, University of California, Berkeley, CA 94720. Partial support from NSF Grant DMS 8802378 is gratefully acknowledged.

k–statistics arises in this context, and we briefly review some known results on this topic. Two related problems then arise: that of finding simplified formulae for the k–statistics, and of expansions for products of k–statistics. For fuller details concerning this material we refer to the relevant papers. Our final section raises a number of problems of both a general and a specific nature relating to this topic.

2. Group actions, orbits and invariant functions. A group* G is said to act on a set I if every element $g \in G$ defines a bijection on I, denoted here by $i \longrightarrow i^g$ ($i \in I, g \in G$), in such a way that (i) the identity element of G defines the identity map on I, and (ii) for every $i \in I$ and $g, h \in G$, we have $(i^g)^h = i^{gh}$. An *orbit* $\mathcal{O}$ of a group action G on I is a subset of I with the following two properties: (i) if $i \in \mathcal{O}$ and $g \in G$, then $i^g \in \mathcal{O}$ (invariance), and (ii) if i and $j \in \mathcal{O}$, then there exists $g = g(i,j) \in G$ such that $i^g = j$ (transitivity). It is not hard to prove that distinct orbits are disjoint, and so the set of all orbits defines a partition of our underlying set I. G is said to act *transitively* on I if there is exactly one orbit, namely I itself. The following simple examples of group actions motivate much of what follows.

Example 2.1. The symmetric group S_n acts transitively on $\mathbf{n} = \{1, \ldots, n\}$. ☐

Example 2.2. Let $I = \mathbf{m}/\mathbf{n}$ denote the disjoint union of m copies of $\mathbf{n}$, to be thought of as m *blocks* each of the n *plots*. We denote elements of I by pairs $(i, j(i))$, $i \in \mathbf{m}, j(i) \in \mathbf{n}$, and where no confusion can result, we simplify this to (i, j). The *permutation wreath product* $G = S_n wr S_m$ acts on $\mathbf{m}/\mathbf{n}$ in the following way: elements of G are pairs (f, h) where $f \in S_m$ and $h : \mathbf{m} \longrightarrow S_n$, and for $i \in \mathbf{m}, j \in \mathbf{n}$, $(i,j)^{(f,h)} = (i^f, j^{ih})$. [We have reversed the usual notation from group theory in order to conform with statistical notation for blocks and plots.] Note that this action is transitive, corresponding to permuting whole blocks and, independently within each each block, permuting plots within blocks. ☐

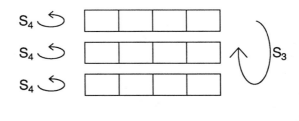

3 / 4

FIGURE 2.1

Example 2.3. The group $G = S_m \times S_n$ acts on $\mathbf{m} \times \mathbf{n}$ in a natural way, namely $(i,j)^{(f,h)} = (i^f, j^h)$ where $i \in \mathbf{m}$, $j \in \mathbf{n}$, $f \in S_m$ and $h \in S_n$. Again it is easy to see that this action is transitive, corresponding to independent permuting of the rows and the columns of the $m \times n$ array of pairs (i,j). ☐

---

*All groups are finite unless otherwise stated.

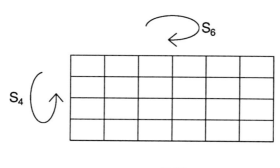

4×6

FIGURE 2.2

Example 2.4. All of the previous examples are special cases of a general class of group actions defined and studied in [2]. The groups in this paper are termed *generalized wreath product groups* and are defined whenever we have a family $((G_p,\ I_p) : p \in P)$ of group actions indexed by a finite partially ordered set P. We refer to [2] for fuller details concerning these groups, but will note the way in which Examples 2.1, 2.2 and 2.3 can be identified with generalised wreath products.

Example 2.1. (ctd) P is a singleton, p say, $I_p = \mathbf{n}$, $G_p = S_n$.

Example 2.2. (ctd) P is the two element chain $\{b, p\}$ say, with $b > p$. (Here b is meant to denote blocks and p plots). The sets and permutation groups associated with b and p are just $\mathbf{m}$ and $\mathbf{n}$, and S_m and S_n, respectively, where m is the number of blocks and n the number of plots, and in this case the generalised wreath product group is simply $S_n wr S_m$ acting as described in Example 2.2 above.

Example 2.3. (ctd) P is the two element anti–chain $\{r, c\}$, having r incomparable with c. (Here r and c are meant to denote rows and columns, respectively). The sets and groups associated with r and c are $I_r = \mathbf{m}$, $G_r = S_m$, and $I_c = \mathbf{n}$, $G_c = S_n$, respectively, and in this case the generalised wreath product reduces to the usual direct product.

We note in concluding that generalised wreath product–groups include all finite (and some countable) iterations of direct and permutation wreath products, and many more groups which cannot be viewed as products of simpler components. The paper [11] describes one such group in its introduction. □

Any action of a group G on a set I extends to an action of G onto the set I^r of all r–tuples ($r \geq 2$) as follows:

$$(i_1, \ldots, i_r)^g = (i_1^g, \ldots, i_r^g), \qquad g \in G, i_1, \ldots, i_r \in I.$$

321

The diagonal $\{(i,\dots,i) : i \in I\} \subset I^r$ is always an orbit of the action of G on I^r and so there are always at least two orbits of such actions. Let us label the set of all orbits of G on I^r by $P_r = P_r(G, I)$, and denote a typical orbit by $\mathcal{O}_\sigma$, $\sigma \in P_r$, where the integer $r \geq 2$ associated with a particular σ will either be clear from the context, or irrelevant.

Example 2.1 (ctd). If the action of S_n on $\mathbf{n}$ is extended to pairs $(i_1, i_2) \in \mathbf{n}^2$, then we readily see that the offdiagonal elements $\{(i_1, i_2) : i_1 \neq i_2, i_1, i_2 \in \mathbf{n}\}$ form an orbit, and so there are precisely two orbits in this case, defined by equality $(i_1 = i_2)$ or inequality $(i_1 \neq i_2)$ of the subscripts. We denote these by $\mathcal{O}_{12}$ and $\mathcal{O}_{1|2}$ respectively, using *partition* notation, where $\pi = \pi_1 | \dots | \pi_b$ denotes a partition of a set $|\pi|$ into *blocks* $\pi_1, \dots, \pi_b$.

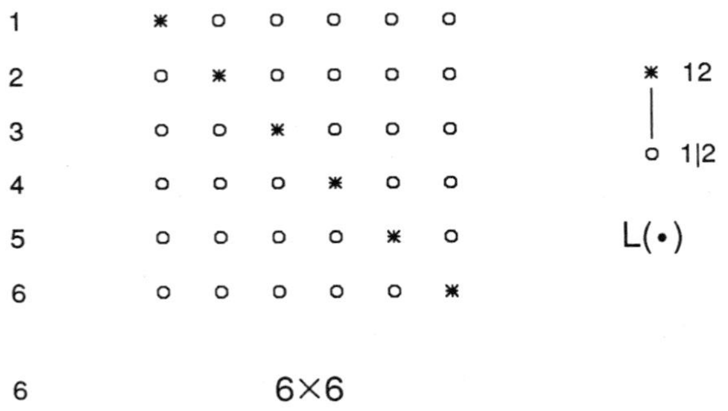

FIGURE 2.3

The notion of refinement or coarseness of partitions defines a partial order on the set $\mathcal{P}(\mathbf{r})$ of all partitions of $\mathbf{r}$: $\pi \leq \rho$ if every block π^a of $\pi = \pi^1 | \dots | \pi^b$ is included in a block ρ^c of $\rho = \rho^1 | \dots | \rho^d$; in other words, π is a refinement of ρ, or ρ is coarser than π.

The orbits of the action of S_n on $\mathbf{n}^r$ are readily seen to correspond to the partitions π of the set $\mathbf{r}$. A simple way to see this is via the kernel $\ker f$ of a map $f : \mathbf{r} \longrightarrow \mathbf{n}$; $\ker f$ is the equivalence on $\mathbf{r}$ defined by $(l_1, l_2) \in \ker f$ if $f(l_1) = f(l_2)$. Viewing elements of $\mathbf{n}^r$ as maps in this way we can write

$$\mathcal{O}_\pi = \{f \in \mathbf{n}^r : \ker f = \pi\} \quad , \quad \pi \in \mathcal{P}(\mathbf{r}).$$

It is easy to check that the subsets $\mathcal{O}_\pi$ of $\mathbf{n}^r$ are disjoint and S_n–invariant, and that S_n acts transitively on them, and so conclude that they are the orbits of S_n on $\mathbf{n}^r$. Thus our set P_r in this case coincides with $\mathcal{P}(\mathbf{r})$. The partial order on $\mathcal{P}(\mathbf{r})$ in fact defines a lattice structure, and we will be making use of this structure in due course. □

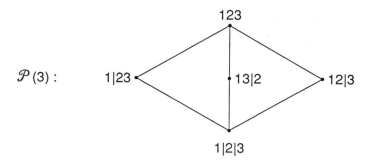

$\mathcal{P}(3):$ with nodes 123, 1|23, 13|2, 12|3, 1|2|3

FIGURE 2.4

Example 2.2 (ctd). The orbits of $S_n wr S_m$ on $(\mathbf{m/n})^2$ turn out to be labelled by pairs (π_b, π_p) of partitions of $\mathbf{2}$ where $\pi_b \geq \pi_p$. This can be seen as follows: (i_1, j_1) and (i_2, j_2) will be in the diagonal orbit if $i_1 = i_2$ and $j_1 = j_2$, and so the diagonal will be denoted $\mathcal{O}_{(12,12)}$. Another orbit comes when $i_1 = i_2$ but $j_1 \neq j_2$: this corresponds to pairs of distinct plots in the same block, and will be denoted by $\mathcal{O}_{(12,1|2)}$. And finally, all pairs of plots in different blocks belong to a single orbit, denoted by $\mathcal{O}_{(1|2,1|2)}$. In Fig. 2.5 we show these orbits for $m = n = 3$, and the lattice ordering the labels.

(1,1)	✳	+	+	o	o	o	o	o	o	
(1,2)	+	✳	+	o	o	o	o	o	o	
(1,3)	+	+	✳	o	o	o	o	o	o	✳ (12,12)
(2,1)	o	o	o	✳	+	+	o	o	o	
(2,2)	o	o	o	+	✳	+	o	o	o	+ (12,1|2)
(2,3)	o	o	o	+	+	✳	o	o	o	
(3,1)	o	o	o	o	o	o	✳	+	+	o (1|2,1|2)
(3,2)	o	o	o	o	o	o	+	✳	+	
(3,3)	o	o	o	o	o	o	+	+	✳	

$L\left(\begin{smallmatrix}\bullet b\\ \bullet p\end{smallmatrix}\right)$

3/3 $\qquad$ (3/3)×(3/3)

FIGURE 2.5

323

The extension of this to $r > 2$ will be discussed below. $\square$

Example 2.3 (ctd). The orbits of $S_m \times S_n$ on $(\mathbf{m} \times \mathbf{n})^2$ turn out to be labelled by pairs (π_r, π_c) of partitions of **2**, this reflecting the patterns of equality or inequality of i_1, i_2, j_1 and j_2 of two ordered pairs (i_1, j_1) and (i_2, j_2) from $\mathbf{m} \times \mathbf{n}$. In Fig. 2.6 we show these orbits with $m = n = 3$ and the corresponding lattice of labels.

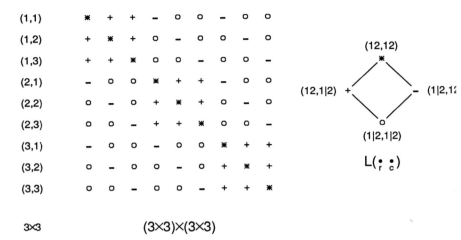

FIGURE 2.6

Again the extension to $r > 2$ will be discussed below. $\square$

Example 2.4 (ctd.). It is shown in [6] that if G is a generalised wreath product of doubly transitive permutation groups acting upon the set I, then the orbits of the action of G on I^r are labelled by elements of the lattice $\mathrm{Hom}(P, \mathcal{P}(\mathbf{r}))$ of all monotone maps from the partially ordered set P in the definition of the wreath product group, into the lattice $\mathcal{P}(\mathbf{r})$ of all partitions of **r**. An explicit description of these orbits is also given, but this need not concern us here. In examples 2.1, 2.2 and 2.3, the partially ordered sets are $\bullet$, $\overset{\bullet b}{\underset{\bullet p}{|}}$ and $\underset{r\ c}{\bullet \ \bullet}$, respectively, and it is easy to check the above assertion in these cases. For example, monotone maps from $\overset{\bullet b}{\underset{\bullet p}{|}}$ into $\overset{\bullet 12}{\underset{\bullet 1|2}{|}}$ are just the pairs (π_b, π_p) with $\pi_b \geq \pi_p$ as described in Example 2.2 (ctd). See [6] and [9] for further discussion of this point. $\square$

Much of our attention will be focused upon the vector spaces $\mathcal{V}_r = \mathcal{V}_r(I)$ of all real-valued functions on $I^r, r \geq 1$, which we will identify with the products $\mathcal{V} \otimes \cdots \otimes \mathcal{V}$ (r terms) of $\mathcal{V} = \mathcal{V}_1 = \mathbf{R}^I$. We will use the standard basis $\{\delta^i : i \in I\}$ of $\mathcal{V}$, where $(\delta^i)_j = 1$ if $i = j$, and zero otherwise, and so $\mathcal{V}_r$ will have as basis the set of all products $\delta^{i_1} \otimes \cdots \otimes \delta^{i_r}$, $(i_1, \cdots, i_r) \in I^r$. The usual inner product $[u|v] = \sum_i u_i v_i$ of $u = \sum_i u_i \delta^i$ and $v = \sum_i v_i \delta^i$ in $\mathcal{V}$ will be extended to the $\mathcal{V}_r$ in such a way that $[u \otimes x | v \otimes y] = [u|v][x|y]$ for $u, v \in \mathcal{V}_k, x, y \in \mathcal{V}_l$.

The action of G on I extends to an action on the vector spaces $\mathcal{V}_r$ as follows: $v^g(i_1, \ldots, i_r) = v(i_1^g, \cdots, i_r^g), g \in G, \ i_1, \cdots, i_r \in I, \ v \in \mathcal{V}_r$. A subspace $\mathcal{W}$ of $\mathcal{V}_r$ will be termed G–invariant if $w^g \in \mathcal{W}$ for every $w \in \mathcal{W}, g \in G$. The $|P_r|$–dimensional subspace $\mathcal{S}_r = \mathcal{S}_r(G, I)$ consisting of all *invariant* functions on I^r will be of central concern to us and much of our attention will focus upon different bases for $\mathcal{S}_r$. The standard basis $\{\delta^{i_1} \otimes \cdots \otimes \delta^{i_r} : (i_1, \cdots, i_r) \in I^r\}$ of $\mathcal{V}_r$ readily gives rise to a basis of $\mathcal{S}_r$ by forming the

$$(2.1) \qquad A_\sigma = \sum_{(i_1, \ldots, i_r) \in \mathcal{O}_\sigma} \delta^{i_1} \otimes \cdots \otimes \delta^{i_r} \quad , \quad \sigma \in P_r \ ,$$

and we call these expressions the *association* tensors. (The reason for this terminology is the following: if $r = 2$ and we formed sums in the same way of *matrices* $\delta^{i_1}(\delta^{i_2})'$, what we would obtain would be the basis matrices of (non–commutative) *association scheme*, see [11].)

It is easy to prove that an element $\gamma \in \mathcal{V}_m$ is invariant if and only if it can be written

$$(2.2) \qquad \gamma = \sum_{\sigma \in P_m} \gamma_\sigma \, A_\sigma$$

for suitable numbers $\gamma_\sigma \in \mathbf{R}, \ \sigma \in P_m$. We hope no confusion will result from our identifying an invariant function $\gamma = (\gamma(i_1, \cdots, i_r))$ on I^r with its coefficients in the representation (2.2).

3. The zeta and Möbius functions on a lattice. In order to keep this paper reasonably self–contained, we recall the definitions of the *zeta* function ζ and the *Möbius* function μ of a finite lattice L. (All of these definitions apply if L is replaced by an arbitrary locally finite partially ordered set.) The function ζ is defined on $L \times L$ by

$$\zeta(a, b) = \begin{cases} 1 & \text{if} \quad a \leq b, \\ 0 & \text{otherwise;} \end{cases}$$

whilst μ has the more complicated recursive definition:

$$\mu(a, a) = 1 \quad ,$$

and if $a < c$ in L,

$$\mu(a, c) = - \sum_{a \leq b < c} \mu(a, b).$$

Here a, b and c vary over L. Clearly μ is defined in such a way that $\mu(a, c) = 0$ unless $a \leq c$, and that $\sum_{a \leq b \leq c} \mu(a, b) = 0$ for every pair a, c with $a < c$, and it is not hard to check that this implies $\sum_{a \leq b \leq c} \mu(b, c) = 0$ when $a < c$. These observations can be summarized in the relation

$$(3.1) \qquad \sum_b \mu(a, b)\zeta(b, c) = \sum_b \zeta(a, b)\mu(b, c) = \delta(a, c)$$

where $\delta(a,c) = 1$ if $a = c$, and $= 0$ otherwise, and the sums are over all $b \in L$. For a general discussion of Möbius functions, see [1]. A fundamental result of great interest to us is the formula for μ on $\mathcal{P}(\mathbf{r})$. We need only consider the case $\sigma < \rho$, and since every interval of $\mathcal{P}(\mathbf{r})$ is isomorphic to a cartesian product of partition lattices of smaller order and μ is readily checked to be multiplicative across cartesian products, we need only consider $\sigma = 1|\cdots|r$ and $\rho = 1 \cdots r$. In this case

$$(3.2) \qquad \mu(1|\cdots|r, \ 1\ldots r) = \mu_r = (-1)^{r-1}(r-1)! \ .$$

4. Moments and cumulants and their generating functions.

In what follows random variables, random vectors or arrays of random variables will be denoted by upper case Roman letters with or without subscripts, e.g. $X, X_i, X(l), X_i(l)$, etc., whilst $t, t_i, t_i(l)$, etc. will denote indeterminates in generating functions. Our random variables will be defined on some fixed probability space, which need not be mentioned; all that we need is the associated expectation operator, to be denoted by $\mathbf{E}$, and the probability, denoted by $\mathbf{P}$.

The *moments* of a random variable X (about zero) are the numbers $\mathbf{E}X^r$, $r = 1, 2, \ldots$, and we will denote these by $\gamma_r = \gamma_r^X$ rather than μ_r' as is usual in statistics, to avoid confusion with the Möbius function μ which will shortly appear. The (exponential) generating function $M_X(t)$ of the moments is known as the *moment generating function* (*m.g.f.*) of X, and so

$$(4.1) \qquad M_X(t) = \mathbf{E}\{\exp Xt\}$$
$$= \mathbf{E}\{1 + Xt + \frac{1}{2!}X^2 t^2 + \cdots\}$$
$$= 1 + \gamma_1 t + \frac{1}{2!}\gamma_2 t^2 + \cdots .$$

The cumulants $\kappa_r = \kappa_r^X$ of X are conventionally defined by their generating function, the cumulant generating function (*c.g.f.*)

$$(4.2) \qquad K_X(t) = \log M_X(t)$$
$$= \kappa_1 t + \frac{1}{2!}\kappa_2 t^2 + \cdots .$$

By expanding the logarithm, we obtain

$$\kappa_1 = \gamma_1 \ ,$$
$$\kappa_2 = \gamma_2 - \gamma_1^2 \ ,$$
$$\kappa_3 = \gamma_3 - 3\gamma_2\gamma_1 + 2\gamma_1^3 \ ,$$
$$\kappa_4 = \gamma_4 - 3\gamma_2^2 - 4\gamma_3\gamma_1 + 12\gamma_2\gamma_1^2 - 6\gamma_1^4, \ldots$$

with inverse relations

$$\gamma_1 = \kappa_1 \ ,$$
$$\gamma_2 = \kappa_2 + \kappa_1^2 \ ,$$
$$\gamma_3 = \kappa_3 + 3\kappa_2\kappa_1 + \kappa_1^3 \ ,$$
$$\gamma_4 = \kappa_4 + 3\kappa_2^2 + 4\kappa_3\kappa_1 + 6\kappa_2\kappa_1^2 + \kappa_1^4, \ldots .$$

In due course we will describe the general form of these non–linear relations. Towards that end, let us suppose now that that X is a random vector $X = (X(1), X(2), \ldots)$. The number of components need not concern us. The joint or mixed moments of X are conventionally defined in statistics to be the numbers $\gamma(m_1, m_2, \ldots) = \mathbf{E}\{X(1)^{m_1}X(2)^{m_2}\ldots\}$ where $m_1 \geq 1$, $m_2 \geq 1, \ldots$, which are the coefficients of $t(1)^{m_1}t(2)^{m_2}\ldots$ in the expansion of

(4.3) $$M_X(t) = \mathbf{E}\{\exp[X|t]\}$$

where $t = (t(1), t(2), \ldots)$ is an array of indeterminates and $[X|t] = X(1)t(1) + X(2)t(2) + \cdots$. The overall *order* of $\gamma(m_1, m_2, \cdots)$ is $m = m_1 + m_2 + \cdots$, and it is in many ways much more convenient to replace this function γ of non–negative integers by a sequence of arrays $\gamma_1, \gamma_2, \ldots$ of moments of order $1, 2, \ldots$, respectively. Thus $\gamma_1(l) = \mathbf{E}\{X(l)\}$, $\gamma_2(l_1, l_2) = \mathbf{E}\{X(l_1)X(l_2)\}$, and so on, and we note that $\gamma_2, \gamma_3, \ldots$ will all be invariant (by definition) under all permutations of their arguments, i.e. under $S_2, S_3, \ldots$ acting on the index set of the arguments. This slightly inconvenient (though essential) consequence of the definitions will be circumvented shortly. In terms of these arrays $\gamma_1, \gamma_2, \ldots$ and using a suggestive notation, we can expand (4.3) obtaining

(4.4) $$M_X(t) = 1 + [\gamma_1|t] + \frac{1}{2!}[\gamma_2|t \otimes t] + \cdots .$$

As before the joint or mixed cumulants are defined via their generating function, $K_X(t) = \log M_X(t)$, and so we would be inclined to define $\kappa(m_1, m_2, \cdots .)$ to be the coefficient of $t(1)^{m_1}t(2)^{m_2}\cdots$ in $K_X(t)$, but again this notation is not the most convenient. As with the moments, it is easier to make use of arrays $\kappa_1, \kappa_2 \ldots$ of cumulants of orders $1, 2, \ldots$ respectively, in effect expanding $K_X(t)$ as

(4.5) $$K_X(t) = [\kappa_1|t] + \frac{1}{2!}[\kappa_2|t \otimes t] + \cdots .$$

These arrays have the same symmetry properties as the $\{\gamma_r\}$ and both reduce to our previous notation if X has exactly one component, i.e. if $X = (X(1))$, for then $\gamma_r(1) = \gamma_r$ and $\kappa_r(1) = \kappa_r$ as defined earlier.

How do the arrays $\{\gamma_r\}$ and $\{\kappa_r\}$ relate in the case $X = (X(1), X(2), \ldots)$? This time the connection is much more transparent, and to highlight it we make a slight change of notation: write $\kappa_l = \kappa_1(l)$, $\kappa_{l_1 l_2} = \kappa_2(l_1, l_2)$, and so on, noting that the order is redundant because it is simply the number of indices! Doing the same thing for the γ_r, we have the relations

$\kappa_1 = \gamma_1$,

$\kappa_{12} = \gamma_{12} - \gamma_1\gamma_2$,

$\kappa_{123} = \gamma_{123} - \gamma_{12}\gamma_3 - \gamma_{13}\gamma_2 - \gamma_{23}\gamma_1 + 2\gamma_1\gamma_2\gamma_3$.

$\kappa_{1234} = \gamma_{1234} - \gamma_{12}\gamma_{34} - \gamma_{13}\gamma_{24} - \gamma_{23}\gamma_{14} - \gamma_{123}\gamma_4 - \gamma_{124}\gamma_3 - \gamma_{134}\gamma_2$

$\qquad - \gamma_{234}\gamma_1 + 2\gamma_{12}\gamma_3\gamma_4 + 2\gamma_{13}\gamma_2\gamma_4 + 2\gamma_{14}\gamma_2\gamma_3 + 2\gamma_{23}\gamma_1\gamma_4$

$\qquad 2\gamma_{24}\gamma_1\gamma_3 + 2\gamma_{34}\gamma_1\gamma_2 - 6\gamma_1\gamma_2\gamma_3\gamma_4, \ldots$

with inverses

$$\gamma_1 = \kappa_1,$$

$$\gamma_{12} = \kappa_{12} + \kappa_1\kappa_2$$

$$\gamma_{123} = \kappa_{123} + \kappa_{12}\kappa_3 + \kappa_{13}\kappa_2 + \kappa_{23}\kappa_1 + \kappa_1\kappa_2\kappa_3,$$

$$\gamma_{1234} = \kappa_{1234} + \kappa_{12}\kappa_{34} + \kappa_{13}\kappa_{24} + \kappa_{23}\kappa_{14} + \kappa_{123}\kappa_4 + \kappa_{124}\kappa_3 + \kappa_{134}\kappa_2 + \kappa_{234}\kappa_1$$

$$+ \kappa_{12}\kappa_3\kappa_4 + \kappa_{13}\kappa_2\kappa_4 + \kappa_{14}\kappa_2\kappa_3 + \kappa_{23}\kappa_1\kappa_4 + \kappa_{24}\kappa_1\kappa_3 + \kappa_{34}\kappa_1\kappa_2$$

$$+ \kappa_1\kappa_2\kappa_3\kappa_4, \ldots .$$

The connection with the partition lattices $\mathcal{P}(\mathbf{r})$, $r = 1, 2, 3, 4, \ldots$ should be unmistakeable, and the appearance of Möbius function values $(-1)^{r-1}(r-1)! = 1, -1, 2, -6, \ldots$ as coefficients should be equally apparent. Note that $\kappa_2 = \gamma_2$, $\kappa_3 = \gamma_3, \ldots$ etc. but that we have only displayed a typical relation, not *all* such.

How do we exploit this connection with the partition lattice? By taking $r \geq 1$ and $\rho \in \mathcal{P}(\mathbf{r})$, and writing

$$\gamma_\rho = \prod_{a=1}^{b} \gamma_{\rho^a} \ , \quad \kappa_\rho = \prod_{a=1}^{b} \kappa_{\rho^a}$$

when $\rho = \rho^1 | \ldots | \rho^b$, and the γs and κs are defined for the blocks ρ^a of ρ as in the preceding paragraph. Thus $\gamma_{12|34} = \gamma_{12}\gamma_{34}$, $\kappa_{123|4} = \kappa_{123}\kappa_4$ and so on. With this notation we can prove that for all $\pi \in \mathcal{P}(\mathbf{r})$

$$(4.6) \qquad \kappa_\pi = \sum_\rho \mu(\rho, \pi)\gamma_\rho$$

with inverse

$$(4.7) \qquad \gamma_\pi = \sum_\rho \zeta(\rho, \pi)\kappa_\rho$$

where the sums are over all ρ in $\mathcal{P}(\mathbf{r})$. The role of partition lattices in the context of exponential generating functions is fully explored in [5], and we refer non–statisticians to [7] for some explanation as to why cumulants are interesting, much more so than moments. For the moment let us just say that variances, covariances, skewness and kurtosis (peakedness or flatness) are cumulants or simple functions of them.

One further level of notational generality is needed before we turn to our main topic: invariant moments and cumulants. There our concern will be with arrays $X = (X_i : i \in I)$ of random variables or random vectors X_i, and so we spend a brief moment explaining how this forces us to consider moment and cumulant arrays $\gamma_1, \kappa_1, \gamma_2, \kappa_2, \ldots$ which are not necessarily symmetric functions of their arguments. Suppose that $X = (X_i : i \in I)$ is an *array* of random variables (i.e. one–dimensional random vectors). Then we could readily use the notation introduced earlier in this section, namely write $\gamma_1(i) = \mathsf{E}X_i$, $\gamma_2(i,j) = \mathsf{E}X_iX_j$, and so on, and a similar notation would be appropriate for cumulants. However, what do we then do if

X_i is itself a random vector, as is the case in many applications of interest to us? Suppose that $X = (X_i) = ((X_i(1), X_i(2), \dots) : i \in I)$. We now have component arrays $X(1) = (X_i(1) : i \in I)$, $X(2) = (X_i(2) : i \in I), \dots$, and a suitable compromise notation for moments seems to be the following:

$$\gamma_1^l(i) = \mathsf{E}\{X_i(l)\}, \quad \gamma_2^{l,m}(i,j) = \mathsf{E}\{X_i(l)X_j(m)\}, \dots,$$

$i, j \in I$, $l, m = 1, 2, \dots$, with $\gamma_1, \gamma_2, \dots$ denoting the resulting array of moments. Take $t = (t_i : i \in I)$ where each $t_i = (t_i(1), t_i(2), \dots)$ is a vector of indeterminates. The notation $t(1) = (t_i(1) : i \in I)$, $t(2) = (t_i(2) : i \in I), \dots$ will be used just as with X. Finally, we will write $[X|t] = \sum_l [X(l)|t(l)] = \sum_l \sum_i X_i(l) t_i(l)$. With this notation, the $m.g.f.$ $M_X(t) = \mathsf{E}\{\exp[X|t]\}$ may be expanded exactly as in (4.4), and the $c.g.f.$ can also be expanded as in (4.5), with the *same* formulae (4.6) and (4.7) connecting the two sets of coefficients. Although this observation is immediate, it proves to be extraordinarily useful in what follows. For example, extending the notational simplifications inherent in (4.6) and (4.7), we have $\kappa_i^l = \gamma_i^l$, and $\kappa_{ij}^{lm} = \gamma_{ij}^{lm} - \gamma_i^l \gamma_j^m, \dots$, with inverses $\gamma_i^l = \kappa_i^l, \gamma_{ij}^{lm} = \kappa_{ij}^{lm} + \kappa_i^l \kappa_j^m, \dots$. It is clear that the symmetry in $\gamma_2, \gamma_3, \dots$ and $\kappa_2, \kappa_3, \dots$ which we observed earlier, does not carry over to arrays of random vectors: we would only have symmetry in a $\gamma_{ij\dots}^{lm\dots}$ or a $\kappa_{ij\dots}^{lm\dots}$ if the i and l, or j and $m, \dots$ were permuted together, or if $l = m = \dots$ or $i = j = \dots$, or some combination of these conditions. In general, if $l, m, \dots$ remain fixed, and $i, j, \dots$ are permuted, or vice versa, then there is no reason to suppose that these moments or cumulants remain the same. However our main interest in what follows will be in those situations in which these further constraints are assumed.

In closing this section, let us note that if $l_1 = 1$, $l_2 = 2, \dots l_r = r$, then $\gamma_{i_1 \dots i_r}^{l_1 \dots l_r}$ may be abbreviated $\gamma_{i_1 \dots i_r}$, whilst the function $\gamma_2 = \gamma_2^{l_1 \dots l_r}$ may safely be abbreviated γ_2 as long as the context is clear.

5. Invariant moments and cumulants. An array $X = (X_i : i \in I)$ of random vectors $X_i = (X_i(1), X_i(2), \dots)$ indexed by a set I on which a group G acts transitively, is said to have a *G–invariant* distribution (or to be G–stationary or G–isotropic) if for every family $(B_i : i \in I)$ of measurable sets in the range of X_i, we have

$$(5.1) \qquad \mathsf{P}(X_i \in B_i \text{ for all } i \in I) = \mathsf{P}(X_{i^g} \in B_i \text{ for all } i \in I)$$

for every $g \in G$. It follows from (5.1) that *all* aspects of the joint distribution are invariant under relabelling the X_i by G and, in particular, the functions $i \longrightarrow \gamma_i^l = \mathsf{E}X_i(l)$, $(i,j) \longrightarrow \gamma_{ij}^{lm} = \mathsf{E}X_i(l)X_j(m), \dots$ are invariant functions on I, $I^2, \dots$ for each $l \geq 1$, $m \geq 1, \dots$. Recalling the notation of §2 above concerning the basis for invariant functions $\mathcal{S}_r = \mathcal{S}_r(G, I)$ on I^r, we see that if X has a G–invariant distribution, then for any $r \geq 1$ and $l_1, l_2, \dots, l_r \geq 1$, we must have

$$(5.2) \qquad \gamma_r^{l_1 \dots l_r} = \sum_{\sigma \in P_r} \gamma_\sigma^{l_1 \dots l_r} A_\sigma$$

for suitable coefficients $\gamma_\sigma^{l_1 \ldots l_r} \in \mathbf{R}$, $\sigma \in P_r$, with a similar representation for the corresponding cumulants:

$$(5.3) \qquad \kappa_r^{l_1 \ldots l_r} = \sum_{\sigma \in P_r} \kappa_\sigma^{l_1 \ldots l_r} A_\sigma \; .$$

Basic problem. Obtain expressions for the cumulants in terms of the moments $\{\gamma_\sigma\}$, *σ here ranging over $P_r, r \geq 1$.* Note that we can suppose that $(l_1, \ldots, l_r) = (1, \ldots, r)$, for if a procedure exists, it will not depend on the ls.

We now give a solution to this problem for Example 2.1: S_n acting on **n**. The solution generalises immediately to cover Examples 2.2 and 2.3; indeed it applies at the level of generality of arbitrary generalised wreath products of symmetric groups.

THEOREM 5.1. *Suppose that S_n acts on n as in Example 2.1. Then for every $r, 1 \leq r \leq n$ and $\sigma \in \mathcal{P}(r)$, we have*

$$(5.4) \qquad \kappa_\sigma = \sum_\tau \mu(\tau, \mathbf{r}) \prod_{a=1}^{b(\tau)} \gamma_{\sigma \cap \tau^a}$$

where $\sigma \cap \tau^a$ denotes the partition of τ^a whose blocks are the non–empty sets from $\sigma^1 \cap \tau^a, \ldots, \sigma^b \cap \tau^a$, where $\sigma = \sigma^1 | \ldots | \sigma^b$ and $a = 1, \ldots, b(\tau)$.

Proof. The idea of the proof is very simple: we change the basis $\{A_\sigma\}$ of S_r to one involving elements $\{R_\sigma\}$ defined by the relations

$$(5.5) \qquad R_\sigma = \sum_{\tau \geq \sigma} A_\tau \; , \qquad \sigma \in \mathcal{P}(\mathbf{r}).$$

By Möbius inversion on $\mathcal{P}(\mathbf{r})$ we immediately obtain

$$(5.6) \qquad A_\sigma = \sum_\tau \mu(\sigma, \tau) R_\tau.$$

We note in passing that the $\{R_\sigma\}$ correspond to the power sum symmetric functions which generate S_r, in the same way that the $\{A_\sigma\}$ correspond to the (augmented) monomial symmetric functions. We call the $\{R_\sigma\}$ *relationship* tensors because for $r = 2$ they correspond to the matrices of equivalence relations. They have an important property which makes them easy to use in generating functions, namely $R_\sigma \otimes R_\tau = R_{\sigma|\tau}$, where σ and τ are partitions of *disjoint* sets. We now note that $\Gamma = \sum_\sigma \gamma_\sigma A_\sigma$ may also be written $\Gamma = \sum_\sigma f_\sigma R_\sigma$, where $f_\sigma = \sum_\rho \mu(\rho, \sigma) \gamma_\rho$, with inverse relation $\gamma_\sigma = \sum_{\rho \leq \sigma} f_\rho$. Temporarily writing $g_\sigma = \sum_\rho \mu(\rho, \sigma) \kappa_\sigma$, the proof continues by proving that

$$(5.7) \qquad g_\sigma = \sum_{\tau \geq \sigma} \mu(\tau, \mathbf{r}) \prod_{a=1}^{b(\tau)} f_{\sigma \cap \tau^a} \; .$$

This result is obtained in the same way as any such formula (e.g. (4.6)): by expanding the series and collecting terms. We omit the details.

The theorem will now be proved by obtaining the coefficients of terms involving the $\{g_\sigma\}$ by expanding the fs in

$$(5.8) \qquad \kappa_\sigma = \sum_{\rho \le \sigma} \sum_{\tau \ge \rho} \mu(\tau, \mathbf{r}) \prod_{a=1}^{b(\tau)} f_{\rho \cap \tau^a} \quad ,$$

the validity of this last formula following from (5.7) and our definitions. Now a typical product of γs in this expression has the form $\prod_{c=1}^{b(\phi)} \gamma_{\theta \cap \phi^c}$ for some θ, $\phi \ge \theta$ in $\mathcal{P}(\mathbf{r})$, and this product will appear in the expansion (5.8) only if $\tau = \phi, \rho \le \phi \wedge \sigma$ and $\theta \cap \phi^c \le \rho \cap \phi^c$ for all $c = 1, \ldots, b(\phi)$. The coefficient of this particular product is $\prod_{c=1}^{b(\phi)} \mu(\theta \cap \phi^c, \rho \cap \phi^c)$ and so the overall coefficient of $\prod_{c=1}^{b(\phi)} \gamma_{\theta \cap \phi^c}$ in (5.8) is thus

$$\sum_{\substack{\rho \le \phi \wedge \sigma \\ \theta \cap \phi^c \le \rho \cap \phi^c, \ c=1,\ldots,b(\phi)}} \prod_{c=1}^{b(\phi)} \mu(\theta \cap \phi^c, \rho \cap \phi^c)$$

$$= \prod_{c=1}^{b(\phi)} \sum_{\theta \cap \phi^c \le \psi_c \le \sigma \cap \phi^c} \mu(\theta \cap \phi^c, \psi_c) .$$

Now the inner sum over ψ_c will be zero by the definition of μ, unless $\theta \cap \phi^c = \sigma \cap \phi^c$, and so the overall coefficient is zero unless this equality holds for all $c = 1, \ldots, b(\phi)$. In this case the coefficient is unity and we get a term $\prod_{c=1}^{b(\phi)} \gamma_{\sigma \cap \phi^c}$. Returning to (5.8), we note that ϕ has replaced τ and that the sum is now unconstrained, thus proving (5.4). $\square$

Let us illustrate (5.4) to see just how close it is to the traditional formula (4.6).

$$\kappa_1 = \gamma_1$$
$$\kappa_{12} = \gamma_{12} - \gamma_1 \gamma_2$$
$$\kappa_{1|2} = \gamma_{1|2} - \gamma_1 \gamma_2$$
$$\kappa_{123} = \gamma_{123} - \gamma_{12} \gamma_3 - \gamma_{13} \gamma_2 - \gamma_{23} \gamma_1 + 2 \gamma_1 \gamma_2 \gamma_3$$
$$\kappa_{12|3} = \gamma_{12|3} - \gamma_{12} \gamma_3 - \gamma_{1|3} \gamma_2 - \gamma_{2|3} \gamma_1 + 2 \gamma_1 \gamma_2 \gamma_3$$
$$\kappa_{12|3} = \gamma_{1|2|3} - \gamma_{1|2} \gamma_3 - \gamma_{1|3} \gamma_2 - \gamma_{2|3} \gamma_1 + 2 \gamma_1 \gamma_2 \gamma_3$$

etc.

If one had to guess at the form of (joint) cumulants of $X_i(1)$, $X_j(2), X_k(3), \ldots$, with various constraints of equality and inequality on $i, j, k, \ldots$, then this is undoubtedly what one would hope for. Indeed a more direct proof is now available, showing that Theorem 5.1 applies with essentially no change to symmetry imposed by generalized wreath products of symmetric groups. The definitions of R, f and g in the proof carry over, but with indexing being by $\pi \in \mathrm{Hom}(P, \mathcal{P}(\mathbf{r}))$, and the analogue of (5.7) is

$$(5.8) \qquad g_\pi = \sum_{\tau \geq \vee \pi} \mu(\tau, \mathbf{r}) \prod_{a=1}^{b(\tau)} f_{\pi \cap \tau^a} \ ,$$

where $\pi, \tau \in \mathrm{Hom}(P, \mathcal{P}(\mathbf{r}))$, and $\vee \pi = \bigvee_{p \in P} \pi_p \in \mathcal{P}(\mathbf{r})$.

Example 5.1. For $S_n wr S_m$ acting on $\mathbf{m/n}$, we have

$$\kappa_{12,12} = \gamma_{12,12} - \gamma_{1,1}\gamma_{2,2} \ ,$$
$$\kappa_{123,123} = \gamma_{123,123} - \gamma_{12,12}\gamma_{3,3} - \gamma_{23,23}\gamma_{1,1} - \gamma_{13,13}\gamma_{2,2} + 2\gamma_{1,1}\gamma_{2,2}\gamma_{3,3} \quad \square$$

6. Invariant k–statistics: unbiased estimates of invariant cumulants.

Fisher introduced classical k–statistics as symmetric unbiased estimators of ordinary cumulants, and later Tukey introduced his polykays to serve the same purpose for products of ordinary cumulants, see [9,§2] for references and some further background on this topic. From our current perspective, it is easy to see how to generalise part of their work, for it is immediate from (5.2) that if $\sigma \in P_r$, and $X = (X_i)$ has a G–invariant distribution, then

$$(6.1) \qquad \mathsf{E}\{\frac{1}{|\mathcal{O}_\sigma|}\,[A_\sigma|X(l_1) \otimes \cdots \otimes X(l_r)]\} = \gamma_\sigma^{l_1 \cdots l_r} \ .$$

This is as far as we can go for general group actions, but for the action of S_n on $\mathbf{n}$ (or for generalised wreath products of symmetric groups) we can do much more. The parameters $\{f_\sigma\}$ introduced in Theorem 5.1 are just linear combinations of the $\{\gamma_\sigma\}$ and so unbiased estimators of them are easily derived: the details are given in [8] and [9]. But the cumulants $\{\kappa_\sigma\}$ are linear combinations of the $\{g_\sigma\}$, which in turn are linear combinations of *products* of the $\{f_\sigma\}$, and so we need unbiased estimators of such products. It turns out that this problem also arises later, when we want the joint moments (and cumulants!) of the symmetric unbiased estimators of these cumulants and their products. But before turning to this, let us define the tensors $\{F_\sigma\}$ which give unbiased estimators of the $\{f_\sigma\}$:

$$(6.2) \qquad F_\sigma = \sum_\rho \mu(\rho, \sigma)\frac{1}{(n)_\rho}\,A_\rho, \qquad \sigma \in \mathcal{P}(\mathbf{r}),$$

where $(n)_\rho = n(n-1)\ldots(n - b(\rho) + 1) = |\mathcal{O}_\rho|$. It is immediate from (6.1) and Theorem 5.1 that

$$(6.3) \qquad \mathsf{E}[F_\sigma|X(1) \otimes \cdots \otimes X(r)] = f_\sigma \quad , \qquad \sigma \in \mathcal{P}(\mathbf{r}),$$

where we have reverted to $l_1 = 1, \ldots, l_r = r$. Examples illustrating these results for S_n acting on $\mathbf{n}$, and more generally, may be found in [8] and [9]. We give only two here.

Example 6.1. S_n acting on **n**. We put $X(1) = X, X(2) = Y, X(3) = Z$ for simplicity.

(a) $F_{12} = \dfrac{1}{n} A_{12} - \dfrac{1}{n(n-1)} A_{1|2}$

and so

$$[F_{12}|X \otimes Y] = \frac{1}{n} \sum_{i=1}^{n} X_i Y_i - \frac{1}{n(n-1)} \sum_{i=1}^{n} \sum_{\substack{j=1 \\ i \neq j}}^{n} X_i Y_j$$

$$= \frac{1}{n-1} \sum_{i=1}^{n} (X_i - X.)(Y_i - Y.) ,$$

after some simple algebra, where $X. = \frac{1}{n} \sum_{i=1}^{n} X_i$, and similarly for $Y.$.

(b) $F_{123} = \dfrac{1}{n} A_{123} - \dfrac{1}{n(n-1)} \{A_{12|3} + 2 \text{ similar terms}\} + \dfrac{2}{n(n-1)(n-2)} A_{1|2|3}$

and so

$$[F_{123}|X \otimes Y \otimes Z] = \frac{1}{n} \sum_{i=1}^{n} X_i Y_i Z_i - \frac{1}{n(n-1)} \sum_{i=1}^{n} \sum_{\substack{j=1 \\ i \neq j}}^{n} X_i Y_j, Z_j - 2 \quad \text{similar terms}$$

$$+ \frac{2}{n(n-1)(n-2)} \sum_{i=1}^{n} \sum_{j=1}^{n} \sum_{\substack{k=1 \\ i,j,k \text{ distinct}}}^{n} X_i Y_j Z_k$$

$$= \frac{n}{(n-1)(n-2)} \sum_{i=1}^{n} (X_i - X.)(Y_i - Y.)(Z_i - Z.) ,$$

again after some algebra. □

One interesting and seemingly difficult problem in this context is the following *simplification problem*: The F_σ are alternating sums of the tensors defining the orbits of G acting on I^r and so (6.2) is not a very convenient form for practical use. However, the expressions $[F_\sigma|X(1) \otimes \cdots \otimes X(r)]$ usually simplify dramatically, see Example 6.1 and [13] for a discussion of this phenomenon. Find an adequate explanation of this simplification.

It is not clear just how difficult it will be to form k–statistics in cases quite different from those involving the symmetric group and its various products. An important example which needs to be studied carefully is the cyclic group $\mathbf{Z}_n$.

Now let us turn to the problem of obtaining unbiased estimators for *products* of the parameters $\{f_\sigma\}$. If we write $|\sigma|$ for the set underlying the partition σ, which has been assumed up until now to be **r**, we can ask about expansions of products $F_\sigma \otimes F_\tau$ in terms of F_ρ for $\rho \in \mathcal{P}(|\sigma| \cup |\tau|)$, where $|\sigma| \cap |\tau| = \phi$. For example, it is easy to prove that $F_1 \otimes F_2 = F_{1|2} + \frac{1}{n} F_{12}$, and in various different forms, many such formulae exist in the literature, see [8] for further details and references to the literature. Note that such expansions are possible because (6.2) is an invertible linear transformation, and so the $\{F_\sigma\}$ are in effect another basis of S_r. More generally, the *product problem* is to calculate the coefficients $c(\tau; \rho, \cdots, \sigma)$ in expansions

$$F_\rho \otimes \cdots \otimes F_\sigma = \sum_\tau c(\tau; \rho, \ldots, \sigma) F_\tau$$

where $|\rho|, \cdots |\sigma|$ are pairwise disjoint sets and $\tau \in \mathcal{P}(|\rho| \cup \cdots \cup |\sigma|)$. The majority of these coefficients vanish, and many *ad hoc* rules for their computation exist, see [8], but there still seems to be no complete understanding of their properties. More insight seems to be required.

7. Extensions and open problems. Let the finite group G act transitively on the finite set I. Our first problem has nothing to do with moments or cumulants, but its solution is necessary before any further analysis along these lines is possible.

Orbit problem. Describe the orbits of the action of G on I^r for $\mathbf{r} \geq 2$.

The next class of problems can be viewed as variants on the classical moment problem which asks for a characterisation of sequences $\mathsf{E} X^r$, $r \geq 1$, or, more generally, of $\mathsf{E} X(1)^{r_1} \cdots X(m)^{r_m}$, $r_1, \cdots, r_m \geq 1$. Here we simply ask after the individual terms in the sequence.

Moment problem. Describe the subsets Γ_r and K_r of $\mathsf{R}^{|P_r|}$ corresponding to the possible parameters $\{\gamma_\sigma : \sigma \in P_r\}$ and $\{\kappa_\sigma : \sigma \in P_r\}, r \geq 1$. More precisely, describe Γ_r (resp. K_r) and, for each $\gamma \in \Gamma_r$ (resp. $\kappa \in K_r$) a G–invariant random array $X = (X_i : i \in I)$ such that $\gamma = \gamma^X$ (resp. $\kappa = \kappa^X$).

For $r = 2$ this problem has been widely studied, at least when $X(1) = X(2)$, for in this case G–invariant cumulants correspond to the non–negative definite elements of the centralizer algebra of the permutation representation of G. This is readily analysed in many cases of interest, and in the case of G a generalized wreath product of symmetric groups acting on the associated product sets, results in [2] and [11] identify the orthogonal idempotents of the association scheme and hence provide a common spectral representation for all G–invariant non–negative definite matrices.

For $r \geq 3$, it seems that little is known about the possible invariant moments or cumulants, even in the case $X(1) = X(2) = X(3) = (X_i : i \in \mathbf{n})$. For example, what is the range of values a, b and c in $\gamma_3 = a\, A_{123} + b(A_{12|3} + A_{13|2} + A_{1|23}) + c A_{1|2|3}$? No doubt the constraints on γ_3 will depend on the values in γ_1 and γ_2, so one should perhaps pose the above question for κ_3 rather than γ_3.

Our main interest is in the problem *obtaining the cumulants* that is, finding expressions for the invariant cumulants $\{\kappa_\sigma\}$ in terms of the invariant moments $\{\gamma_\sigma\}$ which correspond to (4.6) and (5.4).

To our knowledge, this problem has not been solved in the present generality for group actions other than the ones mentioned here: generalised wreath products of symmetric groups. The next case demanding attention would seem to be the cyclic group $\mathbf{Z}_n$ acting on $\{0, 1, \ldots, n-1\}$.

Once we have the cumulants, we have the associated problem of obtaining symmetric unbiased estimators of them, i.e. *obtaining the k–statistics* estimating cumulants and products of cumulants.

Given the k–statistics, it is natural to consider the *problem of moments of moments*: finding the joint moments and cumulants of the k–statistics. The analysis necessary to solve the last two problems will take place in the vector spaces $\mathcal{S}_r(G, I)$, $r \geq 1$, and we note that there are many interesting issues here which have not been fully explored even when S_n acts on **n**. In that case the basis $\{F_\sigma\}$ and another one $\{T_\sigma\}$ defined in [13], differ from the others $\{A_\sigma\}$ and $\{R_\sigma\}$ (which correspond to the augmented monomial and power sum symmetric functions, respectively), have definitions which make explicit use of the underlying cardinality n. This difference becomes important when we seek to expand tensor products of the $\{F_\sigma\}$ or the $\{T_\sigma\}$ and the connection of these expansions with other, more traditional aspects of the theory of symmetric functions, seems worthy of study. Doubilet in [4] introduces a lot more structure onto $\mathcal{S}_r = \mathcal{S}_r(S_n, \mathbf{n})$, and it would be of interest to find analogues of this extra structure (involution, Hall inner product Kronecker product etc.) in the case of $\mathcal{S}_r(G, I)$ where G is a generalised wreath product of symmetric groups.

REFERENCES

[1] M. AIGNER, *Combinatorial Theory*, Springer, New York. (1979).

[2] R.A. BAILEY, CHERYL E. PRAEGER, C.A. ROWLEY AND T.P. SPEED, *Generalized wreath products of permutation groups*, Proc. London Math. Soc. (3) 47 (1983) 69–82.

[3] A.W. DAVIS AND T.P. SPEED, *An Edgeworth expansion for the distribution of the F ratio under a randomization model for the randomized complete block design*, In Statistical Decision Theory and Related Topics, Volume 2, pp. 119–130 Eds S.S. Gupta and J.O. Berger, Springer–Verlag, New York (1988).

[4] PETER DOUBILET, *On the foundations of combinatorial theory VII: Symmetric functions through the theory of distribution and occupancy*, Stud. Appl. Math. 51 (1972) 377–396.

[5] P. DOUBILET, G.–C. ROTA AND R. STANLEY, *On the foundations of combinatorial theory VI: The idea of a generating function*, Proc. Sixth Berkeley Symp. on Prob. and Math. Stat. vol. 2 Univ. of Cal. Press.

[6] CHERYL E. PRAEGER, C.A. ROWLEY AND T.P. SPEED, *A note on generalized wreath product groups*, J. Austral. Math. Soc (Ser. A) 39 (1985) 415–420.

[7] T.P. SPEED, *Cumulants and partition lattices*, Austral. J. Statist. 25 (1983), 378–388.

[8] ——— *Cumulants and partition lattices II: Generalized k–statistics*, J. Austral. Math. Soc. (Ser. A) 40 (1985) 34–53.

[9] ——— *Cumulants and partition lattices III : Multiply–indexed arrays*, J. Austral. Math. Soc. (Ser. A) 40 (1985) 161–182.

[10] ——— *Cumulants and partition lattices IV. A.s. convergence of generalized k–statistics*, J. Austral. Math. Soc. (Ser. A) 41 (1986) 79–94.

[11] ——— AND R.A. BAILEY, *On a class of association schemes derived from lattices of equivalence relations*, In Algebraic Structures and Applications, Ed. P. Schultz, C.E. Praeger and R.P. Sullivan (1982) 55–74. New York: Marcel Dekker.

[12] ——— AND R.A. BAILEY, *Factorial dispersion models*, Internat. Statist. Rev. 55 (1987) 261–277.

[13] ——— AND H.L. SILCOCK, *Cumulants and partition lattices V. Calculating generalized k–statistics*, J. Austral. Math. Soc. (Ser. A) 44 (1988) 171–196.

[14] ——— AND H.L. SILCOCK, *Cumulants and partition lattices VI. Variances and covariances of mean squares*, J. Austral. Math. Soc. (Ser. A) 44 (1988) 362–388.

THE MINIMAL RESOLUTION $3 \cdot k(k = 1, 2)$ PLANS FOR THE 2^4 FACTORIAL EXPERIMENT

JAYA SRIVASTAVA* AND SANJAY ARORA†

Abstract. Consider a 2^m factorial experiment in which it is known that at most k of the interactions are nonnegligible. The individual main effects may or may not be negligible. The designs which identify these nonnegligible interactions, and estimate them along with the main effects (and the general mean, say μ) are called resolution $3 \cdot k$ designs. It is known (Srivastava (1975)) that such designs must have at least $(m + 1 + 2k)$ treatments. In the literature many resolution $3 \cdot k$ designs are available for different values of m. Let N denote the size of a design (i.e., the number of treatments) in a design. It is shown in this paper that (for $m = 4$) the minimal value of N in the class of all resolution 3.1 designs is 10. Also, we present all the nonisomorphic minimal designs of resolution $3 \cdot 1$. We also prove that the minimum possible number of treatments in a design of resolution $3 \cdot 2$ for the 2^4 factorial experiment is 11. A partial bibliography of papers in the area is presented. We await a combinatorial break-through which would help obtain the results of this paper by a shorter process.

1. Introduction. Consider the statistical linear model given by

$$(1.1) \qquad E(\underline{Y}) = A_1 \underline{\xi}_1 + A_2 \underline{\xi}_2, \ \text{var} \ (\underline{Y}) = \sigma^2 I_N$$

where $\underline{Y}(N \times 1)$ is a vector of observations, $\underline{\xi}_1 (\nu_1 \times 1)$ is a vector of unknown parameters (which we are definitely interested in estimating), $\underline{\xi}_2 (\nu_2 \times 1)$ is a vector of parameters about which it is known that at most $k(\leq \nu_2)$ elements are nonnegligible (although it is not known as to which set of k parameters from $\underline{\xi}_2$ are nonnegligible), and $A_i(N \times \nu_i)(i = 1, 2)$ are known matrices.

The problem is to identify the nonzero elements of $\underline{\xi}_2$, and estimate them along with the elements of $\underline{\xi}_1$. Such models are called search linear models.

The choice of a design (say, T) influences the source of observations from which the vector $\underline{Y}$ arises and it influences the matrices A_1 and A_2. A design which allows the identification and estimation of parameters (using the $\underline{Y}$ it gives rise to) is called a "search design".

Such designs were introduced in Srivastava (1975) where the following basic theorem is proved

THEOREM 1. *A necessary condition for a design T to be a search design is that*

$$(1.2) \qquad \text{Rank} \ (A_1 : A_{20}) = \nu_1 + 2k$$

for every $(N \times 2K)$ submatrix A_{20} of $A_2(N \times \nu_2)$.

COROLLARY 1. *We must have: $N \geq \nu_1 + 2k$. In other words, the minimum number of treatments in a search design is at least $\nu_1 + 2k$.*

Remark. In case $\sigma^2 = 0$ (noiseless case), the condition (1.2) is also sufficient. When $\sigma^2 > 0$, the correct identification of nonzero elements of $\underline{\xi}_2$ can be done only

*Department of Statistics, Colorado State University, Fort Collins Colorado 80523.
Supported by AFOSR Grant #830080
†Howard University

with a certain probability which is less than 1. The fact that in practical situations, we have $\sigma^2 > 0$, does not have any influence on the design aspect of the problem.

Consider a 2^m factorial experiment. Let $F_1, F_2, \ldots, F_m$ be m factors each at two levels, where $F_i(i = 1, \ldots, m)$ also denotes the main effect of the ith factor. Let $F_{i_1}, \ldots, i_k$ denote the interaction among the factors $F_{i_1}, F_{i_2}, \ldots, F_{i_k}$, where $2 \leq k < m$, $1 \leq i_1 < i_2 < \cdots < i_k \leq m$. A treatment is denoted by a vector of the form $(t_1, t_2, t_3, \ldots, t_m)$, where $t_i = 0$ or 1 for all i. Any particular set of treatments is referred to as a "design".

In (1.1), let the elements of $\underline{\xi}_1$ be (in order) $\mu, F_1, F_2, \ldots, F_m$, and the elements of $\underline{\xi}_2$ be the set of all distinct interactions. Thus we have

$$(1.3) \qquad \nu_1 = m + 1, \nu_2 = 2^m - (m + 1)$$

Let $A = [A_1 : A_2]$, $\underline{\xi} = [\underline{\xi}_1 : \underline{\xi}_2]$. Then, A is a $(N \times 2^m)$ matrix and $\underline{\xi}$ is $(2^m \times 1)$. The model (1.1) can be written in the form

$$(1.4) \qquad E(\underline{Y}) = A\underline{\xi}, \ \text{var} \ (\underline{Y}) = \sigma^2 I_N.$$

The treatments in a design T correspond, in order, to the observations in $\underline{Y}\cdot$, and hence to the rows of A. Under the usual model for factorial experiments, the column of A (or A_1) corresponding to the element μ of $\underline{\xi}$ (or $\underline{\xi}_1$) has 1 everywhere. Also, for $1 \leq k \leq m$, $1 \leq i_1 < i_2 < i_k \leq m$, the element of A in the row corresponding to the treatment $\underline{t} \equiv (t_1, t_2, \ldots, t_m) \in T$, and the effect $\underline{e} \equiv Fi_1 i_2 \ldots i_k \in \underline{\xi}$ is given by $a(\underline{t}, \underline{e})$ where

$$(1.5) \qquad a(\underline{t}, \underline{e}) = d(t_{i_1})d(t_{i_2}) \ldots d(t_{i_m})$$

and $d(0) = -1$, $d(1) = 1$.

Thus the elements of A are all $+1$ or -1. The above shows that the column of A corresponding to an effect $Fi_1 i_2, \ldots, i_k$ is the product of the columns of A corresponding to the k effects $Fi_1, Fi_2, \ldots, Fi_k$.

A resolution $3 \cdot k$ plan is also called a "main effect plus k" plan. The next question is how to construct a MEP$\cdot$1 plan. We know that such a plan has to satisfy the rank condition (1.2). In other words, we know that there are at least $\nu_1 + 2k(= \nu_1 + 2 = m + 3$, since $k = 1)$ treatments in such a design. A natural way to construct such a design is to take a main effect plan T_1 and extend it by a design T_2 such that $T = [T_1 : T_2]$ is a MEP$\cdot$k plan. This has been the most popular approach in the search design field. Let $\underline{Y}_T$ be the vectors of observations, and let $\underline{Y}\cdot_T$ be partitioned into $[Y_1' : Y_2']$, corresponding to T_1 and T_2. Then the Theorems 1.2 and 1.3 (below) hold; these results are special cases of certain results in Srivastava (1976). These results involve the following concept.

DEFINITION 1.1. A matrix $M(p \times q)$ (over any field) is said to have the property P_t (where $t \geq 1$, and t is an integer) if every set of t columns of M is linearly independent.

It is obvious that if a matrix has property P_t, then it also has $P_s(s \leq t)$.

THEOREM 1.2. *Consider the model (1.1), where $\underline{Y}$ etc., are partitioned as below:*

(1.6)
$$\underline{Y} = \begin{bmatrix} \underline{Y}_1 \\ \underline{Y} \end{bmatrix}, A_1 = \begin{bmatrix} A_{11} \\ A_{21} \end{bmatrix}, A_2 = \begin{bmatrix} A_{12} \\ A_{22} \end{bmatrix}$$

where $\underline{Y}_1, A_{11}$, and A_{12} have N_1 rows each and $N = N_1 + N_2$. Suppose, rank$(A_{11}) = m + 1$. Then, a sufficient condition that T is a MEP·k plan is that the matrix Q given by

(1.7)
$$Q = A_{22} - A_{21}(A'_{11}A_{11})^{-1}A'_{11}A_{12},$$

have P_{2k}.

THEOREM 1.3. *Suppose A_{11} is square and nonsingular. Then, a necessary and sufficient condition for a design $T = [T_1 : T_2]$ to be a MEP·k plan is that the $(N_2 \times \nu_2)$ matrix Q has P_{2k} where*

(1.8)
$$Q = A_{22} - A_{21}A'_{11}A_{12}$$

Thus in order to prove that any plan T is a MEP·k plan, it will be necessary and sufficient to find a saturated main effect plan $T_1 \subseteq T$ (i.e. A_{11} is nonsingular) such that the Q matrix corresponding to $T_2(= T - T_1)$ has P_{2k}. This approach will be utlized throughout this paper.

A computer program (in fortran) is written to generate the matrix Q for a given T_1 and T_2. In what follows, the symbol Q_0 will denote a matrix derived from the matrix Q such that the columns of Q_0 are obtained by multiplying the corresponding columns of Q by appropriate nonzero real numbers, where the numbers are chosen in such a way that Q_0 is easy to inspect. It is obvious that if a set of columns of Q_0 are dependent then so are the corresponding columns of Q, and vice a versa. In particular, if the columns of Q corresponding to the interactions $Fi_1i_2 \ldots i_s$ and $Fj_1j_2 \ldots j_t$ are dependent (i.e., proportional), then the corresponding columns of Q_0 are also proportional. If this happens (for Q or Q_0), then we say that "Δ_0 arises for $(i_1, i_2, \ldots, i_s; j_1, j, \ldots, j_t)$". If the column of Q_0 corresponding to the interaction $Fi_1i_2 \ldots i_s$ is equal to the zero column, then we indicate this fact by saying that Δ_0 arises for $(i_1, \ldots, i_s)$. Also, if the column sum of the columns of Q_0 corresponding to the interactions $Fi_1i_2 \ldots i_p$ and $Fj_1j_2 \ldots j_q$ equals the column corresponding to the interaction $F_{\ell_1\ell_2} \ldots \ell_s$, then it will be expressed by saying that Δ_1 arises for $(i_1, i_2, \ldots, i_p; j_1, \ldots, j_q; \ell_1, \ell_2, \ldots, \ell_s)$.

Let us also introduce the concept of isomorphic designs. This concept is basic to this paper. Let S_m be the permutation group on the m letters $\{1, 2, \ldots, m\}$. Let $\underline{t} = (t_1, t_2, \ldots, t_m)$ be any treatment and let σ be any permutation in S_m. Define $\sigma(\underline{t})$ by

$$\sigma(\underline{t}) = (t_{\sigma(1)}, t_{\sigma(2)}, \ldots, t_{\sigma(m)}).$$

Note that $\sigma(\underline{t})$ is another treatment. Let T be any design for a 2^m factorial experiment. Regard T as a set consisting of treatments. Let $\sigma(T)$ be the design defined by

$$\sigma(T) = \{\sigma(\underline{t}) : \underline{t} \in T\}.$$

DEFINITION 1.2. Let T and T' be two designs for a 2^m factorial experiment. Then T is said to be isomorphic to T', if there exists a permutation $\sigma \in S_m$ such that the designs $\sigma(T)$ and T' (regarded as sets) are identical.

Let $\underline{t} = (t_1, t_2, \ldots, t_m)$ be a treatment for a 2^m factorial experiment so that $t_i = 0$ or 1 for $i = 1, 2, \ldots, m$. Then the weight of treatment vector $\underline{t}$ (written as wt$(\underline{t})$) is the number of nonzero elements in it. Clearly the weight of the treatment $\underline{t}(\equiv t_1, t_2, \ldots, t_n))$ is $\sum_{j=1}^{m} t_j$. Also Ω_{mj}, $(j = 0, 1, 2, \ldots, m)$, will denote the set of all vectors of weight j. Obviously $|\Omega_j| = \binom{m}{j}$, for $(j = 0, 1, 2, \ldots, m)$, and $\sigma(\Omega_{mj}) = \Omega_{mj}$ for any permutation $\sigma \in S_m$.

2. Some Preliminary Results. We start with the following important definitions from Srivastava and Gupta (1979).

DEFINITION 2.1. Let $\underline{t} = (t_1, t_2, \ldots, t_m)$, $t_i = 0$ or $1(i = 1, 2, \ldots, m)$ be any treatment. Let $K = F i_1 i_2 \ldots i_p (1 \leq i_1 < i_2 < \cdots < i_p \leq m, 1 \leq p \leq m)$ be any interaction of order p. Then we define $\theta(\underline{t}, K)$ by

$$\theta(\underline{t}, K) \equiv |\underline{t} \cap K| = \sum_{j=1}^{p} t_{i_j}.$$

Usually $\underline{t}$ and K will be dropped, and $\theta(\underline{t}, K)$ will be written as θ.

DEFINITION 2. Let g be any integer. The $\zeta(\cdot)$ is the function defined by

$$(2.1) \qquad \zeta(g) = \begin{cases} g, & \text{if } g \text{ is an even integer} \\ g - 1, & \text{if } g \text{ is an odd integer} \end{cases}$$

The following result is proved in Srivastava and Gupta (1979).

THEOREM 2.1. Let $T_1 = \Omega_{mm} \cup \Omega_{m1}$. Let $\underline{t}$ be any treatment in T_2, and let $K = F i_1 i_2 \ldots i_p (1 \leq i_1 < i_2 < \cdots < i_p \leq m, 2 \leq p \leq m)$ be any effect from $\underline{\xi}_2 \equiv \xi_{2,m} = \{F_{12}, F_{13}, \ldots, F_{12\ldots m}\}$. The element of $Q_m (\equiv Q)$ corresponding to the treatment $\underline{t} \in T_2$, and the effect K, is $q(\underline{t}, K)$ where

$$q(\underline{t}, K) = 2(-1)p\left[\left\{\frac{(1 - wt(\underline{t}))}{(m-1)}\right\} \zeta(p) + \zeta(\theta)\right],$$

and $\theta = |\underline{t} \cap K|$, and where wt$(\underline{t})$, called "the weight of $\underline{t}$" equals $\sum_{1}^{m} t_i$.

For their designs, Gupta and Carvajal (1984b) took $T_1 = \Omega_{44} \cup \Omega_{41} \cup \Omega_{40}$. We now consider removing Ω_{40} from their T_1.

THEOREM 2.2. Let $T = [T_1 : T_2]$ where $T_1 = \Omega_{44} \cup \Omega_{41}$.

(a) If $\phi \in T_2$, then the minimum number of treatments in T_2 such that T is a MEP·1 plan, is six.

(b) If $\phi \notin T_2$, then the minimum number of treatments in T_2 such that T is a MEP·1 plan, is five. Moreover, there is only one T_2 (nonisomoprhic) for which $T = [T_1 : T_2]$ is a MEP·1 plan, and in this case we have

$$(2.2) \qquad T = \{1111, 1000, 0100, 0010, 0001, 1110, 1101, 1100, 1010, 0101\}.$$

Proof. The part (a) is proved in Gupta and Carvajal (1984b). For part (b) we use the Theorem 1 to obtain the matrix Q for this $T_1 = \Omega_{44} \cup \Omega_{41}$. We have the following expression for the matrix Q_0:

$$(2.3) \quad Q_0 = \begin{array}{c} \\ 12 \\ 13 \\ 14 \\ 23 \\ 24 \\ 34 \\ 123 \\ 124 \\ 134 \\ 234 \end{array} \begin{pmatrix} 12 & 13 & 14 & 23 & 24 & 34 & 123 & 124 & 134 & 234 & 1234 \\ -2 & 1 & 1 & 1 & 1 & 1 & 2 & 2 & -1 & -1 & -1 \\ 1 & -2 & 1 & 1 & 1 & 1 & 2 & -1 & 2 & -1 & -1 \\ 1 & 1 & -2 & 1 & 1 & 1 & -1 & 2 & 2 & -1 & -1 \\ 1 & 1 & 1 & -2 & 1 & 1 & 2 & -1 & -1 & 2 & -1 \\ 1 & 1 & 1 & 1 & -2 & 1 & -1 & 2 & -1 & 2 & -1 \\ 1 & 1 & 1 & 1 & 1 & -2 & -1 & -1 & 2 & 2 & -1 \\ -1 & -1 & 2 & -1 & 2 & 2 & 1 & 1 & 1 & 1 & 1 \\ -1 & 2 & -1 & 2 & -1 & 2 & 1 & 1 & 1 & 1 & 1 \\ 2 & -1 & -1 & 2 & 2 & -1 & 1 & 1 & 1 & 1 & 1 \\ 2 & 2 & 2 & -1 & -1 & -1 & 1 & 1 & 1 & 1 & 1 \end{pmatrix}$$

In (2.3), the matrix in the r.h.s. is bordered by a row of indices on the top, and a column of indices on the left side. These respectively indicate the factorial effects to which the column corresponds to, and the treatments. Thus, for example the 8th column of Q_0 is indexed by (124) which is an abbreviated form of F_{124}. Also, the 7th row of Q_0 is indexed by (123), which is a way of expressing the treatment (1110). (Henceforth a treatment $(t_1, \ldots, t_m)$ will also be sometimes written as $(1_1, \ldots, i_k)$ where $t_j = 1$, if $j \in (i_1, \ldots, i_k)$, and $t_j = 0$, otherwise.) In future, we will omit the indices $12, 13$, etc., from the column headings, because they remain the same for all of the matrices throughout this paper.

Now we will show that if T_2 is any design consisting of five treatments from $\Omega_{41} \cup \Omega_{43}$, then the only choice for T_2 such that $T = [T_1 : T_2]$ is a MEP·1 plan is (2.2). Let v_i be the number of treatments of weight i ($i = 2, 3$) in T_2 where T_2 is any design with five treatments. Because $\phi \notin T_2, v_2 + v_3 = 5$. This gives us the following choices for $(v_2, v_3) : (1, 4), (2, 3), (3, 2), (4, 1)$, and $(5, 0)$.

Case 1. $v_2 = 1$, $v_3 = 4$. For this case we have the following matrix Q_0:

$$Q_0 = \begin{array}{c} 123 \\ 124 \\ 134 \\ 234 \\ \epsilon_2 \end{array} \begin{pmatrix} -1 & -1 & 2 & 1 & 2 & 2 & 1 & 1 & 1 & 1 & 1 \\ -1 & 2 & -1 & 2 & -1 & 2 & 1 & 1 & 1 & 1 & 1 \\ 2 & -1 & -1 & 2 & 2 & -1 & 1 & 1 & 1 & 1 & 1 \\ 2 & 2 & 2 & -1 & -1 & -1 & 1 & 1 & 1 & 1 & 1 \\ * & * & * & * & * & * & a & b & c & d & -1 \end{pmatrix}$$

where $\epsilon \in \Omega_{42}$. Also, $a, b, c, d, \in \{-1, 2\}$ and $*$ means that we have a real number whose value we do not care about. It is now obvious that at least two of the columns

340

of the matrix Q_0 corresponding to the interactions of order three must be identical. For example, if $\epsilon_2 = 12$, then the columns of 134 and 234 are identical. Hence, P_2 does not hold for this case.

Case 2. $v_2 = 2, v_3 = 3$. Without loss of generality, let the treatments of weight three be $123, 124$, and 134. Suppose that the two treatments of weight two have a factor, say x, in common. Then for the matrix Q_0 we obtain that the column for the interaction 1234 equals the column for the interaction $(1234 - x)$. If they do not have any symbol in common, i.e., they are of the type xy and uv where $\{x, y\} \neq \{u, v\}$, then for Q_0 we have:

$$\text{column for the interaction } xyu = \text{column for the interaction } xyv.$$

Thus, P_2 does not hold.

Case 3. $v_2 = 3, v_3 = 2$. Let the two treatments of weight three be 123 and 124. For the three treatments of weight two, we have the following eight nonisomorphic choices: $(12, 13, 14), (12, 13, 34), (12, 13, 23), (12, 14, 23), (13, 14, 34), (12, 23, 34),$ $(13, 24, 34),$ and $(12, 13, 24)$. For the first three cases we find that the column of Q_0 corresponding to the interaction F_{14} equals the column corresponding to the interaction F_{24}. In other words, Δ_0 arises for $(14, 24)$. In the next four cases we find that Δ_0 arises for $(12, 1234)$. But in the last case we have $T_2 = \{123, 124, 12, 13, 24\}$. The matrix Q_0 for this T_2 is

$$(2.4) \qquad Q_0 = \begin{array}{c} 12 \\ 13 \\ 24 \\ 123 \\ 124 \end{array} \begin{pmatrix} -2 & 1 & 1 & 1 & 1 & 1 & 2 & 2 & -1 & -1 & -1 \\ 1 & -1 & 1 & 1 & 1 & 1 & 2 & -1 & 2 & -1 & -1 \\ 1 & 1 & 1 & 1 & -2 & 1 & -1 & 2 & -1 & 2 & -1 \\ -1 & -1 & 2 & -1 & 2 & 2 & 1 & 1 & 1 & 1 & 1 \\ -1 & 2 & -1 & 2 & -1 & 2 & 1 & 1 & 1 & 1 & 1 \end{pmatrix}.$$

Note that Q_0 has P_2. Also, if we delete any row from this Q_0, then P_2 does not hold for the remaining (4×11) matrix. This means that if we drop any element from this T_2, then the remaining treatments do not form a MEP·1 design.

Case 4. $v_2 = 4, v_3 = 1$. Without loss of generality, let the treatment of weight three be 123. Looking at the matrix Q_0 in (2.3), we see that if any one of the treatments from $\{12, 13, 23\}$ is omitted, then the property P_2 breaks down for the columns corresponding to this left-out treatment and the column for interaction 1234. For example, if 12 is not included, then Δ_0 arises for $(12, 1234)$. Now suppose that $12, 13,$ and 23 are in T_2. If any two of the treatments from $\{14, 24, 34\}$ are left out, then the columns of the interactions corresponding to these left-out treatments are identical. Hence, P_2 does not hold for any of the five treatments in this case.

Case 5. $v_2 = 5, v_3 = 0$. Let the treatment 12 be left out. Then Δ_0 arises for $(12, 1234)$. Once again, P_2 does not hold in this case. This proves the theorem.

The design of Theorem 2.1 has the following property, which we will use later. We state this property in the following theorem.

THEOREM 2.3. *Let T be as at (2.2). Then no subdesign of T is a MEP·1 plan.*

Proof. We showed above that if T contains the T_1 of Theorem 2.1, then no treatment can be dropped from $T_2(= T - T_1) = \{1234, 124, 12, 13, 24\}$. Thus, we

341

can assume that the treatments $123, 124, 12, 13$, and 24 are always in the subdesign. But now, if we take $T_1 = \{1234, 123, 13, 34, 124\}$, then we get the following matrix:

$$(2.5) \qquad Q_0 = \begin{array}{c} 123 \\ 1 \\ 2 \\ 3 \\ 4 \end{array} \left(\begin{array}{ccccccccccc} 0 & 0 & 0 & 0 & 0 & -1 & 0 & 0 & -1 & -1 & -1 \\ 0 & 0 & 0 & 1 & 0 & 1 & 1 & 0 & 1 & 0 & 0 \\ -1 & 1 & 1 & 0 & 1 & -1 & 0 & 1 & -1 & 0 & -1 \\ 0 & 0 & 1 & 0 & 1 & -1 & 0 & 0 & 0 & 0 & -1 \\ 0 & 1 & 0 & 1 & 0 & 0 & 0 & 0 & 1 & 1 & 0 \end{array} \right).$$

If we drop any of the treatments from $\{123, 1, 2, 3, 4\}$, then we violate P_2. Hence, none of the treatments from $\{123, 1, 2, 3, 4\}$ can be dropped from T. Thus, no treatment can be dropped from T. This proves the theorem.

Next we consider the case $T_1 = \Omega_{mm} \cup \Omega_{m,m-1}$. We prove the following result about the matrix Q for this T_1.

THEOREM 2.4. *Let* $T_1 = \Omega_{m,m} \cup \Omega_{m,m-1}$. *Let* $q(\underline{t}, \underline{e})$ *be the element of* Q *corresponding to* $\underline{t} \in T_2$ *and* $\underline{e} \in \underline{\xi}_2$. *Then*

$$(2.6) \qquad q(\underline{t}, \underline{e}) = 2\zeta(g)$$

where g *is the number of factors which appear in the effect* $\underline{e}$ *and which are at level zero in the treatment* $\underline{t}$, *and where* $\zeta(g)$ *is defined in (2.1).*

Proof. If the treatments in T_1 are written in the order $(1, 1, \ldots, 1), (1, 1,, \ldots, 1, 0), \ldots, (0, 1, \ldots, 1)$, then A_{11} is given by

$$(2.7) \qquad A_{11} = \left[\begin{array}{ccc} 1 & : & \underline{J}_{1m} \\ \cdots\cdots & & \cdots\cdots \\ \underline{J}_{m1} & : & J_{mm} - 2W \end{array} \right]$$

where

$$(2.8) \qquad W = \left[\begin{array}{ccccc} 0 & 0 & 0 & \cdots & 0 & 1 \\ 0 & 0 & 0 & \cdots & 1 & 0 \\ . & . & . & \cdots & . & . \\ 1 & 0 & 0 & \cdots & 0 & 0 \end{array} \right].$$

Note that $W^2 = I$ and $W^{-1} = W$.

Thus, A_{11}^{-1} is given by

$$(2.9) \qquad A_{11}^{-1} = \left[\begin{array}{ccc} \alpha & : & \beta \underline{J}_{1\ m} \\ \cdots\cdots & & \cdots\cdots \\ \beta \underline{J}_{m\ 1} & : & -\beta W \end{array} \right]$$

where

$$(2.10) \qquad \alpha = 1 - m/2 \text{ and } \beta = 1/2.$$

342

Also, let $\theta = |\underline{t} \cap \underline{e}| = \sum_{k=1}^{\ell} t_{i_k}$. The element of the matrix A_{22} corresponding to the treatment $\underline{t} \in T_2$ and the effect $\underline{e}(= F_{i_1} \ldots i_\ell)$ is $(-1)^{\ell - \theta}$. The row of A_{21} corresponding to the treatment $\underline{t} = (t_1, \ldots, t_m)$ is $(1, 2t_1 - 1, \ldots 2t_m - 1)$.

Let $\underline{v}' = (1 : \underline{v}_0')' = (1, v_1, \ldots, v_m)'$ be the column of A_{12} corresponding to the effect $\underline{e} = F_{i_1 i_2} \ldots i_\ell$. If $\{i_1, \ldots, i_\ell\} = S$, then

(2.11)
$$v_j = \begin{cases} 1, & \text{if } m - j + 1 \in S \\ -1, & \text{if } m - 1 + 1 \notin S \end{cases}$$

for $j = 1, 2, \ldots, m$. Let $S' = \{x : x \notin S\}$. Note that

(2.12)
$$\sum_{j=1}^{m} v_j = m - 2 \times (\text{number of times } (-1) \text{ occurs in the column})$$
$$= m - 2\ell.$$

The element $q(\underline{t}, \underline{e})$ of the matrix $Q = A_{22} - A_{21} \cdot A_{11}^{-1} \cdot A_{12}$, corresponding to the treatment $\underline{t} \in T_2$ and the effect $\underline{w} \in \xi_2$ is thus given by

(2.13)
$$q(\underline{t}, \underline{e}) = (-1)^{\ell - \theta} - (1, 2t_1 - 1, \ldots, 2t_m - 1) A_{11}^{-1} \underline{v}'$$
$$= (-1)^{\ell - \theta} - q_0(\underline{t}, \underline{e})$$

where

(2.14)
$$q_0(\underline{t}, \underline{e}) = (1, 2t_1 - 1, \ldots, 2t_m - 1) A_{11}^{-1} \underline{v}'$$

Now

(2.15)
$$A_{11}^{-1} \cdot \underline{v}' = \begin{bmatrix} \alpha & : & \beta \underline{J}_{1\,m} \\ \cdots\cdots\cdots\cdots\cdots \\ \beta \underline{J}_{m1} & : & -\beta W \end{bmatrix} \begin{bmatrix} 1 \\ \cdots \\ \underline{v}_0 \end{bmatrix}$$
$$= \begin{bmatrix} 1 - \ell \\ \cdots\cdots\cdots\cdots \\ \beta(\underline{J}_{m1} - W_{\underline{v}_0}) \end{bmatrix}$$

Hence,

$$q_0(\underline{t}, \underline{e}) = (1, 2t_1 - 1, \ldots, 2t_m - 1) A_{11}^{-1} \underline{v}'$$
$$= 1 - \ell + \beta(2t_1 - 1, \ldots, 2t_m - 1) \cdot (\underline{J}_{m1} - W_{\underline{e}_0})$$

after appropriate simplification. Hence,

$$q(\underline{t}, \underline{e}) = (-1)^{\ell - \theta} - 1 + 2\ell - 2\theta = 2\zeta(g).$$

where $g(= \ell - \theta)$ is the number of factors which appear in the effect $\underline{e}$ and which are at level zero in the treatment $\underline{t}$. This proves the theorem.

343

THEOREM 2.5. *Let T be a design for the 2^4 factorial experiment such that $|T| = 10$. Let $\Omega_{44} \cup \Omega_{43} \subseteq T$.*

(a) *If $\phi \in T$, then T can't be a MEP·1 plan.*

(b) *If $\phi \notin T$, then there is a unique MEP·1 plan T (up to isomorphism) and this plan is given by*

(2.16) $$T = \{1234, 123, 124, 134, 234, 1, 2, 12, 24, 34\}.$$

Proof. Take $T_1 = \Omega_{44} \cup \Omega_{43}$ and obtain the matrix Q from theorem (2.1) above. We obtain a Q_0 as below:

$$
(2.17) \qquad Q_0 =
\begin{array}{c}
1 \\ 2 \\ 3 \\ 4 \\ 12 \\ 13 \\ 14 \\ 23 \\ 24 \\ 34 \\ \phi
\end{array}
\left(
\begin{array}{ccccccccccc}
0 & 0 & 0 & 1 & 1 & 1 & 1 & 1 & 1 & 1 & 1 \\
0 & 1 & 1 & 0 & 0 & 1 & 1 & 1 & 1 & 1 & 1 \\
1 & 0 & 1 & 0 & 1 & 0 & 1 & 1 & 1 & 1 & 1 \\
1 & 1 & 0 & 1 & 0 & 0 & 1 & 1 & 1 & 1 & 1 \\
0 & 0 & 0 & 0 & 0 & 1 & 0 & 0 & 1 & 1 & 1 \\
0 & 0 & 0 & 0 & 1 & 0 & 0 & 1 & 0 & 1 & 1 \\
0 & 0 & 0 & 1 & 0 & 0 & 1 & 0 & 0 & 1 & 1 \\
0 & 0 & 1 & 0 & 0 & 0 & 0 & 1 & 1 & 0 & 1 \\
0 & 1 & 0 & 0 & 0 & 0 & 1 & 0 & 1 & 0 & 1 \\
1 & 0 & 0 & 0 & 0 & 0 & 1 & 1 & 0 & 0 & 1 \\
1 & 1 & 1 & 1 & 1 & 1 & 1 & 1 & 1 & 1 & 2
\end{array}
\right).
$$

It $\underline{t} = (t_1, t_2, \ldots, t_m)$ is any treatment, then $\bar{\underline{t}} = (1 - t_1, 1 - t_2, \ldots, 1 - t_m)$ will be called the dual to $\underline{t}$. For example, 12 and 34 are duals of each other, when $m = 4$.

Now we consider part (a). There, we have $\phi \in T$. Looking at the matrix Q_0 in (2.17), it is obvious that we need at least two treatments of weight two. If there are exactly two treatments of weight two in T, then they should not be $\underline{t}$ and $\bar{\underline{t}}$. Assume (without loss of generality) that the two treatments are $(12, 13)$. Then by inspection, we find that no two treatments of weight one will work, since by including $(1,2)$, $(1,3)$, $(1,4)$, or $(2,3)$ a column of zeros will result in the matrix Q_0, and by including $(2,4)$ or $(3,4)$, identical columns will result. It is clear that if we only include the treatments of weight two, then also we get identical columns. Let us assume that there are three treatments of weight two and only one treatment of weight one in T. Let $\underline{t}_1, \underline{t}_2$ and $\underline{t}_3$ be three treatments of weight two to be included in T. Then at least two columns of the matrix Q_0 for the interactions corresponding to $\bar{\underline{t}}_1, \bar{\underline{t}}_2$ and $\bar{\underline{t}}_3$ are identical. As a matter of fact, we have the following matrix Q_0:

$$
Q_0 =
\begin{array}{c}
\\ \underline{t}_1 \\ \underline{t}_2 \\ \underline{t}_3 \\ \phi \\ \epsilon_1
\end{array}
\begin{array}{c}
\bar{\underline{t}}_1 \quad \bar{\underline{t}}_2 \quad \bar{\underline{t}}_3 \\
\left(
\begin{array}{ccc}
0 & 0 & 0 \\
0 & 0 & 0 \\
0 & 0 & 0 \\
1 & 1 & 1 \\
x & y & z
\end{array}
\right)
\end{array}
$$

344

where ϵ_1 is a treatment of weight one and $x, y, z \in \{0, 1\}$. Thus P_2 does not hold in any case. This proves part (a).

Now consider part (b). Here we have $\phi \notin T$. Once again, looking at the columns of the interactions of order three and four in the matrix Q_0 at (2.17), it is clear that we will need at least two treatments of weight two. Suppose that there are only two treatments of weight two. There are two nonisomorphic choices for these two treatments. These are (12,34) and (12,13). In the first case, Δ_0 arises for (F_{123}, F_{124}). In the second case Δ_0 arises for (F_{234}, F_{1234}). Suppose that there are three treatments of weight two, and two treatments of weight one in T. Without loss of generality, let the treatments of weight one be 1 and 2. As we look at the matrix Q, we find that if 34 is not in T, then Δ_0 arises for (12). Hence, $34 \in T$. We now need to choose two more treatments from $\{12, 13, 14, 23, 24\}$. The nonisomorphic choices for these treatments are (i) 12, 13, (ii) 13, 14, (iii) 13, 23, and (iv) 13, 24.

In case (i), Δ_0 arises for (13, 14). In case (ii), Δ_0 arises for (13,23), and in case (iii) Δ_0 arises for (124, 1234). In case (iv), the matrix Q_0 is easily seen to have P_2. This give the MEP·1 design (as stated in the theorem). In this case, we have

$$(2.18) \qquad Q_0 = \begin{array}{c} 1 \\ 2 \\ 34 \\ 13 \\ 24 \end{array} \begin{pmatrix} 0 & 0 & 0 & 1 & 1 & 1 & 1 & 1 & 1 & 1 & 1 \\ 0 & 1 & 1 & 0 & 0 & 1 & 1 & 1 & 1 & 1 & 1 \\ 1 & 0 & 0 & 0 & 0 & 0 & 1 & 1 & 0 & 0 & 1 \\ 0 & 0 & 0 & 0 & 1 & 0 & 0 & 1 & 0 & 1 & 1 \\ 0 & 1 & 0 & 0 & 0 & 0 & 1 & 0 & 1 & 0 & 1 \end{pmatrix}.$$

It is easily seen that if we delete any treatment from $T_2 = \{1, 2, 34, 13, 24\}$, then the property P_2 breaks down.

Now suppose that there are four treatments of weight two in T. Thus, we have one treatment of weight one in T, and we leave out two treatments of weight two. Suppose that these two left-out treatments are $\underline{t}_1$ and $\underline{t}_2$. Then the columns of the matrix Q_0 for the interactions corresponding to $\bar{\underline{t}}_1$ and $\bar{\underline{t}}_2$ form a matrix $Q_2(5 \times 2)$ where

$$Q_2' = \begin{bmatrix} 0 & 0 & 0 & 0 & x \\ 0 & 0 & 0 & 0 & y \end{bmatrix} \text{ and } x, y \in \{0, 1\}.$$

Note that if x or y is 0, then P_2 does not hold for Q_0. And if both $x = y = 1$, then the columns are identical. Hence, P_2 does not hold in this case.

Now suppose that all of the five treatments in T are of weight two, and that the left out treatment is 12. Then Δ_0 arises for (34). Thus, in this case, P_2 does not hold for Q_0. Hence, there is only one design of resolution $III \cdot 1$ as stated in the theorem. This completes the proof.

The conclusion of the above theorem is further strengthened in Theorem 2.6.

THEOREM 2.6. *Let T be the unique design of Theorem 2.5. If we take any subdesign T_0 of T with 9 treatments, then T_0 is not a resolution 3.1 design.*

Proof. We have $T = \{1234, 123, 124, 134, 234, 1, 2, 34, 13, 24\}$. We have proved in Theorem 2.5 that we can't drop any of the treatments from the set $\{1, 2, 34, 13, 24\}$.

345

Let us assume that $1, 2, 34, 13$, and 24 are in T. Let $T_1 = \{1234, 1, 2, 34, 13\}$. Then the matrix Q_0 for this case is

$$
Q_0 = \begin{array}{c} 24 \\ 123 \\ 123 \\ 134 \\ 234 \end{array}\left(\begin{array}{rrrrrrrrrrr}
1 & -1 & 1 & 1 & -1 & 1 & 1 & 1 & 0 & 0 & -1 \\
-1 & 1 & 1 & -1 & 1 & 0 & -1 & 1 & 0 & 1 & 1 \\
0 & 0 & 0 & 2 & 0 & 1 & 2 & 0 & 1 & 0 & 0 \\
1 & -1 & -1 & 1 & 1 & 0 & 1 & 1 & 0 & 0 & 1 \\
1 & 1 & 1 & -1 & -1 & 0 & 1 & 1 & 0 & 0 & 1
\end{array}\right)
$$

We see that none of the treatments from $\{123, 124, 134, 234\}$ can be dropped without violating P_2. Hence, no subdesign of T is a MEP·1 plan.

We now know that MEP·1 plans (for the 2^4 factorial experiment) with ten treatments exist. This itself is an improvement on the existing MEP·1 plans in the literature. We also saw that for the MEP·1 plans discovered in Theorems 2.2. and 2.5, there are no subdesigns of those MEP·1 plans which are of resolution III·1. But we have not considered all of the designs with ten treatments to settle the question of minimality. In the next section, we look into the MEP·1 plans (for the 2^4 factorial experiment) with ten treatments. We will make use of the results proved in this section.

3. Enumeration of MEP·1 plans.

In this section, we discuss all of the MEP·1 plans T (for the 2^4 factorial experiment) with ten treatments. Recall that the treatment 1234 is always in T.

Let $n_j (j = 0, 1, 2, 3, 4)$ be the number of treatments of weight j in T. We classify the T's using the values of $n_j (j = 0, 1, 2, 3, 4, 5)$. We have shown in Theorem 2.2 that if $n_1 = 4$, then there is a unique design of resolution 3.1. In Theorem 2.5, we have shown that if $n_3 = 4$, then there is a unique design of resolution III·1. Thus, the cases to consider are

$$
(3.1) \qquad \begin{bmatrix} n_3 \\ n_1 \end{bmatrix} = \begin{bmatrix} 3 & 3 & 3 & 3 & 2 & 2 & 2 & 2 & 1 & 1 & 1 & 1 & 0 & 0 & 0 & 0 \\ 3 & 2 & 1 & 0 & 3 & 2 & 1 & 0 & 3 & 2 & 1 & 0 & 3 & 2 & 1 & 0 \end{bmatrix}.
$$

These are sixteen cases and we discuss each of these cases separately. Note that if T is any MEP·1 plan of order ten, then there is a unique value for the pair (n_3, n_1) for this design T. This value of (n_3, n_1) has to be exactly one of those values listed above. Thus, the discussion of the cases in (3.1) will exhaust all the plans with ten treatments.

Case 1. $n_3 = 3$, $n_1 = 3$. Without loss of generality, let the treatments of weight three be $123, 124$, and 134. The nonisomorphic choices for the three treatments of weight one are **case** (1.1) $1, 2, 3 \in T$ and **case** (1.2) $2, 3, 4 \in T$. For both of the nonisomorphic cases take $T_1 = \{1234, 123, 124, 134, 3\}$. This gives us the following matrix Q_0:

$$(3.2) \qquad Q_0 = \begin{matrix}1\\2\\12\\13\\14\\23\\24\\34\\\phi\end{matrix}\begin{pmatrix} 0 & 0 & 0 & 1 & 1 & 1 & 1 & 1 & 1 & 1 & 1 \\ 1 & 1 & 0 & 0 & -1 & 1 & 0 & 0 & 0 & 0 & 0 \\ 0 & 0 & 0 & 0 & 0 & 1 & 0 & 0 & 1 & 1 & 1 \\ 0 & 0 & 0 & 0 & 1 & 0 & 0 & 1 & 0 & 1 & 1 \\ 0 & 0 & 0 & 1 & 0 & 0 & 1 & 0 & 0 & 1 & 1 \\ 1 & 0 & 0 & 0 & -1 & 0 & -1 & 0 & 0 & -1 & 0 \\ 1 & 1 & 1 & 0 & -1 & 0 & 0 & -1 & 0 & -1 & 0 \\ 0 & 0 & 1 & 0 & -1 & 0 & 0 & 0 & -1 & -1 & 0 \\ 0 & 1 & 0 & 1 & 0 & 1 & 0 & 0 & 0 & 0 & 1 \end{pmatrix}$$

In **case** (1.1) we have $1, 2, 3, 123, 124, 134, 1234, \in T$. We need to choose three more treatments from $\Omega_{40} \cup \Omega_{42}$. Note that the column of F_{14} will be $\underline{0}$ if we don't include at least one of the treatments 24 or 34. In other words, the treatment pair $(24, 34)$ is such that if none of them is included in the plan, then at least one column of the corresponding Q_0 will become zero. This will be expressed by saying that the property L_0 arises for the treatments $(24, 34)$. Note that we now have to discuss the following three possibilities: (i) $24, 34 \in T$, (ii) $24 \in T, 34 \notin T$, (iii) $24 \notin T, 34 \in T$. Each time when the property L_0 arises, we will have to discuss all the possibilities such as (i), (ii) and (iii). Now, if both $24, 34 \in T$ then we need to choose one more treatment from $\{\phi, 12, 13, 14, 23\}$. Choosing any one of the treatments from $\{\phi, 12, 13, 14, 23\}$ (in order), we see that Δ_0 arises for $(23, 1234)$; $(12, 13), (12, 13), (12, 13)$, and $(23, 1234)$ respectively. Thus we assume that only one of the treatments from 24 or 34 is in T. Suppose that $34 \in T$, and 2 and $24 \notin T$. Then we have $\{1, 2, 3, 1234, 123, 124, 134, 34\} \subseteq T$ and $4, 24 \notin T$. We have to choose two more treatments from $\{\phi, 12, 13, 14, 23\}$. If we exclude ϕ, then 23 must be included in T (since otherwise, the column of F_{23} equals the column of F_{123}). But now, if we include any of the treatments from $\{12, 13, 14\}$ (in order), then Δ_0 arises for $(23, 124), (124, 1234)$, and $(23, 1234)$, respectively. Hence, ϕ must be included in T. In this case we have to choose one more treatment from $\{12, 13, 14, 23\}$. If we choose any one of the treatments from $\{12, 14, 23\}$ (in order), then Δ_0 arises for $(134, 234), (123, 1234)$, and $(23, 1234)$, respectively. However, if we choose 13, then

$$(3.3) \qquad T = \{1234, 123, 124, 134, \phi, 13, 34, 1, 2, 3\}$$

is a MEP· plan.

Now suppose that $24 \in T$ and $34 \notin T$. Then $1234, 123, 124, 134, 1, 2, 3, \in T$ and $4, 34 \notin T$. But now, if we interchange 2 and 3, we get the same situation as above. Note that the two MEP·1 plans are isomorphic to each other. Hence, **case** (1.1) is finished.

Below, we present the above discussions of case (1.1) in a shortened form. The reason is this: In the rest of the cases, where a situation like that in case (1.1) arises, we will (for the sake of brevity), provide the discussion in only the shortened form.

347

We now introduce some further condensed notation, which is used in this shortened presentation. Consider the matrix Q_0 corresponding to a given T_1; the rows of Q_0 correspond to all (or some) of the treatments in $\overline{T}_1$, where $\overline{T}_1$ is the set of all possible distinct treatments which are not in T_1. Let u be a positive integer. Suppose there are u distinct treatments (say $\tau_1, \tau_2, \ldots, \tau_u$) corresponding to which there exist rows in Q_0. Now, suppose further that there are two factorial effects (say, F_{α_1} and F_{α_2}), such that if we delete all rows of Q_0 except the u rows corresponding to $(\tau_1, \tau_2, \ldots, \tau_u)$, then (in the resulting u-rowed matrix) Δ_0 arises with respect to the pair $(F_{\alpha_1}, F_{\alpha_2})$. Then, we say (for the given Q_0 (with T_1 implicit in it)) that $(\tau_1, \tau_2, \ldots, \tau_u; \alpha_1, \alpha_2) \in [\Delta_0]$. Also, let v be an integer such that $1 \leq v < u$. Then, the statement "$(\tau_1, \tau_2, \ldots, \tau_u; \alpha_1, \alpha_2) \in [\Delta_0]$" will be dually written as "$(\tau_1, \tau_2, \ldots, \tau_v; \alpha_1 \alpha_2) \in [\Delta_0; \tau_{v+1}, \ldots, \tau_u]$" As an example consider the case (1.1). In this context, "$(1, 2, 24, 34, 12; 12, 13) \in [\Delta_0]$" or, equivalently "$(24, 34, 12; 12, 13) \in [\Delta_0; 1, 2]$" will both mean that if (from the Q_0 at (3.2)) we delete the rows corresponding to all the treatments outside the set $(1, 2, 24, 34, 12)$, then (for the resulting 5-rowed matrix), Δ_0 will arise for the columns corresponding to (F_{12}, F_{13}).

Similar notation is used if only one column is involved. Then, for case (1.2) (to come later), "$(14, 23, 14; 124) \in [\Delta_0; 2, 4]$" means that if we delete all rows of Q_0 (at (3.2)) except the rows corresponding to the treatments $(14, 23, 12, 2, 4)$, then the column corresponding to F_{124} will become zero for the resulting 5-rowed matrix.

Finally, the notation "$(\tau_1, \ldots, \tau_u) \in [MEP \cdot 1]$" or "$(\tau_1, \ldots, \tau_v) \in [MEP \cdot 1; \tau_{v+1}, \ldots, \tau_u]$" will mean that even if we delete all rows of Q_0 corresponding to treatments which are not in the set $(\tau_1, \tau_2, \ldots, \tau_u)$, the resulting u-rowed submatrix will have the property P_2 with respect to columns. In other words, if $T_2 = (\tau_1, \tau_2, \ldots, \tau_u)$, then the treatment set $(T_1 \cup T_2)$ will form an MEP·1 plan. Thus, for example, under case (1.1), we have "$(34, \phi, 12) \notin [MEP \cdot 1; 1, 2]$", which means that if (for the Q_0 at (3.2)) all the rows of Q_0 (except the rows corresponding to the treatments $(1, 2, 34, 12, \phi)$ are deleted, then the corresponding 5-rowed submatrix will still have property P_2. In other words, the set $T_1 \cup (1, 2, 34, 12, \phi)$ forms a MEP·1 plan.

We now proceed with the shortened presentations.

Case (1.1). We have $1, 2, 3, 123, 124, 134, 1234 \in T$. We need to choose three more treatments from $\Omega_{40} \cup \Omega_{42}$. We first note that the property L_0 arises for $(24, 34)$.

We can then check that each of the following belongs to $[\Delta_0; 1, 2]$: $(24, 34, 12; 12, 13)$, $(24, 34, 13; 12, 13)$, $(24, 34, 14; 12, 13)$, $(24, 34, 23; 23, 1234)$, $(24, 34, \phi; 23, 1234)$, $(24, 34, 12; 23, 124)$, $(24, 23, 13; 124, 1234)$, $(24, 23, 14; 23, 1234)$, $(24, \phi, 12; 134, 234)$, $(24, \phi, 14; 123, 1234)$, $(24, \phi, 23; 23, 1234)$, $(34, 23, 13; 23, 134)$, $(34, 23, 12; 134, 1234)$, $(34, 23, 14;$

$23, 1234)$, $(34, \phi, 13; 124, 234)$, $(34, \phi, 14; 123, 1234)$, and $(34, \phi, 23; 23, 1234)$. Also, both $(24, \phi, 13)$ and $(34, \phi, 12)$ belong to $[MEP \cdot 1; 1, 2]$.

This finishes the discussion of case (1.1).

Case (1.2). We have $1234, 2, 3, 4, 123, 124, 134, \in T$ We need three more treatments from $\Omega_{42} \cup \Omega_{40}$. Note that L_0 arises for $(14, 23)$. It is easily seen that each of the following belongs to $[\Delta_0; 1, 2]$: $(14, 23, 12; 124)$, $(14, 23, 13; 134)$, $(14, 23, 24; 134)$, $(14, 23, 34; 124)$, $(14, 23, \phi; 134)$, $(14, \phi, 12; 14)$, $(14, \phi, 13; 14)$, $(14, \phi, 24; 134)$, $(14, \phi, 34; 124)$, $(14, 12, 13; 234, 1234)$, $(14, 12, 24; 24, 13)$, $(14, 23, 34; 12, 34)$, $(14, 24, 34; 123, 124)$, $(14, 12, 34; 124)$, $(14, 13, 24; 134)$, $(23, \phi, 12; 124)$, $(23, \phi, 13; 134)$, $(23, \phi, 24; 134)$, $(23, \phi, 34; 124)$, $(23, 12, 13; 14, 23)$, $(23, 12, 24; 124, 1234)$, $(23, 12, 34; 124)$, $(23, 13, 24; 134)$, $(23, 13, 34; 124, 1234)$, and $(23, 24, 34; 1234)$. Thus we do not get any MEP·1 plan in this case.

Case 2. $n_3 = 3, n_1 = 2$. Let the three treatments of weight three be $123, 124$, and 134. There are two nonisomorphic cases for the treatments of weight one in T. There are **case (2.1)**, $1, 2, \in T$ and **case (2.2)** $2, 3, \in T$. We will now discuss these two cases separately. In both of the cases $1234, 123, 124, 134, 2 \in T$. Thus, we take $T_1 = \{1234, 123, 124, 134, 2\}$ and obtain

$$Q_0 = \begin{array}{c} 1 \\ 12 \\ 13 \\ 14 \\ 23 \\ 24 \\ 34 \\ \phi \\ 3 \end{array} \left(\begin{array}{ccccccccccc} 0 & 0 & 0 & 1 & 1 & 1 & 1 & 1 & 1 & 1 & 1 \\ 0 & 0 & 0 & 0 & 0 & 1 & 0 & 0 & 1 & 1 & 1 \\ 0 & 0 & 0 & 0 & 1 & 0 & 0 & 1 & 0 & 1 & 1 \\ 0 & 0 & 0 & 1 & 0 & 0 & 1 & 0 & 0 & 1 & 1 \\ 0 & -1 & 0 & 0 & 0 & -1 & -1 & 0 & 0 & -1 & 0 \\ 0 & 0 & -1 & 0 & 0 & -1 & 0 & -1 & 0 & -1 & 0 \\ 1 & -1 & -1 & 0 & 0 & -1 & 0 & 0 & -1 & -1 & 0 \\ 1 & 0 & 0 & 1 & 1 & 0 & 0 & 0 & 0 & 0 & 1 \\ 1 & -1 & 0 & 0 & 1 & -1 & 0 & 0 & 0 & 0 & 0 \end{array} \right)$$

Case 2.1. We have $1, 2, \in T$. Thus, $1234, 123, 124, 134, 1, 2 \in T$ and $234, 3, 4 \notin T$. Since $|T| = 10$, we have to choose four more treatments from $\{\phi, 12, 13, 14, 23, 24, 34\}$. Looking at (3.4), we find that if $\phi \notin T$, then $34 \in T$. (otherwise, the column corresponding to F_{12} is $\underline{0}$. Now note that $24 \in T$ (otherwise, Δ_0 arises for (F_{12}, F_{14})). Similar consideration for the columns corresponding to (F_{12}, F_{13}) gives that $23 \in T$. Thus, $23, 24, 34, 2, 1, 1234, 123, 124, 134, \in T$, and we have to choose one more treatment from $12, 13$, or 14. If we include any of the treatments from $(12, 13, 14)$ in order, then Δ_0 arises for $(24, 34), (34, 1234)$, and $(23, 1234)$ respectively. Hence, there is no MEP·1 plan of order 10.

If $\phi \in T$, then looking at the column for F_{14} in (3.4) we see that L_0 arises for $(24, 34)$. Hence (as in case (1.1)). Thus, each of the following cases belongs to $[\Delta_0; 1, \phi]$: $(24, 34, 12; 23, 34)$, $(24, 34, 13; 24, 1234)$, $(24, 34, 14; 23, 1234)$, $(24, 34, 23; 24, 1234)$, $(2, 12, 13; 12)$, $(24, 12, 14; 12)$, $(24, 12, 23; 23, 24)$, $(24, 13, 14; 13)$, $(24, 13, 23; 24, 1234)$, $(24, 14, 23; 23, 1234)$, $(34, 12, 13; 13, 14)$, $(34, 12, 14; 13, 14)$, $(34, 12, 23; 23, 24)$, $(34, 13, 14; 13, 14)$, $(34, 13, 23; 24, 1234)$, $(34, 14, 23; 23, 24)$.

Case 2.2. Let $2, 3, \in T$. Here we have $1234, 123, 124, 134, 2, 3, \in T$ and $234, 1, 4, \notin T$. Since $|T| = 10$, we have to choose four more treatments from $\{\phi, 12, 13, 14, 23, 24, 34\}$. Looking at (3.4), we find that if $\phi \notin T$, then $14 \in T$. Otherwise, the column corresponding to F_{23} is $\underline{0}$. Note that $23 \in T$ (otherwise, Δ_0 arises for (F_{12}, F_{13})). Now we have to choose two more treatments from $\{12, 13, 24, 34\}$. There are six possibilities. These are $(12, 13), (12, 24), (12, 34), (13, 24), (13, 34)$, and $(24, 34)$. For each of these possibilities, Δ_0 arises for $(14), (14, 124), (124), (134), (14, 134)$, and $(23, 134)$, respectively. Hence, no MEP·1 plan of order ten exists in this case. However, if $\phi \in T$, then we have $\phi, 1234, 123, 124, 134, 2, 3, \in T$. Since $|T| = 10$, we need three more treatments from $\{12, 13, 14, 23, 24, 34\}$. Looking at the column of F_{12} in the matrix Q_0 in (3.4), we find that L_0 arises for $(24, 34)$. Then, it can be checked that each of the following belong to $[\Delta_0; 3, \phi]$: $(24, 34, 12; 123)$, $(24, 34, 13; 123)$, $(24, 34, 14; 12, 1234)$, $(24, 34, 23; 23, 1234)$, $(24, 12, 13; 123)$, $(24, 12, 14; 12, 24)$, $(24, 12, 23; 12, 24)$, $(34, 13, 12; 123)$, $(34, 13, 14; 13, 34)$, $(34, 13, 23; 13, 34)$.

Case 3. $n_3 = 3, n_1 = 1$. Without loss of generality, assume that $123, 124$, and $134 \in T$. We have two cases: **case 3.1** $\phi \in T$ and **case 3.2** $\phi \notin T$.

Case 3.1. If $\phi \in T$, then $\phi, 1234, 123, 124, 134, \in T$. Since $|T| = 10$ and $n_1 = 1$, we need to choose four treatments from Ω_{42}. This means that we have to leave out two treatments from Ω_{42}. For the two treatments to be left out, we have four nonisomorphic choices: (i) $12, 13, \notin T$, (ii) $12, 34 \notin T$, (iii) $12, 23 \notin T$, and (iv) $23, 24, \notin T$. Taking $T_1 = \{1234, 123, 124, 134, \phi\}$, we obtain the following matrix Q_0:

$$
(3.7) \quad Q_0 = \begin{array}{c} 12 \\ 13 \\ 14 \\ 23 \\ 24 \\ 34 \\ 234 \\ 1 \\ 2 \\ 3 \\ 4 \end{array}
\left(\begin{array}{ccccccccccc}
0 & 0 & 0 & 0 & 0 & 1 & 0 & 0 & 1 & 1 & 1 \\
0 & 0 & 0 & 0 & 1 & 0 & 0 & 1 & 0 & 1 & 1 \\
0 & 0 & 0 & 1 & 0 & 0 & 1 & 0 & 0 & 1 & 1 \\
-1 & -1 & 0 & -1 & -1 & -1 & -1 & 0 & 0 & -1 & -1 \\
-1 & 0 & -1 & -1 & -1 & -1 & 0 & -1 & 0 & -1 & -1 \\
0 & -1 & -1 & -1 & -1 & -1 & 0 & 0 & -1 & -1 & -1 \\
-1 & -1 & -1 & -1 & -1 & -1 & -1 & -1 & -1 & -1 & -2 \\
0 & 0 & 0 & 1 & 1 & 1 & 1 & 1 & 1 & 1 & 1 \\
-1 & 0 & 0 & -1 & -1 & 0 & 0 & 0 & 0 & 0 & -1 \\
0 & -1 & 0 & -1 & 0 & -1 & 0 & 0 & 0 & 0 & -1 \\
0 & 0 & -1 & 0 & -1 & -1 & 0 & 0 & 0 & 0 & -1
\end{array}\right) .
$$

We have to choose one treatment of weight one. In case (i), if we include any treatment from $\{1, 2, 3, 4\}$ (in order), then Δ_0 arises for $(23, 234)$, $(23, 1234)$, $(23, 1234)$, and $(23, 234)$, respectively. In case (ii), Δ_0 arises for $(234, 1234), (134), (134)$, and (134), respectively. In case (iii), Δ_0 arises for $(13, 14), (13, 14)$, and (12), respectively. But, case (iv) gives a MEP·1 plan if $3 \in T$. For the other choices, Δ_0 arises for $(234, 1234), (234, \dot{1}234)$, and $(13, 134)$, respectively. Thus we have that

$$(3.8) \qquad T = \{1234, 123, 124, 134, \phi, 13, 14, 24, 34, 3\}$$

is a MEP·1 plan.

Case 3.2 $\phi \notin T$. Then $|T| = 10$ and $n_1 = 1$, $n_3 = 3$ implies that T has five treatments of weight two. Thus, we leave out only one treatment of weight two. For this left-out treatment we have two choices (nonisomorhic). These are (i) $12 \notin T$ and (ii) $23 \notin T$. In both of the cases, $34 \in T$ and we take $T_1 = \{1234, 123, 124, 134, 34\}$. We obtain the following matrix Q_0:

$$
(3.9) \qquad Q_0 = \begin{array}{c} 13 \\ 14 \\ 23 \\ 24 \\ 1 \\ 2 \\ 3 \\ 4 \\ 12 \end{array} \left(\begin{array}{ccccccccccc}
0 & 0 & 0 & 0 & 1 & 0 & 0 & 1 & 0 & 1 & 1 \\
0 & 0 & 0 & 1 & 0 & 0 & 1 & 0 & 0 & 1 & 1 \\
-1 & 0 & 1 & 0 & 0 & 0 & -1 & 0 & 1 & 0 & 0 \\
-1 & 1 & 0 & 0 & 0 & 0 & 0 & -1 & 1 & 0 & 0 \\
0 & 0 & 0 & 1 & 1 & 1 & 1 & 1 & 1 & 1 & 1 \\
-1 & 1 & 1 & 0 & 0 & 1 & 0 & 0 & 1 & 1 & 0 \\
0 & 0 & 1 & 0 & 1 & 0 & 0 & 0 & 1 & 1 & 0 \\
0 & 1 & 0 & 1 & 0 & 0 & 0 & 0 & 1 & 1 & 0 \\
0 & 0 & 0 & 0 & 0 & 1 & 0 & 0 & 1 & 1 & 1
\end{array}\right).
$$

We still have to choose one treatment from $\{1234\}$. We note that for case (i), if we choose any treatment from $\{1, 2, 3, 4\}$ (in order), then Δ_0 arises for $(234, 1234)$, $(123, 134)$, (34), and (34), respectively. For case (ii), this happens for $(14), (12, 13), (12, 13)$, and (14), respectively. Hence, we don't get any MEP·1 plan with 10 treatments in this case.

Case 4. $n_3 = 3, n_1 = 0$. Assume that $123, 124, 134 \in T$. Then $|T| = 10$ gives $T \subseteq \{1234, 123, 124, 134, \Omega_{42}, \phi\}$. If $\phi \notin T$, then we get $T = \{1234, 123, 124, 134, \Omega_{42}$. We can use the same Q_0 as in (3.9). Now we see that Δ_0 arises for $(234, 1234)$. If $\phi \in T$, then we use Q_0 from (3.7). We now see that the columns of F_{234} and F_{1234} are always identical. Hence, P_2 can never hold for any five treatments from Ω_{42}. Thus, there is no MEP·1 plan of order 10 in this case.

Case 5. $n_3 = 2, n_1 = 3$. Without loss of generality, let the two treatments of weight three be 123, and 124. We have two case: **case 5.1** $\phi \notin T$ and **case 5.2** $\phi \in T$. We will discuss these separately.

Case 5.1. Let $\phi \notin T$. Then $n_1 = 3$ means that there are two nonisomorphic choices for the treatments of weight one. These are (i) $1, 2, 3, \in T$ and (ii) $1, 3, 4, \in T$. For (i) we have $1234, 123, 124, 1, 2, 3, \in T$. Thus, we take $T_1 = \{1234, 123, 124, 1, 2\}$ and obtain the following matrix Q_0:

$$
(3.10) \qquad Q_0 = \begin{array}{c} 3 \\ 24 \\ 34 \\ 12 \\ 13 \\ 14 \\ 23 \end{array} \left(\begin{array}{ccccccccccc}
1 & 1 & 0 & 1 & 0 & 2 & 1 & 1 & 1 & 1 & 1 \\
0 & 0 & 1 & 0 & 0 & 1 & 0 & 1 & 0 & 1 & 0 \\
1 & 1 & 1 & 1 & 1 & 2 & 1 & 1 & 2 & 2 & 1 \\
0 & 0 & 0 & 0 & 0 & -1 & 0 & 0 & -1 & -1 & -1 \\
0 & 0 & 0 & 1 & 0 & 1 & 1 & 0 & 1 & 0 & 0 \\
0 & 0 & 0 & 0 & 1 & 1 & 0 & 1 & 1 & 0 & 0 \\
0 & 1 & 0 & 0 & 0 & 1 & 1 & 0 & 0 & 1 & 0
\end{array}\right)
$$

Looking at the matrix Q_0, we find that both 24 and 34 can't be left out from T (otherwise, Δ_0 will arise for (14)). Thus, at least one of 24 and 34 must be in T. If both 24 and $34 \in T$, then we note that $23 \in T$ (otherwise, Δ_0 arises for (12, 13)). Similarly $13 \in T$. Since $|T| = 10$, we must have $T = T_1 \cup \{12, 34, 23, 13, 3\}$. Now Δ_0 arises for $(123, 1234)$. Thus, P_2 does not hold in this case.

Now let us assume that $24 \in T$ and $34 \notin T$. The considerations similar to above yield $T = T_1 \cup \{34, 23, 3, 13, 14\}$ and in this case Δ_0 arises for $(12, 1234)$.

Now suppose that we have choice (ii) (i.e., $1, 3, 4, \in T$). Take $T_1 = \{1234, 123, 124, 1, 3\}$. We obtain the following matrix Q_0:

$$
(3.11) \qquad Q_0 = \begin{array}{c} 4 \\ 34 \\ 24 \\ 23 \\ 12 \\ 13 \\ 14 \end{array}
\left(
\begin{array}{rrrrrrrrrrr}
0 & 1 & -1 & 1 & -1 & 0 & 0 & 0 & 0 & 0 & 0 \\
0 & 0 & -1 & 0 & -1 & 0 & 0 & 0 & -1 & -1 & 0 \\
-1 & 1 & -1 & 1 & 0 & 1 & 1 & 0 & 1 & 0 & 1 \\
-1 & 0 & 0 & 1 & 0 & 1 & 0 & 1 & 1 & 0 & 1 \\
0 & 0 & 0 & 0 & 0 & 1 & 0 & 0 & 1 & 1 & 1 \\
0 & 0 & 0 & -1 & 0 & -1 & -1 & 0 & -1 & 0 & 0 \\
0 & 0 & 0 & 0 & -1 & -1 & 0 & -1 & -1 & 0 & -1
\end{array}
\right).
$$

Looking at the column for F_{14} in Q_0 at (3.11) we find that the property L_0 arises for $(23, 24)$. In this case, the following belong to $[\Delta_0; 4, 34]$: $(23, 24, 12; 34, 1234)$, $(23, 24, 13; 12, 1234)$, $(23, 24, 14; 34, 1234)$, $(24, 12, 13; 124)$, $(24, 12, 14; 34, 1234)$, $(23, 12, 13; 12, 123)$, $(23, 12, 14; , 34, 1234)$, $(23, 13, 14; 124, 1234)$, and $(24, 13, 14) \in$ [MEP·1; 4].

Case 5.2. $\phi \in T$. In this case we have $\phi, 1234, 124 \in T$, and $n_1 = 3$. As in case 5.1, three are two nonisomorphic choices for these three treatments of weight one. These are case (i) $1, 2, 3$, and case (ii) $1, 3, 4$. We take $T_1 = \{\phi, 1234, 123, 124, 1\}$. This T_1 works for both of the cases. This gives us the following matrix Q_0:

$$
Q_0 = \begin{array}{c} 12 \\ 13 \\ 14 \\ 23 \\ 24 \\ 34 \\ 2 \\ 3 \\ 4 \end{array}
\left(
\begin{array}{rrrrrrrrrrr}
0 & 0 & 0 & 0 & 0 & -1 & 0 & 0 & -1 & -1 & -1 \\
0 & 0 & 0 & 1 & 0 & 1 & 1 & 0 & 1 & 0 & 0 \\
0 & 0 & 0 & 0 & 1 & 1 & 0 & 1 & 1 & 0 & 0 \\
1 & 1 & 0 & 0 & 0 & 0 & 0 & -1 & -1 & 0 & 0 \\
1 & 0 & 1 & 0 & 0 & 0 & -1 & 0 & -1 & 0 & 0 \\
0 & 1 & 1 & 1 & 1 & 1 & 0 & 0 & 1 & 1 & 1 \\
1 & 0 & 0 & 0 & 0 & -1 & -1 & -1 & -1 & -1 & 0 \\
0 & 1 & 0 & 1 & 0 & 1 & 0 & 0 & 0 & 0 & 1 \\
0 & 0 & 1 & 0 & 1 & 1 & 0 & 0 & 0 & 0 & 1
\end{array}
\right).
$$

Suppose that we have case (i), then $1, 2, 3, 1234, \phi, 123, 124, \in T$. Now looking at the column for F_{23} in the matrix Q_0, we find that the property L_0 arises for $(24, 34)$. Thus, the following belong to $[\Delta_0, 2, 3]$: $(24, 34, 12; 13, 23)$, $(24, 34, 13; 13, 1234)$, $(24, 34, 14; 13, 23)$, $(24, 34, 23; 23, 1234)$, $(24, 32, 13; 24)$, $(24, 12, 14; 13, 23)$, $(24, 12, 23; , 24)$, $(24, 13, 14; 13, 1234)$, $(24, 13, 23; 24)$, $(24, 14, 23; 23, 1234)$, $(34, 12, 13; 2, 124)$, $(34, 12, 14; 12, 123)$, $(34, 12, 23; 14, 24)$, $(34, 13, 14; 13, 1234)$, $(34, 13, 23; 14, 24)$, $(34, 14, 23; 23, 1234)$. Now suppose that case (ii) arises, i.e. $1, 3, 4, \in T$. In this case (by considering the column for F_{12}) we see that the property L_0 arises for $(23, 24)$. This leads to the following member of $[\Delta_0; \quad]$: $(23, 24, 12; 34, 1234)$, $(23, 24, 13; 234)$, $(23, 24, 14; 234)$, $(23, 24, 34; 34, 1234)$, $(24, 12, 13; 1247)$, $(24, 12, 14; 13, 23)$, $(24, 12, 34; 124)$, $(24, 13, 14; 234)$, $(24, 13, 34; 134)$, $(24, 14, 34; 12, 123)$, $(23, 12, 13; 14, 24)$, $(23, 12, 14; 123)$, $(23, 12, 34; 123)$, $(23, 13, 14; 234)$, $(23, 13, 34; 14, 34)$, $(23, 14, 34; 123)$. Thus in this case no MEP·1 plan arises.

352

Case 6. $n_3 = 2, n_1 = 2$. As in case 5, let $123, 124 \in T$. If $\phi \notin T$, then $|T| = 10$ means that there are five treatments of weight two in T. Since there are two treatments of weight one in T, for those we have the following nonisomorphic choices:

$$(3.12) \qquad \text{case } (i) \quad 1, 2, \in T, \text{ case } (ii) \quad 1, 3, \in T, \text{ case } (iii) \quad 3, 4, \in T$$

If case (i) happens, then we have $123, 124, 1234, 1, 2, \in T$ and $\phi, 3, 4, 134, 234, \notin T$. We need to choose five treatments from Ω_{42}. Taking $T_1 = \{123, 124, 1234, 1, 2\}$, we get the following matrix Q_0:

$$(3.13) \qquad Q_0 = \begin{array}{c} 12 \\ 13 \\ 14 \\ 23 \\ 24 \\ 34 \end{array} \begin{pmatrix} 0 & 0 & 0 & 0 & 0 & -1 & 0 & 0 & 1 & -1 & 1 \\ 0 & 0 & 0 & 1 & 0 & 1 & 1 & 0 & 1 & 0 & 0 \\ 0 & 0 & 0 & 0 & 1 & 1 & 0 & 1 & 1 & 0 & 0 \\ 0 & 1 & 0 & 0 & 0 & 1 & 1 & 0 & 0 & 1 & 0 \\ 0 & 0 & 1 & 0 & 0 & 1 & 0 & 1 & 0 & 1 & 0 \\ 1 & 1 & 1 & 1 & 1 & 2 & 1 & 1 & 2 & 2 & -1 \end{pmatrix}.$$

If we drop any treatment from $\{12, 13, 14, 23, 24, 34\}$ (in order), we will have Δ_0 for $(12, 1234), (12, 23), (12, 24), (12, 13), (12, 14)$, and (12), respectively. Hence, P_2 does not hold.

Case (ii). If $1, 3 \in T$, then we take $T_1 = \{1234, 123, 124, 1, 3\}$ and obtain

$$(3.14) \qquad Q_0 = \begin{array}{c} 12 \\ 13 \\ 14 \\ 23 \\ 24 \\ 34 \end{array} \begin{pmatrix} 0 & 0 & 0 & 0 & 0 & 1 & 0 & 0 & 1 & 1 & 1 \\ 0 & 0 & 0 & -1 & 0 & -1 & -1 & 0 & -1 & 0 & 0 \\ 0 & 0 & 0 & 0 & -1 & -1 & 0 & -1 & -1 & 0 & 0 \\ -1 & 0 & 0 & 1 & 0 & 1 & 0 & 1 & 1 & 0 & 1 \\ -1 & 1 & -1 & 1 & 0 & 1 & 1 & 0 & 1 & 0 & 1 \\ 0 & 0 & -1 & 0 & -1 & 0 & 0 & 0 & -1 & -1 & 0 \end{pmatrix}.$$

Dropping any one from $\{12, 13, 23, 24, 34\}$ (in order), will give rise to Δ_0 for $(12, 1234)$, $(12, 23), (12, 13), (13)$, and $(13, 14)$, respectively. If we drop 14, we get a MEP·1 plan with ten treatments. Thus,

$$(3.15) \qquad T = \{1234, 123, 124, 3, 12, 13, 23, 24, 34\}$$

is a MEP·1 plan.

Case (iii). If $3, 4 \in T$, then $1234, 123, 124, 3, 4, \in T$. We can't take $T_1 = \{1234, 123, 124, 3, 4\}$, since this gives rise to a singular A_{11} (i.e., T_1 is not a resolution III plan). Hence, we need to discuss this case a little more. Since we know that $|T| = 10$, there are five treatments of weight two in T. In other words we need to leave out one treatment of weight two. There are four nonisomorphic choices for the treatment to be left out. These are (i) 12, (ii) 13, (iii) 23, and (iv) 34. This gives the following nonisomorphic sets of five treatments to be included: (i) $(13, 14, 23, 24, 34)$, (ii) $(12, 14, 23, 24, 34)$, (iii) $(12, 13, 14, 34, 24)$, and (iv) $(12, 13, 14, 23, 24)$. In each of these nonisomorphic choices, we have $14 \in T$. Thus, we take $T_1 = \{1234, 123, 124, 3, 14\}$, and obtain the following matrix Q_0:

353

$$
(3.16) \qquad Q_0 = \begin{array}{c} 4 \\ 12 \\ 13 \\ 23 \\ 24 \\ 34 \end{array}\left(\begin{array}{ccccccccccc} 0 & -1 & 1 & -1 & 1 & 0 & 0 & 0 & 0 & 0 & 0 \\ 0 & 0 & 0 & 0 & 0 & -1 & 0 & 0 & -1 & -1 & -1 \\ 0 & 0 & 0 & 1 & -1 & 0 & 1 & -1 & 0 & 0 & 0 \\ 1 & 0 & 0 & -1 & 1 & 0 & 0 & 0 & 0 & 0 & -1 \\ 1 & -1 & 1 & -1 & 1 & 0 & -1 & 1 & 0 & 0 & -1 \\ 0 & 0 & 1 & 0 & 1 & 0 & 0 & 0 & 1 & 1 & 0 \end{array}\right).
$$

Since the column corresponding to F_{134} is identical to that of F_{234}, P_2 does not hold for any set of four treatments from Ω_{42}. Thus, in this case, there is no MEP·1 plan with 10 treatments. Recall that all of this was under the case that $\phi \notin T$.

Now suppose that $\phi \in T$. We have the same three nonisomorphic choices for the treatments of weight one as in (3.12).

Case (i): Let $1, 2 \notin T$. Then $\phi, 123, 124, 1, 2 \in T$ and $134, 234, 3, 4, \notin T$. Take $T_1 = \{1234, \phi, 123, 124, 1\}$. We obtain the following matrix Q_0:

$$
(3.17) \qquad Q_0 = \begin{array}{c} 2 \\ 12 \\ 13 \\ 14 \\ 23 \\ 24 \\ 34 \end{array}\left(\begin{array}{ccccccccccc} 1 & 0 & 0 & 0 & 0 & -1 & -1 & -1 & -1 & -1 & 0 \\ 0 & 0 & 0 & 0 & 0 & -1 & 0 & 0 & -1 & -1 & -1 \\ 0 & 0 & 0 & 1 & 0 & 1 & 1 & 0 & 1 & 0 & 0 \\ 0 & 0 & 0 & 0 & 1 & 1 & 0 & 1 & 1 & 0 & 0 \\ 1 & 1 & 0 & 0 & 0 & 0 & 0 & -1 & -1 & 0 & 0 \\ 1 & 0 & 1 & 0 & 0 & 0 & -1 & 0 & -1 & 0 & 0 \\ 0 & 1 & 1 & 1 & 1 & 1 & 0 & 0 & 1 & 1 & 1 \end{array}\right).
$$

Since $|T| = 10 (\phi, 123, 124, 1, 2, \in T$ and $124, 234, 3, 4, \notin T)$, we need to choose four treatments from Ω_{42}. In other words we leave out two treatments from Ω_{42}. There are fifteen possibilities for the two treatments to be dropped out from Ω_{42}. These are: $(12, 13), (12, 14), (12, 23), (12, 24), (12, 34), (13, 34), (13, 23), (13, 24), (13, 34), (14, 23), (14, 24), (14, 34), (23, 24), (23, 34),$ and $(24, 34)$. Correspondingly, Δ_0 arises for $(23, 1234), (24, 1234), (13, 34), (14, 1234), (1234), (23, 24), (13, 23), (23), (14, 23), (13, 24), (14, 24), (24), (13, 14), (13),$ and (14) respectively. Hence, P_2 does not hold in this case.

Case ii. Let $i, 3, \in T$. The matrix Q_0 is the same as in (3.17), and the discussion is also similar to above.

Case iii. Let $3, 4, \in T$. Now $\phi, 1234, 123, 124, 3, 4, \in T$ and $134, 234, 1, 2 \notin T$. Since $|T| = 10$, there are four treatments of weight two in T. Thus, two treatments from Ω_{42} need to be dropped. The following are the nonisomorphic choices for the two treatments of weight two to be dropped: (i) $12, 13$; (ii) $12, 34$; (iii) $13, 14$; (iv) $13, 23$; (v) $13, 24$; and (vi) $13, 34$. This gives the following choices for the treatments of weight two to be included: (i) $14, 23, 24, 23$; (ii) $13, 14, 23, 24$; (iii) $12, 23, 24, 34$; (iv) $12, 14, 24, 34$; (v) $12, 14, 23, 34$; and (vi) $12, 14, 23, 24$. For the choices (i), (ii), (iv) and (v), let $T_1 = \{\phi, 1234, 123, 124, 14\}$. We obtain the following matrix Q_0:

$$(3.18) \qquad Q_0 = \begin{array}{c} 3 \\ 4 \\ 12 \\ 13 \\ 23 \\ 34 \\ 34 \end{array} \left(\begin{array}{ccccccccccc} 0 & 1 & 0 & 1 & 0 & 1 & 0 & 0 & 0 & 0 & 1 \\ 0 & 0 & 1 & 0 & 1 & 1 & 0 & 0 & 0 & 0 & 1 \\ 0 & 0 & 0 & 0 & 0 & -1 & 0 & 0 & -1 & -1 & -1 \\ 0 & 0 & 0 & 1 & 0 & 0 & 1 & -1 & 0 & 0 & 0 \\ 1 & 1 & 0 & 0 & 1 & 1 & 0 & 0 & 0 & 0 & 0 \\ 1 & 0 & 1 & 0 & 1 & 1 & -1 & 1 & 0 & 0 & 0 \\ 0 & 1 & 1 & 1 & 1 & 1 & 0 & 0 & 1 & 1 & 1 \end{array} \right).$$

Since Δ_0 arises for $(134, 234)$, P_2 does not hold for any of the choices (i), (ii), (iv), and (v). For the choices (iii) and (vi), take $T_1 = \{\phi, 1234, 123, 124, 23\}$. We obtain the following matrix Q_0:

$$(3.19) \qquad Q_0 = \begin{array}{c} 3 \\ 4 \\ 12 \\ 13 \\ 14 \\ 24 \\ 34 \end{array} \left(\begin{array}{ccccccccccc} 0 & -1 & 0 & -1 & 0 & -1 & 0 & 0 & 0 & 0 & -1 \\ 0 & 0 & -1 & 0 & -1 & -1 & 0 & 0 & 0 & 0 & -1 \\ 0 & 0 & 0 & -1 & 0 & -1 & -1 & 1 & 1 & 1 & 1 \\ -1 & -1 & 0 & -1 & 0 & -1 & -1 & 1 & 0 & 0 & 0 \\ -1 & -1 & 0 & 0 & -1 & -1 & 0 & 0 & 0 & 0 & 0 \\ 0 & 1 & -1 & 0 & 0 & 0 & 1 & -1 & 0 & 0 & 0 \\ 0 & -1 & -1 & -1 & -1 & -1 & 0 & 0 & -1 & -1 & -1 \end{array} \right).$$

Since Δ_0 arises for $(134, 234)$, P_2 does not hold. Consequently, there is no MEP·1 plan of order ten for this case. Now we got to case 7.

Case 7. $n_3 = 2$, $n_1 = 1$. Without loss of generality we can assume that $1234, 123, 124 \in T$. If $\phi \notin T$, then $|T| = 10$ gives that $\Omega_{42} \subseteq T$. Let $T_1 = \{1234, 123, 124, 13, 24\}$. This gives us the following matrix Q_0:

$$(3.20) \qquad Q_0 = \begin{array}{c} 12 \\ 14 \\ 23 \\ 34 \\ 1 \\ 2 \\ 3 \\ 4 \end{array} \left(\begin{array}{ccccccccccc} 0 & 0 & 0 & 0 & 0 & 1 & 0 & 0 & 1 & 1 & 1 \\ 0 & 0 & 0 & 1 & -1 & 0 & 1 & -1 & 0 & 0 & 0 \\ 0 & -1 & 1 & 0 & 0 & 0 & -1 & 1 & 0 & 0 & 0 \\ 1 & -1 & 0 & 0 & -1 & 0 & 0 & 0 & -1 & -1 & -1 \\ 0 & 0 & 0 & 1 & 0 & 1 & 1 & 0 & 1 & 0 & 0 \\ 0 & 0 & 1 & 0 & 0 & 1 & 0 & 1 & 0 & 1 & 0 \\ 1 & -1 & 1 & 0 & 0 & 0 & 0 & 0 & 0 & 0 & -1 \\ 1 & 0 & 0 & 1 & -1 & 0 & 0 & 0 & 0 & 0 & -1 \end{array} \right).$$

Note that $12, 14, 23, 34 \in T$ and we need one treatment of weight one in T. If we include any treatment form $\{1, 2, 3, 4\}$ (in order), the Δ_0 arises for $(234, 1234), (234, 1234)$, and $(134, 234)$, respectively. Hence no treatment of weight one can be included in T for T to be a MEP·1 plan with ten treatments.

Now let $\phi \notin T$. Here we have $\phi, 1234, 123, 124 \in T$ and $134, 234 \notin T$. Since $|T| = 10$ and $n_1 = 1$, there are five treatments of weight two in T. We have one of the following two possibilities: (i) $23 \in T$, or (ii) $23 \notin T$.

If $23 \in T$, then we get the same situation as (3.19), and if $23 \notin T$, then $14 \in T$ (since T has five treatments of weight two). This corresponds to (3.18). In both of the situations, we saw that no MEP·1 plan with ten treatments exists. This finishes case 7.

Case 8. $n_3 = 2, n_1 = 0$. We assume that $123, 124 \in T$. Since $|T| = 10$, there is only one choice for T, and this choice is $T = \{1234, 123, 124, \phi, \Omega_{42}$. Taking $T_1 = \{1234, 123, 124, 123, \phi, 23\}$, we get the same matrix as in (3.19). Hence, no MEP·1 plan with ten treatments exists.

Case 9. $n_3 = 1, n_1 = 3$. Without loss of generality, we will assume that the treatment of weight three is 123. We will discuss the following two nonisomorphic choices for the treatments of weight one in T:

$$(3.21) \qquad (i) \quad 1, 2, 3, \in T, (ii) \quad 2, 3, 4, \in T.$$

If (i) happens, then $1234, 123, 1, 2, 3, \in T$ and $134, 124, 234, 4, \notin T$. Since $|T| = 10$, T has five treatments from $\Omega_{42} \cup \Omega_{40}$. If we take $T_1 = \{1234, 123, 1, 2, 3\}$, we obtain the following matrix Q_0:

$$(3.22) \qquad Q_0 = \begin{array}{c} 12 \\ 13 \\ 14 \\ 23 \\ 24 \\ 34 \\ \phi \end{array} \begin{pmatrix} 1 & 1 & 0 & 1 & 0 & 0 & 1 & 1 & -1 & -1 & 1 \\ 1 & -1 & 0 & 1 & 0 & 0 & 1 & -1 & 1 & -1 & 1 \\ 0 & 0 & 0 & 0 & 1 & 1 & 0 & 2 & 2 & 0 & 0 \\ 1 & 1 & 0 & -1 & 0 & 0 & 1 & -1 & -1 & 1 & 1 \\ 0 & 0 & 1 & 0 & 0 & 1 & 0 & 2 & 0 & 2 & 0 \\ 0 & 0 & 1 & 0 & 1 & 0 & 0 & 0 & 2 & 2 & 0 \\ 1 & -1 & 0 & -1 & 0 & 0 & 1 & 1 & 1 & 1 & 1 \end{pmatrix}.$$

Since the columns corresponding to F_{123} and F_{1234} are identical, no choice of five treatments from $\Omega_{42} \cup \Omega_{40}$ will give rise to MEP·1 plan with ten treatments.

If (ii) happens (i.e., $2, 3, 4, \in T$), then we take $T_1 = \{1234, 123, 2, 3, 4\}$. We obtain the following matrix Q_0:

$$(3.23) \qquad Q_0 = \begin{array}{c} 12 \\ 13 \\ 14 \\ 23 \\ 24 \\ 34 \\ \phi \end{array} \begin{pmatrix} 0 & 1 & -1 & 1 & -1 & -1 & 0 & 0 & -1 & -1 & -1 \\ 1 & 0 & -1 & 1 & -1 & -1 & 0 & -1 & 0 & -1 & -1 \\ 1 & 1 & -2 & 1 & -1 & -1 & -1 & 0 & 0 & 1 & 1 \\ 0 & 0 & 1 & -1 & 1 & 1 & 1 & 0 & 0 & 1 & 0 \\ 0 & 0 & 1 & 0 & 0 & 1 & 0 & 1 & 0 & 1 & 0 \\ 0 & 0 & 1 & 0 & 1 & 0 & 0 & 0 & 1 & 1 & 0 \\ 0 & 0 & -1 & 0 & -1 & -1 & 0 & 0 & 0 & 0 & -1 \end{pmatrix}.$$

If $\phi \notin T$, then $|T| = 10$ implies that T has five treatments of weight two from Ω_{42}. If we drop any treatment from $\{12, 13, 14, 23, 24, 34\}$ (in order), then Δ_0 arises for $(12, 1234)$, $(13, 1234)$, $(14, 234)$, $(23, 234)$, $(24, 234)$, and $(34, 234)$, respectively. If $\phi \in T$, then we need four treatments from Ω_{42}. In other words we need to drop two treatments from Ω_{42}. For the treatments to be dropped from Ω_{42}, the following are the nonisomorphic choices: (i) $(12, 13)$, (ii) $(12, 14)$, (iii) $(12, 23)$, (iv) $(14, 23)$, (v) $(14, 24)$, (vi) $(23, 24)$, (vii) $(24, 34)$, and (vii) $(12, 24)$. For the choices (i)–(vii), we see that Δ_0 arises for $(12, 13)$, (13), $(12, 23)$, (123), $(12, 24)$, $(34, 1234)$, and $(24, 34)$, respectively. In choice (viii) we get a MEP· 1 plan with ten treatments. This design is

(3.24) $$T = \{1234, 123, 2, 3, 4, 13, 14, 23, 34, \phi\}.$$

This finishes case 9.

Case 10. $n_3 = 1$, $n_1 = 2$. Let the treatment of weight one be 123. There are two nonisomorphic choices for the treatments of weight one in T. There are

(3.25) $$\text{case } (i) \quad 1, 2, \in T, \quad \text{case } (ii) \quad 1, 4, \in T.$$

First, let $\phi \notin T$. Since $|T| = 10$ and $(n_1, n_3) = (2, 1)$ we have $\Omega_{42} \subseteq T$ (for both of the cases in (3.24)). Let $T_1 = \{1234, 123, 1, 23, 34\}$. This T_1 will work for both of the cases in (3.25). This gives us the following matrix Q_0:

$$Q_0 = \begin{array}{c} 12 \\ 13 \\ 14 \\ 24 \\ 2 \\ 4 \end{array} \left(\begin{array}{ccccccccccc} 1 & 0 & 1 & 1 & 1 & 0 & 0 & 1 & 1 & 0 & 0 \\ 1 & 0 & -1 & 0 & -1 & 0 & 1 & -1 & -1 & -1 & -1 \\ 0 & 0 & 0 & 0 & 1 & 1 & 0 & 1 & 1 & 0 & 0 \\ 1 & 1 & 2 & 1 & 1 & 1 & -1 & 2 & 2 & 1 & 1 \\ 1 & 1 & 1 & 1 & 1 & 0 & -1 & 1 & 2 & 0 & 1 \\ 1 & 1 & 1 & 0 & 1 & 1 & 0 & 1 & 1 & 0 & 1 \end{array} \right).$$

If we are in case (i), then Δ_0 arises for $(123, 1234)$. If we have case (ii), then Δ_0 arises for $(123, 234)$. Thus there is no MEP·1 design in this case.

Suppose that $\phi \notin T$. Since $n_1 = 2$, $n_3 = 1$, and $|T| = 10$, we must have five treatments of weight two in T. The following two cases may arise:

(3.26) $$\text{case } (10.1).24 \in T; \quad \text{case } (10.2).24 \notin T.$$

Case 10.1. Let $24 \in T$. Thus, we have $\phi, 24, 1234, 123, 1 \in T$ for both of the cases (i) and (ii) in (3.25). If we take $T_1 = \{\phi, 1, 1234, 123, 24\}$, this T_1 will work for both of the cases in (3.25). This gives us the following matrix Q_0:

(3.27) $$Q_0 = \begin{array}{c} 12 \\ 13 \\ 14 \\ 23 \\ 34 \\ 2 \\ 4 \end{array} \left(\begin{array}{ccccccccccc} -1 & 0 & -1 & 0 & 0 & -1 & 1 & 0 & 0 & -1 & -1 \\ 1 & 0 & 1 & 1 & 0 & 1 & 0 & 0 & 0 & 0 & 0 \\ 0 & 0 & 0 & 0 & 1 & 1 & 0 & 1 & 1 & 0 & 0 \\ 1 & 1 & 0 & 0 & 0 & 0 & 0 & -1 & -1 & 0 & 0 \\ 1 & 1 & 2 & 1 & 1 & 1 & -1 & 0 & 0 & 1 & 1 \\ 0 & 0 & -1 & 0 & 0 & -1 & 0 & -1 & 0 & -1 & 0 \\ 0 & 0 & 1 & 0 & 1 & 1 & 0 & 0 & 0 & 0 & 1 \end{array} \right).$$

If we are in case (i), i.e., $1, 2 \in T$, then Δ_0 arises for $(123, 1234)$. For case (ii), Δ_0 arises for $(123, 234)$. Thus, there is no MEP·1 plan with ten treatments in this case.

Case 10.2. Let $24 \notin T$. Since T contains five treatments of weight two, $34 \in T$. Let $T_1 = P\{\phi, 34, 1234, 123, 1\}$. This T_1 also works for both of the cases in (3.25). This gives us the following matrix Q_0:

357

$$
(3.28) \quad Q_0 = \begin{array}{c} 12 \\ 13 \\ 14 \\ 23 \\ 24 \\ 2 \\ 4 \end{array} \left(\begin{array}{ccccccccccc} 0 & -1 & -1 & -1 & -1 & 0 & 0 & 0 & 0 & 0 & 0 \\ 0 & 1 & 1 & 0 & 1 & 0 & -1 & 0 & 0 & 1 & 1 \\ 0 & 0 & 0 & 0 & -1 & -1 & 0 & -1 & -1 & 0 & 0 \\ -1 & -1 & 0 & 0 & 0 & 0 & 0 & 1 & 1 & 0 & 0 \\ -1 & -1 & -2 & -1 & -1 & -1 & 1 & 0 & 0 & -1 & -1 \\ -1 & -1 & -1 & -1 & -1 & 0 & 1 & 1 & 0 & 0 & -1 \\ 0 & 0 & -1 & 0 & -1 & -1 & 0 & 0 & 0 & 0 & -1 \end{array} \right).
$$

If we have case (i), i.e., $1, 2 \in T$, then Δ_0 arises for $(123, 1234)$, and for case (ii), Δ_0 arises for $(123, 234)$. Thus, in this case, P_2 does not hold for any plan with ten treatments. This finishes case 10.

Case 11. $n_1 = 1$, $n_3 = 1$. Since $|T| = 10$, we must have $\Omega_{42} \cup \Omega_{40} \subseteq T$. Taking $T_1 = \{1234, 12, 13, 14, 23\}$, we get the following matrix Q_0:

$$
(3.29) \quad Q_0 = \begin{array}{c} 24 \\ 34 \\ \phi \\ 1 \\ 123 \\ 234 \end{array} \left(\begin{array}{ccccccccccc} 0 & 1 & 1 & 2 & 2 & 0 & 0 & 0 & 0 & 0 & 0 \\ 1 & 0 & 1 & 2 & 0 & 2 & 0 & 0 & 0 & 0 & 0 \\ 1 & 1 & 0 & 0 & 2 & 3 & 0 & 0 & 0 & 0 & 0 \\ 0 & 0 & 0 & -1 & 1 & 1 & 1 & -1 & -1 & 1 & 1 \\ 0 & 0 & 0 & -1 & 1 & -1 & 1 & 1 & 1 & 1 & 1 \\ 0 & 0 & 1 & 1 & 1 & 1 & -1 & 1 & 1 & -1 & 1 \end{array} \right).
$$

Let the treatment of weight one be 1. There are two possibilities for the treatment of weight three. These are 234, and 123. In these cases, Δ_0 arises for $(123, 124)$ and $(134, 234)$, respectively. This finishes case 11.

Case 12. $n_1 = 0$, $n_3 = 1$. In this case $|T| = 10$ is not possible.

Case 13. $n_1 = 3$, $n_3 = 0$. Let the treatments of weight one be $1, 2$, and 3. If $\phi \notin T$, then we must have $T = \{1234, 1, 2, 3, \Omega_{42}\}$. Using the same Q_0 as in (3.29), we see that Δ_0 arises for $(123, 1234)$. Hence, P_2 does not hold for this T.

If $\phi \in T$, then we take $T_1 = \{1234, \phi, 1, 2, 3, \}$. This gives the following matrix Q_0:

$$
Q_0 = \begin{array}{c} 12 \\ 13 \\ 14 \\ 23 \\ 24 \\ 34 \end{array} \left(\begin{array}{ccccccccccc} -1 & 0 & 0 & 0 & 0 & 0 & 1 & 1 & 0 & 0 & -1 \\ 0 & -1 & 0 & 0 & 0 & 0 & 1 & 0 & 1 & 0 & -1 \\ 1 & 1 & 0 & 1 & 1 & 1 & -1 & 0 & 0 & -1 & 1 \\ 0 & 0 & 0 & -1 & 0 & 0 & 1 & 0 & 0 & 1 & -1 \\ 1 & 1 & 1 & 1 & 0 & 1 & -1 & 0 & -1 & 0 & 1 \\ 1 & 1 & 1 & 1 & 1 & 0 & -1 & -1 & 0 & 0 & 1 \end{array} \right).
$$

Since the columns for F_{123} and F_{1234} are proportional to each other, no five treatments from Ω_{42} can be included in T to give a MEP$\cdot$1 plan with ten treatments.

Case 14. $n_1 = 0$, $n_2 = 2$. Without loss of generality, let $1, 2 \in T$. Then $|T| = 10$ gives

$$
T = \{1234, 1, 2, \phi, 12, 13, 14, 23, 24, 34\}.
$$

Using the same Q as in (3.29), we see that Δ_0 arises for (F_{123}, F_{124}). Hence, T is not a MEP·1 plan.

Cases 15, 16. If $(n_3, n_1) = (0, 1)$ or $(0, 0)$, then $|T| < 10$. Thus, we don't get any MEP·1 plan with 10 treatments in these cases.

This finishes the enumeration of all of the MEP·1 plans with ten treatments for the 2^4 factorial experiment. We obtained six MEP·1 plans with ten treatments. For the plans obtained in section 4.2., we proved that no subdesign of those plans is a MEP·1 plan. In the next section we will prove that there is no MEP·1 plan with nine or less treatments for the 2^4 factorial experiment.

4.4. The Minimal Main Effect Plus One Plans. We now consider all of the MEP·1 plans obtained in section 4.2 and 4.3. We will prove that following result for them.

THEOREM 1. *Consider the following resolution III.1 designs obtained in equations (2.1), (2.6), (3.3), (3.8), (3.15), and (3.24), respectively.*

$$(4.1) \qquad T^1 = \{1, 2, 3, 4, 12, 13, 34, 123, 124, 1234\}$$
$$(4.2) \qquad T^2 = \{1, 2, 13, 24, 34, 123, 124, 134, 234, 1234\}$$
$$(4.3) \qquad T^3 = \{\phi, 1, 2, 3, 13, 34, 123, 124, 134, 1234\}$$
$$(4.4) \qquad T^4 = \{\phi, 3, 13, 14, 24, 34, 123, 124, 134, 1234\}$$
$$(4.5) \qquad T^5 = \{1, 3, 12, 13, 23, 24, 34, 123, 124, 1234\}$$
$$(4.6) \qquad T^6 = \{\phi, 2, 3, 4, 13, 14, 23, 34, 123, 1234\}$$

No subsdesign of the above designs is a MEP·1 plan.

Proof. To prove that no subdesign of the above designs is a MEP·1 plan, it is sufficient to prove that no subdesign of the above designs with nine treatments is a MEP·1 plan. For the designs T^1 and T^2 the result was proved in theorems 2 and 5 (section 4.2), respectively. Now consider T^3. Taking $T_1 = \{1234, 123, 124, 134, 3\}$, we obtain the following matrix Q_0:

$$(4.7) \qquad Q_0 = \begin{array}{c} \phi \\ 13 \\ 34 \\ 1 \\ 2 \end{array} \begin{pmatrix} 0 & 1 & 0 & 1 & 0 & 1 & 0 & 0 & 0 & 0 & 1 \\ 0 & 0 & 0 & 0 & 1 & 0 & 0 & 1 & 0 & 1 & 1 \\ 0 & 0 & 1 & 0 & -1 & 0 & 0 & 0 & -1 & -1 & 0 \\ 0 & 0 & 0 & 1 & 1 & 1 & 1 & 1 & 1 & 1 & 1 \\ 1 & 1 & 0 & 0 & -1 & 1 & 0 & 0 & 0 & 0 & 0 \end{pmatrix}.$$

If we drop any treatment from $\{\phi, 13, 34, 1, 2\}$ (in order), then Δ_0 arises for $(124, 1234)$, $(123, 124)$, $(123, 134)$, (123), and (12), respectively. Thus, none of the treatments can be dropped from $\{\phi, 13, 34, 1, 2\}$ and hence, these treatments are always there in T. Now take $T_1 = \{\phi, 13, 34, 1, 1234\}$. This gives us the following matrix Q_0:

$$(4.8) \qquad Q_0 = \begin{array}{c} 2 \\ 123 \\ 124 \\ 134 \\ 3 \end{array} \begin{pmatrix} -1 & -1 & -1 & -1 & -1 & 0 & 1 & 1 & 0 & 0 & -1 \\ 0 & -1 & -1 & 0 & -1 & 0 & 1 & 0 & 0 & -1 & -1 \\ 0 & 0 & 0 & -1 & 0 & -1 & -1 & 0 & -1 & 0 & 0 \\ 0 & 1 & 1 & 0 & 0 & 0 & -1 & -1 & 0 & 0 & 0 \\ 0 & -1 & 0 & 0 & 0 & 0 & 1 & 0 & 1 & 0 & 1 \end{pmatrix}.$$

359

If we drop any treatment from $\{123, 124, 134, 3, 2\}$ (in order), we get Δ_0 for (12), (234), $(12, 124)$, and $(24, 1234)$, respectively. Hence, none of the treatments from $\{123, 124, 134, 3, 2\}$ can be dropped. We have checked all of the treatments in T^3 and none of them can be dropped so as to give a MEP·1 plan. The proof is similar for the designs T^4, T^5 and T^6.

Now suppose that T is a design of resolution III.1 for the 2^4 factorial experiment with $|T| = 9$. If we add any other treatment, say $\underline{t}$, to this design T, then we will get a design $T^* = [T : \underline{t}]$. Then T^* is a MEP·1 plan with ten treatments, and T^* has a subdesign, T which is of resolution III.1. But, there are only six nonisomorphic designs of resolution III.1 (listed in (4.1)-(4.6)). We have shown that there is no subdesign of these designs which is of resolution III.1. Hence, a MEP·1 plan T with $|T| = 9$ cannot exist. This gives us the following important result.

THEOREM 2. *There are only six nonisomorphic designs of resolution III.1 with ten treatments for the 2^4 factorial experiment; these are listed at (4.1)–(4.6). Furthermore, there is no design of resolution III.1 with nine treatments.*

We know that if a design is of resolution III·2, then it is also of resolution III·1, but not conversely. The six designs (listed in (4.1)–(4.6)) are such that none of them is a resolution III.2 design. Because it is easily seen that the matrixes Q_0 for them doesn't have property P_4. For example the matrix Q_0 for the design T^1 is given in (2.5), and it doesn't have P_4 (sum of columns corresponding to F_{123} and F_{124} is equal the column for F_{14}). This proves the following important result.

THEOREM 3. *The minimum number of treatments required for a MEP·2 plan (for the 2^4 factorial experiment) is eleven and the design $T = \Omega_{44} \cup \Omega_{41} \cup \Omega_{42}$ is a MEP·2 plan with eleven treatments.*

Proof. The result follows from the above remarks and Theorem 2.1 of Srivastava and Arora (1989).

REFERENCES

[1] ANDERSON, D.A. AND THOMAS, A.M., *Weakly resolvable IV·3 designs for the p^n factorial experiments*, JSPI, 4 (1980), pp. 299–312.

[2] CHAKRAVARTI, I.M., *Fractional replication in asymmetrical factorial designs and partially balanced arrays*, Sankhya, 17 (1956), pp. 143–164.

[3] GHOSH, S., *On main effects plus on plan for 2^m factorials*, The Ann. of Stat., 8 (1980), pp. 922–930.

[4] GHOSH, S. ON SOME NEW SEARCH DESIGNS FOR 2^m FACTORIAL EXPERIMENTS, JSPI, 5 (1981), pp. 381–389.

[5] GHOSH, S. AND ZHANG, XIAO, DI, *Two new series of search designs for 3^m factorial experiments*, Utilitas Mathematica (1987).

[6] GUPTA, B.C., *A bound connected with factorial search designs of resolution III·1*, Comm. in Stat. (1988) (to appear).

[7] GUPTA, B.C. AND CARVAJAL, S.S.R., *A necessary condition for the existence of main effect plus one plan for 2^m factorials*, Comm. Stat. Theor. Meth., 13(5) (1984a), pp. 567–580.

[8] GUPTA, B.C. AND CARVAJAL, S.S.R., *A lower bound for number of treatments in a main effect plan for 2^4 factorials*, Utilitas Mathematica (1984b), pp. 259–267.

[9] GUPTA, B.C. AND CARVAJAL, S.S.R., *A lower bound for number of treatments in a main effect plus one plan for 2^5 factorial*, Utilitas Mathematica (1986) (to appear).

[10] GUPTA, B.C. AND SCHEULT, A,, *Some results in search designs with special reference to 2^m factorial experiments*, Metron, 33 (1975), pp. 379–388.

[11] KATONA, GYULA AND SRIVASTAVA, JAYA, *Minimal 2-coverings of a finite affine space based on $GF(2)$*, JSPI, 8 (1983), pp. 375–388.

[12] OHNISHI, T. AND SHIRAKURA, T., *Search designs for 2^m factorial experiments*, JSPI, 11 (1985), pp. 241–245.

[13] SHIRAKURA, T., *Main effects plus k plans for 2^m factorials*, Technical report #205, Hiroshima University, Hiroshima, Japan (1987).

[14] SHIRAKURA, T. AND OHNISHI, T., *Search designs for 2^m factorials derived from balanced arrays of strength $2(\ell + 1)$ and AD optimal search designs*, JSPI, 11 (1985), pp. 247–258.

[15] SRIVASTAVA, J.N., *Designs for searching non-negligible effects*, in *A Survey of Statistical Designs and Linear Models*, (J.N. Srivastava, ed.), North-Holland Publ., Amsterdam, 1975.

[16] SRIVASTAVA, J.N., *Some further theory of search linear models*, in *Contributions to Applied Statistics*, Swiss-Australian Region of Biometry Society, 1976, pp. 249–256.

[17] SRIVASTAVA, J.N. AND GHOSH, S., *A series of 2^m factorial designs of resolution V which allow search and estimation of one extra unknown effect*, Sankhya Ser. B, 38 (1976), pp. 280–289.

[18] SRIVASTAVA, J.N., *Optimal search designs or design optimal under bias-free optimality criteria*, in *Statistical Decision Theory and Related Topics*, (S.S. Gupta and D.S. More, eds.), Vol. II, 1977, pp. 375–409.

[19] SRIVASTAVA, J.N. AND GHOSH, S., *Balanced 2^m factorial designs of resolution V which allow search and estimation of one extra unknown effect*, $4 \leq m \leq 8$, Comm. Stat. Th. Meth., A6 (1977), pp. 141–166.

[20] SRIVASTAVA, J.N., *On the linear independence of sets of 2^q columns of certain $(1, -1)$ matrices with a group structure, and its connection with finite geometries*, in *Combinatorial Mathematics*, (Holton, D.A. and Seberry, J. eds.), Springer-Verlag, Berlin, 1978.

[21] SRIVASTAVA, J.N. AND GUPTA, B.C., *Main effect plan for 2^m factorials which allow search and estimation of one non-negligible effect*, JSPI, 3 (1979), pp. 259–265.

[22] SRIVASTAVA, J.N., *On the inadequacy of customary orthogonal arrays in quality control and general scientific experimentation, and the need of probing designs of higher revealing power*, Comm. Stat. Th., 1987.

[23] SRIVASTAVA, J.N. AND ARORA, S., *A minimal search design of resolution $3 \cdot 2$ for the 2^4 factorial effects*, Jour. Indian Math. Soc., 54 (1989).

361

THE CONSTRUCTION OF NESTED CYCLE SYSTEMS*

D.R. STINSON†

Abstract. In this paper, we prove for any integer $m \geq 3$ that there exists a nested m-cycle system of order n if and only if $n \equiv 1 \bmod 2m$, with at most 13 possible exceptions (for each value of m).

1. Introduction. Let G be a graph, and let $m \geq 3$ be an integer. An m-cycle *decomposition* of g is an edge-decomposition of G into cycles of size m. We will write the m-cycle decomposition as a pair $(G, \mathcal{C})$, where $\mathcal{C}$ is the set of cycles in the edge-decomposition. An m-cycle decomposition of K_n will be called an m-*cycle system* of *order* n. Of course, a 3-cycle system is a *Steiner triple system*; these designs exist for all orders $n \equiv 1$ or 3 modulo 6.

We will say that an m-cycle decomposition, $(G, \mathcal{C})$, can be *nested* if we can associate with each cycle $C \in \mathcal{C}$ a vertex of G, which we denote $f(C)$, such that $f(C) \notin C$, and such that the edges in $\{\{x, f(C)\} : x \in C, C \in \mathcal{C}\}$ form an edge-decomposition of G. Alternatively, we can view a nested m-cycle decomposition as an edge-decomposition of the multigraph $2G$ into wheels with m spokes, where every edge occurs in one wheel of the decomposition as a spoke and in one wheel on the rim.

It is easy to see that a necessary condition for the existence of a nested m-cycle system of order n is that $n \equiv 1 \bmod 2m$. The first examples of nested m-cycle systems to be studied in the literature were nested 3-cycle systems (i.e., nested Steiner triple systems). It was proved by Stinson [5] that there exists a nested Steiner triple system of order n if and only if $n \equiv 1$ modulo 6. In the smallest even-cycle case, $m = 4$, it has been shown by Stinson [6] that the necessary condition $n = 1 \bmod 8$ is sufficient for existence, with the possible exceptions $n = 57, 65, 97, 113, 185$ and 265. More recently, Lindner, Rodger and Stinson [3] showed for each odd $m \geq 3$ that there exists a nested m-cycle system of order n if and only if $n \equiv 1 \bmod 2m$, with at most 13 possible exceptions. Then, Lindner and Stinson [4] proved for any even $m \geq 4$ that there exists a nested m-cycle system of order n if and only if $n \equiv 1 \bmod 2m$, with at most 13 possible exceptions.

In this paper, we give a condensed proof of these existence results.

2. Some constructions. In this section, we present a small number of direct and recursive constructions for nested cycle decompositions that will enable us to prove our existence results in Section 3. Many of these constructions involve nested cycle decompositions of complete multipartite graphs. We refer to the parts of a complete multipartite graph as *holes*. The *type* of a complete multipartite

---

*This research was supported in part by the Institute for Mathematics and its Applications, with funds provided by the National Science Foundation, and by NSERC grant A9287.

†Department of Computer Science, University of Manitoba, Winnipeg Manitoba R3T 2N2 Canada.

graph is defined to be the multiset consisting of the sizes of the holes. We usually use an "exponential" notation to describe types: a type $t_1^{u_1} t_2^{u_2} \ldots t_k^{u_k}$ denotes u_i occurrences of $t_i, 1 \le i \le k$. If T is the type $t_1^{u_1} t_2^{u_2} \ldots t_k^{u_k}$ and m is an integer, then mT is defined to be the type $(mt_1)^{u_1} (mt_2)^{u_2} \ldots (mt_k)^{u_k}$. Also, we will denote the complete multipartite graph having type T by $K(T)$.

First, we give a multiplication construction for nested cycle decompositions of complete multipartite graphs.

Multiplication construction. Suppose there is a nested m-cycle decomposition of a complete multigraph $K(T)$. Let $k \ge 1$. Then there is a nested (km)-cycle decomposition of $K(kT)$.

Proof. Replace every vertex v of $K(T)$ by k independent vertices, (named $v_i, 1 \le i \le k$), thereby constructing $K(kT)$. Let $(K(T), \mathcal{C})$ be an m-cycle decomposition, and let f be a nesting of $\mathcal{C}$. Each cycle $C \in \mathcal{C}$ corresponds to a subgraph of $K(kT)$ isomorphic to the Cartesian product $C \otimes (K_k)^c$ (each vertex of C is replaced by k independent vertices, and each edge is replaced by k^2 edges forming a complete bipartite graph $K_{k,k}$). It is well-known that the graph $C \otimes (K_k)^c$ has an (mk)-cycle decomposition (this is a decomposition into Hamiltonian cycles; see [1] or [2]). The number of (mk)-cycles in this decomposition is k. Suppose these cycles are named $C_i, 1 \le i \le k$. We define a nesting by associating with each C_i the vertex $f(C)_i$. If we do this for every cycle C, we obtain the desired nesting. $\square$

Let S be a set, and let $\{S_1, \ldots, S_n\}$ be a partition of S. An $\{S_1, \ldots S_n\}$-*Room frame* is an $|S|$ by $|S|$ array, F, indexed by S, which satisfies the following properties:

1) every cell of F either is empty or contains an unordered pair of symbols of S,

2) the subarrays $S_i \times S_i$ are empty, for $1 \le i \le n$ (these subarrays are referred to as *holes*),

3) each symbol of $S \backslash S_i$ occurs once in row (or column) s, for any $s \in S_i$,

4) the pairs occurring in F are those $\{s, t\}$, where $(s, t) \in (S \times S) \backslash \bigcup_{i=1}^n (S_i \times S_i)$.

We shall say that F is *skew* if, for any pair of cells (s, t) and (t, s), where $(s, t) \in (S \times S) \backslash \cup (S_i \times S_i)$, precisely one is empty. The *type* of F is defined to be the multiset $\{|S_i| : 1 \le i \le n\}$. As before, we use an "exponential" notation to describe types.

The next construction produces a nested cycle decomposition of a complete multigraph from a skew Room frame.

Skew Room frame construction. [3, Theorem 3.1] Suppose there is a skew Room frame of type T. Let $m \ge 3$ be an integer. Then there is a nested m-cycle decomposition of the complete multipartite graph $K(mT)$.

Proof. Let $r = \lfloor \frac{m}{2} \rfloor$. For $0 \le i \le r$, define $d_i = (-1)^{i+1} \lfloor \frac{i+1}{2} \rfloor$. Let F be a skew Room frame of type T based on symbol set X. We shall define our complete multipartite graph $K(mT)$ on vertex set $X \times \mathbf{Z}_m$. The holes of $K(mT)$ will be $S_i \times \mathbf{Z}_m$, for every hole S_i of the frame F.

363

For any $x, y, z \in X$, define $C(\{x,y\}, z; 0)$ to be the cycle

$$(x, d_0)(y, d_1)(x, d_2), \ldots, (x, d_{r-1})(z, d_r)(y, d_{r-1}), \ldots, (x, d_1)(y, d_0)(x, d_0) \text{ if } r \text{ is odd}$$
$$(x, d_0)(y, d_1)(x, d_2), \ldots, (y, d_{r-1})(z, d_r)(x, d_{r-1}), \ldots, (x, d_1)(y, d_0)(x, d_0) \text{ if } r \text{ is even}.$$

For any $x, y, z \in X$ and $i \in \mathbf{Z}_m$, define $C(\{x,y\}, z; i)$ to be the cycle obtained by adding i to the second coordinate of each point in the cycle $C(\{x,y\}, z; 0)$, and reducing modulo m.

For any unordered pair $\{x, y\}$ from different holes of the frame F, define $\text{Row}(x, y)$ to be the row of F containing $\{x, y\}$ in some cell, and define $\text{Col}(x, y)$ to be the column of F containing $\{x, y\}$ in some cell.

We construct our cycle decomposition as follows. For every unordered pair $\{x, y\}$ from different holes of F, and for every $i \in \mathbf{Z}_m$, take the cycle $C(\{x, y\}, \text{Row}(x, y); i)$, and nest it with the point $\text{Col}(x, y)$. It is not too difficult to verify that this produces a nested cycle decomposition of the complete multipartite graph; the details of the verification are contained in [3]. $\square$

A *group-divisible design*, (or GDD), is a triple $(X, \mathcal{G}, \mathcal{A})$ which satisfies the following properties:

1) $\mathcal{G}$ is a partition of X into subsets called *groups*,

2) $\mathcal{A}$ is a set of subsets of X (called *blocks*) such that a group and a block contain at most one common point, and

3) every pair of points from distinct groups occurs in a unique block.

The *group-type* (or *type*) of a GDD $(X, \mathcal{G}, \mathcal{A})$ is the multiset $\{|G|; G \in \mathcal{G}\}$. As before, we use an "exponential" notation to describe group-types. We will say that a GDD is a K-GDD if $|A| \in K$ for every $A \in \mathcal{A}$.

Our next construction uses group-divisible designs in a recursive construction.

GDD construction. Let $(X, \mathcal{G}, \mathcal{A})$ be a GDD having type T, and let $w : X \rightarrow \mathbf{Z}^+ \cup 0$ (we say that w is a *weighting*). For every $A \in \mathcal{A}$, suppose there is a nested m-cycle decomposition for the complete multipartite graph having type $\{w(x) : x \in A\}$. Then there is a nested m-cycle decomposition for a complete multipartite graph having type $\{\sum_{x \in G} w(x) : G \in \mathcal{G}\}$.

Proof. For every $x \in X$, let $s(x)$ be $w(x)$ "copies" of x. For any subset $Y \subset X$, define $s(Y) = \bigcup_{x \in Y} s(x)$. For every $A \in \mathcal{A}$, suppose that $(s(A), \mathcal{C}(A))$ is a nested cycle decomposition of the complete multipartite graph of type $\{w(x) : x \in A\}$ having holes $s(x), x \in A$. Let f_A be a nesting of $(s(A), \mathcal{C}(A))$. Then $(S(X), \bigcup_{A \in \mathcal{A}} \mathcal{C}(A))$ is a nested cycle decomposition of the complete multipartite graph of type $\{\sum_{x \in G} w(x) : G \in \mathcal{G}\}$ having holes $s(G), G \in \mathcal{G}$. We define a nesting of this cycle decomposition by $f(C) = f_A(C)$ if and only if $C \in \mathcal{C}(A)$. $\square$

Once we have constructed a nested cycle decomposition of a complete multipartite graph, we can produce a nested cycle system by the usual technique of filling in holes.

Filling in holes construction. Suppose there is a nested m-cycle decomposition for the complete multipartite graph $K(T)$, where T is the type $t_1^{u_1} t_2^{u_2} \ldots t_k^{u_k}$. For $1 \leq i \leq k$, suppose there is a nested m-cycle system of order $t_i + 1$. Then there is a nested m-cycle system of order $\sum_{i=1}^{k} (t_i u_i + 1)$.

We also use the following class of nested cycle systems which are constructed by difference methods.

LEMMA 2.1. *For all integers $r \geq 3$, there is a nested r-cycle system of order $2r + 1$.*

Proof. Define $k = \lfloor \frac{r-1}{2} \rfloor$, and define $\mathbf{a} = (a_1, \ldots, a_r)$ by

$$a_i = (-1)^i i, \ \text{if} \ 1 \leq i \leq k - 1$$
$$a_i = (-1)^{i+1} i, \ \text{if} \ k \leq i \leq r,$$

where each a_i is reduced modulo $2r + 1$. Let $\mathcal{C} = \{\mathbf{a} + j : j \in \mathbf{Z}_{2r+1}\}$, where $\mathbf{a}$ represents the cycle $a_1 a_2 \ldots a_r a_1$. Then, it is easy to see that $\mathcal{C}$ is a cycle system of order $2n + 1$. We define a nesting f of $\mathcal{C}$ by $f(\mathbf{a} + j) = j$, for every cycle $\mathbf{a} + j \in \mathcal{C}$. $\square$

LEMMA 2.2. [6, *Lemma 1*] *Suppose $k \equiv 1$ modulo 4 is a prime power. Then there is a nested 4-cycle decomposition of the complete multipartite graph $K(2^k)$.*

Proof. As the vertex set for $K(2^k)$ we take $GF(k) \times \mathbf{Z}_2$, and we let the holes be $\{y\} \times \mathbf{Z}_2, y \in GF(k)$. Let α be a primitive element in $GF(k)$. Write $k = 4t + 1$, and define $\beta = \alpha^t$. For $0 \leq i \leq t - 1$, and for any element $a \in GF(k) \times \mathbf{Z}_2$, define a cycle

$$C(i, a) = (a + (\alpha^i, 1); a + (\alpha^i \beta, 0); a + (\alpha^i \beta^2, 0); a + (\alpha^i \beta, 1)).$$

For each cycle $C(i, a)$, define the nested point to be $f(C(i, a)) = a$. Then, it is not difficult to verify that $\mathcal{C} = \{C(a, i)\}$ is a 4-cycle decomposition of $K(2^k)$ and f is a nesting of $\mathcal{C}$. $\square$

3. The existence results. First, we consider nested m-cycle systems for odd values of m. We shall employ the following known class of skew Room frames.

THEOREM 3.1. [3, *Theorem 2.2*] *For all $n \geq 5, n \notin \{6, 22, 23, 24, 26, 27, 28, 30, 34, 38\}$, there is a skew Room frame of type 2^n.*

LEMMA 3.2. *Suppose $m \geq 3$ is odd and $u \notin \{1, 2, 3, 4, 6, 22, 23, 24, 26, 27, 28, 30, 34, 38\}$. Then there is a nested m-cycle decomposition of $K((2m)^u)$.*

Proof. This follows from applying the skew Room frame construction to a skew Room frame of type 2^u (which exists by Theorem 3.1). $\square$

We now have the following immediate consequence.

THEOREM 3.3. *Suppose $m \geq 3$ is odd, $n = 2um+1$, and $u \notin \{2, 3, 4, 6, 22, 23, 24,$ $26, 27, 28, 30, 34, 38\}$. Then there is a nested m-cycle system of order n.*

Proof. If $u \neq 1$, fill in the holes with nested m-cycle systems of order $2m + 1$ (Lemma 2.1). For $u = 1$, Lemma 2.1 gives the result immediately. □

More generally, we have the following result for even cycle lengths that are not a power of two.

THEOREM 3.4. *Suppose $m \geq 3$ is odd, $n = 2um+1$, $u \notin \{2, 3, 4, 6, 22, 23, 24, 26,$ $27, 28, 30, 34, 38\}$, and $i \geq 0$. Then there exists a nested $(2^i m)$-cycle system of order $2^{i+1} um + 1$.*

Proof. For $u = 1$, the result is given in Lemma 2.1. For $u > 1$, proceed as follows. Apply the multiplication construction to the m-cycle decompositions obtained in Lemma 3.2 using $k = 2^i$. We obtain a nested $(2^i m)$-cycle decomposition of $K((2^{i+1} m)^u)$. Now, fill in the holes with nested $(2^i m)$-cycle systems of order $2^{i+1} m + 1$ which exist by Lemma 2.1. □

Finally, we address the question of constructing nested 2^i-cycle systems. Our construction for nested 2^i-cycle systems ($i \geq 3$) depends on the existence of the following group-divisible designs.

THEOREM 3.5. [4, *Theorem 4.14*] *Suppose $u \geq 5$, $u \notin \{7, 8, 12, 14, 18, 19, 23, 24,$ $33, 34\}$. Then there is a $\{5, 9, 13, 17, 29, 49\}$-GDD having group-type 4^u.*

The existence of the following nested 4-cycle decompositions will prove useful.

LEMMA 3.6. *Suppose $u \geq 5$, $u \notin \{7, 8, 12, 14, 18, 19, 23, 24, 33, 34\}$. Then there is a nested 4-cycle decomposition of $K(8^u)$.*

Proof. Let $(X, \mathcal{G}, \mathcal{A})$ be a $\{5, 9, 13, 17, 29, 49\}$-GDD having group-type 4^u. Apply the GDD construction, giving every point weight 2. For every block A, $|A| \in \{5, 9, 13, 17, 29, 49\}$, so there is a nested 4-cycle decomposition of $K(2^{|A|})$ by Lemma 2.2. We get a nested 4-cycle decomposition of $K(8^{|X|/4})$. □

LEMMA 3.7. *Suppose $u \geq 5$, $u \notin \{7, 8, 12, 14, 18, 19, 23, 24, 33, 34\}$, and $i \geq 2$. Then there is a nested (2^i)-cycle decomposition of $K((2^{i+1})^u)$.*

Proof. Apply the multiplication construction to the m-cycle decompositions obtained in Lemma 3.6 using $k = 2^{i-2}$. We obtain a nested 2^{i+1}-cycle decomposition of $K((2^{i+1})^u)$. □

THEOREM 3.8. *Suppose $u \geq 1$, $u \neq 2, 3, 4, 7, 8, 12, 14, 18, 19, 23, 24, 33$, or 34, and $i \geq 2$. Then there is a nested (2^i)-cycle system of order $2^{i+1} u + 1$.*

Proof. For $u = 1$, apply Lemma 2.1. For $u > 1$, we proceed as follows. Construct a nested (2^i)-cycle decomposition of $K((2^{i+1})^u)$, using Lemma 3.7, and then fill in the holes with nested (2^i)-cycle systems of order $2^{i+1} + 1$ which exist by Lemma 2.1. □

Summarizing the results proved above, we have the following.

COROLLARY 3.9. *Suppose $m \geq 3$ is any integer, $n \equiv 1$ modulo $2m$, and $n \geq 70m + 1$. Then there is a nested m-cycle system of order n.*

4. Further results for small cycle lengths. For some small odd cycle lengths, it is possible to remove most or all of the 13 possible exceptions given in Theorem 3.3. For odd $m \leq 15$, this was done in [3]. We summarize the results from [3] below.

m	spectrum of nested m-cycle systems
3	$n \equiv 1$ modulo 6
5	$n \equiv 1$ modulo 10
7	$n \equiv 1$ modulo 14, except possibly 57 and 85
9	$n \equiv 1$ modulo 18, except possibly 55
11	$n \equiv 1$ modulo 22, except possibly 133
13	$n \equiv 1$ modulo 26, except possibly 105
15	$n \equiv 1$ modulo 30, except possibly 91

REFERENCES

[1] G. HETYEI, *On Hamiltonian circuits and 1-factors of regular complete n-partite graphs,* (in Hungarian), Acta Acad. Pedagog. Civitate Pecs, Ser. 6; Math. Phys. Chem. Tech., 19 (1975), pp. 5-10.

[2] R. LASKAR, *Decomposition of some composite graphs into Hamiltonian cycles,* Proc. Fifth Hungar. Colloq., North-Holland, Amsterdam (1978), pp. 705-716.

[3] C.C. LINDNER, C.A. RODGER AND D.R. STINSON, *Nesting of cycle systems of odd length,* Annals of Discrete Math. (to appear).

[4] C.C. LINDNER AND D.R. STINSON, *Nesting of cycle systems of even length,* preprint.

[5] D.R. STINSON, *The spectrum of nested Steiner triple systems,* Graphs and Combinatorics, 1 (1985), pp. 189-191.

[6] D.R. STINSON, *On the spectrum of nested 4-cycle systems,* Utilitas Math., 33 (1988), pp. 47-50.

GENERALIZED IDEMPOTENT ORTHOGONAL ARRAYS

LUC TEIRLINCK*

Abstract. We show that 2-idempotent t-quasigroups of order v exist for all pairs (t, v) with t odd and $v \notin \{3, 7\}$. They do not exist for even $t \geq 2$ (except when $v \varepsilon \{0, 1\}$) or for odd $t \geq 3$ and $v = 3$. The existence of 2-idempotent t-quasigroups of order 7 remains in doubt for all odd $t \geq 3$. We survey known results on the existence problem for 2-idempotent 3-quasigroups whose conjugate invariant group contains a prescribed subgroup and prove some new results on this topic. The problem is now completely solved (or solved for all orders except 7) for all groups, except the cyclic groups of orders 3 and 4.

Key words. r-idempotent t-quasigroup, orthogonal array, conjugate invariant group, pairwise balanced design.

AMS(MOS) subject classifications. 05B05, 05B15, 20N05

1. Introduction. All notions used, but not defined, in this introduction will be defined in later sections. One can define r-idempotent t-quasigroups as t-quasigroups in which every subset of cardinality at most r is a subquasigroup. It is well known that 1-idempotent t-quasigroups of order v exist for all v if t is odd and for all $v \neq 2$ if t is even. (See section 2). Using folklore arguments, which we will present in section 2, it is easy to see that r-idempotent t-quasigroups of order v with $r \geq 2$, $t \geq 2$ and $v \geq 3$ can only exist for $r = 2$ and t odd. Several papers have been written on 2-idempotent 3-quasigroups, but nevertheless the spectrum for 2-idempotent t-quasigroups remained unknown for all odd $t \geq 3$. In sections 2 and 3, we will show that 2-idempotent t-quasigroups of order v exist for all pairs (t, v) with t odd and $v \notin \{3, 7\}$. No 2-idempotent t-quasigroups of order 3 exist for $t \geq 2$. The existence of 2-idempotent t-quasigroups of order 7 remains open for all odd $t \geq 3$. In section 4, we survey known results on the existence of 2-idempotent 3-quasigroups of order v whose conjugate invariant group contains a specified subgroup. In sections 3 and 6, we obtain some new results on the subject. The problem is now completely solved (or solved up to $v = 7$) for all groups, except the cyclic groups of orders 3 and 4.

Although this paper deals mainly with 2-idempotent t-quasigroups, our main constructions for 2-idempotent 3-quasigroups, especially those in section 6, actually work for more general classes of 3-quasigroups. Thus, they could potentially be useful in the construction of 3-quasigroups, or collections of 3-quasigroups, satisfying all kinds of properties, not necessarily related to 2-idempotence.

We assume that most readers will be somewhat familiar with design theory and orthogonal arrays of strength 2, but may be less familiar with techniques that work specifically for t-quasigroups. Thus, we review in detail all needed folklore and results concerning t-quasigroups and try to make this paper as self-contained

*Department of Algebra, Combinatorics and Analysis, Auburn University, Alabama 36849, U.S.A. This research was supported by NSA grant MDA904-88-H-2005. This research was also supported in part by the Institute for Mathematics and its Applications with funds provided by the National Science Foundation.

as possible in as far as t-quasigroups are concerned. On the other hand, we give references to all used results on designs and orthogonal arrays of strength 2, but do not try to be self-contained or to systematically review known results on these subjects.

2. Definitions, folklore and general results. An <u>orthogonal array</u> $OA(t, k, v)$, t, $k\varepsilon N - \{0\}$, v a cardinal number, $k \geq t + 1$, is a subset q of S^k, S a v-set, such that if $x_{i_1}, \ldots, x_{i_t} \varepsilon S$, $\{i_1, \ldots, i_t\}$ a t-subset of $\{1, \ldots, k\}$, there is a unique $(y_1, \ldots, y_k)\varepsilon q$ with $y_{i_1} = x_{i_1}, \ldots, y_{i_t} = x_{i_t}$. The elements of q are called <u>rows</u>. The number t is called the <u>strength</u> of the orthogonal array. If we want to explicitly mention S, we often consider an $OA(t, k, v)$ to be an ordered pair (S, q). An <u>isomorphism</u> between two $OA(t, k, v)$ (S_1, q_1) and (S_2, q_2) is a bijection $\sigma : S_1 \to S_2$ such that $q_2 = \{(\sigma(x_1), \ldots, \sigma(x_k)); (x_1, \ldots, x_k)\varepsilon q_1\}$. An $OA(t, t + 1, v)$ is called a t-<u>quasigroup</u>. We identify a t-quasigroup with the mapping $q : S^t \to S$ defined by $q(x_1, \ldots, x_t) = x_{t+1}$. Thus, for t-quasigroups, we will use expressions such as $q(x_1, \ldots, x_t) = x_{t+1}$ and $(x_1, \ldots, x_{t+1})\varepsilon q$ completely interchangeably. Using this identification, the 1-quasigroups on S are exactly the permutations of S. A 2-quasigroup is simply called a <u>quasigroup</u>. Moreover, for 2-quasigroups, we often use notations such as $x \cdot y$ or $x + y$ instead of $q(x, y)$.

If q is an arbitrary subset of S^k, S a set, $k\varepsilon N$, then the <u>conjugate invariant group</u> $H(q)$ of q is the set of all $\sigma\varepsilon S_k$ such that $(x_1, \ldots, x_k)\varepsilon q$ iff $(x_{\sigma(1)}, \ldots, x_{\sigma(k)})\varepsilon q$. We call q <u>totally symmetric</u> if $H(q) = S_k$. It is easy to see that an $OA(t, k, v)$ (S, q) with $k > t+1$ can only be totally symmetric if $v\varepsilon\{0, 1\}$ or $t = 1$ and $q = \{(x, \ldots, x); x\varepsilon S\}$. On the other hand, if $(G, +)$ is an abelian group and if $q_{(t, G)} = \{(x_1, \ldots, x_{t+1})\varepsilon G^{t+1}; x_1 + \cdots + x_{t+1} = 0\}$, then $q_{(t,G)}$ is a totally symmetric $OA(t, t + 1, |G|)$. Thus totally symmetric $OA(t, t + 1, v)$ exist for any $t\varepsilon N - \{0\}$ and any cardinal number v.

A <u>subsystem</u> of an $OA(t, k, v)$ (S, q) is a subset D of S such that whenever $(x_1, \ldots, x_k)\varepsilon q$ and $|\{i; 1 \leq i \leq k, x_i\varepsilon D\}| \geq t$, then $x_i\varepsilon D$ for all $i\varepsilon\{1, \ldots, k\}$. Obviously, any intersection of subsystems is a subsystem. A subsystem of a t-quasigroup is often called a <u>subquasigroup</u>. An $OA(t, k, v)$ (S, q) is called r-<u>idempotent</u> if every $D \subset S$ with $|D| \leq r$ is a subsystem. An $OA(t, k, v)$ (S, q) is called <u>totally unipotent</u> <u>with unit</u> x, $x\varepsilon S$, if $\{x, y\}$ is a subsystem for all $y\varepsilon S$. We often use the symbol 1 to denote a unit. We call an $OA(t, k, v)$ (S, q) <u>totally unipotent</u> if it is totally unipotent with unit x for at least one $x\varepsilon S$. (This implies $v \neq 0$.) A 1-idempotent $OA(t, k, v)$ is called <u>idempotent</u>. Obviously, an $OA(t, k, v)$ (S, q) is idempotent iff $(x, \ldots, x)\varepsilon q$ for all $x\varepsilon S$. The only idempotent $OA(1, k, v)$ on a v-set S is $q = \{(x, \ldots, x); x\varepsilon S\}$. All subsets of S are subsystems of q, so that q is r-idempotent for all $r\varepsilon N$. Of course, q is totally symmetric. This takes care of the case $t = 1$. It is easy to check that no $OA(t, k, 2)$ with $1 < t < k - 1$ exists. Thus, if $k > t + 1 > 2$, there are no 2-idempotent or totally unipotent $OA(t, k, v)$ with $v > 1$. Reviewing results on the existence problem for $OA(t, k, v)$ or idempotent $OA(t, k, v)$ would lead us too far.

We have seen that, for r-idempotence with $r \geq 2$ or total unipotence, we can restrict ourselves to the case $k = t + 1$. Assume that (S, q), $S = \{1, x, y\}$, is a totally unipotent $OA(t, t + 1, 3)$ with unit 1, $t \geq 2$. Let $x_i = 1$ for $i \leq t - 2$, $x_{t-1} = x$, $x_t = y$. Then $q(x_1, \ldots, x_t) = x$ would contradict the fact that $\{1, x\}$ is a

369

subsystem, $q(x_1, \ldots, x_t) = y$ would contradict the fact that $\{1, y\}$ is a subsystem and $q(x_1, \ldots, x_t) = 1$ would contradict both. Thus, no totally unipotent $OA(t, t+1, 3)$ with $t \geq 2$ exists. This means that there are no 3-idempotent $OA(t, t+1, v)$ with $t \geq 2$ and $v \geq 3$.

If we want to study 2-idempotent or totally unipotent $OA(t, t+1, v)$, it is obviously important to know how $OA(t, t+1, 2)$ look like. It is easy to see that, for t even, there are exactly two t-quasigroups on a 2-set $S = \{x, y\}$. One is the t-quasigroup q consisting of all $(x_1, \ldots, x_{t+1})$ containing an even number of x's and an odd number of y's. The other one is $S^{t+1} - q$. Note that the permutation (x, y) of S is an isomorphism between q and $S^{t+1} - q$. Both q and $S^{t+1} - q$ are totally symmetric and totally unipotent, but not idempotent. For t odd, there are also exactly two t-quasigroups on S. One is the t-quasigroup q consisting of all $(x_1, \ldots, x_{t+1})$ containing an even number of x's and an even number of y's. The other one is again $S^{t+1} - q$. Both q and $S^{t+1} - q$ are totally symmetric. The t-quasigroup q is 2-idempotent, but the only subsystems of $S^{t+1} - q$ are $\emptyset$ and S, so that $S^{t+1} - q$ is neither idempotent nor totally unipotent.

We now list some consequences of the preceding remarks about $OA(t, t+1, 2)$. First of all, there are no 2-idempotent $OA(t, t+1, v)$ with t even and $v > 1$. Moreover, if t is even, then a totally unipotent t-quasigroup has a uniquely determined unit and this unit is the only subsystem of cardinality 1. When t is odd, then every totally unipotent t-quasigroup is idempotent. Our remarks about $OA(t, t+1, 2)$ also show that, if t is odd, an $OA(t, t+1, v)$ (S, q) is 2-idempotent iff q contains all constant rows as well as all rows containing exactly two distinct elements x and y, both occurring an even number of times. An $OA(t, t+1, v)$ (S, q) is totally unipotent with unit 1 iff q contains the row consisting of all 1's as well as all rows containing an even number i of copies of some $x \varepsilon S - \{1\}$ and $(t+1-i)$ copies of 1.

If $(G, +)$ is an abelian group and I is a set, we will denote by $(G^{(I)}, +)$ the abelian group defined by $G^{(I)} = \{(x_i)_{i \in I}; x_i \varepsilon G, |\{i \in I; x_i \neq 0\}| < \infty\}$ and $(x_i)_{i \in I} + (y_i)_{i \in I} = (x_i + y_i)_{i \in I}$. If v is any infinite cardinal number and if I is a v-set, then for any $t \varepsilon \mathbf{N} - \{0\}$, $q_{(t, \mathbf{Z}_2^{(I)})}$ is a totally symmetric totally unipotent $OA(t, t+1, v)$ with the 0 of $\mathbf{Z}_2^{(I)}$ as unit. If t is odd, $q_{(t, \mathbf{Z}_2^{(I)})}$ is 2-idempotent. For any $t \varepsilon \mathbf{N} - \{0\}$, $q_{(t, \mathbf{Z}_{t+1}^{(I)})}$ is a totally symmetric idempotent $OA(t, t+1, v)$. Thus, in our discussions concerning the existence of idempotent, totally unipotent and 2-idempotent $OA(t, t+1, v)$ whose conjugate invariant group contains some specified subgroup G, it will not be restrictive to assume $v \varepsilon \mathbf{N}$.

It is well known that idempotent $OA(2, 3, v)$ exist for all $v \neq 2$, but not for $v = 2$. Indeed, idempotent quasigroups are equivalent with idempotent latin squares. They can easily be constructed from a pair of orthogonal latin squares [1, pp. 390-391] and a well known theorem of Bose, Parker and Shrikhande [2] asserts that such a pair exists for all $v \notin \{2, 6\}$. (See also [1, Theorem 4.9, page 445].) It is easy to construct an idempotent latin square of order 6.

A quasigroup (S, q) is called <u>commutative</u> if $q(x, y) = q(y, x)$ for all $x, y \varepsilon S$, or equivalently, if $(12) \varepsilon H(q)$. It is easy to see that a finite commutative idempotent $OA(2, 3, v)$ can only exist for odd v or $v = 0$. (Fix $s \varepsilon S$. The 2-subsets $\{x, y\}$

such that $q(x,y) = s$ partition $S - \{s\}$). On the other hand, if v is odd, then the quasigroup $(\mathbb{Z}_v, q)$ defined by $q(x,y) = (x+y)/2$ is commutative and idempotent.

If (S,q) is an idempotent $OA(2,3,v)$, if $1 \notin S$ and if $q_o = (q - \{(x,x,x); x\varepsilon S\}) \cup (\bigcup_{x\varepsilon S \cup \{1\}} \{(x,x,1), (x,1,x), (1,x,x)\})$, then $(S \cup \{1\}, q_o)$ is a totally unipotent $OA(2,3, v+1)$ with unit 1 and $H(q_o) = H(q)$. Conversely, every totally unipotent $OA(2,3, v+1)$ $(S \cup \{1\}, q_o)$ with unit 1 can be obtained in this way from a unique idempotent $OA(2,3,v)$ (S,q). Thus, if S is a v-set and $1 \notin S$, then there is a natural one-to-one correspondence, preserving conjugate invariant groups, between idempotent $OA(2,3,v)$ on S and totally unipotent $OA(2,3, v+1)$ on $S \cup \{1\}$ with unit 1. (This does not generalize to $t \geq 3$.) As a consequence, totally unipotent $OA(2,3,v)$ exist for all $v > 0$, $v \neq 3$, but not for $v = 0$ or $v = 3$. Commutative totally unipotent $OA(2,3,v)$ exist for all even $v > 0$, as well as for $v = 1$, but not for odd $v > 1$.

Let (S, q_i), $i = 1, \ldots, r$, be a collection of t_i-quasigroups and let $t = (\sum_{i=1}^{r} t_i) - 1$. Let (S,q) be an $(r-1)$-quasigroup. Then we can define the t-quasigroup $Q(q_1, \ldots, q_r; q)$ consisting of all $(x_1, \ldots, x_t, x_{t+1})\varepsilon S^{t+1}$ such that $(q_1(x_1, \ldots, x_{t_1}), q_2(x_{t_1+1}, \ldots, x_{t_1+t_2}), \ldots, q_r(x_{(\sum_{i=1}^{r-1} t_i)+1}, \ldots, x_{t+1}))\varepsilon q$. (We will call this construction concatenation.) It is obvious that if $A \subset S$ is a subsystem of all the q_i, $i = 1, \ldots, r$, as well as of q, then A is a subsystem of $Q(q_1, \ldots, q_r; q)$. In particular, if all q_i and q are r-idempotent (totally unipotent, respectively), then $Q(q_1, \ldots, q_r; q)$ is r-idempotent (totally unipotent, respectively).

If S is a set, then $q_{=,S}$, or simply $q_=$, will denote the 1-quasigroup on S defined by $q_{=,S} = \{(x,x); x\varepsilon S\}$. If (S, q_1) is an idempotent (totally unipotent, respectively) $OA(t, t+1, v)$ and if (S, q_2) is an idempotent (totally unipotent, respectively) quasigroup then $Q(q_1, q_2; q_=)$ is idempotent (totally unipotent, respectively) $OA(t+1, t+2, v)$. By induction, idempotent $OA(t, t+1, v)$ exist for all $v \neq 2$ and totally unipotent $OA(t, t+1, v)$ exist for all $v > 0$, $v \neq 3$. (There are other ways of seeing this obvious fact. However, we wanted to prove it in a way similar to the way we will prove less obvious results later on.) We have seen before that there are no totally unipotent $OA(t, t+1, 3)$ for $t \geq 2$. We have also seen that an idempotent $OA(t, t+1, 2)$ exists iff t is odd. This takes care of the existence problem for idempotent and totally unipotent $OA(t, t+1, v)$.

All results mentioned above without reference, are folklore. However, the spectrum for 2-idempotent $OA(t, t+1, v)$ was unknown for all odd $t \geq 3$. One of the main results of this paper is the nearly complete determination of this spectrum. If (S, q_1) is a 2-idempotent $OA(t, t+1, v)$ and if (S, q_2) is a 2-idempotent $OA(3,4,v)$, then $Q(q_1, q_2; q_=)$ is a 2-idempotent $OA(t+2, t+3, v)$. We will show in section 3 that 2-idempotent $OA(3,4,v)$ exist for all $v\varepsilon \mathbb{N} - \{3,7\}$. By induction, this will show that 2-idempotent $OA(t, t+1, v)$ exist for all pairs (t,v) with t odd, $t \geq 3$ and $v \notin \{3,7\}$. We have seen before that no 2-idempotent $OA(t, t+1, 3)$ exist for $t \geq 2$. We have also seen that there are no 2-idempotent $OA(t, t+1, v)$ with t even and $v > 1$. The existence of 2-idempotent $OA(t, t+1, 7)$ remains open for all odd $t \geq 3$.

3. Construction of 2-idempotent 3-quasigroups. In this section, we will

show that 2-idempotent $OA(3,4,v)$ (S,q) with $(13)(24)\varepsilon H(q)$ exist for all $v\varepsilon\mathsf{N}-\{3,7\}$. We also show that finite 2-idempotent $OA(3,4,v)$ (S,q) such that $H(q)$ contains a subgroup conjugate to the dihedral group on 4 elements exist iff v is even or $v=1$.

If (S,q_1) is a commutative totally unipotent $OA(2,3,v)$ with unit 1, or more generally a commutative $OA(2,3,v)$ satisfying $q_1(x,x)=1$ (but not necessarily $q_1(x,1)=q_1(1,x)=x$) for all $x\varepsilon S$, then it is easy to check that $Q(q_1,q_1;q_=)$ is a 2-idempotent $OA(3,4,v)$. Moreover, $H(Q(q_1,q_1;q_=))$ contains the group D_4 of all $\sigma\varepsilon S_4$ such that $\sigma(\{\{1,2\},\{3,4\}\})=\{\{1,2\},\{3,4\}\}$. It is easy to see that the group D_4, as defined here, is conjugate to the dihedral group on 4 elements. (Note that the complement of the graph $\{\{1,2\},\{3,4\}\}$ on $\{1,2,3,4\}$ is a 4-cycle.) Obviously, D_4 contains the permutation $(13)(24)$. As commutative totally unipotent $OA(2,3,v)$ exist for all even $v>0$, 2-idempotent $OA(3,4,v)$ (S,q) with $H(q)\supset D_4$ exist for all even v. Conversely, if (S,q) is a finite 2-idempotent $OA(3,4,v)$ with $H(q)\supset D_4$ and if $a,b\varepsilon S$, $a\neq b$, then, as $(12)\varepsilon D_4$, $\{\{x,y\};(x,y,a,b)\varepsilon q\}$ partitions S into 2-subsets, so that v must be even. Thus, 2-idempotent $OA(3,4,v)$ whose conjugate invariant group contains D_4 exist for all even v, as well as for $v=1$, but for no odd $v>1$.

If (S,q_1) and (S,q_2) are two $OA(2,3,v)$, then it is straight-forward to check that $Q(q_1,q_2;q_=)$ is 2-idempotent iff $q_1=q_2$, q_1 is commutative and $q_1(x,x)=q_1(y,y)$ for all $x,y\varepsilon S$. We already noted the "if" part before. The "only if" part means that the only 2-idempotent 3-quasigroups of the type $(S,Q(q_1,q_2;q_=))$, (S,q_1) and (S,q_2) two $OA(2,3,v)$, are the ones discussed in the preceding paragraph.

An $S(2,K,v)$, $K\subset\mathsf{N}$, v a cardinal number, is a pair (S,β), where S is a v-set and β is a set of subsets of S called <u>lines</u>, such that any 2-subset $\{x,y\}$ of S is contained in exactly one line, denoted by xy, and such that $|L|\varepsilon K$ for all $L\varepsilon\beta$. The symbol $B(K)$ denotes the set of all $v\varepsilon\mathsf{N}$ for which an $S(2,K,v)$ exists. An $S(2,K,v)$ is often called a <u>pairwise balanced design</u> or PBD. If $K=\{k\}$, we often write $S(2,k,v)$ and $B(k)$ instead of $S(2,\{k\},v)$ and $B(\{k\})$.

<u>Construction 1</u>: Let (S,β) be an $S(2,K,v)$, $K\cap\{0,1,2\}=\emptyset$, $v\geq 2$. For every $B\varepsilon\beta$, let (B,q_{1B}) be an idempotent quasigroup. We can define an idempotent quasigroup (S,q_1) by putting $q_1=\bigcup_{B\varepsilon\beta}q_{1B}$. (This is well known). Assume that for each $B\varepsilon\beta$ an idempotent 3-quasigroup (B,q_B) is given. Then we can define an idempotent 3-quasigroup (S,q_o) by putting $q_o=(Q(q_1,q_1;q_=)-\bigcup_{B\varepsilon\beta}Q(q_{1B},q_{1B};q_=))\cup(\bigcup_{B\varepsilon\beta}q_B)$. If $(13)(24)\varepsilon H(q_B)$ for all $B\varepsilon\beta$, then $(13)(24)\varepsilon H(q_o)$. Moreover, (S,q_o) is 2-idempotent iff (B,q_B) is 2-idempotent for all $B\varepsilon\beta$.

We omit the proof of Construction 1, because all details are easy to check. Note that what is going on is the following. The 3-quasigroup $Q(q_1,q_1;q_=)$ contains all elements of β as subsystems. Because we are working with idempotent 3-quasigroups and because no two elements of β intersect in more than one element of S, the rows of these subsystems can be completely independently unplugged and replaced by the rows of another idempotent 3-quasigroup on the same set. If we replace the rows of all subsystems in β by the rows of a 2-idempotent 3-quasigroup on the same set, we obtain a 2-idempotent 3-quasigroup on S. As Construction 1 and related subsequent constructions could potentially be useful in the construction of

3-quasigroups with other prescribed properties than 2-idempotence, we state them in a somewhat more general form than strictly needed for our purposes.

Actually, our proof that 2-idempotent 3-quasigroups exist for all $v \notin \{3,7\}$ will not use Construction 1, but the following, very closely related, Construction 2. We gave Construction 1 first, because it is somewhat simpler and more natural and uses the same basic idea. Again, we do not give a proof, because all details are easy to check.

Construction 2: Let (S, β) be an $S(2, K, v)$, $K \cap \{0, 1, 2\} = \emptyset$, $v \geq 2$. Let q_{1B}, $B\varepsilon\beta$, and q_1 be as in Construction 1. Let $1 \notin S$. Assume that for each $B\varepsilon\beta$ a totally unipotent 3-quasigroup $(B \cup \{1\}, q_B)$ with unit 1 is given. Then we can define a totally unipotent 3-quasigroup $(S \cup \{1\}, q_o)$ with unit 1 by putting $q_0 = (Q(q_1, q_1; q_=) - \bigcup_{B\varepsilon\beta} Q(q_{1B}, q_{1B}; q_=)) \cup (\bigcup_{B\varepsilon\beta} q_B)$. If $(13)(24)\varepsilon H(q_B)$ for all $B\varepsilon\beta$, then $(13)(24)\varepsilon H(q_o)$. Moreover, $(S\cup\{1\}, q_o)$ is 2-idempotent iff $(B\cup\{1\}, q_B)$ is 2-idempotent for all $B\varepsilon\beta$.

To prove that 2-idempotent $OA(3, 4, v)$ exist for all $v \notin \{3, 7\}$, we will need one further construction. Let G be a sharply 3-transitive permutation group on a set S, $|S| \geq 4$. As we can always relabel the elements of S, it is not restrictive to assume that $\{1, 2, 3, 4\} \subset S$. Put $q = \{(x, x, x, x); x\varepsilon S\} \cup \{(x_1, x_2, x_3, x_4); \{x_1, x_2, x_3, x_4\} = \{a, b\} \subset S, a \neq b$, two of the x_i equal a and two equal $b\} \cup \{(\alpha(1), \alpha(2), \alpha(3), \alpha(4)); \alpha\varepsilon G\}$. It is easy to check that (S, q) is a 2-idempotent 3-quasigroup and that $H(q) \supset G|\{1, 2, 3, 4\}$. (If G is a permutation group on a set S and $X \subset S$, we put $G|X = \{g|X; g\varepsilon G, g(X) = X\}$.) Taking $G = A_5$ yields a 2-idempotent $OA(3, 4, 5)q$ with $H(q) = A_4$. Note that A_4 contains $(13)(24)$. Taking $G = PGL(2, p^n)$, p a prime, $n\varepsilon N - \{0\}$, $p^n \geq 3$, yields a 2-idempotent $OA(3, 4, p^n + 1)q$ such that $H(q) \supset K_4$, where K_4 denotes the Klein 4-group. Note again that $(13)(24)\varepsilon K_4$. Choosing $p = 2$ and $n = 3$ yields a 2-idempotent $OA(3, 4, 9)q$ with $(13)(24)\varepsilon H(q)$.

It is well known (see for instance [1, page 438]) that $B(\{3, 4, 5\}) = N - \{2, 6, 8\}$. By our remarks in the beginning of this section, 2-idempotent $OA(3, 4, v)$ (S, q) with $(13)(24)\varepsilon H(q)$ exist for all even v and thus, in particular, for $v = 4$ and $v = 6$. Above, we constructed such a 3-quasigroup for $v = 5$. Thus, Construction 2 yields 2-idempotent $OA(3, 4, v)$ (S, q) with $(13)(24)\varepsilon H(q)$ for all $v\varepsilon N - \{3, 7, 9\}$. We took care of the case $v = 9$ above. Thus, 2-idempotent $OA(3, 4, v)$ (S, q) with $(13)(24)\varepsilon H(q)$ exist for all $v\varepsilon N - \{3, 7\}$. As noted before, no 2-idempotent $OA(3, 4, 3)$ exists. The problem for $v = 7$ remains open, with or without the requirement $(13)(24)\varepsilon H(q)$.

4. A survey of results about 2-idempotent 3-quasigroups with prescribed conjugate invariant group.

In this section, we survey results about the existence of 2-idempotent $OA(3, 4, v)$ (S, q) with $H(q) \supset G$, where G is some prescribed subgroup of S_4. It is easy to see that, once we have solved the problem for a given group G, permutations of the columns of our constructed arrays will solve the problem for all groups conjugate to G.

Before studying our problem for 2-idempotent 3-quasigroups, let us first look at the analogous problem for idempotent quasigroups. The subgroups of S_3 are the trivial group containing only the identity, three subgroups of order 2, which are all conjugate, A_3 and S_3. We have seen that idempotent $OA(2, 3, v)$ exist for all $v \neq 2$, but not for $v = 2$. We also saw that idempotent $OA(2, 3, v)$ (S, q) with $(12)\varepsilon H(q)$ exist iff v is odd or $v = 0$. Idempotent $OA(2, 3, v)$ (S, q) with $H(q) \supset \mathcal{A}_3$ are called Mendelsohn quasigroups. (They are equivalent with combinatorial structures known as Mendelsohn triple systems.) It was proved by N. S. Mendelsohn [7] that an idempotent $OA(2, 3, v)$ (S, q) with $H(q) \supset \mathcal{A}_3$ exists iff $v \equiv 0$ or $1 \pmod 3$ and $v \neq 6$. It is well known and easy to see that idempotent $OA(2, 3, v)$ (S, q) with $H(q) = \mathcal{S}_3$ are equivalent with $S(2, 3, v)$. An $S(2, 3, v)$ is called a Steiner triple system. It is well known that an $S(2, 3, v)$ exists iff $v \equiv 1$ or $3 \pmod 6$ or $v = 0$ [6]. By our remarks in section 2, totally unipotent $OA(2, 3, v)$ (S, q) with $H(q) \supset G$, $G \subset \mathcal{S}_3$, are equivalent with idempotent $OA(2, 3, v-1)$ (S, q_o) with $H(q_o) \supset G$. Thus, the above mentioned results can easily be retranslated in terms of totally unipotent quasigroups.

An $S(\lambda; 3, 4, v)$ is a pair (S, β), where S is a v-set and β is a collection of 4-subsets of S, called blocks, such that any 3-subset of S is contained in exactly λ blocks. Note that we allow repeated blocks, i.e. β may contain several copies of the same 4-subset. The number of times a 4-subset B of S occurs in β is called the multiplicity of B. We usually write $S(3, 4, v)$ instead of $S(1; 3, 4, v)$. An $S(3, 4, v)$ is called a Steiner quadruple system. A well-known necessary condition for the existence of an $S(\lambda; 3, 4, v)$, $v \geq 4$, is that λ must be divisible by $gcd(v - 3, 12)$. (This condition is also sufficient [4].) If (S, q) is a 2-idempotent $OA(3, 4, v)$, then it is easy to check that, if β_q denotes the collection of 4-subsets obtained by replacing each $(x_1, x_2, x_3, x_4)\varepsilon q$ by $\{x_1, x_2, x_3, x_4\}$ and then discarding all $1-$ and $2-$ subsets, then (S, β_q) is an $S(24; 3, 4, v)$. The multiplicity of a 4-subset B of S in β_q is divisible by $|H(q)|$. Dividing, in β_q, the multiplicity of all blocks by $|H(q)|$ yields an $S(24/|H(q)|; 3, 4, v)$. Thus, if (S, q) is a 2-idempotent $OA(3, 4, v)$, then $|H(q)| \cdot gcd(v - 3, 12)$ must divide 24.

If $q \subset S^k$, if $x\varepsilon S$ and $i\varepsilon\{1, \ldots, k\}$, put $q[x, i] = \{(x_1, \ldots, x_{i-1}, x_i, \ldots, x_{k-1});$ $(x_1, \ldots, x_{i-1}, x, x_1 u, \ldots, x_{k-1})\varepsilon q\}$. Note that $H(q[x, i])$ contains a subgroup conjugate to $(H(q))_i$, where $(H(q))_i$ denotes the stabilizer of i in $H(q)$. We call $q[x, i]$ the derivation of q at i with respect to x. If (S, q) is an $OA(t, k, v)$, then $(S, q[x, i])$ is an $OA(t-1, k-1, v)$. If (S, q) is a totally unipotent $OA(t, t+1, v)$ with unit 1 and $i\varepsilon\{1, \ldots, t+1\}$, then $(S, q[1, i])$ is a totally unipotent $OA(t-1, t, v)$. In particular, if (S, q) is a 2-idempotent $OA(3, 4, v)$, if $x\varepsilon S$ and $i\varepsilon\{1, 2, 3, 4\}$, then $(S, q[x, i])$ is a totally unipotent $OA(2, 3, v)$ with unit x such that $H(q[x, i])$ contains a subgroup conjugate to $(H(q))_i$ and, from $(S, q[x, i])$, we can obtain an idempotent $OA(2, 3, v-1)$ $(S - \{x\}, q_o)$ with $H(q_o) = H(q[x, i])$. This gives some further necessary conditions for the existence of 2-idempotent $OA(3, 4, v)$ (S, q) with $H(q) \supset G$, where G is a fixed subgroup of $\mathcal{S}_4$. (Remember that, given a 2-idempotent $OA(3, 4, v)$ (S, q), we can apply the preceding arguments for all $i\varepsilon\{1, 2, 3, 4\}$.)

We now can review known results about 2-idempotent $OA(3, 4, v)$ (S, q) where $H(q) \supset G$, G some subgroup of $\mathcal{S}_4$. It is well known and easy to see that a 2-idempotent $OA(3, 4, v)$ (S, q) with $H(q) = \mathcal{S}_4$ is equivalent with an $S(3, 4, v)$. It was proved by Hanani [3] that a necessary and sufficient condition for the existence of an $S(3, 4, v)$ is that $v \equiv 2$ or $4 \pmod 6$ or $v\varepsilon\{0, 1\}$. A recent result of Hartman and Phelps [5] states that a 2-idempotent $OA(3,4,v)$ (S,q) with $H(q) \supset \mathcal{A}_4$ exists iff $v \equiv 1, 2, 4, 5, 8$ or $10 \pmod{12}$ or $v = 0$. In section 3, we showed that a 2-idempotent $OA(3,4,v)$ (S,q) with $H(q) \supset D_4$ exists iff v is even or $v = 1$. Moreover, we showed that a 2-idempotent $OA(3,4,v)$ (S,q) with $H(q) \supset \{(1)(2)(3)(4), (13)(24)\}$ exists for all $v \neq 3$, except maybe $v = 7$, and that no 2-idempotent $OA(3,4,3)$ exists. In section 6, we will show that a 2-idempotent $OA(3,4,v)$ (S,q) with $H(q) \supset K_4$ exists iff $v \equiv 0, 1$ or $2 \pmod 4$. It is easy to check that combined with the necessary conditions given above and the obvious fact that if $H(q) \supset G$ and $G \supset G_o$, then $H(q) \supset G_o$, the above results solve the problem completely, except when $v = 7$ or G is conjugate to C_3 or C_4, where C_3 is the group generated by (123) (4) and C_4 is the group generated by (1234). If (S,q) is a 2-idempotent $OA(3,4,v)$ with $H(q) \supset C_3$ and if $x \varepsilon S$, then $(S, q[x,4])$ is a totally unipotent $OA(2,3,v)$ with $H(q[x,4]) \supset \mathcal{A}_3$. This show that a necessary condition for the existence of such an $OA(3,4,v)$ is that $v \equiv 1$ or $2 \pmod 3$ or $v = 0$ and that $v \neq 7$. On the other hand, as $C_3 \subset \mathcal{A}_4$, such $OA(3,4,v)$ exist for all $v \equiv 1, 2, 4, 5, 8$ or $10 \pmod{12}$, as well as for $v = 0$, leaving open only the cases $v \equiv 7$ or $11 \pmod{12}$, $v \neq 7$. The obvious necessary condition for the existence of 2-idempotent $OA(3,4,v)$ (S,q) with $H(q) \supset C_4$ is $v \equiv 0, 1$, or $2 \pmod 4$. On the other hand, C_4 is contained in a group conjugate to D_4. Thus, such $OA(3,4,v)$ exist for all even v. This leaves open the cases $v \equiv 1 \pmod 4$. There are no 2-idempotent $OA(3,4,5)$ (S,q) with $H(q) \supset C_4[8]$. On the other hand, a 2-idempotent $OA(3,4,9)$ (S,q) with $H(q) \supset C_4$ is constructed in [8]. As C_3 and C_4 are the only remaining cases, we believe that a complete solution to either of the two would be interesting.

5. Orthogonal arrays with holes. Before studying 2-idempotent 3-quasigroups (S,q) with $H(q) \supset K_4$, we need to review some results on orthogonal arrays with holes.

If S is a set, $P(S)$ will be the set of all subsets of S and $P_k(S)$ the set of all k-subsets of S. If $\delta \subset P(S)$, a $\delta - OA(t, k, S)$ will be a subset q of S^k such that for every $(x_1, \ldots, x_k)\varepsilon q$ and every $D\varepsilon\delta$, we have $|\{i;\ 1 \leq i \leq k,\ x_i \varepsilon D\}| < t$ and such that, for any $\{i_1, \ldots, i_t\} \in P_t(\{1, \ldots, k\})$ and any subset $\{x_{i_1}, \ldots, x_{i_t}\}$ of S not contained in any $D\varepsilon\delta$, there is exactly one $(y_1, \ldots, y_k)\varepsilon q$ with $y_{i_1} = x_{i_1}, \ldots, y_{i_t} = x_{i_t}$. (We do not assume that $x_{i_1}, \ldots, x_{i_t}$ are pairwise distinct.) In other words, a $\delta - OA(t, k, S)$ is an $OA(t, k, |S|)$ with holes, the holes being the elements of δ. If δ is a set of subsystems of an $OA(t, k, v)$ (S,q), then erasing all rows that are completely contained in an element of δ, yields a $\delta - OA(t, k, S)$. However, not every $\delta - OA(t, k, S)$ can be completed into an $OA(t, k, |S|)$. If q is a $\delta - OA(t, t+1, S)$, we often write $q(x_1, \ldots, x_t) = x_{t+1}$ instead of $(x_1, \ldots, x_t, x_{t+1})\varepsilon q$. Of course, $q(x_1, \ldots, x_t)$ is only defined if $\{x_1, \ldots, x_t\}$ is not contained in an element of δ.

If $q_1 \subset S_1^k$ and $q_2 \subset S_2^k$, the direct product $q_1 \otimes q_2$ of q_1 and q_2 is defined by $q_1 \otimes q_2 = \{((x_1, y_1), \ldots, (x_k, y_k));\ (x_1, \ldots, x_k)\varepsilon q_1,\ (y_1, \ldots, y_k)\varepsilon q_2\}$. Note that if $q_1 \neq \emptyset$ and $q_2 \neq \emptyset$, then $H(q_1 \otimes q_2) = H(q_1) \cap H(q_2)$. If q_1 is a $\delta_1 - OA(t, k, S_1)$ and q_2 is a $\delta_2 - OA(t, k, S_2)$, then $q_1 \otimes q_2$ is a $(\delta_1 \otimes \delta_2) - OA(t, k, S_1 \times S_2)$, where $\delta_1 \otimes \delta_2 = \{A \times S_2;\ A\varepsilon\delta_1\} \cup \{S_1 \times B;\ B\varepsilon\delta_2\}$.

An $OA(t, k, v)$, $v = u \cdot w$, with holes of size u, $u \neq 0$, is a $\delta - OA(t, k, S)$, $|S| =$

$u \cdot w$, where δ is a partition of S into w holes of size u. There is an obvious one-to-one correspondence, preserving conjugate invariant groups, between $OA(t, k, v)$ with holes of size 1 and idempotent $OA(t, k, v)$. If (S_1, q_1) is an $OA(t, k, v)$ and (S_2, q_2) is an $OA(t, k, uw)$ with holes of size u, then $(S_1 \times S_2, q_1 \otimes q_2)$ is an $OA(t, k, uvw)$ with holes of size uv. In particular, if (S_1, q_1) is an $OA(t, t+1, u)$ and (S_2, q_2) is an $OA(t, t+1, w)$ with holes of size 1, then $(S_1 \times S_2, q_1 \otimes q_2)$ is an $OA(t, t+1, uw)$ with holes of size u. Remember that $OA(t, t+1, u)$ exist for all u and that $OA(t, t+1, w)$ with holes of size 1 exist for all w if t is odd and for all $w \neq 2$ if t is even. This means that an $OA(t, t+1, uw)$ with holes of size u exists for all u and w if t is odd and for all $w \neq 2$ if t is even. It is not difficult to see that an $OA(t, t+1, 2u)$, $u \neq 0$, with 2 holes of size u does not exist for even t.

In section 6, we will need commutative $OA(2, 3, uw)$ with holes of size u. If (S, q) is a commutative $OA(2, 3, uw)$ with holes of size u and if $z \varepsilon Y$, Y a hole, then $\{\{x, y\}; (x, y, z) \varepsilon q\}$ is a partition of $S - Y$ into 2-subsets, which forces either w to be odd or u to be even. Of course, we must also have $w \neq 2$. On the other hand, if w is odd, then there is a commutative $OA(2, 3, w)$ (S_2, q_2) with holes of size 1. A totally symmetric $OA(2, 3, u)$ (S_1, q_1) exists for all u. But then $(S_1 \times S_2, q_1 \otimes q_2)$ is a commutative $OA(2, 3, uw)$ with holes of size u. If w is any positive integer different from 2, then there is a commutative $OA(2, 3, 2w)$ (S, q) with holes of size 2. There are several ways of seeing this well known fact. Our own favorite is to use the fact that if $2w + 1 \equiv 1$ or 3 (mod 6), then there is an $S(2, 3, 2w + 1)$ (S_o, β) and if $2w + 1 \equiv 5$ (mod 6), then there is an $S(2, \{3, 5\}, 2w + 1)$ (S_o, β) having exactly one line of size 5 [10]. Choose $s \varepsilon S_o$. In the case $2w + 1 \equiv 5$ (mod 6), choose s outside the line of size 5. (Here, we use $w \neq 2$.) Put $S = S_o - \{s\}$. The holes will be the 2-subsets $\{y, z\}$, where $\{s, y, z\} \varepsilon \beta$. The rows of q will consist of all ordered 3-subsets (a, b, c), where $\{a, b, c\} \varepsilon \beta$, $s \notin \{a, b, c\}$, as well as, in the case $2w + 1 \equiv 5$ (mod 6), the rows of a commutative $OA(2, 3, 5)$ with holes of size 1 on the line of size 5. Now, if $w \varepsilon \mathbf{N} - \{2\}$ and u is even, let (S_1, q_1) be any commutative $OA(2, 3, u/2)$ and let (S_2, q_2) be a commutative $OA(2, 3, 2w)$ with holes of size 2. Then $(S_1 \times S_2, q_1 \otimes q_2)$ is a commutative $OA(2, 3, uw)$ with holes of size u. To summarize, commutative $OA(2, 3, uw)$ with holes of size u exist except when $w = 2$ or when u is odd and w is even, $w \neq 0$.

Let us conclude this section by noting that $P_r(S) - OA(t, k, S)$, $0 \leq r \leq t - 1$, $|S| > r$, are a natural generalization of r-idempotent $OA(t, k, v)$. Of course, a $P_o(S) - OA(t, k, S)$ is exactly the same thing as an $OA(t, k, |S|)$ on S. Also, $P_1(S) - OA(t, k, S)$ are the same thing as $OA(t, k, |S|)$ with holes of size 1 on S and thus, are in one-to-one correspondence with idempotent $OA(t, k, |S|)$ on S. If t is odd, there also is an obvious one-to-one correspondence between $P_2(S) - OA(t, t+1, S)$ and 2-idempotent $OA(t, t+1, |S|)$ on S. If $t \geq 2$, then the $P_{t-1}(S) - OA(t, k, S)$ are exactly the $OD(t, k, S)$ studied in [9]. All finite $P_r(S) - OA(t, k, S)$ with $0 \leq r \leq t-1$, $t \geq 2$ and $|S| > r$ known to us satisfy either $r \varepsilon \{0, 1, t - 1\}$ or $r = 2$, $k = t + 1$ and t odd.

6. On 2-idempotent 3-quasigroups whose conjugate invariant group contains K_4.

If (S, q) is a 2-idempotent $OA(3, 4, v)$ with $K_4 \subset H(q)$, then, as we have seen in section 4, $gcd(v - 3, 12)$ must divide $24/|K_4| = 6$, i.e. we must have